Paul C. Helmreich
9/4/07

Wheaton College,
1834–1957

Wheaton College, 1834–1957

A Massachusetts Family Affair

Paul C. Helmreich

Cornwall Books
New York • London

Cornwall Books
2010 Eastpark Boulevard
Cranbury, NJ 08512

The paper used in this publication meets the requirements of the American National Standard for Permanence of Paper for Printed Library Materials Z39.48-1984.

Library of Congress Cataloging-in-Publication Data

Helmreich, Paul C.
  Wheaton College, 1834–1957 : a Massachusetts family affair / Paul C. Helmreich.
    p.   cm.
  Includes bibliographical references and index.
  ISBN 0-8453-4881-7 (alk. paper)
  1. Wheaton College (Norton, Mass.)—History.   I. Title.

LD6040 .H45   2002
378.744'85—dc21   2002023860

SECOND PRINTING 2007
PRINTED IN THE UNITED STATES OF AMERICA

For Dorolee
and
For Jim, Alan, and Kristen

Contents

Illustrations

Preface

During the academic year 1984–1985, Wheaton College celebrated 150 years as the oldest continuing institution for the higher education of women in New England. As part of that sesquicentennial celebration, the College published Part I of this volume under the title, *Wheaton College, 1834–1912: The Seminary Years.* To my great surprise, one day that spring I was approached by President Alice Emerson, who told me that the Board of Trustees had formally designated me College Historian. Noting the sly smile on her face, I responded that I supposed it was meant as an inducement to continue my work, to which she laughingly replied, "Of course!" Part II of this book is the result.

Wheaton Female Seminary, like its nineteenth century counterparts, Ipswich, Troy, Hartford, Abbot, and Mount Holyoke, was founded in order that young women of the middle classes might obtain the same level of education as that provided at the colleges for men, albeit only in those subjects deemed suitable for women to study. From the very beginning the seminaries sought to distinguish themselves from the so-called finishing schools in terms of subject matter taught, seriousness of purpose, and quality of instruction.

As the nineteenth century progressed, female seminaries found themselves trapped between the pressures exerted by an expanding public school system and the appearance of new full-fledged colleges for women—most notably in the East, Vassar, Smith, and Wellesley. These were followed shortly thereafter by Pembroke and Radcliffe, the coordinate colleges for women established by Brown and Harvard Universities. For most seminaries the consequences were decline and demise, reduction to preparatory school status, or ultimate designation as a two-year junior college. Only a handful of seminaries nationwide successfully made the transition from seminary to four-year women's college. Two were located in New England—Wheaton and Mount Holyoke, which had opened its doors two and one-half years after Wheaton.

Shortly after Wheaton received its college charter in 1912, President Samuel Valentine Cole established five hundred students as the appropriate size for a "small college." This outlook was accepted out of both educational preference and fiscal necessity until the mid-1950s, when the College's Board of Trustees overcame the initial opposition of President A. Howard Meneely and embarked in 1955 upon a planned program of expansion and growth. Part II examines this first and clearly defined period in Wheaton's history as a very small liberal arts college for women.

From its founding in 1834 up until 1957, Wheaton Female Seminary and College operated very much within the confines of the financial legacy provided by the family whose members had personally watched over the growth and development of the institution from 1834 to 1905. Wheaton was not alone in having received its initial start as a result of the vision and funds provided by a single family. Vassar, Wellesley, and Smith come readily to mind. But in all those cases the contribution was primarily in the form of a one-shot, start-up infusion of capital, and the supervision and control of the "founding family" turned out to be quite short-lived. Such was not the case with the Wheatons.

Judge Laban Wheaton, the most prosperous citizen in the early nineteenth-century small town of Norton in southeastern Massachusetts, established Wheaton Female Seminary as a memorial to his recently deceased daughter. He did so at the suggestion of his daughter-in-law, Eliza Baylies Wheaton, who subsequently watched over the growth and development of the Seminary from her home across the street until her death in 1905. Time and again infusions of cash from the Wheatons served to balance an annual operating budget, fund the construction of new facilities, or repair old ones. The Wheaton family did not seek, nor were they particularly receptive to, monetary contributions to the Seminary from outside sources. Wheaton was *their* institution, and its success was *their* responsibility.

When Eliza Baylies Wheaton died heirless in 1905, the bulk of the Wheaton family estate was left to the Seminary, which was at that time halfway through a fifteen-year period of preparation to become a chartered college. After decades of supporting an institution that rarely had balanced its annual operating budget, and also having financed the construction of eight new buildings to create a college campus, the resulting legacy of just over $1 million, which became almost the total amount of Wheaton's endowment, was relatively small.

During the first half of the twentieth century, the College was singularly unsuccessful in its attempts to raise funds through solicitations of alumnae or general capital fund-raising campaigns. In part this was because all colleges for women historically had much more trouble securing gifts than their male counterparts. But even more it was the result of the fact that Wheaton had never really asked before for outside support from alumnae, private individuals, businesses and corporations, or charitable foundations. The general public perception was that the College was financially secure because of the Wheaton family legacy, and during the period covered by this volume attempts by College officials to convince potential donors otherwise were almost always unsuccessful.

The result was that until the mid-1950s Wheaton consciously made

decisions based upon the necessity of living within the gentle, but binding, fiscal ties that the Wheaton family had created—ties that indeed
provided essential financial sustenance and support, but which also in
various ways involving size, curriculum, and staff proved ultimately to
be restrictive. The 1955 decision to expand the size of the College was
done with the conscious knowledge, as trustee Gilbert Hood later put it,
that the Wheaton family era was coming to an end. The College, as an
educational institution that had been nurtured, but also bound, by the
fiscal, attitudinal, and emotional ties created by the Wheaton family and
its legacy, would exist no longer.

This volume examines the period during which the Wheaton family
influence, extended through its fiscal legacy beyond the death of Eliza
Baylies Wheaton in 1905, was the dominating force in determining the
developmental path followed by the Seminary and College. Part I traces
the growth and development of Wheaton during its seventy-five years
as a female seminary, and examines the gradual and carefully planned
transition process to full collegiate status, initiated in 1897 and completed in 1912. At all times an effort has been made to place the history
of Wheaton in the larger perspective of the changing status of women
during the nineteenth century, particularly as this affected attitudes regarding the higher education of young women. During this period seminaries for young women, more than any other type of educational
institution, provided examples of liberalizing changes and conservative
reaction regarding the proper place of women in middle-class society
and the appropriate form their education should take.

Part II chronicles the first years when the recently chartered College
sought to establish for itself a new niche in the academic world. It examines the challenges and responses necessitated by two World Wars and
the intervening Great Economic Depression. Attitudes toward both academic requirements and the social rules and regulations governing the
lives of college women are discussed, as well as the constantly changing
views that college women had of themselves and their futures. The shifting patterns of engagement between administrative officers and faculty
are scrutinized, as well as the growing unrest of women faculty over
their second-class status vis-à-vis those members of the teaching staff
who were male. It investigates in some detail a crisis dealing with the
proposed construction of an Arts Center, which had its roots in the pre-
World War II period, but which shook the College to its very foundations
in the immediate postwar years. And it concludes with a discussion of
the changing set of circumstances that led the Board of Trustees in the
mid-1950s to engineer what Board Chairman Richard Chapman later referred to as a "revolution from above"—the decision to begin a process
of expansion which has seen Wheaton in the past four and one-half decades expand from five hundred to sixteen hundred students and make
the transition from a single-sex to coeducational institution.

Writing a history of one's own academic institution involves both considerable risks and pleasures. But overall, the experience has been a refreshing and rewarding one, particularly since shifting my scholarly endeavors to the American scene after years of researching European history provided what can in many ways be regarded as a recharging form of mid-life career change. Although this volume concludes at the very point when my association with Wheaton commenced, many of the people I have written about in the final seven chapters were and are friends and colleagues, and in some cases, personal mentors. And a great many of the events, issues, tensions, failures, and successes are ones that I have heard about at great length from many participants over the years. I have tried at all times to impose on myself and this account the professional objectivity of a trained historian. I hope those who read this book will find that I have succeeded in that endeavor.

Readers of this volume will note that it is documented extensively and that the chapter endnotes include a good deal of supplemental information, as well multiple source identifications. Experience has shown that a volume covering the history of a college serves two distinct purposes. On the one hand, alumnae/i and other interested parties seek a readable general account of the growth and development of the institution. On the other, the book quickly becomes a source of first reference for the many college administrative offices seeking specific information about a wide variety of events, buildings, persons, traditions, financial costs, etc. Thus the extensive endnotes in this volume are intended to provide further informational data and also the directional arrows to enable the archives staff and others to find additional facts quickly, or to move to the specific collections of papers where further information about a particular issue can be found. This becomes especially important when one is researching twentieth-century events. For example, the Wheaton faculty files for the nineteenth century occupy less than one foot of shelf space, while those covering faculty since 1910 currently take up 48 linear feet.

I wish to express my appreciation to the Wheaton College Board of Trustees for granting me permission to review all papers and materials in the College Archives designated as restricted by general Board policy. However, all access restrictions imposed by donors of papers, or by those who were interviewed as part of the Wheaton Oral History Project, have been scrupulously observed. Nor have I sought permission to examine any files labelled as "sealed" by the College.

Over the years I have been fortunate in receiving financial aid for my research from a number of sources. Funds from a Mellon Foundation Grant, administered by Wheaton College, allowed me to extend one of several sabbatical leaves to a full year. In addition my election to a term as William C. H. and Elsie D. Prentice Professor provided me with additional released time. Finally, the College's willingness to make available a computer, printer, and private study in the College Library following my retirement from teaching in 1999 greatly facilitated my ability to complete this project.

I am deeply grateful for the strong support provided at all stages of my research by Presidents Alice Emerson and Dale Rogers Marshall, by Provosts Hannah Goldberg and Susanne Woods, and by Vice Presidents for Development Ann Caldwell, Catherine Conover, and Eric Snoek. To the staffs of the Bowdoin, Mount Holyoke, and Smith College archives, and to the officers of the Norton Historical Society, I express my appreciation for their courtesy and helpfulness. Wilma Slaight, Archivist at Wellesley College, cheerfully undertook to investigate and provide me with information regarding Portia Washington. And to all the members of the staff of the Wheaton College Library I can only express inadequately my gratitude for their interest and help in assisting me at all times over the many years this project has consumed.

My colleague, Professor of History Emerita Nancy Norton, generously made available the results of her investigation of the history of physical education and athletics at Wheaton. I am also grateful for the contributions of Megan McKeown Folker (W1989) and Rachael K. Class-Giguere (W1991), who served in different years as my research assistant. And to Nancy Allen of the Faculty Secretarial Staff I owe a special note of thanks for the many hours she spent wrestling with the Seminary portion of the manuscript in the years before I was introduced to the blessings and challenges of the computer age.

To the many alumnae, faculty, friends, and students of Wheaton College who have expressed their interest in this project, I can only say that I hope the end result justifies the encouragement they have given me. In particular I am indebted to my colleagues, Alexander Bloom, Katherine Burton, Frances Maher, and Nancy Norton, who read Part I and made many valuable suggestions. Professor of Art History Emerita Mary Heuser was kind enough to read and comment on the material dealing with the Art Center Crisis. My parents, Professor Emeritus Ernst C. Helmreich of Bowdoin College and Dr. Louise Roberts Helmreich critiqued Part I, and the first chapters of Part II. Until their deaths they were always my best and most thorough critics, and always my enthusiastic supporters.

To my good friend and colleague Professor of Philosophy Emeritus Holcombe Austin and his wife Ethelind, whose joint association with Wheaton began in 1941, I am deeply indebted for their careful reading of the entire manuscript, their astute editorial comments and suggestions, and for the many insights they were able to provide concerning events and persons at Wheaton during the wartime and postwar years.

Above all, from the very beginning of my research Wheaton College Archivist Zephorene Stickney has been a source of constant help and assistance. Her ability to find the materials I needed, her many comments and suggestions as she read each chapter of the manuscript, her

assistance in selecting the photographs to be included, and her willingness to help solve problems, large and small, has been nothing short of
extraordinary. Both her professional expertise and supportive friendship
have been indispensable in enabling me to complete this work.

I am also greatly indebted to Julien Yoseloff, Director of Associated
University Presses, and to Christine Retz, Managing Editor, for their enthusiastic support, unceasing patience, and careful editorial assistance in
bringing the publication of this volume, under the Presses' Cornwall
Books imprint, to completion.

Finally, my wife Dorothy, whose unerring nose for foggy prose and
trite clichés has saved me over the years from many a disaster, has as
always provided editorial assistance and total support. Everything substantial I have written during the past forty-five years, beginning with
seminar papers in graduate school, has benefited from her fine sense of
style and proportion. To her this book is dedicated, with love and gratitude for the more than forty-five years we have spent together. Equally,
however, this book is also dedicated to the most important project the
two of us have shared—our three children, for whom our affection has
no bounds.

P.C.H.

Wheaton College,
1834–1957

Part I
The Seminary Years, 1834–1912

1

The Family

WHEATON FEMALE SEMINARY

A new School by this name is to be opened next spring in Norton. A commodious building has been erected by the liberality of the Hon. Laban Wheaton, and the following gentlemen have been appointed Trustees. Hon. Laban Wheaton of Norton, Rev. Sylvester Holmes of New Bedford, Rev. Orin Fowler of Fall River, Rev. Erastus Maltby and Dea. William Reed of Taunton, Major Jonathan Bliss of Attleborough, and Samuel Perry, Esq. and L. M. Wheaton Esq. of Norton.

It is designed that the general character of this school shall be similar to that of the Ipswich Female Seminary. It is well known, that the Seminary at Ipswich is rendered much more pleasant and profitable to adult young ladies by the exclusion of younger misses. As schools adapted to the wants of little girls are so much more numerous than those designed particularly to benefit young ladies of mature age, it is thought that the rejection of younger scholars will render this new institution a greater blessing to the community, even though the number of pupils should in consequence be much smaller at first. Miss EUNICE CALDWELL, who has been a teacher several years in the Ipswich Female Seminary, is to take charge of the school. Competent assistance will be furnished when needed.

The first term will commence the last Tuesday in April. A more particular notice of the school will be given a few weeks before the commencement. Any inquiries may be addressed to the Secretary of the Board of Trustees.

Jan. 23   LABAN M. WHEATON, *Secretary*[1]

THIS NOTICE, PUBLISHED in the January 23, 1835 issue of the *Boston Recorder,* announced to the general public plans which had been developing since the early summer of 1834 for the establishment of a seminary for young ladies in the small town of Norton, Massachusetts. And indeed, on April 22, 1835 the fledgling school opened its doors and commenced a twenty-two week summer term. Three teachers and fifty pupils gave reality to a dream that had already become deep rooted for the members of the family whose direct personal involvement in Wheaton would continue until 1905. Conceived initially as a means to help assuage the grief of a father for his recently deceased daughter, Wheaton

23

Female Seminary would become a living memorial not so much for the daughter in whose memory it was established, as for the daughter-in-law, Eliza Baylies Wheaton, who first suggested its founding and who would live to watch over and nurture its development well into the twentieth century.

Wheaton was not unique in being founded through the generosity of a single person or family. In fact such an origin was more normal than not for private women's educational institutions in the nineteenth century. Vassar, Smith, and Wellesley each owed its inception to the generosity of a single person. However, none of them remained dominated by their founders for so long or so completely as did Wheaton. The land, buildings, operating expenses (whenever not met by charges to students), fiscal endowment, and the educational and social philosophy—all these were primarily derived from Wheaton family resources and leadership during the first seventy years of the institution's existence. Even the final transition from seminary to four-year liberal arts college in 1912 was undertaken with the knowledge, approval, and possibly at the instigation of Eliza Baylies Wheaton, though she did not live to see the change actually take place. And from 1912 until 1957 the College continued to live within the limits of the Wheaton family's fiscal legacy to the institution, which constituted all but the most miniscule portion of the College's entire endowment.

The location of the Seminary, in an isolated, 28.5-square-mile country town in southeastern Massachusetts, hardly seemed felicitous. Originally part of Taunton, which was the westernmost settlement of Plymouth Colony, Norton petitioned for recognition as a separate township in 1708 and after three years of political lobbying received approval from the General Court, Council, and Governor of Massachusetts on June 12, 1711. The main reason advanced for this separation was the great distance inhabitants of Taunton North Purchase had to travel in order to attend church in Taunton Center. For some it was nearly twenty miles each way. Subsequently, in 1725, a part of Norton was further divided to create what is today the town of Easton, while in 1770 the North Precinct of Norton became the southern two-thirds of the present town of Mansfield.[2]

As a town, Norton was different from most New England communities in that it did not have a cohesive center. Because of its early history as an outlying section of Taunton, it developed as four distinct villages: Barrowsville, Copper Works Village, Winnecunnet, and Norton Center. This division engendered a lack of cohesiveness that continued well into the twentieth century. Although the Copper Works Village disappeared and new areas known as Chartley and Norton Grove made their appearance, the lack of a true town center has always remained a characteristic of Norton.[3]

Of the four villages that comprised Norton in the 1830s, Norton Center was the largest, although since the population of the entire town never reached 2,000 in the nineteenth century "largest" is a relative term. In addition to Wheaton Seminary, Norton Center consisted of about sixty houses, two churches, one public house, two stores, and a couple of one-room schools.[4] By the 1830s the Town had seen the establishment of a number of small saw and grist mills, but the only major industries augmenting its dominant agricultural economy were several mills devoted to making cotton cloth and yarns, and a copper works. The latter was engaged in manufacturing copper blanks which were sent to the United States mint for coinage into pennies. The town, and its 1500 inhabitants, constituted in 1835 a quiet, relatively prosperous community, inhabited primarily by families who had lived there a long time, were somewhat suspicious of outsiders, but who were extremely loyal to their own. The Wheatons were one of these families.[5]

Members of the Wheaton family had lived in the Rehoboth/Swansea area of southeastern Massachusetts since the middle of the seventeenth century when Robert Wheaton had left Salem, Massachusetts, to seek a more receptive religious climate in an area then being settled by those sympathetic to the teachings of Roger Williams. Robert Wheaton had come to Massachusetts in the mid-1630s from Swansea, Wales, and undoubtedly he was influential in giving the town of Swansea, Massachusetts, its name when it was ceded to the Baptists and set off from Rehoboth in 1667. It is recorded that he was instrumental in creating the first officially recognized Baptist parish in Massachusetts.[6]

The first Wheaton to take up residence in Norton was Robert Wheaton's great-grandson, Dr. George Wheaton, who came to Norton in 1749 at the age of 21 to set up practice as a "Practitioner of Physick." In 1750 he married Elizabeth Morey, the daughter of a man of such prominence in Norton that he was one of the few residents who could afford slaves. The young couple purchased the property of a doctor who had recently died, located on Essex Street straddling the present Mansfield-Norton line. They had six children, all of whom lived to maturity, a rarity in that era.[7]

Their second son was named Laban. Like two of his brothers, he attended Harvard University, graduating in 1774.[8] He studied for the ministry and preached for a number of years, including four years at a parish in Framingham where he was invited to settle, but declined, partly on account of his health. He then entered into mercantile business with another Harvard graduate, a business that entailed journeying with a wagon-load of miscellaneous goods from Boston to Northampton, selling materials as he went. He was, in fact, a typical "Yankee peddlar" of the day. He also made several journeys to Canada to trade for furs with the Indians. A story survives that Laban's sled was shot at by Indians while he was crossing frozen Lake Champlain and that he was forced to stop up the bullet hole in a barrel of whiskey with his finger until he reached the other side of the lake. Here he made a permanent plug, but only after draining off enough of the liquid to ensure that he could warm himself well. Although this story seems too much like that of the Dutch boy and the dike to be blithely accepted, it is certainly true that young Laban led a rather unusual and highly adventurous life for four years, years that left him with restored health, but $500 in debt.[9]

Having given up one career and essentially failed in another, Laban resourcefully turned to a third. In 1785, at the age of thirty one, he began to read law with a Watertown lawyer named William Hunt. In return for board and instruction he performed clerical work in Mr. Hunt's office and wrote what were known as "justice writs," an activity that provided an additional small source of income. After two years of study he moved to Milton where he undertook the additional two years of law practice required by the Commonwealth before admission to the Court of Common Pleas.

This was done in the law office of Samuel Swift, the most important lawyer in that town. Late in 1788, having completed his term in Milton, Laban returned to his native town of Norton, ready to begin the practice of law, though he was required by state law to wait until November 10, 1789, before he was officially admitted to the bar.[10]

During the years Laban had been away from Norton much had happened. The town of Mansfield had separated from Norton. His parents had moved from the family farm, turning it over to Laban's brother Calvin, and now lived in a house in Norton Center. His older brother George had died while Laban was still in college, and a sister, Elizabeth, had passed away a couple of years before his return in 1788. His younger sister Abigail had married John Hodges (a member of another prominent Norton family), and his youngest brother Daniel was a student at Harvard.[11]

During the first years after his return to Norton, Laban lived with his parents at their home in Norton Center. But in order to have any real status in the community, he had to become a registered voter, and in order to do that he had to own property. It was for this reason mainly that he purchased approximately thirty-two acres, including a house and barn, on the road to Taunton in May, 1789, although he did not go to live there until his marriage to his double cousin, Fanny Morey on June 1, 1794.[12]

About Fanny Morey we know little, except that she was a member of the same Morey family to which Laban's mother belonged, and that she was 30 years old at the time she married her 40-year-old husband. They had four children, two of whom died at birth. The older of the two survivors, Elizabeth (later known as Eliza), early won a place in her father's heart that the second child, Laban Morey, did not, a fact the father admitted to years later.[13]

During the next several decades, Laban Wheaton's career broadened and prospered. His law practice extended to the courts of several counties, and he repeatedly received Governor's appointments to terms as Justice of the Peace for Bristol county. In 1810 he was appointed Chief Justice of the Court of Common Pleas for Bristol County, and in 1819 Chief Justice of the Court of Sessions. Over the years he was elected Moderator of the Town of Norton twenty times, and also served on occasion as Selectman and Town Treasurer. He represented Norton in the state legislature from 1803 to 1808, and again in 1825. From 1809 to 1817 he was a member of the United States House of Representatives, where he was counted as a Federalist and developed a reputation as an outspoken opponent of slavery.[14]

As his career prospered, so did his financial position. He invested wisely in real estate and was known for driving a hard, though honest, business bargain. In 1815 he was able to purchase one of the finest homes in Norton, located on the corner where the road from Mansfield to Taunton intersected the road from Easton to Attleboro. The fifty-two acres that went with this property, added to his already substantial holdings, made the Judge one of the major landholders in Norton, and provided the land upon which, twenty years later, he would found the seminary for young women that would bear his family name.[15]

In 1820, one year after he was appointed Chief Justice of the Court of Sessions, that court was dissolved by the state legislature and Judge Wheaton returned to private practice, from which he retired in 1827. There are accounts which indicate that as his law practice lessened, he opened a general store in Norton that sold "oats to the farmer, and the mechanic, rum and molasses and to their daughters straw bonnets and calico." As one writer put it: "I do not know that he absolutely stands behind the counter himself, but he will do it, and I have no doubt of seeing Laban with a yardstick in his hand, and as expert, as civil a shopman, as ever cut an inch short of measure."[16] Clearly his talents as a shrewd businessman were well known!

Early in his retirement two major events occurred which permanently affected the course of his remaining years. For most of his life the Judge, though not known for intense religious devotion, had accepted the doctrines of Unitarianism. Around his seventy-fifth year he attended for several months in Boston what his daughter-in-law would later describe as an "Evangelical Ministry" and as a result converted to Orthodoxy (Trinitarianism). It was shortly after this time that the majority of the members of the Congregational Church in Norton opted for the Unitarian view, and the Wheaton family, along with several others, left the Norton Unitarian Congregational Church in 1832 to found a new Trinitarian Congregational Church.[17]

The second event was clearly the single most tragic episode in the Judge's life. On March 25, 1834, his beloved daughter Elizabeth (Eliza) died after a long, lingering illness. Always holding a special place in the

Judge's affections, he had been overjoyed when in 1826, at the rather advanced age of thirty-one, she had married a highly regarded Boston doctor, Woodbridge Strong. During the first year and a half of their marriage they lived on Devonshire Street at the corner of Congress Square in Boston, but on June 27, 1827, the Judge purchased for their use a recently built brick house on Winter Street. It was regarded as one of the best houses in a very exclusive residential section of the city, to which was added an additional distinction that it stood on the same site as the wooden house in which Samuel Adams had lived during his years as Governor. The cost to the Judge was $12,540, an enormous sum for a residential building in that day.[18]

The Judge never actually turned the deed to the property over to the Strongs, although clearly it was intended as a belated wedding present. Apparently he intended to maintain it during his life and will it to his daughter along with enough money to ensure its continued maintenance during her lifetime. Elizabeth's death in 1834 totally altered the situation. The property that was to have been the legacy to a beloved daughter still belonged to Judge Wheaton. Dr. Strong was well-off in his own right. The grief-stricken father initially contemplated the erection of an immense white marble monument in Elizabeth's memory. However, another suggestion was put forward by Eliza Baylies Chapin Wheaton, the young wife of Judge Wheaton's only living child, Laban Morey Wheaton. She proposed that a living monument be created in the form

Judge Laban Wheaton, 1754-1846. All photos courtesy of the Marion B. Gebbie Archives, Madeleine Clark Wallace Library, Wheaton College, Norton, MA.

Elizabeth (Eliza) Wheaton Strong, 1795-1834, in whose memory Wheaton Female Seminary was founded.

of a school for the education of young women. Within a matter of weeks, plans were underway and from that time until his death in 1846 at the age of 92, the development of Wheaton Female Seminary became the primary concern of the Judge and his wife Fanny, who would outlive the Judge by nearly four years.[19]

If the motivating force for creating the new school remained the Judge's desire to establish a permanent testament to the memory of his daughter, the responsibility of planning, organizing, and overseeing all the arrangements and details necessary for opening an educational institution fell to the Judge's son, Laban Morey Wheaton. Laban Morey and the Judge had never been close. Their relationship had developed in quite a different way from the one the Judge had established with his daughter. In fact young Laban led for many years a life of indulgence that apparently scandalized much of the small country town. Only the prestige and position of his father, and perhaps at times his father's money, served to keep him from serious trouble.

A significant number of stories about the young man, involving everything from gambling, drinking, and horse racing to forgery of checks and murder can be found, none of them verifiable today. But even making considerable allowance for small town gossip and the natural tendency toward exaggeration of stories oft told, it seems evident that Laban Morey was both a distinct problem and an embarrassment to his family. His father, though repeatedly distressed with his son, could not find it in his heart to deny Laban Morey anything, the result being that Laban Morey was never lacking in funds with which to fuel his escapades.[20]

The Judge did manage to get his son prepared for college and in the fall of 1813, against Laban Morey's wishes, enrolled him as a freshman at Brown University, apparently hoping that institution would provide a stricter discipline than would the Judge's alma mater, Harvard, and that the distractions of Providence would be less than those of Cambridge. Laban Morey did survive, graduated from Brown in 1817, and returned home to Norton. Although he studied law for a while with his father, he never evinced any serious interest in a legal career, much to Judge Wheaton's dismay. In fact, Laban Morey did not indicate an interest in pursuing anything as a career; rather he chose to live the life of a youthful spendthrift, enjoying the pleasures that Boston and Providence had to offer.[21]

During the Judge's last year in Congress, he had been influential in obtaining a federal post office for Norton. A year later, in 1818, he was able in turn to have his son appointed postmaster, a position Laban Morey would hold until 1845. This apparently was mainly an effort to create some sort of respectable situation for his son. In 1827 and 1828 Laban Morey, again primarily because of his father's influence, was chosen as the town's representative to the General Court; he was elected again on his own in 1838. In later years he served terms as Town Moderator, Tithing Man, and Town Surveyor (in charge of highways and of collecting highway taxes). He was chosen by the state legislature to serve on the Governor's Council in 1857 and 1858, and ran unsuccessfully for the 29th and 30th Congresses on the abolitionist Liberty Party ticket. He was Justice of the Peace from 1828 until his death in 1865, became involved in a number of manufacturing enterprises as an investor, both in Norton and in Providence, and served as a Trustee of the State Industrial School for Girls in Lancaster, Massachusetts. And, of course, he played a preeminent role in the founding and continuing operation of Wheaton Seminary from 1834 until his death.

In other words, Laban Morey Wheaton, rapscallion, became rather suddenly Laban Morey Wheaton, solid citizen, whose behavior and stature befitted his ultimate position as the wealthiest resident of the small town of Norton. What prompted this metamorphosis?[22]

Undoubtedly, maturation had its effect, but more important than anything else was his marriage in 1829, at age 33, to Eliza Baylies Chapin of Uxbridge. The Chapins were a large, respected, though not wealthy family of Puritan stock, who lived mainly around Springfield and Chicopee in the central part of Massachusetts. Eliza's father, Henry Chapin, however, grew up in Uxbridge, and thus it was not strange that he married into one of the more prominent and well-to-do Uxbridge families, the Baylies. He and his wife had ten children, two of whom died in infancy.

Eliza's first years were spent in Northbridge and Sutton, but in 1823, when she was fourteen, the family moved about a mile into Uxbridge to Baylies Hill, near her grandfather's house. It is not clear whether Eliza had already started studying at Uxbridge Academy prior to this move; we do know that she attended the school, and that for at least some of the time she studied there she boarded with her father's cousin, Amariah Chapin, a successful Uxbridge merchant. It was while she was living at his home that she met her future husband Laban Morey Wheaton, though what circumstance threw them together is not known. Subsequent to the Academy at Uxbridge, Eliza attended the Young Ladies High School in Boston, a private school with a very high tuition—$80.00 per year, a sum provided by her elder brother, Adolphus. This school was noted for the strength of its academic curriculum, but since Eliza had already attended for several years an academy taught by a Harvard graduate, Abiel Jacques, she clearly was prepared and able to sample from the best that was offered. She remained at the school until the spring of 1829, leaving it to marry Laban Morey Wheaton on June 25, 1829.[23]

The marriage was based neither on social standing or practical convenience, but rather on mutual attraction and an affection that would continue unabated for the next thirty-six years. From the time of their marriage until Laban Morey's death in 1865, there is overwhelming evi-

Laban Morey Wheaton, 1796-1865.

Eliza Baylies Chapin Wheaton, 1809-1905, at the time of her marriage to Laban Morey Wheaton in 1829.

dence that the couple, individually so different, remained devoted to one another and found in each other's company a close friendship that never waned. Nineteen-year-old Eliza Chapin was all that the elderly Judge Wheaton could have wished as a suitable partner for his gadabout son. Not that Laban Morey ever completely lost his love for the "good life." He was, after all, "an Epicurean, dropped by mistake into a Puritan nest."[24] Nevertheless, it is very evident that his life took on a totally different character from the time of his marriage to the attractive, yet very dignified, young woman he brought to Norton in the summer of 1829.

Eliza's initial reaction on arriving in Norton was delight in the large and well-appointed home that had been built for her by her husband (with her father-in-law's money), and dismay at the town in which it was located. Mrs. Wheaton later commented that when she first came to Norton she wondered why her husband had built a house in such a place—it was "nothing but a swamp."[25] Yet she grew to love it. Though she and her husband traveled often, and she summered away from Norton regularly after her husband's death, she always returned with a sense of happiness in being home.

Norton, of course, also changed over the years and the largesse of the Wheaton family both before and after Laban Morey's death in 1865 contributed much to its development. There was the Seminary to be looked after, and in addition the Trinitarian Congregational Church, of which Eliza and Laban Morey were charter members from the time of its founding in 1832. Most of the funds for building its sanctuary, as well as for later substantial remodeling, were provided by the Wheatons. A public library was built with Wheaton funds on Wheaton land in the 1880s and given by Mrs. Wheaton to the town. She also gave land for the building of a public high school at the turn of the century. In these and in many other less public ways, the fiscal beneficence of the Wheaton family was bestowed upon the inhabitants of Norton.

Laban Morey was the only surviving child of the venerable Judge. He and Eliza had no children. They did adopt a three-year-old cousin of Laban Morey's and named him Laban Morey Wheaton, Jr. He proved a difficult child to raise, constantly rebelling against the strictly regulated and disciplined household of Eliza Wheaton. Ultimately, he ran away from home at the age of sixteen and went to live with his uncle in Newark, New Jersey, where he apparently found responsible work with a New York wholesale firm. Shortly thereafter he contracted typhoid pneumonia, and died in 1853 at age 18, but not before becoming reconciled with Mr. and Mrs. Wheaton, who journeyed to New York to be with him at the end.[26]

Thus, there were no Wheaton heirs. Had there been, the history of Wheaton Seminary and College and the town of Norton would certainly have been different, although given Eliza Wheaton's deep religious commitment, it is highly likely the strong fiscal support she provided the Trinitarian Church would have been forthcoming under any circumstances.

During her husband's life, Mrs. Wheaton devoted herself to running the house, teaching Sunday school, and working for the church in many other ways. Most important, she successfully created a genteel and respectable lifestyle befitting the wealthiest family in Norton. One of the first things she did when married was to insist that Laban Morey's local friends and cronies ask for "Mr. Wheaton" rather than "Laban" whenever they came seeking him at home. This must have been a bitter pill for those whose friendship with Laban Morey was of several decades standing and with whom he had participated in many a party and escapade. The Wheaton household for many years not only observed the strict traditional Puritan Sabbath but also the customs of Sabbath-even, which demanded that no frivolous activity take place on Saturday night. Frivolous activity might include sewing or fancy work. What one did in one's own room was a private affair, but in the downstairs sitting rooms, total and solemn decorum prevailed.[27]

The house had a large contingent of servants, whose duties Mrs. Wheaton oversaw. But she was hardly a lady of leisure; for someone of her New England Puritan upbringing such an existence would have been considered sinful. She took part actively in all aspects of cleaning, cooking, preserving food, making clothes, etc., and was accomplished in all these areas. After her husband's death forced her to take over management of the family finances (for which she kept meticulous records), she participated far less in regular household activities. Nonetheless, almost to the time of her death in 1905, she insisted every night in personally making sure the windows were shut, locked, or open to a specified height before she retired.[28]

She entertained warmly, but formally. Not only did Eliza Wheaton wean her husband away from his former intemperate ways, but both became active participants in the Norton Temperance Movement and participated many times in parades and demonstrations by the "Cold War Army" of the Massachusetts Temperance Union. She was the epitome of caution, always wanting to leave for the railway station early enough to allow time to call another carriage if the first broke down. Having experienced first hand as a child the devastating effects of the hurricane of 1815, she kept a place cleared in her cellar as potential refuge against the time another storm might come.[29]

If caution, pride, piety, and dignity were four watchwords in Mrs. Wheaton's life, practicality would be a fifth. Aware of the world around her, she never lamented what was not possible, but concentrated instead on seeking realistic solutions to present problems. Whether the problem involved the literal survival of Wheaton Seminary or dealing discreetly with the minimal carving skills of Mr. Wheaton, Eliza Baylies was up to the challenge. The story is told of a dinner party at which Mrs. Wheaton skillfully carved a roast of beef, while Mr. Wheaton at his end of the table made "ineffectual efforts" to deal with a boiled fowl. Seeing this, Mrs. Wheaton quietly instructed the waiter to exchange the two platters,

The Wheaton Homestead, home of Laban Morey and Eliza Baylies Wheaton. Since 1905 it has served as the President's residence for Wheaton College.

and on receiving the fowl, proceeded to separate the joints in a quick and easy fashion—all the while carrying on a lively and uninterrupted conversation.[30]

Proud, dignified, cautious, pious, practical—Eliza Baylies Chapin Wheaton was well suited in every respect for the role of protectress of the reputation of the wealthiest, most prominent family in Norton. But those who knew her testify also to the warmth of her caring for individuals and for the community in which she lived. Steadfast in her friendships, she evidenced time and again compassion for the needs and problems of others. Used to having her own way and quick to anger if displeased, she nonetheless possessed, according to those who knew her well, many of the tactful skills of a diplomat and a quiet, rather wry sense of humor that only those most close to her really saw. Her great love in her later years was the Seminary and to it she dedicated not only her considerable financial assets but also her constant interest and concern. Never apologetic for her wealth or station in life, she sought only to live according to the maxim she set late in life for the young women being educated in the Seminary across the street from her home: "It is my wish and hope that as they come in contact with the world, it shall be the better and happier for their having lived in it."[31]

NOTES: CHAPTER 1

Note: In Part I, an underlined year indicates the twentieth century; in Part II an underlined year indicates the nineteenth century.

Abbreviations used in Notes

HWC	Helen Wieand Cole
SVC	Samuel Valentine Cole
EBW	Eliza Baylies Wheaton
LMW	Laban Morey Wheaton

1. Wheaton Histories, Seminary: Seminary.

2. G. F. Clark, *A History of the Town of Norton, Bristol County, Massachusetts: From 1669 to 1859* (Boston: Crosby Nichols and Company, 1859), pp. 16–26, 546–58.

3. Ibid., pp. 37–38.

4. Ibid., pp. 37, 268; Leonard, Jacob, "A Brief Historical Sketch," in *Town of Norton Bi-Centennial, 1711–1911, Souvenir Program.*

5. Clark, *Norton History*, pp. 325–43.

6. W. G. Hill, *Family Record of Deacons James W. Converse and Elisha S. Converse, including some of the descendants of . . . Robert Wheaton. . . .* pp. 43–46. Extracts in Wheaton Family: History.

7. Wheaton Family: Copeland, "Judge Laban Wheaton," Unpublished manuscript, pp. 10–12; *Vital Records of Norton, Massachusetts, to the Year 1850* (Boston: New England Historic Geneological Society, 1906), pp. 152–63.

8. Norton was rather surprising in the number of its sons who attended and graduated from college in this period, especially since the town offered no educational facilities beyond the common schools in each district. Between 1749, when George Wheaton Jr. graduated from Harvard, and 1791, when Laban's youngest brother Daniel did the same, ten young men from Norton graduated from Harvard, four from Dartmouth, and two from Yale and Brown respectively. Clark, *Norton History*, pp. 482–90.

9. Wheaton Family: Copeland, "Judge Wheaton," pp. 45–63; Services and Funeral Oration: E. B. Wheaton, "Incidents in the Life and brief account of the death of Hon. Laban Wheaton."

10. Wheaton Family: Copeland, "Judge Wheaton," pp. 64–71; Services and Funeral Oration: E. B. Wheaton, "Hon. Laban Wheaton."

11. Wheaton Family: Copeland, "Judge Wheaton," p. 72.

12. Ibid., p. 75.

13. Ibid., p. 78; H. E. Paine, *The Life of Eliza Baylies Wheaton: A Chapter in the History of Higher Education of Women* (Cambridge, MA: Riverside Press, 1907), p. 49. Both birth and death records indicate that the daughter's name was Elizabeth, though the record of her marriage gives her name as Eliza. Copeland notes that fourteen months after her birth, Laban's brother Calvin and his wife had a daughter they also named Elizabeth. It was probably to avoid confusion between the two Elizabeth Wheatons, living within five miles of each other, that led the Judge and Fanny to begin calling their daughter Eliza. See also *Norton Vital Records*, p. 152, 335, 400; Wheaton Family: Correspondence: A. Elizabeth Lincoln to S. V. Cole, 5/28/<u>19</u> and 6/4/<u>19</u>.

14. Wheaton Family: Judge Wheaton: G. Allen, notice published in *The Congregationalist* at the time of Judge Wheaton's death; S. Holmes, *Sermon Preached at the Funeral of the Honorable Laban Wheaton at Norton, March 26, 1846* (Boston, 1846), p. 14; Clark, *Norton History*, pp. 483–84; "Judge Laban Wheaton," *Biographical Directory of the American Congress, 1774–1971* (Washington D.C.: U.S. Government Printing Office, 1971), p. 1904.

15. Wheaton Family: Copeland, "Judge Wheaton," p. 76.

16. Ibid.: Judge Wheaton: Manuscript of Samuel W. Baylies; Clark's *Norton History* records that in 1835 a store owned by Judge Wheaton burned. See p. 351.

17. Wheaton Family: Services and Funeral Oration: E. B. Wheaton, "Hon. Laban Wheaton." This was a period of religious revivalism throughout America. Many "evangelicals" in New England found Unitarianism too rational, impersonal and unemotional. For more information regarding this religious division in Norton, see E. J. Knapton, ed., "The Harvard Diary of Pitt Clarke, 1776–1791," in Publications of the Colonial Society of Massachusetts, vol. 59, *Sibley's Heir* (Boston 1982), pp. 236–37.

18. Wheaton Family: Copeland, "Judge Wheaton," pp. 6–7.

19. Ibid.: pp. 1, 3; Services and Funeral Oration: E. B. Wheaton, "Hon. Laban Wheaton"; Holmes, *Funeral Sermon*, pp. 15–17; L. Larcom, *Wheaton Seminary: A Semi-Centennial Sketch* (Cambridge, MA: Riverside Press, 1885), pp. 6, 17–18; Paine, *E. B. Wheaton*, pp. 64–69. There is no document extant that states clearly that the initial suggestion to found a seminary came from Eliza Baylies Wheaton. However, comments and testimony in subsequent years from many who knew the Wheatons personally and who were alive in 1834–35 lend unanimous support to this view of Eliza Wheaton's role as the person responsible for initiating the concept of the Seminary.

20. Wheaton Histories, Shepard "Reference History" Notes: Vose: Comment by William I. Cole; Wheaton Family: Correspondence: Diman to Park, 12/4/<u>41</u>; Copeland, "Judge Wheaton," pp. 2–4; Clark, *Norton History*, p. 180; Grace Shepard, in her "Reference History of Wheaton College," takes the position that the stories about Laban Morey Wheaton's escapades are not credible. See pp. 3–4. Perhaps it should

also be noted that it was during the years of Laban Morey's adolescence that the Judge was away for long periods of time in Washington, serving as a member of the House of Representatives.

21. Wheaton Family: Copeland, "Judge Wheaton," pp. 2–4; Clark, *Norton History,* p. 496.

22. Wheaton Family: Laban Morey Wheaton (hereafter referred to as LMW); Copeland, "Judge Wheaton," p. 77; Clark, *Norton History*, pp. 279–312 passim, and 496.

23. For more information on Eliza Baylies Chapin's life in Uxbridge, see Paine, *E. B. Wheaton*, Chs. 1, 2. The Young Ladies High School was opened in December, 1827, by Ebeneezer Bailey. Bailey had previously been principal of the ill-fated public Girls High School, established by the Boston School Committee in February, 1826. This school was closed after a year and a half of operation, due to an overabundance of applicants and the reluctance of the school committee to expend public funds on girls' education to the extent required to meet the demand. Paradoxically, the school's "alarming success," to quote the Mayor of Boston, Josiah Quincy, was the cause of its failure. See T. Woody, *A History of Women's Education in the United States* (New York: Science Press, 1929), vol I, pp. 520–21; "Ebeneezer Bailey," American Council of Learned Societies, *Dictionary of American Biography* (New York: Scribners, 1928–1936).

24. Mary Chapin Smith, quoted by Paine, *E. B. Wheaton*, p. 26.

25. Ibid., p. 207.

26. Ibid., pp. 33–37; Wheaton Family: LMW: Family.

27. Paine, *E. B. Wheaton*, pp. 39, 50.

28. Ibid., p. 206.

29. Ibid., pp. 53, 86.

30. Ibid., p. 172.

31. Ibid., p. 248; Wheaton, Eliza Baylies (hereafter referred to as EBW): Alexander portrait: *Attleboro Sun*, 5/13/04.

2
Mary Lyon and Wheaton
1834–1837

THE DECISION TO found an educational institution for young women was, for the Wheaton family, an intensely personal one, arising as it did out of a family crisis brought on by the death of Elizabeth Wheaton Strong. But though the Wheatons may not have been aware of it, the times in general were highly propitious for such a venture. The first decades of the nineteenth century witnessed an explosive growth in opportunities for female education, reflecting major shifts in popular attitudes on the status of women. Nowhere were these changes manifested more strongly than in Massachusetts.[1]

Until the early nineteenth century, educational opportunities for women had been few. For those families that could afford it, private tutors provided boys with the classical training needed for college entrance, while girls concentrated on artistic endeavors and social graces. For persons dependent on public education, however, the options were minimal.[2]

In most Massachusetts communities the amount raised for education by town meeting vote was divided among several school districts, each of which then had the responsibility for providing a school and supplying it with a teacher. In the latter part of the eighteenth century, girls, if they were allowed to attend at all, did so whenever time could be fitted around the boys' schedules. Thus many a young girl trudged to school for one hour early in the morning, or attended on Thursday afternoons, traditionally a half-holiday for the boys. Often too, a thrifty district school committee, wishing to keep its teacher occupied during the summer months when boys were needed in the fields, instituted a summer session for the daughters of families in the district. But it would be fair to say that in education, girls got whatever was left over after the needs of boys were met.[3]

Not that district school education was very rigorous in any case. At best it provided what we would regard today as basic literacy. For boys who evidenced interest or talent, larger communities offered further education, either in public grammar schools, or in semi-private academies that charged tuition but also were funded partially by state, town, or private grants. Although by the second decade of the nineteenth century a few of these schools were open to young women, most were not, or admitted only an occasional particularly persistent female student.[4]

In the public sector, resistance to providing more than elementary education for women was often high. Women, after all, would never enter the productive world of business or the professions. To municipal officials it seemed both rational and politic to spend public money raised through taxation on educating those who would in turn be the breadwinners, taxpayers, and voters of the future.[5]

Thus, educational opportunities for the majority of young women were clearly defined. For the poor there were none, or at best the basic literacy provided by the common schools. For the rich there were finishing schools or private tutors in French, drawing, music, dancing, and social graces, studies that seminaries such as Ipswich, Wheaton, and Mount Holyoke would refer to as "ornamental branches." But there was another rapidly growing constituency whose educational needs were being redefined and for whom the existing system did not adequately provide. This was the economically rising and numerically expanding business and professional middle class.[6]

The period 1815–1840 was one of rapid growth and expansion in the United States. Recovered from the pains of revolution and having survived the initial tests of organizing a functioning political and economic structure, the new republic exuded confidence after having successfully met its first military challenge in the War of 1812. The acquisition from France of the central part of the continent in the Louisiana Purchase of 1803 opened new vistas of greatness and ever expanding opportunities. A steady influx of immigrants, many of them skilled machinists, helped create a rapidly developing industrial base, particularly in the Northeast. The Presidency of Andrew Jackson seemed to affirm the concept that the United States did indeed provide unlimited opportunities for all, and that established wealth did not necessarily mean permanently established economic or political power.[7]

The result was the creation of an upwardly mobile, highly ambitious middle class. The ablest sons of New England farmers, machinists, and small shopkeepers prepared for and were accepted at colleges such as Harvard, Yale, Brown, Dartmouth, Bowdoin, Amherst, and Williams. Many became ministers, lawyers, and doctors; others sought their fortunes in the expanding world of industry and commerce. To their number were added those who prospered without the benefit of formal education, who sought to create lifestyles befitting their new prosperity and to provide for their children the educational opportunities they had not received.

In essence, the early nineteenth century was a period when traditional stereotypes regarding economic class, social position, and political leadership appeared to be crumbling before the energy and exuberance manifest in what truly seemed to be a land of unlimited opportunities. And part of this attitudinal metamorphosis was the growing conviction that women not only had the right, but indeed *ought* to be educated in all things useful to them.[8]

What did this mean? Of course it did not enter many minds, male or female, that women should be doctors, lawyers, or ministers. Nor was it expected that women would enter into any of the business professions. Thus there was no need to consider admitting women to the several New England colleges, not because they would be unable to do the work, but because there was no point to it. The traditional college curriculum, with its heavy emphasis on Greek and Latin, seemed totally unsuited to women's needs. Yet at the same time there was growing sentiment that in what were referred to as the English branches—science, philosophy, mathematics, rhetoric, history, composition, logic, and religious studies, women ought to have available to them the same quality of education that was provided for men in colleges and universities. The underlying motivation for this shift in attitude stemmed from three sources.[9]

First, teachers were needed in abundance. Not only were they needed in Massachusetts, but they were needed in the expanding western territories from which new settlements were continually advertising back east for persons able to provide education for their families. Women were in great demand for these positions, for they could be hired at half the rate paid a man. Also, because other means of self-support were closed to women, they tended to remain in the teaching profession longer than men, until they found the opportunity to enter into what was openly regarded as the only really legitimate female occupation—marriage, the maintenance of a household, and the raising of a family. It has been estimated that by 1837 one out of every five Massachusetts-born white females who reached adulthood had taught school at some point in her life.[10]

The second force promulgating higher education for women was provided by the churches. By the second decade of the nineteenth century churches had ceased to receive support from general tax revenues and were forced to depend solely on voluntary contributions to finance their activities. This in turn led to a growing emphasis on volunteerism and the turning over of many church activities, both traditional and fund-raising, to the women of the parish, who were more likely than their bread-winning husbands to be able to allocate time to these activities. Moreover, during the great evangelical revival that peaked in the 1830s, many more women than men experienced a spiritual rebirth, and parish records indicate that church membership, more than ever before, was dominated by women. Men might continue to preach from the pulpit and shepherd their flocks, but at every other level the work of God was carried on increasingly by women. And for this work it was desirable that at least some women have a solid grounding in theology, moral philosophy and logic, a competency in mathematics, an awareness of the new discoveries of science, and the ability to write and speak well.[11]

Finally, there was marriage itself. There was growing demand for better education of daughters in the new rising middle class, daughters who would in turn marry practical, ambitious, educated, professional and business men who had little or no interest in old style feminine graces (often scornfully referred to in the Northeast as "southern feminine gentility"). These women would more than likely be called on to lend behind-the-scenes practical help in their husbands' work. Even if this were not the case, they would be expected to provide an appropriate, sober, cultured home environment in an efficiently managed household. Most important would be the raising of children, and what could better prepare a woman to undertake this task than spending several years as a teacher? The woman of the household would evidence moral leadership for her children through good works in the community of the church, and cultivate a literate and cultured atmosphere at home that would stimulate them to develop inquisitive minds and lofty ambitions, to become moral and virtuous members of the new Republic. She would, in other words, be a teacher in the home, and teachers, everyone agreed, needed to be well educated.

Thus, by the 1830s women held consciously recognized important roles which in one way or another centered on the home, the church, and the nurturing of the young. Taken together, these created, as Nancy Cott has put it, "a constellation of ideas regarding women's roles that we call domesticity."[12] The duties were not new, but the public and social definition of their purpose and import was. And all this, combined with the requirements inherent for success in school teaching, the one professional area increasingly open to women, justified a new and more serious approach to the education of young women.

It was to meet these middle-class perceptions and needs that Wheaton Female Seminary was founded. The Wheatons, somewhat cosmopolitan themselves, were part of a rapidly developing rural middle class in southeastern Massachusetts and were certainly aware that few real educational opportunities for young women existed in that area. From the beginning the family's overall educational purpose was the same as it was for Mary Lyon when she opened the doors of Mount Holyoke Seminary in South Hadley, Massachusetts in November, 1837—to provide a broad, serious, higher education for women equivalent to that available for men. It would be done, however, only in those fields that were practical for women to study as they prepared for lives in their allotted spheres of domesticity or teaching. Never did it occur to the Wheatons, or for that matter to the founders of the seminaries at Troy, Ipswich, or South Hadley, that the concept or limiting nature of those spheres should be challenged. Rather, they sought their preservation and, by providing tough, serious, educational opportunities, to improve the quality of women's performance within them.[13]

Judge Wheaton, in the deed that conveyed the Seminary Building to the Board of Trustees, succinctly stated his views:

> I Laban Wheaton of Norton in the County of Bristol Esquire, convinced that the increase and diffusion of knowledge in the Community is greatly to be desired, and that the safety and happiness of the rising generation, will very much depend on affording to Females the means of an early, virtuous, pious, and liberal education, have caused a building to be erected in said Norton, well accommodated as a place for Female instruction, which has received the name of the Wheaton Female Seminary. . . .[14]

At another time the Judge commented that since "the promotion of female education is now considered by the wise and good an object of high importance to the rising generation," the object of Wheaton Female Seminary would be "the education of females in all branches of Science and Literature that are suitable and proper for them to attend to."[15] This meant a curriculum similar to that being offered at men's colleges at that time, exclusive of the intensive training in Latin, Greek, and on occasion, Hebrew, that still took up close to half of the four-year curriculum at those institutions.

Eunice Caldwell Cowles, first principal of Wheaton wrote years later:

> The whole spirit of this institution . . . has been as we all know, solid rather than superficial, useful rather than fashionable and vain. This was according to the spirit and plan of all the Wheatons—the father, the son, and their wives . . . Their absorbing and abiding desire has been to lift our race higher by lifting its women.[16]

In her study, *Woman's Education Begins,* Louise Schutz Boas entitled her first chapter, "Colleges for Men: Seminaries for Ladies." The title is apt, not so much for the difference it implies as for the similarity. The term "seminary" was a traditional one, long in use as a designation for institutions of higher learning. The founders of Bowdoin College referred to it as a seminary or college interchangeably. In his annual report, the President of Harvard during the 1830s consistently referred to himself as "The President of the Seminary." Ministers in church customarily offered prayers for "our seminaries of learning," and it was after hearing many such prayers that Emma Willard decided to apply the term to her own school in Troy, New York. Though "academy" and "seminary" were at times indiscriminately adopted by various educational institutions, it became the general custom to reserve the word academy primarily for those institutions that offered a curriculum specifically designed to prepare young boys for admission to the established seminaries of higher learning, or colleges as they were coming more generally to be known.[17]

By the 1820s and 1830s the term "college" carried with it a sense of preparation for a career or profession. Since women were not training for specific professions other than teaching, it seemed more appropriate to use "seminary" rather than "college" for their institutions of higher learning. There was, after all, no idea of providing for women a college of law, a college of medicine, or vocational preparation for the ministry. The concept of the "seminary" had always been somewhat general and broad. It implied that the education provided was not preparatory, like that found in an academy, but terminal in the sense of providing an education that enabled graduates to go into the world well equipped to undertake the life expected of them. The founders of the seminaries at Troy, Hartford, Ipswich, Norton, or South Hadley adopted the term consciously and avowedly. The female seminaries, as distinct from the academy or the finishing school, were regarded as providing higher education for women equivalent to that available for men. But they did so only in those fields that were regarded as practical and beneficial for women to study.

Once the decision had been made to memorialize his daughter by founding a seminary, Judge Wheaton wasted no time. During the summer of 1834, a building to house the new school was constructed directly across the street from the home that Laban Morey Wheaton had recently erected for himself and his wife. Though Judge Wheaton provided the funds, it was his son who watched over the construction. Solidly built, the rectangular two and one-half story wooden frame structure would serve as the main classroom building for twenty-five years.[18]

For many new schools, generating start-up funds and creating teaching space were the two most severe problems faced in getting under way. More often than not, those who started schools were the teachers themselves, so questions of curriculum and instruction were not the main concern. For Wheaton Female Seminary, just the reverse was true. The Wheatons, though well educated, were not, and had no desire to become, educators. The money, the land, the buildings—these they could provide. But clearly they needed help and advice from someone who would know how to go about attracting students, developing a curriculum, and finding teachers. Aware of this they turned for guidance to a woman widely recognized as a leader in female education, whose plans for founding a new seminary for young women were already well known. That person was Mary Lyon.

Along with Catherine Beecher, Zilpah Grant, and Emma Willard,

Mary Lyon stands as one of the great leaders in the development of higher education for women in the first half of the nineteenth century. Having attended Sanderson Academy and the pioneering school of Joseph Emerson in Byfield, Massachusetts, she drew from the two ministers who headed these institutions views and concerns that would serve to direct the whole course of her future life. From Rev. Emerson she absorbed the conviction that permanent educational institutions for women were greatly needed, that the highest occupation to which a woman could aspire was that of a teacher, and that the training of teachers was a task of consummate importance for the survival of society. Rev. Emerson's fervent belief that women were far better suited than men to teach the young became a cornerstone of Mary Lyon's philosophy.[19]

Rev. Emerson also "talked to ladies as if they had brains"[20] and emphasized serious study of academic subjects at his school, using a technique based heavily on discussion and analysis rather than lecture and recitation, a radical approach for that day. Most important for Mary Lyon, however, was the conviction drawn from her experiences at both Sanderson and Byfield that it was the role of the teacher to be as concerned for the "spiritual prosperity" of her pupils as for their academic development. "Ministers encouraged female teachers like Mary Lyon to exercise spiritual authority and leadership in their schools, transforming their task of instilling 'virtue' in their pupils from a nominal to a vital responsibility, and viewing the training of female teachers as a sacred as well as secular undertaking."[21]

It was at Byfield that Mary Lyon formed a life-long friendship with Zilpah Grant, who was preceptress there when Mary Lyon attended in 1821. From 1824 to 1828 she joined Miss Grant during the summers as a teacher on the staff at Adams Female Academy in East Derry, New Hampshire, while in the winter she operated her own academy in her home town of Buckland, Massachusetts. Then in 1828 she joined Zilpah Grant on a full-time basis at Grant's newly founded female seminary in Ipswich, Massachusetts.

Miss Grant had left Adams Academy, where she was preceptress, because of a serious philosophical difference of opinion with the trustees of that school. Like Mary Lyon, who was a Baptist converted to Congregationalism, Zilpah Grant was a firm believer in the need to encourage students to seek a personal religious experience that would lead to conscious and full dedication of their lives to the service of Christ. In this both Miss Lyon and Miss Grant were part of the great evangelical revival of the first decades of the nineteenth century. But not all religious groups were so enthusiastic. Chief among these were the Unitarians, whose eighteenth-century rationalistic views tended to make them sceptical of too great a reliance on sudden, personal, emotional experiences. It was this group that controlled the board of trustees at Adams Academy, and when they insisted that less emphasis be placed on attainment of personal religious commitment and that the curriculum be expanded to include such social graces as drawing and dancing, Zilpah Grant resigned in protest. Her new seminary at Ipswich, in which Mary Lyon soon became essentially an equal partner, continued to reflect the serious academic purpose and quest for spiritual growth that would later characterize both Wheaton and Mount Holyoke Seminaries.[22]

However, Adams Academy possessed one important attribute, the absence of which was sorely felt by the leaders of Ipswich Female Seminary. It had an endowment, modest indeed, but one which seemed to ensure the institution against the vagaries of fluctuating student enrollment and the steady costs of plant maintenance. Ipswich did not have such funds, in fact the building housing the seminary was rented by Miss Grant from businessmen who looked for a profitable return on their investment. Almost from the day the seminary was founded, Miss Lyon and Miss Grant began appealing for an endowment, including buildings that would be owned by the institution. Only by achieving this, they argued, could there be hope for the permanence of the seminary. However, their requests to the trustees met with no success.[23]

It was the failure of these appeals that led Mary Lyon to begin formulating plans for a new institution, primarily intended for the education of middle and lower middle-class girls, that would have as its main purpose the training of women for teaching careers. She was determined that this institution should be endowed, at least in terms of owning its buildings, before it began operating. Only this, she believed, could give it the independence and security needed for long-term survival. Moreover, she became convinced that the new venture should take place in the area of her birth, central-western Massachusetts. Not only was there need for an educational institution for women there, but it was far enough away from Ipswich so as not to be a direct competitor for that seminary's clientele. This was important to Mary Lyon, for Zilpah Grant despite her disappointment over lack of a permanent endowment, intended to remain at Ipswich.

Several years of indecision, soul-searching and anxiety culminated in February, 1834, when Mary Lyon, while still at Ipswich, issued a printed appeal for funds for the new school. Addressed to the "Friends and Patrons of Ipswich Female Seminary," it outlined the main features of the proposed new seminary: buildings permanently endowed through gifts from public citizens; control by an independent board of trustees, not local merchants or ministers; and low tuition, lower by at least a third than that charged at Ipswich. This last would be made possible by seeking teachers who would render their services out of missionary zeal rather than concern for pecuniary gain, and by requiring students to perform most of the domestic work, thereby making the hiring of housekeeping and kitchen staff almost, if not totally, unnecessary. Excess income would be used to reduce tuition further in subsequent terms.[24]

Thus, when the Wheatons were looking for someone to assist them in starting their proposed seminary, it was logical that they should turn to Mary Lyon. She was assistant principal of Ipswich Seminary, an institution acknowledged as the leader in serious female education in eastern New England. She had indicated her desire to leave that institution and to found a new one. Her views on education, both secular and religious, corresponded with those of the Congregationalist Wheatons. And she sought an institution whose physical plant and equipment would be permanently endowed. Aware of Mary Lyon's plans from the printed circular she had issued, the Wheaton family turned to her, not just for advice and help, but with the hope she might find in Norton the appropriate site for her new venture.

Therefore, in the early summer of 1834 Laban Morey Wheaton journeyed to Ipswich, where he put the matter before Miss Lyon. We have no direct record of the meeting, but years later Eunice Caldwell Cowles, first principal of Wheaton, wrote to Eliza Baylies Wheaton succinctly summarizing events during the months leading to the Seminary's opening, as well as Mary Lyon's role in them.

> It is now nearly twenty six years since Miss Lyon called me, one morning, to her private parlor, and said to me, that a _young_ man had been to see her, the day before, about starting a school in Norton; that he seemed timid and not very abundant in talk, but, from what she could gather, there was no lack of money for the enterprise, and that there seemed to be no selfish motive in the undertaking. The gentleman wanted her, she went on to say, to embark in it herself, but she had assured him that she was engaged for another field, yet if he would go on and erect a suitable building and provide for boarding scholars, she would find him a teacher—"Now,"

Mary Lyon, consultant to the Wheatons and teacher at Wheaton Female Seminary, 1834-1837.

she added, "I think this may be the place for you; you are perhaps the one to commence that school. It will be a year or two before I shall need you in my institution, and since you are pledged to go with me then, you will not exactly want to remain in this [the Ipswich] School, after I leave." I shrunk from a work that looked to me then far beyond my ability.

"Oh I will go and help you," she replied. "I shall want some place for the sole of my foot, while I am flitting about here and there, getting ready for our great Institution, and I will make my home partly with you and help you a little. You can do well enough if you only think so. Light and help will be given as you need it and ask for it."

Accordingly I went, under her escort, to Norton that Autumn to survey the land, and to settle the preliminaries in the case. Then and there I for the first time saw you and Mr. Wheaton. In the spring following, 1835, she again accompanied me to Norton, and, as you will remember, took the lead in making arrangements for the boarders; assumed, in short, all the drudgery, and left to me what I knew best how to do and even delighted in doing, the care and instruction of the school as such. We began with thirty nine pupils. The average number of that year was between forty and fifty and a large majority all the time were boarders. They were all above thirteen years of age. Never was a lovelier, more teachable class of pupils. There was no need of law. They studied my wishes. The slightest preference I expressed became to them a statute. It used to seem as though, if it were possible, they would pluck out their own eyes and give them to me.[25]

Indeed, Laban Morey's visit did come at a propitious time for Mary Lyon. Having publicly started her fund-raising campaign, she found it impolitic to remain much any longer at Ipswich. The same was true for her young colleague, Eunice Caldwell, who had already agreed to take on the position of associate principal at Mary Lyon's new seminary when it opened. Both needed somewhere to go. Miss Caldwell also needed experience organizing and directing an academic program (the same duties she would later fulfill at Mount Holyoke). A couple of years heading the seminary in Norton would ideally serve that purpose. Moreover, Mary Lyon needed a base of operations in eastern Massachusetts from which she could continue her fund-raising activities in that area.

Therefore, although she refused the job herself, Mary Lyon wrote to Laban Morey Wheaton on July 8, 1834, recommending Eunice Caldwell to serve as Principal. In describing her to the Wheatons, Miss Lyon painted a picture of her own ideal view of a teacher and the teacher's role in society:

Miss Caldwell wishes to devote herself to the business of teaching, not to promote mainly her own interests, and happiness, but to promote the present and future and eternal welfare of the rising generation. She does not wish to engage in any place, without knowing so much of the situation, as to know that it would be favorable to the promotion of those objects.[26]

Miss Lyon also recommended that the opening of the seminary be delayed until the spring of 1835, for Miss Caldwell could not assume the position until that time.[27]

This last must have come as a disappointment for the Wheatons, since the seminary building would be ready for use that fall, and plans for boarding accommodations were well under way. However, Mary Lyon's suggestion was accepted, and planning went forward with a target date of April, 1835, for the beginning of classes.

Mary Lyon continued to serve as both consultant to the Wheatons and employment agent for Miss Caldwell. On September 25, 1834, she sent to the Wheatons a set of conditions under which Miss Caldwell would accept the position of Principal. It specified that her appointment was to be sanctioned by the Trustees, once they were established, and that her connection with Wheaton could be dissolved with six months' notice by either party. She would receive the tuition fees ($10.00 for a twenty-two week term) as compensation, but would be responsible for paying out of that all operating expenses connected with running the academic program or operating the seminary building. This would include compensation paid to other teachers.

A major stipulation was that the seminary building itself, with all its furnishings and equipment, was to be supplied free of rent. Board charges and type of accommodations were to be similar to those provided at Ipswich. In particular Mary Lyon insisted that no more than two students should occupy any room and recommended that the age of entering students be no less than fourteen, again following the policy established at Ipswich.

> The school is to be conducted on the same general principles as Ipswich Female Seminary. This is in compliance with the request of Mr. Wheaton, & in accordance with the wishes of Miss Caldwell. . . . It is proposed, that under their [the Trustees] general oversight, the responsibility of the course of instruction, & mode of government, the formation & execution of the plans of the school, be committed directly to Miss Caldwell, till the system pursued shall be tested to the satisfaction of the Trustees.[28]

The academic plan advanced by Mary Lyon was also modeled on that of Ipswich, and was similar to the one she would later institute at Mount Holyoke.[29]

An independent Board of Trustees for the new seminary was convened on November 17, 1834, consisting of Judge Wheaton, Laban Morey Wheaton, and six others from the southeast Massachusetts area, three of whom were Congregational ministers. At its meeting the Board approved a series of resolutions implementing Mary Lyon's proposals, with only one exception. That exception was the approval of a special committee's recommendation to reduce the minimum age of admission from fourteen to thirteen. This change was undertaken with the advice and consent of Eunice Caldwell.[30]

Since the aim of both the Wheatons and Mary Lyon was the creation of an institution of higher education for young women, it may well be asked why the age requirement was lowered, particularly since we have evidence that in the first entering class the age of students ranged from fifteen to twenty-five.[31] Though we cannot know for certain, there is reason to believe that the reduction in the minimum age required for entrance was undertaken mainly to accommodate local residents of Norton. One of Eliza Wheaton's main concerns was to provide a means by which the girls of Norton could continue their education beyond the level available in the common schools. Over the years the majority of thirteen-year-olds admitted to Wheaton came from Norton itself and attended as day, rather than boarding, students. Occasionally a student as young as thirteen was admitted as a boarder, but this seems to have been a rare enough happening to cause comment from other students in their letters home, as well as problems in finding a suitable roommate for someone so young.

A more interesting question is why Mary Lyon did not accept the Wheatons' proposal that she abandon her own plans and take on the principalship of the Norton seminary. Certainly, much that she was seeking was there for the asking in Norton. Instead of a long and uncertain fund-raising campaign to endow an educational plant, in Norton Mary Lyon would have a wealthy family, ready to provide the needed facilities, with every indication that there was more money available from the same source, should it be needed. Judge Wheaton and his family clearly did not seek any fiscal gain from the institution, nor did they evince any pretensions as educators. Aside from the normal oversight of an independent Board of Trustees, the Principal would have a free hand in developing the curriculum and overseeing the quality of instruction. Finally, the religious commitment of the Wheaton family, especially of the young Mrs. Wheaton, must have enhanced Mary Lyon's views as to the worthwhile nature of the project.

The reasons for her rejection of the Wheatons' suggestion were several, and in the long run, probably wise. Her own plans, of course, were already well advanced at the time she received the initial Wheaton offer.[32] She remained convinced that the suitable place for her new school was in central-western Massachusetts. This was an area lacking in higher educational facilities for young women; moreover, she had originally come from there. She had many acquaintances and connections in the Amherst region, particularly Professor and Mrs. Edward Hitchcock of Amherst College—close friends of long standing. By the time Mary Lyon talked with the Wheatons in 1834, she also had arranged the formation of a planning committee which would begin the process of determining the location of the new seminary, as well as aiding in soliciting funds for it.[33]

Moreover, several differences in outlook between herself and the Wheatons undoubtedly became apparent to Miss Lyon. Although the Wheatons and Mary Lyon shared a common outlook regarding women's spheres of occupation and the desirability of providing appropriate college-level education in preparation for fulfilling these roles, a difference in emphasis was clearly evident. Mary Lyon always was aware that ultimately many of her pupils would marry and settle down to raise and educate their own families. Nonetheless, her seminary was, as a prospectus issued shortly before the opening of Mount Holyoke bluntly stated, "principally devoted to the preparing of female teachers."[34] For the Wheatons, the emphasis was reversed. Though they recognized that many Wheaton students would teach, and always encouraged those who did, they saw the primary purpose of the seminary as educating young women for useful and creative lives as wives of the middle class professionals, businessmen, and prosperous farmers of southeastern Massachusetts and Rhode Island.[35]

One of the most striking features of Mount Holyoke when it opened was the requirement that all students perform domestic tasks to the degree that the seminary could dispense with hiring domestic help. This program was designed to allow the setting of tuition at no more than two-thirds of that required at any other female institution, thus attracting students from lower middle-class families who otherwise could not afford to attend. To assure an equitable sharing of responsibilities, Mary Lyon required all students to live and board at the seminary; no day students were allowed at Mount Holyoke.[36]

The Wheatons wanted no part of such a plan. They believed strongly that the place for domestic training was in the home, and that the limited time spent at their institution should be devoted exclusively to the academic and moral training unattainable elsewhere. Since the general economic prosperity of the southeastern Massachusetts area was relatively high at that time, concern for lower tuition rates was not one that the Wheatons shared with Mary Lyon or thought necessary. Moreover, day students from Norton were not only allowed, they were encouraged.[37]

In a letter written to Catherine Beecher in 1836, Mary Lyon discussed how best one could raise the money to endow "a permanent seminary in New England for educating female teachers. . . . I am convinced there are but two ways to accomplish such an object. First, to interest one, two, or a few wealthy men to do the whole: second, to interest the whole New England community, beginning with the country population, and in time receiving the aid and cooperation of the more wealthy in our cities."[38] She went on to comment that the first had the advantages of speed and efficiency, while "the second would require vastly more time and labor; but if it were accomplished, an important and salutory impression would be made on the whole of New England."[39] No public relations expert could have said it better. With the example of the recent public community funding of Amherst College before her, Mary Lyon obviously realized that communities, church parishes, and individuals who contributed funds to bring an institution into existence would retain an interest in its well-being and would be likely to send their young women to study there. Moreoever, reliance on the beneficence of one or two families might lead to subsequent donor interference, while a wide contributory base would obviate that particular concern.[40]

Both Wheaton and Mount Holyoke were unusual to their day in beginning as permanently endowed institutions for the higher education of females, but the method through which each achieved that independence was different. Before Mount Holyoke opened, Mary Lyon conducted public and private fund raising campaigns. Subsequently, she and others connected with Mount Holyoke continued soliciting churches, businessmen, alumnae—any group or person that would lend an ear. Wheaton existed for over sixty years before it sought outside funds, even from alumnae. Much of the difference in the history of the two institutions stems from this fact. From its beginning Mount Holyoke, though in any technical or legal sense a private institution, developed in both its basis of support and in its image a public quality and constituency. Wheaton might have done so, but chose not to because there was no need, and because the family that supported the Seminary clearly did not wish it.[41]

There was, finally, one other circumstance that may have entered into Mary Lyon's reluctance to become permanently involved with Wheaton. It must not have taken her long to recognize that though it was the Judge and his son who officially were organizing the new seminary, the power behind the scenes rested in the hands of Eliza Baylies Wheaton. A strong woman in her own right, as strong as Mary Lyon in many ways, it is, as Louise Boas put it, "doubtful if, even had Mrs. Wheaton been sympathetic with all Mary Lyon's plans, the two women could have fitted into the same seminary."[42]

Aside from their shared religious fervor and their commitment to education of women, the two were very different. Both accepted the "women's spheres of occupation" as defined by society, but Mary Lyon had chosen the teaching sphere for herself, and sought primarily to train more teachers. Conversely, Eliza Baylies Wheaton, also well educated, had chosen the sphere of cultured wife and home manager, and thus resisted a philosophy that seemed too narrowly directed toward motivating students for teaching careers. Mary Lyon had come from a family with modest economic resources, and was extremely concerned with making education more readily affordable to young women from similar circumstances, witness her emphasis on the required domestic work program. Eliza Wheaton, though hardly born to wealth, had been part of the more prosperous southeastern Massachusetts middle class, had married into

wealth, and was not ashamed of it. She saw nothing wrong with maintaining a seminary in which young women would lead the cultured and
mannered existence they would be expected to know and practice when
they married.[43]

In one of the frequent talks Miss Lyon was wont to give to the assem-
bled students at Wheaton she discussed her views on teaching and personal financial gain. Commenting that nine-tenths of the teaching in the
world was done by females, she asserted that women should be very
thankful for this field of labour. Teaching provided a way in which
women could cultivate Christian benevolence in others, which was important, since women did not possess the financial means to provide benevolence in other ways. And this was as it should be. "It seems as if
Providence had designed that men should have the care of money, and
the pecuniary concerns, and that females should have the care of minds.
. . . We are to act on the principle that the mind will exist forever," wrote
Hannah Richmond, a student whose notes of this lecture we have.[44]

Moreover, earning money should never be the concern of a teacher,
or, for that matter, of any lady. We have the first two manuscript pages
of this talk, written in Mary Lyon's own hand. "A lady who designs to
teach should not suffer her mind to be engrossed with the lower motives,
and least of all by pecuniary motives," she wrote. "That last *may come
into* the list but it should be least thought of. A lady bent on making
money is always *low* and *degrading.* They may dress pretty and *act the
lady* among a ceartain [sic] circle, but if we look into the mind, we shall
find a barren waste."[45] Later, according to Hannah Richmond, she asserted: "The love of making money in a lady is calculated to destroy all
that is feminine, tender, and benevolent. Ladies that have large salaries
generally spend it about as soon as they get it and to no purpose; or else
they become one of those narrow contracted souls and think of nothing
but hoarding up wealth, and from *this* intelligent minds would shrink."[46]
One can see that in some ways Mary Lyon's outlook on the world differed from that of Eliza Wheaton, who had no aversion to making money
and had a sharp eye for business affairs. She would manage with great
care and skill her husband's considerable property and investments for
nearly forty years after his death.

The two women also differed in another way. Mary Lyon apparently
never evidenced great concern with neatness of dress or carefulness of
manners. In a woman who had to travel as extensively and inexpensively
as Mary Lyon did, this was probably a great virtue. But this must have
contrasted sharply with Eliza Wheaton, whose near obsessiveness with
proper manners, personal neatness, and household cleanliness is well
documented.[47] In fact, this difference led to an amusing set of negotiations between Mary Lyon and the Wheatons as to the living arrangements for the new principal, Eunice Caldwell. The Wheatons were
anxious to have Miss Caldwell board with students, the better to promote

what today would be called faculty-student relations. However, Miss Caldwell was very reluctant to do so, and eventually Mary Lyon arranged with the Wheatons that she should have a private room in Laban Morey and Eliza's home. One of the special privileges that Mary Lyon was very insistent in negotiating for Eunice Caldwell was the right to "receive a friend as a visitor several days, to occupy the chamber with herself without charge."[48] Clearly Mary Lyon made this arrangement with herself in mind. The Wheatons apparently had no objection, but after visiting their house Mary Lyon did. On February 25, 1835, she wrote Miss Caldwell:

> At Norton I settled it that you were not to board with the scholars. But Mrs. Wheaton's particularity & excessive fear of a speck of dirt, makes me afraid that you could not be comfortable. I have just been talking about it with Miss Grant, and she thinks it would be vastly more trying to you than to board in the boarding house, and I am nearly of her opinion. . . . Now will you be willing that Miss Grant and I should look this over and have you board at the boarding house if we think best.[49]

Writing on the same day to Mr. and Mrs. Wheaton, Miss Lyon presented the situation in a different light. She stated she had talked with Zilpah Grant about the Wheatons' desire to have the Principal board with the students, and that Miss Grant "attaches more importance to her boarding with them, than I have. Since convening with her, I have inclined to reconsider the subject. . . . Just before the mail went today, I decided to write a few lines to Miss Caldwell, requesting a reply immediately."[50]

Miss Caldwell was hardly enthusiastic, and consented reluctantly to Mary Lyon's pressure on the matter. In fact, given the long and firm friendship, lasting over many decades, that subsequently developed between Eliza Wheaton and Eunice Caldwell Cowles it seems unlikely that the young Miss Caldwell would have found boarding in a home where the mistress of the house was only three years older than she anything but a pleasant experience. It is much more likely that it was Mary Lyon, rather than Eunice Caldwell, who would have regarded living with the Wheatons as a chore, and Miss Lyon's sudden reversal on the matter seems to indicate this fact.[51]

In her role as consultant to the Wheatons Mary Lyon performed many important functions. Not only did she secure a Principal, but she and Miss Caldwell collectively devised the academic curriculum, as they would subsequently do at South Hadley. A comparison of the catalogues of Wheaton and Mount Holyoke indicates that for many years both institutions used the same curriculum and texts, drawn from what was clearly the academic parent institution, Ipswich Female Seminary.

The notices that appeared under Laban Morey Wheaton's name in the

Boston Recorder in January and March, 1835, announcing the April opening of classes, were drafted by Mary Lyon. In one area above all others, the Wheatons and Mary Lyon saw eye to eye. Wheaton was to offer serious education, essentially equal in the "English branches" to that available to men in the colleges of the day. Thus Wheaton, and Mount Holyoke two and a half years later, both directed their education toward "young ladies of mature age" rather than "younger scholars," to "adult young ladies" rather than to "younger misses."[52]

During the first year, Wheaton students found their room and board in various homes in the village center. In addition, Judge and Mrs. Wheaton vacated their spacious "Mansion House," which was converted by means of temporary partitions into a boarding house for Miss Caldwell and a number of students. Several others lived with the younger Wheatons. Neither Mary Lyon nor Eliza Wheaton found this arrangement acceptable, and Eunice Caldwell recalled later that "it was during that first year, that Miss Lyon, encouraged by you [Eliza Wheaton] may be said to have talked that boarding house into being; while Mr. Wheaton and I, timid and fearful, were all the while giving way to doubts and discouragements. She and you had the faith that never wavered, and Mr. Wheaton found the money, and I yielded, overborne by a mind which used all common minds as the current does floating straws."[53] Recognition that erection of a boarding house would allow Judge and Mrs. Wheaton to return to their own home must also have been a factor influencing the Board of Trustees to approve its construction, which began in December, 1835, with students taking up residence sometime in late 1836 or early 1837.[54]

During that first year, Mary Lyon spent considerable time in Norton, and often participated in the work of the Seminary. The following year her time at Wheaton diminished substantially. Never around long enough to take up the teaching of a regular course, she participated actively, even frantically, in instructional activity whenever she was able. Records reveal the indelible impression she made upon students, who regarded her whirlwind appearances, turbanned head, and unbounded energy with a mixture of awe, fear, and admiration. At one point she instituted a crash course in arithmetic, in which for three weeks the students did nothing else and covered what normally would have been the work of a twenty-two week term. Students remark most on how she was always urging them to move quickly from one place and activity to another. "Lose none of the precious time God has given you," one student quotes her as saying. "Remember for every second wasted on these stairs, God will bring you to account."[55]

For all her services to Wheaton, what did Mary Lyon get in return? Apparently no monetary remuneration, although the Seminary students, aided undoubtedly by the Wheatons, did contribute $235.00 to furnish a parlor at Mount Holyoke. Rather, just as the Hitchcock residence in Am-

West View of the Wheaton Female Seminary, Norton, Mass[?]

Wheaton Female Seminary, ca. 1840.

herst served as a home for Mary Lyon in western Massachusetts during the 1834–1837 period, so did Wheaton Female Seminary provide a base of operations for her fund-raising work in eastern Massachusetts. In Norton she was always welcome; her right to stay with Miss Caldwell free of charge had been established from the beginning. Here she could rest, write, and occasionally teach, which she did, as one student later put it, "when she was not out on Begging Tours."[56]

One can see that Mary Lyon played a major role in the founding of Wheaton; certainly, she did much to shape the course the institution would take in succeeding years. Yet it would not be correct to say that Wheaton can attribute its existence to the work of Miss Lyon, as is the case with Mount Holyoke. In all likelihood Wheaton Seminary would have been founded with or without her aid, and at least in one respect it might have had an easier time. Just as it is necessary to recognize the tremendous positive contributions Mary Lyon made to Wheaton, it is also important to note that she was responsible for creating the first major crisis the young institution faced, one that nearly caused its demise.

That crisis was generated by the departure of Wheaton's Principal, Eunice Caldwell, at the end of the 1837 summer term in order that she might fulfill her long-time commitment to Mary Lyon to become her Associate Principal when Mount Holyoke Seminary opened. Although we know it was this commitment that in part engendered Mary Lyon's initial recommendation of Eunice Caldwell to the Wheatons, it is not at all evident they were aware of it at the time Miss Caldwell was retained. But if indeed they were not, they certainly learned of it in short order.

By the winter of 1836–1837, the imminent departure of Miss Caldwell was known throughout the Seminary. As one student wrote her sister, "I expect Miss Caldwell will go to the South Hadley school next fall, and then I won't give much for this school after she is gone."[57]

Persis Woods, a Wheaton student who would follow Miss Caldwell (with whom she roomed for a time at Wheaton) and become a member of Mount Holyoke's first graduating class, recorded how happy Miss Caldwell was in Norton and how reluctant she was to leave her own enterprise to take up an associate position with Mary Lyon. Both Mary Lyon and Zilpah Grant urged her to leave Wheaton at the end of the winter term in March, 1837, and indeed thought they had convinced her to do so. However, Miss Caldwell remained for the summer term, as a result arriving at South Hadley tired and with her nerves on edge. Within a year she retired to marry Reverend John Cowles and went to live with him in Oberlin, Ohio. Subsequently the Cowles returned to Massachusetts and in 1844 took over the reins of Ipswich Seminary, which they administered jointly for thirty-three years. Mrs. Cowles' friendship with Eliza Wheaton grew ever closer and stronger, and for years she served as private confidante and consultant to Mrs. Wheaton regarding the affairs of the Seminary.[58]

Not only did Eunice Caldwell leave Wheaton, but eight students followed her to Mount Holyoke in November, 1837. In at least one case this was the result of active recruiting by Mary Lyon. "Miss Lyon invited me to go to South Hadley as one of her first senior class," wrote Persis Woods, "and love for Miss Caldwell decided me to do so."[59] In addition, Miss Caldwell took with her Mary Smith, one of two other full-time teachers at Wheaton and the only other teacher who had been in Norton since the opening of the Seminary. Persis Woods, who had served as an "assistant pupil" at Wheaton, performing tutorial services, fulfilled a

Eunice Caldwell Cowles,
Principal, 1835-1837.

similar rôle during her senior year at Mount Holyoke. Thus, in the winter of 1837–1838, Wheaton found itself under the leadership of the one remaining full-time teacher, Miss Susan Palmer, who served a term as head teacher while the Board of Trustees searched for a permanent principal.[60]

Enrollment dropped precipitously. The winter term always had lower enrollment than the summer, but the decline from 69 to 18 was catastrophic, especially when one notes that the first two winter terms had had enrollments of 49 and 59 respectively. Morale was extremely low; one student wrote home in December, 1837: "It is uncertain whether the school will keep next quarter."[61] Eliza Wheaton, in a long letter to Eunice Caldwell, pleaded with her to return to Norton:

> Ever since you left us my heart has been burdened with anxiety for it [the seminary]. . . . The school seems to excite but little interest. . . . The state of my feelings may be summed up in a few words—I am altogether disheartened about the school. I see no prospect of its taking the stand it has heretofore held—I do feel its glory has departed. . . . Indeed! Miss Caldwell, we had almost as lief have the Seminary closed entirely as to have the little number there is now here. We love Miss P. [Palmer] . . . but she is not Miss Caldwell. . . . If you were married or if you were dead it would be comparatively nothing tho. the loss would then be irreparable— But to have you here in New England in an Institution that has just begun to exist, O it is aggravating. . . . Shall this Institution, that has already done so much good, Shall it live, or shall it die? We feel that it rests with you to decide this question. Will you not, my dear Friend, say that you will turn to this Institution? O this is a question of vast moment and I do feel that upon your decision hangs the future destiny of this Seminary.
>
> We know that you were engaged to Miss Lyon for one year, was it not? And then you could leave, if you chose to do—Will you not take as early an opportunity as possible to examine the question whether you will return to Norton, and let us know the result. . . . Words do fail to express what we feel on the subject.[62]

To this eloquent plea, Laban Morey Wheaton added a calmer, but equally imploring note, pointing out how her return would "alleviate the feelings of a distressed parent [Judge Wheaton], whose glass is almost run but whose days I believe would be prolonged upon earth by your so doing."[63]

The words of Eliza Baylies Wheaton convey the deep despair for the future that had set in at the Seminary during the winter of 1837–1838. For a fledgling school to lose its Principal and one of its two additional teachers after only two years of existence was a blow of major proportions. Mary Lyon's impact on Wheaton clearly had its negative as well as positive aspects. Given the commitment Eunice Caldwell had made to Mary Lyon before coming to Norton, Miss Lyon's recommendation of Miss Caldwell for the principal's position almost insured this ultimate crisis. One must at least consider whether Wheaton would have been better off had it opened its doors with a teaching and administrative staff that could have provided a more stable, long-term foundation upon which to construct a thriving educational enterprise.

However great Wheaton's debt to Mary Lyon may be, it must be recognized that Wheaton also, in a specific and unique sense, had special problems surviving the founding of Mount Holyoke Female Seminary. The opening of classes at Mount Holyoke in November, 1837, would not have created the extreme difficulties for Wheaton that resulted had the Seminary not tied itself so closely in its formative years to Mary Lyon and Eunice Caldwell. Their prior and absolute commitment to the South Hadley project meant that in the winter of 1837–1838, Wheaton found itself facing a situation in many ways equivalent to starting anew.

NOTES: CHAPTER 2

1. G. H. Martin, *The Evolution of the Massachusetts Public School System* (New York: D. Appleton, 1902), p. 130.

2. S. Delamont, "The Contradictions in Ladies Education," in S. Delamont and L. Duffin, eds., *The Nineteenth Century Woman: Her Cultural and Physical World* (New York: Barnes and Noble, 1978), p. 138.

3. Martin, *Massachusetts School System*, p. 13; N. F. Cott, *The Bonds of Womanhood: "Woman's Sphere" in New England, 1780–1835* (New Haven: Yale University Press, 1977), pp. 102–93; M. F. Katz, *The Irony of Early School Reform: Educational Innovation in Mid-Nineteeth Century Massachusetts* (Cambridge, MA: Harvard University Press, 1968), p. 53; C. F. Thwing, *A History of Higher Education in America* (New York; D. Appleton, 1906), p. 334.

4. L. S. Boas, *Woman's Education Begins: The Rise of Women's Colleges* (Norton, MA: Wheaton College Press, 1935), pp. 4–5; Cott, *Bonds of Womanhood*, pp. 112–13; Martin, *Massachusetts School System*, pp. 120–22.

5. Boas, *Woman's Education Begins*, pp. 13–14; Martin, *Massachusetts School System*, pp. 130–32.

6. Thwing, *Higher Education*, p. 336; Boas, *Woman's Education Begins*, p. 95; E. Green, *Mary Lyon and Mount Holyoke: Opening the Gates* (Hanover, NH: University of New England Press, 1979), p. 65.

7. B. Bailyn, D. Davis et al., *The Great Republic: A History of the American People* (Boston: Little, Brown, 1977), pp. 425–63.

8. Cott, *Bonds of Womanhood*, pp. 117–20.

9. Boas, *Woman's Education Begins*, pp. 105–6; C. Degler, *At Odds: Women and the Family in America from the Revolution to the Present* (New York: Oxford University Press, 1980), p. 310.

10. Boas, *Woman's Education Begins*, p. 3; Cott, *Bonds of Womanhood*, pp. 121–122; Delamont, "Contradictions," in Delamont and Duffin, *Nineteenth Century Woman*, p. 138; K. K. Sklar, "The Founding of Mount Holyoke College," in C. R. Berkin and M. B. Norton, eds., *Women of America, A History* (Boston: Houghton Mifflin, 1979), p. 181; Woody, *Women's Education*, I, pp. 457–505 passim.

11. Sklar, "Mount Holyoke," in Berkin and Norton, *Women of America*, pp. 184–88; Boas, *Woman's Education Begins*, ch. 3, passim; Cott, *Bonds of Womanhood*, ch. 4, passim; Degler, *At Odds*, p. 302; P. Bunkle, "Sentimental Womanhood

and Domestic Education, 1830–1870," *History of Education Quarterly*, 14:1, pp. 13–30; M. P. Ryan, "A Woman's Awakening: Evangelical Religion and the Families of Utica, New York, 1800–1840," in J. James, ed., *Women in American Religion* (Philadelphia: University of Pennsylvania Press, 1980), pp. 89–110.

12. Cott, *Bonds of Womanhood*, p. 8, see also pp. 62, 94–100, 104–5, 122–23; Degler, *At Odds*, pp. 306–7; Boas, *Woman's Education Begins*, ch. 2, passim; J. Conway, "Perspectives on the History of Women's Education in the United States," *History of Education Quarterly*, 14:1 (Spring, 1974), pp. 4–5.

13. Boas, *Woman's Education Begins*, p. 48; Paine, *E. B. Wheaton*, pp. 70–71; Wheaton Histories, Seminary: Seminary: Park to Palmer, 5/12/42; M. Lyon, *Mount Holyoke Female Seminary*, September, 1835, Old South Leaflets, No. 145, pp 425–35, n.d.

14. Shepard, "Reference History of Wheaton College" (Unpublished manuscript, 1931), p. 4; Trustees Minutes: 10/18/36.

15. Paine, *E. B. Wheaton*, p. 81.

16. Principals: Cowles: Speech at semi-centennial celebration, 1885.

17. Boas, *Woman's Education Begins*, pp. 6–9; see also, for example, passages in L. Hatch, *The History of Bowdoin College* (Portland, ME: Loring Short and Harmon, 1927), p. 11; R. Guild, *Early History of Brown University . . . 1756–1791* (Providence: Snow and Farnham, 1897); P. Monroe, ed., *A Cyclopedia of Education* (New York: MacMillan, 1913), "Seminary Grants"; M. Newcomer, *A Century of Higher Education of American Women* (New York: Harper, 1959), p. 11; E. Hitchcock, *The Power of Christian Benevolence: Illustrated in the Life and Labors of Mary Lyon*, 3rd ed. (Northampton, MA: Hopkins, Bridgman, 1852), "Z. Grant and M. Lyon to Trustees of Ipswich Female Seminary," 2/17/31, p. 159; "M. Lyon to Miss W.," 8/1/34, p. 198.

18. The original cost of the building was $1,142. Subsequently it survived several moves and many uses, until it arrived at its present location on Howard Street and was remodeled into two faculty apartments. LMW, "Day Book"; Anniversaries: 75th anniversary: Draft of speech by S. V. Cole; Trustees Minutes: 10/1/35; 10/18/36.

19. Sklar, "Mount Holyoke," in Berkin and Norton, *Women of America*, pp. 184–85; S. R. MacLean, "Mary Lyon," in *Notable American Women* (Cambridge MA: Belknap Press, 1971), vol. II, p. 444.

20. MacLean, "Mary Lyon," in *Notable American Women*, vol. II, p. 444.

21. Sklar, "Mount Holyoke," in Berkin and Norton, *Women of America*, p. 182; also 188–90; see also E. Hitchcock, *Christian Benevolence*, pp. 262–66; B. Gilchrist, *The Life of Mary Lyon* (Boston: Houghton Mifflin, 1910), pp. 69–83.

22. Green, *Lyon and Mount Holyoke*, pp. 55–56.

23. Ibid., pp. 83–89; Boas, *Woman's Education Begins*, pp. 35–36.

24. Green, *Lyon and Mount Holyoke,* pp. 113–14; Hitchcock, *Christian Benevolence*, pp. 187–89.

25. Principals: Cowles: Cowles to EBW, 6/6/60.

26. Lyon, Mary: Correspondence: Lyon to LMW, 7/8/34; Shepard, "Reference History," pp. 8–10.

27. Lyon, Mary: Correspondence: Lyon to LMW, 8/18/34.

28. Ibid.: Lyon to Trustees, 9/25/34. See also Lyon to LMW, 12/23/34.

29. Mount Holyoke College Archives. A printed circular by Mary Lyon, 9/8/34, proposed a new school "similar in character to the Ipswich Seminary." Another document, *Mount Holyoke Female Seminary* (Sept., 1835) stated, "Mount Holyoke Female Seminary will take the Ipswich Female Seminary for its literary standard." And again, in 1837, a pamphlet issued by the Trustees of Mount Holyoke entitled *General View of the Principles and Design of Mount Holyoke Female Seminary*, stated: "General course of study and the general character of instruction is to be like that at Ipswich." For a general discussion of the Wheaton Seminary curriculum, see ch. 7.

30. Trustees Minutes: 11/17/34. The median age for entering freshmen at Harvard in 1810 was 15.5; by 1845 it had reached 17. See S. E. Morison, *Three Centuries at Harvard, 1636–1936* (Cambridge, MA: Harvard University Press, 1946), pp. 183–84. Bowdoin College admitted a fourteen year old freshman in 1825. See Hatch, *Bowdoin*, p. 73.

31. Larcom, *Semi-Centennial*, p. 13; Principals: Cowles: Memorandum to EBW, 6/6/60.

32. At approximately the same time Mary Lyon turned down an offer from the trustees of Abbot Academy to take direction of their faltering institution. See S. Lloyd, *A Singular School: Abbot Academy, 1828–1973* (Andover, MA: Phillips Academy, 1979), p. 41.

33. Green, *Lyon and Mount Holyoke*, pp. 120–23.

34. Mount Holyoke Trustees, *Principles*, p. 3; or, as the same document stated on page 8, "of supplying our country with well qualified female teachers."

35. Paine, *E. B. Wheaton*, pp. 70–71; Boas, *Woman's Education Begins*, p. 48; Wheaton Histories, Seminary: Reminiscenses: Memorandum by M. Merrill, n.d.; Seminary: Park to Palmer, 5/12/42.

36. The domestic work program was also justified as providing opportunities for daily exercise, for sociability, and for generation of concern for the welfare of all. See Mount Holyoke Trustees, *Principles*, p. 6–7; Hitchcock, *Christian Benevolence*, pp. 198–99, 253, 291, 302–4; Green, *Lyon and Mount Holyoke*, pp. 114, 181; A. Cole, *A Hundred Years of Mount Holyoke College: The Evolution of an Educational Ideal* (New Haven: Yale University Press, 1940), pp. 39–43; Woody, *Women's Education*, I, p. 416; Thwing, *Higher Education*, pp. 210–11.

37. Paine, *E. B. Wheaton*, pp. 70–71; Wheaton Histories, Seminary: Seminary: Park to Palmer, 5/12/42; Reminiscences: Memorandum by M. Merrill.

38. Hitchcock, *Christian Benevolence*, Lyon to C. Beecher, 7/1/36, p. 226; also M. Lansing, ed., *Mary Lyon Through Her Letters* (Boston: Books, Inc., 1937), p. 196.

39. Hitchcock, *Christian Benevolence*, Lyon to C. Beecher, 7/1/36, p. 226.

40. Mount Holyoke College Archives, Printed circular re proposed Seminary, 9/8/34; Hitchcock, *Christian Benevolence*, Lyon to Grant, 2/24/33, pp. 175–76; S. Stow, *History of Mount Holyoke Seminary, South Hadley, Massachusetts, during its First Half Century, 1837–1887* (South Hadley, MA: Mount Holyoke Female Seminary, 1887), pp. 48–60; Green, *Lyon and Mount Holyoke*, p. 88.

41. The Town of Norton contributed $50.00 for the purchase of "philosophical [scientific] apparatus" shortly after Wheaton was founded. But aside from this gift, "all needs were met by the Wheaton purse." Boas, *Woman's Education Begins*, p. 39.

42. Ibid., p. 38.

43. Wheaton Histories, Seminary: Seminary: Park to Palmer, 5/12/42; Boas, *Woman's Education Begins*, p. 49; Green, *Lyon and Mount Holyoke*, pp. 6–13. The difference in emphasis seen in the views of Eliza Wheaton and Mary Lyon reflected a general debate regarding women's education at that time, a debate that included such outstanding educators as Catherine Beecher and Emma Willard.

44. General Files: 1835–36: Hannah Richmond Notebook.

45. Lyon, Mary: Correspondence.

46. General Files: 1835–36: Hannah Richmond Notebook.

47. See Paine, *E. B. Wheaton*, passim; Hitchcock, *Christian Benevolence*, pp. 283–85; Green, *Lyon and Mount Holyoke*, pp. 19, 29.

48. Lyon, Mary: Correspondence: Lyon to EBW and LMW, 2/25/35.

49. Mount Holyoke College Archives. Lyon to Caldwell, 2/25/35; see also Green, *Lyon and Mount Holyoke*, p. 165.

50. Lyon, Mary: Correspondence: Lyon to EBW and LMW, 2/25/35.

51. Ibid.: Lyon to EBW and LMW, 3/4/35; Green, *Lyon and Mount Holyoke*, pp. 165–66.

52. See ch. 1. Also Wheaton Family: original draft of announcmement of 3/1/35; Lyon, Mary: Correspondence: Lyon to LMW, 12/23/34; Paine, *E. B. Wheaton*, pp. 77–80; Mount Holyoke Trustees, *Principles*, p. 6.

53. Principals: Cowles: Cowles to EBW, 6/6/60.

54. Cost of the boarding house was $5,735. It accommodated forty students and three teachers. LMW, "Day Book." See also Trustees Minutes, 10/1/35; 11/17/35; General Files: 1834–35; Anniversaries: Cole Draft Speech for 75th anniversary; Shepard, "Reference History," p. 27. Room and board for the first year cost $1.67 per week, "including washing and lights." See C. Clewes, *Wheaton Through The Years: 1835–1960* (Norton, MA: Wheaton College, 1960), p. 3.

55. Shepard, "Reference History," p. 54. For more information regarding Mary Lyon at Wheaton, see pp. 53–59; also General Files: 1835–1836: M. Robinson letter, n.d.; and composition by Mary Paine, "Three Weeks in Arithmetic"; 1836–37: Agnes Wardrop letters.

56. General Files: 1836–37: Mary Robinson letter, n.d.; Mount Holyoke Archives, Lyon to Caldwell, 4/3/36; Paine, *E. B. Wheaton*, p. 91.

57. General Files: 1835–36: P. Lewis to sister, 2/19/37.

58. Mount Holyoke College Archives. Lyon to Grant, 3/13?/37; 3/17/37; "Memorabilia of Mary Lyon-Presented by Amelia Woodward Truesdall, Class of 1858," unpublished manuscript, statement of P. Woods Curtis, p. 144.

59. Ibid., "Lyon Memorabilia," P. Woods Curtis statement, p 144.

60. The eight students were: senior Persis Woods; middle class members Hannah Brigham, Lucy Brigham, and Elizabeth Mann; junior class members Mary Caldwell, Rachel Hathaway, Louisa Packard, and Elizabeth Tyler. See also Boas, *Woman's Education Begins*, p. 182; Cole, *Hundred Years*, p. 35; E. Cunliffe, "History of Wheaton College and the Class of 1868," unpublished manuscript, pp. 42–43.

61. General Files: 1837–38: Blackinton to Hodges, 12/7/37; also enrollment data. See also Principals: Palmer; Shepard, "Reference History," p. 190.

62. Principals: Cowles: EBW to Caldwell, 12/2/37.

63. Ibid.

3

Perils and Prosperity
1838–1876

IN 1840 THERE were 1,446 private academies and seminaries operating in Massachusetts, of which 78, Wheaton among them, were incorporated. Only if an educational institution held property or other fiscal assets in its own right was it necessary to obtain a charter of incorporation from the state. The many academies and seminaries that had no permanent endowment were not under any obligation to obtain a charter, or for that matter to have a board of trustees.[1]

The fact that a board of trustees for Wheaton Female Seminary was established well before the institution opened its doors to students indicates Judge Wheaton's intention from the outset to endow the Seminary with land and buildings, and ultimately to seek a charter. But the need to apply to the Commonwealth for a formal act of incorporation did not become pressing until October, 1835, when Judge Wheaton proposed to the trustees that he convey to them the seminary building that had been constructed in the summer of 1834. The trustees initially submitted the matter to their Prudential Committee for review. However, one year later, on October 18, 1836, the Board followed the Committee's recommendation and accepted the deed of gift that Judge Wheaton had drawn up the previous March. Not coincidentally, at the same meeting they voted to petition the legislature for an Act of Incorporation.[2]

The incorporation was speedily obtained, passing the House on March 9 and the Senate on March 10, 1837. For reasons unknown, the formal name on the document was Norton Female Seminary. Since the Board of Trustees in November, 1834, had chosen the name Wheaton Female Seminary, and the deed conveying the seminary building used the same name, the new designation must have resulted from some clerical error made during the incorporation process in Boston. The discrepancy, however, apparently did not bother the trustees, for no effort was made to rectify it until the Board's fall meeting in 1838. Even then, the decision to obtain a new charter was brought on primarily by fiscal needs rather than by concerns about the name.[3]

The original act had limited the power of the Board to hold personal and real property to $10,000 in each instance. In terms of personal prop-

erty this limitation remained adequate, but the deeding of the new boarding house to the Board of Trustees in early 1838 brought the real estate
holdings of the Seminary perilously close, if not over, the limit. Thus the
new act of incorporation, which was obtained on March 16, 1839, not
only changed the name to Wheaton Female Seminary, but also expanded
the permissible value of holdings to $30,000 in each category. These
new limitations would be sufficient for the needs of the institution for
the next fifty years.[4]

The crisis generated by the departure of Eunice Caldwell in October,
1837, lasted approximately six months. Unable to find a suitable person
to replace her, the trustees were forced to appoint one of the teachers,
Susan Palmer, to administer the Seminary during the winter term. It was
during that term, when enrollment had dipped to eighteen students, that
Mrs. Wheaton wrote frantically to Miss Caldwell pleading with her to
return. However, with spring came rejuvenation. A new principal, Eliza
Knight, was secured from Ipswich Seminary, and enrollment for the
summer term totalled 48 students. The following winter 29 pupils attended, and in the summer of 1839 the Seminary was overwhelmed with
75 students. It was over a decade before such numbers were attained
again, but even though enrollment dipped alarmingly in the mid-1840s,
not until the 1890s would the future of the Seminary appear as perilous
as it had in that dark winter of 1837–1838.[5]

In 1839, Wheaton finally produced its first degree recipients.[6] Nothing
attests better to the rigorous standards and demands of the academic program than the fact that it was more than four years after the Seminary
opened its doors before any student completed the prescribed course of
study. One of the four who received degrees, Julia Pond, had completed
her work in four terms. The others had attended five or more terms, not
all of them consecutively. The record shows that during the first five
years of its existence, the Seminary enrolled a large number of students
who attended in three or even four academic years without receiving a
degree.[7]

The reasons for this were several. Many parents, of course, chose to
enroll their daughters only for two to three terms, believing that the
amount of education provided during that time should more than suffice.
Some students chose to spend part of their time taking courses in music,
drawing, Latin or French, which were available at extra cost but did not
count in the regular degree program. A number received offers of teaching positions before they completed the required course of study. But the
most important factor was that Wheaton, like Ipswich and Mount Holyoke, had a rigorous system of examination requirements both for admission into classes, and for advancement to the next level. It does not

appear that students were asked to withdraw because of academic deficiencies; however, a student whose performance was inadequate would find that she was prohibited from advancement to senior class status in one or more areas of the curriculum. It was through this procedure, more than by admissions standards per se, that Wheaton made sure that those who were admitted out of the primary studies program into upper class standing were serious, able and academically qualified students.

The years between 1838 and 1850 can best be categorized as ones of stabilization and survival. Enrollments fluctuated, morale soared and plummeted. But overall there was growth and, as the century reached its midpoint, the Seminary could point with pride to what it had accomplished. A new wood-frame Seminary Hall, so sturdily constructed that 130 years later the Wheaton trustees would remodel it in anticipation of many further years of use, lent an aura of permanence to the developing institution, as did a small gymnasium, constructed in 1844.

But the prosperity indicated by the growth in physical plant, while real in one sense, was illusory in another, for it did not mean that the Seminary had generated the income needed to built these new facilities. In many years, though not all, the income from student fees did serve to cover normal operating expenses, but both the new Seminary Hall and the gymnasium were built with special infusions of Wheaton family money. The boarding house was leased to a private individual, who in turn collected the charges for room and board and was required to operate the boarding house and pay his rent out of that income.[8] Tuition fees went for payment of teaching staff and incidental expenses, such as obtaining a library collection and purchasing pianos.[9] It is interesting to read Trustees Minutes in 1842 that describe the fiscal condition of the Seminary as satisfactory at the same time the Treasurer reported a positive balance of $12.62. Similarly, the balance in July, 1844, was $357.45; a year later it was $173.44; and in July, 1847, a negative balance was avoided by the receipt of a $500.00 gift from Laban Morey Wheaton. There was obviously no surplus capital for physical plant or grounds improvement. Whenever this did occur it was due to the Wheaton family's willingness to supervise construction and pay the bills. Although occasional small gifts were received, aside from one abortive short-lived effort to raise $2000 by general subscription it does not appear that any attempt was made to obtain money from any source other than the Wheatons.[10]

Perhaps the greatest problem the young Seminary faced, however, was an inability to retain teaching and administrative staff for any length of time. Between 1838 and 1850 five different women served Wheaton as Principal, and on one occasion in the winter of 1846–47, the trustees were forced to repeat the procedure of 1837–38 and appoint a teacher as interim Principal for a term.[11]

When Eliza Knight agreed to take over the position of Principal at

Wheaton in the spring of 1838, she brought with her as a teacher her prize pupil from Ipswich Seminary, Martha Vose. Thus it was only natural that Miss Vose should succeed Eliza Knight in 1840. Martha Sawyer, one of the first class of Wheaton graduates in 1839, remained at the Seminary as a teacher and was chosen in turn to replace Miss Vose in 1842, despite the fact that it was only three years since she had been a pupil. Her tenure lasted through the fall term of 1846, when she was compelled to resign for reasons of ill-health. Following the ensuing winter term, Elizabeth Cate, a teacher in the school of Reverend Hubbard Winslow in Boston was retained. Under her administration the Seminary, which had declined in enrollment and reputation during the tenure of Miss Sawyer, made a remarkable recovery and it was with real regret that the Board of Trustees accepted her resignation in 1849. Their regret only deepened as it became apparent that her successor, Margaret Mann, was not all they had hoped for. The result was the sudden, and more likely than not forced, resignation of Miss Mann in the summer of 1850.[12] Her successor, Mrs. Caroline Metcalf, finally brought administrative stability to Wheaton. She remained for more than a quarter century, and her tenure constituted a completely different era in the history of the Seminary.

Except in the instance of Margaret Mann, one cannot blame the Board of Trustees for the rapid administrative turnover. If anything, the Board was more reluctant in acquiescing to change than it should have been. Probably it was unwise to place women as young as Martha Vose and Martha Sawyer in charge of a school whose pupils included some nearly the same age as they were. The job was an exhausting one, particularly for Martha Sawyer, yet when she sought to resign prior to the summer term in 1846 the Trustees insisted that she take a leave of absence instead.[13] When in October she informed them that she would be unable to continue for the winter term, something the Board must have long suspected, they had no Principal in mind. It is hardly surprising that when Elizabeth Cate assumed the position in the spring of 1847 she found an institution, as she put it, that "was not in a prosperous condition, its numbers had decreased, its prestige was declining."[14] This was a fact that Martha Sawyer had herself recognized when she commented in her letter of resignation that "the influence of the Institution is greatly limited, and its growth retarded by the ill health and absence of its Principal."[15]

All of Wheaton's first six principals married ministers, either immediately upon leaving Wheaton or within two or three years. The attraction was logical—ministers, well educated themselves, sought young women who could provide intellectual as well as domestic companionship. Moreover, one of the prime requirements for heading Wheaton Seminary was a deep religious commitment on the part of the Principal, for the Seminary, though non-sectarian in outlook, was deeply committed to

the concepts of Christian moral, spiritual, and educational training and
leadership.

Equally noteworthy is the fact that, with the exception of Margaret
Mann, all the principals from Eunice Caldwell to Elizabeth Cate maintained strong ties with the Seminary after their departure as well as close
personal friendships with Eliza Wheaton. Like Mrs. Wheaton they all
lived for many years, and in 1885 all, including Miss Mann, were able
to return and address the gathering at the fiftieth anniversary celebration
of Wheaton's founding. Three—Eliza Knight, Martha Sawyer and Elizabeth Cate later lived part of their lives in Norton, and their husbands,
Samuel Beane, Franklin Holmes, and William Barrows all served terms
as trustees of the Seminary. A fourth, Martha Vose, married Alfred Emerson, son of Joseph Emerson, the famous educator of Mary Lyon. Her
husband would become one of Wheaton's most influential trustees; two
daughters would graduate from Wheaton and teach there; one would become a trustee herself; the family would be memorialized by having the
main dining facility of the college named in their honor.

In retrospect one gets the distinct impression that the period 1838–
1850 was one of "marking time" in the history of Wheaton's development. The Seminary survived, and of course for a new school that was
an accomplishment in itself. But prosperity and real success eluded it.
That it continued at all was probably due more than anything else to the
leadership and financial resources provided publicly by Laban Morey
Wheaton and privately, behind the scenes, by his wife Eliza. The two
most important long-term developments for the Seminary were the result, it would appear, of their initiative as well as their financial munificence. These were the erection of the gymnasium in 1844 and the
replacement of the old seminary building with a new Seminary Hall in
1849.

The decision to construct a free standing building for the sole purpose
of providing an indoor gymnasium for Wheaton students is particularly
intriguing, for it appears that no other educational institution in the
United States, male or female, had undertaken such a step prior to
Wheaton's doing so. Outdoor gymnasiums, which essentially were open
fields with gymnastic apparatus placed on them, had been in existence
for some time. Harvard had for a period in the 1820s allowed one of its
dining rooms to be used for indoor gymnastic and calisthentic activity,
but student enthusiasm for this project had quickly waned. There is no
record in the Wheaton Board of Trustees minutes of their ever discussing
the erection of a gymnasium—yet we know that in the summer and fall
of 1844 Laban Morey Wheaton paid for and supervised its construction,
which he specifically labeled as being a "Gymnatium" in his day book.
Why the Wheatons decided to build a structure specifically for this purpose when all other institutions at that time used corridors, or classrooms
with desks pushed back, we do not know. But in some sense this action

symbolized the commitment to leadership in the area of physical conditioning and athletic activity for women that has characterized Wheaton
during much of its history.[16]

The decision to replace the original Seminary Hall with a larger, finer
structure was a much more obvious one. Miss Cate brought to the principalship a degree of maturity and experience that her immediate predecessors had not had. During her relatively brief term in office a number
of curricular changes were introduced, and enrollment and teaching staff
both increased. It also became painfully apparent that if the Seminary
were to grow and prosper it would need better teachng facilities, as well
as some sort of space specifically set aside for a library and for work in
the sciences. Therefore, in July, 1848, the Board of Trustees gratefully
accepted a gift of $10,000 from Mr. Wheaton and immediately ap-
pointed a Committee on Repairs and Grounds for the purpose of preparing plans for erecting a "new Academy Building."[17]

Two months later the committee reported that it was "expedient to
proceed to the erection of a new Seminary building which shall cost not
more than four thousand dollars."[18] Plans were sought, and in November, 1848, a building committee was established and authorized to spend
up to $5,000 in erecting a new seminary hall, to be placed immediately
adjacent to the old building, which in turn would be removed as soon as
the new structure was ready for occupancy.[19]

As had been the case with the first seminary hall, the boarding house,
and the gymnasium, oversight of the construction was left in the hands
of Laban Morey Wheaton, despite the fact that he was nominally only
one of a three-person building committee. The final cost was $624 over
the allocated $5,000. The building was dedicated on December 27, 1849
(the Seminary was in session) with formal ceremonies that began in the
original hall erected in 1834, from which students, faculty and trustees
solemnly processed to the new structure for the conclusion of the program. Designed in Greek Revival style, the building included five or six
small classrooms on the first floor and a single large assembly hall on
the second level. It would serve as the main academic building for the
next thirty years.[20]

The fall of 1850 ushered in what may properly be called the Metcalf
era in Wheaton history. Caroline C. Metcalf brought to the principalship
both the firm hand and the creative leadership Wheaton had long been
seeking. Widowed after only one year of marriage, she apparently never
was tempted again in that direction. The result was that Wheaton, after
experiencing six Principals and two Head Teachers in its first fifteen
years, now entered a period of uninterrupted administration by one individual that was to stretch over more than a quarter century.

Seminary Hall, erected in 1849, with the Gymnasium, built in 1844.

Caroline Metcalf was a strong-willed woman. Deeply religious, she encouraged students to seek a personal religious experience that would result in a serious commitment to Christ. At least once, in the early 1860s, the Seminary underwent an epidemic of religious enthusiasm and soul-searching aimed at obtaining a "second conversion" or "sanctification"—all this part of a general revivalist movement sweeping New England at the time. As Mrs. Metcalf commented early in her tenure: "What I desire to see in the Seminary is aggressive Christian work, having definitely in view the salvation of souls."[21]

Yet she was nothing if not a tough, conscientious, able administrator. She soon established her dominance over the Board of Trustees; if all else failed, she was not above using the threat of resignation as a means of gaining their acquiescence to her desires. Twice she used this technique: the first time to obtain changes in the management of the boarding house as well as a personal vacation for a term; the second to demand an increase in salary for herself and the hiring of her niece, Ellen Plimpton, as full-time instructor in Physical Education.[22]

Students viewed her with a mixture of awe, fear, and respect, as well they might a woman who, when faced with a student who had become hysterical, calmly seized the pitcher of cold water found in each student's room and threw it over her, remarking, "Girls never have hysterics but once where I am."[23] She needed, as one of her teachers put it, "but a glance at a face, a handwriting, a companionship—any trifle,—to recognize mischief as readily as Cuvier could an animal from one bone, Agassiz a fish from one scale."[24]

Large lecture hall and assembly room, Seminary Hall, 1850s.

Mrs. Metcalf was famous for her sharp tongue. "You must learn, young ladies," she told a group of students being sent to scavenge the lawn for peanut shells carelessly dropped, "that you can't have all creation for your slopbowl."[25] It is generally agreed that what she lacked in diplomacy and tact, she made up in commitment, energy, and ability. "Eminently fitted for her position, she was quick and decided, peremptory but kind, helpful to those who had come there for work, unsparing in her sarcasm towards those who were negligent or indifferent," wrote Caroline Stickney Creevey, a student during the Metcalf years.[26]

Her greatest strength, however, was her ability to find and retain superior teachers. Committed totally to educational growth and innovation, she sought teachers who were not constrained by tradition or custom, and when she found them, gave them the greatest possible latitude as to teaching methods as long as the final results met the exacting standards she demanded. Unwilling to tolerate mediocrity, she had no compunction about terminating faculty appointments after only one term if she believed the teaching to be inadequate or ineffective. Yet she did not demand conformity in outlook and approach, and this freedom extended to a degree even into the area of religious matters. She was willing to tolerate on her staff disparate personalities, "women with whom she was personally neither in tune nor touch."[27] The result was that teachers such as Lucy Larcom, Ann Carter, Mary Cragin, Sarah Cole, and Clara Pike developed programs in literature, mathematics, and science that became widely recognized for their creativity in teaching and excellence in standards.[28]

Caroline Cutler Matcalf,
Principal, 1850-1876.

Standards indeed remained high. When Mrs. Metcalf arrived, the regular academic program embraced a three-year course of study, although the catalogue noted that many students would "require more than one year on the studies of a single class."[29] By 1854–55, the regular course included four years, and in 1870–71 a preparatory year was added as well. The result was that only the best, most ambitious students, with parents who were both willing and able to support extended endeavors, received the diploma. The average size of the graduating classes during the Metcalf era was seven, and of the six classes that numbered ten or more members, five occurred between 1868 and 1876, when the total enrollment was considerably less than in earlier years.

Overall, the Metcalf years also saw considerable growth and subsequent stabilization in the student population of the Seminary. During the 1850s enrollment achieved record numbers, so sizeable that they were not attained again until the first decade of the twentieth century. The peak year was 1854–55, in which 226 different students attended Wheaton, with 138 enrolled in the fall term, 128 in the spring, and 151 in the summer. While the whole number of students annually attending declined by nearly a hundred during the next twenty years, the enrollment by term for the most part remained between 100 and 125. In fact, one of the striking changes was the decline in the seasonal fluctuation of term enrollments, the deviation by the early 1860s being no more than ten to fifteen students. Fewer and fewer Wheaton students were sent by their parents for only part of the year, a fact that must have made fiscal and staff planning on the part of Mrs. Metcalf and the trustees a good deal easier.

An explanation for these changes in enrollment patterns can be found by examining the general development of public education during these years. Public high schools in the United States had their beginning in Massachusetts as the result of an 1827 state law that required towns with over 500 families to establish such a school. Compliance, however, came very gradually. There were only 18 public high schools in Massachusetts by 1840 and the number grew slowly to 47 in 1850. Fifteen years later the total had reached 108, but still only 68% of those communities required to have high schools had complied with the law. But by 1875, 202 public high schools existed in the state, including forty in towns not required to have them, while only six communities that met the census requirements had failed to comply. These new schools offered a viable, far less costly, alternative to private education beyond the district or grammar schools, which for so many years had been all that was available in the public sector.[30]

However, the slowness with which public officials implemented the 1827 legislative mandate meant that public demand for education during the 1840s and 1850s vastly outstripped the pace at which high schools were being established. A multitude of private seminaries and academics filled that gap, presenting variations of educational quality almost as great as their numbers. The best academies, however, continued to provide solid training for entrance into college, while the leading seminaries supplied young women with much of the college-level education that was not available to them anywhere else. But in the long run, competition from the public sector proved disastrous for many a private school. The number of incorporated academics and seminaries decreased from 78 in 1840 to 63 in 1875. Even more striking was the decline in unincorporated private schools, academies and seminaries, which fell from 1,368 in 1840 to 369 in 1875.[31]

For Wheaton, however, the growth of high schools had only minimal impact. In fact in many ways it may have been beneficial, for it was probably the availability of public high school education that led to a rapid decline in the number of students who attended only one or two terms of the three-term year. By the mid-1860s, young women who came to Wheaton tended to commit themselves for a year at a time, thus keeping enrollments for all terms at over 100 though the whole number of students attending was not nearly as great as during the mid-1850s. In other words, the more casual student remained in the local school system.

Not all high schools were required to have the same curriculum; many offered only two or three-year programs rather than the full four. Even the best rarely approximated more than the first two years of Wheaton's four-year seminary curriculum. Thus, more serious students, wishing to continue beyond what their local high school provided, turned to Wheaton as the leading institution for women's education in southeastern Massachusetts. Yet at the same time, the Seminary also continued to attract students from the many small rural towns of the area, including

Norton, that had no high school at all. It was in response to the resultant great diversity of preparation among its applicants that Wheaton expanded its offerings in 1870 to include a preparatory class prior to the regular four-year course of study. The official seminary curriculum continued to approximate in its final years the curriculum in the "English branches" and modern languages offered at colleges and universities open only to men.[32]

There was also a new challenge looming on the horizon, but its impact on Wheaton during Mrs. Metcalf's years was not noticeable. In 1865 Vassar College in Poughkeepsie, New York, opened its doors as the first college for women in what may be loosely defined as the New England area. An examination of its collegiate curriculum indicates considerable similarity between the last two and one-half years of Wheaton's course offerings and Vassar's program in the freshman, sophomore, and parts of the junior year.[33] Clearly Vassar's program went beyond what Wheaton offered, but its existence (at a goodly distance from Norton) apparently did not pose any real threat to Wheaton's image as an institution of higher education for women. Much more important would be the opening of Wellesley and Smith Colleges in 1875, but their impact on Wheaton would only be felt by Mrs. Metcalf's successors.

The increased demand for women's education, coupled with Wheaton's growing reputation for excellence, put extreme pressure on the Seminary to provide adequate boarding facilities. The result was the addition in 1851 of two wings to the original boarding house, designed to accommodate several additional teachers plus twenty more students. However, within a year the number of additional students had increased to twenty-five, so that the boarding house now took in 65 rather than the planned 60 students. This was accomplished by having an occasional student room with an accommodating teacher, and by allowing three students to occupy some of the larger rooms, thus breaking Mary Lyon's rule of only two students per room.[34]

Even that was not enough. In 1853 Laban Morey Wheaton donated an additional $10,000 to the Seminary and immediately was authorized by the trustees to expend it by erecting a new free-standing boarding house. The building was completed in 1857 and then connected to the old boarding establishment, thus earning itself the name of "West Wing," though a wing it really was not. The boarding house now consisted of two distinct, but connected, houses, one of which had two wings attached to the back of it, accommodating in all 95 students and the teaching staff. To this structure was added, in 1868, the original seminary building. Since its removal to Howard Street following the construction of the new Seminary Hall in 1849, the old Seminary Hall had served for a time as a straw hat factory, then as a tenement house with two apartments, and finally as a meeting hall for the Sons of Temperance. Upon its return to the seminary grounds and attachment to the westerly of the two rear wings of the boarding house it was outfitted to become the laundry for the Seminary. To all of this an indoor toilet system was added in the 1870s.[35]

The expansion of the boarding facilities led also to a change in their management. For several years Mrs. Metcalf had complained regularly about the food, heating, and preparation of rooms prior to the start of terms. "I have no sympathy with those who live to eat," she wrote in November, 1855, "and when there is no just cause for complaining, I can put a stop to it, but when we have poor bread, I cannot say to the young ladies, 'Your complaints are groundless.' "[36] The trustees, understandably, were not anxious to terminate a system which not only relieved them of management responsibility of the boarding house, but also generated a rental figure equivalent to $.25 per student per term. However, so insistent were Mrs. Metcalf and her teaching staff that in May, 1856, using as justification the anticipated addition of the new boarding house, the Board of Trustees voted to hire the existing tenant and his wife as steward and matron rather than rent to them, in hope that removal of a profit motive would solve the problems of quality. This compromise did not suit Mrs. Metcalf and the next year, faced with her threatened resignation, the Board capitulated, and agreed to seek new personnel for the position. The basic authority of the Principal over the administration of the boarding facilities had been established once and for all.[37]

With the exception of a few years in the 1850s, these accommodations proved sufficient to house the vast majority of those attending Wheaton as boarding students in any given semester. The enrollment of the middle fifties taxed the boarding capacities of the private homes in Norton

Wheaton Female Seminary, 1860.

Center to the utmost, and the temptation to build even more dormitory facilities must have been great. But in a sense the fiscal well ran dry, though as it turned out, only temporarily. The national bank panic of 1857–58, triggered initially by over-expansion of investments in railroad construction, created a short, but very serious, nation-wide fiscal crisis, which was reflected in a brief, but severe decline in enrollment at the Seminary. This in turn led the Board of Trustees to reduce the size of the faculty and limit the range of offerings in music, French, and calisthenics, a decision vehemently protested by Mrs. Metcalf. But most important of all was Laban Morey Wheaton's statement to the trustees that he wished to be paid back the $5,085.16 that the new boarding house had cost over the $10,000 he had originally given for that purpose. The note would run without interest as long as it was paid up within five years, a term he later extended. The trustees readily assented, but clearly were apprehensive, for they suddenly found their source of extra revenue not only cut off, but the institution faced with the need to generate surplus income of its own in order to pay back this unanticipated debt.[38]

Fortunately, the decline in enrollment was short lived. Student attendance in the 1860s, despite the turmoil of the Civil War, remained steady and even increased somewhat as the war progressed. While the loan was never entirely paid off, it had been reduced to $3500 at the time of Laban Morey Wheaton's death in January, 1865. The remainder of the debt was forgiven by Eliza Wheaton shortly afterwards. Though she would not resume substantial giving to the Seminary until the mid-1870s, never again would the Wheaton family's fiscal support take any form other than outright gifts.[39]

Another major addition to the resources of the Seminary during the Metcalf years was the gift in 1874 from Mrs. Wheaton of a telescope made by the famed London firm of John Browning. At a cost of $261.81, a small observatory, labeled the "Cheesebox" by the students, was built to house it. The growth of the library collection also necessitated its removal to the gymnasium in 1869; gymnastics and calisthenics classes were relegated to a classroom in Seminary Hall.[40]

During the 1850s, the trustees for the first time organized themselves in a more formal fashion than that initially established at their first meeting in 1834. The stimulus for this was the erection and acceptance of the new Seminary Building in 1849. The trustees suddenly discovered that they had never formally accepted the Acts of Incorporation granted by the legislature in 1837 and 1839. This was voted in March, 1851, along with a new set of by-laws creating a corporation and establishing five-year terms for the members of the Board of Trustees, two to be elected each year. Subsequently, in 1858, the Board, after what were apparently some rather intense deliberations, passed a series of resolutions drafted by Rev. Franklin Holmes, the husband of former principal Martha Sawyer, establishing four permanent committees, each responsible for administering one aspect of the life of the Seminary, each required to report at the three annual meetings of the full Board. These committees, Instruction, Boarding, Repairs, and Finance, regularized the work of the Board and made the continued smooth functioning of its operation easier when the trustees found themselves forced to take on more responsibility after Mr. Wheaton's death in 1865.[41]

During the last years of the Metcalf administration a new organization made its appearance—the Wheaton Alumnae Association. Plans for the association were formulated in the fall of 1869 by members of the Class of 1870, and the first meeting of the fledgling organization was held at the time of graduation exercises on July 13, 1870. In general the Association concerned itself only with holding a social reunion each year at commencement time. Limited to graduates, principals, teachers, and Mrs. Wheaton, its numbers remained necessarily small for many years. Mrs. Metcalf was elected its first President, and it is therefore not surprising that on her retirement in 1876 the Association collected money to establish an endowed scholarship fund in her name.[42]

This was the first such fund in Wheaton's history, though not, in a sense, the first scholarships. Since 1840 the Seminary had remitted tuition to daughters of clergymen and missionaries, a practice that would continue until 1906. In addition, students from Norton had been granted a partial remission of tuition since 1850. In 1876, this meant a charge of

Founders of the Alumnae Association in 1870, ten of fourteen graduates returned for their 50th reunion in 1920.

$11.00 per term rather than the normal $15.00. In 1877, there are records of remission of fees to some students in return for their undertaking general light janitorial work in Seminary Hall. Finally, in 1880 Mrs. Wheaton undertook to add six $100.00 scholarships annually for students who otherwise would be unable to continue their education. These funds apparently were paid out of pocket, rather than endowed with any permanent principal.[43]

The 1870s also witnessed an educational experiment long forgotten in Wheaton's history, but one which, if continued, would undoubtedly have altered the course of its development more than any other possibly could have. The July, 1872, issue of the student literary magazine, *Rushlight,* records that Mrs. Metcalf had tutored the son of the Steward and Horsemanship Teacher, Harry Cobb, plus a "young lady and gentleman" from Norton, in her office every morning. This experiment had been a great success, so much so in fact, "that with the approval of the trustees the halls of Wheaton will probably soon be opened wide to both sexes."[44]

Such enthusiasm hardly fitted the situation, but in 1873–74 Harry Cobb was allowed to enroll formally in regular courses in French and drawing, and in the fall of 1874 Wheaton began a period of four years in which a substantial number of young men from the town of Norton were registered in the regular program of the Seminary, several of them advancing from the preparatory level through the junior and junior middle classes. None went beyond the second year, which is understandable, since completion of that program would generally have been enough for them to gain admission into any college or university in the country. These students were listed in the Wheaton catalogue, but, unlike the women, only with initials—no first names. Occasionally however, in the sublistings of students taking French, Latin, or drawing, first names were inadvertently inserted, so that a Frank, George, Harry, or Laban suddenly appeared among the many female names listed.[45]

In 1874–75, five young men attended full-time and one part-time; the next year four were full-time students. In 1876–77 enrollment increased to six full-time and two part-time, and in 1877–78 the numbers were five and one. In subsequent years, however, male students were few, with single persons attending full-time in five of the next nine years, plus two part-time in one year. Clearly the ending of this phase in Wheaton's history was almost as sharp and sudden as its beginning.

What prompted this coeducational interlude and how serious was it? The evidence is at best very slim, and circumstantial at that. Nowhere in the Trustees Minutes is there the slightest mention of the presence of young men in the classroom. In a letter written on March 7, 1875, a student commented that Wheaton, "is not a Female Seminary any longer, for they take small boys."[46] Even more interesting was the sudden offer made by Eliza Wheaton in April, 1873 to the Board of Trustees to give $12,000 toward new or enlarged boarding facilities. The trustees deferred action, but three months later they did pass a rather cryptic resolution to the effect that "steps be immediately taken to enlarge the accommodations in this Seminary as the emergences of the institution and progress of education demand."[47] What this meant is hard to say. Enrollments at Wheaton, though remaining constant at slightly more than 100 per term, were not increasing in any way that would have warranted consideration of new boarding facilities. However, a policy change that involved admitting young men would certainly have called for such construction. And with the knowledge that two new institutions were soon to open their doors, Wellesley and Smith Colleges, the Board and Mrs. Wheaton may well have felt that a move toward coeducation might be necessary for Wheaton. The problem, however, was that few young men, if any, would be interested in completing the full seminary program, since they could enter male colleges upon completion of most, not even all, of the junior middle year curriculum. In retrospect it seems clear that had Wheaton adopted coeducation at that time, forces would have been put in play that probably would have meant the ultimate emergence of the Seminary as purely a college preparatory school.

The temptation, however, must have been a real one. The Wheaton family, and the Seminary in general, had always had as one of its special aims the furtherance of educational opportunities for the young women of Norton, witness the willingness to admit day students and to charge reduced tuition to children of Norton citizens. Norton, however, remained a small town, and while communities to the north, east, and west (Mansfield, Easton, and Attleboro) all had public high schools, Norton and towns to the south such as Dighton, Rehoboth, Berkley, and Swansea had none.[48] The concept that Wheaton might fill this educational gap for the young men of Norton and other small towns, as well as for young women, must have been an attractive one.

And there was another factor. A cousin of Laban Morey Wheaton, George Wild Sr., an elder brother of the boy whom the Wheatons adopted in 1838, had lived with his family for many years in Norton. Mr. Wild served as Mr. Wheaton's business agent and secretary, a function he and later his son continued to perform for Mrs. Wheaton after her husband's death. Eliza Wheaton and Mrs. Wild became friends, and the childless Eliza lavished much affection on the Wild children, in particular a daughter, Mary, and one of the young sons, who had the same name as her husband, father-in-law, and adopted son, Laban. It hardly seems coincidental that the four years when a number of young men attended Wheaton were the four when Laban E. Wild attended, spending one year in the preparatory class, two in the junior and one in the junior middle. With his departure from Wheaton, the attendance of other Norton youths quickly declined, though a few, including one more Wild son, attended for a year or so. Had there been more young men for whose education Eliza Wheaton was personally concerned, perhaps the course of Wheaton's history would have been substantially different.[49]

In any case, no new boarding house was ever built. By the mid-1880s males had ceased to attend, and the issue of coeducation had been laid to rest for the next eighty years.

NOTES: CHAPTER 3

1. Katz, *School Reform*, p. 224.

2. Shepard, "Reference History," p.14; Trustees Minutes: 10/1/35; 10/18/36; see also unused draft of Incorporation, written by Judge Wheaton, n.d., in Wheaton Histories, Seminary: Seminary.

3. Trustees Minutes: 10/18/38. The Trustees Minutes covering 1848–1849 has copies of the two incorporating charters in the front of the volume. See also Shepard, "Reference History," pp. 73–74.

4. Shepard, "Reference History," pp. 73–74; Trustees Minutes, 2/13/38; Paine, *E. B. Wheaton*, p. 65.

5. Principals: Sawyer: Memorandum re 1837–39; Knight: Memorandum written in 1860.

6. From 1839 to 1845, Judge Wheaton personally presented the diplomas at each graduation ceremony. Shepard, "Reference History," p. 74.

7. Ages ranged from 13 to 25. Since breakdowns of attendance by term are not available for all years, it is impossible to tell whether individual students attended for both terms of the years they appear in the general list in the catalogues. Given the lower attendance in the winter terms which always occurred, though not as drastically as it did in 1837–38, it is obvious than many only attended during the summer. Wheaton Female Seminary, *Annual Catalogues*, 1835–1849; Principals: Knight: Grade Book; Sawyer: "Report of Years 1842–1846."

8. General Files: 1844–45: "Conditions of Leasing Boarding House and Renting Furniture to Mrs. Putnam," 3/5/45; 1848–49, "Provisions for Renting Boarding House." 11/21/48; Shepard, "Reference History," pp. 93–96.

9. The library collection was started with a $100.00 gift from Judge Wheaton's wife, Fanny, in 1840. She also donated the first piano in 1839. Trustees Minutes, 4/23/39; 10/20/40.

10. Trustees Minutes: 2/13/38; 4/23/39; 10/22/39; 10/25/42; 7/10/44; 7/15/45; 7/26/47; Treasurer: Treasurer's Statement: 1847–1848.

11. This was Sarah B. Putnam, Teacher in English Branches and Latin. Miss Sawyer's resignation became effective at the end of the fall term and Elizabeth Cate did not begin her duties until April, 1847.

12. It appears that the Board, concerned about a perceived lack of serious personal religious commitment in the Seminary, initiated a search for a new principal unbeknownst to Miss Mann. On July 23, 1850, the Board approved the engagement of Mrs. Metcalf at $500.00 per year, "she bearing her own expenses in every particular." The next day the trustees received a one-sentence, cold, formal letter of resignation from Miss Mann. No letter of thanks or appreciation was voted by the Board members, the first time in the Seminary's history they had failed to do so. Trustees Minutes: 7/23, 24/50; Principals: Mann: letter of resignation, 7/24/50; for other materials relating to the resignation and retention of principals, see Trustees Minutes: 4/10/37; 10/3/46; 2/22/47; 7/27/47; 5/21/49; 7/25/49; 7/8/50; Principals, Mann: Mann to Metcalf, 6/5/60.

13. It appears that Maria Browne, Associate Principal, served as administrative head of the Seminary during the summer term, 1846. Trustees Minutes, 7/14/46.

14. Paine, *E. B. Wheaton*, p. 94. See also Principals: Cate: Cate to Thurston, 10/3/47.

15. Principals; Sawyer: Sawyer to Barrows, 10/8/46. Elizabeth Cate originally declined the invitation to become Principal when it was offered by the Board of Trustees. "I supposed that the question was definitely and finally settled," she later wrote, "but I had reckoned without—Mrs. Wheaton." Eliza Wheaton journeyed to Boston to visit Miss Cate, and turned on all her persuasive forces. "I had not been particularly impressed by what I had heard of Mrs. Wheaton . . . but, at once, I knew her for a remarkable woman. . . . In the glamour of her presence and personality all obstacles seemed to disappear. In her vocabulary there was no such word as 'fail' and of course I yielded. What could I do but lower my colors to a superior force." Paine, *E. B. Wheaton*, pp. 93–94.

16. LMW, "Day Book," entries on 9/30/44; 12/10/44; plus entry in back of book. See also Principals: Cate: Cate to Thurston, 10/3/47; Morison, *Harvard*, p. 207.

17. Trustees Minutes: 7/26/48.

18. Ibid.: 9/15/48.

19. Ibid.: 11/21/48. See also Wheaton Histories, Seminary: Administration: Tyler to Barrows, 10/30/48. This letter indicates that it is possible the plans used for Seminary Hall were originally drawn for a chapel at the Young Ladies Institute in Pittsfield, Massachusetts, and may also have been used to build an Academy building in Hinsdale, Massachusetts.

20. Principals: Mann: Mann to Metcalf, 7/5/60; LMW, "Day Book"; Shepard, "Reference History," erroneously cites Mann's letter as the "1849 catalogue." See also Preservation Resource Group, Inc., "Initial Evaluation for Preservation and use of Mary Lyon Hall," p. 4.

21. Shepard, "Reference History," p. 112; see also C. Creevey, *A Daughter of the Puritans* (New York: G. Putnam's, 1916), pp. 235–46.

22. A description of the first incident is included subsequently; for the second, see Trustees Minutes: 11/24/63; 4/15/64; 7/12/64; Principals: Metcalf: Report to Trustees, 1866.

23. Shepard, "Reference History," p. 104.

24. Ibid., p. 103. The Metcalf "maxim" most remembered by students was "Be fertile in expedients." See p. 107.

25. Ibid., p. 104.

26. Creevey, *Daughter*, p. 225.

27. Paine, *E. B. Wheaton*, pp. 161–63.

28. Shepard, "Reference History," pp. 123–25; Creevey, *Daughter*, pp. 225–26; Paine, *E. B. Wheaton*, pp. 161–63.

29. Wheaton Female Seminary, *Annual Catalogue, 1849–1850*. In 1843, Wheaton had shifted from a two-term to a three-term annual calendar. See ch. 7.

30. Katz, *School Reform*, pp. 224, 228, 231; Commonwealth of Massachusetts, *Thirty-Ninth Annual Report of the Board of Education . . . 1874–1875* (Boston: Massachusetts Board of Education, 1876), pp. 139–40.

31. Katz, *School Reform*, p. 224; Commonwealth of Massachusetts, *Annual Report, 1874–1875*, p. 122.

32. Katz, *School Reform*, pp. 228–30. The curriculum included Latin (through Horace), plus the options of French, German, or Italian. See Wheaton Female Seminary, *Annual Catalogue, 1870–1871*.

33. J. M. Taylor and E. Haight, *Vassar* (New York: Oxford University Press, 1915), pp. 61–66. Despite its announced beginning as a college, Vassar found it necessary for the first twenty-two years of its existence to run an auxiliary preparatory division.

34. Trustees Minutes: 11/19/50; 12/11/50; 5/17/51; 11/25/51; also Wheaton Female Seminary, *Annual Catalogue*, 1849–1852.

35. Trustees Minutes: 7/19/53; 11/20/53; 3/14/55; 3/12/56; 12/15/68; 6/28/76; 3/20/77; 12/18/77; LMW, "Day Book," 1828–1859; EBW, Letters, 1865–73: 2/25/68; 6/9/68; Wheaton Female Seminary, *Annual Catalogue, 1856–1857.*

36. Principals: Metcalf: Metcalf to Trustees, 11/19/55.

37. Ibid.: 11/25/56; 3/18/57; Trustees Minutes, 11/20/55; 3/12/56; 5/10/56; 11/25/56; 3/18/57; 4/28/57; General Files: 1855–1856: notes of two Trustees Meetings; Treasurer's Office: Trustees Correspondence: Teachers to Trustees, 5/10/56.

38. Trustees Minutes: 7/13–14/58; 3/18/62; Principals: Metcalf: Metcalf to LMW, 12/29/59.

39. Trustees Minutes: 7/12/64; 11/22/64; 7/12/65.

40. Ibid.: 11/27/67; 3/24/74; 7/1/74; *Rushlight,* 19:2 (March, 1874); General Files: Class of 1871: Lucy Dodge letters, To Mother, 9/19/69.

41. Trustees Minutes: 3/25/51; 3/17/58. See also revised by-laws in Trustees Minutes: 11/22/64.

42. H. Harris, "No Backward Steps: The Wheaton Alumnae Association, 1870–1970," *Wheaton Alumnae Bulletin,* 49:2 (Summer, 1970), p. 5; Trustees Minutes: 9/14/75; 3/20/77; 6/27/77; Treasurer's Office: Reports: December, 1875.

43. General Files: 1839–1840: C. W. Allen to Editor, *Boston Recorder,* 4/29/40; Trustees Minutes: 11/19/50; 3/25/71; 12/12/70; 12/18/77; Shepard, "Reference History," p. 20.

44. *Rushlight,* 17:3 (July, 1872). This same issue forecast a population of 50,000 for Norton by 1900! (The population in 2000 was slightly more than 18,000.)

45. See Wheaton Female Seminary, *Annual Catalogue,* 1873–1887, in particular the catalogue for 1874–1875.

46. General files: 1874–1875: Comments on a picture of the Seminary by Marion Holpine, 3/7/75. Lucille Zwicker told the author that her uncle, Frank Clapp (pictured in the *Town of Norton Bi-Centennial, 1711–1911, Souvenir Program*), had always told of attending Wheaton—and indeed, a F. A. Clapp is listed as having advanced to junior class status.

47. Trustees Minutes: 7/2/73. See also 4/15/73.

48. Norton did not open a public high school until 1904.

49. Paine, *E. B. Wheaton,* pp. 33–34; Wheaton Female Seminary, *Annual Catalogue,* 1874–1878.

4

Troubled Times
1876–1895

THE DEATH OF Laban Morey Wheaton in 1865 removed the direct participation of the Wheatons in the work of the Board of Trustees. Initially, however, there was little apparent change in its mode of operations, aside from the fact that the Board now received communications directly from Eliza Wheaton, where before she had exerted influence through her husband. Immediately following Laban Morey's death, the trustees wrote Mrs. Wheaton indicating their desire that she should "be consulted in reference to the appointment of the new trustees, and all other matters of importance to the Institution," an opportunity Eliza Wheaton gratefully accepted and regularly exercised.[1] No one connected with the Seminary during the next forty years would be under any illusion as to the leadership role, both in terms of fiscal support and general policy, that she exerted as she watched over the institution whose existence she had initially proposed in the spring of 1834.[2]

Only in one area did Mr. Wheaton's passage have an immediate effect on the duties of the Board of Trustees. The old Wheaton family property on Winter Street in Boston suddenly became an item of concern. In his will, following the wishes of Judge Wheaton, Laban Morey designated that upon the death of Eliza the Boston property should go to the Seminary as residuary legatee. Therefore, Eliza Wheaton felt it necessary to consult the Board regularly regarding the property, which by that time was being leased to a Boston business firm. Trustees records show that the Board from that time on became heavily involved in negotiation and settlement of lease renewals when they periodically came due.[3]

Otherwise, matters generally went on as they had before. The Seminary remained in the firm, competent, and well-established control of Caroline Metcalf. But her resignation, originally tendered in 1875 but only effected in 1876, changed all that.[4] During the next two decades the work and importance of the Board of Trustees increased dramatically, and the influence of certain key members greatly affected the affairs of the Seminary. The Board remained dominated by Congregational ministers, a fact which in great part reflected Eliza Wheaton's own deep personal religious commitment. Many trustees were elected at the direct suggestion of Mrs. Wheaton. A few emerged as her particular confidants. Pressure from alumnae to include women as members of the Board was successfully resisted for nearly a decade before two were finally elected in June, 1896.

During these years four trustees in particular devoted themselves intensively to the work of the Seminary. Rev. Mortimer Blake, Pastor of the Winslow Trinitarian Congregational Church in Taunton, had served on the Board from 1854 to 1859. He was reelected in 1868 and served as Board President from 1872 until his death in 1884. Though his position as President was never challenged, he proved at times to be a source of vexation to other Board members. This problem became particularly acute during the period when Blake's daughter attended Wheaton and he took special interest in every aspect of its operation. Living in Taunton, it was easy for him to visit Norton, and so greatly did he seek at times to direct policy, both social and academic, that Mrs. Wheaton and several of the Trustees consulted as to ways by which his "interference . . . in the affairs of the school," as one trustee put it, could be curbed.[5] An old-fashioned Puritan in belief and outlook, Rev. Blake decried any lessening of religious intensity in the atmosphere of the Seminary, or any tendency to modify its strictly Congregationalist outlook.

Much more moderate and progressive in outlook were two other minister-trustees. Rev. Alfred Emerson, husband of former Principal Martha Vose, served from 1872 to 1893, eleven of those years as Treasurer. He and Rev. Albert Plumb (1873–1907), who succeeded Blake to the Presidency of the Board in 1885, provided, along with Mrs. Wheaton, the fundamental leadership for the Seminary during the last quarter of the nineteenth century. While Plumb handled policy and personnel issues, Emerson took over Laban Morey Wheaton's role of supervising major construction projects and safeguarding the Seminary's finances. To these men should be added the quiet, more retiring figure of Edwin Barrows, who served forty-three years on the Board, the last seventeen as Treasurer following the resignation of Alfred Emerson from that position in 1891. Barrows, along with Rev. Plumb, played a central role in the rejuvenation of the Seminary at the turn of the century.

Though the trustees prevailed upon Mrs. Metcalf to remain for a year following the celebration of her twenty-fifth (and Wheaton's fortieth) anniversary, the selection of a new Principal did not proceed easily. The heir-apparent was Mary Briggs, who had taken over much of the routine administrative duties of the Seminary during the last years of Mrs. Metcalf's administration. A rather large, plump, very jovial woman, she was loved by the students, who found in her a friend, confidante, and pleasing antidote to the usually stern and rather forbidding Caroline Metcalf. She also enjoyed a well-deserved reputation as an excellent teacher, with intense religious convictions. Yet, perhaps because of her appearance and less than stern manner, the trustees did not consider her for the position. Instead, after more than a year of searching, they appointed Ellen Haskell to become the eighth Principal of Wheaton, with Miss Briggs again serving in an unofficial assistants capacity.[6]

About Ellen Haskell and her term of three years at Wheaton we know very little. Apparently her coming brought some needed fresh air to Wheaton; in particular many of the multitude of daily behavior rules that had accumulated during the years of Mrs. Metcalf's regime were either abolished or modified. One student later remembered Miss Haskell as a "Christian Gentlewoman" who won the hearts of all the students with her quiet grace and charm.[7] "She carried with her an atmosphere of high living and thinking and changed the conduct of the school from the many-ruled boarding school to one where self government was almost established, a great change for us who experienced it."[8]

But perhaps it was just this relaxation of requirements that led to the problems Ellen Haskell faced. Though personally deeply religious, she, unlike Mrs. Metcalf, did not believe it part of her duty (or even her right) to pursue the sort of public manifestation of conversion or calling that had characterized the earlier period. As a result, it appears that some members of the Board of Trustees, particularly President Mortimer Blake and Secretary Albert Plumb, along with Mrs. Wheaton, became concerned for a time that there might be a falling away from religious commitment at Wheaton. Eliza Wheaton even sought out some of the teachers for their opinions. As one former student wrote years later, "I have always had a feeling that Miss Haskell was not fully appreciated at Wheaton," adding, however, that there was "nothing by which to prove it."[9]

This sense of uncertainty about Ellen Haskell may well have become particularly important in the last part of her administration when the Seminary suddenly found itself faced with an unexpected crisis. As usual, this concerned enrollment figures, which declined precipitously from 122 in 1877–78 (70 in the regular four year program), to 80 with only 45 in the seminary degree curriculum in 1878–79.[10] Perplexed by this sudden decline, and stung by a meeting with Rev. Plumb who intimated that several trustees believed it was due to a lessening of the religious tone and intensity at Wheaton, Miss Haskell suddenly resigned in the fall of 1878. This offer was refused at the express wish of Mrs. Wheaton who declared she was satisfied with Miss Haskell's leadership and instead asked the trustees to curb the interference of Rev. Blake, President of the Board, in the day to day operation of the Seminary. But the next spring, as current and projected enrollment figures continued to plummet, Miss Haskell again wrote to the Board: "In view of this great decrease the Principal is ready to receive any suggestions which the Trustees may make and to confer with them concerning methods of reducing expenses. She wishes the utmost frankness to be used towards her and if there is reason to suppose that her conduct of the school has operated to produce this state of things that it be fully made known to her."[11] This time, the Committee of Instruction, which was headed by Rev. Blake, decided that indeed a change of leadership was necessary. On April 26th the Committee advised Miss Haskell that they would now accept the letter of resignation that had been refused earlier, a decision that was confirmed somewhat reluctantly by the full Board on May 26.[12]

In retrospect, it seems that Ellen Haskell was the victim of circumstances and forces beyond her control. The sudden decline in enrollment was most likely attributable to the implementation of a construction project that in the long run would assure new prosperity for the Seminary in the 1880s and early 1890s. This was the extensive remodeling and expansion of Seminary Hall undertaken in the spring, summer, and fall of 1878. In the short run, however, the construction had a serious negative impact, for the fact that three wings were being added to the existing classroom building meant that for the whole of one term and part of another the facilities and accommodations for academic work were anything but felicitous. And with the boarding house so close to Seminary Hall, the piles of dirt, noise of construction, and general turmoil must have made for anything but pleasant living conditions. It seems likely that the precipitous drop in enrollment in the fall of 1878 (construction had started before the end of the spring term) was primarily due to these conditions—conditions that would have made any parent think twice about sending a daughter to Wheaton.[13]

The trustees undoubtedly were aware of this and were prepared to accept low enrollment that fall. What they probably did not understand was that recovery from this period of chaos would be slow—that it takes time for public knowledge and opinion to recognize changing circumstances. Thus, when the student body remained small in the spring semester of 1879 despite the fact that the new facilities were in use, it appears the Board became overly concerned and decided a change in leadership was necessary.[14]

Two considerations had prompted the decision to remodel and expand Seminary Hall. The first was the ever more apparent need for larger and better equipped facilities for science laboratories. The second was the expansion of the library holdings to the point where space in the old gymnasium, to which the library had been moved in 1869, was no longer adequate. Under the constant prodding of Clara Pike, head of the science department, the trustees had for some years been considering means for an expansion of facilities, but to no actionable conclusion. As had been the case in the past, and as it would be again in the future, it was Mrs. Wheaton who stepped in to break the logjam. Despite the fact that she had for several years been funding an annual operating deficit for the Seminary out of her own purse, she sent a letter to the Board of Trustees on March 31, 1878, in which she stated: "I wish to inquire if you are willing to give me the Library building on condition that I put in its place a larger one suitable for Gymnasium and Library and perhaps Laboratory if on further reflection I think best."[15] With what seems, even today, almost an audible sigh of relief, the trustees unanimously agreed and subsequently on May 14, voted to "submit the entire project to the judgement of Mrs. Wheaton to be done either by erecting a separate structure or by annexing wings to the Seminary building, as she may see fit."[16]

It was the latter of these two options that Eliza Wheaton ultimately chose. Under the watchful eyes of Trustee Alfred Emerson, three wings were added to the existing structure, transforming its shape from that of a rectangle to a cross. In accordance with Mrs. Wheaton's wishes, the old gymnasium, in use since 1869 as the library, was moved from the grounds to the Trinitarian Congregational Church. Subsequently, it was attached to the main sanctuary during a major remodeling of that edifice undertaken by Mrs. Wheaton in 1882. One of the wings of the expanded Seminary Hall was designed specifically to serve as a chemistry and biology laboratory, while other rooms for a physics laboratory, library, art studio, and gymnasium were specially constructed in addition to regular classroom space. Although the building was threatened by a fire which broke out just as construction had finished and which delayed the opening for several weeks, it was available for occupancy at the beginning of the second term in January, 1879. Exterior and grounds work, plus some minor interior furnishing, continued into the summer of 1879.[17]

The decision to add to the old Seminary Hall rather than construct a new building was a fortunate one, for it provided a large, solidly built structure that could house in one convenient location all the academic activities of the Seminary except astronomy. Available space for academic purposes was nearly tripled and the old facilities greatly modernized. The building continued in use with only minor interior renovations for another century, when it was again deemed worthy of a major renovation.[18]

During the late spring and summer of 1879, the Board of Trustees undertook an extensive search for a new Principal, for the first time with the assistance of a commercial employment bureau. In the latter part of August the appointment of Martha Sprague was confirmed, an appointment which soon proved to be nothing less than a disaster. Without trying, indeed probably with no idea of what she was doing or why it was happening, Miss Sprague managed within the course of one term to alienate completely the entire teaching staff, a number of trustees, and to a lesser extent, Eliza Wheaton. From the first, she and her new assistant, Alice King, were regarded as outsiders. The failure of the trustees to offer the Principalship to Miss Briggs a second time had led to her resignation in July, 1879; the Board had then chosen to hire a new chief assistant rather than promoting one of the existing staff. As a result, Wheaton opened that fall with two persons in charge who had no knowl-

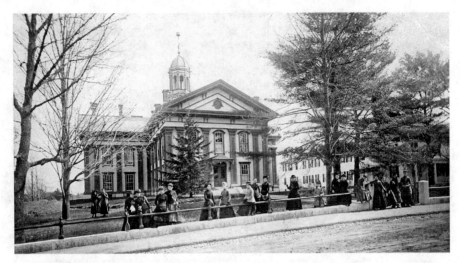

Seminary Hall after the 1878 addition of three wings. In 1912 the building was renamed Mary Lyon Hall.

edge of the traditions and customs of the Seminary. Moreover, they faced a suspicious and somewhat disgruntled teaching corps, one not about to allow passively great changes initiated by a couple of outsiders.[19]

Nor did Miss Sprague's appointment solve questions relating to religious activity. Deeply religious herself, she from the beginning suspected that her views did not coincide with those of some members of the Board of Trustees. Prior to her appointment she told Rev. Blake, President of the Board of Trustees, that her concerns were with daily life, rather than words, and indicated that she "was not in favor of revivals among school girls," which too often led to conversions of emotion that were not really genuine. "One needs," she wrote to Trustee Albert Plumb, "to guard against <u>excitement merely</u> among excitable school girls."[20]

On the other hand, when she asked the teaching staff to participate in leading morning and evening devotions, she met with stiff resistance, for this was a task that had been reserved mainly for the Principal since the time of Mrs. Metcalf. In the same way she was astounded when the music teacher refused to lead singing in devotional exercises, stating that the terms of her engagement did not require her to do so. As Miss Sprague wrote later, "I found it very difficult to learn what the terms of agreement were. Teachers seemed injured and offended because I wished to know."[21]

She also managed to alienate several members of the Board (and probably Eliza Wheaton) by altering one of Wheaton's most hallowed traditions. The morning half-hour private devotions, required since the

Central stairway and gallery, Seminary Hall, 1899.

Seminary had opened in 1835, were made optional. "The girls who do not choose to use it for devotions may use it for their studies—that kills it," wrote Trustee William King in a high fit of dudgeon. Noting that when his daughter had attended Wheaton it was impossible to study during devotions because everybody around one was praying, King commented, "Miss Sprague has . . . many excellent qualities, but she was not reared and educated in New England."[22]

Perhaps that was the nub of the problem. Never the epitome of tact and diplomacy, Miss Sprague, who came from the brash and less tradition-oriented Middle West, indeed did not understand New England, or at least that part of it still steeped in and clinging to Puritan traditionalism. As Rev. Blake put it in February, 1880, "it is a question of West and East in seminary management."[23]

The result was that by the middle of October, 1879, Eliza Wheaton expressed her concern to Albert Plumb, the secretary of the Board. "If our old and valued teachers should be so disgusted as to leave it would be disastrous. Miss Sprague seems to lack discretion as things have developed."[24] Plumb, however, felt very much in the middle, for he and Alfred Emerson had become very concerned over Rev. Blake's continual unwarranted interference in the daily affairs of the Seminary, so much that they and others were casting about for means to control his actions. Indeed, in her final letter to the Board the following May, Miss Sprague alluded directly to having "received letters at different times from a member of the Board, expressing great dissatisfaction with the work done. . . . [letters] which pained me deeply, indeed made me ill, and induced me to resign the position."[25]

But the ultimate telling force to the Board of Trustees was the opposition of the entire staff of teachers—opposition which became so severe that at the end of December, 1879, Clara Pike and Ellen Stanton sought out a member of the Trustee Committee of Instruction, Rev. Michael Burnham, and presented him with a list of grievances on behalf of the entire staff. In addition to complaints that the teachers were being required to perform tasks they had never had to do before, they lodged a series of specific charges against Miss Sprague. She had assigned the writing of a business letter as a Sunday exercise. She was unwilling to have teachers assign topics that would require students to use the library, in fact she discouraged use of the library and believed that students should not be encouraged to go beyond their textbooks. The teachers were convinced that Miss Sprague was not well educated herself, for she had stated before a class and its teacher that oil and water had a chemical affinity for each other and that it was possible to see the twelve signs of the zodiac at once. Her ungrammatical expression had been commented upon by students, as well as her coarse, rough, unladylike ways of speaking. Moreover she had had the temerity to suggest that Mrs. Wheaton's role in reviewing and approving the appointment of teachers went beyond what was proper for a person not officially connected with the administration of the Seminary.[26]

Rev. Burnham was clearly disturbed and impressed, and from that time on general support for Miss Sprague faded. Only Albert Plumb remained her loyal supporter, and even he was forced to recognize that a change was due. When, much to everyone's surprise, Miss Sprague voluntarily tendered her resignation on March 30, there was a great sense of relief. Before accepting the resignation, the Board decided it should ask for reasons, but this was purely pro forma. In fact, Mrs. Wheaton was afraid that Rev. Plumb's letter asking for reasons was "so kind and gentle in its remarks to Miss Sprague . . . that I am afraid she will relent and propose to you to withdraw her resignation. . . . It seems a merciful interpretation of providence that she should resign rather than that the Trustees have to ask her to do it. . . . I will write you again soon, but must now close with the hope you Trustees will soon accept of the resignation."[27]

With such an explicit expression of opinion, Miss Sprague's fate was sealed. But that created new problems. If Miss Sprague left, so obviously would her assistant, Alice King. The trustees were thus faced again with the prospect either of bringing in a whole new administration, or of appointing someone from the very staff that had successfully engineered the rebellion against Miss Sprague. Many trustees were not happy with either alternative, for they recognized the pitfalls of the first, but were equally disturbed by what they regarded as the unwillingness of the faculty to lead the regular devotional services. Moreover, they were distressed that some members of the staff were not of strictly Congregational religious persuasion.

The leading candidate from within the Seminary was Ellen Stanton, one of the two teachers who had gone to see Rev. Burnham in December, and who had taught French at Wheaton since 1871. However, she faced stern opposition from the President of the Board, Mortimer Blake, who wrote regarding her and another teacher, Eva Tappan:

> In regard to Miss Stanton, I cannot think that she is at all fitted for the position of Principal. . . . She fails <u>especially</u> in that religious interest for the piety of our pupils which I consider a sine-qua-non in the head of the Seminary, and whatever interest she may feel, she has never been willing to lead the devotions, or conduct a prayer meeting. I could <u>not</u> vote for a Methodist or Episcopalian. Ours <u>is</u> a Congregational school and patronized widely because it <u>is</u>. If we depart from it we lose our place in the ranks. There must be somewhere existent a Congregational Lady fitted to our needs. We cannot be so short of material as to hand our school over to other hands. For this very reason, I shall move to exchange Miss Tappan for someone in sympathy with our polity. Divers facts suggest it.[28]

Clearly the Board of Trustees was at a crossroads. Miss Sprague had been hired, it would appear, in part to reexert the kind of religious influence and tone that had existed in the Metcalf era and which the Board believed had disappeared during the Haskell administration. While there was never any question that the Seminary should continue to require attendance at church, Bible study, and the maintainance of a thoroughly "Christian atmosphere," the emphasis on what one trustee called public personal commitment as opposed to private, individual involvement had become a major issue.

The ultimate resolution was a compromise. Despite the objections of the President of the Board, and the doubts of others, Miss Stanton was indeed chosen to be Principal, albeit at a salary $200.00 lower than her predecessor. However, Eva Tappan, who taught Latin and German, was forced to resign.[29] It turned out that Ellen Stanton was Mrs. Wheaton's personal choice, and that she, along with Martha Vose Emerson, had worked long and hard to ensure Miss Stanton's selection by the Board. Not only did Eliza Wheaton discuss the matter privately with several Board members, but, in a move clearly designed to strengthen her influence on this issue, she sent a letter on May 8 to the Board offering to donate annually six $100.00 scholarships for able and needy students. This letter was received by the Board at the same meeting at which they were scheduled to act on the candidacy of Miss Stanton. There were, of course, no conditions attached to the scholarship offer, nor did there need to be. Mrs. Wheaton still controlled the purse strings that allowed the Seminary to operate, a fact which both she and the trustees recognized full well.[30]

Miss Stanton's appointment brought to the Principal's position another strong personality, who always maintained a close and cordial relationship with Mrs. Wheaton, going to great lengths to defer to her in many ways. Described as tall and distinguished looking, "she wore trained dresses, in the morning, to school; indeed, she was always the dignified and grand, although gracious, lady."[31] She was regarded as a rather stern, though always fair, administrator by the students who "took great pride in her, but . . . did not exactly love her."[32] Miss Stanton was also firm in the sense of her own worth, as witnessed by her threat to resign in March, 1883, if the $200.00 she had lost from her predecessor's salary was not restored for the next academic year. Under her leadership and with the able help of her chief assistant, Clara Pike, the Seminary experienced a return to full enrollment and academic, if not fiscal, prosperity for more than a decade. By the end of 1881 the very trustees who had most doubted her appointment were singing her praises.[33]

One of the most positive developments during the 1880s and early 1890s was the growth and expansion of the Alumnae Association. Officially the Association remained small, with its headquarters located in Norton, and its membership limited to the relatively small numbers who were graduates of the Seminary. But the Association did serve to bring together Wheaton's most loyal supporters, who in turn developed the idea of forming Wheaton Clubs open to all who had attended Wheaton, whether they had graduated or not. This was the great era of social and business clubs in America. Women, following the example of men, and often because they were denied admission into professional societies, were busy forming a myriad of social, civic and professional clubs of

A. Ellen Stanton, *Principal*, 1880-1897.

their own. The idea for Wheaton Clubs was not novel, but its timing was fortuitious for the Seminary.[34]

The New York Wheaton Club was organized in 1886 and was followed in 1888 by the formation of the New England Wheaton Seminary Club based in Boston. These clubs met monthly during the fall, winter, and spring for programs of serious lectures, poetry readings, and recitals, as well as the opportunity to socialize and receive news of the Seminary. Attendance was large, the Boston meeting averaging 100 persons per session for many years. Because their membership was more broadly based, the clubs soon came to overshadow the formal Alumnae Association in terms of influence and impact on the Seminary. But, though they were self-supporting in terms of dues, the concept of financial support of the parent institution, long established among alumni associations of men's colleges, seems not even to have been considered. Nothing of the sort was offered nor was it expected. This was probably due in part to the Wheaton family's view that the Seminary was a personal and family fiscal responsibility. However, an equally important factor was undoubtedly the lack of independent financial resources available to women. Those who were married were totally dependent on their husbands for funds—those who were not were almost always living on very slender means, since salaries for women were much lower than for men.[35]

The impact of the Alumnae Association and the Clubs was felt rather quickly in another area. On June 20, 1888, the Board of Trustees received a letter from the New York Wheaton Club asking that they "fill the next vacancy occurring in their ranks from among the Alumnae in the vicinity of the school."[36] Obviously nonplussed, the Board voted to defer the matter and to "assure the Association that the subject would receive due consideration."[37] And consider it they did; on January 14, 1889, the Board voted that it was "expedient to admit ladies to the Board of Trustees and that the secretary be requested to make known this action to the alumnae association, asking them to make nominations."[38]

Two months later, however, at the next meeting of the Board, this action was summarily rescinded. The minutes of the Board record that "inasmuch as the Secretary (by request) had not yet communicated with the alumnae association with regard to electing women to the Board of Trustees, the action concerning this at the previous meeting be revoked and that the matter be indefinitely postponed."[39]

Postponed it was—for more than seven years! What had led the Board members to change their minds so suddenly and so completely? Evidence points to the hand of Eliza Wheaton. James Lane, Secretary of the Board of Trustees and pastor of the Trinitarian Congregational Church in Norton, met regularly with Mrs. Wheaton, the church's most prominent member, to discuss church and seminary matters. It seems highly likely that the request to delay writing to the New York Club, a request specifically referred to in the Board of Trustees' minutes, came from her.

This view gains credibility when one notes a letter written to Mrs. Wheaton on January 31, 1889, by former principal Eunice Caldwell Cowles. Mrs. Wheaton had long been accustomed to consulting Mrs. Cowles on Seminary affairs, as extensive correspondence during the Haskell-Sprague crises of a decade earlier testifies. In her letter Mrs. Cowles commented at length on the advantages and dangers of organized alumnae associations:

> So long as they have good times, bless and cheer one another, carry forward their own culture, and laud the old, dear old, school, they are a joy. When they take in hand the oversight and care of the Institution and pass resolves as to what Alma Mater should do they are an unmitigated nuisance. I think they have proved a plague to one college, and I am awfully afraid they will be nothing less to Mt. Holyoke Seminary. As the Wheaton [Seminary], God be thanked, asks for none of their money, they may never feel it incumbent on them to dictate who shall be added to the trustees, who to the faculty, and what to the course of study or system of discipline.[40]

It is not illogical to conclude that the rather lengthy postponement of a decision on admitting women to the Board was Mrs. Wheaton's doing. Only she had the kind of influence that would bring the Board to reverse itself so swiftly and completely on an issue of such major import.[41]

The sudden resurgence in enrollment and morale experienced by the Seminary in the early 1880s was in part due to the fact that from the beginning Ellen Stanton enjoyed the confidence of her staff. Moreover, she had taught during the last years of the Metcalf administration and

Eliza Baylies Chapin Wheaton in 1887 at age 78. She continued to watch over and financially assist the Seminary until her death in 1905.

therefore understood the traditions and religious concerns so important
to Mrs. Wheaton and many of the trustees. Although the Seminary
moved forward in many ways, at the same time a sense of continuity was
established that had been lost during the Haskell and Sprague years.

In addition, Wheaton began to reap the fruits of the major upgrading
in academic facilities that had caused such chaos during the construction
period in 1878–1879. The scope and nature of the new facilities gradually became known throughout the area, and the landscaping finally took
hold. The result was that the Seminary projected a new and modern
image, one that signified its intention to stay abreast of the times. Enrollment quickly responded; in 1884–1885, when the Seminary celebrated
its fiftieth anniversary with a gala week-long celebration, ninety-three
students were in attendance.[42] In fact, from 1882–83 to 1891–92, when
enrollment peaked at 100, student attendance held consistently in the
nineties. Then a precipitous slide began; five years later only 38 students
were registered during the winter term, and that number decreased to 25
in the summer. For the first time since the winter of 1837–38, the very
existence of the Seminary seemed in doubt.[43]

What had happened? If the resurgence in the 1880's can be traced
mainly to internal changes and stabilization, the answers as to the decline in the 1890s can be found only by examining developments in education for women that were taking place throughout New England.
Certainly, these changes were not unique to New England, but since
Wheaton drew more than 90% of its student body from that area, it is
there we must look for factors exerting an influence strong enough to
generate such a mammoth student defection.

It is not hard to find the answer: a growing number of colleges open
to women—colleges authorized to confer bachelor of arts degrees and
offering a curriculum basically identical in all respects to that available
to men. Vassar had opened its doors in 1865. Smith and Wellesley had
followed a decade later.[44] Yet their immediate impact on Wheaton had
been minimal. The severe crisis Wheaton experienced in the last half of
the 1870s was probably unavoidable, but it was generated primarily by
internal problems of various types. Once these were resolved, and the
turmoil of major construction ended, the Seminary quickly rebounded
for another decade. The curriculum, though improved in quality by the
availability of brand-new facilities and a vastly expanded guest lecture-
ship program, remained the same in its format—a preparatory year plus
a four-year seminary curriculum, the last two of which went beyond anything offered in the public high schools. Clearly, despite the existence of
three colleges for women, two of them located in Massachusetts, the appeal of Wheaton's type of education remained strong throughout the
1880s and into the 1890s. Many parents shied away from the concept of
a full college education for their daughters. This would, it was thought,
make them too "mannish." Moreover, the colleges, larger than the semi-

naries, could not provide the individual moral and spiritual guidance and training so necessary for women to fulfill their assigned roles in the traditional spheres of teaching, missionary work, and domesticity. Eunice Caldwell Cowles was far from alone when she expressed the sentiment to Mrs. Wheaton that "I value more and more the schools that fit girls for companionship and contentment in the spheres for which women are designed, and from which it is impossible they can en masse be withdrawn. . . . A school which aims to make companionable, reasonable, unpretentious and unassuming women is better for the race than the one that talks about careers. The career of wife and mother is surely ample for most of us; is it not?"[45]

Earlier, in 1883, in response to Mrs. Wheaton's expressed concern about the future of the Seminary, Mrs. Cowles had written: "I agree fully with you, that there are many of the daughters of our land to whom the rounded and adequate education which the Wheaton Seminary furnishes is a better outfit for life than the preparatory course in a college [the first two years], and vastly better than the strain which often attends the full college course."[46]

Despite the fact that more and more women's colleges such as Bryn Mawr and Wells appeared on the scene, as well as coeducational or coordinate institutions like Tufts, Cornell, and Pembroke, Wheaton continued to enjoy relative prosperity and stability under the leadership of Ellen Stanton. Then the bubble burst. It was not unexpected. Eliza Wheaton had been worrying about the collegiate issue for some time. But the impact, when it came, was more swift, more devastating than anyone had anticipated.

Two independent, but related, events in the world of women's education may have served as the catalyst that triggered the abrupt change in Wheaton's fortune between 1892 and 1896. The first was the decision by the Board of Overseers of Harvard University to recognize the women's educational program known as the "Harvard Annex" as a coordinate but separate institution, to be called Radcliffe College. From 1894 on the diplomas of Radcliffe, awarded upon completion of courses taught almost without exception by Harvard faculty, would be counter-signed by the President of Harvard University. More than any other single event in the history of higher education for women, this action by Harvard University lent credibility to a movement that had been growing rapidly for some time, but had continued to be regarded by most as avant-garde and not the normal form of education for women. The seal of approval given by Harvard to collegiate education for women almost immediately created a totally new attitude. Collegiate education became the norm to be aspired to, not the exception. It suddenly became the fashion for middle and upper-class young women to go to college if they possibly could.[47]

But for Wheaton Female Seminary, the biggest problem may have been that by 1893 it found itself isolated, a growing anachronism in a day when seminaries were closing, or reverting exclusively to a curriculum designed to prepare young women for admission to college. This had been happening across the country for some time, but in Massachusetts one other seminary had remained—bigger, stronger, and with a wider reputation than Wheaton, yet offering in its academic curriculum a program very similar to that offered by Wheaton in its own four-year seminary schedule of courses. As long as Mount Holyoke Female Seminary remained, the concept and legitimacy of a seminary education was sustained. But in 1888 Mount Holyoke obtained a charter to operate as both a Seminary and College, and in 1893 it dropped the seminary curriculum completely and announced that it would operate only as a college from that time onward.

Other seminaries such as Troy and Abbot Academy had already decided to emphasize special college preparatory programs. In addition, in 1893 the nation plunged into a severe depression that was to last nearly four years. Nonetheless, Wheaton clung to its tradition of offering a viable alternative to collegiate education, perhaps hoping that the defection of Mount Holyoke from the ranks would result in less competition for a larger pool of seminary students. Whatever the reasons, the results were not auspicious, and in April, 1896, when Miss Stanton resigned, the trustees found themselves in the position of having to find new leadership at a time when the institution's future seemed very much in doubt.

Wheaton also was faced with severe fiscal problems in addition to those posed by sharply declining student enrollments. During the Haskell-Sprague-Stanton years the Seminary did not prosper financially. In fact, not once during those twenty-one years did the Seminary operate in the black. In every year Wheaton family money, to a greater or lesser extent, was needed to balance the books. Tuition, room, and board fees for the regular course rose from $255.00 per year in 1876–77 to $300.00 in 1885–86, where they remained without change for the next decade.[48] The result was an ever increasing annual deficit, which was covered year after year by gifts from Mrs. Wheaton. In addition she provided funds for physical plant maintenance and academic scholarships. Finally, she bore the cost of all major building programs, though in the fifteen years following the renovation of Seminary Hall the only major changes were the building of a bowling alley in 1884 and the installation of central steam heating in 1885. The financial drain of the Seminary on Wheaton family resources had never been heavier or steadier. Exclusive of the cost of the Seminary Hall additions and the bowling alley, Eliza Wheaton gave at least $100,000 to the Seminary during the years 1875–1897, plus some 37 acres of land. At the end there was little to show for it except ever increasing annual deficits and rapidly decreasing student enrollments.[49]

In a very real sense the majority of the Stanton years provided a happy and relatively quiet hiatus before the storm, a storm that was

The Public Library, which was given to the town by Mrs. Wheaton in 1888, and Norton Common.

clearly approaching during the last years of her administration, but for which neither the Board of Trustees nor Mrs. Wheaton had made any real preparation, despite their awareness of its existence. Yet it must be noted that it was the modern facilities built in 1878–79, plus a dynamic and dedicated teaching corps led by an able administrator, that enabled the Seminary to withstand for so long the pressures that were buffeting similar institutions during the 1880s. The magnitude of the crisis of the mid-1890s should not overshadow the inherent basis of strength that had been created at Wheaton over the years, one that had been severely tested in the latter 1870s but which had been consolidated anew under the quiet but steady leadership of Ellen Stanton.[50]

NOTES: CHAPTER 4

1. Wheaton Family: Letters to EBW, 1848–78: King to EBW, 2/25/65; Trustees Minutes: EBW to Trustees, 7/12/65.

2. For an example of Mrs. Wheaton's method of influencing Seminary affairs, see her letter to the Board of Trustees in their Minutes: 12/13/69. In it she suggested possible new members of the Board; donated money for the library; suggested an increased Seminary contribution to the Trinitarian Church; asked that a particular student be granted free tuition; and commented that she thought the Board should fund travel expenses for Trustees attending Board meetings or visiting the Seminary in term. Other examples will be cited in subsequent sections.

3. Ibid.: 10/6/65; 10/23/65; 6/26/75, and continuing, passim. Wheaton family revenue from this source was: $1,700 annually from 1856–1865 (C. King); $8,000 from 1865–1878 (W. Lane); $21,000 from 1878–1903; $24,000 from 1903–1913; $32,000 from 1913–1917; and a minimum of $32,500 from 1919 until the property was sold in 1924 to the firm that had leased it since 1878, A. J. Stowell Co. Prior to 1856, the property was leased for at least five years to A. H. Blanchard, who ran a boardinghouse and paid $1,100 rent annually. Whether the lease to Mr. Blanchard extended earlier than 1851 is not known, although record of a rent payment from someone is noted in LMW's receipt book in 1849. See also LMW and EBW, "Account Books," and Wheaton Family, Winter Street Property.

4. Trustees Minutes: 3/23/75.

5. Principals: Sprague: A. Emerson to Plumb, 8/22/79.

6. A cryptic note in pencil in the Trustees Minutes indicates that Miss Haskell received $1,200 plus room and board to start, while Mrs. Metcalf earned only $700 in her final year. Trustees Minutes: 5/2/76; 6/14/76; Cunliffe, "History," p. 117; Wheaton Histories, Shepard "Reference History" Notes: F. V. Emerson notes, pp. 2–3.

7. Principals: Haskell: French to Shepard, 5/9/29.

8. Private letter quoted by Shepard, "Reference History," p. 231.

9. Principals: Haskell: French to Shepard, 5/9/29; Stanton to EBW, 9/22/78. For examples of trustees' attitudes relating to "revivals of religion," see Trustees Minutes: 3/23/75, or Wheaton Family: Letters to EBW, 1848–1878: Plumb to EBW, 9/21/78, in which he comments on the Seminary's tradition of "decided and active efforts for the conversion of the pupils and the development of an earnest and consecrated type of piety."

10. The students listed as not being enrolled in the degree curriculum were either in the preparatory program offered for those not yet ready for the regular course work, or were special students taking a few courses with no intention of conforming to or completing the standard curriculum.

11. Principals: Haskell: Report to Trustees, 3/25/79. See also Wheaton Family: Letters to EBW, 1848–1878: Plumb to EBW, 9/21/78; copy of EBW to Plumb, 9/32/78.

12. Trustees Minutes: 5/19/79; 5/26/79; Principals: Haskell: Haskell to Plumb, and enclosed letter of resignation, 4/28/79; Trustees to Haskell, 5/26/79.

13. See *Rushlight* account of studying and classroom space problems in the fall of 1878, 24:1 (Fall, 1878), pp. 35–36.

14. Theoretically, it could also be argued that the opening of Smith and Wellesley Colleges in 1875 might be blamed in part for enrollment problems, but this seems unlikely. The drop was too sudden; moreover the subsequent return to prosperity during the 1880's belies such a conclusion. The impact of colleges for women on Wheaton would not become acute for at least another decade.

15. Trustees Minutes: 3/27/78.

16. Ibid.: 5/14/78. See also 3/18/73; 7/1/74; 12/18/77; Trustees, 1834–1911: Seminary: Pike reports, 1872; Shepard, "Reference History," pp. 237–38.

17. C. Dahl, "Mary Lyon, 1878," *Wheaton Alumnae Magazine* (Fall, 1978), pp. 6–7; *Rushlight*, 23:3 (Summer, 1878), p. 30; 24:1 (Fall, 1878), p. 36; 24:2 (Winter, 1879), p. 25; General Files: 1878–1879: Program for the rededication of Seminary Hall, 1/15/79.

18. Architect Gridley J. F. Bryant's fee was $525; the main builder, Crassy and Noyes, charged $12,064; the plans for the grounds were developed by Percy Blake, a civil engineer. The entire cost, including furnishings, extensive landscaping, and construction of street curbings, concrete sidewalks, and an iron fence along East Main Street came to approximately $22,600. Trustees Minutes: 9/17/78; EBW, "Account Book," Houses and Repairs, 1866–1885, pp. 104–8.

19. Principals: Cowles: Cowles to EBW, 6/23/79; Trustees Minutes, 6/25/79; 7/22/79; 8/21/79; 12/23/79; Faculty Before 1910: Wells: Wells to Plumb, 12/11/79.

20. Principals: Sprague: Sprague to Plumb, 8/879.

21. Ibid.: Sprague statement to Board of Trustees, 5/8/80.

22. Trustees, 1834–1911: King: King to Plumb, 12/9/79; see also King to Plumb, 12/11/79.

23. Ibid.: Plumb: Blake to Plumb, 2/10/80.

24. Principals: Sprague: EBW to Plumb, 10/21/79.

25. Ibid.: Sprague statement to Board of Trustees, 5/8/80. None of the plans advanced for curbing the actions of the President of the Board were ever implemented. See Trustees, 1834–1910: Emerson: Emerson to Plumb, 8/22/79; also Principals: Sprague: Sprague to Plumb, 4/1/80.

26. Trustees, 1834–1910: Burnham: Burnham to Plumb, 12/15/79; Principals: Sprague: Burnham to "My dear Br" (Plumb), 12/15/79; Notes of meeting re complaints of teachers, n.d.

27. Principals: Sprague: EBW to Plumb, 3/31/80. See also Sprague to Trustees, 3/30/80; 5/8/80; Trustees Minutes: 3/30/80; 5/10/80; Trustees, 1834–1910: Plumb: Blake to Plumb, 2/10/80.

28. Principals: Sprague: Blake to "My Dear Bro"(Plumb), 5/1/80.

29. Miss Tappan went on to receive a Ph.D. in 1896 from the University of Pennsylvania, became a well-known author supporting herself by her writings, and ultimately endowed a number of scholarships at her alma mater, Vassar College.

30. EBW: Correspondence, 1839–1899: EBW to Plumb, 4/5/80; EBW to Trustees, 5/8/80; Wheaton Family: EBW correspondence, 1879–1890: M. V. Emerson to EBW, 5/5/80; 5/14/80; Trustees Minutes, 5/10/80; 5/30/80; 7/7/80; Principals: Stanton: Stanton to Plumb, 6/8/80.

31. Shepard, "Reference History," p. 234.

32. Ibid.: p. 235.

33. Trustees, 1834–1910: Blake: Report of Committee on Instruction, 6/29/81; Trustees Minutes: 3/27/83; Wheaton Family: EBW correspondence, 1879–1890: King to EBW, 11/17/81; Burnham to EBW, 12/5/81; Principals: Stanton: Stanton to Board of Trustees, 3/26/83.

34. The history of the Wheaton Alumnae Association has been thoroughly researched by Miss Hilda Harris, former Librarian of Wheaton College, whose article in the summer 1970 *Wheaton Alumnae Quarterly* entitled "No Backward Steps: The Wheaton Alumnae Association, 1870–1970," along with her research notes preserved in the Alumnae Association Boxes, provide the best compiled sources of information on the growth and development of the Association.

35. Scrapbook, New England Wheaton Seminary Club; Alumnae Association: NY Wheaton Club and New England Wheaton Club files. See also Shepard, "Reference History," pp 325–28.

36. Trustees Minutes: 6/20/88.

37. Ibid.

39. Ibid.: 1/14/89.

40. Ibid.: 3/14/89.

41. Hilda Harris suggests a similar interpretation in her article, which was read by the author only after he had come to the same conclusion based on examination of the available evidence. See Harris, "No Backward Steps."

42. For materials relating to the semi-centennial, see Anniversaries; and Wheaton Histories, Seminary: Seminary.

43. Principals: Stanton: Stanton (?) letter, spring 1897; Wheaton Histories, Seminary: Seminary to College #1: Samuel Valentine Cole (hereafter referred to as SVC): *Why Did Wheaton Change From Seminary to College?* (Norton, MA; Wheaton College, 1920); Shepard, "Reference History," p. 250.

44. According to Kate Upson Clark (WS1869), and later a trustee, "Mr. Durant [Henry F. Durant, founder of Wellesley College] was planning a college then and meditated for a while, I was told, to make Wheaton the beneficiary of his millions. He was often here to talk to us on Friday nights and was always paying the tuition of one or more girls here. But he finally concluded to leave Wheaton to the Wheaton family and to found Wellesley himself." General Files: Class of 1869: K. U. Clark memoir, "At Wheaton Seminary in 1867–69."

45. Principals: Cowles: Cowles to EBW, 2/10/85. See also Boas, *Woman's Education Begins*, ch. 5, passim.

46. Principals: Cowles: Cowles to EBW, 8/6/83.

47. Shepard, "Reference History," p. 235; Paine, *E. B. Wheaton*, pp. 221–229; Boas, *Woman's Education Begins*, ch. 5, passim.

48. Contributing to the fiscal deficit was the continuing policy of remitting the tuition of all clergy and missionary daughters, and granting reduced rates to students from Norton. Together these students often totalled nearly 30% of the total enrollment. Tuition and fees for regular students were finally raised to $350.00 in December, 1895. Trustees Minutes: 4/1/91; 7/1/91; 6/13/92; 6/26/95; 12/18/95.

49. Cost of the bowling alley was $2,544.33. It was located between and to the rear of Seminary Hall and the dormitory complex. Part of it remains today as an ell on the faculty house at 5 Pine Street. EBW, "Account Book," p. 167; Shepard, "Reference History," p. 355; Treasurer's Office: Seminary; Trustees Minutes: 8/10/85; 12/21/87; *Rushlight,* 40:1 (December, 1894).

50. Trustees Minutes: 4/9/88, Committee on Instruction Report.

5
Challenge and Response
1895–1900

THE RAPIDITY WITH which Wheaton Seminary moved, over a course of three years, from apparent stability and relative prosperity in 1891–92 to a financial, educational, and enrollment crisis of major proportions in 1895 shocked the Board of Trustees. Clearly some new course of action was necessary; to the Board its direction seemed obvious. Without a specific set of courses designed to attract students who wished to prepare for admission to college, it seemed the Seminary could not hope to survive. Therefore, on June 26, 1895, the Trustees requested the Committee of Instruction to prepare a special course of college preparatory studies.[1]

This decision had serious implications for the future of the Seminary. A college preparatory program would mean the addition of considerable staff and many new courses, in particular the reintroduction of Greek into the curriculum. Moreover, since entrance requirements and examinations differed for every college, considerable tutoring would be required in the final two years of the program, tutoring geared to ensure that a student would be drilled in the specific materials necessary to gain entrance to the college of her choice. The general experience of other preparatory institutions had been that encouragement of individual initiative, creativity, and the development of analytical skills tended to give way to intensive cramming designed to ensure mastery of specified data.

What the adoption of such a program would mean for the future of the seminary curriculum was not clear. While the final years of the preparatory program would parallel in some ways the subject matter covered in the first two years of the seminary course, the approach to subjects would often be different. For both programs to co-exist would probably require additional physical facilities and would certainly necessitate increased staffing. These changes would be possible only if enough additional students could be attracted to bring annual income into line with operating expenses. Wheaton family funds could then be diverted to capital expenditures. Even so, future prospects would be risky at best, and in the long run it could be expected that Wheaton would have to choose either to let the preparatory program become ever more dominant, or follow the path taken by Mount Holyoke and expand its seminary program into that of a four-year college.[2]

That the Board of Trustees recognized all this in the summer of 1895 is not apparent. But at least some members were aware of the problem, even if they were not certain as to the solution. In this they were joined by Eliza Wheaton, whose worries about the challenge of women's colleges had been evident for more than a decade in her private correspondence with Eunice Caldwell Cowles.

The Committee of Instruction proceeded slowly with its task. The 1895–96 catalogue (published in March, 1896) did not mention a specific college preparatory course though for the first time it indicated that students might elect a concentration in a special Literary, Scientific, or Classical program, with corresponding diplomas awarded. But continued decline in enrollment in 1895–96 indicated ever more clearly that major program changes would be needed if the Seminary were to survive.

How much the steady drop in student registration and the decision to create a college preparatory course affected Ellen Stanton's decision to resign on April 14, 1896, we do not know. Her letter of resignation was brief and pro forma. By the time the Trustees met to consider it on April 27, resignations from Clara Pike and Sarah Palmer, the two academic teachers with the longest tenure (and most committed to the seminary tradition) were also in hand. The Trustees agreed to accept Miss Stanton's resignation while tabling the other two. In their letter of reply to Miss Stanton they commented that they accepted her resignation, "it being understood that her desire to be relieved of her cares at the close of the current year fully coincides with her judgement."[3] They went on to thank her for her many years of service "and especially her tender and thoughtful consideration always of the obligations the Seminary is

Students in 1895. The Bowling Alley is in the background.

under to its patroness, Mrs. Wheaton, and the esteem and honor which she has uniformly cherished and shown to this most worthy and reverend friend of the school."[4]

If, in retrospect, the resignation of Ellen Stanton and the choice of her successor can be seen as a major turning point in the history of Wheaton, it does not appear that the Board of Trustees recognized it as such at that time. A committee to select a new principal was immediately convened and empowered by the full Board to offer the position to the senior teacher and assistant principal, Clara Pike. There seems to have been little doubt in the minds of the Board that Miss Pike would accept and it must have been with some considerable surprise that it heard the report of the Committee on May 29 informing them that she had refused.[5]

The Committee then recommended that the board approach Miss Mary Woolley, an 1884 graduate of the seminary, who in 1894 had become one of the first two women to receive a Bachelor of Arts degree from Brown University. Before her entrance to Brown in 1891 she had taught for five years at Wheaton, and had returned in 1894–95 on a part-time basis while successfully pursuing a Master of Arts degree at Brown. In 1895 she had accepted a position on the Wellesley College faculty, where she had been promoted to associate professor of Biblical history and literature after one year. She was, in 1896, Wheaton's most distinguished alumna in the field of education, ideally qualified to direct either a college preparatory or seminary curriculum. It was only logical that the Board of Trustees should seek her out.[6]

Miss Woolley, well embarked on a successful career in a flourishing college, evidently had no desire to return to Norton and the problems of a seminary that gave every appearance of steady and permanent decline.[7] On June 24, 1896, the selection committee once again reported its failure to the full Board. One senses that by this time the magnitude of the problems facing the Seminary and the serious question of its future survival had become quite apparent. The Trustees abruptly decided to cease their search for an immediate replacement, and instead voted to request Miss Stanton's continuance in the position for another year, taking great care to note both in their minutes and in their communication to Ellen Stanton that their request was made with Mrs. Wheaton's special concurrence.[8]

Meanwhile the trustees suddenly chose this moment to address an issue that had lain dormant for over seven years—the admission of women to membership on the Board. At the same May 29th meeting when the decision was made to invite Mary Woolley to be Principal, the names of Jeannie Woodbury Lincoln (WS1866), the wife of former trustee Annes Lincoln, and Estelle Hatch Merrill (WS1877), well-known Boston journalist, club-woman, and first President of the New England Wheaton Club, were placed in nomination as trustees. They were routinely elected at the June 26th meeting, and since both were present in Norton for the graduation ceremonies, they took part in the further deliberations of the Board. Mrs. Merrill resigned after only seven months and was subsequently replaced in March, 1897, by Annie Kilham (WS1870), who remained on the Board for the next 34 years. All three of these initial female trustees had either taught or lectured at Wheaton and had been very active in the work of the alumnae organizations. One other alumna would join the Board during the seminary years: Kate Upson Clark (WS1869), founder of the New York Wheaton Club, was elected in 1907 and remained a member until 1934.[9]

There is considerable reason to believe that the decision to admit women to the Board was part of a larger policy shift triggered by the crisis enveloping the Seminary and, more specifically, by the leadership problems brought on by the resignation of Ellen Stanton. One suspects that it may have been initiated by Eliza Wheaton; certainly we can be sure that it had her prior approval, for the Board of Trustees never took action on a major policy or fiscal issue without first ascertaining her views. The fact that women were already serving as trustees at Vassar, Smith, Wellesley, and Mount Holyoke Colleges must also have been an influencing factor. By the spring of 1897, the Trustees were publicly pointing to the introduction of women trustees as indication of the Seminary's progressive and forward looking attitude toward the education of women. Moreover, having two positions occupied by prominent alumnae in all likelihood lessened alumnae resistance to the proposed curricular changes, plans for which were already well underway in the spring of 1896.[10]

Throughout the summer and fall of 1896, the selection committee continued to search out potential candidates for the Principal's position. In December they made another recommendation to the Board, but again, when an invitation was extended it was declined.[11] Meanwhile student registration continued to fall. "At present," Ellen Stanton wrote in the beginning of March, 1897, "we are reduced to thirty-eight pupils including day-pupils, and the outlook indicates fewer still for next term."[12]

As had so often been the case before, it was Eliza Wheaton who took the initiative, proposing a new and radical solution. A handwritten, signed memoir tells the story:

> About the 19th of Feb. 1897 I wrote Edwin Barrows in expressing my desire to have the Trustees call Rev. S. V. Cole to be President of Wheaton Seminary and to offer him a salary of $2500 and a home in the Boarding House for himself and wife. I said I would pay his salary while I lived.[13]

That a man should be sought to head the Seminary evidently had not occurred to the selection committee, and when the trustees convened in special session on February 22 to consider the principalship issue, the three-person committee clearly was not aware of the existence of Mrs.

Wheaton's letter. After a lengthy presentation of their report, which included discussion of the qualifications of several potential female candidates, Mrs. Wheaton's letter was brought to the attention of the Board, probably by Edwin Barrows, the Treasurer. In swift succession the selection committee voted to include Mrs. Wheaton's recommendations in its formal report, the trustees accepted the report, and then voted to elect Rev. Cole to the position.[14]

Who knew about this in advance? Obviously Edwin Barrows, and most likely the president of the Board, Albert Plumb. Samuel Cole himself, who had been a member of the Board since 1893 and currently was secretary, either chose to stay away from the meeting or was not notified of it—in any case he was conveniently absent. It is equally evident that Mrs. Wheaton's initiative came as a surprise to some Board members, though one may suspect, remembering Mrs. Wheaton's lobbying techniques at the time Miss Stanton was elected Principal, that certain individuals may have been canvassed in advance. Be that as it may, the vote was unanimous and a letter inviting Cole to assume the leadership of the Seminary was immediately dispatched.

At the time Samuel Valentine Cole was minister of the Broadway Trinitarian Congregational Church in the neighboring city of Taunton, Massachusetts. An 1877 graduate of Bowdoin College, where he had served as tutor and instructor for several years, Rev. Cole had also taught classical languages in public high schools in Bath, Maine and Williamstown, Massachusetts. He had assumed his pastoral duties in Taunton in 1889 after completing the course of study at Andover Theological Seminary. His position as minister of a large Congregational church in a nearby community had brought him to Mrs. Wheaton's attention, and she had personally recommended him for membership on the Wheaton Board of Trustees in 1893. By 1896, having served several years as a member of the Trustee Committee of Instruction, he was well aware of the serious nature of the problems facing the Seminary. We do not know to what extent Mrs. Wheaton had discussed these issues with him, though in his role as Secretary of the Board he had the opportunity to communicate with her frequently on Seminary matters. Nonetheless, subsequent events indicate strongly that Eliza Wheaton knew exactly what she was doing, and why, when she wrote to Edwin Barrows recommending a man instead of a woman, the title of President rather than Principal, and a salary that was considerably higher than the $1800.00 Ellen Stanton was receiving in her seventeenth year as Principal.[15]

But whatever shared views existed between Eliza Wheaton and Samuel Cole, they did not extend to a commitment to accept the position, for there is abundant evidence of the considerable internal reservations and doubt Rev. Cole experienced before finally deciding to accept his new post. It seems probable that he and Mrs. Wheaton had discussed the problems facing the Seminary and possible solutions for them, but Rev.

Samuel Valentine Cole,
President, 1897-1925.
Under his leadership
Wheaton made a successful
transition from Seminary to
College.

Cole apparently had not entertained the thought that he might be selected as the one to put those solutions into effect. Happy in the position
he occupied, he was deeply admired and respected by his parishioners.
In accepting the Trustees' offer, he commented about the difficulties he
had experienced in arriving at his decision.

> For me to reach this conclusion has been no easy thing—at first I
> thought it would be an impossible thing—owing in part to the strength of
> the ties and the character of the opportunity which bind me to my present
> sphere of work, and in part to the uncertainties involved in such a change
> as your action contemplates.
> The problem which confronts Wheaton Seminary is a difficult one, and,
> while my acceptance of the important trust which you offer to place in my
> hands would indicate my belief that the problem is not impossible of solu-
> tion, I feel that it will require the united wisdom and effort of all the
> friends of the Seminary.[16]

In the draft of his address given at the seventy-fifth anniversary celebration in 1910, President Cole stated that Mrs. Wheaton's suggestion to
the Board was done "without my knowledge." He went on to comment
that "at first, the proposition seemed an impossible one for me to consider, but in the end I yielded; though when I mailed my reply, it would
pretty nearly have indicated my state of mind, if I had taken two letters
in my pocket, the first accepting and the second declining the position,
and then drawn one of them out and mailed it without looking to see
which one it was."[17]
On the whole, the decision to place a man in the former principal's
position seems to have been greeted favorably by alumnae and faculty.
Certainly Ellen Stanton was pleased. Writing to Kate Upson Clark

shortly after Rev. Cole had been invited to take the position she commented that the idea to hire him was a "far better scheme" than that of looking elsewhere for another principal. "Mr. Cole is a poet, scholar, and gentleman in the highest sense of the term," she went on. "He is a natural born teacher, and if he will only accept the position . . . we feel that it would be the best possible thing for the school."[18]

If Samuel Cole had not imagined that he might be asked to lead the Seminary, he nonetheless had ideas about how Wheaton might escape the pressure of the colleges and high schools, a pressure which constituted, as he later wrote, "the upper and nether millstones between which the old academies and seminaries seemed likely to be crushed."[19] How specific he was initially in presenting his views is hard to tell, for the minutes of the Board of Trustees meeting at which he accepted the position state only that he "indicated briefly the general lines along which he thought the policy of the Seminary should proceed."[20] However, the announcement of his appointment as President, which was issued shortly thereafter in lieu of a catalogue for the ensuing year, gave some general hints when it mentioned not only that a thorough revision of the curriculum was underway and that a college preparatory course existed, but that the Seminary, with "anticipated improvements in its buildings and equipment to be realized at no distant day, has before it enlarged possibilities of usefulness, which may well excite the ambition of its managers, and awaken the warmest hopes of its friends."[21]

Rev. Cole was equally cautious in his inaugural address—although he outlined the problem facing Wheaton clearly enough:

> You are aware of the problem which confronts a school of this grade. The rise of the high schools on the one side and the rise of the colleges on the other have squeezed us thin. What shall we do to be saved? Shall Wheaton Seminary be an institution to which its graduates will want to send their daughters, or only an institution which they will recommend to the daughters of other people? Shall it be a place for preparing a young woman for her life work, or a place to prepare her for going somewhere else to get prepared? What will you do with Wheaton Seminary? . . .
>
> It is a fact that a larger educational equipment is required for a young woman today than was the case fifty or twenty-five years ago. And, so far as Wheaton Seminary is concerned, I believe it is the desire and purpose of its trustees and friends to adapt the institution to the needs of the times.
>
> In just what way this should be done is a subject to be carefully studied. . . . I, for one, do not feel like rendering a verdict till the evidence is all in.[22]

Undoubtedly President Cole was wary of expressing his views publicly. But it seems very likely that even at the time he accepted his new office he had a "verdict" in mind, and it was one with which Mrs. Wheaton concurred. Years later, when Wheaton was preparing to announce its intention to apply to the Massachusetts legislature for permission to institute a full collegiate degree program, Rev. Cole commented that Mrs. Wheaton had specifically expressed her desire to him that Wheaton become "a small college."[23]

And indeed that is what President Cole had in mind. Within six months of taking office he was so sure of the course he wished to pursue that he laid it before the full Board of Trustees on December 21, 1897. The minutes of that meeting deserve extensive quotation:

> The next item of business referred to the general condition of the Seminary, the outlook for the future, and the line of policy which might be followed in view of the changed conditions in the educational life of women.
>
> The President of the Seminary, as a result of his investigations, made a statement of considerable fullness on the various points involved, and this was followed by a careful discussion, under the leadership of the President of the Board, in which every member participated. At the conclusion of the discussion, although no formal vote was taken, the unanimous opinion of the Board, as expressed by each member individually at the call of the President of the Board, was found to be in favor of shaping the policy of the Seminary toward the introduction of a college curriculum, with a view to applying for a college charter at some future time if circumstances shall seem to warrant.[24]

Even though no formal vote was taken, the decision effectively had been made. Wheaton would aspire to the same solution already achieved by Mount Holyoke. But the methods it would use to achieve this end would be very different from those employed by its former sister seminary. Mount Holyoke Seminary, with its larger student enrollment, greater physical plant, and wider reputation, had been able to make the change relatively quickly. For Wheaton the road would be much longer, much slower, and for nearly fourteen years cloaked in such total secrecy that no mention of the ultimate goal can be found, even in Trustee records, during all that time.

Why the secrecy? Why the long delay? The reasons were several. First, the physical plant and the size of the student body in 1897 (registration during the summer term when Rev. Cole took office dipped to twenty-five) would scarcely have encouraged the General Court of Massachusetts to greet an application for a college charter with anything but scorn. A massive revitalization program had to be undertaken before Wheaton could hope to be taken seriously in terms of its ultimate ambition. Moreover, President Cole was well aware that Mount Holyoke had run into unexpected and stiff opposition from both Wellesley and Smith when it applied for a college charter, opposition contending that there was no need for another women's college in Massachusetts.[25] The same objection had subsequently been raised when Simmons College in Boston was founded, though in more muted form, given Simmons' specific mission of vocational training required by the terms of its endowment. President Cole knew that the groundwork would have to be laid carefully and the final public changeover initiated only after a position of great strength had been quietly achieved.

How much the teaching staff knew about the initial decision relating to future college status is not clear; certainly students and the public in general seem to have had no idea of it. In the months immediately after President Cole's appointment there was some sentiment expressed in student and alumnae circles favorable to college status, but this soon subsided as no encouragement was forthcoming from trustee or administrative sources.

In retrospect, however, we can see that there was a plan—a plan carefully developed and adhered to by President Cole in the years between 1897 and 1912. It had three components.

The first was the belief that the demand for collegiate education for women would continue to increase. In the eastern part of the United States, where the tradition of single-sex male colleges was already well established and new land grant state universities did not dominate as they did in the mid-west, it was logical to assume that families who looked to colleges such as Dartmouth, Williams, Bowdoin, Amherst, or Yale for their sons' education would seek similar women's institutions for their daughters. In time there should be room for another to stand alongside Wellesley, Vassar, Smith, Mount Holyoke, and the coordinate colleges of Harvard (Radcliffe) and Brown (Pembroke). In the meantime, since it could be demonstrated clearly that a seminary education constituted a distinct step beyond anything offered in high school or college preparatory programs, there should continue to be enough demand to make a seminary curriculum viable—a curriculum that in time would form the basis on which a full four-year college program could be built.

Secondly, funds would be needed to build the dormitories, classrooms and athletic facilities required for successful implementation of a college program. President Cole was fortunate in having someone to whom he could turn for such revenue. Eliza Wheaton had been subsidizing the operation of the Seminary heavily for years. With no heirs of her own, she intended to leave her own personal estate, as well as the Boston Winter Street property of which the Seminary was already residuary legatee, to the educational institution that had become the focal point of her life. And she was willing, as she had already demonstrated, to part with much of her wealth before her death if it were needed for this cause.

But in order to have Mrs. Wheaton's funds available for capital investment it was necessary that the Seminary regain fiscal solvency in its annual operational expenses, which were running at an annual deficit ranging between five and ten thousand dollars. These deficits had been met by regular transfusions from the purse of Mrs. Wheaton plus the sale of some $6000 worth of Seminary-held stocks and bonds. The key to stopping this drain and making her funds available for building purposes lay in attracting enough students so the Seminary could become operationally self-supporting.[26]

Therefore, the third component of President Cole's plan involved a full-scale implementation of the college preparatory program which he believed would create this needed financial stability. Within a year the Seminary dropped the three-term format it had used for decades and adopted a two-semester calendar that paralleled those of colleges in the area. A six-year academic schedule was carefully worked out involving a four-year college preparatory program and a four-year seminary program, with the last two years of the former and the first two years of the latter overlapping to some degree. Students were admitted into either course of study and allowed to shift from one to the other. In addition the Seminary actively recruited special students who did not enter any particular program but enrolled in those courses which suited their own tastes or needs for any number of semesters they chose.[27]

The results were highly dramatic. By the end of the 1899–1900 academic year enrollment had increased to 85 students and the Seminary was operating some $3500 in the black. This was partially due to increased student revenues but also reflected the fact that President Cole's $2500 salary was paid separately by Mrs. Wheaton, who also had given $60,000 worth of bonds to the Seminary in 1899 with the express instructions that only the interest drawn on them could be used for general expenses. This gift constituted the first real nucleus of a permanent endowment, something which Wheaton Seminary had been notably lacking, despite the generosity of the Wheaton family over the years. The achievement of basic and sustained operational solvency meant that Mrs. Wheaton's annual gifts, which the Seminary continued to receive, could be turned to other concerns.[28]

During the first three years of President Cole's administration, no major plant expansion was attempted. Instead, funded by gifts from Mrs. Wheaton, a large number of improvements and additions to existing facilities were undertaken, the most important of which were the installation of a long-distance telephone, the wiring of both the dormitory and Seminary Hall for electricity, and the drilling of an artesian well and the erection of a water tower on Mrs. Wheaton's property. This last allowed the installation of piped drinking water into the dormitories and ended dependence on attic storage tanks for water pressure for toilet facilities. Buildings were repainted, lounges refurbished—in other words a concerted attempt was made to modernize existing facilities. In addition, in 1898 electric trolley lines were extended to Norton. In time these linked the small town directly to Attleboro, Taunton, and Mansfield, thus greatly improving access to the Seminary from the railroad lines that passed through those communities.

By the turn of the century the combination of plant modernization,

Rear view of the Seminary, 1899.

improved travel facilities, and successful implementation of the college preparatory program had brought renewed prosperity to Wheaton. Particularly important was a change in general public perception of Wheaton Female Seminary. Writing in the spring of 1897, an alumna from the class of 1888 sadly commented: "I very much fear that Wheaton's best days are over."[29] One year later her view had totally changed: "The *gentleman* who reigns there as *President* is Mr. Cole. He has changed the management very greatly; no half-hours, six o'clock dinner, shorter study hours and longer recreation hours and very few rules. They have a long distance telephone in the office. I have a young cousin in there this year from Nebraska and she enjoys the new order of things. . . ."[30]

The college preparatory program continued to be a major component of Wheaton's academic curriculum during the first decade of the 1900s. But President Cole had also been right in thinking that there would be a steady market for a seminary curriculum whose final two years designedly and specifically went beyond anything required for those preparing for college certification elsewhere. In fact, the annual number of graduates from the seminary course steadily increased, particularly as each year several students who had originally enrolled in the preparatory program shifted courses and decided to remain at Wheaton rather than go to college.

The temptation must have been great to continue relying on the successful blend of college preparatory, special, and seminary programs that had brought about the rejuvenation of the Seminary from the dark days of 1895–1897, but the course had already been set toward a different goal. Once operational stability was achieved, President Cole, with the enthusiastic support of Mrs. Wheaton and the Board of Trustees, embarked on a major expansion program that continued for more than a decade, a program which is understandable only in terms of the long-range plan to change again the nature of the institution, this time to full-fledged college status.

From its inception in 1834–35, the founders of Wheaton had sought to provide the highest level of education deemed appropriate for women. By the turn of the century this meant a four-year college program. It seems evident that Eliza Wheaton had come to recognize this by the mid-1890s, and she consistently encouraged and liberally supported Samuel Cole's policies and plans toward that end. It can be confidently assumed that Mrs. Wheaton was aware and supportive of Rev. Cole's plan to bring the matter of future college status before the Trustees well before he actually did so in December, 1897. In fact, her personal selection of Rev. Cole as the person to head the Seminary, and her suggestion that the title of the office be changed from Principal to President, indicates that she understood and was in agreement with his ideas at the time she nominated him.

Support for this view also can be found in a passage in the statement prepared for the State Board of Education and the Massachusetts legislative committee that conducted hearings on the Seminary's petition to become a college in 1912: "The last survivor of those who endowed and fostered it [the Seminary] signified her desire in expressed words that the Seminary should become a small college, and, with that end in view, committed it, through the Trustees, to the present administration."[31] One can only marvel at the progressive vision of a woman, already in her middle eighties, who could adapt to and promote changes so far advanced over what she had known for so much of her life.

NOTES: CHAPTER 5

1. Trustees Minutes: 6/26/95.
2. SVC, *Why Change?*
3. Trustees Minutes: 4/27/96.
4. Ibid. See also Principals: Stanton: Stanton letter of resignation, 4/14/96.
5. Trustees Minutes: 4/27/96; 5/29/96.
6. Ibid.: 5/29/96; A. M. Wells, *Miss Marks and Miss Woolley* (Boston: Houghton Mifflin, 1978), pp. 23–48.
7. In 1900, having declined an offer to become Dean of Pembroke College, Mary Woolley accepted the Presidency of Mount Holyoke College, a position she held until 1937.

8. Trustees Minutes: 6/24/96.

9. Ibid.: 5/29/96; 6/24/96; 12/16/96; 3/24/97; 1/21/07.

10. Wheaton Female Seminary, *Annual Catalogue*, "Announcement by the Board of Trustees of Wheaton Seminary. Sixty-Third Year, 1897–1898," p. 3.

11. The offer was made to Ada G. Wing, who decided to remain at Brown University, where she had recently been appointed Assistant Professor of Physiology and Sanitary Science. G. Hawk, *Pembroke College in Brown University* (Providence: Brown University Press, 1967), pp. 47–48; Principals: Stanton: Stanton letter, Spring, 1897; Trustees Minutes: 12/16/96; 2/22/97.

12. Principals: Stanton: Stanton to K. U. Clark, March, 1897; see also Trustees Minutes: 12/16/96; 2/22/97.

13. SVC: EBW Memorandum.

14. Trustees Minutes: 2/22/97; also 3/24/97; and Paine, *E. B. Wheaton,* p. 229. This meeting took place in Boston.

15. Trustees Minutes: 3/29/93; SVC: College Business: SVC to Trustees, 7/17/93; Bowdoin College, *General Catalogue of Bowdoin College, 1794–1950* (Brunswick, ME: Bowdoin College, 1950), p. 139.

16. SVC: College Business: SVC to Trustees, 3/24/97; Trustees Minutes: 3/24/97.

17. Anniversaries: SVC draft of 75th Anniversary Speech, p. 31.

18. Principals: Stanton: Stanton to K. U. Clark, March, 1897.

19. SVC, "Historical Address" (Extracts), *Wheaton Bulletin*, 6:3 (June, 1910), pp. 8–9.

20. Trustees Minutes: 3/24/97. These minutes were, of course, written by President Cole, who continued to serve in his elected position as Secretary of the Board.

21. Wheaton Female Seminary, *Annual Catalogue*, "Announcement of Sixty-Third Year, 1897–1898."

22. SVC: Printed Material: *Concerning Education: Inaugural Address of Rev. Samuel V. Cole as President of Wheaton Seminary, given June 23, 1897*, pp. 17–18.

23. Ibid.: College Business: Report to Trustees, 3/21/11.

24. Trustees Minutes: 12/21/97.

25. Wells, *Marks and Woolley*, p. 55; A. C. Cole, *Hundred Years*, ch. 9.

26. Trustees Minutes: 3/27/95; 12/18/95; 12/16/96; 12/21/97; 3/12/98; 3/29/99; SVC: College Business: Report to Trustees, 3/21/11.

27. Wheaton Female Seminary, *Annual Catalogue*, 1898–1912; Shepard, "Reference History," pp. 250, 345–47; Trustees Minutes: 12/21/97.

28. EBW: EBW Letters: Letter conveying bonds to Seminary; SVC: College Business: SVC to EBW, 6/15/99; Trustees Minutes, 6/14/99; 3/28/00; 11/26/00; 11/20/01. Aside from the Carter and Metcalf Scholarship Funds, the Seminary held only $8000 worth of stocks prior to this gift from Mrs. Wheaton. See Trustees Minutes: 12/16/96.

29. General Files: 1887–1888: H. Thompson letter (spring, 1897).

30. Ibid.: Thompson to Dickey, 1/16/98.

31. Wheaton Histories, Seminary: Seminary to College #2: "Wheaton Seminary," p. 4. In 1912, and again in 1920, President Cole stated that Mrs. Wheaton had expressed this view to him shortly before her death in 1905. Undoubtedly she did reiterate this position then, but the evidence is overwhelming that it was not a new conviction, but rather one she had held since the mid-1890s. See SVC, *Why Change?*; Shepard, "Reference History," p. 288.

6
From Seminary to College
1900–1912

THE EARLY DECISION to become a college, along with the concomitant delay in the implementation of that step, meant that Wheaton dealt with most of the problems of transition while still a seminary and preparatory school, rather than experiencing them after becoming a college. By the time the formal decision to seek a new charter was made in November, 1911, so well had the ground been prepared that in four months' time the change was fully effected and announcements had been sent out to recruit a freshman class for the fall of 1912. The first two years of the college preparatory program were dropped immediately; the last two years (which coincided with the first two of the seminary curriculum) were eliminated a year at a time. The third and fourth years of the Seminary curriculum served, with almost no alteration, as the curriculum for the college freshman and sophomore years; advanced courses appropriate for the junior and senior years were swiftly added. By September, 1914, the entire college preparatory program and the first two years of the seminary curriculum had been eliminated. The whole formal transition process seemed incredibly smooth and easy when compared to what Mount Holyoke had experienced or in contrast to the birth pains felt in their early years by Vassar, Smith, and Wellesley.[1]

The reason for this rapid and relatively problem-free final transition lay in years of careful preparation and planning under the leadership of Samuel Valentine Cole. Many of these earlier years were anything but easy, yet the plan of action devised by President Cole when he assumed office in 1897 not only worked, but worked exceedingly well. The college preparatory and special student programs attracted students. More students meant a balanced operating budget. A balanced operating budget allowed Wheaton family funds to be turned to capital expenditures for new dormitory and classroom facilities. Bigger, better, and newer facilities in turn attracted more students, and as each dormitory filled its beds, the justification for a further addition was created.

An upward spiral of this sort, especially when there is a source of outside money to provide additional energy, tends to feed itself and generate additional growth. So long as this growth can be controlled and

112

coordinated within an understood, comprehensive vision of the future, it can often be perpetuated for a considerable period of time. Such was the case with Wheaton. Incredibly rapid as the expansion of the first decade of the twentieth century must have appeared then, and still appears today, in retrospect it can all be seen as part of a meticulously designed plan to reach a well defined end. Nowhere is this more evident than in two of the earliest steps taken during the carefully orchestrated growth process.

Within months after the decision had been made to become a college President Cole entered into discussions with the well known Boston architectural firm of Cram, Goodhue and Ferguson regarding the erection of a new dormitory. This prospect enticed Ralph Adams Cram, the senior partner, to come to Norton to view the site first-hand. Mr. Cram would ultimately become famous as the planner of college campuses such as Princeton and West Point, as well as architect of the Cathedral of St. John the Divine in New York. He looked at the small campus and discussed not only the contemplated dormitory, but also the larger vision which President Cole held for the future of Wheaton. Writing several years later to the architectural firm, President Cole commented:

> The day of Mr. Cram's first visit here, as he may recall, I stated that Mrs. Cole and I had often talked the matter over and wondered whether buildings could not be grouped around a central court on our grounds. He at once said they could and on returning to my office he made a rough pencil diagram of the way it could be done. I said that everything was in the air as to the future and that we could not bind ourselves in any way as to what would be done or as to whom would do it. All we contemplated at the time was the erection of a dormitory. . . . I understood that the "rough scheme for the entire development of the school" which you subsequently laid out was in order to [establish] the proper location and construction of Chapin Hall, for we should have been unwilling, as I explained, to proceed with the building without some such scheme.[2]

The original rough sketch hastily drawn by Mr. Cram indeed showed the basic concept of a large open space bordered by a rectangular walkway and surrounded by a series of impressive buildings (doodles of which also can be found on the sketch).[3] The long axis would run north and south with Mrs. Wheaton's house serving as the focal point at the north and Seminary Hall and the Boarding House occupying the northeast and northwest corners respectively. Interestingly enough, the first dormitory to be built was placed slightly away from this central court, which in concept resembled a traditional New England Common or Green. Chapin Hall, named for Mrs. Wheaton's brother Samuel Chapin, was completed early in 1901. Designed by Cram, Goodhue and Ferguson, it was the first of twelve buildings and one major building addition for which the firm would serve as architect between 1900 and 1934. In

1907 the Seminary accepted the firm's proposal that it be named supervising architect for the campus as a whole, a position it would hold for approximately three decades.[4]

During the final eleven years that Wheaton existed as a Seminary, six more buildings were constructed, only three of which were designed by Mr. Cram's firm. In fact, the decision to utilize a different architect, the firm of Rotch and Tilden, to design a new gymnasium elicited a vigorous protest from Cram, Goodhue and Ferguson, which contended that the tentative campus plans it had drawn, plus several preliminary sketches prepared for a new gymnasium, entitled the firm to the commission. While President Cole vigorously disputed that assertion, he did admit that the decision to utilize a different firm stemmed from a "special reason" which "made it wise" for Wheaton to do so.[5] That reason is not difficult to discover.

One of the most important decisions President Cole made was to build, at the very outset of his expansion program, a large, ultra-modern gymnasium designed to accommodate many more students than currently were attending the Seminary. In 1899 he convinced the Board of Trustees to launch the Seminary's first coordinated capital campaign in order to raise funds for this structure. The appeal, sent to all alumnae and former students, used Mrs. Wheaton's approaching ninetieth birthday as the focal point for this solicitation. The response was disappointing; only "a few hundred dollars" were received, but President Cole was undeterred. He sought out his long-time acquaintance from Bowdoin College days, Dr. Dudley Sargent of Harvard University, who had become nationally recognized as a leading expert on physical training in colleges and schools. Director of Hemenway Gymnasium at Harvard, as well as the head of his own private normal school and gymnasium in Cambridge, Sargent has been described as "a man of strong convictions, very loyal to those who shared his views but often intolerant toward those who opposed him."[6]

Samuel Cole was well aware of the favorable publicity that could accrue to the Seminary if he could associate Dudley Sargent's name with a building. But one of those to whom Dr. Sargent was loyal was George Tilden, the man who had designed his normal school and gymnasium. Sargent readily agreed to serve as consultant for the Wheaton gymnasium, but apparently insisted that the architect be Mr. Tilden. This was undoubtedly the "special reason" President Cole referred to as governing the choice of the architect for the gymnasium. However, the resultant publicity for Wheaton at the time the building was dedicated (with Dr. Sargent giving the major address), as well as the use of Dr. Sargent's name in Seminary public brochures in succeeding years, more than justified the limited embarrassment that the seemingly arbitrary rejection of Ralph Cram caused for Mr. Cole.[7]

The gymnasium was opened in 1903. It was placed at a considerable

Calisthenics in the new Gymnasium, ca. 1915. Note the overhead running track.

distance from the other existing structures, at the southeastern corner of
what was still merely a contemplated rectangular walkway. It was a situation that only made sense in terms of a major long-term scheme of plant
expansion; to the students and most observers at the time its location
seemed capricious. But they did not have to wait long for further developments. In rapid succession a new power plant (1904), a large dining
and kitchen facility (1908), two dormitories (1908 and 1911), and a
building providing science classrooms and a large assembly hall (1911)
were constructed.[8] The dining hall, named in honor of the Emerson family, and the two dormitories, named for two of Wheaton's most famed
teachers, Lucy Larcom and Mary Cragin, essentially filled the west side
of the quadrangle, while the science building balanced the gymnasium
on the eastern side.[9] Thus, by the time the Seminary applied to the legislature in January, 1912, for permission to offer college degrees, visiting
members of the Joint Committee on Education found a well-designed
campus consisting of eight major buildings, six of them very recently
constructed, as well as athletic fields, tennis courts, a small observatory,
and houses surrounding the campus that provided a separate infirmary
plus additional living space for students, faculty, and the President.[10]

The period of simultaneous construction of Emerson Dining Hall and
Larcom dormitory in 1907–1908 was a particularly trying one for President Cole. Recently bereaved by the death of his wife, Annie Talbot
Cole, in 1906, he faced for the only time in his career serious, even for
a brief period, majority opposition from the Board of Trustees. The issue
was the location of the new buildings. The President insisted that they
be placed the same distance as the gymnasium from the long axis of the
projected rectangular court of honor. But the trustees, concerned that the
land in back of the structures would go to waste, argued vigorously that

the buildings ought to be moved back some sixty feet and constructed as close as possible to the street that bordered the campus. Supported strongly by the teachers, President Cole adamantly resisted. Although the controversy caused him "sleepless nights," as he put it, and created a rift between him and a long-time trustee, Judge William Fox, that never fully healed, President Cole's will prevailed and the concept of a visually-balanced campus was maintained.[11]

The financing for much of this construction was made possible, paradoxically, by the death of the Seminary's great patron, Eliza Baylies Wheaton, in June, 1905, at the age of 95. For more than seventy years she had watched over and served as the great benefactress of the institution whose creation she had suggested to her father-in-law. In her last years she had strongly supported, both personally and financially, Samuel Cole's expansionist goals. Although the Seminary had achieved an annual operational budget surplus by 1900, the major part of the funds for Chapin dormitory, the gymnasium, and the powerhouse had come from Mrs. Wheaton's annual gifts, gifts that had heretofore been used to balance operational deficits. Her death meant that not only her personal estate, but the Boston Winter Street property, for which the Seminary had been designated residuary legatee in the will of Laban Morey Wheaton, became the property of the Seminary.

In monetary terms, Mrs. Wheaton's personal estate proved to be relatively modest. After her executors (of whom Samuel Cole was one) made provisions for the many beneficiaries and projects she specified in her will and its several codicils, the Seminary received only $28,124.60 in shares of stock, promissory notes, and cash. However, the income from the Boston property, $24,000 annually, now came directly to the institution and was used primarily to finance new construction. In addition the Seminary inherited Mrs. Wheaton's fine homestead and the more than fifty acres that surrounded it, along with considerable acreage in the vicinity (none of it bordering on the campus), as well as several frame buildings along East Main Street and Howard Street that were contiguous to Seminary property.[12]

Until the time of Mrs. Wheaton's death, President Cole and his wife had lived in a suite of rooms in Metcalf Hall, as the rambling boarding house was now called. However, in June, 1905, the trustees designated Mrs. Wheaton's house as his residence, a function it would continue to serve for succeeding presidents. The Seminary also proceeded to purchase Judge Wheaton's original Mansion House, which had been sold in 1876 and operated by various owners as an inn. In 1907, however, it became apparent that the current proprietors were selling liquor to customers, and the Board enthusiastically endorsed the repurchase in order, as the President put it in the draft of his 75th anniversary address, "to control the selection of the tenant, since the building had become a menace to the morals of the town."[13] In addition, the trustees adopted a policy of acquiring, whenever possible, additional parcels of land in the block surrounded by Howard Street, Taunton Avenue, and East Main Street.[14]

But the changes in the Seminary during the first decade of the twentieth century were not confined to its facilities. Along with the new buildings came both an increase and a change in the composition of the faculty. Again, this shift, gradual though it was, was not free from tension and moments of crisis. Chief among them was the growing rift between Clara Pike and Samuel Cole, a rift that ultimately led to her forced resignation, a consequent outcry from students, parents, and many alumnae, and a full-scale investigation by the Board of Trustees that required the filing of a twenty-five page, single-spaced report to the Trustees from the President. It ended ultimately with a formal vote of confidence by the Board in support of President Cole.[15]

The issues appear to have been several, some overt, others hidden. Clara Pike, unlike the newer faculty who were being hired, did not have a college degree. Yet for students both current and past, she, more than any other faculty member, symbolized Wheaton Seminary. An outstanding teacher since 1869, she had developed over the years an excellent science program. She had wheedled, badgered, and coaxed the trustees into providing science facilities and equipment unusually sophisticated for a female seminary. During the last years of Ellen Stanton's administration Miss Pike had served as unofficial, but fully recognized vice-principal. Offered the position of Principal when Ellen Stanton retired, she had declined, but one senses that she was not happy with the selection of Rev. Cole and that her relationship with him and Mrs. Cole was

The Mansion House (home of Judge Wheaton), and the First Congregational Church Unitarian, Norton Center, ca. 1900. From 1876 to 1963 the Mansion House served both the seminary/college and the Norton community as the Wheaton Inn. The building was razed in 1965.

never good. In part this may have been because President Cole hired Annette Munro to the newly created position of Librarian and Registrar and placed her in charge of student accounts and records, in which she was assisted by Mrs. Cole, who handled the kitchen billings.[16] Most of the work designated to this early version of a business office had always been the task of the Principal and her chosen assistant, and it is likely that Clara Pike disapproved of the shift in organizational structure. Even more important was the role Miss Pike had assumed as senior teacher in the last years of Ellen Stanton's administration. This included the scheduling of all courses and determining what subjects each faculty member would teach in a given term. This authority President Cole was not willing to delegate to anyone, and as new faculty members hired by him were added to the teaching staff, they often found themselves caught between what they understood they had been hired to do and the mold into which Miss Pike wished them to fit.

In no case was this problem more clear than that of Helen Swain. A graduate of Dr. Sargent's normal school, she had been hired in 1898–99 by President Cole specifically to upgrade Wheaton's program in physical training and culture—this in anticipation of the new gymnasium, for which plans were already well under way.[17] A devotee of Dr. Sargent's modern curriculum of physical training and an advocate of athletic participation and gymnastics for women, President Cole sought to de-emphasize what had been known as physical culture (modern rhythmic movement and mild calisthenics) and devote more time to instruction in personal hygiene and physical fitness.

In seeking to implement her new program, Miss Swain often came in conflict with Clara Pike, who was entrusted with the general health of the students. Apparently Miss Pike took a dim view of programs that included cold sponge baths every morning and exercise that promoted a high state of facial flushing and bodily perspiration. But in a real sense this issue was only symbolic of the larger one. In his report to the trustees, President Cole spelled the matter out quite clearly.

> I came here wholly unprepared to find that a teacher in order to hold her place and do her work in peace must satisfy any other member of the faculty than the head of the school. The situation was one that I did not bring about, and one that I could not control. Again and again I found that my responsibility exceeded my authority. The result was finally a divided allegiance and a confusion in the minds of parents as to what was and what was not the truth.
>
> I desired of all things that Miss Pike should remain in the school, occupying the most honorable position and having almost any privilege which she might desire, provided she was willing that I should arrange the work and decide on the qualifications of the other teachers. The matter was absolutely in her hands from first to last. It was in the spirit of perplexity, even of sadness, that I conferred with some of the Trustees—as I felt I

ought to be able to confer with my natural advisers and supporters—when I saw that two different policies were emerging so distinctly into view as to destroy and endanger the safety of the school. A house divided against itself cannot stand.

I do not wish to open the case before the public or before this Board in detail, unless circumstances force me to do so; but the evidence for what I have said is simply overwhelming.

Let me add that personally I could get along with Miss Pike to the end of time. No one recognizes her excellent qualities and valuable service more distinctly than I, or regrets more deeply the circumstances of her withdrawal. But I do not see how I could have helped it. . . . As one of our most influential alumnae has said to me, in substance, "It is a wonder that it could be out of sight so long."[18]

Privately, President Cole clearly saw the confrontation as one of personal rivalry. Writing to Kate Upson Clark in January 1902, he commented: "I have protected Miss Pike to a greater extent than her friends are aware of. When the matter finally got beyond my control and reduced itself to the plain question as to whether Miss Pike or I was the head of the school, of course the break had to come, as much as I deplored it."[19]

In retrospect, the importance of this confrontation seems even greater than it may have appeared to those at the time, for it was in a real sense the final stage in the break between the seminary concept and that of a modern college. From the time of its inception the Seminary had been administered, both fiscally and in terms of curriculum, by its teaching staff. The Principals were hired from the ranks of teachers, either at Wheaton or elsewhere, and they all continued to teach. They regarded themselves more as the leader of a group of colleagues than as administrative head of an institution in which the teachers, like other members of the staff, were employees of a different type and at a different level. It truly could be said that there was minimal separation between administration and faculty in any of the day-to-day running of the Seminary.

With President Cole's appointment, matters changed. Previously the Board of Trustees had had little or no internal impact on the daily affairs of the Seminary. Now one of their number, a male who was not by profession a teacher, had taken control. Moreover, he was accompanied by a wife who was eager and able to assist him in dealing with some of the more routine business affairs of the Seminary, as she had undoubtedly done in the administrative side of his Taunton parish work.

Creating a separate registrar's office and placing the librarian in charge of it, President Cole removed from the hands of teaching faculty many student record and business matters. Though he annually taught a Bible course, and regarded himself as chief academic officer, the result, nonetheless, was the creation of separate categories of administration and faculty in a manner hitherto unknown at Wheaton.

Finally, President Cole's policies of emphasizing the college preparatory program and physical plant expansion must have seemed to Clara
Pike and the other senior teachers most committed to the traditional seminary as highly threatening to the very educational system they held
most dear. Undoubtedly President Cole was correct in characterizing the
clash between himself and Miss Pike as personal and a basic challenge
to his authority. His response was probably the only one open to him,
but he also seems to have been remarkably indifferent to the emotional,
educational, and psychological impact his policies were having on the
fabric of the old Seminary. Ailing as it may have been, the Seminary
still engendered extreme loyalty and devotion from those who had long
been a part of its existence, or who deplored the changing nature of education for women, as many still did when they surveyed the drive
towards collegiate education and the concept of adopting "men's ways."

Perhaps the saddest result of this clash of iron wills was that over the
next thirty-five years, as the Seminary and College systematically sought
through naming its new buildings to recognize those former teachers,
administrators, and trustees who had contributed greatly to the educational development of Wheaton, the name of Clara Pike, who had graduated from Wheaton in 1866 and returned to teach and oversee the
development of a strong science program for more than thirty years, was
never included in that list. Only a bird feeder in the form of a Chinese
Pagoda, along with a concrete bench and a small endowment for bird
seed provided by Wheaton alumnae, served to memoralize a woman
who contributed in so many positive ways throughout her adult life to
the well-being and growing academic reputation of Wheaton Female
Seminary.

Two major organizational changes occurred during the first years of
the twentieth century. Wheaton had for decades brought male guest lecturers to the campus, and often retained noted professors from Harvard,
MIT, and Princeton to spend some time at the Seminary giving a series
of talks on their academic specialties. Beginning in 1879, the Seminary
employed on a permanent basis Hiram Tucker, organist of the Handel
and Haydn Society of Boston, as teacher of piano and head of the Music
Department. But the Seminary had never hired a man to teach any of the
courses that counted for credit toward either the seminary degree or the
college preparatory certificate. So major was such a step perceived to be
that President Cole felt obliged to consult the Board of Trustees specifically regarding it. Only after tabling the issue for some time, plus sub-
jecting the matter to committee review and the most "careful
consideration and discussion" by the full Board, did the trustees vote on
May 2, 1906, that "in the judgement of the Board it is desireable to employ a man as suggested. . . ."[20] The result was that in the fall of 1906,
George Sherman, who held B.A. and M.A. degrees from Amherst College, assumed the position of teacher of natural science. Though Mr.

Sherman would remain the sole male faculty member teaching courses in the credit curriculum until after the transition to college status occurred in 1912, the issue itself had been decided once and for all.

The second major organizational change occurred in 1908, following the death of the President of the Board of Trustees, Albert Plumb, who had served on the Board since 1870. The trustees proceeded to elect President Cole in his place. This choice was probably not so much due to his being President of the Seminary as to the fact that as Secretary of the Board and member since 1893, he was obviously the next in line for the position.[21]

Wheaton was not unique in having its President serve also as Head of the Board of Trustees. Many colleges, including Mr. Cole's alma mater, Bowdoin, followed this practice, but the position was ex officio rather than independent, and usually carried with it minimal power within the elected Board, whose chief officer was in effect the vice-chairman. President Cole's position was somewhat different. He had been a member of the Board before assuming the administrative leadership of the Seminary, and had continually been reelected to five-year terms. His position on the Board thus stemmed from that fact rather than from being President of the Seminary. Until his appointment as President, no administrative head of the Seminary had served on the Board and one may wonder if even Rev. Cole would have been admitted had he not already been there. But the manner in which these two offices became combined served to give President Cole unusual authority and control over all aspects of seminary and subsequently college affairs, a tradition that would be continued by his successors until the Board chairmanship was relinquished by President-elect A. Howard Meneely in 1944.

By June of 1910, when Wheaton celebrated its seventy-fifth anniversary, President Cole could point with pride to an institution with a modern campus and an enrollment of more than 200 students, with more seeking admission than could be accommodated. Only one trustee, Judge Fox, and two faculty members, musicians Hiram Tucker and Louise Brooks, remained from among those associated with Wheaton when Rev. Cole had joined the Board of Trustees in 1893. Throughout the gala celebration that June, no mention was made of any potential changes, but clearly the time was right. In September, the President asked for and received authorization to begin the planning necessary for erection of another dormitory and a new science and assembly hall. Both these structures were well underway when, at a Board meeting held on March 21, 1911, President Cole formally initiated the process that would culminate one year later in the complete transition from seminary to college.[22]

To give up an educational system that was prospering so well must have given more than one person some doubts, but for the President, who had been working steadfastly toward this moment for fourteen years, there were none. His arguments, presented both in a formal statement and in general discussion, proved so persuasive that the Board quickly agreed to create a subcommittee, composed of the President, George Smart, and Annie Kilham, which would "consider the future policy of the school."[23] Permission was also granted for President Cole to invite President William DeWitt Hyde of Bowdoin College and Dr. David Snedden, Commissioner of Education for Massachusetts, to serve in an advisory capacity to the Trustees.[24]

In brief, the President stated that the Seminary had grown to the point where the number of students made its two-track, overlapping, six-year curriculum of college preparatory and seminary studies totally unwieldly, hard to administer and almost impossible to teach. Further problems were created by the number of special students enrolled, each of whom desired her own course program. President Cole expressed dissatisfaction with the "machine process" of preparing students to meet the varied admissions requirements of different colleges. "Very little," he wrote, "is left to the judgement of the school. . . . We have been forced to separate the college preparatory students from the seminary students even in the same studies, because the methods are different as well as the ends in view."[25]

The most satisfactory educational work, the President continued, was being done in the last two years of the seminary program, where Wheaton was free to do what it thought best in preparing a young woman for her life work. "This work is truly educational, aiming as it does, not so much to impart a vast deal of information as to wake up the mind, give it ideals, and stimulate it to further and life-long activity."[26] Yet these same students could not subsequently gain admission to college, because they had not fulfilled all the exact requirements for admission. "One division, therefore, of the Seminary work is done as the colleges prescribe; another division as the parents prescribe; and the

Graduation procession returning from the Trinitarian Congregational Church, 1908.

third division, in which our judgment has freer play, is done under such limitations as to leave the graduate unable to use her acquirements to the best advantage in the effort to earn a livelihood."[27]

Admitting that what Wheaton was doing, it was doing well, the President nonetheless asked if the Seminary as presently constituted were indeed "making the best use of the resources which it has accepted as a sacred trust for implanting the ideals of the Founders in the life of the community."[28] His view was that it probably was not. Citing Mrs. Wheaton's expressed wish that Wheaton ultimately become "a small college," and pointing to the intent of the institution from the day of its founding to provide the best education available for "older rather than younger girls," President Cole also noted that there was ample room for another women's college in Massachusetts, citing as evidence that "those now existing are crowded to the doors and Mount Holyoke, by no means the largest, advises in its latest catalogue that prospective students apply two or three years in advance to make sure of admittance."[29]

But the President had no desire that Wheaton follow exactly in the footsteps of its predecessors:

> Whatever the Seminary becomes I feel sure that it should be something unique, and not a trespasser on fields already occupied; that its numbers should be so strictly limited that it will never lose the home idea and the educative power that lies in personal associations; that character and culture should hold the prime place in its ideal; that its aim should be women's education for woman's work, and its basic principle, "that they may have life and may have it abundantly."[30]

At its June meeting, the Board was presented with a thorough report prepared by Ida Everett, a teacher of English and Literature, who later would become the first Dean of Wheaton College.[31] In it she detailed the history of the transition periods from seminary to college as experienced by Mount Holyoke and Mills. A report by the Trustee subcommittee was accepted and it was authorized "to continue their work of formulating a scheme of reorganization with a view to making application for a college charter."[32]

That scheme was not hard to create, for all the pieces had already been carefully crafted by Samuel Cole. Chief among them, of course, was the prospering educational institution Wheaton had become, with a student body, physical plant, and fiscal stability that would stand examination by legislative committees and the State Board of Education. But President Cole's planning went well beyond this. He recognized that the two chief arguments against the change were likely to be the termination of Wheaton's highly regarded college preparatory program and the concomitant objection that Massachusetts did not need another carbon copy of the collegiate offerings for women already provided by Smith, Mount

Holyoke, Wellesley, and Radcliffe, to say nothing of Pembroke, located only eighteen miles away in Providence, Rhode Island.

The former of these two concerns was dealt with in what can only be described as a highly enterprising and innovative way. In the spring of 1911, President Cole wrote to Gertrude Cornish, a graduate of Middlebury College and former member of the Wheaton teaching staff, suggesting that she return to Norton and establish a private secondary school for girls in the "house in the pines" situated just east of the Wheaton Seminary property. Miss Cornish, then teaching at Miss Porter's School in Connecticut, readily assented and that fall, in conjunction with Althea Hyde, former superintendent of the Training School for Teachers in Portland, Maine, she opened the school, taking as its name the phrase "House in the Pines" first used by President Cole to describe the main building to her. In undertaking this venture she received considerable support and help from President Cole, who not only was instrumental in helping negotiate the purchase of the property, but who also instructed the Seminary manager of buildings and grounds, John Dorety, to solicit bids for the general renovation work that was needed before the school could begin operation. Thus, when Wheaton undertook the transition from seminary to college, there already existed as next-door neighbor a secondary school which offered both general secondary education and college preparatory programs, providing a ready place for referral of those from the area who no longer would be able to turn to Wheaton. As the *Boston Transcript* noted in a February, 1912 article, "The Pines and Wheaton have maintained the most harmonious of relations and there are some well-informed persons in Norton who think that the former will eventually become a 'prep' for the latter."[33]

The second potential objection, that there was no need for another women's college, was met with equal directness. To President Cole that answer was obvious. Wheaton, unlike other colleges for women, would not seek specifically to prepare its graduates for professional careers or jobs in the market place. That some would aspire to and attain such positions would undoubtedly be true, but Wheaton's main emphasis would be directed elsewhere, toward the fullest possible education for "the business of being a woman."

This last phrase became, during the critical transition period, the basic slogan by which Wheaton sought to differentiate itself from other women's colleges. Women's business, as President Cole saw it, still remained primarily that of wife and homemaker, and it was to those ends that the new college and its curriculum would be dedicated. It was with this in mind that he had persuaded the Board of Trustees in November, 1908, to fund a new Domestic Science department in which students could take courses in nutrition, sanitation, and the "household arts." As Wheaton moved toward submitting its petition to the legislature, this program became ever more central to the concept that Wheaton was unique in what it was trying to do. "The proposed college," read the prospectus prepared for the Massachusetts General Court and the Board of Education, "will aim to educate a woman, body, mind, and soul, for a woman's life, keeping especially in view her efficiency in the home and her usefulness in the social order with its varied interests."[34]

> The object of all education is life; and to say that a woman's education should be identically the same as a man's does not quite meet the case. While it should largely be the same, the differences between her life and his are too important for any system of education to ignore.[35]

Thus, though the initial public announcement of the college in 1912 denied any desire to discourage women from entering the professions, it specifically advocated the necessity of every student's receiving training in subjects ranging from hygiene, nursing, and child life to household accounts and business law:

> Wheaton College will, within its own field, regard a liberal education for women from the point of view of the intelligent woman who wishes to magnify the calling of wife, mother, and neighbor. This it expects to do without lessening the opportunities it will provide for those who aim ultimately at professional work.[36]

In promulgating this educational program and philosophy, President Cole placed Wheaton in the vanguard of a movement that was gathering momentum throughout the United States, and which had its origin and driving force in the person of Ellen Swallow Richards, the first woman to be hired as a member of the Massachusetts Institute of Technology faculty. Mrs. Richards, who taught courses in the sanitary engineering department, advocated the study of domestic science as a separate academic discipline. She believed that new scientific knowledge regarding hygiene and nutrition could thereby be integrated into the work of the household. The homemaker would also be trained to make use of the vast array of new labor saving devices made available by the technology of a newly industrialized society. "The educated woman," she wrote, "longs for a career, for an opportunity to influence the world. Just now the greatest field offered to her is the elevation of the home into its place in American life."[37] One of the founders of the National Household Economics Society in 1893, Mrs. Richards initiated annual meetings of professionals in 1897 which evolved in 1908 into the formation of the American Home Economics Association, for which she served as President from 1908 until shortly before her death in 1911. She pioneered in introducing domestic science into college curriculums in the East, helping to organize the first such program, located at Simmons College. She also advised Clara Pike regarding the science program at Wheaton. Both she and her views had been well known in educational, professional and social circles in the Boston area for several decades. President Cole, whose personal views regarding educated women and the family clearly coincided with those of Mrs. Richards, undoubtedly was well aware of and influenced by her work.[38]

To say that President Cole's concept was well received would be understating the case. The phrase "the business of being a woman" caught the public fancy and, for the two or three critical years during which the seminary-to-college transition was taking place, it engendered highly favorable commentary in articles and editorials, not only locally but in such papers as the *New York Times* and the Grand Rapids, Michigan, *Sunday Herald.* Typical was an editorial in the *Boston Herald* written in February 1913, at the time the college issued its first catalogue. Other women's colleges, the *Herald* said, were conformist, "so paralyzing is the dread of violating classic college standards." Wheaton, however, was a real pioneer, its approach more courageous than those of other women's institutions. Conceding that if household economics came to dominate the curriculum Wheaton would not be able to call itself a college, the *Herald* agreed that if used properly as a means to widen perspective and give to other parts of the curriculum a special unity and integrative purpose, then "it ought not to be missed in any woman's college which aims toward real culture."[39]

"Women's colleges so far as I know them educate women for the work of men. You propose to educate them for the work of women," enthusiastically wrote Dr. Albert Getchell, father of a seminary graduate of 1910.[40] Without further ado he transferred his daughter from Radcliffe back to Wheaton where she became one of its first two college graduates in 1914.

The domestic science requirement for the B.A. in reality was quite minimal, the equivalent of a one-semester, 3 credit course. It would remain until 1927, when both the department and the requirement would quietly disappear. Despite the fact that President Cole always remained philosophically committed to the concept of providing an extensive program in what came to be known as Household Economics, within two years of Wheaton's becoming a college he was instructing the College's advertising agent to eliminate references to homemaking in its releases, since "we receive quite a good many letters that seem to lay undue emphasis on the Domestic Science business, and we do not want it to appear that that is the prominent thing connected with the institution."[41]

The domestic science program never actually played a vital or major role in the curriculum of either the Seminary or the College. But it did provide a means by which President Cole was able to present to the legislature and the State Board of Education a rationale for Wheaton's existence that was sure to appeal to those all-male bodies, and which also engendered considerable favorable publicity that appears to have aided in recruiting students in the College's early formative years. To say that the program was instituted solely for this purpose would be incorrect. President Cole clearly believed very strongly in the general educational concepts that justified it. But the central focus that household economics was given in the case presented for college certification, and its subsequent publicity, was definitely much greater than was warranted by the actual role it played in the overall academic structure of the Seminary or College. In a letter to Kate Upson Clark written at the height of the petitioning process, President Cole commented: "During these many weeks I have been obliged to try playing the role of educator, diplomat, politician and various other things."[42] The degree of utilization, even manipulation, of the domestic science format may have reflected President Cole's sense of practical politics every bit as much as it did the sincerity of his personal educational philosophy.[43]

Of all those from whom President Cole sought counsel during the transition period, none was more consistent in his help and encouragement than William DeWitt Hyde, President of Bowdoin. The ties between the two ran deep and strong. Bowdoin awarded Samuel Cole an honorary D.D. at the time he assumed the Presidency of Wheaton, and granted him an LL.D. in 1912. Appointed to the Bowdoin Board of Trustees in 1901, Rev. Cole became Chairman of the Visiting Committee that prepared the college's annual budget. In 1912, he became Vice President of the Board, thereby serving as President Hyde's chief conduit to the other Trustees. President Hyde had long encouraged Samuel Cole in his plans to turn Wheaton into a college, and when President Cole finally decided to take the plunge, Mr. Hyde wrote him on December 20, 1911: "The sooner the thing is launched the better it will be in every way. The women's colleges are overflowing, and if you do not catch the overflow, somebody else will."[44] In 1911, in what clearly was a favor to President Cole, Bowdoin awarded Wheaton's soon-to-be-Dean, Ida Everett, an honorary M.A., only the fourth time Bowdoin had conferred a degree on a woman in its 110-year existence.[45]

Although President Hyde may have been the most important adviser to President Cole, his was hardly the only aid enlisted. Even before the Board of Trustees formally approved the petitioning action to the legislature, President Cole, George Smart, and Edwin Curtis were hard at work drumming up support. By the time the Joint Legislative Committee on Education met to conduct hearings on the matter, all the pieces were carefully in place. Not only did the Committee receive written testimony of support from the Presidents of Radcliffe, Smith, and the University of Wisconsin,[46] but both David Snedden, Massachusetts Commissioner of Education, and A. Lawrence Lowell, President of Harvard, came personally to testify on Wheaton's behalf. A subsequent visit to the campus by the Joint Legislative Committee went equally smoothly and on February 12, 1912, the bill approving college status for Wheaton sailed through both houses of the Massachusetts General Court without opposition, and was immediately signed into law by Governor Eugene Foss.[47] Although the State Board of Education still had to give final certification that a faculty and curriculum were ready and in place, the battle, such as it was, had been won, for President Cole through individual canvassing had long since assured himself of a positive reception from that Board. Privately, Mr. Cole could not resist crowing a little:

> There was absolutely no opposition, a fact that is very gratifying when we remember the fierce opposition which Mount Holyoke encountered and the difficulty which Simmons had in getting the power to grant degrees. ... The preliminary work which we have been doing for a long time with the Board of Education and others, in showing them our plans and discussing with them the situation, doubtless has helped to bring about this result.[49]

Writing to Kate Upson Clark, he commented with evident satisfaction, "It is really something of an achievement to have gotten our bill through the legislature and the new plans before the public without meeting opposition from any quarter. We have met the 'enemy' in detail and he is ours."[49]

To say there was no opposition is hardly correct, though certainly what little there was had been muted and never allowed to come to the attention of those in whose hands the ultimate decision rested. Of the educators consulted, only President William Faunce of Brown University voiced serious reservations, which were echoed in various forms by local elements in Norton and the neighboring city of Taunton. Essentially these centered on Wheaton's giving up a prospering system for something untried and untested, though President Faunce was probably also concerned about the effect that a new women's college, located only a few miles from Providence and Brown's coordinate college, Pembroke, might have on the latter's enrollment.[50]

The only other opposition came from the Norton Board of Assessors and was not directed at the change to college status per se. One member in particular objected to a companion bill that was simultaneously working its way through the chambers of the General Court that would authorize an increase in the value of real and personal property held by the Seminary/College to $1,000,000. Coupled with the advent of the House-in-the-Pines School, it is easy to understand the reluctance of the Assessors to support further potential loss of valuable land, located in the center of town, from the property tax rolls. However, when town officials met to discuss the matter, President Cole and others overwhelmed them with reassurances and evidence of the benefits provided to Norton by having Wheaton in its midst. Opposition disappeared and when hearings on the bill were held in Boston, no adverse testimony was received.[51]

It is interesting to note that when the original petition to the legislature was published in newspapers throughout the state, as required by law, it stated that the name was to be changed from Wheaton Female Seminary to Laban Wheaton College. President Cole was blunt about the reason: there was a Wheaton College already in existence in Illinois. Apparently he initially thought no two colleges could have the same name, but he soon discovered otherwise and the petition was changed before it was formally submitted. As President Cole wrote to Mrs. Clark: "The name of the institution will not need to include the word 'Laban'. It will be simply Wheaton College, which, I understand, you and the other trustees really preferred. I find on looking the matter up that nothing is more common than duplicate names among educational institutions."[52]

Common it may have been, and certainly in 1912 the geographical distance between the two institutions seemed to indicate that there was little reason not to use the same name. But in subsequent decades, as both Wheaton Colleges became more nationally known, the confusion created caused from time to time certain problems, for the most part minor and often amusing, but on occasion more substantial. For the two institutions were markedly different, the one liberal and restricted to women—the other coeducational and church-related, fundamentalist in its religious orientation, and extremely conservative in its social outlook.

Certification that "courses of college grade for Wheaton College have been laid out and a college organization effected" was received from the State Board of Education on March 8, and on March 23, 1912, the final step was completed when the certification was registered in the office of the Secretary of the Commonwealth. On March 14, the Seminary Board of Trustees held its last formal meeting and voted to accept the acts of the Legislature, to change the institution's name on all stocks and bonds, and to reconstitute themselves as Trustees of Wheaton College. The formal transition was complete; academically the process would take two years, at the end of which the first two graduates would receive their degrees, a full college curriculum would be in place, and the college preparatory and first two years of the former seminary program eliminated from the curriculum.

But in President Cole's mind, one final step was needed to facilitate the changeover. On March 27, 1912, he wrote to the Board of Trustees expressing concern that in the new forthcoming announcement of the College it seemed imperative to call the main classroom building "by some other name than 'The Seminary' or 'Seminary Hall'. . . . The word 'Seminary' attached to a separate building in this way is likely to prove misleading and to have the effect of deterring some prospective college students."[54] Noting that the trustees had tried some years past to find a new name for the building, he now proposed that it be called Mary Lyon Hall. "The building stands on the site and takes the place of the original building in which the school was organized and for two years conducted

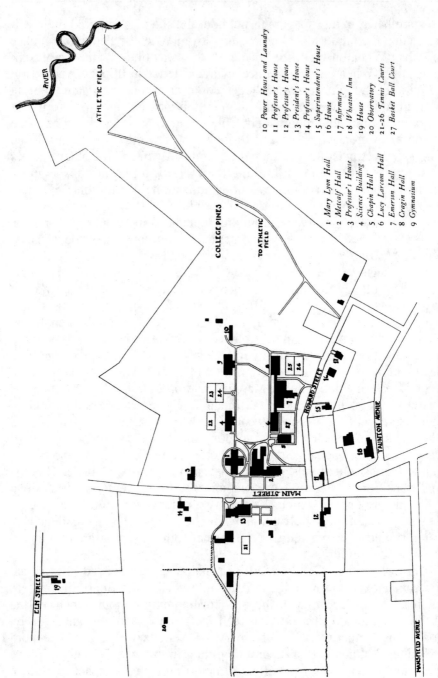

1 Mary Lyon Hall
2 Metcalf Hall
3 Professor's House
4 Science Building
5 Chapin Hall
6 Lucy Larcom Hall
7 Emerson Hall
8 Cragin Hall
9 Gymnasium

10 Power House and Laundry
11 Professor's House
12 Professor's House
13 President's House
14 Professor's House
15 Superintendent's House
16 House
17 Infirmary
18 Wheaton Inn
19 House
20 Observatory
21-26 Tennis Courts
27 Basket Ball Court

RIVER

ATHLETIC FIELD

COLLEGE PINES

TO ATHLETIC FIELD

HOWARD STREET

TAUNTON AVENUE

MAIN STREET

ELM STREET

MANSFIELD AVENUE

Map of Wheaton Female Seminary (Wheaton College), 1911-1912

under Mary Lyon's supervision. We have no building, and are never likely to have a building, which could so appropriately bear her name."[55]

The proposal was enthusiastically endorsed by all who were consulted. Thus, this final symbolic step in effecting the change that would ensure the future history of Wheaton as a college also appropriately returned to the heritage that had begun on the summer day in 1834 when a young man, representing his wife and father, first met with Mary Lyon to consult about the dream upon which all had fixed as the appropriate memorial to a dearly loved daughter and sister, Elizabeth Wheaton Strong.

Notes: Chapter 6

1. Trustees, 1834–1911: K. U. Clark: SVC to Clark, 2/14/12. See also Wheaton Female Seminary, *Annual Catalogue*, 1899–1911.

2. SVC, Letterbook, 1900–1908: SVC to Cram, Goodhue and Ferguson, 3/26/02, pp. 317–18; also "Chapin Hall," 3/4/01, p. 54; Trustees Minutes: 5/17/00.

3. Buildings: Miscellaneous.

4. Ibid.: Cram, Goodhue and Ferguson to Cole, 7/17/07; Trustees Minutes, 9/21/07; SVC, Letterbook: "Chapin Hall," 3/4/01, p. 54; By 1901 President Cole was referring to the central court or green as a "Court of Honor."

5. SVC, Letterbook: SVC to Cram, Goodhue and Ferguson, 3/26/02, p. 317. See also SVC to Cram (not sent), 2/11/02, p. 296.

6. *Dictionary of American Biography*, vol. 16, "Sargent, Dr. Dudley A.," p. 356. See also Trustees Minutes: 3/29/99; 11/20/01; General Files: 1888–1889: printed appeal for funds, 1899; Shepard, "Reference History," pp. 391–91b; Anniversaries: SVC Draft of 75th Anniversary speech, p. 38.

7. Trustees Minutes: 3/3/02; SVC, Letterbook: SVC to Clark, 4/1/02, p. 320. Adding fuel to the controversy was the fact that Cram had served an apprenticeship in the firm of Rotch and Tilden prior to establishing his own office in 1889.

8. This building program necessitated removing the bowling alley and relocating the observatory to a site behind the President's house. Trustees Minutes: 6/19/07; 3/19/08; *Wheaton Bulletin*, 4:3 (June, 1908), p. 24.

9. The architects for Larcom and Emerson Dining Hall were Ripley and Russell, while the plans for Cragin dormitory, the Powerhouse (presently Doll's House), and the Science/Assembly Hall (now Knapton) were drawn by Cram, Goodhue and Ferguson. The depression located in front of Emerson Dining Hall, which would become a campus landmark known as the Dimple, began as the cellar hole for a barn, and was sloped into its present form at the time the dining hall was constructed. Originally intended by Cram, Goodhue and Ferguson to serve as a reflecting pool, later plans called for its use as a formal garden and/or site for a Greek amphitheater. None of these metamorphoses took place, though for years the Dimple has been used for graduation exercises, providing an excellent natural amphitheater for that event. See Trustees Minutes: 11/20/07.

10. The statement of worth for Wheaton Seminary, prepared in January, 1912, set the value of the Seminary's land and buildings at $426,600; Stocks and Special Funds, $125,000; Private Lands, $22,500; and the Boston Winter Street Property, $686,000—totalling $1,260,200. Almost all of this was a direct result of Wheaton family munificence. If one adds to this the funds given by the Wheatons that were used repeatedly to cover annual operational deficits, the extent of the Wheaton fami-

ly's contribution over seventy years becomes readily apparent. Trustees: Curtis: SVC to Curtis, 1/15/12.

11. Trustees Minutes: 1/21/07; SVC, Letterbook: SVC to Dr. Clark, 3/21,25/07, pp. 721–722; Trustees, 1834–1911: Barrows: Barrows to SVC, 3/23/07; Fox: Fox to Dr. Clark, 3/21/07; Vose: Vose to SVC 3/22/07; Buildings: Miscellaneous: Fox to SVC, 3/21/07; Eight Faculty Members to SVC, 3/23/07.

12. EBW: Receipts of gifts in Will of EBW: Seminary receipt as residuary legatee, 2/22/07.

13. Anniversaries: SVC Draft of 75th Anniversary Speech, p. 40.

14. Trustees Minutes: 6/26/05; 1/21/07; 6/19/07; 11/20/07; 6/13/10; 3/21/11; *Wheaton Bulletin*, 4:1 (December, 1907), p. 18. The renaming of "The Home," as the rambling wooden boarding house had been called, to honor Caroline Metcalf had occurred in 1901.

15. C. Marshall Letters, 1900–1904: Marshall to Mother, 1/23/01; 5/2/01; Trustees Minutes: 3/20/01; 6/19/01; 7/11/01; SVC, Letterbook: SVC to Farnsworth, 3/19/01, p. 63; SVC to Snow, 6/24/01, p. 105; SVC Report to Trustees, 7/11/01, pp. 122–46.

16. Marshall, Letters: Marshall to Mother, 2/21/01. Annette Munro would subsequently become Dean of Women at the University of Rochester.

17. See *Rushlight*, 44:1 (January, 1899), Essay by Helen Swain.

18. SVC, Letterbook: Report to Trustees, 7/11/10, p. 142.

19. Ibid.: Cole to Clark, 2/12/01, p. 299.

20. Trustees Minutes: 5/2/06. See also 3/21/06; and SVC, Letterbook: Cole to Dr. Vose. 4/24/06, p. 695. Hiram Tucker taught at Wheaton for forty-three years, including ten years after the Seminary became a College.

21. Trustees Minutes: 3/29/08.

22. Ibid.: 9/20/10; 11/9/10; 2/24/11; 3/21/11; Anniversaries: SVC Draft of 75th Anniversary Speech, p. 49.

23. Trustees Minutes: 3/21/11.

24. Ibid.; also Wheaton Histories, Seminary: Seminary to College #1: Hyde to SVC, 1/6/12.

25. SVC: College Business: Statement read to Trustees by SVC, 3/21/11, p. 5.

26. Ibid., p. 7.

27. Ibid.

28. Ibid., p. 5.

29. Ibid., p. 9. Writing to the alumnae of the Seminary years later, President Cole stated his views succinctly: "We have no moral right to use the money of the Founders for any other purpose than the one for which they gave it—the higher education of women. What they would approve for their purpose, and through Mrs. Wheaton did approve is the college—and no longer the seminary—owing to the changed conditions in education." SVC, *Why Change?*

30. SVC: College Business: Statement read to Trustees by SVC, 3/21/11, p. 9. It was at this meeting that the Trustees adopted this last phrase as the formal motto for Wheaton, replacing the old motto devised by Eliza Knight in 1838, "Who drinks will thirst for more."

31. Miss Everett, a graduate of Mount Holyoke College, had studied at Oxford and completed all course work, but not the dissertation, for the Ph.D. from Yale.

32. Trustees Minutes: 6/14/11.

33. Wheaton Histories, Seminary: Seminary to College #1: *Boston Transcript*, 2/17/12. See also *Wheaton News*, 4:25 (May 26, 1925), Statement by Gertrude Cornish; *Wheaton Bulletin*, 7:3 (July, 1911), pp. 16–17.

34. Wheaton Histories, Seminary: Seminary to College #2: "Prospectus for Massachusetts General Court," p. 9.

35. Ibid., p. 6. See also Wheaton College, *Announcement of Wheaton College, Nor-*

ton, Massachusetts, 1912, pp. 11–14; *Wheaton Bulletin*, 6:1 (December, 1909), p. 13; Trustees Minutes: 11/30/<u>08</u>; 11/17/<u>09</u>.

36. Wheaton College, *Announcement of Wheaton College, 1912*, p. 11.

37. E. S. Richards, as quoted in R. S. Cowan, "Ellen Swallow Richards: Technology and Women," in C. W. Pursell, Jr., ed., *Technology in America: a History of Individuals and Ideas* (Cambridge, MA: MIT Press, 1981), p. 146.

38. Ibid., pp. 142–50; J. W. James, "Ellen Henrietta Swallow Richards," in *Notable American Women, 1607–1950*, vol. 3 (Cambridge, MA: Belknap Press, 1971), pp. 143–46.

39. Wheaton Seminary and College, "Scrapbook of Clippings," 1899–1917, passim; and in particular *Boston Herald*, 2/19/<u>13</u>. Also *Wheaton Bulletin*, 8:2 (March, 1912), pp. 12–15; Shepard, "Reference History," pp. 368–69.

40. Wheaton Histories, Seminary: Seminary to College #1: Getchell to SVC, 2/21/<u>12</u>.

41. Quoted by Shepard,"Reference History," p. 375. Wheaton was not alone in offering a domestic science program. Courses in domestic science also received credit at Smith College during the 1920s.

42. Trustees, 1834–1911: K. U. Clark: SVC to Clark, 2/2/<u>12</u>.

43. See, for example, Cole's long interview in the *Boston Post*, 2/25/<u>12</u>, in Wheaton Histories, Seminary: Seminary to College #1; or article in the *Boston Transcript*, 2/17/<u>12</u>.

44. Ibid.: Seminary History: Hyde to SVC, 12/20/<u>11</u>; see also Cole to Woolley, 1/3/<u>12</u>.

45. *Wheaton Bulletin*, 7:3 (July, 1911), p. 17. President Cole remained on the Bowdoin Board of Trustees until his death in 1925. Another Wheaton trustee, Edwin Curtis, served with President Cole as a Bowdoin trustee from 1912 to 1922. Curtis, former Mayor of Boston and later to gain renown as Commissioner of Police at the time of Boston's famed police strike of 1919, was a member of the three-person committee designated to shepherd the Wheaton College charter petition through the General Court of Massachusetts. So close did the ties between Bowdoin and Wheaton become that years later undergraduates at both institutions would speak in puzzled tones of some undefined, mythologized, special relationship between the two colleges, maintained by a tradition whose source had long since been forgotten.

46. Charles R. van Hise was drawn into Wheaton's plans by the accident of his having spoken with President Lowell of Harvard just prior to George Smart's meeting with Mr. Lowell to discuss Wheaton's plans. Van Hise apparently had been urging upon Lowell the need to establish more women's colleges in the East to balance the men's institutions. The Mid-West, Van Hise maintained, did not need women's colleges, since all colleges and universities in that area were coeducational. Wheaton Histories, Seminary: Seminary to College #1: Smart to SVC, 11/14/<u>11</u>; Van Hise to Cole, 2/9/<u>12</u>.

47. Ibid.: SVC to Briggs. 1/20/<u>12</u>; SVC to Trustees, 1/22/<u>12</u>; SVC to Smart, 1/26/<u>12</u>; SVC to Hyde, 2/2/<u>12</u>; SVC to Kilham, 2/2/<u>12</u>; Journal of George Smart, quoted by Shepard, "Reference History," pp. 371–372; Trustees Minutes, 11/23/<u>11</u>; *Wheaton Bulletin*, 7:2 (March, 1912), pp. 18–21. The petition was filed in the Legislature by President Cole. It was moved in the House of Representatives by Rep. Edward Sweeney and in the Senate by Senator Charles Chase. Representative Joseph Martin of North Attleboro, who would later become Speaker of the US House of Representatives during the Truman and Eisenhower administrations, was at this time a newly elected member of the Massachusetts House, and as such played a minimal, though supportive role, in furthering the cause of Wheaton's petition for college status.

48. Wheaton Histories, Seminary: Seminary to College #1: SVC to Trustees, 1/22/<u>12</u>. See also SVC to Fish, 1/18/<u>11</u>; SVC to Cabot, 12/15/<u>11</u>; Cabot to SVC, 12/19/<u>11</u>;

SVC to Hyde, 12/18,22/11; Seminary to College #2: Cole private statement to Board of Education; Trustees, 1834–1911: K. U. Clark: SVC to Clark, 2/2/12; Journal of George T. Smart, as quoted by Shepard, "Reference History," pp 371–72.

49. Trustees, 1834–1911: K. U. Clark: SVC to Clark, 2/28/12.

50. Wheaton Histories, Seminary: Seminary to College #1: SVC to Faunce, 1/8/12; SVC to Curtis, 1/24/12; Trustees, 1834–1911: K. U. Clark: SVC to Clark, 2/2/12; Wheaton Seminary and College, "Scrapbook of Clippings," 1899–1917, *Boston Transcript* editorial, 1/9/12.

51. General Files: 1911–1912; Wheaton Histories, Seminary: Seminary to College #1: Senate Petition #59, January, 1912; SVC to Curtis, 1/19/12; SVC to Apsey, 1/19,20/12; SVC to Trustees, 1/22/12; SVC to Chase, 1/19/12; SVC to Sweeney, 1/19/12.

52. Trustees, 1834–1911: K.U. Clark: SVC to Clark, 3/17/12. Also SVC: College Business, and Wheaton Seminary and College, "Scrapbook of Clippings, 1899–1917," contain copies of the original petition to change the name to Laban Wheaton College. See also Wheaton Histories, Seminary: Seminary to College #1: Senate Petition #50, January, 1912.

53. A copy is in Wheaton Histories, Seminary: Seminary to College #1. See also SVC to Board of Education, 2/17/12; Snedden to SVC 3/8/12; Trustees Minutes: 3/4/12.

54. SVC: College Business: SVC to Trustees, 3/27/12.

55. Ibid.

7

And Gladly Would They Learn,
And Gladly Teach

Let me recall the seminary building. On the first floor was a small recitation room, a large room for the whole school, another small room in which were a lead colored sink and pump, a water pail and a tin dipper. On the second floor were one large room and two recitation rooms furnished with settees and blackboards. . . . The desks were painted lead color, those for the use of the teachers, as well as the others, being straight up-and-down boards. . . . There was no apparatus and no library; but we were patiently and thoroughly taught.[1]

So WROTE A student who was present the day Wheaton Seminary commenced classes in April, 1835. The building she described, located directly across the street from the residence of Eliza and Laban Morey Wheaton, hardly provided what one could call a comfortable or elaborate environment for learning. But there is no doubt that rigorous education took place, with a quality and intensity of instruction and a seriousness of educational purpose that set Wheaton apart from the general run of finishing schools for young ladies. An overview of admissions policy, calendar, special programs, curriculum, and the faculty provides a picture of the educational work and atmosphere of the Seminary in the years between 1835 and 1912.

Admission to the Seminary over the decades was open for the most part to any young woman whose parents wished her to attend. Because Wheaton for most of those years offered a preparatory year in addition to the formal seminary curriculum, it could afford to follow this policy. Students were subjected to testing and placement after admission. Progression into the seminary program and subsequently through the various years of the curriculum was controlled by a rigorous series of examinations.

Although Wheaton did admit thirteen and fourteen-year-old students, most of these younger girls were either day students from Norton or sisters of older students already enrolled in the Seminary. The policy

135

allowing these younger girls to attend reflected the uneven quality of educational opportunities in Norton and the other small towns of southeastern Massachusettss. Norton, for example, did not have its own public high school until the first decade of the twentieth century. Most of the students in the thirteen to fifteen age group spent a year or more in the preparatory program before entering into the regular seminary curriculum.

Between 1879 and 1884 the age of students at Wheaton ranged from 10 in one case to 23 in another. However, there were no boarding students younger than thirteen and both the average and median age of all students, including those in the preparatory class, was seventeen.[2]

By the turn of the century only students who had completed a full grammar school education could enter Wheaton, and then only into the college preparatory program. Admission directly into the four-year seminary course of study required completion of either two years of high school or the first two years of the college preparatory program at Wheaton. Most high school graduates were able to enter the seminary program's third year and complete their work for the seminary diploma with two years of study.

Admission of African-American students became an issue only twice between 1835 and 1912. In the first case, the matter was easily resolved, for the student made it abundantly clear that she was applying only at her parents' behest, and that she hoped Wheaton would refuse her because she really wanted to attend Abbot Academy in Andover. Thus William Barrows, the Secretary of the Board, was able to reply on March 14, 1848, that since "as you say,-'it would be no disappointment to me if not accepted,' and 'if not accepted I can go to'-another place, we would prefer to have you go to some other Institution."[3]

The second case occurred more than half a century later. In the summer of 1902, Booker T. Washington, nationally recognized leader of Tuskegee Normal and Industrial Institute, regarded then and now as the most influential and powerful African-American at the turn of the century, applied to have his daughter Portia attend Wheaton. She had attended Wellesley College as a special student the year before, but had left at the end of the year.[4]

Wheaton was not unknown to Mr. Washington. Over the years student donations had been sent to Tuskegee as part of the missions work annually undertaken by the Wheaton community. On at least one occasion, Mr. Washington had visited the Seminary, accompanied by the Tuskegee Jubilee Singers, and spoken about the "growth and progress of the Tuskegee Normal School." Perhaps his warm welcome, plus the frequent contributions made by Wheaton both to Tuskegee and to his alma mater, Hampton Institute, encouraged Mr. Washington to see Wheaton as an appropriate place for his daughter.[5]

The application, however, prompted President Cole to write each member of the Board of Trustees, asking their advice on the issue. "As this question involves some practical difficulties," he wrote, "and might seriously disturb a portion of the patronage of the school, I do not feel authorized to give an answer without knowing the mind of the Trustees. Of course in a home school of this kind there would be complications which would not arise in a college. I have had a frank talk with Mrs. Washington and I think she fully understands the situation."[6]

Five days later, President Cole wrote Wellesley asking for information regarding Portia's leaving Wellesley and also inquiring as to the impression she had made there. "I would esteem it a great favor if you would kindly write me a word about her character, ability, scholarship, general appearance and bearing—anything, in fact, that would aid us in deciding the question of admitting her here. The race question aside, was she a desirable student? May I ask also whether the race question caused any difficulty? Was Miss Washington on the same footing with the other students?"[7]

While waiting for replies, President Cole wrote to Mr. Washington, who was then in South Weymouth, Massachusetts, asking to meet personally with him and offering to come to Boston at Mr. Washington's convenience. "I need a little further information about your daughter," he wrote, "and there are some facts in the situation here of which you ought to be informed. All this, it seems to me, could be managed much more satisfactorily by personal interview than by correspondence."[8]

Apparently, the requested meeting never took place. Nor do we know the reaction of any of the Trustees. But the letter that President Cole wrote to Mrs. Washington on July 25 gives some indication of the response that was received from Wellesley:

> In order to save time—as it was uncertain when I could see Mr. Washington—I wrote to Wellesley College for some statement in regard to your daughter, our rules requiring a testimonial in every case and preferably from the last school. The Wellesley statement, while speaking in high terms of your daughter's character, leads us to feel, however, that her attainments in her studies are not such that the conditions here at the present time would meet her case. Our number is limited, and the roll for the coming year is so nearly complete that, for the remaining places, we are obliged at this season to give preference to students of good scholarship who apply for the regular courses. Only a few days ago we declined the application of a girl from Pennsylvania on this ground, and I have thought that if Mr. Washington knew the circumstances he would probably not wish to enter an application.[9]

It is true that every applicant to Wheaton was required to provide a testimonial regarding her character as a condition of admittance. It is also true that on July 23 an applicant from Pennsylvania had been denied admission on the grounds stated by President Cole.[10] During the previ-

ous academic year Wheaton had for the first time in its history received
more applicants than it could accommodate, and the same situation occurred in the summer of 1902. By the latter part of July, the Seminary
was indeed seeking to use the last few available spaces to admit students
who would become part of the "regular" course of studies, i.e., candidates for the regular Seminary degree, rather than the college preparatory or special student programs. Given the fact that Miss Washington
had been a special student at Wellesley, not enrolled in the regular degree program, it seems likely she sought the same status at Wheaton,
and President Cole's comments appear to substantiate this conclusion.

All this having been said, it is also relevant to note that on the same
day he wrote Mrs. Washington denying admission to her daughter, President Cole accepted as a special student on scholarship a young woman
from Maine whose level of achievement placed her only in the beginning
year of the college preparatory program, despite the fact that she was
considerably older than students normally studying at that level. "Our
roll is nearly full," he wrote, "and we are giving the preference among
new applicants to those who can enter the regular courses. But we are
glad to make this exception with a view to helping you solve the problem you are trying to meet. I hope you will not feel discouraged. There
will surely be a work and a place for your daughter somewhere in this
great world."[11]

It should also be recognized that at the time the Washingtons first applied in early July, the level of applications had not yet reached the point
where distinctions between the study programs of applicants were being
made. Had it not been felt that special consultation with the Trustees and
others was necessary, it seems likely a place would have been routinely
available at some level for Portia Washington. Whether that would have
been at an academic level acceptable to her parents is not ascertainable.

It is impossible to escape the conclusion that the issue of race entered
strongly into the decision as to whether Portia Washington should attend
Wheaton. To have the daughter of a person already popularly recognized
as the preeminent African-American leader in America would have been
no small feather in Wheaton's cap. Clearly, concerns about dormitory
residence and racial relations overshadowed everything else. At Wellesley, Miss Washington had lived off-campus with two faculty members.
At Wheaton, all the faculty, including President Cole and his wife, lived
in one of the dormitories, so the Wellesley solution to the issue of housing was not available. The stated reasons regarding Miss Washington's
academic performance at Wellesley and her desire for special student
status, valid as they may have been, must be seen as telling only half the
tale. Given the fact that Wheaton, unlike Wellesley, offered a college
preparatory program whose courses were basically comparable to a high
school curriculum, it seems highly unlikely that had Wheaton wished to
accept Portia Washington, an appropriate schedule at some level could

not have been found for her. In any case, her candidacy was rejected: Portia Washington enrolled at Bradford Academy, from which she received a degree in 1905. Although one African-American student attended Wheaton in 1919–1920, only in 1945 did the Board of Trustees authorize the regular acceptance of qualified African-American applicants.[12]

In 1835, the calendar of the Seminary called for two terms of 22 weeks, with a one-week recess in the middle of each, and a three-week vacation separating each term. In December, 1843, the Seminary shifted to a three-term calendar, with Winter and Summer terms of fourteen weeks duration, while the Fall term was shortened to twelve weeks. Although the three-term configuration remained until President Cole installed a two-semester calendar as one of the first steps in the long preparation by the Seminary to become a college, the length of the terms was gradually reduced over the years. In the final year of the three-term system, 1896–97, the fall term ran for fourteen weeks, the winter term for twelve, and the spring for eleven, with two-week vacations between the terms and a long summer recess from the last week in June to the second week in September. Thus the shift to a two-semester calendar in 1897–98 did not necessitate a major change in the broad configuration of the academic year.

During its existence as a seminary, Wheaton tried a number of educational experiments with varying degrees of success. In addition to the college preparatory program and the short-lived flirtation with coeducation which have already been discussed, three others deserve mention.

Over the years many Wheaton students had gone from the Seminary to assume teaching positions at all levels. In 1838, the Commonwealth of Massachusetts became the first state in the nation to authorize the establishment of state-supported normal schools for training teachers. One of the first three to open, in September, 1840, was situated in Bridgewater, about twenty miles from Norton. Perhaps the success enjoyed by this school was the catalyst that stimulated Wheaton to establish its own teacher-training program. Whatever the cause, the Wheaton catalogue for 1867–68 contained the following brief announcement:

Normal Class

Many of the pupils of the Institution become Teachers. For the benefit of such, a Normal Class has been organized, so that those who desire may have the advantages of special preparations for their work, in connection with a more extended course of study than that afforded by the State Normal Schools.

Eight students were listed as participants in the Normal Class. The catalogue for 1869–70 provides five more names, including Annie Kilham, who graduated from the Seminary in 1870, taught at Wheaton from 1871 to 1875, and served as a member of the Board of Trustees from 1897 to 1931. But the formal program itself was short-lived. Although the notice concerning it remained in the catalogues for three more years, there were no students listed as taking part in the program. Just what kind of course of study was involved we do not know, but clearly it did not catch on, and was quietly discarded after six years.

However, the Normal Class experiment was replaced by another innovative educational program which commenced in 1873–74 and again ended only three years later. In response to alumnae demand, which may have been generated in part by the formation of the Alumnae Association in 1870, the Seminary began offering what would today be known as correspondence courses or an alumnae enrichment program. Alumnae were invited to send for an outline of independent study in a number of subjects, plus a list of books to be used. These ranged from the natural sciences to history and literature. Completion of an examination on the work assigned in two of these "courses" would earn the participant a certificate of achievement. Apparently a number of alumnae did begin work in a variety of subjects; whether any actually completed the assigned work is not known. The demise of the program coincided with the retirement of Caroline Metcalf as Principal, which was probably not a coincidence, since her successors, Ellen Haskell and Martha Sprague, did not have the many ties to alumnae that Mrs. Metcalf had garnered during the twenty-six years of her administration.[13]

The final curricular experiment that deserves mention was an attempt to award diplomas that distinguished between a student's completion of a Literary, Scientific, or Classical course of study. This was an outgrowth of an expanding policy that allowed students to replace prescribed courses with a limited number of electives as part of the degree curriculum. During the 1880s, French and German began to be allowed as substitutes for courses in what was technically still a fully defined four-year seminary curriculum. By 1892–93 the catalogue specifically noted that certain elements of the prescribed course had been made elective in order to allow students to tailor their programs more closely to their interests and needs, "thus practically constituting two courses, classical and scientific, according to the predominance of the studies pursued in each case."

Three years later this concept had been expanded to include a literary course of study as well as the scientific and classical. Though the idea of awarding diplomas that specified a field of concentration was continued until 1908–09, and the curriculum of the Seminary allowed a concomitant degree of flexibility, the vast majority of students apparently continued to complete a "general" program that did not qualify for the awarding of a specific area diploma. Nonetheless, by instituting these options Wheaton was falling in step with changes in academic curricular philosophy pioneered initially by President Charles W. Eliot of Harvard University during the 1870s and 1880s. While Wheaton's elective program remained far more circumscribed than the freewheeling system introduced by President Eliot at Harvard, the influence of this new approach to education, which was sweeping the colleges and universities of the nation, clearly also had its impact in Norton, and helped pave the way for the smooth transition from seminary to college.[14]

The development of the curriculum to its position in 1912 as equivalent to the first two years of college study was not the result of a sudden, conscious effort to alter or upgrade a lesser program of study. Rather it was the outgrowth of a concept of education and set of standards that had been in effect since the day the Seminary opened its doors, and which responded to and grew with the evolution of thinking regarding higher education for women as it developed during the nineteenth and early twentieth century.

From the beginning, Wheaton dedicated itself to providing a level of education in the "English branches" comparable, if not completely identical, to that provided for young men in the colleges and universities of that day. As has been discussed earlier, this included all subjects other than classical languages and literature, modern languages, studio art, and music.[15] Instruction in Latin and on occasion, Greek, plus drawing, piano, and French was also provided, but only on a special fee basis, and without degree credit.

Wheaton's curriculum, like that of Mount Holyoke, was initially derived from that offered at Ipswich Female Seminary, which in turn had modeled its curricular structure and teaching methods on those pioneered by Joseph Emerson at his seminary in Byfield, Massachusetts. The subjects taught, and in many cases the texts used, were the same as those at men's colleges such as Harvard, Amherst, or Bowdoin.[16] Algebra, Plane Geometry, Geology, Chemistry, Astronomy, Logic, Moral Philosophy, English Grammar, Rhetoric, Natural History, Natural Philosophy, and Evidences of Christianity were as much requirements of the men's colleges as they were at Ipswich, Wheaton, or Mount Holyoke. Neither type of institution offered any English literature.

The educational programs at Wheaton and Mount Holyoke in the late 1830s coincided down to the scheduling of courses in certain years. Each had a three-year curriculum. Mount Holyoke, because of its required domestic work program, set a slightly less rigorous academic schedule. However, Mount Holyoke did require that all entering students be prepared in Adams' *Arithmetic,* Watts' *Improvement of the Mind,* United States history, and basic English grammar. These subjects constituted about one-half of the curriculum in Wheaton's first-year program, but since Wheaton students, free of any domestic work requirements, studied a few more topics each year than did the Holyoke women, the end result for those who completed the full course at each institution was the same. In nineteen different courses the same text was used by both seminaries.

This similarity did not disappear as the years progressed. A comparison of the curriculums of Wheaton and Mount Holyoke in 1875–76 indicates that they remained very much alike, although Wheaton placed somewhat more emphasis on history and English literature, and Mount Holyoke on Latin. The seminary program at both institutions had long since become a four-year course of study. Both began the study of mathematics with Algebra and proceeded through Geometry to Trigonometry. Both offered Botany, Physiology, Chemistry, Physics, Astronomy and Geology, as well as Rhetoric, Ancient and Modern History, Moral Science, English Literature, Latin and that capstone of any proper seminary or college education, the required study of Butler's *Analogy of Religion, Natural and Revealed, to the Constitution and Course of Nature.* Wheaton, however, also offered a fifth year, designated as the "Preparatory Class," for students not prepared sufficiently to enter the regular four-year seminary curriculum. Mount Holyoke had no such program.

During the first half of the nineteenth century, the Wheaton educational program emphasized four broad areas, with a fifth added in the 1870s. The first of these can be identified as writing and public speaking, to which in the mid-1850s were added several courses in English literature. Symbolic of the Seminary's success in its instruction in composition was the much-treasured compliment paid to Wheaton in 1874 by the nationally known editor of *Old and New,* Rev. Edward Everett Hale, when he commented: "As Editor of *Old and New* I have seen many papers written by Wheaton Seminary ladies, and have never seen one that was not well written. I have recommended that school I know not how many times. They teach their students to write good English. Please tell Mrs. Metcalf this for me."[17]

Equally important was the emphasis placed on science and mathematics. A report to the trustees by Principal Martha Vose indicates that in 1841–42, of the 52 classes taught that year, 14 were in mathematics and 9 in science, including astronomy, botany, chemistry, geology and natural history (physics.)[18] In 1849 the *Gazateer of Massachusetts* commented that the scientific equipment at Wheaton was much more elaborate than that in other seminaries.[19] That this did not always remain the case is evidenced by Clara Pike's intense lobbying for improved science facilities in the early 1870s, efforts that were rewarded when the major expansion of Seminary Hall in 1878–79 provided extensive additional space for chemistry, biology, and physics laboratories. In addition, the purchase of a telescope and the erection of an observatory, combined with a biennial series of lectures given by Professor Charles Young of Princeton, provided Wheaton students with expert instruction in astronomy. Clara Pike regularly attended, with Board of Trustees approval and financial support, classes at the Women's Laboratory of the Massachusetts Institute of Technology, founded in the 1870s by Ellen Swallow Richards. In turn Miss Pike brought many MIT professors to Norton to give lectures, and engaged the help of Mrs. Richards in planning the science courses taught at Wheaton.[20] Whether it involved Mary Cragin's nationally recognized pioneering techniques of teaching geometry without a textbook, performing a dissection on a chloroformed live rabbit, extensive field observation in botany and ornithology, or working with a compound microscope or chemicals in the laboratory, Wheaton Seminary, from the first classes in botany and algebra taught in the summer of 1835, resolutely pursued the study of science and mathematics throughout the years of its existence.[21]

No less thorough and even more all-encompassing was the Seminary concern with the spiritual life of its students. Wheaton never had a specific denominational affiliation. In his funeral oration upon the occasion

Clara Pike conducts a class in one of the science laboratories constructed in Seminary Hall in 1878.

of the death of Judge Wheaton, Reverend Sylvester Holmes, Seminary trustee from 1843 to 1851, noted:

> The views of Judge Wheaton were ever decidedly against every thing exclusive or denominational, in the character and government of the Seminary he founded. On this subject, his opinions have often been heard by the Board. With these views, the guardians of the Institution, and its teachers, have most fully accorded. None of the vexed and exciting questions of the day are introduced into the school, and every young lady has, and ever has had, the unrestrained privilege of attending church, where she, or her parents, desired. The general influence over the young ladies, is, as it should be, of a high moral character.[22]

While it is true that Wheaton never assumed a rigidly denominational stance, nor rejected applications on the basis of religion, it can hardly be said that its philosophy or outlook was ecumenical in nature. Religion—Christian, Protestant, Trinitarian, Congregational religion—was the dominating force and influence on the life of the Seminary throughout the nineteenth century.[23] Students were required to attend church, and for years a fee for their pews at the Trinitarian Congregational Church was part of the term charges levied. Whether all students had to attend that church is not clear—certainly the First Congregational Church, Unitarian, was located even closer to the Seminary. By the twentieth century we know that Roman Catholic students were provided with a horse and carriage in order to attend Catholic services, but the earliest students who can be identified as Roman Catholics, Sarah Flaherty (WS1878), and her sister, Ellen (WS1881), apparently conformed willingly to the requirements to attend the Trinitarian Church as part of the rules for attending the Seminary.[24]

For decades the Seminary kept the practice of "half-hours," in which each student had a half hour per day by herself in her room expressly for the purpose of personal religious devotion and prayer. All students were required to attend Bible classes on Sunday. Though religious studies were not part of the regular curriculum, and were thus in a sense extra-curricular, they were hardly voluntary. The Sabbath was rigidly kept. No visitors, including parents, were allowed, and students were expected to spend the time they were not at Bible class or church quietly in their rooms, unless they applied for and received permission to take a walk for a couple of hours during the afternoon.[25]

Above all, there was a steady concern, which reached almost epidemic proportions in the 1840s and again in the 1860s, with what was known as sanctification, or second conversion. Not unlike the experience of being "born again" which characterized much of the evangelical movement in the 1970s and 1980s, the process of sanctification involved much effort, and was usually a very personal, intense, and emotional process. "What I desire to see in the Seminary is aggressive Christian

Trinitarian Congregational Church, 1895. Wheaton students regularly attended this church, and graduation exercises were held there until the College Chapel was built in 1917.

work, having definitely in view the salvation of souls," Mrs. Metcalf wrote.[26] Caroline Stickney Creevey, who participated in one of the most intense periods of concern for second conversion, commented later:

> The desire for sanctification shook our school to its center. For days teachers and pupils strove mightily for it. Classes were suspended, and prayer-meetings took their place. Deacon King [a Trustee] was with us most of the time. At all hours of the day, supplication could be heard as a few gathered together in the small music and study rooms. We wept, we struggled. All faces were awe-struck. A solemn hush instead of the cheerful hum of girl's voices was everywhere. As one and another emerged from this sorrowful state and announced with joy that she had become sanctified, those who were still in darkness crowded around and asked how she had done it. . . . Those to whom no light was vouchsafed were wholly miserable.[27]

This kind of intensity could, of course not be maintained for very long, as Mrs. Creevey subsequently and somewhat ruefully commented: "When I went back to Wheaton after vacation everything was as usual; everybody sinned as of yore, and the word 'sanctification' became obsolete."[28]

Not all faculty were enthusiastic about these sessions, which had much of a revivalist element to them. Lucy Larcom, who was a teacher at the time Mrs. Creevey attended, commented in her journal:

> There is a 'revival' of religious feeling here; it is hard to take such a time in the right way. There is good in it,—for true reviving is coming to

life; but there is great danger that it may be spasmodic, emotional merely.
. . . I will say it to these pages, because I feel it so bitterly sometimes, that
there is too much of the "tearing open of the rosebud" in talking with
those who are seeking the truth. Some are thought to be indifferent or untrue, because they will not speak of their deepest feeling to anybody that
asks them. . . . The deeper depths of the soul are sacred to one Eye alone.
. . . Why cannot we leave our friends to find God in the silence of the soul,
since this is his abode?[29]

Though the intensity of the religious atmosphere at Wheaton ebbed
and flowed over the decades, and in general reflected similar movements
throughout New England and New York state, without question the comment made by trustee Albert Plumb in a letter to Mrs. Wheaton in 1878
can serve as an accurate summation of the religious purpose that per-
vaded Wheaton Female Seminary during the nineteenth century. The
Seminary, Plumb wrote, "had always enjoyed the reputation of a school
where decided and active efforts for the conversion of the pupils and the
development of an earnest and consecrated type of piety were put forth.
. . . It was founded and fostered chiefly for this end of seeing a high
religious culture and promoting a high order of female education and
exalted character."[30] It was no accident that trustee concerns about the
religious atmosphere at Wheaton played a major role in the Haskell-
Sprague controversies of the late 1870s. Nor is it surprising that the
Board of Trustees, in accepting Mrs. Metcalf's resignation after more
than twenty-five years of service as Principal, chose above all to congrat-
ulate her "especially upon the degree of divine favor shown to the school
in the numerous revivals of religion which have been enjoyed and by the
general religious influence which has here prevailed."[31]

The fourth broad area of emphasis was again, like the concern for
spiritual life, technically extracurricular but omnipresent and required of
all. The physical well-being of Wheaton students was regarded as criti-
cally important from the day the Seminary opened its doors. Wheaton
students were being prepared to live active, influential lives in their families, their communities, and their church. Neither Mary Lyon nor Eliza
Baylies Wheaton, no matter how they differed on some issues, accepted
for a moment the restrictive physical concepts regarding women that so
often dominated middle-class attitudes during much of the nineteenth
century. For both women, the preeminent word was "usefulness," and
to be useful, women also had to be strong and healthy. In this the trustees
of Wheaton also agreed wholeheartedly. "We would suggest," a Trustee
committee commented in 1859, "that the whole subject of physical exercise be more thoroughly attended to by the pupils. The grand defect of
the female constitution in the country demand [sic] the prompt and earnest attention of families and schools."[32]

It was this attitude that prompted the Seminary to become in 1844 the first educational institution in the United States to erect a freestanding building specifically designed to serve as a gymnasium for its students; to add to its staff in 1862 a graduate of the first normal school for physical education in America, founded in Boston by Dio Lewis in 1861; and to erect as the second building in its massive expansion program at the turn of the century a new gymnasium designed by the person acknowledged as the national leader in the field of physical education, Dr. Dudley Sargent of Harvard.[33]

Whether in the 1840s or the first decade of the twentieth century, Wheaton consistently remained in the forefront among those institutions that advocated organized physical activity for women. Calisthenics and required outdoor walks, instituted in 1835, were replaced in time by various forms of gymnastics. These in turn were supplemented by the appearance of competitive sports—tennis in the 1880s, baseball and basketball in the 1890s and field hockey and track (both running and field events) in the first years of the twentieth century. To these were added skill activities such as golf, fencing, archery, and horseback riding, plus recreational activities ranging from croquet to ice skating. For a period of time the bowling alley provided a source of much entertainment, but as the popularity of outdoor activities increased, the appeal of bowling diminished, and the alleys were finally torn down in 1908.[34]

Beginning in the 1890s the Seminary, in accordance with the policies advocated by Dr. Sargent, annually subjected every student to some forty different measurements, primarily of strength and lung capacity. Students were grouped in classes according to ability, with particular ac-

Sports, ca. 1904. Note the basketball stanchion with no backboard. The observatory known as the "Cheesebox" is behind the tennis court.

tivities prescribed in order to rectify perceived deficiencies. At the end of each year the measurements were repeated. Along with these attempts to institute a scientific method of physical development, at the turn of the century a strong program in personal hygiene was established. Students could earn half their physical education credit each term by taking a cold sponge bath every morning. Further instruction covering items ranging from sleeping apparel to healthful foods was also provided.[35]

Without question the expansion of athletic opportunities was popular with Wheaton students. In particular the advent of gym suits created a sense of physical freedom that was almost overwhelming. "I was on the hockey team," wrote Catherine Small Keesey, who attended Wheaton in 1902. "We played in our gym suits which had short skirts over bloomers and we wore long black stockings. I had always played tennis in a skirt to my ankles and my new golf skirt was as heavy as lead, so that to play a game in a gym suit was bliss, for you felt so free and unhampered."[36]

Equally enthusiastic was Carrie Marshall, who wrote home in 1901: "I am limberer now than I was when I was five years old. I just begin to realize now that I have missed half my life in not playing more games and running around more."[37] Every bit as important was the sense of accomplishment, along with a spirit of independence, that participation in a wide range of athletic activities provided. For most of the Seminary years, the hours following the noon meal were reserved for physical exercise, with classes resuming in the late afternoon and continuing until the supper hour. The formation of a student Athletic Association in 1904 also provided many opportunities for experience in organizational and administrative roles, and the Association quickly became the biggest and most active student group on the campus.[38]

Perhaps the words of Professor Nancy Norton best sum up the role of physical education at Wheaton during the Seminary years:

> Though the Trustees may not have thought of it specifically in these terms, their policies in relation to physical education reflected the attitudes of the times and the changing position of women over the years. At the beginning nothing more strenuous than calisthenics and walking were required. Then came gymnastics, which made more demands on women's bodies. Tennis showed that women could run and furthermore that it was proper to do so. Basketball opened the pores and made them sweat—not a very Victorian concept. Hockey introduced violence and pain when sticks and ankles met and ladies became black and blue. To complete the picture, the introduction of the "dangerous" game of baseball and the ultra-masculine shotput indicates how much the image of women's capabilities had changed. And imbued in all of this was the concept of competition, and also that of sportsmanship.[39]

One other major area deserves some consideration. During the first few decades of the Seminary's existence the study of foreign languages, either classical or modern, did not count toward the attainment of a diploma. It was here that the seminaries parted sharply from the men's colleges, institutions that they sought to emulate in most areas of the curriculum. Though instruction in Latin, and occasionally Greek, was available to Wheaton students for an extra fee from 1840 on, it was only in 1868–69 that students were permitted to elect courses in Latin as part of the regular degree curriculum. In 1876–77 with the advent of Miss Haskell's principalship, Latin became a required part of the regular curriculum, and the number of required courses in the subject increased steadily in subsequent years.[40]

French was also introduced as an "extra-fee" subject in 1840, but it was only in 1871–72, when it was joined by German and Italian, that students could substitute modern language courses for some of those still listed as part of the regular curriculum.[41] Although Italian soon disappeared, and there were occasional lapses in the availability of German, French took its place along with Latin as a graduation requirement in 1876–77. However, while the separate charge for Latin instruction was removed in 1870–71, students continued to pay an extra fee for modern language courses until 1885–86.

Courses in music performance and studio art were available to students as early as 1838–39, but even in the final years of the Seminary curriculum could only be taken upon payment of a special fee and generally did not count toward the Seminary degree.

One of the oldest and most used cliches of the academic world is the saying that an educational institution is "only as strong as its faculty." In the twentieth century, "faculty" was probably joined by "library collection" and "science facilities," all perhaps to be replaced by "computer center" in the twenty-first century. However, the truth of the original concept is unchallengeable when one considers the Seminary period in Wheaton's history. It is true that repeated attempts were made to provide suitable and up-to-date science facilities; the library collection, however, remained small, numbering only some 8000 volumes in 1912. The strength and quality of the Wheaton educational experience, attested to again and again by former students, lay without question in the dedication, energy, and excellence in teaching exhibited by the faculty.

The academic preparation demanded of Wheaton faculty reflected accurately the educational opportunities available for women in any given period of the nineteenth and early twentieth centuries. Initially, instructors were seminary graduates drawn from the teaching staffs of similar educational institutions, or were recent Wheaton graduates who had excelled as students and who often had served as "assistant pupils" or tutors during their final year of study for the degree. The opening of state normal schools for teacher training led Caroline Metcalf to be sure that at least one member of the staff was a normal school graduate, thus insuring that Wheaton students would benefit from the latest knowledge and practice in the teacher-training field. With the advent of colleges for women, new appointees to the Wheaton faculty usually held a Bachelor of Arts or Bachelor of Science degree, and by the turn of the century President Cole was seeking faculty who also held a Master of Arts diploma. One faculty member, Martha Austin, who taught natural science in the fall semester of 1901–02, possessed a full doctorate.[42] Only after Wheaton received its collegiate charter in 1912, and began regularly to hire men as well as women as faculty members did the Ph.D. become the usual, though not absolute, requirement for attainment of permanent tenured-faculty rank. What is evident is that at any period in its history, Wheaton Female Seminary drew its faculty from among the small number of women who had reached the top educational level and attained the highest formal diploma generally available to women at that particular time.

At no period in the Seminary's history was teaching excellence more thoroughly exemplified than during the administration of Caroline Metcalf. A strong administrator and an exacting taskmistress, she also believed strongly in giving her faculty free rein in the classroom, holding them responsible only for the end results. Because of this she was able to bring together an amazing group of teachers, two of whom, Mary Cragin in mathematics and Lucy Larcom in literature and composition, would in time attain national recognition for their achievements.[43]

Five years after her death, the *National Teachers Monthly* lauded Mary Cragin as having been "a woman who came as near the ideal of true teacher, everything considered, as any that we have known."[44] During her years at Wheaton she developed her special technique of teaching geometry without benefit of a textbook. One student, Ella Fisher Luther, commented later:

> I never saw a text book on Geometry until one of my sons came to study it. We each had a blank book and were first given definitions, axioms, etc. A problem was put on the blackboard, we copied it in our blank book, and if we did not solve it the first day, we were not marked for it, but after it was once explained in the class, we were, and each day a new proposition was given. As we went on into Natural Philosophy and Astronomy we were not only required to understand what our textbook gave us, but to prove geometrically everything that could be. The course would have been called severe, but we had an exceptional teacher and I loved it.[45]

Known to the students as "Miss Why?," Mary Cragin's development of a teaching technique that made each student responsible for thinking through and solving mathematics problems on her own won national acclaim when she left Wheaton to teach at the St. Louis, Missouri, Normal School. Later Seminary students attest to the fact that her particular approach to mathematics was perpetuated in the classroom at Wheaton by the instructors who followed in Mary Cragin's footsteps.

Writing years later to President Cole at the time the Seminary was considering naming a dormitory in honor of Miss Cragin, Mary Briggs, herself an outstanding teacher of history and assistant principal for many years, commented: "I suppose that for a good many years Miss Cragin was the most potent force in the school, both from an ethical and an educational point of view. She was a woman whose like in all my years of teaching and of social life I have never known."[46]

However, it is Lucy Larcom who today remains the best known of Wheaton's nineteenth century teaching staff. As a young girl, Miss Larcom had worked in the Lowell textile mills, subsequently graduating from Monticello Seminary in Illinois where she had gone to live with her sister. Aside from one year teaching at Bradford Academy, Miss Larcon's teaching career was confined to Wheaton, where she was a member of the faculty from 1854 to 1862, returning again from 1865 to 1867. A close friend of John Greenleaf Whittier, she served as compiler of several anthologies published under his name, from which she received steady royalty income. After leaving Wheaton she was able to support herself entirely through the proceeds from her writing and poetry, which was published extensively in childrens magazines and in religious and ladies journals.

Her work at Wheaton had the same profound long-term effect on the teaching of history and literature as that of Mary Cragin in mathematics and Clara Pike in science. Not only was Lucy Larcom responsible for founding the student literary magazine *Rushlight,* but she was also the inspiration for organizing the intellectual discussion group known as

Lucy Larcom, teacher of writing, literature and history, 1854-1862, 1865-1867.

"Psyche," which in time became the senior honor society.[47] Her views on teaching history and English literature were contrary to the standard recitation practices of the day. "I find," she wrote in her journal, "that the young girls are more interested in ideas than in mere facts, they follow me well; but then it makes me feel my own ignorance so much!"[48]

> Tomorrow a class in Rhetoric is to be examined. Twelve weeks is altogether too short a time for this study, with that of the principles of general Criticism; but it is a satisfaction to know that some new ideas have been gained; and that these pupils will know a little better how to judge books. I am more and more inclined to a liberal spirit in these things; to judging by the spirit of the writer than by his conformity to rules. Good taste is a good thing, but good sense and great truths are far better.[49]

Like superior teachers in any age, Lucy Larcom complained that her many duties and the variety of courses to be taught left her little time for the serious study and course preparation she wished to make. "I wish the days longer, and the nights shorter, and my head a great deal stronger," she wrote, "so that I might teach and study to some purpose. . . . Wisdom cannot be hurried, crowded, or driven. . . . Girls will be ill-educated, till their teachers are allowed the time and thought which teachers of *men* are expected to take. . . . I am glad to be busy, but I dislike to be superficial."[50]

To the names of Mary Cragin and Lucy Larcom can be added many others—Ann Carter, Clara Pike, Mary Blair, and Mary Briggs in particular come to mind. Required to live and eat in the sprawling dormitory with the students, they and the other teachers became the students' friends and confidantes as well as their teachers, supervisors, and occasional disciplinarians. Expected to provide a daily example of proper spiritual and intellectual life, theirs was truly a taxing existence, physically, intellectually, and emotionally. But the end result was to create an atmosphere not only of learning and intellectual stimulation, but also of self-confidence and personal commitment to excel. "I think," wrote a student who attended the Seminary in 1860, "that the dominant influence was an excitement to *be* and do my *best,* whatever the task assigned."[51] What teacher could ask for more!

NOTES: CHAPTER 7

1. General Files: 1834–1835: Memoir, "One who was a Pupil at the first opening the the School."

2. Wheaton Female Seminary, "Grade Books" (2), 1879–1884.

3. Wheaton Histories, Seminary: Admissions, 1835–1899: Barrows to Zerviah Mitchell, 3/14/48. See also Mitchell to Barrows, 3/7/48. It does appear that, unbeknownst to Wheaton, Mary E. Stafford of Cumberland Island, Georgia, the child of a mixed racial liaison, attended Wheaton in 1856–1857. See General Files: 1856–1857:

J. Ehrenhard and M. Bullard, "Stafford Plantations, Cumberland Island National Seashore, Georgia," p. 16.

4. I am grateful to Ms. Wilma Slaight, Archivist at Wellesley College, for providing information and materials regarding Portia Washington.

5. See *Rushlight*, 30:1 (Fall, 1884); 3 (June, 1885); 38:1 (December, 1893); 40:2 (February, 1895); Treasurer's Office: Contributions by Wheaton, 1881–1923. Portia Washington had celebrated her nineteeth birthday in June, 1902.

6. SVC, Letterbook: Cole to Trustees, 7/10/02, p 363.

7. Ibid.: Cole to Secretary, Wellesley College, 7/15/02, p. 369.

8. Ibid.: Cole to Mrs. Washington, 7/16/02, p 320.

9. Ibid., 7/25/02, p. 378. Ruth Ann Stewart, in her biography of Portia Washington Pittman, confirms that Portia, despondent in her isolation at Wellesley, did poorly in her courses other than music, and voluntarily withdrew. See *Portia: The Life of Portia Washington Pittman, The Daughter of Booker T. Washington* (Garden City, NY: Doubleday, 1977) p. 42.

10. SVC, Letterbook: Cole to Spencer, 7/23/02, p. 375.

11. Ibid.: Cole to Mrs. Bird, 7/25/02, p. 377. Ironically, one week after denying admission to Miss Washington, President Cole sent a $70.00 check to Hampton Institute on behalf of the Wheaton students and faculty, to be used for scholarship purposes. SVC, Letterbook: Cole to Frizzel, 8/1/02, p. 388. According to Ruth Stewart, Portia Washington lived in an off-campus boardinghouse at Wellesley. Wellesley sources indicate that she lived with two faculty members. It should be noted that *all* special students at Wellesley were required to live off-campus. Dormitory space was reserved for degree candidates.

12. President's Reports to Trustees: 6/3/45; Trustees Minutes: 6/3/45. The student who enrolled as a freshman in 1919–1920 was Elizabeth Baker Lewis from Cambridge, Massachusetts. The following year she transferred to Radcliffe College, to which she was recommended by President Cole. Miss Lewis graduated from Radcliffe in 1924, earned an M.A. degree in 1925, and died less that a year later in March, 1926. For discussion of the decision to admit African-American students on a regular basis to Wheaton, see ch. 18.

13. See Wheaton Female Seminary, *Annual Catalogue*, 1873–1876.

14. Morison, *Harvard*, pp. 341–47.

15. See ch. 2; also Clewes, *Wheaton Through the Years*, p. 5.

16. See appropriate catalogues for Wheaton, Mount Holyoke, Bowdoin and Amherst; also Morison, *Harvard*, p. 235; J. S. Pond, *Bradford, A New England Academy* (Bradford, MA: Bradford Academy Alumnae Association, 1930), ch. 10; Green, *Lyon and Holyoke*, pp. 219–21.

17. Principals: Metcalf: Beach to Metcalf, 11/11/74.

18. Ibid.: Vose: "Report for year ending October 25, 1842"; also in Shepard, "Reference History," pp. 79–84.

19. Wheaton Histories, Seminary: Reminiscenses: Merrill manuscript; see also Shepard, "Reference History," p. 277.

20. G. Shepard, "Female Education at Wheaton College," *New England Quarterly*, 6:4 (1933), pp. 819–20; Shepard, "Reference History," pp. 236–38, 286; Wheaton Histories, Shepard "Reference History" Notes: F. V. Emerson memoir; Paine, *E. B. Wheaton*, pp. 146–54; Cowan, "E. S. Richards," pp. 143–44.

21. *Rushlight*, 25:2 (March, 1880), 27:2 (June, 1883); General Files: Class of 1870: Ella Luther memoir, 1/7/28.

22. Wheaton Family: Judge Wheaton: "Holmes Funeral Sermon," pp. 18–19; Shepard, "Reference History," p. 20.

23. In 1900–1901, a recruiting circular sent to Congregational ministers by President Cole asserted that "Wheaton Seminary is one of our Congregational institutions." General Files: 1900–1901.

24. Trustees Minutes: 5/31/55; General Files: 1877–1878: "In Memoriam, Sarah Flaherty"; 1905–1906: Gracia Harrington memoir. By 1901, fish was served every Friday night, presumably out of deference to students who were Catholic. Marshall, Letters: to Mother, 4/28/01.

25. Principals: Cate: "Regulations for the Sabbath," 4/26/49; Shepard, "Reference History," pp. 113–14.

26. *Rushlight*, 33:1 (November, 1888); Shepard, "Reference History," pp. 88–89, 112; Principals: Sawyer: "Report for 1842–1846"; Metcalf: "To the class of 1870," 2/28/70; *Wheaton Bulletin*, 6:3 (June, 1910), p. 27.

27. Creevey, *Daughter*, p. 242. See also General Files: 1837–1838: Blake to Hodges, 9/2/37; Blackinton to Hodges, 9/21/37; 1848–1849: Smith to Brother, 7/2,5/48; 1866–67: Prouty to Mother, n.d.; Class of 1871: Dodge to Brother, 2/28/69.

28. Creevey, *Daughter*, p. 245.

29. L. Larcom, Journal II: 3/5,6/62. See also P. Helmreich, "Lucy Larcom at Wheaton," *New England Quarterly*, 63:1 (March, 1990), p. 118.

30. Wheaton Family: Letters to EBW, 1848–1878: Plumb to EBW, 9/21/78.

31. Trustees Minutes: 3/23/75. For more on religious influence at Wheaton, see Shepard, "Reference History," pp. 14–18, 112–21, 255–58, 366–67.

32. Trustees Minutes: 7/12/59.

33. The instructor hired in 1862 was Ellen Plimpton, Mrs. Metcalf's niece. To get her reappointed in 1864, Mrs. Metcalf had to use the threat of her own resignation. See Trustees Minutes: 4/15/64; also 12/16/73; and chs. 3 and 4.

34. General Files: 1835–1836: H. Richmond Notebook; Principals: Knight: Grade Book, 1838–1840; Trustees Minutes: 12/15/74; 3/23/75; C. Marshall Letters: to Mother, 10/17/01; N. Norton, "Physical Education and Athletics at Wheaton Female Seminary," Unpublished manuscript, pp. 3–6, 16–17. Nationally and internationally known experts were brought to Wheaton to give clinics and lectures on calisthenics, golf, and field hockey.

35. Norton, "Physical Education and Athletics at Wheaton Seminary," pp. 13–14, 23–24; Marshall, Letters: to Mother, 10/4,29/00; 11/1/00. Carrie, who wrote enthusiastically about the hygienic virtues of cold sponge baths, also commented to her mother on January 20, 1904, that she had washed her hair for the first time since Thanksgiving. "It needed to be washed badly. It was so oily that I could do nothing with it. Now it is pretty and wavy."

36. General Files: 1901–1902: "Wheaton, 1902," by C. S. Keesey. See also *Rushlight*, 22:3 (Summer, 1877), p. 29.

37. Marshall, Letters: to Mother, 2/14/01.

38. *Rushlight*, 49:1 (June, 1904); Norton, "Physical Education and Athletics at Wheaton Seminary," p. 21.

39. Norton, "Physical Education and Athletics at Wheaton Seminary," pp. 25–26.

40. An interesting side-note to the growth of Latin in the curriculum was the advice given to President Cole by President Burton of Smith College, himself a classicist, in 1912. Counseling President Cole regarding the process of the Seminary's becoming a college, President Burton advised that Wheaton stay away from a Latin entrance requirement. He stated that he wished he could give it up at Smith, but politically was not yet able to do so. President Cole did not follow President Burton's advice; the Latin admissions requirement remained until 1930–1931. Shepard, "Reference History," pp. 371–72; Wheaton Histories, Seminary: Seminary to College #1: Cole to Hyde, 2/12/12.

41. German had been offered for one or two-year periods twice earlier. Shepard, "Reference History," p. 271.

42. SVC, Letterbook: Cole to Gooch, 5/30/01, p. 91; Announcement of new faculty, July, 1901, p. 176; Payroll for term ending 12/18/01, p. 273.

43. See ch. 3; also essay by Julia Osgood in *Rushlight*, 34:1 (November, 1889); Creevey, *Daughter*, pp. 226–29; Paine, *E. B. Wheaton*, p. 148.

44. R. Edwards, "Mary Jane Cragin," *National Teachers Monthly*, 1:6 (April, 1875), pp. 161–62.

45. General Files: Class of 1870: Memoir of Ella F. Luther, 1/17/<u>28</u>. See also 1869: K.U. Clark memoir.

46. Faculty Before 1910: Briggs: Briggs to SVC, 6/13/<u>11</u>.

47. See articles by Lucy Larcom in *Rushlight*, 28:2 (June, 1883). *Rushlight* commenced in 1855; "Psyche" in 1857.

48. Larcom, Journal II: 1/25/62. See also S. Roller, "Lucy Larcom: A Portrait of 19th Century America," Wheaton College Honors Thesis #182, (1982), ch. 4.

49. Larcom, Journal I: 11/21/59; see also Helmreich, "Larcom at Wheaton," p.112.

50. Larcom, Journal II: 1/19,25/62; 5/23/62; also Helmreich, "Larcom at Wheaton," pp. 117, 120. For discussion of Miss Larcom's work and contacts in the wider literary world, see D. Addison, *Lucy Larcom: Life, Letters and Diary* (Boston: Houghton Mifflin, 1894), and S. Marchalonis, *The Worlds of Lucy Larcom, 1824–1893* (Athens, GA: University of Georgia Press, 1989). Chs. 6–8 in the latter volume deal specifically with the years Miss Larcom was teaching at Wheaton.

51. Quoted by Shepard, "Reference History," p. 129.

8

We Lived in a Woman's World, Yet Triumphed With Gaiety

"IF I WERE to describe Norton to you I should say it is as flat as a meadow, not a hill to be seen, a few large houses at some distance from each other, and the stillest place I was ever in, and on that account very favourable to study. . . ."[1] So wrote Hannah Richmond in the fall of 1835. Commenting that the students were given enough to eat and drink, she went on to heap praise upon the Principal, Eunice Caldwell, and pronounced herself "perfectly satisfied."

> My time is wholly occupied. We stay at school 7 hours each day but there is such a variety in the exercises that it does not seem long. . . . School is done at 4 o'clock, and we have one hour to walk and make calls on each other, we have tea at 5 o'clock. At 6 the bell is rung for study hour and we have only 10 minutes during that time till 9 o'clock to talk with each other. If we have got our lesson at 9 we can sit up and talk until half past 10. Miss Caldwell advises us not to talk after we go to bed, for she says young ladies will say a great many foolish things in the dark that they would be ashamed to say in the light and when looking at each other.[2]

Throughout the nineteenth century, life at Wheaton Female Seminary was regulated to the minute of every hour and every day. A student in 1836 complained that "there are 31 bells regularly here and sometimes several more," and students in subsequent decades commented repeatedly regarding the number of bells that regulated all aspects of their lives, from rising to lights out.[3] Only in the first decade of the twentieth century, under the administration of President Cole, was the number of bells rung during the day drastically reduced.

Compared to today's college students, those of the nineteenth century brought very few clothes with them when they came to Wheaton. We have a list of the items brought by one student in 1838–39. It totals 48 pieces, including seven dresses, four pairs of shoes, two bonnets, a cape, and seven pairs of stockings. The rooms were sparsely but adequately furnished. A double room contained two bureaus, a wash stand, a wash pitcher and basin, perhaps a screen for the washstand, a table, a small bookcase, two wooden chairs and a double bed. Only in the 1880s did

156

institutions such as Wheaton, Mount Holyoke and Vassar switch from double to single beds.[4]

Although in many ways student life differed dramatically from that in the twentieth century, some things were much the same. "You must excuse me for not writing to you before for I don't have any time to write home, have to study almost all the time," wrote one early Seminary student.[5] Homesickness and the adjustment of roommate to roommate also has a timeless quality:

> I suppose you would like to know by this time how I get along here. . . . If you want to know how I like it, I can tell you I don't like it very well, and I don't know the reason either. I have got acquainted with some of the girls. I expect it will take a good while to get acquainted with them all as there are fifty-two that board here and eight more expected to come next week.
>
> My room-mate is rather a pleasant girl I should think, although she does not stay with me much, and when she is with me she acts as if she wanted to be somewhere else.[6]

Equally universal, whatever the decade, were problems of class scheduling. In 1901, a student wrote home with a complaint familiar to college students of any generation. "I have a new schedule now. It is very hard to make out a schedule in a school like this when no two people have exactly the same studies. It is hard not to have conflicts with the scholars. . . . I had my drawing period changed. That came at the same time my English did according to the new schedule."[7]

Sketch by Emma Cunliff (WS1868), of the room she shared with Mary Lincoln (WS1868). Note the double bed.

Musicians, ca. 1899.

Rules abounded. The following list of "Rules and Regulations of Wheaton Seminary," recorded in 1875 by one student, Amelia Pond, can be considered typical of the whole Seminary period.

Rule I   Pupils must not go to the Post Office without permission.
Rule II   Promptness in everything is required of the pupils.
Rule III   Rooms are to be visited only in recreation hours.
Rule IV   Teachers must not be interrupted in study hours except in the case of necessity.
Rule V   Pupils under 18 years of age are not to go to the store without permission.
Rule VI   All must keep Cash Accounts.
Rule VII   Must not go riding without Mrs. M's permission.
Rule VIII   Can't go ride without permission from home.
Rule IX   No gentleman callers who do not bring letters of introduction are received.
Rule X   Must not answer the doorbell.
Rule XI   No one to go out of their room to sleep without Mrs. M's permission.
Rule XII   Pupils do not receive their gentlemen friends in their bedrooms.
Rule XIII   Must not talk in the library.
Rule XIV   Not to talk from windows.
Rule XV   Nothing to be thrown from windows.
Rule XVI   Must not borrow money or wearing apparel.[8]

Rules for the Sabbath were strict. In the early decades no visitors, including parents, were allowed on Sunday, and students were expected to remain quietly in their rooms except for Bible study, church, meals, and evening devotions. With special permission, it was possible to take a walk with another student for an hour or two in the afternoon. No school work could be done on Sunday, and only reading of approved material was allowed. In the earlier decades even letter writing was prohibited, though there is ample evidence that this rule was often ignored.[9]

Equally well regulated was students' social life, particularly when it came to members of the opposite sex. Even at the beginning of the twentieth century letters could be sent to or received from persons only if their names were on an approved list provided to the Seminary by parents. Any young man who wished to call on a student had to present a card of introduction from her parents. If he wished to meet or be introduced to a roommate or friend of a student he knew, he was required to procure first a card of introduction from that girl's parents as well. No visitors or telephone calls, in or out, were allowed on the Sabbath.[10]

The result was that the social life of the students was almost completely self-contained. "We lived in a woman's world, yet triumphed with gaiety," commented Gratia Harrington (WS 1906).[11] Saturday evening sewing bees, corn popping and molasses pulls, sleigh-rides, making "orange sherbet" out of oranges, milk, and fresh fallen snow were favorite occupations. Special "dinners" and masquerade parties with elaborate costumes also broke the monotony, as did occasional trips to Boston for lectures, concerts, or plays. "One gala costume party happened in my senior year," wrote a student who attended in the 1880s. "The Sun and Moon on a throne watched the planets and some constellations and famous stars pass by in their glory. One girl appeared in a wholly masculine costume for "Mars," imported for the occasion. She endured the mortification of being told it was immodest and she must add a short skirt that would at least cover her knees. With no gentlemen invited . . . we girls felt aggrieved."[12]

By the 1870s students were occasionally allowed to invite young men to campus for carefully regulated receptions or dances. "I had two dances with real men," Carrie Marshall wrote in ecstasy to her mother in 1903.[13] Yet the threat of administrative curtailment of these particularly treasured events was never far removed, witness this communication from Caroline Metcalf to the Class of 1873 regarding a proposed reception to be held at the time of graduation.

> My dear young friends,
> In compassion for your great disappointment in view of my decision respecting a reception, on the evening of our anniversary, I am moved to grant you permission to invite your friends, on the following conditions, viz. that you give me an <u>assurance</u> that your guests will leave <u>promptly</u> at the time stated in your invitation without the necessity of <u>two</u> bells, also that they leave the yard and have no serenading.

May Day celebration, 1904. Seminary Hall is in the background. Begun in 1889, the ceremony was moved in the 1920s to the athletics field in back of the Chapel. Subsequently, May Day festivities were held in the Dimple until 1960.

I am forced to make these conditions, on account of the great annoyance experienced last year, not only by the guests at the Mansion House, but by all the dwellers in this usually quiet neighborhood. If these terms can be complied with, I cheerfully reverse my decision, although it had the sanction of the Trustees and all the patrons of the school with whom I have conversed.

Wishing you a pleasant reception.

I am very truly your friend,

C.C. METCALF

The appearance of a "gentleman caller" was likely to excite great interest among the friends of the student so favored. "I would rather J.B. did not come to Norton," wrote Sally Jarvis in 1843, "for when a Gentleman comes near the house, the girls act as if they were crazy or had never seen a man before. And, another thing, I don't care about seeing him much."[15]

An account concerning another male visitor sixty years later indicates that things had not greatly changed.

Wheaton never encouraged visits from beaux. Not many men had the courage to call on a girl there. One day, to my amazement, I received a note from Charlotte Keesey's older brother Vincent. He was a senior at

Harvard. I hardly knew him and thought his mother had probably asked him to come to see me. He was very good-looking, exceptionally bright, very quiet and scared me to death. I asked permission to have him call and it was granted and the time set. I got more nervous and more nervous as the time arrived. The windows in Metcalf Hall were full of girls watching for Vincent, for we were not allowed to introduce the caller to anyone, but had to entertain him in a formal reception room. At last Vincent came and we were seated in stiff chairs facing each other and I was doing my best to be entertaining when suddenly there was a knock at the door. I said, "Come in," and who should appear but Jeannette with her hair pulled back tight in a knot and dressed as a maid with a white apron and said in the most awful Irish brogue, "You're wanted at the telephone, Mum." I tried not to look amazed and excused myself and left the room presumably to answer the telephone. When I got outside I found no one in sight so in a few minutes I returned. Not long afterwards there was another knock at the door and when I said, "Come in," Nell appeared in a black dress with a dainty sheer white apron and cap, looking pretty as could be, with a tray with tea and said, "Would you like some tea, Miss?" I thanked her and she put down the tray and I poured tea. I tried to act as if this was what happened when a man called on a girl at Wheaton. The girls were determined to see Vincent and he and I laughed many times over his visit to Wheaton, for I married him a few years later.[16]

Male visitors could easily run afoul of an ever-watchful Principal. Such was the case of a young man, Joseph Hamblin, who in 1849, accompanied by a friend, drove a carriage with a team of horses down from Cambridge in order to visit Sarah Judson and two of her friends. In the course of the visit the young ladies apparently got soaked in a sudden rainstorm and Hamblin and his team of horses incurred the wrath of Miss Cate for reasons not totally clear. In a delightful letter to Miss Judson, one that a Wheaton student of any era would certainly treasure, Hamblin asked:

> Was Miss Cate very angry? If so we humbly beg of you to plead our cause, confident that your appeal will be irresistable.
>
> We have to thank you for the most delightful visit it has ever been our fortune to experience, particularly our last evening in Norton, which is beyond our powers of description—we look forward with impatient eagerness to a repetition of the same.
>
> By the way, do you intend remaining at the seminary during the 4th of July next, as heretofore. Boston is so <u>stupid</u> and <u>monotinous</u> [sic] a place that <u>possibly</u> we may visit Norton on that day, should matters remain as at present.
>
> We sincerely hope you suffered no physical derangement by your exposure to the storm on Monday evening, or moral lectures from Miss Cate, occasioned by our imprudence Tuesday morning.

Please present our regards to Misses Lydia Smith and Jo. Peckham and let us hope that occasionally a thought is wasted upon

Your Devoted and Obt Servants
Jo. E. Hamblin
Geo. West

Life in the sprawling dormitory, with its two main sections and several additions could at times become hectic, and was particularly trying for the teachers who lived amidst their students. "I have got a pleasant room on the third story," wrote one student. "As the wildest girls room up here, we intend to have real fun after we get our compositions done."[18] "Fun with the atomizer after lights out," recorded another in her diary more than half a century later.[19] "Life in a crowd of girls has become almost a torment to me," wrote Lucy Larcom plaintively in her diary. "Not that the genus *girl* is disagreeable to me; I should like them all, separately in their homes, but so much pent-up life is painful. I cannot *love* boarding-schools. . . . The French *a la maison* is the only proper term for this great lodging-and-studying-house; *home* is another thing altogether."[20]

By the last decade of the nineteenth century student life had been considerably modernized. Indoor plumbing for toilets and bathtubs had been in existence for some time, though students until the turn of the century drew pitchers of water each night from a well in the dormitory basement to be used for drinking and washing in their rooms. Central heating with steam heat for all seminary buildings began in 1885. A long-distance telephone was installed in 1897. In the same year the dining rooms and classrooms were first lighted by electricity, and one over-head bulb was placed in each room. However, students continued to study by kerosene lamps for more than a decade, on the theory that electric light was trying to the eyes.[21]

Norton in the nineteenth century was far less isolated in terms of available public transportation than it would be for much of the twentieth. By the end of the century trolley lines connected Norton with Mansfield, Taunton, and Attleboro. The Norton railroad station, located approximately one mile east of the Seminary, saw eight or nine trains to and from Boston each day, with almost equally good connections to Providence and Fall River. Mail was delivered to the Norton post office seven times a day. A livery service provided easy transportation to the railroad depot, which was also a favorite destination of Wheaton students on their "walks" from the time the railroad began service in August, 1836. Then in 1908 the Trustees voted to purchase the Seminary's first automobile, little realizing that in doing so they were contributing in a small way to the process that would lead in the twentieth century to greater, rather than less difficulty on the part of students in gaining easy access to the urban centers that seemed both tantalizingly near and distressingly far.[22]

Relations between the Seminary and the Town of Norton over the years may be classified as cooperative, if not warm. For those who lived in one of the small village clusters of Norton other than the Center, the existence of the Seminary had minimal if any impact, unless a daughter in the family chose to attend the institution. The prosperity of the Wheaton family apparently led to occasional feelings of jealousy among the townspeople, and hard feelings engendered by the break with the Unitarian Congregational Church on the part of the Wheatons and other families took a long time to heal. But it is also clear that the citizens of Norton recognized the many benefits, ranging from a public library to the site for a public high school, that resulted from Wheaton family munificence.

For able young women from the town Wheaton Seminary proved a boon, especially because Norton residents were always granted partial remission of tuition fees. The presence of the Seminary was greatly influential in getting trolley lines to neighboring towns installed, and the willingness of the Seminary to participate in and subsidize the building of a town water system had much to do with its creation at the turn of the century. And of course, the Seminary served as a place of employment for Norton residents, and its students were customers for the few shops located in the Center.

Although from time to time there were grumblings over the exclusion from property and real estate taxes enjoyed by the Seminary, they were not very loud or widespread. Real confrontation on this issue, at one

"Off for Vacation," ca. 1900.

point carried to the Massachusetts Supreme Court by the Town of Norton, occurred only after the transition to full collegiate status. This affair, plus the building of the college chapel in 1917 and the resultant attendance of Wheaton students at Sunday services there, rather than at churches in Norton, served to alienate much of the town from the college and created problems of "town-gown relations" for Wheaton College that did not exist in the Seminary era.[23]

What impact did the events of the outside world have on Wheaton Seminary, located as it was in a quiet rural town not normally subject to the turbulence of major public concerns? To a great extent the answer depended on the attitudes and concerns of the teaching staff, and probably to some extent, of the Wheaton family. Certainly this was true of Wheaton's involvement in the evangelical religious fervor that developed and intensified during much of the nineteenth century. The impact of this movement on Wheaton has already been discussed. Equally active was the Seminary's commitment to the Temperance movement, a cause to which Eliza Wheaton was particularly dedicated. Wheaton students marched en masse in Temperance parades in Norton, and attended Temperance meetings and lectures, both locally and in Boston.[24]

Other than Temperance and spiritual re-birth, the only concerns that seemed to affect the faculty and students at Wheaton deeply were the abolitionist movement and the Civil War. Central to the Seminary's involvement were the convictions of Lucy Larcom. A confirmed and active abolitionist, Miss Larcom found a receptive audience at a Seminary whose founder, Judge Wheaton, had been known as an abolitionist when he served in Congress half a century earlier. Shortly after she came to Wheaton to teach, Lucy Larcom won a major contest for a song aimed at recruiting abolitionist northerners to go to Kansas and insure that the territory became free rather than slave-holding. Copies of Miss Larcom's song were distributed by the thousands, and the fame it brought her must certainly have helped to inspire the strong resolution supporting the cause of freedom in Kansas that was passed unanimously by the faculty and students at a meeting held on July 4, 1856.[25]

The outbreak of the Civil War caused great excitement at Wheaton. The Seminary immediately advised the few students who came from the South to withdraw, and made every effort to ensure their safe return home. The war itself was greeted with enthusiasm and public displays of patriotic fervor.

> Norton is comparatively quiet, yet we Seminary girls are wild with excitement. The front of our boarding house is decorated with the Stars and Stripes, and last night a large flag of our own was raised on the Seminary building, and unfurled to the breeze, where it flies proudly.
> We had a glorious time at the raising, sang patriotic songs, and cheered loud and long. We have finished 120 flannel shirts for the noble volunteers,

and have bought yarn, and are knitting socks for them. Each girl sewed a motto in the sleeve of the shirt she made, with her name and that of the Seminary. I hope mine will cheer some manly heart as he goes forth to battle for his country. God bless them. I admire their noble spirit, and were I a young man, I would share their glory—yea, would fight for my country's honor, and if need be, give my life to save it."[26]

A year later Lucy Larcom wrote in her diary: "Yesterday morning the news came of the surrender of Norfolk, and in a sudden burst of patriotism, the school went out and marched round the Liberty-pole, under the Stars and Stripes singing 'Hail, Columbia,' and cheering most heartily."[27]

The coming of the Civil War also brought the first appearance of student interest in political affairs, along with a slight stirring of sentiment supportive of voting rights for women. What is striking about this development is that it seems to have been almost entirely student sponsored rather than led or nourished by faculty, as had been the case with religious conversion, Temperance, and abolition. The right to vote was something in which neither Mrs. Wheaton nor the Seminary staff was particularly interested. Nonetheless, beginning in the 1860s, political debates and mock elections became the rule in every presidential election season.[28] The freeing of the slaves stirred in some student minds the idea that political rights for women might be the next item of reform on the national political agenda,

> Now that the cruel war is o'er, and the poor slave, a slave no more, the rights of the downtrodden, oppressed woman, are brought, for the first time, before the minds of this mighty nation. . . . Republican principles are gaining ground, and our experienced (?) editorial eye has to glance down the vista of only a few of the coming generations to foresee the day when the whole world shall be one vast republic, and an American citizen (possibly a woman) shall be its President! . . .
>
> People are growing, now-a-days, and casting off as they progress the old cramping customs. One day, and that not far off, men will grow to this. The female sex are always a decade in advance of the men. We are ready for both the ballot and the bureau: they will soon be ready to grant them and when they come with their own free will to offer us what so many are trying to wrest by force, then we shall have the first of all rights.[29]

A poll of the six graduating seniors of the class of 1869 indicated that two "insisted" on getting the right to vote, two would be "willing" to vote if it were possible to do so, one did not care, and one would have felt "disgraced by touching the ballot."[30] Yet throughout the Seminary era one finds little to indicate that, aside from serving as an element of occasional discussion, the enfranchisement of women was given serious attention. There is certainly no indication that Wheaton students or faculty took any active role in the growing movement for women's political

A mock political rally, held in front of Larcom Hall in the fall of 1912.

rights that characterized the decades at the turn of the century. The emphasis placed upon traditional views of women as housekeepers, wives, and mothers, which served as the basis for President Cole's statement to the Massachusetts Legislature that the new Wheaton College would concentrate on educating its students for "the business of being a woman," definitely reflects the atmosphere that existed at Wheaton throughout the Seminary years.

Despite the sheltered, secure, and disciplined environment that the Seminary provided, students still managed on occasion to get into trouble. One whose name was Helen Potter, affectionately and appropriately nicknamed "Old Hellpot" by her compatriots, was expelled for cooking fudge in a closet after lights out. The porch roofs connecting sections of Metcalf Hall were regarded as a good way to escape detection on the way to "midnight spreads." The rule noted by the student of Mrs. Metcalf's era that nothing was to be thrown from windows apparently stemmed from an incident in which students successfully doused a number of young male callers from Taunton with pitchers of water thrown from second and third story windows.[31]

Amazingly, given the close proximity in which residents lived in the crowded dormitory, it was not until 1907 that the Seminary experienced a serious health problem. That year a major outbreak of scarlet fever occurred, forcing the Seminary to cancel classes and send most students home for nearly two months. Since the infirmary on Howard Street, which had been opened in 1894, was too small to accommodate all who had contracted the disease, twenty-six students and two maids were quarantined in the West Wing of Metcalf Hall. Other than this one incident, however, the Seminary always was remarkably free of either major or minor health problems—so much so that the healthfulness of the Norton air and climate was often touted by the Seminary and attested to by others as one of the advantages to be gained by attending Wheaton.[32]

From time to time groups of students formed what they always referred to as secret societies. Generally these involved a close circle of friends who would design a logo, have a pin made, write a charter, or perform some combination of such activities, all designed to cement the friendships formed at Wheaton. Only once did such a society become self-perpetuating, with each year's members selecting five to seven persons to replace them the following year. Apparently this organization continued for several years before President Cole found out about its existence, whereupon the society was summarily terminated, despite some protests from alumnae and bitterness among the student members that lasted for many years after.[33]

There were, of course, many recognized clubs and organizations. The student literary magazine, *Rushlight,* and the literary discussion society, Psyche, both founded by Lucy Larcom in the 1850s, were among the earliest and certainly the most permanent.[34] A missionary society and a glee club existed from the 1870s, a YWCA club was founded in the 1890s, and the Athletic Association and a student council were formed shortly after the turn of the century. Other approved groups, among them the Clytie and Sappho societies, the *Chrysalis* magazine, and the Reading Club, were all created for the younger students and led briefer, more tenuous existences. Despite the obvious social element involved, all of these organizations always had as their central focus serious academic, physical, or spiritual concerns.[35]

From its inception, Wheaton Female Seminary did everything within its power to avoid any action that would tarnish it with the image of being a "finishing school." This fact was recognized in March, 1875, when a national journal commented: "Two people are sure to be disappointed at Norton—the young lady who goes there to fashionably idle away a year or two, and the parent who expects that, at a stipulated time, his daughter will be sent home finished and labeled with no need or desire to open another book as long as she lives, and with no desire to make her life a test of her learning."[36]

Speaking at the fiftieth anniversary celebration in 1885, Eunice Caldwell Cowles, first Principal of Wheaton, noting the growth and prosperity of the Seminary, commented:

Because it has advanced, it lives. The most stable of all things is change. We must go backward or forward, advance every moment toward life or toward death. What we call standing still is stagnation, sure death. Some of you will doubtless be permitted to see this Institution's hundredth birthday. Whether it shall then be as vigorous and promising as today, depends upon whether the trustees, in time to come as in time past, still march forward. May it always go in the way of truth and holiness, and always, as now, leave a trail of glory behind it.[37]

"Wheaton Seminary was founded in 1834 for the higher education of young women," read the opening statement in the annual catalogues at the turn of the century. From this purpose the Wheaton family and the many trustees, administrators, and teachers who served the institution had never deviated. In 1912, as the fledgling Wheaton College stood poised to face the challenges of a new century, the overriding concern of those who guided its destiny remained steadfastly the same—to remain true to the mission for which, seventy-five years earlier, Wheaton had been founded.

NOTES: CHAPTER 8

1. General Files: 1835–1836: H. Richmond to Mother and Sisters, Fall 1835.
2. Ibid.
3. General Files: 1836–1837: G. Whitwell to Sister, August, 1836. See also Shepard, "Reference History," p. 141; *Rushlight*, 33:6 (April, 1889), pp. 103–8.
4. General Files: 1838–1839: list of items brought to Wheaton; 1876–1877, Belle Hammond memoir; Faculty Before 1810: F. V. Emerson: Emerson to S. B. Young, 5/14/35.
5. General Files: 1838–1839: B. Packard to Almira, 6/1/39.
6. Ibid.: Packard to Mother, 5/17/39.
7. Marshall, Letters: to Mother, 2/21/01.
8. General Files: 1874–1875. See also 1838–1839 and 1853–1854; Shepard, "Reference History," p. 87.
9. Principals: Cate: "Regulations for the Sabbath," 4/15/49. Also S. Jarvis, Letters, 1843–1850: to Father, 9/10/43; General Files: 1843–1844: S. Kempton to Bailey, 4/28/44; Marshall, Letters: to Mother, 2/3/01. Not only was Sunday recreational reading a concern, but light reading at anytime. As late as 1875 one set of rules stated: "No work of fiction must be read without permission of the Principal." General Files: 1874–1875. See also Trustees Minutes: 3/12/56.
10. Marshall, Letters: to Mother, 1/18/03; Shepard, "Reference History," pp. 358 and n. 1.
11. General Files: Class of 1906: Notes on interview by Ann Caldwell with Gratia Harrington, August, 1981.
12. Shepard, "Reference History," pp. 254, 258–60; *Rushlight*, 22:1 (Fall, 1876), p. 15; General Files: 1850–1851: E. Morville, Journal, 1850–1851: 10/8/50; 1872–1873: Bachelder to Mother, 2/17/73; 1883–1884: E. B. Dawes, Journals, 1883–1884; Marshall, Letters: to Mother, 11/1/00.
13. Marshall, Letters: to Mother, 2/5/03.
14. Principals: Metcalf: "To the Class of "73," 6/14/73.

15. Jarvis, Letters: to Father, 8/10/43.

16. General Files: 1901–1902: C. S. Keesey memoir. The Jeannette referred to was Jeannette Kittredge (WSX1902), who later married Thomas Watson, founder of IBM Corporation. In the latter 1950s Mrs. Watson provided the funds for the Fine Arts Center at Wheaton that bears her name.

17. General Files: 1848–1849: Hamblin and West to Judson, 6/6/49. Hamblin later became an artist and illustrator of considerable repute.

18. Jarvis, Letters: to Father, 8/29/43.

19. General files: 1903–1904: E. Bates Bird, Journal, 4/21/04.

20. Larcom, Journal II: 10/9,26/61.

21. *Rushlight*, 31:1 (December, 1885); Trustees Minutes: 9/14/75; 12/21/87; 7/7/98; 11/17/09; Shepard, "Reference History," pp. 259, 354–55.

22. Shepard, "Reference History," p. 353; Trustees Minutes: 6/16/08; Marshall, Letters: to Mother, 3/5/03. In 1909 another battle was joined; the Trustees bought "a spraying instrument to save the elm trees." Trustees Minutes: 6/15/09.

23. Shepard, "Reference History," Appendix, pp. b–d; also SVC, *The President's Report, 1921–1922*, pp. 38–42.

24. *Rushlight*, 39:2 (April, 1894); Shepard, "Reference History," pp. 91–92.

25. Shepard, "Reference History," Larcom to friend, 6/2/56, pp. 170, 147–48; Larcom: "Kanzas Prize Song"; *Rushlight*, 1:4 (July, 1856), pp.19–20; Marchalonis, *Lucy Larcom*, p. 95; H. Austin and N. Budd, eds., *Alive and Well Said: Ideas at Wheaton—A Sesquicentennial Anthology* (Norton, MA: Wheaton College, 1984), p. 8.

26. SVC: Miscellaneous: Hutt to Cole, 6/4/21, includes a section from *Taunton Gazette*, 5/16/61, with a passage from a letter written by a student at Wheaton to her father. Lucy Larcom wrote a special song for the flagraising ceremony. See Shepard, "Reference History," pp. 149–50.

27. Larcom, Journal II: 5/13/62. See also her description of July 4, 1861, in Journal I; and *Rushlight* editorials, 6:3 (July, 1861); 9:3 (July, 1864).

28. *Rushlight*, 6:1 (November, 1860); 21:1 (Fall, 1876); 29:1 (December, 1883). Occasionally these straw votes caught the public eye. *The Revolution*, 2:19 (11/12/68), a women's rights news-journal, reported Wheaton's 70–2 vote in favor of Ulysses Grant with the comment, "O, no, . . . the women don't want to vote! Not they!"

29. *Rushlight*, 13:3 (July, 1868); 14:1 (December, 1868).

30. *Rushlight*, 14:3 (July, 1869). For an interesting comment at a much later date see Marshall, Letters: 3/18/02.

31. E. Cunliffe, "History," p. 94; General Files: 1867–1868: Capen to Father, 1/26/65; 1902–1903: article re Helen Potter; Marshall, Letters: to Mother, 2/15/03; SVC, Letterbook: 1901ff, passim, letters to parents.

32. *Rushlight*, 40:1 (December, 1894), p. 23; General Files: 1906–1907: SVC to parents, 2/28/07; 3/18/07; Trustees Minutes: 3/1/07; SVC, Letterbook: SVC to Trustees, 2/12/07, p. 715; G. Hubbard, "Wheaton Seminary, Norton, Mass." *New England Magazine*, 18:1 (March, 1898), pp. 113, 115.

33. Jarvis, Letters: to Father, 9/9/43: General Files: 1901–1902: Keesey memoir; Class of 1906: Notes of Ann Caldwell interview with G. Harrington, August, 1981; SVC, Letterbook: Cole to Bonney, 12/2/06, p. 701.

34. Larcom: Miscellaneous: "To the Editors of Rushlight"; "Psyche at Wheaton"; Larcom, Journal II: 7/9/62; Shepard, "Reference History," pp. 193, 207; *Rushlight*, 28:2 (June, 1883).

35. General Files: Class of 1871: Dodge to Brother, 2/27/70; *Rushlight*, 34:8 (June, 1890); 35:1 (November, 1890); *Wheaton Quarterly* (*Rushlight*) 1:1 (December, 1897); 1:2 (March, 1898); General Files: 1901–1902: Keesey memoir; SVC, Letterbook: SVC Memorandum, 1/9/02, p. 284; SVC to K. U. Clark, 4/2/02, p. 320; Shep-

ard, "Reference History," pp. 227–229; Marshall, Letters: to Mother, 11/17/<u>02</u>; *Wheaton Bulletin,* 6:2 (March, 1910).

36. "Where Some of Our Girls are Educated: Wheaton Seminary, Norton, Mass." *Phrenological Journal,* 11:3, new series (March, 1875), p. 178.

37. Principals: Cowles: Speech at 50th anniversary celebration, 1885.

Part II
The Wheatons' College

9
Transition Years: Institutional Metamorphosis, 1912–1922

WHEATON COLLEGE

This new college for women is located in Massachusetts, thirty miles from Boston and seventeen miles from Providence. Like most good things it began as something else. Founded in 1834 under the superintendence of Mary Lyon before she entered upon her work at Mount Holyoke, it was a pioneer school in women's education—the oldest endowed institution in New England which began its work exclusively for girls and has continued without interruption until the present time.[1]

So READ THE FIRST PARAGRAPH of an announcement designed to publicize Wheaton College in the spring of 1914. After only two years of offering a formal college curriculum, Wheaton that spring had 48 students enrolled in its college program and was about to confer its first Bachelor of Arts degrees on two young women who had transferred as juniors in the fall of 1912.[2] Two years later, when 14 of the original 16 students who had arrived as freshmen in September, 1912, received their degrees, the College had grown to 117 students. The successful transition from seminary to college was clearly proceeding at a vigorous pace.

Between 1912 and 1914, students in the last two years of the Seminary program were allowed to continue, but the last Seminary degrees were conferred in 1914.[3] For the next five years the College offered a two-year associates certificate to students who wished to enroll in only the first two years of the college program, but as enrollment in the full four-year college degree program escalated rapidly, this was discontinued. By 1921–22, Wheaton's tenth year as a college, 309 students were in attendance and the graduating senior class numbered 40. Thirty-three full-time and three part-time faculty ensured a ten to one student/faculty ratio. In November, 1922, Wheaton received full accreditation from the Association of American Universities. The years of transition were clearly over, and Wheaton's future success as a liberal arts college for women seemed assured.[4]

Outwardly, this transition would certainly seem to the casual observer

173

to have been characterized by a smoothly accelerating process of growth and change, almost completely free of the bumps and potholes one might reasonably expect to experience in traveling such a new road. And in the broadest sense this was certainly the case. The long years of careful development and planning by President Cole had fairly well ensured that the basic transition would be steady and successful. However, a closer examination of this period indicates that beneath the surface there was indeed much *Sturm und Drang*, that there was much that was not easy in the transition, and that the process in some ways had an extremely stressful impact on many aspects of the work of the College, its various constituencies, and on the College's relations with the town of Norton.

The initial petition to the state legislature for permission to grant college degrees had stated that the institution would be called Laban Wheaton College, a reflection of Dr. Cole's concern over the existence

May Day, circa 1914. The unfinished "Court of Honor," with the new Gymnasium and the Power House standing in lonely isolation from the rest of the campus buildings, provides evidence of the far reaching vision of President Cole and architect Ralph Adams Cram when they first drafted a plan for a college campus in 1898.

of another Wheaton College located in Wheaton, Illinois. However, having discovered that it was not uncommon to have two colleges with the same name, President Cole and the Board of Trustees reverted to their original plan to call the institution Wheaton College, and the enabling legislation encompassed in Chapter 84 of the Acts of the 1912 General Court of Massachusetts referred to it in this form.[5] Moreover, although the legislation gave permission to confer Bachelors, Masters, and Honorary Degrees, it made no reference to the gender of those who would receive those degrees. Nor did the Board specify gender exclusivity when it formally accepted the Acts of the Legislature at a meeting on March 14, 1912. It was only three years later, with the creation of the first set of College Statutes, that the College defined itself as specifically existing for the purpose of "the education of women." In addition, the Statutes asserted, "the education contemplated, in accordance with the evident desire of the founders of the Institution, shall keep service as well as culture constantly in mind."[6]

This concept of a dual purpose, of inculcating "personal culture and service to the world,"[7] became during the first years of the College's existence a recurring theme, particularly in the writings and speeches of President Cole. For Cole, the primary vehicle through which these two attributes could be evidenced was the home. Time and again, he emphasized that a Wheaton education sought not the rejection of homemaking in favor of a professional career, but rather was intended to make life in the home the center for all activities, including both community service and many forms of professional development. Although President Cole also stated that the College would prepare and encourage students who sought professional graduate training and careers, his primary emphasis in discussing the mission of Wheaton always focused on preparation for an enlightened role for Wheaton graduates in the home and in public service to the community. Nonetheless, it should be noted that of the forty graduates in 1922, twelve immediately entered the teaching profession, while thirteen went on to some form of graduate study.[8]

"The aim of the college," Cole wrote in 1915, "is culture. It does not educate for any specific vocation, unless you call life itself a vocation." Homemaking, he went on, did not mean housekeeping. "Nothing is farther from the fact. Homemaking is an intellectual, moral and spiritual exercise and service. It requires knowledge, literary appreciation, aesthetic refinement, mental alertness, judgment, tact, sympathy, self-denial. In fact, no culture is broad enough or deep enough to have its possibilities exhausted for employment in the home. To supply this general culture is the function of the college, and to adapt it to use in the home is peculiarly the office of women."[9] Wheaton would not follow the paths of other women's colleges, which tended to emphasize careers; instead it would seek to meet the needs of "the intelligent woman who wishes to magnify the calling of wife, mother and neighbor."[10]

This theme was in fact a continuation in modified form of the concept that had dominated Wheaton's attempt, in the months leading to the attainment of a college charter, to distinguish itself from colleges such as Wellesley, Smith and Mount Holyoke, and also from those with a specific vocational mission such as Simmons. Wheaton, Cole had maintained at every opportunity in 1911 and 1912, would emphasize "the business of being a woman."[11] This would involve combining a standard liberal arts education with a program in domestic science that would demonstrate the relevance of information and skills learned in other courses to the specific problems of running a household, nurturing children and supporting a husband in the development of his professional career.

In actual fact, the domestic science program at Wheaton never came close to being a major component of the curriculum. Students were only required to complete one three-credit course in it to obtain their degrees, though more were available. And within a couple of years after the charter was obtained, President Cole specifically ordered references to the program eliminated from college brochures, on the grounds that "we received quite a good many letters that seem to lay undue emphasis on the Domestic Science business, and we do not want it to appear that that is the prominent thing connected with the institution."[12] Eventually, in 1927, the requirement was dropped from the curriculum and the department quietly abolished.

On March 13, 1913, the ten-member Board of Trustees formed four major committees—Administration, Finance, Faculty Appointments, and Grounds and Buildings, to which they later added a Committee on Degrees. They also established a temporary Committee on Rules and Regulations whose task was to draft the first set of Statutes for the College. These were presented and formally accepted by the Board on March 18, 1915. All full professors were to receive three-year appointments; the duration of all other appointments was to be at the Board's discretion, which in reality meant that of the President. Reaffirming the nonsectarian religious cast of the College, the trustees placed the internal administration of the College "in the hands of the President, Dean and the Academic Council."[13]

This last was to consist of the President, Dean, Registrar, and all professors and associate professors, plus such other members of the teaching faculty as the Board of Trustees wished to designate. Seven women faculty holding the rank of assistant professor or instructor were added by appointment to the Academic Council, along with William I. Cole, the President's brother, who served as College Treasurer as well as Lecturer in Applied Sociology. The Council's function was to determine and set the academic policy of the College, including degree and admissions requirements (in consultation with the Trustee Administration Committee), and also to establish and monitor the curricular course of instruction. It was required to meet at least once a month during the academic year. In practice, the Academic Council came to include all continuing full-time members of the faculty and administration, and for the remainder of President Cole's administration its meetings routinely took the place of meetings of the faculty as a whole.[14]

During these early years the Board also concerned itself with the creation of a College Seal. Conceived by President Cole, and produced by the College's supervising architect, Ralph Adams Cram, the seal was originally cast in an oval form, but had become round by 1914. Carefully designed to reflect the official motto of the College, "That they may have life, and may have it abundantly," the interior of the seal consisted of a shield (reflecting faith and courage) on which was centered the tree of life bearing the fruits of knowledge. In the left-hand upper corner of the shield was the star of aspiration and noble ideals, while a small cross reflecting sacrifice and unselfishness was placed just above the shield. Two dates, 1834 and 1912, were also included, reflecting the founding of Wheaton Female Seminary and its transition to college status; the name and location of the College, plus its motto, encircled the whole. The Board also authorized the use of standard academic regalia for the first commencement in 1914, and shortly thereafter entered into lengthy discussions with the firm of Cottrell and Leonard which resulted in the crafting of a distinctive blue and white hood, worn by graduating seniors ever since.[15]

The most striking change in the role of the Board of Trustees during President Cole's tenure as chief administrator of the Seminary and College was the complete disengagement of the trustees, either collectively or as individuals, from the day-to-day affairs of the institution. Although

Wheaton College Seal.

the Board retained its formal right to approve the granting of degrees, as well as faculty appointments and promotions, in fact on all but financial issues the Board's involvement became routinely pro forma. This contrasted greatly with the Seminary period before 1897, when trustees routinely visited the campus, attended classes, often personally expressed their opinions on the religious and moral character and atmosphere of the campus, critiqued the curriculum, and strongly advised the administration and faculty regarding issues dear to their hearts. It seems likely that this major shift in the role of the trustees was due to the advent of a male leader of the institution, chosen in 1897 from among their own ranks. With a man rather than a woman in charge, the attitude of the Board regarding administrative autonomy for the leader of the College became noticeably different from what it had been in the past.[16]

In the years following his appointment as President of Wheaton in 1897, Dr. Cole had restored the Seminary to a point of financial stability and equilibrium by instituting the college preparatory and special programs. These attracted enough students so that in its final years the Seminary's annual operating costs were covered entirely by income from tuition, room, board and a few special fees. In fact, income from these sources exceeded expenses by approximately $14,000 in 1911–12, the last year of the Seminary's existence.[17]

In that final year Wheaton was filled to capacity; some 225 students were enrolled in one or another of the several educational tracks being offered. The change to college status, which brought an immediate discontinuation of the college preparatory program and a two-year phasing out of the seminary curriculum, led to a substantial, though anticipated, decline in enrollment. However, this reduction was not as great as it would have been had the College consisted only of candidates for the four-year Bachelor of Arts Degree. In 1914–15, out of 175 students attending Wheaton, only 91 were enrolled in the four-year degree program. Though the last Seminary degree had been awarded the previous spring, and the college preparatory program had been gone for two years, Wheaton continued for some years to admit students in two other categories that were holdovers from the last years of the Seminary.[18]

Qualified female high school graduates were allowed to enroll in courses for a year or two as they wished. Listed as "unclassified students," they were under no obligation other than to perform as responsible citizens of the Wheaton community. More interesting, and relatively unique for that day and age, was the decision to offer a structured two-year associates degree program for able high school graduates who did not want to pursue a full four-year course of study. This was in many ways the continuation of a two-year course for high school graduates that the Seminary apparently had been offering for those students who did not wish to fulfill all the requirements for the Seminary degree.

Courses were prescribed in English, History, Philosophy, Bible, Foreign Language and Science, with about one-third of the program left free for electives.[19]

In 1914–15 a total of 43 students were registered in the associates degree program, along with 41 who were listed as unclassified. During the next several years, as the numbers in the regular college course increased, those in the other two programs gradually declined. By September 1919, there were only 10 students seeking an associates degree, and the Board of Trustees authorized the President to discontinue the program whenever he deemed it advisable to do so. Cole, with unanimous support from the Faculty Academic Council, immediately did exactly that. By 1920–21 no students were enrolled in the Associates Program and the following year unclassified students also disappeared from the roster of those attending Wheaton. The 309 students in the four college classes enrolled at Wheaton in its tenth year as a college filled every available bed the institution could provide, and represented a 37 percent increase over the number who had attended Wheaton in its final year as a Seminary.[20]

However, this relatively swift and in some ways astounding success in converting to a full college program did not bring with it the same fiscal

"The Home," as the sprawling dormitory was called, was renamed in honor of Caroline Metcalf in 1901. It continued to serve as a student residence and the College's administration center until 1932.

stability that had graced the Seminary in its last years. Although the Board of Trustees had recognized that it would be necessary during the first years of the transition to supplement income from tuition, room, board and fees with revenues derived from income generated by the Wheaton estate, it was not prepared for the continuation of this operational deficit even after student enrollments rebounded and then surpassed those of the Seminary period. Not only did the annual deficit remain, but it steadily increased, peaking at $45,623 in 1920–21, an amount which represented 22.7 percent of the total operating budget of $201,235. Covering this negative balance in annual operations became an ever-increasing burden placed upon the Wheaton family estate.[21]

During the last decade of the Seminary's existence, having attained an operating budget balanced by revenues from tuition and fees, President Cole had been able to use revenue derived from the Wheaton estate to fund the ambitious building program that had created the new college campus. But the attainment of a college charter did not mean that Cole's plans for expanding the campus had been concluded. The need for additional student and faculty living quarters, including off-campus housing for male faculty, necessitated the systematic purchase and remodeling of private residential houses contiguous to the campus as they came upon the market.[22] During the first ten years of the College's existence the long-planned addition of a swimming pool to the gymnasium was also completed; an astronomical observatory was built in the field behind the President's House; the College Chapel was erected, along with a new dormitory named after the last principal of the Seminary, Ellen Stanton; and in 1922 construction was begun on a new library.

Financing for all of these capital improvements came primarily from revenue generated by income received from the Wheaton family estate, a source that by 1920 was greatly imperiled by the annually accruing deficits in the operational budget. Despite the rapid growth in the number of students attending Wheaton, operational expenses continued to escalate more rapidly than nonendowment income. The reasons for this were several.

Until 1920–21 all revenues from whatever source in a given year were ultimately lumped together in the final ledger and shown as available funds. Thus it was all too easy to be taken in by a bottom line that showed a very acceptable surplus of revenue over operating expenditure. Minimal attention was paid to the fact that the annual operating budget was actually being balanced only by a transfusion of funds generated either by securities owned by the College, or by rent from real estate property located on Winter Street in the heart of the Boston business district, which constituted the majority of the legacy inherited by the College from the Wheaton family. It was only when diversion of these funds to sustain the operational budget began to have a severe negative impact on the building program sought by President Cole that the Board of Trustees became concerned about the long-term implications of this problem.

The issue was driven home to the Board in 1920 when the College, at the urging of Treasurer William I. Cole, for the first time engaged a professional auditing firm in Boston to conduct a review of the books and assets of the College. During this process a discrepency of over $32,000 was discovered; this was described as essentially untraceable and probably due to many smaller bookkeeping errors over the years. The accountant, E. E. Stackpole, insisted on setting up a bookkeeping system that clearly separated operational revenue and expenses from what he termed the general fund, which constituted all revenues derived from sources other than those connected with the normal yearly operation of the College. Transfers could then be authorized from the general fund to cover operational deficits, fund new buildings, or pay for major maintenance or development projects.[23]

The second reason for the growing fiscal crisis was the painfully obvious decline in the purchasing power of the Wheaton endowment. The Wheaton family had never wanted the Seminary to engage in outside fundraising. In fact they had for the most part systematically discouraged it, preferring that the institution remain totally a family project.[24] In the first decade of the College's existence, although there was occasional talk about the need to obtain new sources of revenue, nothing of a substantive nature was done to attract such capital. Since all the revenue generated by invested endowment funds and by the rental of the Winter Street property was used either for plant expansion or funding the annual operational deficit, there was little appreciable new growth in the total amount of funds generating revenue. The value of the combined portfolios increased only 20.5 percent during these ten years.[25]

But what did grow steadily during the decade was the cost of living. Pressures created by World War I forced wages up for domestic and maintenance help, though it did not do the same for teachers' salaries. Scarcity of goods during wartime led to a general increase in prices, and the postwar period of national inflation that ensued led to a steady decline in the purchasing power of the dollar. While the consumer price index grew by only 4.8 percent between 1912 and 1915, over the next five years it increased 97.3 percent.[26]

All of this was compounded by the Board of Trustees' reluctance to raise charges. From 1912 to 1917 tuition and room/board fees were held constant at $150 and $300 respectively. In January, 1917, the College reluctantly raised its room and board fee by $50 for the following fall. Even then, this increase was only applied to students not yet enrolled, on the grounds that the lateness of the announcement did not make it fair to impose it on those already attending or enrolled to attend. Thus this minimal increase did not fully go into effect until September, 1918. Only in 1920–21 did the Board authorize the first of what, during the 1920s, would be for the most part annual increases in the comprehensive fee, usually between $50 and $100 per year. In justifying his requests for these increases to the trustees, President Cole noted that Wellesley, Mt. Holyoke, and others were charging even more. Not only was the increased revenue desperately needed at Wheaton, he maintained, but if the College's fees remained too far below those of its competitors the quality of Wheaton's education was likely to be called into question in the eyes of the public.[27]

The reason that the Board was disinclined to increase charges is not hard to perceive. Anxious to attract students to the College, and having only about $1000 in scholarship funds designated to assist those with need, the trustees were understandably wary of pricing the institution at a level that would discourage applications. But the result was that at the end of a decade in which the cost of goods and services had doubled, the College's comprehensive fee had increased only from $450 to $650.

As Wheaton's first decade as a college drew to a close there was growing concern on the part of both the administration and the Board of Trustees about the institution's increasingly precarious financial situation, one that seemed to threaten the continued growth and development proposed by President Cole. Although the assessed value of the College buildings and land in Norton had risen by 87.5 percent to $800,256 over the ten year period, the 20.5 percent increase in the value of the endowment had not even come close to keeping up with the pace of the general inflationary growth in the cost of goods and services. The situation certainly did not bode well in light of the College's perceived need to continue to grow and expand its facilities. Particularly distressing was the decision reluctantly made by the Board on March 15, 1922, to authorize the borrowing of up to $200,000, using the Winter Street property as collateral. Not coincidentally, it was at this same meeting that an Investment Committee was created as a subcommittee of the Trustee Finance Committee.[28]

In a letter to W. Irving Bullard, President of the Merchants National Bank of Boston, President Cole outlined the perilous state of the College's finances in the most explicit terms.

> We shall end the fiscal year July 1st with a recently incurred debt of $40,000 and with all bills paid up to that date. $25,000 of the debt has been incurred for payments on the library building. There will be due and the treasury will receive on July 1st $9,500 from our Winter Street property so that at that date we should be really only $10,500 behind. But we must continue borrowing in order to finance the library. We have recently purchased with money contributed to our Building and Endowment Fund a large dwelling with the building adjoining it which can easily be made into a small overflow dormitory. It adjoins the college land and therefore is conveniently located. This arrangement will enable us to take thirty or thirty-five additional students and so help to some extent the financial situ-

ation. But the college is in great need of funds for additional equipment and especially for piecing out inadequate salaries and for making additions to the number of the faculty and staff of workers to say nothing of other expenses which have been constantly growing. The college is in splendid condition but at so critical a stage in its development that we must continue to appeal for help.[29]

Educational success and fiscal crisis!—a story oft told during the Seminary years, and one which apparently was to continue despite the successful transition to college status. But there was one major difference. No longer was there a ready and willing benefactor, who could be turned to time and again to provide funds for buildings, scholarships, and to fill the gap between operational revenue and expenditures. The legacy provided by the Wheaton family no longer seemed adequate to the task. After ninety years of being supported almost totally by the direct munificence of the Wheaton family, the College was now faced with the daunting prospect of having to seek new and creative ways to maintain its fiscal stability.

In his annual reports, President Cole consistently emphasized the virtues of Wheaton being a "small college," and used this distinction to separate Wheaton and its sense of community from the larger or coordinate colleges for women in New England, which he stated time and again Wheaton had no desire to emulate. But as the years passed and the College continued to grow, the issue of defining a maximum size to which the College could expand and still preserve the unique virtues associated with smallness became ever more pressing.[30]

As it became evident that Wheaton could indeed expect to attract an increasing number of students, and as the financial pressures on the College steadily increased, President Cole's view as to the appropriate size of a small college changed. While in 1914 two hundred had seemed to him a size that was appropriate both for Wheaton and many other colleges throughout the country, by 1918–19 he was advancing a strong case in his annual report for building additional residence halls that would allow the college to grow to 350–400. Citing the enormous rise in the cost of providing services, President Cole also noted that the purchasing power of faculty salaries had declined by almost 50 percent despite an average 17 percent increase over those in effect when Wheaton had begun operation as a college. Moreover, Cole asserted, the College had an immediate need for a new library, the one major academic building still lacking on the campus. Not only were there efficiencies of scale to be gained by enlarging the size of the institution, but the revenue generated by expansion was absolutely necessary. To regard expansion as destroying the ethos of a small college would in his opinion only lead to "arrested development."[31]

Three years later, in his report signalling the end of the College's first decade, Dr. Cole brought the issue of size to a point of closure. Remarking that "when Wheaton sought and obtained the authority to grant degrees, it announced its purpose to become and remain a small college," Cole asserted that he "saw no reason why that purpose should be changed either now or at any future time."[32] However, noting that a survey conducted by the President of Hamilton College had resulted in educators across the country specifying five hundred as the maximum size for a small college, Cole indicated his acceptance of that number for Wheaton. "While it [Wheaton] may properly become somewhat larger than it is, in the interests of economic and academic efficiency, I am convinced that we should keep the numbers well within the limit of five hundred. Such is both my judgment and my personal preference, and I believe it to be the policy that commends itself to the alumnae and other friends of the college."[33]

This policy, established as the College ended what can be regarded as its transition period, would remain in effect for the next three decades. It represented both educational philosophy and the restrictions imposed by the relatively small remaining Wheaton family financial endowment. Only in the mid-1950s would Wheaton, as a matter of both policy and necessity, decide that it was appropriate to venture beyond the five hundred student limit established by its first President.

If escalating annual operational costs were one part of the fiscal crisis generated during Wheaton's early years, an equal and in some ways greater problem was created by the continuing need to expand facilities, both residential and academic. The purchase and remodeling of houses contiguous to the campus, the completion of the swimming pool and the erection of an observatory and new dormitory have already been noted. But far more costly and very central to President Cole's vision for Wheaton was the need for a college chapel and a new library.[34]

From Cole's perspective the chapel took precedence, understandable when one remembers that he had come to Wheaton from a position as minister of the Broadway Trinitarian Congregational Church in nearby Taunton. A chapel would not only serve as the architectural capstone and centerpiece for the campus, Cole maintained, it would also "exert a refining and unifying influence on the college life."[35] At the second meeting of his new faculty in October, 1912, the President received overwhelming support for his assertion that a chapel was the most pressing need facing the new College, and an all-male committee of three faculty members and the President was created to further the project.[36]

Although President Cole prevailed upon the Board of Trustees in November, 1912, to authorize the hiring of an architect to draw preliminary plans for a chapel, two years later matters had proceeded no further, and Cole was becoming desperate. "We must have a chapel," he wrote trustee Kate Upson Clark (WS1869), "It has become an absolute necessity, and we have as yet no money to build it with." "If Wellesley, Smith and Mount Holyoke can raise funds," he lamented, "why not us?"[37]

Not only was a chapel needed to enhance the moral and spiritual qualities of the campus, but the space currently used for chapel meetings and assemblies in the Science Building was desperately needed for expanded laboratories. The transfer of the library from its current location in Mary Lyon Hall to the basement of the proposed chapel also would make available much needed classroom space. With all this in mind, the Board of Trustees in April, 1916, authorized the firm of Cram and Ferguson, the College's supervising architects since 1907, to prepare the necessary drawings and specifications. On June 16, the plans were approved, and the Board authorized the Building Committee to put the project out to bid. To fund the construction the trustees also authorized the use of any moneys not needed for current operations, approved the sale of unrestricted securities, and authorized the Building Committee to borrow funds if necessary.[38]

The cornerstone for the new ediface was laid at the Founders Day celebration in October, 1916. One year later at a similar celebration on October 27, the Chapel was dedicated. Built in traditional early nineteenth century Colonial style by a local contractor, Witherell and Sons of Taunton, the interior reflected early Puritan simplicity and dignity. It provided seats for nine hundred persons, albeit many of them with considerably obstructed views. Set between the Science Center and the Gymnasium, the brick building, with its soaring white columns and spire reaching 147 feet above the ground, indeed dominated the campus quadrangle and completed the east side of the central court that Rev. Cole and Ralph Adams Cram had designed together nearly two decades before. Blending naturally with the Georgian style of architecture that characterized all of the buildings erected since 1900, the Chapel was topped by a gold weathervane in the shape of a peacock. For President Cole this must have seemed a highly appropriate symbol for a college, for the peacock was an early Christian symbol of immortality. The flesh of the bird was traditionally viewed as "incorruptible;" Christian decorators had long used the peacock as a symbol of resurrection because it lost and renewed its splendid plumage annually.[39]

The final cost of the Chapel was $86,875, not including the organ, which was purchased separately. The strain that paying this amount created on the fragile finances of the College was indeed considerable. But for President Cole it was more than worth it. Daily brief, though required, chapel services were supplemented by a program of Sunday church services presided over by a coterie of guest ministers recruited personally by Rev. Cole. For the first time since Wheaton's founding, students attended Sunday church services on campus rather than walking en masse to the old Wheaton family church, the Trinitarian Congregational, located across the street from the northeast corner of the campus.[40]

"It has proved," Cole wrote of the building that would later bear his name, "to be . . . a spiritual asset of vast importance."

> Not only does it add to the campus an architectural feature both dominating and beautiful but, set apart for the highest uses, the building itself is an effective though silent preacher, and its message is not lost. Merely to look upon it or to sit within its walls helps to direct one's thoughts to the better things of life. . . . The college is unsectarian and puts forth no effort to turn a student from one form of religious faith to another, but it always cultivates the religious spirit and systematically endeavors to create in its students a loyalty to truth, righteousness, humanity, and God—the four great verities for the service of which the chapel stands."[41]

Faced with the rapidly escalating costs of inflation, the substantial expenditures on the Chapel which had left the College without any accumulated reserves, and the urgent need for both a new dormitory and a library, the Board of Trustees, after considerable urging from President Cole, agreed in the fall of 1920 to mount the College's first capital campaign.[42] This was only the second time in Wheaton's history that an organized appeal to alumnae and others for financial support had been made. In 1899 a request to alumnae and former students for funds to help build the gymnasium had produced a disappointing "few hundred dollars."[43] Recognizing that it would be necessary to attract funds from business sources as well as Wheaton alumnae, the College hired a professional fund raising firm from New York, Tamblyn and Brown, and embarked on a drive to raise $1,000,000. The "Calling 2–6–0" campaign stressed that an average contribution of $260 ($5 per week for 52 weeks) from 2000 former students or alumnae would ensure a net revenue of $500,000 after expenses, which could be used for College purposes. If fully successful, the campaign would nearly double the value of Wheaton's endowment, and presumably generate enough income to allow not only the construction of the contemplated new buildings, but also a modest improvement in faculty salaries.[44]

On the same day that the trustees authorized the capital campaign, they also voted to proceed immediately with the construction of a dormitory which would be named after the last principal of the seminary, Ellen Stanton. It was, Cole noted, a terrible time to build a dormitory, the "cost of labor and material is beyond all reason."[45] But the risk to the

Subsequently named for the College's first President, Cole Memorial Chapel, constructed in 1917, filled the gap between the Science Center and the Gymnasium on the eastern side of the "Court of Honor."

College of not building it was greater than that of going ahead. "Some very serious problems confront us, as you know," he wrote to Kate Upson Clark, "for it will never do to let the development of the college stop at this point."[46]

Unfortunately, the capital campaign was anything but a success. Despite the formation of impressive Executive and Advisory Campaign Committees, which included the names of Boston and New York businessmen, publishers and bankers, the two-year campaign brought in only $132,122 in cash gifts and pledges. Tamblyn and Brown, which had originally signed a three-year contract, was dismissed after one year, departing with the comment that the failure of the trustees and the advisory committees to support the campaign in any substantial way made it very difficult to make a meaningful appeal to the "girls."[47]

Actually it turned out that 50 percent of the 624 "living and located" college and seminary graduates did contribute to the campaign, though in small amounts because most were relatively recent graduates with limited available assets. But only 14.5 percent of the 1660 nongraduates whose location was known and who were therefore solicited chose to contribute, despite the obvious inducement provided by the opening of membership in the Wheaton Alumnae Association in 1922 to all who had ever attended Wheaton.[48]

After campaign expenses were deducted, only $85,588 had made its way into College hands by the end of January, 1924. Giving up any idea of using the funds to enhance endowment principal, the College used the moneys to fund in part the construction costs of Stanton dormitory and the library. Even so, in order even to begin construction of the library, Wheaton was forced in the spring of 1922 to borrow $40,000 in short-term notes. Faced with the need for additional funds to build yet another dormitory, plans for which were well underway in 1922, plus anticipated future costs for the expansion of both power plant and dining facilities, it is little wonder that President Cole commented somewhat ruefully and sadly in his report for 1921–22 about a popular misconception regarding the financial affluence of Wheaton College.

> An obstacle with which the college has been obliged to contend in all its financial efforts is the rather widespread belief, inherited from the days when the institution had a patron, that Wheaton is abundantly supplied with funds. A perusal of the Treasurer's Statements and of the section in the report describing the needs of the college should remove that impression.[49]

The transition from Seminary to College, plus the ever-present need for additional funds inevitably brought about significant changes in Wheaton's relations with its alumnae. Interestingly enough, there appears to have been minimal serious negative response on the part of Seminary alumnae to the announcement that Wheaton had decided to apply for a charter as a college. This was undoubtedly partially due to the fact that relatively few students who attended Wheaton over the years had actually completed work for the degree. Moreover, in the last decade of the Seminary's existence, the number of students enrolled in the college preparatory or individualized programs had vastly exceeded those who sought to complete the full seminary curriculum. Thus women who, as graduates, had the fullest personal investment in Wheaton's status as a degree granting institution were comparatively few in number.

Nonetheless, it appears that reaction from former students to the change was initially more reserved than positive. In his *President's Report* celebrating the conclusion of the College's first decade, Rev. Cole commented: "The seminary alumnae were naturally hesitant in regard to the college idea when it was first broached, but as fast as they learned the circumstances and the reasons for the change, hesitation generally developed into enthusiasm and opposition into cooperative service."[50] In an effort to inculcate a positive outlook, President Cole sent a special letter to all alumnae and former students in April, 1913, assuring them that they were still, and always would be, an integral and important part of Wheaton, and stressing that they would always be warmly welcomed whenever they chose to return to Norton.[51]

Even more important was the reorganization of the Wheaton Alumnae Association undertaken between 1920 and 1922. Founded in 1870, the Association's membership had been restricted to graduates of the Seminary or College. Conversely, membership in the seven regional Wheaton Clubs, of which the largest and most important were those in Boston and New York, had always been open to anyone who had attended Wheaton and was willing to pay nominal membership dues. Recognizing that there were more than twice as many nongraduates as graduates, and encouraged by the substantial participation of the former in the various clubs, the Alumnae Association voted in 1922 to admit nongraduates to associate membership in the organization. An Alumnae Office was established at the College, and in November, 1921, the Board of Trustees approved the appointment of Sylvia Meadows (W1918) as the first Alumnae Secretary, her salary to be paid by the Association. It was also in the Fall of 1921 that the first official Fall Alumnae Day was held in conjunction with the Founders Day ceremonies that traditionally were held each year on the anniversary of Mrs. Wheaton's birth.[52]

Subsequently Harriet Hughes (W1918), who headed the New York Wheaton Club, was elected President of the Association. In May, 1922, the first issue of the *Wheaton Alumnae News* was published; the journal would be renamed the *Wheaton Alumnae Quarterly* in 1926.[53] Much of this renewed interest in and expansion of the Alumnae Association undoubtedly stemmed from the expected role that contributions from alumnae and former students would play in the 1920–22 capital campaign. Unfortunately, the response was minimal, and the capital campaign an unmitigated disaster. But the changes engendered in the structure of the Alumnae Association, as well as the creation of a permanent Alumnae Office and the position of Alumnae Secretary, would endure.[54]

In 1915, administrative representatives of Smith, Mount Holyoke, Vassar, and Wellesley formed an informal organization which they called the Four College Conference. Its basic premise was that it would

On May 6, 1922, President Cole and his wife, Helen Wieand Cole, attended a meeting of the New York Wheaton Club at the Hotel McAlpin.

be useful for presidents or academic deans occasionally to discuss together matters of mutual interest or concern. Joined by Bryn Mawr in 1925 and Radcliffe and Barnard in 1926, the group, now known as the Seven College Conference, assumed a new role in 1927. Concerned that lack of publicity regarding colleges for women was a major factor in the evident lack of major gifts to such institutions, it was decided to sponsor jointly a series of dinners in major cities throughout the country at which the presidents of all seven colleges would be present. These dinners, conducted throughout 1927, brought a favorable response, not only in increased giving from foundations and private citizens, but also in terms of raising general public knowledge of the existence and needs of the seven colleges. "We found," wrote Virginia Gildersleeve, Dean at Barnard, "that whereas one college president arriving in Chicago or St. Louis might not achieve much of a headline, seven of us together distinctly seemed something worth photographing and writing up."[55] Committees composed of alumnae from all seven colleges also organized luncheon meetings with bank and trust company lawyers and officials, the goal being to encourage them to promote bequests from their clients.[56]

Although these cooperative publicity and fundraising efforts lasted only about ten years, meetings of the representatives of the seven colleges continued, and the image of the "Seven Sisters" as representing the elite of women's colleges became firmly entrenched in the public mentality. Wheaton, to the great chagrin of succeeding generations of alumnae, was never included in this group, nor is there any indication that President Cole or his successors ever sought such an affiliation.

The explanation for Wheaton's exclusion seems to have been based on issues of size. For a short period of time the Seven College Conference was popularly labeled the "Big Seven," "which suggests," Elaine Kendall comments, "that size may have had something to do with inclusion."[57] This seems particularly likely when one remembers that in September, 1915, the year when the three Massachusetts colleges and Vassar first organized, Wheaton's total enrollment was 206, of which only 117 were in the four-year college degree program. The decision made at the end of the College's first decade to limit enrollment at Wheaton to 500 students confirms that President Cole saw Wheaton's smaller size as an important distinctive feature. "Wheaton," he commented, in a letter to Irving Bullard, "is the only small separate college for women in the Commonwealth and, of its type, in all New England."[58] In his annual *President's Report* for 1921–22, Cole reiterated this point: "Wheaton fills a distinct place in the educational system of this Commonwealth. . . . I am convinced that we should keep the numbers well within the limit of five hundred."[59]

Thus, in 1926, when the final additions were made to create the Seven College Conference, Wheaton's enrollment stood at 466 students. Although Bryn Mawr, with just over 400 students, was smaller, it was still considered the preeminent women's college, both for the numbers and quality of its faculty and because it was the only independent women's institution offering graduate degree programs at the Ph.D. level. The other six "sisters" ranged in size from 728 students at Radcliffe to 2158 at Smith, while the five that were independent colleges were supported by endowments in the $4–6.5 million range as opposed to Wheaton's $1,050,000. It seems likely that the leaders of these colleges believed that there was little their institutions had in common with a brand new college in Norton, still struggling to get its feet firmly on the ground.[60]

Moreover, there is definite evidence that this feeling was reciprocated by President Cole. Rather than sending overtures to the Four College Conference, in 1919 Cole set about trying to create a separate consortium of colleges he considered similar to Wheaton. In a letter to trustee Kate Upson Clark, Cole noted that he had invited the presidents of "the smaller colleges for women to come together and compare notes, as the problems in all these college are strikingly similar."[61] The presidents of Wilson, Wells, and Connecticut College for Women were approached and all accepted. "It seemed best," Cole noted, "to begin with only three or four and then later on arrange a larger conference."[62]

At least one meeting did take place. Between December 7 and December 10, 1919, the presidents of the three invited colleges all visited Norton. There is no record of the results, but one must conclude that they were not positive, since there is no indication of subsequent discussions among the four, nor of any attempt to implement joint policies or invite others to participate. Nonetheless, it seems evident that President Cole's initiative was most likely inspired by the creation of the initial Four College Conference which included the larger private liberal arts colleges for women in Massachusetts. A similar grouping of smaller, less prestigious institutions undoubtedly seemed at the time a sensible avenue to pursue.[63]

Throughout the nineteenth century, relations between the Seminary and the town of Norton were generally cordial. Daughters of residents of Norton were allowed to attend at reduced tuition rates. The presence of the Seminary was an influential factor in getting trolley lines to the neighboring towns of Mansfield, Attleboro and Taunton installed. But in most ways the Seminary had little or no impact on the citizens of the town as a whole, especially if they lived in one of the several village clusters other than Norton Center.

What tied the town and the Seminary to each other was the Wheaton family. Without doubt the wealthiest and most influential of Norton's citizens, both Judge Wheaton and his son, Laban Morey Wheaton, played an active role in the politics and governance of the town. It was also the Wheatons who led the break with the Unitarian Congregational Church in the early nineteenth century, with the resultant founding of the Trinitarian Congregational Church, whose place of worship was built and later remodeled primarily with Wheaton family money.

After Laban Morey's death in 1865, the direct role of the Wheaton family in town government ended, but its influence did not. Not only did Mrs. Wheaton continue to serve as the exclusive patron of the Seminary and chief benefactor of the Trinitarian church, her largesse extended to the town as well in the form of an iron fence surrounding the town common, a new public library built with Wheaton funds on land she donated to the town, and the gift of the land upon which Norton's first public high school was erected.[64]

The death of Eliza Baylies Wheaton in 1905 severed the primary ties that bound the Seminary and town together. As the Seminary prepared for its transition to college status, the gap between the expanding institution and the largely farming and blue-collar working class community which surrounded it gradually widened. The rapid development of Wheaton's physical plant, with its many impressive but tax-exempt buildings, engendered considerable local resentment. In fact, the only real protest against the granting of the college charter came from the Norton Board of Assessors, a protest that Cole successfully defused by demonstrating the many advantages to the town of having Wheaton in its midst. Yet overall it can be said that in 1912, as the College embarked on its new educational adventure, relations with the town were coopera-tive, if not warm.[65]

All of this changed radically during the next ten years. Conditions steadily deteriorated to the point that when the College's first decade ended, Norton and Wheaton found themselves in a distinctly adversarial relationship. The general attitude of the townspeople toward the College could only be described as hostile, an attitude clearly reciprocated by the administrative leadership of the College.

This is not to say that the lines of demarcation were fixed and abso-lute. In 1913 President Cole felt called to comment on the need for fac-ulty to have an "interest in the civic life of Norton."[66] Wheaton continued to charge students from Norton considerably less than the standard tuition rate. President Cole served as an appointed member of the Norton Finance Committee in 1921; his wife and brother reviewed books at the behest of the Norton Public Library, acting as unofficial and official censors respectively. The College agreed to donate a parcel of land for a new high school, but because Town Meeting refused to appro-priate funds to build the school the transfer never took place. During World War I, many of the lectures and discussions at Wheaton were de-signed specifically to include the general public. The College, at its ex-pense, rebuilt the sidewalk running along East Main Street from the campus to the Wheaton Inn, and donated a section of Neck Woods to the State in order to allow a major straightening of the road to Taunton. Nonetheless, by 1922 the view held by Wheaton and Norton toward each other was bitter and acrimonious.[67]

Three main issues combined to create the rift, which extended beyond town officials to the populace at large. The central one was that of taxes, and the claims of the College to tax-exempt status for its land and build-ings. This was nothing new; the Seminary had never paid taxes on its buildings and grounds. But between 1902 and 1922 ten new brick build-ings were added to the original two wooden ones that had graced the Seminary, and a new library was in the process of being constructed. Moreover, many of the houses surrounding the campus now belonged to the College, and were used to house male faculty and their families. Even the substantial Wheaton family residence, since it now was the President's home, had been removed from the tax rolls.

For years the Seminary/College had observed an informal voluntary arrangement with Norton by which it paid taxes on most of the college-owned property on the northerly side of Main Street, and also on the Wheaton Inn, without questioning whether or not it was legally obliged to do so. But in 1913, new personnel on the Norton Board of Assessors sought to impose real estate taxes on all frame houses owned by the Col-lege, including the Infirmary on Howard Street. When the College refused to pay on houses occupied by Wheaton employees, the Board threatened in January, 1915, to take the properties for taxes, despite the fact that no hearing on the College's application for an abatement had been held. Subsequently it was learned that the Assessors had in fact abated entirely the tax imposed on the Infirmary but had neglected to inform Wheaton of this action.

By April, 1915, a new ingredient had been added to the already simmering pot. Town officials claimed that they had the legal right to tax wood and farm land owned by Wheaton because the College competed with local farmers by selling wood, excess produce from its vegetable farm, and pigs from the piggery run by the College for the purpose of disposing of dining hall garbage. Despite warnings from legal counsel that these claims were probably legitimate, plus the fact that under the voluntary agreement Wheaton had previously paid taxes on its farm property, the College administration was now loathe to comply. The College did not undersell area farmers, Treasurer William I. Cole asserted. Moreover, it hired Norton people on its farm, unlike an unnamed Norton industry which imported "a very low grade of Italian labor," whose presence in town increased the school budget and "the expense of maintaining law and order."[68]

Ultimately the matter wound up in Taunton before a court-appointed Master, whose findings in January, 1917, supported the College's case with the exception of the piggery. Subsequent negotiations between Norton and the College broke down and in April, 1917, Town Meeting voted unanimously to take the matter to court, despite the private observation of the Chairman of the Board of Selectmen that he believed the town was making a mistake in doing so. Interestingly, and indicative of the general atmosphere, no representative from the College bothered to attend the Town Meeting.

To the College's great delight, the results of the court proceedings were even more favorable than the original Master's report had been. Only the Wheaton Inn and the property purchased with it were ruled as subject to taxation. But the town government did not give up easily. In January, 1918, it filed an appeal to the Massachusetts Supreme Court, a process which ultimately resulted in the Court essentially upholding the findings of the lower court.

Finally, on August 1, 1919, after several more months of negotiation regarding abatements for past years, the College paid taxes plus interest for the years 1914–18 totalling $922.34, only slightly larger than its legal fees for the whole case. The principle that Wheaton was legally bound to pay taxes only on income-producing property not connected with the College plant had been firmly established. The result, as President Cole pointed out in his annual report for 1921–22, was that from 1919 on Wheaton actually paid several hundred dollars less per year than it had under the old voluntary agreement. Given the circumstances, this was undoubtedly a battle that had to be fought. But the legacy of town-gown bitterness that remained for years would prove a difficult obstacle to overcome for those on both sides who subsequently had to attempt to pick up the pieces.[69]

A second serious, though less public area of conflict with town officials resulted from a major dispute with the Norton Water Company over water rates. The Norton Water Company was a private company, formed in 1911 to provide water service to the residents and industries in the vicinity of Norton Center. This included the Seminary. In order for the company to sell its initial construction bonds, however, it needed a guarantee of $2000 annual revenue from the Town of Norton, and $1500 from the Seminary. The town swiftly approved, and on November 3, 1911, the Seminary agreed to the stipulated sum for a period of five years, with the understanding that in return Wheaton would receive an unlimited supply of water.[70]

All went well for those five years. The company began operation as scheduled in the summer of 1912. For Wheaton, the new system was extremely welcome, for the rapid growth of the campus since 1900 had put severe demands on the Seminary/College's water delivery system. Nonetheless, when the issue of rates came up for renegotiation in the summer of 1917, a total impasse soon developed. Convinced that it was paying more for the actual amount of water used than other consumers, Wheaton offered to pay $1000 per year, and threatened to return to using its own system if this were not agreed to. The College was a "charitable institution," William I. Cole wrote to Henry Symonds, President of the Norton Water Company, and as such had "no right to devote any considerable part of our income to enterprizes, however desireable they might be in themselves, which would primarily benefit the town rather than advance the interest of the college."[71]

The Water Company held out for an annual payment of $1800. The result was that the College severed its ties with the company and in the fall of 1917 returned to using its own system. But the loss of the company's largest customer put its very existence in jeopardy, a possibility which led the Norton Board of Health to take action. Turning to the State Board of Health, they asked that an analysis be made of the College's water supply. The results were not satisfactory, which left Wheaton with no option but to reenter negotiations with the Water Company. The issue became even more pressing when the College received notice of substantial increases in its fire insurance premiums, since the elevated tanks in Wheaton's own system did not provide suitable pressure for the fire hydrants on campus. The Water Company, anxious to regain Wheaton's business, offered to restore its water service immediately, and to submit the question of rates to arbitration, a proposal which the College instantly accepted.

Although the question of rates was never formally settled, in March,

1918, the College tacitly accepted the demands of the Water Company by increasing its payment from $1500 to $1800 per year. There matters remained until February, 1920, when the Water Company announced that it would be increasing its charge to $2580 per year. Both President Cole and his brother were furious. On February 20, 1920, they responded by charging the company with rate discrimination, notifying Symonds that the matter had been placed in the hands of the College's lawyers, who in turn filed a formal petition with the Massachusetts Department of Public Utilities on February 28.

There was at least some measure of legitimacy in the College's position. Noting that the two major industries in town, Talbot Mills and the Sweet Company, were charged only twenty-five cents per 100 cubic feet with a $300 minimum guarantee, the College protested that it was being asked either to subscribe to an unreasonably high guarantee or to pay thirty-three and one-third cents per hundred cubic feet without a minimum guarantee. Either policy, the College argued, amounted to an unfair and discriminatory rate, especially if one noted the common custom of charging a lower rate to high consumption customers.

There was also the matter of amount used. Since in the past the water had not been metered, company and college estimates of consumption differed greatly. In April, 1920, with meters now installed, much of that mystery was solved when a major leak in the piping on campus was discovered and plugged, one which cut daily consumption to 15,000 gallons per day, a far cry from the 35,000 that the Water Company maintained that Wheaton was using, a figure the College had never accepted.

In an effort to obtain an independent analysis of the quality of its water supply, the College hired the Cambridge firm of Arthur D. Little, whose tests produced good readings. But when Wheaton then requested a retest by State examiners, the results were again negative. It turned out that when there was only a light draw upon the College wells the water tested positively, but when the wells were used heavily water was drawn in from a distance that contained high bacteria counts. In addition the water itself was very hard and contained an excessive chlorine count. The State could not prohibit its use, the College was informed, but if Wheaton did so and trouble then ensued, the State's findings could be used in any public or private legal action against the College.

Given all this, the administration suggested a compromise, which the Norton Water Company accepted. Wheaton would pay for water at the rate of 25 cents per 100 cubic feet, measured at the main meter where company water entered the College's piping system. However, Wheaton would guarantee a minimum payment of $1500 per year, even if the amount of water used did not come to that amount on the basis of the agreed-upon rate.

The agreement went into effect on August 1, 1920. The College immediately connected the President's House and the faculty houses on Pine and Main Street directly to the Norton Water Company system. Faculty houses on Howard Street were forced to remain on the College system, for there was no company main on the street. The agreement remained in place until 1924, when the Norton Water Company sold all its physical assets to the Town of Norton. The result was the creation of a municipally owned water department, from which Wheaton continued to purchase water, and with which it continued an on-going dialogue, though with far less rancour, concerning the rates charged by the town.

The water rates dispute had little of the impact on general public attitude toward Wheaton that had resulted from the tax issue. The Norton Water Company was, after all, a private business concern, not a town department. But because the company's services to Norton were predicated on it also having the College as a customer, for those in town government the question of Wheaton's continued participation was an issue of great concern. Coupled with the fight over tax assessments, it is easy to see why town officials saw the "new Wheaton" as having diverged substantially from the supportive interrelationship that had existed as long as the Wheaton family provided close linkage between the two.

For many citizens of the town, however, including some of the most influential, the event that did most to destroy good town-gown relations permanently was the building of the College Chapel. Ever since the Seminary's inception, students had been required to attend Sunday church services at the Trinitarian Congregational Church, located at the corner of Pine and East Main Street. Mrs. Wheaton and her husband had been instrumental in founding the Church in 1832, and had paid most of the costs of building the original sanctuary and of a major renovation in 1882. The Seminary's graduation ceremonies were conducted in the Church until 1910; College baccalaureate services continued there through 1917.

In the later years of the Seminary and during the first few College years, students were allowed to attend Sunday services at the Unitarian, Methodist or Roman Catholic churches in Norton, but the vast majority still attended services at the Trinitarian Congregational Church. Not only did they attend each Sunday, but the Seminary/College continued its long-standing practice of paying pew fees to the Trinitarian Church, based on the number attending. This ranged in the twentieth century from $700 to $1100 per year, a substantial contribution to the annual operating budget of the church.[72]

All this ended in 1917–18 with the completion of the College Chapel. Sunday services were now conducted on campus; moreover, they were attended not only by the members of the Wheaton community, but also by the students and faculty from the House in the Pines School. This meant that the College gained the pew fees from that institution that the Trinitarian Church also lost.[73]

But the emotional and psychological shock to the members of the
Trinitarian Church and the wider Norton community was far greater than
the financial hardship that this religious separation imposed. The Trinitarian Congregational Church had been the Wheaton family church. For
nearly eighty years the church and the Seminary had been Eliza Baylies
Wheaton's greatest concerns. To break this connection seemed to many
to be a direct insult to her memory, and an action they were sure she
would never have countenanced. Moreover, for a man such as Rev. Cole,
a Congregational minister himself, to lead the College away from its
Congregational heritage by instituting church services that were avowedly nondenominational was regarded as almost blasphemous.

The strained relations that developed between the church's congregation and President and Mrs. Cole because of this break never healed.
Once the Chapel opened, neither Rev. Cole nor his wife ever again attended Sunday services at the Norton church. On March 18, 1918, Mrs.
Cole commented in a letter to her family that she and the President had
not attended church on Easter Sunday because the college was on vacation and "the people of the town do not love us."[74] Two years later she
noted to her sister on June 6, "After next Sunday no more church for a
long time, for us! Heathen!"[75] And in 1921 she lamented, "It is too bad
to be in a community and to be so little of it, as we are."[76] Even in 1923
the rift was as strong as ever. "This is the one Sunday each summer we
go to church," Mrs. Cole wrote her sister, "SVC is preaching at his old
church in Taunton."[77]

The split between the Coles and the Norton church was even more
apparent in the comments made by Mrs. Cole to new faculty who inno-
cently inquired about churches in the community. "Norton is a rather
pretty New England village," Mrs. Cole wrote to Helen Manning. "The
life of the college, however, does not touch the life of the town. . . . We
even have our own college church."[78] To Agnes Riddell she responded
that there were indeed two churches located on the edge of the campus,
"but it is hardly probable that you would care to connect yourself with
either."[79]

Even more telling was the furious reaction of both Coles to Dean Mina
Kerr's announcement that she planned to become a member of the Congregational Church. "By doing so," Mrs. Cole wrote her sister, "she ut-
terly disregards all that S. V. went through when he decided it was wiser
for the college to separate from that church. She says she thinks she
ought to support the local church, and lend her help to its growth; when
she will merely be making a laughing-stock of herself. She, like some
other people, hopes to heal the gap between the town and the college;
and she says that she has always needed the inspiration which comes
from contacts outside the college in which her work is placed. We do not
exactly know where she expects to get that uplift in Norton. But she may
go her own sweet way to the fall, which we think is before her."[80]

Bitter as this attitude might have been, it was reciprocated by numbers of town residents. Arthur Cutler, the College's business manager, was confronted by one angry resident in the fall of 1922, who alleged that just as Wheaton had broken up the town church by building its own, so now it was planning to break up the town library by erecting its own separate library. "Did you ever hear of such stupidity?" Mrs. Cole commented. "And then New Englanders boast of their intellectual superiority over other parts of the country!"[81]

Whatever the reasons, the end result of the transformation of a small seminary into a thriving college within the confines of a small rural and working-class community was one of growing hostility and a sense of disconnection between the two entities. Perhaps such a split was inevitable, and part of a process resulting from the fact that the College was changing far more rapidly than the town. But the confluence of the tax, water, and church issues within the short period of ten years permanently eroded the sense of community which had in many ways characterized the relationship of Wheaton and Norton during the Seminary decades. It would be many years before the scars created by these conflicts faded, and even longer before relations between the College and the Norton community substantially improved.

Notes: Chapter 9

1. Wheaton Histories, Seminary: Seminary to College #2.

2. The College's first two graduates were Margaret Getchell and Eleanor Lord. General Files: Class of 1914.

3. Ruth Skinner (W1916) was the only student to complete the college preparatory, seminary and college degree programs. General Files: Class of 1916.

4. Provost/Registrar: Enrollment Statistics; Trustees 1834–1910: K. U. Clark: Cole to Clark, 2/14/12; SVC, *President's Report, 1921–1922,* pp. 9, 15.

5. See ch. 6.

6. Trustees Minutes: 3/14/12; 3/18/15; Wheaton Histories, Seminary: Seminary to College #1, 2; Incorporation Papers, Statutes and Seal: Statutes: Mass. General Laws, ch. 84 of 1912.

7. SVC, *President's Report, 1914–1915,* p. 9.

8. SVC, *President's Report, 1921–1922,* p. 28.

9. SVC, "Connecting the College with the Home," *The Congregationalist,* (July 29, 1915).

10. *Wheaton Seminary, 1912,* p. 7; see also SVC, *Why Change;* SVC, *President's Report, 1912–1913,* pp. 48–49; *1913–1914,* pp. 47–48; *1914–1915,* pp. 26–32; *1918–1919,* pp. 35–36.

11. See ch. 6; also Wheaton College, *Announcement of Wheaton College, 1912.*

12. Quoted in Shepard, "Reference History," p. 375.

13. Trustees Minutes: 3/18/15.

14. Faculty Meeting Minutes: 9/14/15; see also, Trustees Minutes: 3/17/13; 5/26/13; 11/18/14; 3/18/15; SVC, *President's Report, 1912–1913,* p. 29; *Wheaton Bulletin,* 9:3 (June, 1913).

15. The motto was officially adopted by the trustees at their meeting on March 21,

1911. See Trustees Minutes: 3/21/11; also 3/16/14; General Files: Class of 1916: Correspondence with Cottrell and Leonard; Academic Council Minutes: 4/25/16; Incorporation Papers, Statutes, and Seal: College Seal: R. Fletcher to P. Dougall, 4/10/70; Shepard, "Reference History," appendix, p. d.

16. In November, 1920, the trustees increased the size of the Board from ten to fifteen persons. The President of the College was always, in this period, considered a regular, rather than ex officio, member of the Board. This reflected the fact that Rev. Cole had been a trustee for some years before he became President. Trustees Minutes: 11/17/20.

17. Bursar's Office Correspondence, 1889–1940: #3, Treasurers and Miscellaneous, 1910–1920: "Treasurer's Report for the Year ended July 10, 1912."

18. SVC, *President's Report, 1913–1914*, p. 14; Provost/Registrar: Student Enrollment Statistics.

19. General Files: Class of 1914: "Announcement of Two-Year Associates Diploma Course"; SVC, *President's Report, 1912–1913*, pp. 34–37; *1913–1914*, p. 14; *1915–1916*, p. 13.

20. SVC, *President's Report, 1913–1914*, p. 14; *1918–1919*, p. 33; *1921–1922*, p. 6; Wheaton College, *Catalogue of Officers and Students*, 1914–15; 1920–21; 1921–22; Trustees: J. W. Lincoln: SVC to Lincoln, 4/17/19; Trustees Minutes: 3/3/19; Academic Council Minutes: 3/24/19.

21. Wheaton College Financial Reports, 1920–21; see also Bursar's Office Correspondence, 1889–1940: #3, Treasurers and Miscellaneous, 1910–20.

22. Trustees Minutes: 11/20/13; 3/16/14; 6/12/22.

23. Up until 1920, the annual audit was done by a member of the Board of Trustees, usually someone who was a banker. See Wheaton College Financial Reports, Assets and Liabilities, 1920–22; also Bursar's Office Correspondence, 1889–1940: #3, Treasurers and Miscellaneous, 1910–20; #36, E. E. Stackpole; Treasurer: Reports, 1912–32.

24. See chs. 2, 6 and 6, n. 10.

25. During this decade the College received only two sizeable gifts, one a bequest of $1,000 from a former Seminary pupil, Mary French Porter; the other from Calista Mayhew, aunt of President Cole's first wife, Annie Talbot Cole, who gave $10,000 in 5 percent bonds in return for which the College agreed to pay her the annual interest of $500 as long as she lived. See Trustees Minutes: 3/27/14; 11/23/16.

26. *Historical Statistics of the United States: Colonial Times to 1970* (White Plains, NY: Kraus International Publications, 1989), vol. 1, pp. 210–11. The 1920 index of 60, based on 1967 = 100, was not reached again until 1946–1947.

27. *Wheaton College Bulletin: Catalogue and Announcements,* 1912–27; Smart/Park: Smart: SVC to Trustees, 12/2/20; Trustees: Kilham #3: SVC to Kilham, 5/3/20; Trustees 1834–1910: Hervey: SVC to Hervey, 5/3/20.

28. Trustees, 1834–1910: Curtis: SVC to Curtis, 1/5/12; Trustees Minutes: 3/15/22; Wheaton College Financial Reports, 1921–22.

29. SVC: Correspondence: SVC to Bullard, 6/9/22.

30. SVC, *President's Report, 1912–1913*, p. 10; *1913–1914*, pp. 13–14, 39–42; *1918–1919*, p. 35; *1921–1922*, pp. 22–23.

31. Ibid., *1918–1919*, pp. 35–36.

32. Ibid., *1921–1922*, p. 24.

33. Ibid.

34. Regarding the swimming pool, see Shepard, "Reference History," p. 360. Commenting that a pool was regarded at the best places as a necessary adjunct to a gymnasium, Cole observed that the students wanted it, and that it would "prove for us a good drawing card." Trustees: Lincoln: SVC to Lincoln, 7/31/13; also Smart/Park: Smart: SVC to Smart, 7/31/13; Trustees 1834–1910: Curtis: passim, summer

1913. For data on the construction of the Observatory, see Buildings: Observatory; Trustees Minutes: 4/20/16; 6/12/16; Trustees 1834–1910: K. U. Clark: SVC to Clark, 8/26/16; SVC, *President's Report, 1915–1916*, pp. 16–17.

35. SVC, *President's Report, 1912–1913*, p. 46.

36. Faculty Meeting Minutes: 10/17/12.

37. Trustees: K. U. Clark: SVC to Clark, 1/13/15.

38. Trustees Minutes: 4/20/16; 6/12/16; Trustees 1834–1910: K. U. Clark #2: SVC to Clark, 7/18/16; Smart/Park: Smart: SVC to Smart, 7/5,11,12/16.

39. Buildings: Chapel 1916–30. See this and succeeding files for changes and remodeling of the Chapel over the years. Also, SVC, *President's Report, 1916–1917*, pp. 15–16.

40. SVC, *President's Report, 1918–1919*, pp. 19–20; Bursar's Office Correspondence, 1889–1940: #10, Cole Chapel, 1910–20.

41. SVC, *President's Report, 1918–1919*, pp. 19–20.

42. Cole was undoubtedly encouraged by the success of a recent similar campaign at Smith College, which had raised $4,000,000 in one semester, with 85 percent alumnae participation. See M. Thorp, *Neilson of Smith* (New York: Oxford University Press, 1956), pp. 284–85.

43. See ch. 6.

44. Academic Council Minutes: 5/28/20; Trustees Minutes: 9/2,23/20; Trustees 1834–1910: K. U. Clark #2: SVC to Clark, 9/17/20; 11/1/20. At the close of the 1920–21 fiscal year, the value of Wheaton's endowment, including the Winter Street property, was $1,066,118. Wheaton College Financial Reports, 1920–21.

45. Trustees 1834–1910: Curtis: SVC to Curtis, 9/13/20; Smart/Park: Smart: SVC to Trustees, 12/7/20; Trustees Minutes: 9/2/20; 11/17/20.

46. Trustees 1834–1910: K. U. Clark #2: SVC to Clark, 9/17/20; see also Buildings: Stanton Dormitory.

47. Bursar's Office Correspondence, 1889–1940: #39, Tamblyn and Brown, 1920–30; Trustees Minutes: 11/17/20; 9/22/21; SVC, *President's Report, 1921–1922*, pp. 54–55; Trustees 1834–1910: K. U. Clark #3: SVC to Clark, 8/31/21.

48. The location of 71 graduates and 673 nongraduates was not known. Shepard, "Reference History" pp. 439–40; Alumnae Affairs Office, 55: Endowment campaign, 1920–22; Bursar's Office Correspondence, 1889–1940: #30, Miscellaneous, 1920–30: "Analysis of Donors to the Wheaton College Building and Endowment Fund, from its Beginning to January, 1924."

49. SVC, *President's Report, 1921–1922*, pp. 56–57. See also Bursar's Office Correspondence, 1889–1940: #30, Miscellaneous, 1920–30: "Analysis of Donors to Building and Endowment Fund," p. 2; Wheaton College Financial Reports, 1921–22; Trustees Minutes: 11/17/20; 3/16/21; 3/15/22.

50. SVC, *President's Report, 1921-1922*, p. 27.

51. General Files: 1912–13: SVC to former students and alumnae, 4/15/13.

52. In the spring of 1922 the college listed 512 living graduates of the Seminary, and 183 from the College. In addition there were 1738 former students who had not completed either degree program. SVC, *President's Report, 1921–1922*, p. 26; Harris, "No Backward Steps," pp. 8, 10; Shepard, "Reference History," pp. 323–24; Trustees Minutes: 11/17/21.

53. Harris, "No Backward Steps," pp. 8, 10.

54. Alumnae Affairs Office, 55: Endowment campaign, 1920–22.

55. V. Gildersleeve, *Many a Good Crusade: Memoirs of Virginia Crocheron Gildersleeve* (New York: MacMillan, 1954), p. 90.

56. Ibid., p. 91; L. Baker, *I'm Radcliffe! Fly Me!: The Seven Sisters and the Failure of Women's Education* (New York: MacMillan, 1976), p. 2, n..

57. Kendall, *Peculiar Institutions: An Informal History of the Seven Sister Colleges* (New York: G. Putnam's, 1976), p. 29.

58. SVC: College Business: Cole to Bullard, 2/15/22.

59. SVC, *President's Report, 1921–1922*, p. 24.

60. *World Almanac and Book of Facts for 1927*, pp. 385–92.

61. Trustees, 1834–1910: K. U. Clark #2: SVC to Clark, 11/26/19.

62. Ibid.

63. HWC: Letters to Family: to Sister, 12/7/19.

64. SVC, *President's Report, 1921–1922*, pp. 39–40.

65. For further discussion of the Wheaton family and town-gown relations during the Seminary years, see chs. 1, 6, 8. For relations between the College and the Town of Norton, see Shepard, "Reference History," appendix, pp. b–d.

66. Faculty Meeting Minutes: 9/17/13.

67. Trustees Minutes: 3/14/12; 6/15/14; 1/30/15; Trustees 1834–1910: Hervey #2: Hervey to SVC, 5/9/14; Curtis #1: Cole to Curtis, 11/9/14; K. U. Clark #3: Cole to Clark, 3/3/21; Wheaton Histories, Wheaton in World Wars I and II: World War I; HWC, Letters to Family: to Sister: 12/7/19.

68. Bursar's Office Correspondence, 1889–1940: #14, Warner, Warner and Stackpole, 1910–20: Stackpole to SVC, 4/13/15; W. I. Cole to Stackpole, 4/15/15. President Cole also asserted to the faculty that "the Italians" had been "speaking to students and in other ways molesting them," and urged all faculty to do whatever they could to assist in "putting a stop to such proceedings." Faculty Meeting Minutes: 2/27/13.

69. For extensive correspondence relating to this case, see Bursar's Office Correspondence, 1889–1940: #11, Tax Returns, 1910–20; #14, Warner, Warner & Stackpole, 1910–20; see also Trustees Minutes: 11/23/16; 11/21/17; 3/15/18; 3/13/19; SVC, *President's Report, 1921–1922*, pp. 38–42.

70. Additional materials relating to the College's dealings with the Norton Water Company can be found in Bursar's Office Correspondence, 1889–1940: #12, Norton Water Company, 1910–20; #34, 1920–30; See also Town of Norton: Town Meeting: Norton Water and Fire districts.

71. Bursar's Office Correspondence, 1889–1940: #12, W. I. Cole to Symonds, 6/29/17.

72. Treasurer, "Cash Disbursements Ledger," July, 1913-September, 1918: passim.

73. Bursar's Office Correspondence, 1889–1940: #8, House in the Pines: Bursar to G. Cornish, 1/8/19.

74. HWC, Letters to Family: to Family, 3/31/18.

75. Ibid.: to Sister, 6/6/20.

76. Ibid., 3/27/21.

77. Ibid., 7/30/23.

78. Faculty: Manning: HWC to Manning, 4/13/21.

79. Ibid.: Riddell: HWC to Riddell, 4/29/22.

80. HWC, Letters to Family: to Sister, 1/6/22.

81. Ibid., 10/1/22.

10
Transition Years:
The Human Dimension
1912–1922

IF ADMISSIONS GROWTH and the physical plant were President Cole's primary concerns during Wheaton's first decade as a college, the creation of a new administrative structure and the recruitment of a college faculty did not come far behind. Here, as in the case of planning the curricular transition and developing a suitable campus, Rev. Cole had begun planning and implementing policies during the last years of the Seminary's existence.

For several years prior to obtaining a college charter, President Cole had known that he would appoint Ida Everett, a teacher of English, as his new Dean of the College. To this end he had prevailed upon President Hyde of Bowdoin College (where Cole was Vice President of the Board of Trustees) to grant Miss Everett an honorary Master of Arts degree. Miss Everett, who had ranked first in her graduating class at Mount Holyoke, studied for a year at Oxford, and completed all requirements but the dissertation for her Ph.D. at Yale, became a central figure in developing and instituting the plan for Wheaton's transition from Seminary to College.[1]

Similarly, in 1909 the President retained a recent Colby College graduate, Sarah Belle Young, to serve as Registrar and to teach some English classes. Until that time both the position of Registrar and that of Librarian had been filled as adjunct duties by persons hired first and foremost as teachers. With Miss Young's appointment, the emphasis was reversed. Her predecessor as Registrar, Mary Converse, continued at Wheaton as a member of the English department, but from the beginning it was clear that Miss Young was regarded primarily as an administrative officer, who would also teach an occasional course. In 1912, with the beginning of the first college year, Miss Young was also designated as Secretary to the Faculty, and her formal connection with the English department was discontinued.[2]

President Cole dealt with the position of College Librarian in a distinctly different manner. For decades some member of the Seminary

Ida J. Everett, Professor of
English Literature, served as the
first Dean of Wheaton College
from 1912 to 1921.

teaching staff had also managed the library and held the title of Librarian. After the transition to college status, Dr. Cole continued the practice, but changed the title to Acting Librarian. Most often held by a member of the Classics Department, the position moved through several hands during the first years of the College's existence. Only when a new library building was completed did the President in 1923–24 remove the "Acting" designation from the title, while at the same time hiring a full-time librarian with no departmental designation.[3]

The final official member of the college administration during these first years was the President's brother, William Isaac Cole, known informally to one and all as "Billy Ike." An ordained minister, Rev. Cole had been involved for nearly twenty years with the founding and operation of the South End Settlement House and the South End Improvement Association in Boston. A recognized expert in the field of social work, he came to Norton in 1912 to live with his widower brother and serve as Resident Lecturer in Applied Sociology. In 1913 he became College Treasurer, and in 1916 was appointed Professor of Applied Sociology. Working closely with President Cole, he took over supervision and control of the day-to-day fiscal operations of the College, a job which up until then had been included in the tasks of the President.[4]

These three persons, Ida Everett, Sarah Belle Young and William I. Cole, plus the President, constituted the administrative officers of the College. The President remained very much the chief academic officer who dealt with all matters relating to curriculum and the faculty. He also personally reviewed and authorized expenditures ranging from library book orders to any form of plant repair or renovation, no matter how small. A bookcase for a faculty suite, new linoleum for a hall—each had to gain presidential approval.[5] Dean Everett, though still affiliated with the English department, functioned mainly in the student life and services capacity that one would today associate with a Dean of Students. Review of admissions credentials and the decision as to the applicant's qualifications rested with the Registrar, who also dealt with class scheduling and keeping the academic records for all students.

In reality, however, there emerged during this period a fifth, totally unofficial, but very much de facto member of the administrative team, a person whose role raised considerable comment among the faculty, as well as envy, concern, and some jealousy on the part of the Registrar and Dean, particularly the latter. This person was Helen Wieand Cole, the President's second wife, who married Dr. Cole, thirty-three years her senior, in the summer of 1917, and came to live with the President and his brother in the impressive President's House located adjacent to the campus across East Main Street.

A 1906 graduate of Mount Holyoke, Helen Wieand had come to Wheaton initially in 1911, having received her M.A. and completed additional course work toward the Ph.D. at Bryn Mawr. After teaching Latin and Greek for four years she resigned to return to Bryn Mawr to complete her Ph.D. Two years later she returned to Norton, dissertation not completed, but as the wife of the College President.[6]

To have one of their former number return in this exalted position created a situation to which many of the faculty had trouble adjusting. The same could be said for the new Mrs. Cole. Widowed since 1906, President Cole remained steadfastly devoted to the memory of his first wife, with the result that his unconscious comments about her often cut the second Mrs. Cole to the quick. Moreover, Helen Wieand Cole came

Samuel Valentine Cole and Helen Wieand Cole on their wedding day, August 22, 1917.

from a reasonably well-to-do Philadelphia family and had been used to earning her own income as a teacher. At times she found it difficult to live with a husband so much older, whose lack of interest in fashion and style, along with his parsimonious attitude toward the expenditure of money, never ceased to prove a source of frustration. In turn, her practice of exchanging clothes with her sister, and also accepting gifts of clothing from the same source, irked her husband considerably, for he considered these actions an unfavorable reflection on his ability to "keep" his wife in a suitable fashion. Since "Brother William" also lived with them, Mrs. Cole found the task of maintaining a household for the two men occasionally quite irksome, though she often commented that William Cole at times served as an understanding ally in her differences with her husband.[7]

For Ida Everett, having a former junior faculty member return as the President's wife was especially disturbing. When the new Mrs. Cole first arrived in Norton, the President's brother warned her that Dean Everett was used to summoning the President across the street to Metcalf in the evenings to discuss College affairs, and commented to Mrs. Cole that Miss Everett "in reality feels as if I had supplanted her in confidential relations with SV."[8] Subsequently told by the Dean that she looked "too young for my place,"[9] Mrs. Cole wrote to her family: "I find as I had anticipated a little chill in the greeting of some of the Faculty—may I whisper it, especially of Miss Everett, but from the security of my present position I can ignore that."[10] Noting that Miss Everett also seemed jealous of the growing power and influence of Sarah Belle Young, Mrs. Cole observed: "She [Dean Everett] is so tenacious of her position and her prerogatives. It is extremely hard for her to admit that consideration for me [on the part of President Cole] comes before her own now."[11] Miss Everett was apparently particularly upset when Mrs. Cole insisted to her husband that a Dean and President should be able to arrange things so as to have evenings free. Cole agreed, but said that he would have to get Miss Everett used to the idea gradually.[12]

Beginning in 1918, Mrs. Cole again held a faculty appointment, though never on a full time basis, teaching courses in Latin, Greek and Archaeology. She organized monthly faculty gatherings at which the members of one or another academic department would give a presentation and lead a general discussion. She also completed her doctoral thesis and in 1918 received her Ph.D. degree, but was not allowed by Bryn Mawr "to wear my gown or to use my degree, until I have my thesis printed."[13]

But most of all Helen Wieand Cole served as her husband's confidante, adviser, and executive secretary in terms of implementing and carrying through much of the business of the President's office. This was particularly true in the area of hiring new faculty. In August, 1918, she commented in a letter to her family that she was handling all of her husband's correspondence regarding vacancies on the faculty. Telling her only to whom she should write, Cole generally let her "say just what I please; to be sure it is largely due to laziness and aversion to writing letters; but then I am getting more power into my hands thereby and as you know, I am not averse to being a boss myself, on occasion. The only person who does not seem to relish it is Miss Everett, and she cannot say anything."[14]

The result was that not only was all correspondence, except the formal appointment letter, carried out between Helen Wieand Cole and women candidates for teaching positions (President Cole handled all dealings with men), but Mrs. Cole also on occasion journeyed to Smith, Mount Holyoke, Swarthmore, and other locales to interview candidates. Her most important work in this area occurred in the spring and summer of 1921, when she was in charge of all correspondence, from initial inquiry to negotiations concerning salary, teaching load, and administrative duties with the woman eventually hired to replace the retiring Dean Everett. This was Mina Kerr, who came to Wheaton from a similar position at Milwaukee-Downer College.[15]

In addition to recruiting Dean Kerr, Helen Wieand Cole's work that year involved seeking replacements for six faculty and six other persons, of whom she noted she had "managed the getting of all except Dr. Shook's assistant and the assistant in Physical training."[16] Commenting with relief to her sister on August 3 that she and the President had filled the last vacancy, she wrote: "My work is over, except to answer such questions as the new people write about. From January 9—July 29 I was busy in the job, and in that time wrote 273 letters. And what do I get for it except a certain feeling of power? And unpopularity! I should worry!"[17]

Part of the reason that Mrs. Cole was given such responsibility undoubtedly came from the President's growing concern with fiscal matters and the enormous time demands put on him by the abortive capital campaign of 1920–22. In addition, having only one "typewriter" [typist] in his office, and sharing a stenographer with both Dean Everett and Miss Young, Cole undoubtedly found it a great relief to have someone to whom he could turn over completely the correspondence part of a recruitment process.

Finally, there is considerable evidence that from 1919 on Samuel Valentine Cole's health was somewhat in decline. His wife time and again expressed concern over a condition that was not life-threatening in the short run but dangerous in the long run, correctable only by a major operation that carried its own risks. Although the specific nature of the problem was always discreetly avoided in any of Mrs. Cole's letters to her family or sister, she noted that the death of Senator Henry Cabot Lodge of Massachusetts came in the wake of an operation for the same condition from which her husband suffered. That President Cole found himself the victim of problems connected with an enlarged prostate is hardly surprising, since in December, 1921, he celebrated his seventieth birthday.[18]

All of this was not lost on the faculty, and became a matter of apprehension and concern, as Mrs. Cole found out in November, 1921, from the outspoken Sarah Belle Young.

> Today I had quite a revelation from Miss Young. I went over to the office to see about some Endowment Fund business; for I am going to help the Alumnae Secretary with that, for a while. And I said to Miss Young that I might be criticised for it, as people might think that the college was being too much managed by the Cole family. And she told me that some of the Faculty were very hot when they came back in the fall, and had heard about the new appointments on the Faculty, and that it was generally understood that Dr. Cole was preparing to retire, and that he was planning for me to take his place; and that so I had had the appointment of the new people, so that the new Faculty would be people of whom I approved.
>
> I asked her whether she did not think that I would make a fine college president,—for I was so amazed and disgusted. She said, yes, but she would not receive the appointment that way if she were in my place. So it does not matter what one does, or what one omits to do, one is criticised anyway. And it seems my going to Swarthmore was very much criticised, and was also considered a definite proof of my prospects. Such rot! And yet, as you know and what makes it funny to myself, is that the prospect was not one which I had failed to think of. Only long ago I realized that it would never do, nor would it be desirable.[19]

The "retirement" of Miss Everett from the office of the Dean undoubtedly exacerbated tensions between the faculty and administration. As early as 1919, Mrs. Cole reported to her sister that the President was finding it "increasingly hard" to work with Miss Everett, who apparently was finding it difficult to focus on specific problems and had an increasing tendency in meetings to digress extensively from the business at hand.[20] By 1920, President Cole had persuaded a reluctant Miss Everett that she should return to full-time teaching as Head of the English Department. "I think," Cole wrote trustee Annie Kilham in April, 1921, "that she understands that I greatly appreciate her service and have her interest at heart. As Head of the English department we will have her here longer than otherwise at the college. . . . Miss Young and others here besides myself feel that Miss Everett would be in danger of a breakdown in health if she is not relieved in this way."[21]

Despite being awarded an honorary L.H.D. degree at the time of her retirement from the Deanship, Miss Everett remained disgruntled at what she clearly perceived as an unwarranted demotion. Mrs. Cole, admittedly no great friend of the former Dean, commented in September, 1921, that Miss Everett had assumed "a sort of aggrieved dowager air, with every other remark prefaced with the phrase 'for sixteen years I did thus and so.' "[22]

Central to ensuring the successful establishment of Wheaton as a college was the creation of a creditable college faculty. For President Cole this meant that most of those holding the rank of professor, and in particular those serving as department heads, should have the Ph.D. degree. In addition, Cole was adamant in his insistence that it was important to recruit a goodly number of men. Though the President had persuaded the Board of Trustees to approve the hiring of men to full-time teaching positions in 1906, in 1911–1912 only George Sherman and Hiram Tucker, who taught natural science and music performance respectively, were members of the teaching staff. No member of the faculty held a Ph.D.

Cole immediately set out to rectify the situation. When Wheaton opened its doors as a college in September, 1912, five men, four of them new, including two with Ph.Ds, were part of the faculty. Although two left within a couple of years, one to a department at a western university, the other dismissed due to incompetence, Cole continued to reserve new positions, particularly those as heads of departments, for men with both experience and a Ph.D. Perhaps the most notable of these early appointments was a newly-minted Harvard Ph.D., Walter McIntire, who was hired in 1914 as Professor of Philosophy and Education. His success as a teacher was instantaneous; "Dr. Mac" would remain one of Wheaton's most popular instructors for nearly three decades.[23]

In his pursuit of male faculty members Cole sometimes encouraged current female members of the faculty to leave, indicating bluntly that their hope of promotion was negligible, since he was reserving a full professorship in their field for a man. At times he was thwarted in implementing this policy by lack of suitable off-campus housing for men, and on one occasion was forced to retain a woman because the only living accommodations available were in a dormitory.[24]

Nor were salaries at all equitable, even taking into account the amount that could be written off for women faculty as consisting of room and board. Men were married, had wives and children who must be supported, and for whom year-round living accommodations must be found. Women faculty, who were required to live in the dormitories, vacate them during vacations, and take their meals with the students, were by definition single. That many of them might find it necessary to contribute to the support of parents or other family members, might want to have an elderly parent come to live with them, or just might not want to live year after year in a dormitory, was conveniently disregarded.[25]

This is not to say that President Cole regarded the salaries paid to any of his faculty as adequate. Increases did not come annually. In general they were awarded only when a new contract was issued, and not always then. In fact there was little change in salaries during the first years of College operation. But in the face of the rampant inflation of the wartime and immediate postwar years, President Cole time and again pressed upon the trustees the need for major increases in faculty compensation, going so far as to state publicly a targeted salary scale in his annual report for 1918–19. This ranged from $1200–$2000 for an assistant professor to $3000–$4000 for a full professor. Achieving this, he noted, would require a minimum 25 percent raise across the board for faculty. While this goal was not attained, increases were provided in the last several years of the decade, and coincided with the reluctant decision by the Board of Trustees to increase tuition, room, and board charges on a nearly annual basis. Nonetheless, at times Cole had to be at his persuasive best to convince prospective faculty to accept a position paying considerably less than what could be obtained as a public high school teacher.[26]

By the end of the College's first decade the composition of the faculty had been transformed. Twenty-nine full-time and two part-time faculty provided a student/faculty ratio of ten to one. Of the nine full professors five were men; there were no associate professors and all the assistant professors, instructors, and assistants were women. Five professors and three assistant professors held the Ph.D. degree. Most of the other faculty members had attained at least a Masters degree, and many had continued their graduate work beyond that level. Of the full-time teaching faculty only Hiram Tucker in Music and Ida Everett in English remained from those who had taught in the last year of the Seminary.

For some who had loyally served the Seminary, the transition to college status brought an end to the need for their services at Wheaton. Those faculty whose teaching loads had primarily involved students in the college preparatory curriculum or the first two years of the Seminary degree program suddenly found themselves without jobs. Only in one case, that of Miriam Converse, who served as Registrar prior to the hiring of Sarah Belle Young, and who had directed the English classes for the college preparatory students, was President Cole willing to retain the services of a person who did not nominally qualify for membership on a college faculty. Commenting that she was such an asset that he was prepared to find a place for her in college work, even if it meant a salary increase, Cole wrote in a letter of recommendation, "She strikes me as having a peculiarly sane view of things."[27] But Miss Converse, anxious to continue teaching and recognizing that she was not prepared to instruct at the college level, chose instead to depart.

Faculty turnover during the College's first decade was great, but the overall quality of academic preparation continued to improve. Full professors were invariably brought in at that rank. Only one faculty member, Grace Shepard in the English department, made her way up through

Twenty-five of the 35 members of the administration and faculty gathered for a photograph in the final year of President Cole's administration, 1924-1925. Front Row: Mary Tenney, *Classics*; Marion Jenkins, *Household Economics*; Ida Everett, *English*; Mabel Rice, *Biology*. Second Row: Glen Shook, *Physics*; Grace Shepard, *English*; Mathilde Lange, *Biology*; Nesta Williams, *Music*; Minnie Yarborough, *English*; Agnes Riddell, *Romance Languages*; Auguste Pouleur, *Chemistry*. Third Row: Walter McIntire, *Philosophy*; Kathleen Bruce, *History*; Mary-Louise Hubbard, *Psychology*; Mary Armstrong, *Librarian*; Marjorie Preston, *Art*; Amy Otis, *Art*; Ellen Webster, *Biblical Literature*. Back Row: Elizabeth Morgan, *French*; Theresa Lammers, *Physical Education*; Alice Abbott, *Spanish*; Iola Eastburn, *German*; Pearl Wallis, *Physical Education*; Sarah B. Young, *Registrar*; Allen West, *History*. Missing: Flora Amos, *English*; Helen W. Cole, *Classics*; Samuel V. Cole, *President*; William I. Cole, *Sociology*; Helen Falkner, *Economics*; Enrico Leboffe, *Vocal Music*; Marguerite Metivier, *French*; Eleanor Randall, *Art*; Violet Robinson, *Oral English*; Martha Watt, *Mathematics*.

the ranks, moving over a course of nine years from instructor to professor, despite the fact that she did not hold the terminal academic degree. New male professors with a Ph.D. were always given the rank of professor, but the same was not necessarily true for women. In fact President Cole was forced to go back on his initial appointment of Mathilde Lange as Professor of Biology, professing to have made a mistake. The Board of Trustees, he explained, did not like new appointments to be given the rank of professor. Instead, clearly embarrassed, he asked her to accept the rank of assistant professor with no difference in salary, pointing out that there were other heads of departments with the Ph.D. at that rank. Lange accepted, but her insistant demands for promotion subsequently bedeviled both Cole and his successor, J. Edgar Park.[28]

A study of eleven women's colleges, not including Wheaton, seven of them in the New England or Middle Atlantic areas, indicates that in 1920 they averaged 74.4 percent women on their faculties, with the highest being Milwaukee Downer at 94.7 percent and the lowest Bryn Mawr with 55 percent. All of these institutions had been functioning as colleges before 1890. Wheaton, with a faculty that was 83.9 percent female, had in one decade brought itself basically within the range already created by other women's colleges. The difficulties in recruiting faculty with Ph.D. degrees for all academic institutions, not just Wheaton, can readily be seen when one recognizes that in 1900–1901 the doctoral degree was awarded nationally to 312 men and 31 women, figures which grew only minimally by 1919–20 to 439 and 93 respectively. With over 25 percent of his faculty holding that degree, President Cole had every reason to believe that faculty development between 1912 and 1922 had kept pace with the other facets of the College's growth and development.[29]

In the process of recruiting and hiring faculty, many procedures were followed that would be both unthinkable and illegal today. Age and marital status were routinely discussed, it being even more important for men to be married than it was for women to be single. The "fit" of a person into the community was of extreme import in terms of contract renewal, and there are several cases on record of faculty members who were asked not to return for reasons having nothing to do with performance in the classroom. This concern weighed far more heavily on women faculty than on men, for the women, living among the students as they did, often found the social and supervisory expectations placed on them more than a little wearing. Noting that one teacher seemed to "chafe" under the restraints of community life, President Cole commented, "you give the decided impression in the faculty and the student body that you are not in sympathy with the aims, methods, and management of the college."[30] Unquestioning personal loyalty to him and to his administration was something Cole felt strongly about, and faculty who fell short ran the risk of having the question of loyalty raised in confidential letters of recommendation, even if it did not lead to actual forced termination of services.[31]

Nowhere was the double standard applied to men and women more evident than in the area of housing. Male faculty were allocated houses for themselves and their families. Women were required to live in the dormitories, where they served as supervisor of a floor or administrative head of the house, fulfilling as well the function of social adviser, role model, and confidante that had been regarded as one of the strong points of Seminary life. They ate in the dining rooms with the students, where they were required to host a table, carving and serving the chosen meat for the evening meal, a prospect that at least one new faculty member found far more daunting than the challenges of the classroom.[32]

While male faculty could live in their houses year round, women faculty had to vacate their lodgings during vacations, and were permitted to occupy their quarters only a couple of days before the students returned each fall. Thus every female member of the faculty had to have a readily available place to go at Thanksgiving, Christmas, spring break, and during the summer. For most this meant, of course, either returning to the parental home, or finding a brother or sister willing to provide accommodations. These policies were nothing more than a continuation of practices that had been followed since Wheaton opened its doors in 1834. But the addition of a contingent of male faculty during the College's first decade created and brought into focus discrepencies that would endure into the post World War II era, becoming an ever increasing source of irritation for women faculty, who chafed at the limited privacy and added duties and responsibilities that this system imposed upon them.[33]

Interestingly enough, religious persuasion rarely seems to have been a primary consideration in hiring faculty. Wheaton was officially nonsectarian in terms of student admissions; President Cole appears to have been equally open in terms of faculty recruitment. Only after a faculty member had been hired and appointment letters sent was a person asked to identify both religious affiliation and whether or not that included actual membership in a church. Helen Wieand Cole, aware of her husband's personal prejudices, was surprised when the President offered a midterm emergency fill-in position to a friend of hers from Bryn Mawr who was a Russian Jew. She was even more astounded when Cole, highly pleased with Lillian Soskin Rogers' work, subsequently offered her the position of department head for the following year and even offered a house so her husband could come and live in Norton too. "I was much amazed," wrote Mrs. Cole, "for I thought he would object to her race."[34]

For Cole, who was after all a Congregational minister, religion was a matter to be taken very seriously. But one also senses in his later years a growing impatience with the formal structure of organized denominational practice. Unwilling to attend the Norton Trinitarian Congregational Church because of its members' bitter hostility to the building of the College Chapel, Cole and his wife came to relish the summers, when the lack of services on campus meant that they did not have to attend church at all. Nor was Cole in step with Congregational thinking on other matters. Approached by a Reverend Warren Landers, who urged him to support an organized drive in favor of prohibition and to urge his faculty to do likewise, Cole replied that he would of course distribute the proffered enrollment cards to the faculty. However, he would not support the movement himself, for he believed that the enactment of prohibition would only lead to "evasion of the law and the fostering of a spirit that disregards law in general."[35] By taking this position, Cole put himself out of step with the army of clergy throughout America who supported prohibition, and also divorced himself from a principle that had been at the moral center of Eliza Baylies Wheaton's personal life and beliefs. At the same time, though never a political activist himself, Cole encouraged his wife in her active membership in the Women's Republican Group of Norton, and welcomed the national enfranchisement of women in the fall of 1920.[36]

The outbreak of war in Europe in 1914 appears to have passed almost unnoticed in terms of concerns or attitudes on the Wheaton campus. However, the sinking of the *Lusitania* in May, 1915, with the resultant loss of American lives, stirred considerable anti-German feelings on campus, sentiments that were clearly supported and even encouraged by the President. United States entry into the war in April, 1917, galvanized the College community to undertake a wide range of war-supportive activities. The dining hall scrupulously observed the nationally recommended "two wheatless and two meatless days" per week. Red Cross courses in first aid, elementary hygiene, and home care of the sick were provided on campus, and noncredit courses in stenography and typewriting were offered through the College's Bureau of Vocational Opportunities. Slings, bandages and other items were made in workshops; wool distributed by the Red Cross was returned in the form of countless sweaters and stockings knit by students. Supported by financial contributions from their compatriots, a group of students created and staged three musical and dramatic productions as part of the entertainment program at Camp Devens in central Massachusetts.[37]

Cash donations from the Wheaton community totalled over $1000 to the Red Cross, and $2235 to the Students' Friendship War Relief Fund. During three days in November, 1918, exhilarated both by news of the armistice and the presence of a combat-wounded British army major who was touring college campuses on behalf of the United War Work Fund, students and faculty contributed nearly $2700 to that cause. In addition, the Wheaton community subscribed to more than $40,000 in Liberty Loan Bonds.[38]

At the urging of and in cooperation with the Federal government, a series of ten lectures open to the general public was presented on campus. Five of these dealt with the economic condition of the country, while the other five focussed on issues relating to food conservation and preservation. All-college forums were regularly held to discuss the latest war developments. At the suggestion of the United States Food Administration, materials provided by it were incorporated into courses already offered by the domestic science program, and a new household economics course was added to the curriculum. The College took particular pride in the fifteen former students and alumnae who were serving in some support capacity, usually nursing, in France.[39]

Perhaps the most bizarre initiative undertaken by the College community as a whole was a resolution passed in a community meeting on May 28, 1918, to urge the President of the United States and the Massachusetts congressional delegation to support legislation imposing "complete prohibition during the period of the war and of the subsequent demobilization."[40] Such action, it was argued, would free 289,000 men for jobs in other industries, create available grain supplies sufficient to furnish bread for 3,000,000 men, and render some 3,200,000 tons of coal available for other purposes.

Availability of coal was of particular great concern to President Cole. In February, 1918, coal supplies in New England were at an all-time low, and the allocation of what little was available lay in the hands of a federal fuel administrator. At the beginning of the month the College had only a two-week supply. As a conservation measure the heat was initially turned off in the Chapel, but this brought an urgent warning from the firm which had recently installed the new organ. It was imperative, Hook and Hastings wrote, that there be both heat and air circulation in the building to prevent the reeds from corroding and other parts from rusting.[41]

By February 28, the College's coal supply was exhausted. "We have no coal," Mrs. Cole wrote to her father, "and are apprehensive, for it is hard to get wood and the mouth of the furnace in the power-house is wide and cavernous. No help is in sight, so if a cold wave comes upon us we may have to have our spring recess early."[42] Two weeks later the President wrote to Kate Upson Clark, "For nearly two weeks we have had to depend on green wood, but owing to the difficulty of finding choppers we must soon get some coal or close the doors. I have sent an urgent appeal to Mr. Storrow, the fuel administrator for New England, and I hope it will bring some result."[43]

Indeed it did, and the immediate crisis was resolved, but the scarcity of coal continued well into the post-war period. In March, 1920, Wheaton was forced to shut down all classroom buildings and the Chapel for a weekend, forcing the cancellation of Sunday church services, although a carload of coal was obtained from New Bedford in time to prevent any interruption of classes.[44]

But a shortage of heating fuel was not the only problem that President Cole faced as a result of the war. The military draft, plus a booming economy generated by the war effort, resulted in a shortage of reliable workers, both male and female, to serve as housemaids, cooks, or on the grounds and buildings crew. Workmen came one day and left the next, Mrs. Cole complained. "It is simply impossible to get a young woman for the wages we offer, even though I went up to eight dollars a week."[45]

Even more serious and frustrating was the loss of two male members of the faculty to the war effort. Dr. William Warren, who had headed the Chemistry department since 1912, was also a member of the military reserve. Called for active duty the day before the fall term opened in 1917, he was commissioned a captain, and served first in Georgia, then in Washington D.C., and finally as a research scientist in a laboratory

"Wheaton Clothes Line," 1914. The laundry was located in the Powerhouse, later to become known as the Doll's House.

investigating poison gasses in Paris. Dr. Arthur Klein, who had chaired the Department of History and Economics since its inception in 1915, left in January, 1918, to assume a military position connected with the Committee on Public Information in Washington. Although the trustees, at Cole's request, officially voted to grant faculty in government service a leave of absence, neither Warren or Klein returned to Wheaton, a blow to President Cole, who was actively trying to increase both the number of men and holders of the Ph.D. degree on the faculty.[46]

News of the Armistice prompted a 7:00 A.M. chapel service before breakfast on November 11, 1918. That was followed in the evening by a student torchlight parade to the hockey field in the Wheaton woods, where, according to Mrs. Cole, "they tormented an effigy of the Kaiser."[47] Overall the war had had minimal impact on the fortunes and well-being of the College, unlike President Cole's alma mater, Bowdoin, where, Mrs. Cole commented, Class Day in June, 1918, was "a forlorn occasion, as there were only seventeen out of a class of sixty there, the rest being in the service."[48]

In the fall of 1916, a member of the class of 1918, Catherine Filene, approached the Wheaton administration with the proposal that Wheaton host a conference dealing with vocational opportunities for college women. Daughter of the owner of one of Boston's largest and most prestigious department stores, Miss Filene was backed by the willingness of her father to contribute $500 to the college for the purpose of financing this project. Permission was readily granted, and in February, 1917, the first intercollegiate Women's Vocational Conference was held at Wheaton. The program and arrangements were undertaken by a committee of the Alumnae Association, chaired by Catherine Filene despite the fact that she would not graduate for another year and a half. Invitations were sent to colleges east of the Mississippi, and some twenty responded by sending delegates. For two days an impressive program of distinguished speakers, drawn primarily from the Boston/New York area discussed a wide range of professional, business, and community service options for women.[49]

So successful was this program that a second conference was held a year later, in March, 1918, again with financial support from the Filene family. This time over thirty colleges attended, and the proceedings were published in the May, 1918, issue of *Education*. As a result, the organizing committee received commendatory letters and requests for information from across the United States and from England.[50]

But the very success of the program, and the evident interest on the part of many colleges in pursuing this endeavor, meant that the movement rather quickly outgrew Wheaton's capacity to organize and sponsor it. At the 1918 conference an informal Intercollegiate Vocational Guidance Association was created, with representatives of Smith, Radcliffe and Wheaton designated to serve on the Executive Committee. The 1919 conference, held at Radcliffe, resulted in the expansion of the organization, with forty-three institutions assuming formal membership. The purpose of this Association, according to its new constitution, was "to facilitate the interchange of vocational information; to hold an annual conference on vocational subjects of interest to college women; to study vocational opportunities for college women; and to further the cooperation of appointment bureaus and students."[51] By the spring of 1920, when the next conference was held at Cornell, membership had grown to fifty colleges and universities. As the Association grew, however, Wheaton's role declined, nor did it much benefit Wheaton students, especially as the annual conferences, held now at large universities with appropriate facilities, moved farther away from Norton.[52]

For Wheaton, the most immediate impact of the vocational conferences was the creation on campus in the spring of 1917 of the Bureau of Vocational Opportunities, a student-run organization limited primarily to dispensing information and material relating to jobs and careers for college women. The Bureau was headed by Catherine Filene until her graduation in June, 1918. Under the auspices of the Bureau a series of lectures on career opportunities was established in addition to an annual on-campus vocational conference open only to Wheaton students.[53]

Although Catherine Filene left Wheaton after graduation for a position as special agent in the Employment Service of the Federal Department of Labor, she continued to serve as official, though off-campus, vocational adviser until 1924. As such she played a major role in the activities of the Bureau of Vocational Opportunities. Not only was she influential enough to be able to obtain speakers such as Mary Anderson of the Children's Bureau in Washington and Helen Bennett of the Chicago Bureau of Operations, but, as Mrs. Cole noted to her sister, "she probably foots the bill too."[54]

In the fall of 1922, recognizing that the work of the Bureau of Vocational Opportunities was not in itself enough to gain entry for Wheaton graduates in the job market, Cole approved the establishment of an Appointments Bureau which would serve both seniors and alumnae seeking job placements. Administration of the the Bureau, which became operational in 1924–25, was allocated to the Alumnae Office. In 1927, having lost the direct guidance and support of Catherine Filene, the student-run Bureau of Vocational Opportunities voted to merge with the Appointments Bureau. From that time forward all matters connected with vocational information and job placement were placed under the supervision

Flanked here by two undergraduate members of her staff, Catherine Filene (W1918) founded and headed the Bureau of Vocational Opportunities. In later years Catherine Filene Shouse donated the land for and became the chief benefactor of the Wolf Trap Farm Park for the Performing Arts, located in Vienna, VA, outside of Washington D.C.

of the Alumnae Secretary, and Wheaton's efforts to find career placements for its graduates became similar to those of other institutions.[55]

But the College's pioneering role in hosting the first-in-the-nation intercollegiate conferences on vocational opportunities for college women should not be overlooked. Nor should the fact that it was done with the full support of the same president who, a decade earlier, had sought to distinguish Wheaton's mission from that of other colleges for women through his emphasis on the "home" and the preparation of women for their lives within it.

By 1921–22, admission to the College as a student could be achieved in a wide variety of ways. Those who had attended a school on a list approved either by Wheaton, the College Entrance Examination Board, or one of a number of state or regional accrediting agencies, could submit a certificate attesting to courses successfully completed. Students could also take a series of subject examinations offered by the College Entrance Examination Board. These in turn could be supplemented or replaced by examinations given by Wheaton in September just prior to the opening of college. A further alternative lay in taking four broad comprehensive examinations in English, a foreign language, biology or physics or chemistry, and one from a wide range of elective topics. These again could be administered either through the auspices of the College Entrance Examination Board or at Wheaton just prior to matriculation. Students who failed to satisfy all of the prescribed entrance requirements were often admitted with a "condition" in one or two subjects, which had to be removed by passing an examination at a later date before college credit for courses in that area could be granted. Designed to provide various means of gaining entrance and to account for the wide varieties of candidates' preparation, often in school systems unknown to the College, the hurdles of the admission process today seem daunting, to say the least.[56]

Once enrolled, students chose one of several four-year curriculum tracks, referred to as "groups." In 1913–14 these consisted of Latin, Modern Languages, English, History, Art, Biology-Chemistry, and Chemistry-Physics-Mathematics. Within a year the Art Group had disappeared and been replaced by Philosophy. By 1919–20, the options had increased to nine, with the separation of Mathematics and the three sciences into individual categories. Incorporated in each of these curriculum groupings were basic requirements common to all of them, including at least one course in English, French or German, Latin, Biblical Literature, History, History of Art, Household Economics, Psychology and Ethics, and Biology, Chemistry or Physics. By 1922, courses were also offered as electives in Studio Art, Astronomy, Economics, Sociology, Greek, Italian, Music (both theoretical and practical), and Spanish. Programs in "Physical Training" were required of freshman and sophomores and were available as options for juniors and seniors. Attendance at noncredit lecture "courses" presented on American Citizenship, Business Law, and two dealing with Hygiene was required of all students.[57]

The Hygiene courses deserve a word of comment. Personal Hygiene, required of freshmen and sophomores, was a conventional course in personal cleanliness, exercise and first aid. But the course on Public Hygiene, mandated for upperclass women, dealt with health issues relating to the community, ranging from sewage and water supplies to foods and public conveyances. It also included a section on sex hygiene, including material on birth control and abortion. In providing such information the College was backed by the Federal Government, which in 1919, prompted by its success in instructing men on sex hygiene and regulating houses of prostitution during World War I, urged the YWCA to send lecturers to colleges and schools to instruct women on "such knowledge as will both help them to take better care of themselves and to help their brothers."[58]

Another unique aspect of Wheaton's curriculum was the inclusion from 1912 on of credit courses in Sociology. This was undoubtedly due to the presence on campus of William I. Cole, the President's brother, who came to Wheaton from years of work at the South End Settlement House in Boston. At that time Sociology was a new discipline, offered at only a few educational institutions and generally looked at askance by the majority of New England colleges and universities. In fact, many of the most prestigious New England liberal arts colleges did not begin to offer courses in this field until well after World War II. Wheaton, more by accident than design, became a front-runner in the development of Sociology as an academic discipline.

Not all subjects prospered equally as a result of the transition to a college curriculum. Art, which was initially included as one of the concentration groups, was quickly downgraded to elective status. President Cole commented in January, 1917, that the number of music pupils had declined greatly. "College students as a rule, whether elsewhere or at Wheaton, give less time to music than the seminary girls used to do."[59]

Initially, although faculty were required to turn in numerical grades for students in their courses, satisfactory work was recorded by the Registrar with a grade of either Pass or Credit; in 1916 the designation High Credit was added. At least half of the required sixty units for graduation needed to be above the Pass level.[60] Unsatisfactory work was designated by the terms Condition or Failure; those receiving a Condition were given the opportunity to remove it by passing a special examination given at the end of each semester or at the opening of college in September. Entering students who were classified as deficient in a specific subject area were also required to remove this "condition" through special examination by the end of their first year in order to gain promotion to sophomore status.[61]

During the College's first two years of operation, classes were held all day on Monday, Tuesday, Thursday, Friday and Saturday, with no academic meetings on Wednesday. However, beginning in September, 1914, Wheaton turned to a five-and-one-half day schedule with classes ending at noon on Saturday, a change that met with overwhelming approval from both students and faculty, and which remained in place for nearly fifty years.[62]

Throughout the College's first decade the issue of student housing was of constant concern. In the early years the problem was one of finding suitable ways to group students in the various degree programs. In 1912–13, those in the college program were placed together on one floor in Chapin, but by the next year their numbers had increased sufficiently for all of Larcom to be designated for them. Subsequently, as the Seminary and Associate programs were phased out, students were assigned to the various residence halls on the basis of their class. It was only in the fall of 1922 that spaces for members of all four classes were reserved in each residence hall.[63]

As Wheaton continued to grow, issues of space became of preeminent concern. Frame houses originally intended for male faculty and their families were pressed into service as dormitories. Late but admissable applicants, or those with "conditions" attached to their admission, at times were housed in the infirmary during the first weeks of the fall semester, and assigned eventually to fill the spaces created by the inevitable withdrawal of some students in the first days of the college year. So critical did the space issue become that on several occasions Mrs. Cole made plans to house several students temporarily in the President's House, though this never actually proved to be necessary.[64]

Applicants for admission who were deemed unprepared in more than one area were sometimes allowed to come to Norton in September to try to remove these "conditions" through special examination. They did so at their own risk, for the College would not admit or reserve a dormitory space for applicants with more than one entrance condition. Even if they succeeded in removing all, or all but one condition, these students were admitted officially only if a space in a dormitory became available because of student attrition in the first couple of weeks of classes.[65]

Exacerbating the housing crisis was the lack of an option employed regularly by both Smith and Wellesley during their formative years. Both of these institutions made extensive use of private accommodations available in the towns of Northampton and Wellesley; in 1917 more than

55 percent of Smith's two thousand students resided in college-approved off-campus boardinghouses. "Conditions in Norton," wrote President Cole, "are such that all our students must live in dormitories and houses of the college."[66] Moreover, student use of college-owned off-campus houses prevented these facilities from being available for their intended purpose. "We are debarred," Cole complained, "from adding more men to our faculty until we can provide houses for them to live in."[67]

The result was the erection of a new dormitory, named after the last principal of the Seminary, Ellen Stanton, which was dedicated in May, 1921. But that was not enough. Pointing to the need to remove students from smaller frame houses, and to the disrepair of Metcalf Hall, the rambling wooden dormitory and administration center whose oldest section had been constructed in the 1830s, Cole in 1922 outlined the need for a new dormitory which would house twice the usual number of students, along with the erection of a separate administration building. The strain that such construction would place on the College, which had recently completed the new Chapel, had commenced building a new library, and would soon need a new powerhouse, was readily apparent, especially in light of the total failure of the $1,000,000 capital campaign.[68]

Approximately half of the three hundred students enrolled at the end of the College's first decade were drawn from Massachusetts. Maine was a distant second, followed by the rest of the New England states, New York and New Jersey. Other states were represented sporadically and rarely with more than five persons. An occasional foreign student from China, Japan, Turkey or elsewhere made her appearance. A wide variety of religious preferences was represented, including both Catholic and Jewish students, but 36 percent indicated that they were Congregationalists.[69]

Of the nine curricular groups from which students chose an area of concentration, two-thirds selected English. About twenty-five students received scholarships ranging from $50 to $200, while ninety were able to earn various amounts of money in the College's self-help work program. But the lack of funds for scholarships and for the establishment of a student loan fund was a major concern for President Cole.[70]

Much of the food consumed in the dining halls was produced on the College farm. Wheaton maintained its own poultry barn, from which both chickens and eggs emanated for College use. A specially constructed root cellar provided cold storage for a year's supply of apples, potatoes, cabbages, carrots, beets, and onions. Milk was purchased from the dairy farm run by the House in the Pines School. When the College loaned House in the Pines $3000 in 1919, the loan was secured by twelve of the Pines' cows, each valued at $250.[71]

The appointment of Edith Lincoln to head the Domestic Services Department in the fall of 1921 proved to be the most long-lived of any made by President Cole, other than that of Registrar Sarah Belle Young. For the next 29 years Miss Lincoln presided over the dining halls, determining the menus, and personally journeying to Boston to purchase the food needed from the various Fanieul Hall markets. Years later, recalling President Cole's methods of hiring female staff members, she commented that he would often interview persons at his home on Saturday afternoon and evening. This enabled him to see "whether, when you took off your gloves, you were wearing an engagement ring and to get a view of you minus your hat. Then, if you didn't eat the Saturday night beans with your knife, and said you were a Congregationalist, you were as good as hired."[72]

Social and extracurricular life at the new College continued much in the way it had existed during the latter years of the Seminary. As was the case at other women's colleges, myriad rules and regulations governed the lives of the young women attending Wheaton, with freshmen restricted even more by various rules of behavior imposed by upperclasswomen. Students were required to turn their lights out at 10 P.M., though four exceptions for study purposes were allowed each month. For every unexcused class absence a secret fixed percent known only to the Registrar was deducted from the final numerical course grade submitted by the instructor; the penalty was doubled for absences immediately before or after holidays. Attendance at chapel services during the week, and church and vespers on Sunday, was mandatory.

The presence of young men at campus events was carefully regulated, though as the decade progressed rules relating to individual dating were gradually relaxed. There were a few formal dances, of which by far the

Dinner in Emerson Dining Hall, 1914.

Junior Prom, 1915, held in the Gymnasium.

most important was the Junior Promenade. To style one's hair in bangs was considered the height of daring. While the College did not permit students to have cars on campus, rules concerning "motoring" with others were continually being changed and revised.[73]

Students were allowed to leave campus during the day, or go home on weekends, but were required to register their names whenever they left, if only to walk or shop in Norton. In October, 1920, Mrs. Cole wrote to her sister that the Chapel had seemed full for Sunday services, despite

For generations of Seminary and College students the Norton Railway Station, located one mile east of the campus, provided frequent rail access to Boston, Fall River, New Bedford, Providence, and New York.

the fact the one hundred girls were away from campus for the weekend. Evidently the "suitcase college syndrome" as it would later become known among all women's colleges, was already becoming a problem, so much so that in 1921 President Cole asked the faculty to help persuade students to remain on campus during weekends so that they could discover that "there is much of value in college leisure."[74]

Sororities were banned, but a wide range of clubs with an ostensible academic purpose existed, as well as the Young Women's Christian Association and its off-shoot, the "Sub-Settlement Chapter," whose function was to promote community service activities by Wheaton students in Norton and surrounding communities. "State" clubs for students from a specific state or general region were popular, purely social organizations. A Chapel Choir, Glee Club, and an instrumental organization known as the Mandolin Club all thrived. The Athletic Association provided the structure for both varsity and intramural athletic activities. Students were limited in the number of offices they could hold in various campus organizations by a point system that assigned a value to every position and then imposed a maximum total beyond which a student could not go.[75]

One major issue of national import for women seems to have aroused little active interest and concern on the Wheaton campus. Despite the fact that the constitutional amendment giving women the right to vote was ratified during these years, there is no indication that Wheaton stu-

Mandolin Club, 1915.

dents were particularly interested or participant in the rallies and demonstrations that preceded final ratification. The *Wheaton Record* did note on one of its back pages in November, 1920, that Wheaton students who were twenty-one had gone to the Norton Town Hall to register to vote, but overall this issue seems to have created little stir on campus.[76]

In 1916 an epidemic of infantile paralysis swept the nation, followed in 1918 and again in 1919 by widespread and deadly attacks of influenza. Although Wheaton decided to delay its fall opening by two weeks in 1916, the College completely escaped the outbreak of polio, and emerged relatively unscathed from the ravages of the influenza epidemics that claimed so many lives across the nation. At its peak in October, 1918, the College recorded fifty cases of influenza, but none proved serious. Despite the severe ravages of the disease felt in the surrounding communities of Attleboro, Taunton, and Brockton, Wheaton managed to isolate itself effectively by restricting student travel and cancelling public events.[77]

With the opening of the Chapel and its availability for all-college events, a number of new practices developed that were to become Wheaton traditions. In 1916, the custom of a recurring cycle of four class colors was first adopted. Initially these were red, yellow, green, and purple, but the purple was subsequently changed to light blue. The Class of 1918 was the first to use the symbol of Pegasus, and the first to hold commencement in the Chapel. The symbol of Pan was appropriated by the Class of 1919. In 1920 the seniors, with the permission of the Class of 1918, also adopted Pegasus, thus putting into motion the alternating class symbols that became, like the class colors, a permanent part of Wheaton tradition.[78] Beginning in 1918, class rings, which until then had been designed every year by the class that would wear them, became regularized, with the symbols of Pan and Pegasus alternating in successive years.[79]

The annual May Day pageant, which dated from Seminary days, proved to be an ever more popular public event. In 1921, President Cole reported in some amazement to Kate Upson Clark that it had attracted some six to eight hundred guests and approximately one hundred cars.[80] Dramatic productions, often very elaborate in their costuming and sets, were produced annually by each of the four classes.

One tradition that proved to be relatively short-lived was that of the senior class serenading every residence hall at 5:00 A.M. on the morning of the final day of classes before the Christmas recess. "They were all carrying candles, dressed in white, and in the bright moonlight it looked very lovely," Mrs. Cole wrote to her sister.[81] The practice was repeated the night before the Easter vacation break, with Easter hymns substituted for Christmas carols.

Of all the various extracurricular clubs and organizations, perhaps the one that assumed the greatest importance was the Athletic Association.

Senior Play, "The Chinese Lantern," 1921.

Under its auspices varsity teams in tennis, basketball, and field hockey were formed to compete against Radcliffe, Pembroke, and the Sargent Normal School of Physical Training in Boston. Victories over both Sargent and Radcliffe in field hockey in 1920 and 1921 engendered enormous excitement on campus. Even more important were the numerous class teams in a wide variety of sports ranging from baseball and soccer to archery, along with intramural competition between dormitories in sports such as touchball and volleyball. A hiking club, formed in 1916, proved quite popular. In addition the Athletic Association was responsible for staging the May Day Pageant. A show sponsored by the Athletic Association known as *Vaudeville*, consisting of student-written and performed songs, dances and comedy skits, emerged on the scene and quickly became an eagerly anticipated annual event. *Vaudeville*, for which an admission charge was allowed, proved to be the Association's biggest fundraising event.[82]

All students were required to take four years of physical education, or "physical training" as it was called until 1921–22. This included required courses in "apparatus work, vaulting, jumping, running, marching tactics, folk dancing, and games" during the freshman and sophomore years, plus mandatory swimming instruction. A total of four hours per week in physical training was required, with at least two of them outdoors, no matter the season of the year.[83]

Of all the physical education requirements, the only one that seems to have engendered considerable student complaint was the swimming program. The reason for this was clearly the pool, which though new in 1913 proved to be neither appealing nor adequate. Measuring only 12 by 36 feet, the water initially was changed only twice a year, creating a situation so unpleasant that Pearl Wallis, the Director of Physical Education, commented that she "could not blame the students for not wanting to go in." By 1921–22 the water was being changed four or five times a year, still "not nearly enough to be sanitary."[84]

The advent of the first college classes in the fall of 1912 brought the November formation of a Student Government Association. The organization was empowered to "control registration, church and chapel attendance, chaperonage, the maintenance of order and quiet in the halls and on the campus, in fact, all matters concerning the conduct of the students and all matters that are not strictly academic."[85] To this was subsequently added the organization and running of fire drills.[86]

However, the Student Government Association was not the preeminent undergraduate organization during Wheaton's first college decade that it became in later years. Rather it was seen as one of many campus organizations, rivaled in particular for popularity and influence by the Young Women's Christian Association and the Athletic Association. Only in 1922–23 did a restructured College Government Association absorb all student-run campus organizations within its constitutional framework.[87]

∞

For many years the leaders of the Young Womens Christian Association campus organizations from several colleges gathered each fall prior to the opening of college for a retreat at Silver Bay on Lake George in upstate New York. This is the Wheaton contingent, 1921.

As Wheaton celebrated the close of its first decade as a four-year college, the on-going members of the community—teaching, administrative, trustee, or alumnae—could take considerable pride in what had been achieved. An impressive campus, consisting primarily of new facilities, a remolded faculty, and an expanded administration all provided solid support for a student body rapidly approaching four hundred. True, relations with officials and citizens of the town of Norton had worsened considerably, but this seemed a price which, if unfortunate, was well worth paying. From all outward signs, the College was prospering and moving steadily forward toward bigger and better things.

Only for those intimately familiar with Wheaton's financial situation did the College's future existence seem precarious. Because of rampant inflation and a high institutional draw on generated income, the real value of the small Wheaton family legacy that served as invested endowment had declined substantially. This, coupled with the failure of the relatively modest $1,000,000 capital campaign, had created a financial situation which the President and others regarded as severe enough to threaten the very survival of the College. Openly envious of the endowment strength and fundraising success of many of the independent and coordinate women's colleges, Cole could not help but give vent to his frustration in his 1920–1921 *President's Report*:

> I cannot believe that the earnest effort expended during these years to make Wheaton College what it has become must finally go for nothing; that at the very moment when the battle is won and there emerges the opportunity for which we strove—I cannot believe, I say, that at this critical moment of decision the people who should be most interested will allow the splendid opportunity for perpetual service of the noblest kind, such as this college represents, to pass and be lost forever through lack of appreciation and cooperative support.[88]

NOTES: CHAPTER 10

1. Faculty: Everett: Mead to SVC, 3/03/03; Notes to Bowdoin Trustees, n.d.; see also ch. 6.

2. Wheaton Female Seminary, *Annual Catalogue,* 1907–13; *Wheaton Female Seminary, Trustees, Faculty, Students, 1834–1912;* Wheaton College, *Catalogue of Officers and Students,* 1912–29.

3. *Wheaton College Bulletin: Catalogue and Announcements,* 1912–24; Wheaton College: *Catalogue of Officers and Students,* 1912–24.

4. Trustee Minutes: 6/12/16; SVC, *President's Report, 1912–1913,* pp. 29–30.

5. See Staff: Arthur Cutler, 1921.

6. SVC, *President's Report, 1914–1915,* p. 16.

7. HWC, Letters to Family: to Sister, 4/24, 28, 29/19; 5/18/20; 6/6/20; to Family, 9/9/17; 1/3/18. "Brother William" also at times presented a problem for Mrs. Cole, who described him in 1918 as conceited, and concerned only with "his own sweet comfort." to Family, 11/17/18.

8. Ibid.: to Family, 9/9/17.

9. Ibid., 9/20/17.

10. Ibid., 10/15/17.

11. Ibid.

12. Ibid., 9/9/17; see also 2/24/18.

13. Ibid., 6/13/19; also 1/4/18; 2/2/18; to Sister, 10/30/19; 1/18/20; 10/31/20.

14. Ibid.: to Family, 8/4/18.

15. Faculty: Kerr: HWC to Kerr, 3/23/21; 4/7,15/21; 6/8,21/21; Kerr to HWC, 4/11/21; 6/10,26/21; SVC to Kerr, 4/26/21; HWC, Letters to Family: to Sister, 3/24,27/21; 4/5/21; travel letters, July, 1923.

16. HWC, Letters to Family: to Sister, 9/13/21.

17. Ibid., 8/3/21; see also Faculty: Lange: Correspondence with HWC, spring, 1921.

18. Faculty: Kerr: HWC to Kerr, 4/15/21; HWC, Letters to Family: to Sister, 9/12/20; 11/21/21; 11/9,17/24; to Family, 7/31/18; see also J. Garraty, *Henry Cabot Lodge: A Biography* (New York: A. A. Knopf, 1953), p. 423. President Cole also suffered occasionally from bouts with rheumatism and sciatica. See HWC, Letters to Family: to Sister, 4/10/19; 2/13/21; 12/23/21.

19. HWC, Letters to Family: to Sister, 11/21/21.

20. Ibid., 12/14/19.

21. Trustees: Kilham #3: SVC to Kilham, 4/30/21; see also HWC, Letters to Family: to Sister, 9/16/21.

22. HWC, Letters to Family: to Sister, 9/19/21; Trustees Minutes: 6/13/21.

23. Faculty: West: SVC to West, 5/29/19; McIntire: passim; W. Warren: passim.

24. Ibid.: Richards: SVC to Richards, 10/27/14; 11/17/14; Manning: SVC to Young-Fulton, 7/15/21; Lundin: Lundin to SVC, 1/29/18; SVC to Lundin, 1/31/18; M. Fraser: Summer 1918, passim; Kennedy: SVC to R. Woods, 7/7/14; SVC to Kennedy, 4/20/14; SVC, *President's Report, 1913–1914*, p. 13; *1914–1915*, pp. 16–17.

25. See salary scale in Trustees Minutes, 11/26/18. Mrs. Cole commented that getting Wheaton recognized by the AAUW (American Association of University Women) was problematic, "for there are some requirements, like equal salaries for men and women, which S.V. does not meet." HWC, Letters to Family: to Sister, 5/23/22.

26. SVC, *President's Report, 1915–1916*, p. 21; *1918–1919*, pp. 37–38; *1921–1922*, pp. 53, 56; Trustees Minutes: 11/26/18; 11/25/19; 3/10/20; 9/22/21; Faculty: Rice: 5/16/22. In November 1918, President Cole's salary was increased from $4000 to $4400, plus the use of the President's House.

27. Faculty: Converse: SVC letter of recommendation, 5/20/12; Goodrich: passim.

28. Ibid.: Lange: SVC to Lange, 5/18/21; Trustees Minutes: 3/13/19; 3/16/21.

29. L. Pollard, *Women on College and University Faculties: A Historical Survey and a Study of Their Present Academic Status* (New York: Arno Press, 1977), pp. 158–160; Woody, *Women's Education*, 2: pp. 337–38; Wheaton College, *Catalogue of Officers and Students*, 1912–13; 1921–22; For an example of the difficulty Cole had in finding persons with the Ph.D. to fill faculty positions, see Faculty: Manning: SVC to Manning, 6/30/21.

30. Faculty: Fergus: SVC to Fergus, 6/21/13; see also Richards: Klein to SVC, 2/7/18.

31. Ibid.: W. Warren: SVC to Harvard Appointment Bureau, 1919; see also HWC, Letters to Family: to Family, 3/8/18.

32. Faculty: Manning: Manning to HWC, 8/2/21; HWC to Manning, 8/4/21.

33. Ibid.: Wallis: S. B. Young to Wallis, 9/10/19; Metivier: Metivier to HWC, 7/29/21; Shook: Shook to SVC, 7/3/18; Manning: Manning to HWC, 9/6/21.

34. HWC, Letters to Family: to Family, 4/13/18; to Father, 3/13/18. Mrs. Rogers

accepted, only to be replaced a year later by Allen West, who had the Ph.D. that Mrs. Rogers did not.

35. SVC: Personal Correspondence: SVC to Landers, 2/2/18.

36. HWC, Letters to Family: to Sister, 9/12/20; 10/31/20.

37. SVC, *President's Report, 1918–1919*, pp. 24–27; Wheaton Histories, Wheaton in World Wars I & II: World War I, 1913–16; 1917; 1918; General Files: Class of 1918.

38. SVC, *President's Report, 1918–1919*, pp. 26–27; Wheaton Histories, Wheaton in World Wars I & II: World War I, 1917; HWC, Letters to Family; to Family, 11/17/18.

39. SVC, *President's Report, 1918–1919*, pp. 25–27; Wheaton Histories, Wheaton in World Wars I & II: World War I, 1917: SVC to Warren, 12/10/17; Academic Council Minutes: 2/14/18; General Files: Class of 1914: Grace Marling.

40. Wheaton Histories, Wheaton in World Wars I & II: World War I, 1918.

41. Trustees, 1834–1910: K. U. Clark #2: SVC to Clark, 2/4/18; Bursar's Office Correspondence, 1889–1940: #7, Hook & Hastings, 1910–1920: Hook and Hastings to Bursar, 2/5/18.

42. HWC, Letters to Family: to Father, 2/28/18.

43. Trustees, 1834–1910: K. U. Clark #2: SVC to Clark, 3/12/18.

44. HWC, Letters to Family: to Sister, 3/7/20.

45. This cash wage would, of course, be in addition to room and board. HWC, Letters to Family: to Family, 5/21/18, 9/18/19.

46. Wheaton Histories, Wheaton in World Wars I & II: World War I, 1918; Trustees, 1834–1910: Curtis: SVC to Curtis, 9/24/17; Faculty: W. Warren: Warren to SVC, 11/29/17; SVC to Warren, 8/8/18; Warren to SVC, 8/13/18; SVC to Warren, 8/17/18; A. Klein: passim; B. Jennings, *Chemistry at Wheaton* (Plymouth, MA: Jones River Press, 1999), pp. 31–32; SVC, *President's Report, 1918–1919*, p. 11.

47. HWC, Letters to Family: to Family, 11/17/18.

48. Ibid., 6/23/18.

49. Much of the information in this section was compiled by Rachael Class-Giguere (W1991), who served as the author's research assistant in the summer of 1990. See SVC, *President's Report, 1918–1919*, pp. 21–23; Vocational Conference 1917–1952: Vocational Conferences, 1917–1926; Trustees Minutes: 12/15/16; 3/22/17; Shepard, "Reference History," pp. 434–435; Oral History Project: C. Filene Shouse interview, 1983.

50. SVC, *Presidents Report, 1918–1919*, p. 23; Trustees Minutes: 3/15/18.

51. As quoted in Woody, *Women's Education*, 2: p. 212.

52. C. Filene, ed., *Careers for Women* (1920, reprinted Boston: Houghton Mifflin, 1924), p. vi; SVC, *President's Report, 1918–1919*, p. 23; Trustees Minutes: 3/13/19; General Files: 1917–18: C. Filene Shouse, Vocational conferences, 1917–18.

53. Alumnae Affairs Office, 50: Wheaton Bureau of Vocational Opportunities; General Files: 1917–18; Wheaton College, *Catalogue of Officers and Students, 1912–29.*

54. HWC, Letters to Family: to Sister, 3/8/22.

55. SVC, *Presidents's Report 1921–1922*, pp. 27–28; *Wheaton News*, 2/21/25; *Wheaton Alumnae News*, 5:1 (December, 1925), p. 7; *Wheaton Alumnae Quarterly*, 6:3 (May, 1927), p. 17.

56. Faculty: Shook: S. B. Young to Shook, 7/26/22; HWC, Letters to Family: to Family, 8/17/19; *Wheaton College Bulletin: Catalogue and Announcements, 1920–1921.*

57. Curriculum: Group System, 1914–28; Faculty Meeting Minutes: 5/2/14; *Wheaton College Bulletin: Catalogue and Announcements, 1912–22.*

58. HWC, Letters to Family: to Sister, 11/21/19; see also Faculty: Dr. M. Southard: Course outline for Public Hygiene lectures.

59. Faculty: Bagg: SVC to Bagg, 1/4/17.

60. A year course, meeting three times a week for fifty minutes, was worth three "units." A normal student course load for a year was fifteen units.

61. Faculty Meeting Minutes: 12/5/13; Academic Council Minutes: 12/19/16; SVC, *President's Report, 1921–1922,* p. 19.

62. SVC, *President's Report, 1913–1914,* p. 43; Wheaton College Handbook, 1912–26, passim in Wheaton College Handbook. The College abandoned Saturday classes and moved to a five-day class schedule in 1961–62.

63. *Wheaton News,* 10/10/22; SVC, *President's Report, 1912–1913,* p. 22.

64. HWC, Letters to Family: to Sister, 4/29/20; 5/23/20; 9/15/20.

65. See Faculty: Shook: S. B. Young to Shook, 7/26/22; Trustees 1834–1910: K. U. Clark #3: Young to Clark, 5/13/21; Kilham #3: SVC to Kilham, 9/16/22.

66. SVC, *President's Report, 1921–1922,* p. 48.

67. Ibid.; see also Thorp, *Neilson of Smith,* p. 255; H. Horowitz, *Alma Mater: Design and Experience in the Women's Colleges from their Nineteeth Century Beginnings to the 1930s,* 2nd ed. (Amherst, MA: University of Massachusetts Press, 1993), pp. 308–10.

68. SVC, *President's Report, 1921–1922,* pp. 46–49, 55–56. The basement of Stanton dormitory was used to feed overflow students from Emerson dining room until a second dining facility was built as part of the construction of Everett dormitory in 1925.

69. SVC, *President's Report, 1921–1922,* pp. 20–21.

70. The employment of student waitresses in the dining hall was begun as "an experiment" in September, 1917. Academic Council Minutes, 9/18/17; SVC, *President's Report, 1921–1922,* pp. 21–22, 55–56; Bursar's Office Correspondence 1889–1940: #4l, Miscellaneous, 1920–30.

71. SVC, *President's Report, 1913–14,* pp. 18–19; Bursar's Office Correspondence 1889–1940: #3, Treasurers and Miscellaneous, 1910–20: Wheaton College Farm, Income and Expense, 7/l/18–11/1/18; #8, House In the Pines, 1910–20; #22, House in the Pines, 1920–30.

72. *Wheaton Alumnae Quarterly,* 30:3 (July, 1951), pp. 9–10, interview with E. Lincoln. Miss Lincoln estimated that she supervised the preparation and serving of 1,900,000 meals during her twenty-nine years at Wheaton.

73. Faculty Meeting Minutes: 2/26/14; Wheaton College, *Rules and Regulations,* 1912–1921, passim, in Wheaton College Handbook. Catherine Filene Shouse remembered that she was restricted to campus for a month because she went driving with a young man on Sunday in a convertible. Oral History Project: C. F. Shouse interview, 1983. See also Academic Council Minutes: 4/18/19; 4/25/19.

74. Academic Council Minutes: 9/13/21; General Files: Class of 1918, #1; HWC, Letters to Family: to Sister, 10/10/20; Clewes, *Wheaton, 1835–1960,* p. 12.

75. *Nike,* 1917; SVC, *President's Report, 1921–22,* p. 22; *Students' Handbook, 1919–1920,* in Wheaton College Handbook.

76. *Wheaton Record,* November, 1920, p. 8.

77. General Files: Class of 1917; SVC, *President's Report, 1918–1919,* pp. 17–18; HWC, Letters to Family: to Family, 10/2, 6/18; Trustees, 1834–1910: Hervey: SVC to Hervey, 9/18/16; K. U. Clark #2: SVC to Clark, 9/24/18; Academic Council Minutes: 10/11/16; 10/17/18; L. R. Shea, "Sudden, Swift, Silent, and Deadly—80 years ago, Flu ravaged New England," *Boston Sunday Globe,* 11/1/98.

78. Academic Council Minutes: 1/17/16; General Files: Class of 1918, #1, 2; Student Groups and Activities: Wheaton Traditions: *Wheaton Traditions.*

79. The earliest reference to class rings is found in the recollections of Emily Hartwell (WS1883). The three members of her graduating class designed a ring using the symbol of a triangle to cement their friendship. See Student Groups and Activities: Societies and Traditions: Rings.

80. Trustees 1834–1910: K. U. Clark #3: SVC to Clark, 5/24/21.

81. HWC, Letters to Family: to Sister, 12/19/18.

82. Ibid.: 4/16/20; 11/14/20; 11/90/21. For an in-depth discussion of physical education and athletics at Wheaton between 1912 and 1941, see the unpublished manuscript by Professor of History Emerita Nancy P. Norton, "Physical Education and Athletics at Wheaton: The College and the Intercollegiate Years, 1912–41." Begun in 1906, an early picture of *Vaudeville* shows the 1916 cast performing in blackface. In 1946 *Vaudeville* became *Vodvil*. See *Wheaton,* 1916; General Files: Class of 1919; HWC, Letters to Family: to Family, 11/21/18; *Nike,* 1946; *The Wheaton Bulletin,* 2:3 (June, 1906), p. 18.

83. *Wheaton College Bulletin: Catalogue and Announcements,* 1921–22, pp. 95–97.

84. SVC, *President's Report, 1912–1913,* p. 45; Wallis, Annual Reports, 1919–1920, 1921–1922, as quoted by Norton, "Physical Education and Athletics, 1912–1941," p. 3; *Nike,* 1922, student biographies, passim; *Wheaton Record,* November, 1921, p. 19.

85. *Students' Handbook, 1914–15,* p. 6, in Wheaton College Handbook.

86. *Wheaton,* 1916; Faculty: W. Warren: Warren to SVC, 2/19/13; Shepard, "Reference History," p. 409; General Files: Class of 1918.

87. *Wheaton News,* 10/10/22; *Wheaton College Government Association, 1923,* in Wheaton College Handbook; *Nike,* 1923; Academic Council Minutes: 5/29/22.

88. SVC, *President's Report, 1920–1921,* p. 41.

11

Presidential Succession and Administrative Turmoil 1922–1930

Every college of serious aims, real service, and respectable standing follows a receding goal. No sooner is one thing achieved than something else appears on the horizon. . . . The college that does not constantly improve its methods, enlarge its opportunities, and meet the ever-changing conditions of life with the proper means, so far as they lie within its power, is no longer alive. Adaptability in ways and means with inflexibility in the one great and final purpose for which colleges exist, should be kept unfailingly in view. The work must go on forever.[1]

JUNE, 1922, SIGNIFIED the completion of twenty-five years of service by Samuel Valentine Cole as Wheaton's president. The goal that he and Eliza Baylies Wheaton had privately agreed upon before she suggested his name to the Board of Trustees in February, 1897, had been achieved. The transition from Seminary to College was complete; all vestiges of the former had been eliminated and a vibrant, expanding four-year college with an almost all-new campus stood in its place.[2]

Throughout the remainder of the 1920s, the themes of transition and change that had dominated Wheaton's first decade as a college were replaced by policies aimed more at completion and consolidation. By the midtwenties student enrollment approximated the five-hundred-level maximum that Cole had specified in his 1921–22 *President's Report*. The completion of the Library, the erection of an oversized "double-dormitory," and the building of a new powerhouse concluded construction of the self-contained residential college campus that had begun in 1901. No longer so concerned with filling beds, the College was able to turn its attention in the latter 1920s to issues of admissions standards, student quality, and curriculum improvement. The College's affairs, Cole could report to Trustee Kate Upson Clark in April, 1925, were going "wonderfully well. . . . Our problem just now is not how to get students, but how to keep them out and still seem gracious."[3]

Much of this was undoubtedly made possible by the dramatic general growth in the numbers of young men and women seeking a college education in the 1920s. The number of women enrolled in colleges nation-wide increased from 283,000 in 1919–20 to 480,000 in 1929–30, while the number of men went from 317,000 to 520,000. The percentage of women between the ages of eighteen and twenty-one who attended college increased from 3.8 percent in 1910 to 7.6 percent in 1920, and to 10.5 percent in 1930. While the vast majority of this expanded cohort matriculated at coed public institutions, the added numbers also increased the pressure for admission to the established private colleges for women, a situation which made it easier for newer and still growing institutions such as Wheaton to fulfill their expanded admissions goals.[4]

Even the College's financial situation seemed to improve considerably. The drain on annual revenue imposed by successive building projects subsided, and efficiencies of size began to have a favorable impact on operational costs. The trustees regularly approved increases in the comprehensive fee, which assured a positive revenue flow. While increased costs did create a larger number of requests for scholarship aid, the College was able to limit the number of students requiring such support to a relative few, though many more were able to help finance their college costs by engaging in one of the rapidly expanding number of available campus self-help jobs.

Although admissions issues, curriculum change, faculty development, fiscal constraints, and the attitudes and mores of the "flapper" generation all provided intriguing challenges during the years between 1922 and 1930, perhaps the events which had the greatest impact on the College occurred in the administrative sector. Of these, by far the most important was the sudden and unexpected death of President Cole in 1925, the resultant one-year interim administration of Trustee George Smart, and the installation and initial "shake-down" years of Wheaton's second president, John Edgar Park.

In December, 1921, Samuel Valentine Cole celebrated his seventieth birthday. Facing the likelihood of major surgery, and worn down from nearly twenty-five years as Wheaton's chief administrator, he began to talk privately about the possibility of retirement. Rumors that he was planning his retirement were rife among the faculty; in fact, as Helen Wieand Cole noted in a letter to her sister, many assumed that he was grooming her as his successor. While it seems evident that Mrs. Cole might well have responded positively to such an eventuality, there is no indication that she and Dr. Cole ever discussed it. But although Cole was determined to see his building program through to completion, he also began actively considering who should succeed him.[5]

One of the main reasons that the President became, over the next two years, increasingly concerned about his successor was his growing displeasure with the person he had selected to replace Ida Everett as Dean. Mina Kerr, who held a Ph.D. in Psychology and had come to Wheaton from a similar position at Milwaukee-Downer College, soon proved to be, at least from Cole's perspective, a perfect example of a square peg who would make little effort to adjust smoothly into a round hole. Just as her decision to join the Trinitarian Congregational Church was viewed by the Coles as a personal affront to them, so her take-charge attitude and authoritarian manner rubbed the Coles and many members of the faculty the wrong way. "Kerr," wrote Helen Wieand Cole no more than a month after her arrival on campus, "is a born boss, and we all foresee where we will not have to do much ourselves."[6]

"If only Miss Kerr were the sort of person that we needed, or that saw our needs, and could realize the difference in conditions in places and circumstances," commented Mrs. Cole on November 21, 1921. "But she is increasingly more and more a problem. And the end must be a smash-up!"[7] Part of Dean Kerr's problems, at least from the Coles' perspective, was that she was "terribly provincial in many ways; and I think expected to find us so, and got a shock. . . . She returns tomorrow from the meeting of Deans in Chicago and I suppose will be ready to make over the college; for she wrote S.V. that she was gathering many new ideas."[8]

By the end of her first year at Wheaton, both Samuel Valentine and Helen Wieand Cole were convinced that Miss Kerr would have to be replaced. Nonetheless, it was decided to "give her as long a trial as possible" and thus to continue her for another year.[9] But in fact the die was already cast. Mrs. Cole wrote to her sister that the President did not feel that he could leave campus for very long because he did not trust what Miss Kerr would do in his absence. Commenting that Dean Kerr was "no judge of persons" and was easily swayed by flattery, she noted that "the sort of persons whom she has recommended S.V. would not tolerate. So it is quite a mess! Her opinionatedness and lack of insight and adaptability make it much harder."[10]

In retrospect, it is hard to determine to what degree Mina Kerr deserved the castigation she received in Mrs. Cole's private correspondence. A perusal of College records indicates no major changes in policy or attempts to remake any aspect of Wheaton's existence, either academic or extracurricular. One suspects that the conflict was more one of personality and manner of operation than of real substance. Mina Kerr, a Smith graduate with a doctorate from the University of Pennsylvania, teaching experience at Hood, and several years as a college dean, undoubtedly had a confidence in her own experience and capabilities that allowed her to believe she could operate relatively independently from President Cole. It does appear that she "took charge" from the moment she set foot on campus, and made little or no attempt to spend some time tactfully trying to learn about Wheaton or its manner of operation. That such an attitude would be seen as a direct challenge to his authority by the person who had driven Wheaton forward for twenty-five years is hardly surprising. President Cole had time and again indicated that above all he demanded "loyalty" from those who worked at Wheaton, a

term which to him clearly meant an absolute and unquestioned acceptance of his leadership and policies. Adaptability ideally should be a
two-way street, but there is abundant evidence that President Cole did
not view it that way.

What is clear is that concern over his health problems, plus "worry
about the college and the Kerr-complications," led Cole to begin actively, though very privately, looking for his successor in the fall of
1922.[11] At the suggestion of his wife, President Cole approached a member of the religion department at Smith College, Robert Smith, whose
wife, the former Emma Kingsley, had graduated from Wheaton in 1905,
where she had been a particularly favorite student of President Cole's.
Professor Smith had come to Wheaton annually since 1918 to take one
of the Sunday church services in the new Chapel; he and his wife were
always welcomed as houseguests at the Cole residence, and the two cou-
ples had become good friends. Mrs. Cole described the discussion as follows:

> The minister whom we had on Sunday is the man whom we have se-
> lected as S.V.'s successor. It was my suggestion, and he suits our family
> well. Of course no one else hereabouts knows that we are on the look-out.
> But I assure you if we do not, Mina Kerr will eat up the whole place. Mr.
> Smith is a Yale man, and a minister; he agrees with so much that S.V. be-
> lieves in; he was first assistant pastor in a big church at Montclair; then he
> had a church at Poughkeepsie; has often been an instructor at Silver Bay;
> is now on the faculty at Smith, and one of the members of the Administra-
> tive Board. And his wife is an old Wheaton girl, whom S.V. knew well,
> and who adores him. They would be ready to carry out his ideals and
> would always be friendly; so that we could feel like coming back. And that
> means a lot. S.V. approached Mr. Smith on Sunday, and he was one
> amazed man! But he was not averse to thinking of the possibility. S.V.
> thinks of resigning this coming June, announcing the appointment of his
> successor, so that there can not be any underhanded work anywhere; and
> his resignation to take effect at the end of next year. That would give him
> a year to work and prepare Mr. Smith. Of course this is a dead secret. . . .
> And something may turn up to spoil it all. In the meantime we'll be look-
> ing for a house somewhere near Boston.[12]

Something did indeed turn up which changed, though hardly spoiled,
the plan. In November, 1922, President Cole was advised by a Boston
specialist that since his prostate condition had not worsened over the past
year, he could safely put off the contemplated operation, should he wish
to do so. Since surgery would involve a six to seven week stay in the
hospital during which the College would be in the hands of Dean Kerr,
as well as a 10 percent chance he would not recover, the President
quickly chose to continue living with what his wife delicately described
as "the inconvenience."[13]

Given this reprieve, Rev. Cole instead decided to attack what Mrs. Cole was now referring to as the "cur" problem head on.[14] In early February, 1923, he asked for Dean Kerr's resignation, which to his consternation was not immediately forthcoming. His anxiety was intensified by the fact that Miss Kerr was the official delegate from the Boston Board of the American Association of University Women to its regional convention in Philadelphia. Wheaton was applying for formal admission to that body, and it was feared that Miss Kerr might do her best to derail this project.[15]

In fact, only after the regional conference had approved Wheaton's candidacy did Dean Kerr tell her friends in the organization about her situation. While the application itself was not affected, the College was forced to deal with an official on-campus investigation by an appointed representative of the AAUW, which created a situation on campus that Mrs. Cole likened to a volcano, "seething underneath" and waiting to explode. One faculty member, Mary Hough, refused to sign a new contract unless assured that Dean Kerr would remain. Cole rejected her request out of hand, gave her a month to decide, and required her to sign, if she wished to stay, a formal statement that read: "In doing this I signify my intention to be loyal to the Administration so long as I remain connected with the college."[16]

Miss Hough capitulated, but subsequently in June asked for and received her release to assume a position as Chair of the Department of Romance Languages at the Women's Annex of Rutgers University. Protesting her devotion to Wheaton in her letter of resignation, she commented cryptically: "One comes to understand, after much difficulty, that the unfairness and lack of appreciation are only signs of a necessary conservatism in the first years of a growing college, hard as it may be to comprehend."[17] For Miss Hough, and one senses for many of the younger women on the faculty, the patriarchal authority of a seventy-two-year-old President, who recruited men for the top teaching positions and was unwilling to tolerate anything less than blind loyalty and devotion from his staff, was becoming increasingly difficult to accept.

Faced with Dean Kerr's obstinate refusal to resign, Dr. Cole took the matter to the Board of Trustees, which on March 14 expressed its full confidence "in the wisdom and discretion of Dr. Cole in arriving at the right decision."[18] "Would you stay if it were known that you weren't wanted?," Mrs. Cole asked her sister. "I cannot understand the sort of person she is. I'm not sure she is a lady."[19] Ironically, both Dean Kerr and Wheaton were rescued from this dilemma by the AAUW. In June, Mina Kerr accepted an appointment as Executive Secretary to the National Board of AAUW in Washington, D.C.. Breathing a sigh of relief, President Cole appointed Professor of Romance Languages Agnes Riddell as Acting Dean, and mentioned nary a word about retirement to the Board of Trustees.[20]

This is not to say that discussions with Professor Smith did not clandestinely go forward. Meetings continued periodically; Smith apparently was willing to accept, but was in no hurry to assume his duties. Cole, while looking ever more longingly toward retirement, was determined to complete the building program he had started in 1900, now defined as a physical plant capable of supporting a resident student body of five hundred.

With the dedication of the new Library as part of the Commencement celebration in June, 1923, the final ediface surrounding the rectangular "Court of Honor," first envisioned and designed by President Cole and Ralph Adams Cram twenty-five years earlier, was put in place. True to the original concept, the long axis of the "town common" type open green featured the former Wheaton family homestead at one end and the Library, with its rising, columned entrance at the other. Obviously designed to represent in its frontal exterior a miniature version of the Widener Library at Harvard, the Library featured above its entrance the official College motto, "That they may have life and have it abundantly," a phrase which, however well-intentioned, consistently amused and bemused the male dates of Wheaton undergraduates in subsequent decades.[21]

The basic educational plant was now complete. What remained to be achieved was the erection of dormitory space for another 150 students, plus the unanticipated construction of a new powerhouse. A new heat and light distribution system had not been envisioned in any of the long-range planning for the development of the campus, and the sudden but

Wheaton College Library, 1923-1924, taken from the Emerson Dining Hall terrace. The construction of the Library completed the ring of major buildings enclosing the "Court of Honor" designed twenty-five years earlier.

absolute need for it came as a considerable surprise to both Cole and the Board of Trustees. But it was evident that the old powerhouse, constructed in 1904, was no longer adequate to service the existing campus, much less a contemplated new oversized dormitory. "What an engine is to an automobile, what the heart is to the human body, such the central power system is to the physical life of the college," President Cole proclaimed. "If this stops, the college stops."[22] The trustees were persuaded, and in the spring of 1925 the new Powerhouse and laundry, connected to all buildings by an upgraded underground steam distribution system, went on line. The old powerhouse, renamed Tower Hall, initially was designated to be renovated for academic purposes; instead it was ultimately converted into a small dormitory which proved to be very popular, since it consisted of a number of two-room suites.[23]

One large task remained—the construction of the new dormitory. With all the major academic and support infrastructure in place, it seemed obvious to President Cole that the efficiencies of size that would come with 150 more students made immediate construction of additional residential facilities necessary. But although the trustees had agreed to the development of architectural plans for the project, they were reluctant to authorize actual construction. The cost of Stanton dormitory, just opened in the fall of 1921, plus the substantial amount of money borrowed to complete both the Library and the Powerhouse undoubtedly contributed to the Board's hesitation. Thus, in the spring of 1925, President Cole almost literally girded himself for a battle to achieve what he saw as the final step to the completion of his long-term vision of the transition from Seminary to College.

Time and again in the preceding few years, Helen Wieand Cole had noted in letters to her family that Cole was becoming ever more desirous of retirement. But each comment was also always linked to the final completion of his building projects. "Then our record as the 'Builder' of the college will be complete," wrote Mrs. Cole. "That means S.V.'s, of course."[24] As a means of encouraging the trustees to faster action, Cole even contemplated announcing his resignation, effective in two years, to the Board of Trustees in February, 1924.[25]

However, he did nothing of the sort. The result was that when President Cole died unexpectedly of bronchial pneumonia on May 6, 1925, after a brief five-day illness, no plans relative to his succession were in place. Moreover, the situation regarding Robert Smith had changed dramatically. During 1924 his wife's health, which had never been strong, declined dramatically, so much so that in October Professor Smith indicated that he was somewhat hesitant about giving up his position on the faculty at Smith for one which would put far greater demands upon his wife. Sadly, in January, 1925, Emma Smith died, and shortly thereafter Professor Smith received and accepted an offer to join the Yale faculty in the fall of 1925. With his Wheaton alumna wife deceased, and a new prestigious academic position in hand, Smith's willingness to consider the future presidency of Wheaton apparently diminished considerably, though he did accept an appointment to the Wheaton Board of Trustees in March, 1925.[26]

There is some evidence to suggest that immediately following President Cole's death, his brother and wife made a last-ditch effort to persuade Mr. Smith to let his name be brought before the Board as Samuel Valentine Cole's choice as his successor. But nothing came of it, and on May 11, William I. Cole wrote to trustee George Smart that both he and his sister-in-law hoped that Smart would assume the duties of Acting President for a year. Smart accepted, and on May 14, the Board of Trustees confirmed the appointment and designated him, along with Robert Smith and Frances Vose Emerson as the search committee for a new president. Mrs. Cole was allotted one-third of the remainder of President Cole's annual salary and the use of the President's House through the summer.[27]

Born in England in 1863, George Smart had come to the United States at the age of eighteen. He subsequently attended Harvard College and received his divinity degree from Middlebury College. Retired from his position as minister of the Congregational church in Newton Highlands, Massachusetts, he had been a member of the Wheaton Board of Trustees since 1908, and was currently serving as its vice-president.[28] Rev. Smart had thus participated in the long process of the transition from Seminary to College, and was fully cognizant of the successes, problems, policies and traditions which had developed over the preceding decades. With no ambitions to the office himself, he was the ideal person to serve in an interim capacity, and his year as Acting President proved felicitous for the institution and all concerned with it.

In a calm, relaxed, fashion Rev. Smart carried on the policies of the Cole administration, particularly in terms of dormitory construction, dealt forthrightly with some of the problems left on his table, and quietly tried not to intensify those which of necessity would be passed on to his successor. His personal, rather self-effacing view of himself is evidenced by his wry comment to trustee Annie Kilham that after taking his first driving lesson the previous night "the car is uninjured."[29] Informing a prospective member of the French department that he would meet her at the Mansfield train station, he commented: "Please look for a rather short man with a gray overcoat and hat and hair."[30]

During the summer of 1925, Mrs. Cole and her brother-in-law dealt with all the various business and administrative affairs required in preparation for the opening of the fall term.[31] Mrs. Cole took on sole reponsibility for hiring new staff as needed. This included retaining the services of Eunice Work as Head of the Department of Latin and Greek, a position Mrs. Cole had held for the previous two years.[32] Only in one personnel case was Rev. Smart required to make a decision. This involved what

George T. Smart, *Acting President*, 1925-1926.

had begun as a salary dispute between Iola Eastburn and President Cole, but which had escalated into a conflict involving issues of loyalty to the administration and conformity to the traditions of the institution.

Iola Eastburn had been Professor of German at Wheaton since 1915. Holder of a Ph.D. from the University of Pennsylvania, she had, during the 1920s, become increasingly dissatisfied with her salary of $1200 per year plus room and board. In turn, President Cole had become disenchanted with Miss Eastburn, who as an avowed pacifist refused to sing hymns with martial content at church and vespers services, was a friend and supporter of Dean Kerr, and was also at times openly critical of Dr. Cole. The upshot was that Cole had denied her any increase in pay, using low enrollments in German as the formal reason, and had suggested strongly that Miss Eastburn might be happier employed elsewhere. Taking him at his word, in 1925 Miss Eastburn made enquiries concerning other positions through Dean Kerr, who was now with the AAUW in Washington, and through a colleague at Swarthmore who coincidentally was chair of the AAUW committee on salaries of women professors. This in turn brought a threat that Wheaton might be dropped from its just recently attained position on the Association's approved list of colleges because of low salaries paid to women. All of this further strained Professor Eastburn's relations with the President.[33]

During the summer of 1925, Miss Eastburn appealed her salary case to Rev. Smart, but to no avail. Refusing to accede, she wrote a second time to the Acting President requesting an increase to $1800. This time Smart took a new tack, offering a one-year increase to $1500 with the proviso that she would leave Wheaton at the end of that year. The reasons were made crystal clear.

I think you must surmise that the reason Dr. Cole could not advance your salary was because he felt that you would be happier and less perplexed if you could find a position where things were ordered differently. A resident college is a large family where individuals must sink some of their personal preferences for the good of the whole and where one cannot do or say things that are perfectly legitimate when one lives at home, and where personal qualities cannot be pushed to an extreme. I know that he thought you would be happier in some other instititution and probably most happy in a school where the social and teaching lives were more separate and I am inclined to agree with him.

Teaching is not all there is in college work. There are also the intangible qualities which make or mar one's work and these are the most important when one considers the family life of the college.[34]

Miss Eastburn, obviously stunned, pleaded her case in a lengthy interview with Rev. Smart, in which she admitted that she had been indiscreet, professed willingness to remain at the old salary level, and promised that she would "keep from criticizing and would work with me heartily and try to avoid conflicts."[35] Smart was unmoved. On August 4, Iola Eastburn capitulated and accepted the provisions of the one-year terminal contract.[36]

The termination of Professor Eastburn's tenure at Wheaton was significant for a number of reasons. In one sense it gave clear indication that Wheaton had come of age as a college. Recruiting faculty with Ph.D. degrees was not the problem it had been in the College's early years, and thus the loss of a person with that degree was no longer seen as critical. However, what did continue to be regarded as fundamentally important was loyalty and conformity to the leadership and traditions of the College. Continued employment, raises in salary (usually given only in the first year of a multiyear contract), residence assignments—all these depended not only on one's effectiveness in the classroom, but also on how a faculty member was viewed by the President relative to the smooth running of the total College operation.[37]

Never, during the Cole or subsequent administrations, is there the slightest evidence that the College administration tried in any way to infringe upon the academic freedom of Wheaton's faculty in the classroom. Effectiveness and competence as a teacher were monitored, but not ideological or philosophical outlook. However, a similar level of freedom was not always reflected in tolerance of attitudes or behavior which seemed to challenge the administration's holistic view of the nature and purpose of the college experience, or the role each faculty member was expected to play in supporting and furthering it.

The power to define and enforce this community ethos remained firmly in the hands of the President, who was both guided and supported by the Board of Trustees. This authoritarian, patriarchal structure was not unique to Wheaton. Small, private liberal arts colleges throughout the country were led by presidents who were expected to serve both as academic leader and chief financial officer of the college. This meant on-campus oversight directly and personally of everyday operations. Presidents defined the philosophy and perspective from which the colleges operated, and retained exclusive authority over wages, promotion, tenure, termination and a host of other faculty-related issues. He (and very occasionally she) also directed and wielded final decision-making power over curricular and extracurricular matters.

All this had worked well in the late nineteenth and early years of the twentieth century. But the world was changing in the 1920s and 1930s. Just as the advent of cars, cigarettes, women's right to vote, and the jazz age all produced challenges to the traditional views of college as providing a substitute "home environment" for its students, so the development at Wheaton of a faculty with professional training and degrees at the Ph.D. level created a sense of professional entitlement among its members that had not existed in earlier years. This was further enhanced by the addition of male faculty, who were better paid and exempt from many of the onerous duties that befell the single women who were required to live in the dormitories, where they served as constant advisers and role models to the students who surrounded them twenty-four hours a day. Submission to the paternalistic, patriarchal authority and outlook of the President, though required of faculty of both genders, created a much harsher and all-encompassing aura for women than it did for men. Resistance and reaction to these conditions at Wheaton would increasingly be a factor in presidential dealings with women faculty members over the next several decades.

Rev. Smart's main accomplishments during his one-year tenure were two-fold. Determined to see President Cole's building plans completed, Smart pushed the Board of Trustees to authorize construction of the new "double dormitory," that had been so dear to Cole's heart, and for which preliminary plans had been drawn by the College architects, Cram and Ferguson. This approval was given on May 14, 1925, the same meeting at which Smart's appointment as Acting President was confirmed. A relieved Mrs. Cole commented in a letter to Eunice Work that completion of the new dormitory would allow the College's enrollment to reach five hundred, which was "the maximum of our plans."[38] Seventeen months later, two weeks after J. Edgar Park assumed the duties of President, Everett Hall, complete with its own dining hall, was dedicated in the presence of former Dean Ida Everett at the same Founders day celebration at which the College Chapel was officially named in honor of President Cole.[39]

Rev. Smart's other main obligation was to chair the Trustee Committee charged with finding a new president. It did not have to look very far. John Edgar Park was minister of the Congregational church in West Newton, and thus well known to George Smart as a professional colleague. Raised in Ireland, and a graduate of the Royal University in Dublin, Park had done postgraduate study at Belfast, Leipsig, Edinburgh,

Oxford, and Princeton. Recipient of an honorary Doctor of Divinity degree from Tufts, he also held an appointment as Professor of the Theory of Worship at Boston University. He was the author of several books and a regular contributor to the *Atlantic Monthly* and other magazines. Married, with four children, Dr. Park seemed ideally suited for Wheaton's presidency, and there is little indication that the Committee ever seriously considered any other candidate.[40]

It is clear that Rev. Smart's influence with Park was the decisive factor in leading him to accept the offer. "As you know," Park wrote to trustee Robert Smith in September, 1927, "I entered the position without any very extended knowledge of the institution. It was chiefly upon the assurance of Acting President Smart that he considered it the most hopeful educational enterprize with which he was acquainted."[41] Years later, when asked why he had given up the ministry to come to Wheaton, Park replied that as a minister he was not sure he was opening the gates of heaven to adults, and he thought he might do better with young people.[42] His salary was set at $10,000, plus a $300 car allowance and use of the "Homestead" rent free, including heat and light.[43]

The advent of J. Edgar Park to Wheaton's presidency marked at least a small step in the College's slow transition away from regarding itself exclusively as a Wheaton family enterprise. Nonetheless, although Mrs. Wheaton had been dead for twenty years, her influence and legacy, both financial and philosophical, remained dominant in the development of the College. President Cole had been handpicked by Eliza Baylies Wheaton to be Wheaton's President, and the path that Cole had followed over the years in moving Wheaton from Seminary to College status was one with which she had concurred in the initial planning and development stages. Dr. Park, who was not a member, as Cole had been, of Wheaton's Board of Trustees before becoming President, by his own admission knew little or nothing about the institution before he was approached about assuming the office. However, he clearly understood the basic premises upon which the College had been built, and during the years of his administration Wheaton continued to live within the fiscal means provided almost exclusively by the Wheaton family legacy. "With your cooperation," he wrote the Board in his letter of acceptance, "I hope that I may be able to carry on the fine traditions of the College and help to build up at Wheaton a home of simple culture and sound learning, which may inspire its students to live lives of serenity and high endeavor."[44]

Dr. Park's administrative style, both similar to and more relaxed than Cole's, was later described cryptically by one member of the faculty as "despotism tempered by epigram."[45] "He used humor as a weapon," commented another, who, while professing to have idolized Park, also characterized him as a "holy terror as a tyrant."[46] One of his most loyal admirers, French professor and long-time Dean of Freshmen Dorothy

John Edgar Park, *President*,
1926-1944.

Littlefield, described him in 1983 as a "nineteenth century paternalistic president."[47] Renowned for his wry sense of humor and somewhat off-beat perception of the human condition, Park possessed an unparalleled ability to turn a phrase in memorable fashion. He was, Professor Hol-combe Austin recalled, the "absolute master of the four-minute speech;" his chapel talks both inspired and amused generations of Wheaton students.[48] Characterized by Robert Frost as "a poet in an office,"[49] President Park delighted in shocking the sensibilities of others, witness his announcement at the opening faculty meeting in September, 1941, that the first paychecks would be distributed that Friday "to enable you to pay your summer racing and gambling bills."[50] With his unconventional comments he proved to be an able publicist for Wheaton, for he was widely sought after as a speaker. His talks more often than not attained considerable attention in the press.

One of Dr. Park's more notable addresses, given first in Cleveland, but repeated elsewhere and disseminated nationally through the press wire services, was entitled "How to Get Along With Our Daughters." Positing the thesis that heavily chaperoned girls made poor wives, Park, according to the news dispatch, stated:

> Boyfriends, and plenty of them, are necessary if a girl is to know how to select a husband. . . . Eve got into trouble without a buggy or an automobile. Virtue that cannot survive the automobile doesn't amount to much. Mothers can't sit in the middle of an automobile seat between their daughter and her boy friend, so they might as well stop worrying and go to sleep.[51]

Perhaps even more startling was Park's assertion, as reported in the *Boston Evening Transcript*, that he felt "certain that women are to be the men of the future, or, in other words, that men have had their chance in the world and that women are just beginning to find themselves and are destined to greater and greater things in the world's affairs."[52]

Two anecdotes in particular concerning President Park became part of faculty lore for as long as those who served under him remained part of the Wheaton community. As President, Dr. Park not only appointed all members of faculty committees, he also sat on all committees himself. This included the so-called "Low Grade Committee" whose function was to deal with students in severe academic difficulty. Faced with a student record of four Fs plus an A in an Old Testament course, Park was prompted to remark, "Thank God she has her religion."[53] When his own daughter's academic record proved totally unacceptable, the tension in the committee meeting was enormous. According to members of the committee, no one dared to put forward the motion that she be dismissed. The President swiveled in his chair and stared silently out of the window. "I'll tell you what's wrong with that girl," he said finally, "poor family background." With that the tension was broken, and the committee voted to allow her to "resign" from the College.[54]

One of Park's favorite personal anecdotes was of the visit to campus by a Seminary graduate of the late nineteenth century. The President, having some free time, gave her a tour of the campus with all its new buildings, which seemed to impress her mightily. Upon concluding the tour, as they stood in front of the Chapel, the elderly woman turned to Dr. Park with tears in her eyes. "God, how I hated this place!" she said with vehemence.[55]

While more able than his predecessor to delegate some authority in routine matters of day-to-day management, and considerably more willing than Cole had been to tolerate discussion and debate on issues, Park nonetheless kept all academic matters and most other policy decisions within his tight control. The Dean continued to deal almost exclusively with student services and affairs; the President, as in times past, functioned as the day in, day out supervisor of academic matters, as well as the ultimate decision maker on any and all aspects of the operation of the College.

It was in his relations with the Dean of the College, Emma Denkinger, that President Park found his greatest challenge in the early years of his administration. Following the forced resignation of Dean Kerr in the spring of 1923, Agnes Riddell, a member of the English department had served as Acting Dean for two years. Even though both President and Mrs. Cole found it "so pleasant to deal with a lady," a characteristic they had not ascribed to Mina Kerr, by May of 1924, Mrs. Cole was describing Miss Riddell as being "too slack." "She lets things go, is almost a Kerr in reverse," Mrs. Cole wrote to her sister.[56] The need for a permanent Dean who would be able to wield more effective control in the area of student life and services seemed apparent. Therefore, in

March, 1925, President Cole appointed Emma Denkinger, a Radcliffe Ph.D. who had taught English at both Mount Holyoke and Wellesley, to the position.[57]

In Emma Denkinger Wheaton obtained an administrator with boundless energy and enthusiasm for her work. Never one to waste a moment of time, Dean Denkinger imprinted all correspondence, even to the President, with a large stamped signature of her full name. Faced with the daunting prospect of dealing with the problems of an ever-expanding student body, she prepared a detailed list of the duties of her office for Dr. Smart. In it she suggested that serving as academic adviser to the three lower classes and recorder of all student class absences made it impossible for her adequately to take full reponsibility for the social life of the College and the workings of the College Government Association. With no administrative and little secretarial help it was not possible, she maintained, for either her or the Registrar to function effectively.[58]

The Dean clearly was right, a point reinforced by the fact that the Registrar, Sarah Belle Young, had been forced to take an extended leave of absence in the fall of 1925 because of a nervous breakdown caused by overwork.[59] The result was that one of President Park's first administrative decisions, in December, 1926, was to create a separate Admissions Office, and to appoint Edith White, who had come to Wheaton the previous January as Assistant Professor of Economics, to the new position of Secretary to the Board of Admissions. The removal of the enormous burden of the admissions process from the Registrar allowed President Park in turn to divert many of the Dean's duties relating to class absences and registration for courses to the Registrar's office, while still ensuring that the overall functioning responsibilities of both the Dean and the Registrar were substantially reduced.[60]

In an effort to balance further the work load between the three offices, the task of supervising and advising each new class during the freshmen year was removed from the Dean's purview in September, 1928, and given over on a trial basis to the Secretary of the Board of Admissions, Miss White. The following year the position was formalized when Miss White was given the additional title of Dean of Freshman. "Wheaton, like many colleges, has found that it is desirable for the admission officer to follow the records of students through the first year since such experience is helpful in evaluating the standards of schools who are sending students to Wheaton," Miss White wrote in a report to Dr. Park. "Moreover, the fact that the admission officer is familiar with the entrance records of weak students makes it easier for her to advise such students than it would be for the Dean of the College."[61] Miss White held these dual positions until her untimely death in March, 1935. Her replacement, Barbara Ziegler, assumed only the role of Secretary of the Board of Admissions, while the position of Dean of Freshmen was entrusted to Dorothy Littlefield, who also held an appointment in the

French department. These two would jointly oversee the admittance and first-year guidance of all students entering Wheaton during the remaining years of the Park administration.

Relieved of many of her former recording, scheduling and advising duties, Dean Denkinger set out to bring regulation and order to the social situation at Wheaton. Not given to the view that matters ought to be evaluated on a case by case basis, she sought to regularize all social activities through reliance on recorded precedent and regulated procedure. To be caught offguard in any situation with neither precedent or procedure to refer to was for her a scenario to be avoided at any cost, especially when it related to the workings of the College Government Association.

The result was that by 1929 Dean Denkinger had created a six-volume reference source entitled "History and Procedure." It contained 161 alphabetized topic headings under which were recorded the results of any and all actions taken by her office in the years between 1925 and 1929, along with elaborate rules and procedures regarding how every conceivable situation should be handled. Woe betide the faculty member, administrative official, or undergraduate officer in any campus organization who wittingly or unwittingly failed to act in accordance with these regulations.[62] Not content with this elaborate compendium of rules and procedures, Miss Denkinger also compiled an equally thorough confidential record of how previous cases had been handled, complete with names and dates, including issues as minute as "Bathrooms," "Bicycles," "Gum Chewing," "Walking on the Grass," and "Manners in the Dining Room."[63] By 1928, the control exerted over every aspect of College life by Emma Denkinger had reached a point where faculty and student morale was being severely and adversely affected.

For no one was this more true than President Park. There is evidence to indicate that Rev. Smart, in his one year as Acting President, had come to have reservations regarding Dean Denkinger, reservations which he passed on to the new President. Yet Dr. Park, knowing little about Wheaton, had been hesitant to act summarily regarding staff already in place. Moreover, he had immediately recognized that administering a college of five hundred students with a staff that had been overworked when the enrollment was two hundred was not possible, and had readily acceded to the plans for expansion of administrative staff and offices suggested by Dean Denkinger and endorsed by the Registrar, Sarah Belle Young.[64]

Nonetheless, by the fall semester of 1928, Park had decided that he must act. With the support of the Board of Trustees, he demanded the resignation of Miss Denkinger, effective the end of the academic year. Though resistant at first, ultimately she acceded. "We are agreed," Park wrote her, "that it is best for your career and for the college that the engagement should end in June, 1929." Promising that she would go out "with flags flying," he suggested that she should resign in order to pursue "further study." Assuring her that she could count on a favorable letter of recommendation, he commented, "You have so great ability that if the proper environment were found there is no limit to the eminence you are able to attain."[65]

In his Chapel announcement to the College community of Denkinger's impending departure, Park was as good as his word, heaping lavish praise on the Dean's contribution to Wheaton. Privately, his relief and that of several members of the Board of Trustees was palpable. "Hallelujah," wrote William I. Cole to President Park. "With her going, what I have considered as one of your most serious and urgent problems will be solved." The charge, Cole went on, that we are "throwing away the academic future of the college" is nonsense, rather her leaving "is the essential condition of recurring it."[66] To which Sylvia Meadows added that it was essential to find the right person as Miss Denkinger's successor, for "it would be fatal if we got another poor dean after Miss Kerr and Miss Denkinger."[67]

Park wasted no time. He turned for help in identifying suitable candidates to a long-time acquaintance, Miriam Carpenter, who was Registrar, Adviser of Women, and Head of the Appointment Office at the Harvard Graduate School of Education, only the second woman in the history of Harvard University to receive a Corporation appointment. Miss Carpenter suggested a number of persons, and in early February, 1929, Park met with her to discuss their credentials. Park later reported to the trustees:

> As I went over these applications with her I was more and more convinced that she herself was the real person for the position. At last I made up my mind to suggest to her that instead of trying to get us somebody else she take it herself. She was the first and only person asked to take the position. It was a clear case of the office seeking the person.[68]

Following this meeting, Miss Carpenter wrote a remarkable letter to Park, which is both indicative of her nature, and of Park's approach as he sought a person who could work compatibly with him.

> No matter what the final outcome may be, I want to tell you how much good our talk Saturday afternoon did me. It added enormously to my self-respect to think that with all my perfectly obvious and well recognized limitations for a dean's job, you still saw something in me to balance them. . . . I have been through a curious series of reactions about the possibility of this work, and am now inclined to believe that your confidence in me might enable me to grow up mentally. I never thought it through before, and I do not know the origin of the difficulty now, but I do see for the first time, since our talk Saturday, how I have refused to try to think, fearing always I should make a spectacular failure. Accordingly I have pushed the intuitive and personal end of my work up high. People have

constantly cried, "Of course you can think!" But no one was willing to gamble on it before. . . . [Even if someone else is hired] I shall have had a glimmer of sense break through my delusion, and nothing so important as that has happened to me in several years.

Thank you for being willing to wake me up![69]

Whether by design or not, Miss Carpenter's letter cemented her candidacy in Park's eyes, and he wrote by return mail confirming his offer. "We shall hope for many fruitful differences of opinion held in a good open friendly spirit," he wrote, "and issuing in results better than hoped for by either side."[70]

Wheaton was not a total unknown to Miriam Carpenter. A close friend of Edith White, recently appointed to head the new Admissions Office, she had also, as head of the Harvard School of Education Appointment Bureau, often recommended persons for positions at Wheaton. As quiet and unassuming in personality as Kerr and Denkinger had been outgoing and domineering, Carpenter nonetheless brought firm resolve and an ability to control matters to the Dean's office. It hardly seems coincidental that Park described Miss Carpenter's first year as Dean as having been "without doubt the happiest year since I became connected with Wheaton."[71] She and President Park worked easily and well with one another, and the resulting partnership remained in place until both left Wheaton at the end of the 1943–44 academic year.[72]

Only one thing was lacking in Miss Carpenter's credentials from President Park's perspective, and he quickly set about rectifying this deficiency. Just as President Cole had persuaded his alma mater, Bowdoin College, to grant the first Dean of the College, Ida Everett, an honorary M.A. degree, so Dr. Park actively solicited Miss Carpenter's alma mater, Colorado College, and indirectly planted a suggestion at Mount Holyoke, where Wheaton alumna Mary Woolley was President, regarding the conferral of honorary degrees from those institutions. In both instances he was successful, with the result that Miss Carpenter was soon able to add L.H.D. and Litt.D. to the earned B.A. that followed her name in the college catalogue.[73] Park was equally successful in a similar suggestion to the President of Colby College regarding Wheaton's Registrar, Sarah Belle Young, who was awarded an honorary Doctorate in Humane Letters from Colby in August, 1931.[74]

One final major change remained for President Park in the administrative restructuring that took place in the first years of the new administration. In the spring of 1929, Mary Armstrong, who had been appointed by President Cole as College Librarian, resigned because of ill health. Miss Armstrong had implemented the reclassification of the library collection according to the Dewey Decimal system, survived a bitter struggle with the Classics department which had fiercely resisted that change, and supervised the establishment of a special room to house the books

Miriam F. Carpenter, *Dean of Wheaton College*, 1929-1944, with Paula Stevenson (W1936), President of the Senior Class, and her fiancé.

of President Cole (donated to the College with the proviso that they be maintained as a separate collection). She had so endeared herself to President Park that in the fall of 1927 he had rewarded her work by abolishing the supervisory faculty library committee and appointing her to the faculty with the rank of full professor.[75]

Six months after her retirement, in severe pain and distress, Miss Armstrong took her life in Philadelphia. The circumstances of her death, coupled with her round-the-clock devotion to the Wheaton Library during her years in Norton, soon led to a student-perpetuated myth that the ghost of "Aunt Mary" had returned to haunt the alcoves and stacks of the Library, a part of Wheaton lore that still existed seventy years later as the twentieth century drew to a close.[76]

With the appointment of Marian Merrill to replace Mary Armstrong, President Park had in place by September, 1929, an administrative structure and team whose personnel, with the exception of the replacement of Edith White by Barbara Ziegler and Dorothy Littlefield, would remain virtually intact throughout the subsequent fifteen years of his presidency. A decade of considerable administrative turmoil and uncertainty was about to give way to an extensive period of stability in the governance and administration of College affairs. Given the considerable stress that the Great Depression and World War II would impose on all institutions of higher learning, President Park's accomplishment in putting together what would turn out to be such an effective, long-term administrative team seems in retrospect to have been one of his greatest achievements.

During the 1920s, the College's relations with the various alumnae organizations remained cordial but passive. In February, 1924, the first meeting of the newly organized Alumnae Council was held on campus, and that summer the Association was admitted into membership in the American Association of University Women (AAUW). The on-campus Secretary of the Alumnae Association also continued to head the College's Appointment and Vocational Bureaus. More important than the umbrella Alumnae Association were the eight regional clubs, of which the New York Club undoubtedly wielded the most influence. Until 1930, the Association was not involved in systematic fund-raising of any sort; the failed capital campaign in the early 1920s had almost completely killed any organized attempts by the College to raise money.[77]

One of the problems faced by the Alumnae Association during these years was a certain amount of tension within the various clubs between recent graduates of the College and those who had either graduated or attended during the Seminary years. The younger alumnae tended to move to the forefront in the operation of the clubs and the Association. At times, their more aggressive mode of operation did not sit well with older alumnae, including some who served on the Board of Trustees.[78]

In June, 1930, spurred by a fund-raising initiative begun by students in 1928, the Alumnae Association did begin a long-term campaign to raise funds for the eventual erection of a Student Alumnae Building, which would serve as a center for on-campus student clubs and organizations and also as headquarters for the Alumnae Association. By the end of the year, and in the face of disastrous national economic conditions, over $25,000 had been raised, the first even modestly successful attempt at fund-raising in the College's history.[79]

Aside from her own home, and various parcels of real estate located in Norton, the one major bequest that had accrued to Wheaton from the will of Eliza Baylies Wheaton was the property located on Winter Street in Boston that had originally been purchased in 1827 by Judge Wheaton as a home for his daughter Elizabeth and her husband, Dr. Woodbridge Strong. Throughout the nineteenth century the property had been leased to various companies; since 1878 it had been held by the prominent Boston jewellers, A. Stowell and Company. Beginning in 1921, the Board of Trustees had restricted the use of income from this property to the construction and equipping of campus buildings.[80]

Despite the fact that the property generated over $30,000 annually in rental income, in 1923 the trustees decided that it would be advisable to sell it and use the cash received to create Wheaton's first substantial portfolio endowment fund. Since 1916 the College had been receiving inquiries relative to the Winter Street property, and in the fall of 1923 a serious bid was received from a company other than Stowell. Stowell's reaction was one of considerable concern, with the result that Wheaton was able to leverage the selling price up from the initial offer of $950,000 to $1,025,000. The sale between the College and Stowell was negotiated in December, 1923, and ratified by the Board of Trustees on February 26, 1924. Three days later the formal purchase and sales agreement was signed. However, due to complexities connected with the title search, which finally had to be ruled on in Land Court, final conveyance did not occur until January 3, 1927. Stowell by that time had paid the College $300,000; Wheaton accepted a ten-year, 5 percent mortgage for the remaining $725,000.[81]

Why did the Board and President Cole decide to sell? The linkage between the abysmal failure of the capital campaign in the early 1920s and the decision to create an endowment fund by selling the Winter Street property, though nondocumentable, seems obvious. A 5 percent return on the $1,025,000 selling price, certainly a reasonable estimate at that time, would generate considerably more than the amount being received as rental income. Desperate for funds to pay off debts incurred in constructing Stanton dormitory and the Library, and anxious to begin building the residential complex that would become Everett Hall, President Cole saw the immediate fiscal needs of the College as outweighing the desirability of holding a prime piece of Boston real estate for its long-term growth potential.

In a letter to her sister in October, 1923, Mrs. Cole commented that Ralph Adams Cram, the College architect, had come for lunch in order to discuss the contemplated new double-sized dormitory. "It is possible," she wrote, "that we may start it soon, since a deal has been made with the jewellry people whereby we could get funds for the erection of the buildings. This is a secret at present, but things are on the way."[82] While it is hard to quarrel with the decision made at that time, one can only wistfully contemplate the impact selling the Winter Street property might have had on Wheaton's fiscal position had it occurred in the last decade of the twentieth century rather than in 1923.[83]

The initial payments received from Stowell for the Winter Street property made it possible to proceed with the construction of the new residence hall. The opening of Everett dining hall and dormitory in the fall of 1926 brought to a conclusion the massive thirteen-building construction program that had commenced in 1901 with the erection of Chapin dormitory. Samuel Valentine Cole's vision of a small college campus was in essence complete. Of course there were still many further needs, but the main construction period was over. Cole's place in history as the "builder of Wheaton" was secure. But the price in other ways had been considerable. In his report to the Board of Trustees in 1930, President Park succinctly stated the situation:

> When I became President of Wheaton there was one situation which was and remained a mystery to me. Every other college of which I knew had a larger endowment than Wheaton and yet had a deficit. Wheaton not only had no deficit, but actually was able to build its own buildings out of its surplus. Gradually in these years I have discovered the reasons for this situation.[84]

Wheaton, Park maintained, was a no-frills college. Its campus was compact, with no "show" buildings. It did not have any luxuries—there were no professional heads of houses, no elevators, and few maids. No provision had been made up until that time for a retirement fund for faculty and staff; moreover, "Wheaton has not paid salaries to faculty large enough to attract first-rate teachers or hold promising young instructors more than one or two years."[85] Money had been spent "almost exclusively for bricks and mortar to the detriment of the library and academic equipment."[86] While the rambling wood-frame Metcalf Hall would have to be replaced in the near future, it was even more important, Park emphasized, to recognize that more must be spent on education and less on buildings.

The result was that in the early years of President Park's administration, Wheaton experienced its first hiatus in major "bricks and mortar" construction since the beginning of the century. Smaller projects were indeed undertaken. Walks were paved and filter beds rebuilt. A tennis court and three-hole golf course were constructed, and a new vegetable cellar was dug into the sloping bank next to the carpenter shop. The former "coal hole" of the old powerhouse was whitewashed for use by the Dramatics Association. Trees in the Wheaton woods were cut and the money from their sale used to landscape the main campus. All but one team of horses were sold and College transportation was motorized. Renovations were made to the Wheaton Inn, and garages for its patrons' cars and for rental to faculty and students were built close by. Finally, a building on Taunton Avenue was purchased to serve as a boarding house for unmarried male help.[87]

In addition the College accepted a proposal from Admissions Director and Dean of Freshmen Edith White that she be allowed to build at her expense a house on College land, which would be leased to her for $1.00 for her lifetime. Miss White would pay taxes on the house to Norton and insure the property, while the College in turn would maintain the grounds and the building, provide electricity during the academic year, shovel the walks and include the house in the patrol route of the night watchman. Upon Miss White's death the house would become the property of the College. Through this mechanism Hollyhock House (so named as the result of a contest run in the *Wheaton News*) became part of the campus and a future residence for academic and student deans for decades to come.[88]

But during the first five years of his administration, President Park and the trustees authorized only one major building project. This was the construction of what would in time become known as Peacock Pond. First envisioned by George Smart, the plan to create a two-acre pond by excavating the marsh on the eastern edge of the campus was presented to the Board of Trustees by President Park in November, 1928. The project, he suggested, would provide good loam for the campus lawns and gravel for the filter beds. It would become the center around which future buildings could be constructed to create a campus of lasting beauty. It would be a resource for swimming in the summer and ice-skating in the winter, and could provide a ready water supply for "flushing, heating, and fire control." Moreover, it would rid the College of one of its major sources of mosquito infestation.[89] Finally, Park argued, "Whether it be rational or not, parents choose colleges largely upon their appearance. A college which takes enough pride in itself to look nice is in their opinion more than likely to take pride also in the type of education which it gives to young people."[90]

With income now available from the invested proceeds of the Winter Street property sale, the trustees were persuaded. Construction proceeded throughout the winter, spring and summer of 1929; by December of that year Park could report to trustee Annie Kilham that "Eliza Lakelet or Peregrine Lake (call it what you wish)" was frozen and providing excellent skating opportunities for the campus community.[91] Covering about two acres and showing "a good sandy or clay bottom everywhere," the pond also provided an outdoor swimming facility which was used extensively by students, faculty and staff.[92]

In an effort to extend an olive branch to the Norton community, President Park wrote to Superintendent of Schools L. G. Nourse, asking him to announce in the schools that "Wheaton College is very happy to have the pond on its campus used for swimming or skating by the girls of the Norton schools. The College is sorry not to be able to extend this invitation to boys also."[93] Well intentioned as the offer may have been, it evidenced a surprising lack of political acumen on the part of President Park. To the dismay of many townspeople, the placement of fill dredged from the pond, and the new pond itself, had altered enormously and diminished effectively the steep slope known as Mary Lyon Hill. This hill, along with the frozen swamp at its base, had been the favorite winter sledding spot for generations of girls and boys from Norton Center. Far

Bridge across Peacock Pond, 1937. The small Greek temple was built from the pillars of Old Metcalf, Wheaton's original dormitory, which was razed in 1932.

from improving relations between the town and College, the gender-based inclusion of some, but not all, children to the benefits of the new pond, only served to increase the suspicion and hostility evidenced by many members of the Norton community toward the new and seemingly ever-expanding institution that was growing in its midst.[94]

NOTES: CHAPTER 11

1. SVC, *President's Report, 1914–15*, p. 7.

2. See ch. 5.

3. Trustees, 1834–1910: K. U. Clark #3: SVC to Clark, 4/9/25.

4. B. Solomon, *In the Company of Educated Women: A History of Women and Higher Education* (New Haven: Yale University Press, 1985), pp. 63, 64, 142; Thorp, *Neilson of Smith*, p. 253; H. Horowitz, *Campus Life: Undergraduate Cultures from the End of the Eighteenth Century to the Present* (New York: A. A. Knopf, 1987), pp. 5–6; HWC, Letters to Family: to Sister, 9/21/24.

5. HWC, Letters to Family: to Family, 9/19/21; to Sister, 3/16/22; 9/19/22. Regarding faculty anticipation of Cole's retirement and Mrs. Cole's personal views on holding an administrative position, see ch. 10; also her comment to her sister that while she enjoyed teaching, should she ever again seek a permanent job she would prefer a deanship. See Letters to Family: to Sister, 10/14/23.

6. HWC, Letters to Family: to Sister, 9/16/21. Muriel Reynolds (W1924), later a Wheaton Trustee, vividly remembered Dean Kerr's most famous motto directed at students: "A bath a day is the lady's way." Oral History Project: M. Reynolds interview, 1984.

7. HWC, Letters to Family: to Sister, 11/21/21.

8. Ibid., 12/14/21; 2/28/22.

9. Ibid., 3/19/22.

10. Ibid., 4/21/22.

11. Ibid., 11/2/22.

12. Ibid., 10/11/22; see also to Family, 5/5/18.

13. Ibid.: to Sister, 11/2,9/22.

14. Ibid., 2/4/23.

15. Ibid. Technically, it was the Wheaton Alumnae Association that would be admitted to AAUW, but in order for that to occur the College had to be recognized as meeting the standards of the Association.

16. Faculty: Hough: Hough to SVC, 2/21/23; SVC to Hough, 2/21/23; HWC, Letters to Family: to Sister, 2/15,20/23. Wheaton was admitted into the corporate membership of AAUW in June, 1923. Ibid., 6/18/23; Trustees: Kilham #2: SVC to Kilham, 6/18/23.

17. Faculty: Hough: Hough to SVC, 6/23/23.

18. Trustees Minutes: 3/14/23.

19. HWC, Letters to Family: to Sister, 3/21/23.

20. Ibid.: 6/5/23; Trustees Minutes: 6/17/23.

21. The motto had been adopted officially, at President Cole's suggestion, by the Trustees in March, 1911. See Trustees Minutes: 3/21/11; and ch. 9. For details of the Cole/Cram discussions, and the rough sketch of the "Court of Honor" created by Mr. Cram, see ch. 6 and 6, n. 4. The cost of the Library was $152,060. See Treasurer: "Trial Balance Ledger," 1919–33; Trustees Minutes: 11/17/21; 12/9/21; 2/20/22; Trustees: Hersey: SVC to Hersey, 3/6/22.

22. SVC, *President's Report, 1921–1922*, p. 46.

23. All telephone and electric lines were placed underground in the summer of 1923. The cost of the new Powerhouse, laundry, and steam distribution system was $166,681, while the renovations to Tower Hall, later known as the Doll's House, came to $30,183. Treasurer: "Trial Balance Ledger," 1919–33. See also Academic Council Minutes: 9/18/23; Trustees Minutes: 11/21/22; 3/14/23; 2/26/24; 3/20/24; 6/16/24; 11/20/24; Smart/Park: Smart: Park to Smart, 12/31/26; Bursar's Office Correspondence, 1889–1940: #40, Walworth-English-Flett, 1920–30: contract and blueprints for underground steam distribution system, 4/2/23, revised 4/23/23; General Files: Class of 1926: Clippings, 1926; HWC, Letters to Family: to Sister, 7/30/23.

24. HWC, Letters to Family: to Sister, 9/19/21; see also 3/16/22; 2/26/23; Trustees: R. Smith #5: Wood to SVC, 4/7/24.

25. HWC, Letters to Family: to Sister, 2/25/24.

26. *Wheaton News*, 5/16/25; HWC, Letters to Family: to Sister, October (nd), 1924. See also Trustees: R. Smith #4: passim.

27. Trustees: R. Smith #4: W. I. Cole to Smith, 5/6/25; Smart/Park: Smart: W. I. Cole to Smart, 5/11/25; Trustees Minutes: 5/14/25. Smart was appointed at the same $6000 salary that Dr. Cole had received, plus the use of the President's House and "expenses for two."

28. In the tradition of many New England colleges of the time, the President of the College also served as the President or Chairman of the Board of Trustees. At Wheaton this practice continued until 1944, when the Board decided to elect its own chair, although incoming President A. Howard Meneely continued as an ex officio member.

29. Trustees: Kilham #2: Smart to Kilham, 5/11/25.

30. Faculty: Parker: Smart to Parker, 5/12/26; Shepard, "Reference History," p. 446.

31. William I. Cole remained in his position as Treasurer until October, 1926, resigning as soon as the new President, J. Edgar Park, took office. Having been elected to his brother's slot on the Board of Trustees, Cole continued, however, on the Board until his death in 1935, when the again-vacant "Cole" position was filled by the election of Helen Wieand Cole, who in turn served as a Trustee until 1965. With her resignation the formal involvement of the Cole family came to an end, and the College's last direct connection with the Wheaton family was terminated. Trustees Minutes: 6/15/25; 7/14/26.

32. Faculty: Work: HWC to Work, 6/17/25.

33. Ibid.: Eastburn: Eastburn to SVC, 3/4/25; S. B. Young to Clippinger, 5/3/33; see also Kerr: SVC to Kerr, 3/2,14/25.

34. Ibid.: Eastburn: Smart to Eastburn, 7/29/25.

35. Ibid.: Smart memo re Eastburn interview, 7/31/25.

36. Ibid.: Eastburn to Smart, 7/16/25; 8/4/25; Smart to Eastburn, 7/29/25.

37. For other examples of Cole's concern with faculty "loyalty," see ibid.: L. Soskin Rogers: SVC to A. Bates, 5/27/24; W. Warren: SVC to Harvard Appointment Bureau, 1919.

38. Ibid.: Work: HWC to Work, 6/17/25.

39. A groundswell of alumnae, faculty, and student sentiment in favor of naming these two buildings in honor of Ida Everett and President Cole was responded to favorably by the Board of Trustees at their meeting on July 14, 1926. See ibid.: Everett: passim, 1925–26; Trustees Minutes: 7/14/26; also 3/15/22; 5/14/25; *Wheaton Alumnae Quarterly*, 6:1 (December, 1926), pp. 2–3. The cost of Everett Hall was $340,684. Additional accoustic work in the dining room costing $3,313 was completed in 1930. See Faculty: Everett: clipping from *N.Y. Times*, 10/17/26; Buildings: Everett Hall; Treasurer: "Trial Balance Ledger," 1919–33; President's Office, Dormitories/Practices: Dormitories 1926–29: Everett, 1/10/28; Bursar's Office Correspondence, 1889–1940: #19, Cram and Ferguson, 1920–30; President's Reports to Trustees: 6/11/32.

40. Smart/Park: Park Correspondence: "Dr. John E. Park New Wheaton Head," 6/14/26.

41. Trustees: R. Smith #4: Park to Smith, 9/22/27.

42. Oral History Project: D. Littlefield interview, 1983.

43. Trustees Minutes: 5/24/26; 7/14/26, and appended letter, Park to Board of Trustees, 7/3/26; 9/28/26.

44. Trustees Minutes: Letter, Park to Trustees, 7/3/26, appended to minutes of 6/17/26.

45. Quoted by E. J. Knapton, Oral History Project: E. J. Knapton interview, 1983.

46. Ibid.: K. Burton interview, 1983; see also C. White interview, 1983, in which she describes Park as a "benevolent despot."

47. Ibid.: D. Littlefield interview, 1983.

48. H. Austin, interview with author, 3/28/96.

49. Oral History Project: R. Park interview, 1984.

50. Faculty Meeting Minutes, 9/24/41.

51. Smart/Park: Park, 26–44: *Boston Herald* clipping, wire service report, 5/7/29.

52. Ibid.: *Boston Evening Transcript* clipping, 12/3/29.

53. Oral History Project: E. J. Knapton interview, 1983.

54. Oral History Project: M. Hidy interview, 1985; E.J. Knapton interview, 1983; E. J. Knapton, *Small Figure in a Large Landscape: An Autobiography* (Privately published, 1987), p. 163; see also Faculty Meeting Minutes: 9/20/34.

55. Oral History Project: H. Austin interview, 1983; Austin and Budd, *Alive and Well Said,* p. 13.

56. HWC, Letters to Family: to Sister, 9/20/23; 5/1/24.

57. Trustees Minutes: 3/18/25.

58. Faculty: Denkinger: Denkinger to Smart, 4/3/26.

59. Staff: S. B. Young: Smart/Young correspondence, Fall, 1925; Trustees: Meadows #13: Smart to Meadows, 10/12/25. For a summary of the duties performed by the Registrar's Office, see Staff: S. B. Young: Young to Smart, 7/17/25; 1/23/26.

60. Faculty: E. White: passim; Staff: Spaulding: Denkinger to Greene, 12/16/26; 1/6/27; Park memorandum, 12/13/26; Trustees, General Information: Miscellaneous, 1925–45: Park to R. Smith, 1/6/27. Apparently Edith White was able to memorize the picture and file of every incoming freshman to the point that she would greet each one

immediately by name when the student first appeared to register in the fall. Faculty: Carpenter: Carpenter to Meneely, 6/14/54.

61. Dean's Office, Admissions: "Summary of Changes in Wheaton's Admission Policy, January, 1927–January, 1932."

62. Dean's Office, Denkinger: "History and Procedure, 1925–1929," vols. 1–6. This collection actually is contained in six file folders, but since they are described in the table of contents as "volumes" I have followed that designation in the citations.

63. Ibid.: "Study of College Government in Wheaton College, 1920–1928," 6 files.

64. Trustees: R. Smith #4: Smith to Park, 12/4/28.

65. Faculty: Denkinger: Park to Denkinger, 11/27/28.

66. Ibid.: W. I. Cole to Park, 1/4/29.

67. Trustees: Meadows #12: Meadows to Park, 2/17/29; see also R. Smith #4: Park to Smith, 12/4/28; Faculty: Denkinger: undated letter of resignation from Dean Denkinger; Chapel address by Park, 1/24/29.

68. Trustees Minutes: 4/4/29.

69. Faculty: Carpenter: Carpenter to Park, 2/13/29.

70. Ibid.: Park to Carpenter, 2/14/29; see also Carpenter to Park, 2/17/29; 2/27/29.

71. Trustees Minutes: 3/10/30.

72. The President's memos to Miss Carpenter were usually headed simply, "Dear Dean," with the result that she often signed her replies to him "DD."

73. Faculty: Carpenter: Carpenter to Park, 2/27/29; Park to Mierow, 2/28/29; Mierow to Park, 3/11/29; Holmes to Woolley, 4/26/30.

74. Staff: S. B. Young: Johnson to Park, 10/28/30.

75. Ibid.: Armstrong: Park to Armstrong, 9/22/27.

76. Ibid.: passim; Faculty: Work: Work to Park, 10/5,15/28; 11/28/28; 1/26/29; Park to Work, 10/5/28; 10/17/28. The Cole collection of more than 1500 volumes constituted a major part of the Library's modest collection of 18,500 volumes in 1929. See Staff: Amrstrong: Armstrong to Park, 2/4/29; Trustees Minutes: 11/23/25.

77. General Files: Class of 1924: Historic Data 1923–25; Alumnae Affairs Office, 64: AAUW.

78. See Trustees, 1834–1910: K. U. Clark #3: Clark to SVC, 5/31/22.

79. Trustees Minutes: 3/12/28; *Wheaton Alumnae Quarterly*, 9:4 (August, 1930), p. 21; 10:2 (February, 1931), p. 12.

80. See chs. 1, 4, n. 3; Trustees Minutes: 6/31/21; 9/8/21; 9/22/21.

81. Trustees: Plimpton #4: SVC to Plimpton, 11/1/23; Trustees Minutes: 6/12/16; 11/21/22; 6/17/23; 11/23/23; 2/26/24; 12/11/26; Wheaton Family, Winter Street Property: Bursar's Office, 1920–30; 1922–1926, passim; Cook to W. I. Cole, 12/1/23; Letter to Cook, 12/10/23; Trustees: Soliday #5: Soliday to Jackson, 12/11/26; Park to Soliday, 12/13/26; Soliday to Park, 12/17/26.

82. HWC, Letters to Family: to Sister, 10/23/23.

83. In 1927, the College also sold to the Wading River Reservoir Corporation for $1000 the land formerly owned by Mrs. Wheaton which lay beneath the man-made Norton Reservoir. This body of water had been created in the latter nineteenth century to assure an adequate year-round water supply for industries located on the Ten-Mile river downstream in Taunton. Bursar's Office Correspondence, 1890–1940: #23, Land Transactions, 1920–30: Crapo to Smart, 2/19/26; #32, Norton Taxes: Witherell to College Treasurer, 10/20/27; Trustees Minutes: 3/17/26; 3/22/27; 6/18/27; Trustees: Kilham #2: Kilham to Park, 3/28/27; Park to Kilham, 3/30/27.

84. Trustees Minutes: 3/10/30.

85. Ibid.

86. Ibid.

87. Trustees Minutes: ll/15/26; 3/22/27; 11/15/27; 3/12/28; 11/18/29; 3/10/30; 6/

16/30; Staff: Cutler: Park to Cutler, 9/29/28; Bursar's Office Correspondence, 1889–1940: #37, Soliday 1920–1930: Park memorandum, 1/5/29; #30, Miscellaneous, 1920–30: Park to Dunkle, 5/21/29.

88. Trustees Minutes: 4/4/29; Faculty: E. White: Agreement with Wheaton College, 5/6/29; Carpenter: Carpenter to Meneely, 6/14/54; *Wheaton News*, 11/16/29; 2/15/30.

89. Trustees Minutes: 11/26/28.

90. Ibid.: 4/4/29.

91. Trustees: Kilham #2: Park to Kilham, 12/16/29.

92. Though the original low bid was $8,542, the final cost of constructing the pond was $16,932. President's Reports to Trustees: 6/11/32; Trustees Minutes: 3/12/28; 11/6/28; 4/4/29; Trustees: Crapo #1: Park to Crapo, 1/26/29; Smart/Park: Smart: Park to Mrs. Smart, 2/2/29. Grace Shepard notes that in addition to Eliza Lakelet and Peregrine Pond, the pond was also referred to "facetiously" as the Peacock's Mirror, presumably because on calm days one could see the Chapel steeple with its peacock weathervane reflected on its surface. See Shepard, "Reference History," p. 408.

93. Staff: Cutler: President's secretary to Cutler, 6/26/30, copy of letter sent to L. G. Nourse.

94. Oral History Project: J. Yelle interview, 1983.

12

Settling In: The Not-So-Roaring Twenties

In his *President's Report* for 1921–22, President Cole had set 500 students as an upper limit for the size of the College. In the fall of 1926, as J. Edgar Park assumed the administrative leadership of Wheaton, enrollment for the first time passed that magic number; 510 students were registered as classes opened. Within two years, however, the number had fallen to 450; it would remain between 450 and 475 until the end of World War II, only returning permanently to numbers exceeding 500 in 1949–50.[1]

The reasons for this turnaround and subsequent stabilization at a level lower than originally contemplated were several, and for the most part reflected changes in College policy, rather than outside forces at work. Although the national economic depression undoubtedly was a contributing factor in determining enrollment in the 1930s, the initial downturn was almost exclusively the result of a series of admissions, curricular, and facilities policy changes undertaken in the first years of the Park administration.

Although the College had for some years allowed students to qualify for admission through examinations administered either by the College Entrance Examination Board or by Wheaton, the most popular method for gaining admission was by "certification." This meant that any student from an "approved" school, who was certified as having successfully completed a program of study conforming to Wheaton's entrance requirements, could gain admission without taking any form of examination.[2] The problem was that preparatory schools, anxious to place their graduating seniors in college, were not always as careful in awarding this certification as Wheaton or other colleges might have liked. Now, with the growing acceptance of the national College Entrance Examination Board (CEEB) testing process, a new and much more objective evaluation process seemed to be at hand.[3]

Issues of student quality, compounded by the ever ongoing drive to increase the size of the student body, came to a head just as J. Edgar Park assumed the presidency. Wheaton opened in the fall of 1926 with 510 students, only to witness the withdrawal for various reasons—voluntary, social and academic—of 37 students during the academic year. Although in June, 1927, President Park was anticipating 521 students in September, the College actually opened with 497 and the following year the number had been reduced to 450. In his report to the Board of Trustees in November, 1928, President Park asserted that this reduction had been both anticipated and planned. In order to upgrade other areas of the College's work, he stated, he had found it necessary to take rooms that had accommodated some 66 students out of use. This space had been utilized to provide more administrative and office secretarial space, music practice rooms, larger reception rooms, more bathrooms, a few two-room suites in the dormitories for senior faculty, and the conversion of the smallest student doubles to single person status. All of this was necessary, Park asserted, to put Wheaton "in line" with other women's colleges, and the anticipated drop in numbers had been dealt with by raising the tuition for freshmen and sophomores by $50.[4]

All of this was undoubtedly true, but it is evident that in many ways the driving force behind this reduction was concern with the academic ability of some of the students matriculating at Wheaton. Believing that the admission by certification process was primarily responsible for the increasing numbers of students with academic problems, Registrar Sarah Belle Young advocated in 1925 that the College consider admission by examination only. This change was strongly supported in 1927 by the head of the newly created Admissions Office, Edith White. Beginning with the class admitted in the fall of 1928, entrance by certification was no longer allowed, and all candidates for admission were required at a minimum to take the CEEB Scholastic Aptitude and English examinations. The result was a substantial drop in applications, from 336 the previous year to 272, and an even more drastic reduction in those admitted, because of a high failure rate on the English examination. Whereas 171 freshmen had entered in September, 1927, only 117 were admitted in the fall of 1928.[5]

The change in admissions policy apparently did have the desired effect on student quality. Of the 171 members of the last freshman class allowed admission through the certification process, 13 had been dropped from the College for academic reasons by the end of the first year, and 3 more were required to attend summer school in order to return in the fall. A substantial number of others were denied full sophomore standing until they could remove through special examination the "conditional failure" grades they had received in one or more courses. The next year far fewer entering students were dropped at midyears. Park was able to report to the trustees that the faculty seemed to believe that the overall academic quality of the student body had improved, an opinion in which Edith White concurred.[6]

Nonetheless, in an effort to increase enrollment, the College in 1929 began to enroll a selected number of students whose grades on the CEEB English exam had been unsatisfactory, but whose credentials in other

ways seemed promising. The performance of these students was carefully monitored, and the results were reported as quite positive—only 3
out of 25 in this risk category failed to survive the freshman year. Conversely, the Admissions Office reported poor results from an experimental admission of 16 students from the waiting or rejected lists of other
colleges, for their obvious disgruntlement had a negative effect on those
students for whom Wheaton had been the first choice.[7]

Despite the Admissions Office's best efforts, and a gradual but steady
increase in the number of applicants from the low point experienced in
1927–28, total enrollment permanently leveled off in the range between
450 and 475. Much of this can be attributed to the small amount of
money available for scholarships, a matter that became increasingly important as the national economic situation worsened beginning in 1929.
Although the College continued to provide many on-campus self-help
work opportunities for students, only $4250 was available in the fall of
1927 for direct grants to students, a sum that was apportioned among
thirty applicants. In addition students from Norton continued to receive
a 50 percent tuition remission. The means by which additional money
for scholarships might be generated was one Dr. Park discussed time and
again with the trustees, but with no perceptible result.[8]

One positive side effect of Wheaton's decision to accept applicants
exclusively through the examination process was that it gained admission into a new elite group. "Although not one of the 'Seven Colleges'
cooperating to raise funds," Miss White wrote to President Park, "we
are now one of 'The Nine Examination Colleges'."[9] Consisting of the
now well-known "seven sisters," plus Wells and Wheaton, this group
annually held a joint meeting with delegates from the National Association of Principals of Schools for Girls, and participation in it demonstra-
bly enabled Wheaton to become better known in areas of the South and
Midwest from which it had hitherto had little success in attracting students.[10]

In the spring of 1918, several trustees suggested to President Cole that
the College should consider awarding honorary degrees at commencement. Cole was cool to the idea. Pointing out that Boston University had
yet to grant honorary degrees despite having been in existence for fifty
years, Cole replied that while Wheaton certainly should not wait that
long, he believed that as a young and not well-established institution it
should proceed cautiously in this regard. Nonetheless, it was only a year
later that Wheaton conferred its first honorary degree upon trustee and
alumna Kate Upson Clark (WS1869). This was followed by similar
awards to Dean Ida Everett in 1921, and to well-known alumna missionary Emily Hartwell (WS1883) in 1922. But the College stepped beyond

its own ranks only in 1923, when Vice President of the United States Calvin Coolidge accepted Wheaton's invitation to serve as Commencement speaker and to receive an honorary Doctor of Laws degree. Graduating its largest class ever of fifty seniors, the events of the weekend proved to be an enormous public relations coup for Wheaton.[11]

A public relations issue of a far different nature was the College's name, which became a major concern for President Park and the Board of Trustees in the first years of his administration. This was not a new problem; it will be recalled that in his original petition to the Massachusetts legislature for a college charter in 1912, President Cole had given the name of the institution as Laban Wheaton College in order to avoid

Vice-President Calvin Coolidge and President Cole at the Commencement ceremonies in 1923 during which the Vice-President received an honorary degree.

confusion with another Wheaton College, located in Wheaton, Illinois. However, having discovered that "nothing is more common than dupli- cate names among educational institutions," President Cole had quickly changed his mind, and the charter, as granted, listed the name as Wheaton College.[12] Despite the fact that the two colleges were markedly different, one relatively liberal and restricted to women—the other coed- ucational and church-related, fundamentalist in its religious orientation, and extremely conservative in its social outlook, Cole was convinced that there would be no long-term problem. "There is no comparison be- tween the two catalogues," he wrote trustee Kate Upson Clark. "What- ever confusion there is, I am sure will be temporary. In a short time the word Wheaton will suggest to most people only the Wheaton we have in Norton."[13]

In terms of New England, New York, and the central Atlantic coast states, Cole was fundamentally correct. But as Wheaton sought to ex- pand its recruiting into the Midwest, it discovered that the "other" Wheaton had established its name as firmly there as the Norton Wheaton had done in its own region. As a result, in November, 1927, President Park initiated discussion within the Board of Trustees regarding a possi- ble name change. Time and again, he told the Board, he had encountered instances of confusion between the two institutions on his speaking trips. "We have a student here whose parents thought she was going to the other college, and Illinois has written that they have two who thought they were coming to us," Park reported to trustee Annie Kilham.[14]

While indeed the natural confusion resulting from two institutions having the same name was a matter of concern, it was not the real issue. Trustee Robert Smith, who supported changing the College's name, wrote privately to Park in 1928, "I do not see how we can, in public print, really set before our constituency the main reason for the change—that is to say, the particular character of Wheaton College, Illi- nois, and its insistence upon certain points of view with which we have no sympathy. But that could be tactfully brought to the attention of our alumnae in conversation and, I think, even in alumnae meetings."[15]

That was the nub of the situation. Wheaton had responded to the social and cultural changes of the 1920s by removing Bible Study from its de- gree requirements, becoming more relaxed in its attitudes toward dating, automobiles, and smoking, instructing the teacher of the required sex- hygiene class to answer student questions about birth control, and em- ploying a consulting psychiatrist who would see every week "one or two students who for one reason or another have not come to satisfactory terms with themselves."[16] The resultant clash in philosophies between the College and an institution which prohibited dancing or card playing, and emphasized the teaching of fundamentalist religious principles throughout its curriculum, was becoming ever more apparent.[17]

However, even those who believed a change in name was desirable could not find one that pleased them. Both Park and the Board recognized that total elimination of the name Wheaton would meet with overwhelming alumnae disapproval. Thus the name Old Colony College, perhaps the best of those suggested, was deemed unacceptable. Laban Wheaton College, Eliza Wheaton College, and Wheaton Massachusetts College, were among those considered. However, when the Trustee Committee on Instruction, to whom the matter had been referred, polled the full Board and a selected number of alumnae, they encountered massive resistance to any change whatsoever. As a result on April 4, 1929, the trustees formally voted to drop the matter, adding to their resolution a directive that the word Massachusetts should be emphasized on the letterheads of all Wheaton College correspondence.[18]

The final years of President Cole's administration and the one year of George Smart's leadership saw few significant changes in the curricular structure of the College. Perhaps the most noteworthy were the creation of a new academic department, Economics and Sociology, which was separated from History and Political Science, and the addition of a new discipline, Education, which was combined into a single department with Psychology (previously coupled with Philosophy). In 1922, the College began awarding "degrees with distinction" based upon work done in general studies, while special honors in a concentration was reserved for those who had excelled in work within one of the nine groups into which the curricular program had been organized since 1914–15. In addition, an academic honor roll similar to a Dean's List was created. On the other end of the scale, in 1925 the faculty voted, with Rev. Smart's approval, that students whose written work in any course proved deficient should be remanded to the English department for further tutoring in writing, even if they had already successfully completed the basic writing program.[19]

In the fall of 1922 the old grading system of High Credit, Credit, Pass, Condition, and Fail was replaced by a six letter scale ranging from A to F. A through D was considered passing, but students were required to accumulate at least thirty-four of the sixty credits required for graduation at the level of C or above.[20] The grade of E indicated that a student had received a "condition" in the course, which subsequently could be removed by passing a special examination given either at the opening of College in the fall or immediately following spring vacation.[21]

Although there was no recognized system of permitted class cuts during this period in Wheaton's history, students were allowed to apply for a limited number of "special leaves" (different for each class year), which involved absences from campus that would include missing a class or classes. Excused absences for health reasons, field trips, or offi-

cial extracurricular activities were also granted. All absences were reported daily, and, in accordance with faculty legislation, at the end of
the semester the Registrar's office imposed a proportionate reduction in
the grade for any course in which unexcused absences had occurred.
This reduction was doubled if the absences involved the class meetings
directly before or after a vacation period. The percentage of this reduction was a carefully guarded secret, but since faculty were required to
hand in numerical grades based upon a 100 point scale, it undoubtedly
was not hard to administer the process uniformly and fairly.[22]

One of the first things President Park did upon taking office was to
undertake a systematic personal review of both the admissions requirements and the curriculum as a whole. By the end of his first academic
year in office, he felt comfortable enough to begin instituting unilaterally
a number of substantive changes. His mode of operation was to inform
the academic departments affected, giving them a chance to discuss the
matter with him privately before the changes were publically announced.
Though he always listened to comments from the various department
heads, and was open to student suggestions for curricular change, the
general thrust of Park's approach was that he was sure whomever he
consulted would of course agree with whatever alterations he was about
to make.

The first of several such changes occurred in the spring of 1927, when
Park decided to close down the program in Household Economics and
abolish the requirement, which had existed ever since President Cole had
created it as a means of justifying to the State Board of Education
Wheaton's unique mission of training students in the "business of being
a woman." In his report to the Board of Trustees, Park commented that
students universally disliked the courses offered, it was difficult to find
competent teachers, and the equipment required was very expensive.
Household Economics was "an impossible side of college life to accommodate in a liberal arts college."[23] It was far better to leave courses of
this type to colleges "better constituted to specialize in them," unquestionably an indirect reference to Simmons College in Boston, which emphasized vocational training. In place of the offerings in Household
Economics, Park proposed, and the faculty and students approved, an
elective course in the chemistry of foods.[24]

In the same manner, in the fall of 1927 Park made the decision to drop
the Biblical Literature and Art History requirements for the degree. His
letter to Amy Otis, Head of the Art Department, is illustrative of his operational technique.

> In reviewing the catalogue I am changing some of the requirements for
> the A.B. degree in order to make our requirements correspond more with
> those of other colleges of our type. I am proposing not to require Art as
> one of the subjects which <u>must</u> be taken for the degree. I imagine that you
> will approve of this step.[25]

On a visit to Middlebury College in the spring of 1927, Park was favorably impressed by the existence of a "French House" in which resident faculty and students conversed only in French. Upon his return to Wheaton he immediately set about organizing a similar facility with such determination that the next fall Wheaton's *Maison Blanche*, located on Howard street, opened under the direction of Agnes Riddell. Arrangements were also made for there to be exclusively French-speaking tables in the dining room.[26]

Several other major changes went into effect between 1928 and 1930. Seeking to bring Wheaton's curriculum more in line with that of other colleges, Park was the driving force in gaining faculty and student approval for abolishing the so-called "group system" in which students were required to concentrate in one of nine groups, each of which incorporated a planned four-year course program. This was replaced by a broadly defined fifteen credit-hour general education requirement, plus a mandate that each student complete a major program of study in a particular subject, such as History, English Literature, French, or Chemistry. In addition a minor in either a single subject or a combination of subjects relevant to and approved by the student's major department was required. A Dean's List was established by the faculty, originally limited to seniors, but soon extended to all students who had received an honor rating (85 average) for the previous two semesters. Students on the Dean's List were free from class-cutting regulations except for the so-called "calendar days" before and after vacations, and were not required to take quizzes, only final examinations, in courses in which they were enrolled.[27]

At the request of the Classics department, President Park also authorized the institution of individualized independent studies honors programs. At first he considered seeking faculty approval for this program, but then changed his mind. "It seems to me," he wrote the Head of the Classics Department, Eunice Work, "that with the approval of the President it is entirely a matter for each department to decide." While it would be necessary to monitor each program carefully, "I am perfectly sure that it is along the right educational lines."[28] In a similar vein he enthusiastically supported the English department's creation in 1930 of an honors program for selected majors in the junior and senior years, as well as the department's plan to institute a comprehensive examination for all English majors in the spring of their senior year.[29]

Two further changes were implemented in the admissions process. Openly admitting that he was following the example of Vassar College, which he regarded as a leader in progressive education, President Park authorized dropping the entrance requirement in Latin, and approved a system of proficiency examinations, passage of which would allow well-prepared students to be excused from fulfilling one or another of the general education requirements for the degree. This option, Park asserted, would provide more academic freedom for the better students. It was based on the assumption that secondary schools were providing the necessary general background required in many areas, and that it was therefore "the function of the college to inspire a student to attain real knowledge in her field."[30]

In one other area President Park differed noticeably from President Cole. Undoubtedly urged in this direction by Dean Denkinger, President Park was clearly much more willing to accept and even seek student input into a wide variety of questions that until then had been regarded as beyond their legitimate purview. Early in his administration he accepted a suggestion that seniors be allowed to make suggestions regarding the curriculum, and it was a faculty/student committee that, at the President's initiative, reviewed the group system and recommended the change to a system of major and minor subject concentrations.[31]

But in 1929 Park went even further. In a meeting with Louise Barr, student editor of the the *Wheaton News*, Park suggested that the newspaper initiate a College-wide undergraduate course evaluation process. At the same time he made it crystal clear that he would never acknowledge publicly that this was *his* idea. Knowing, however, that he would not disapprove, the students proceeded. A standardized questionnaire was developed; the results for each course were tabulated and given to the course instructor along with the general overall averages for the College as a whole. In his report to the Board of Trustees, Park indicated clearly that he saw this as a good thing, but he also felt compelled to comment that "some faculty resented this very keenly, feeling that the dignity of the office of professor was threatened by any such freedom of criticism on the part of the students, or that the source of error would not be covered by the law of averages."[32]

Overall, as in the area of administrative staff and structure, the first four years of the Park administration encompassed substantial alterations in the academic curriculum and in requirements for both admission and graduation. In a statement to the faculty in September, 1927, Park asserted his belief that it was necessary to "conduct here an experiment in education which will make Wheaton stand for something other than a second-rate minor edition of the larger colleges. . . . The only hope of the small college," he went on, "lies in the adventurous spirits in its faculty who dare to try educational experiments."[33] Aware that major changes were occuring nationwide in the educational landscape as colleges sought to attract an ever increasing percentage of high school and preparatory school graduates, Park obviously saw his rapid and often highhanded implementation of changes in the academic program as necessary in order to bring Wheaton in line with what was being done in other colleges and universities. In doing so he at times trod somewhat heavily on faculty sensibilities regarding due process, though one senses that at the same time many of the newer faculty found his willingness to approve innovative and experimental initiatives such as independent studies, advanced level seminars, and departmental honors programs highly refreshing.

The one problem President Park did not have to face immediately upon taking office was the continued stress, both fiscal and in terms of time and energy, of a major building program. This allowed him during his first years as President to turn the major part of his attention to matters long neglected. In addition to curricular and administrative issues, one of these was faculty compensation and development.

While President Cole had lobbied for modest increases in faculty and staff salaries from time to time, his overriding concern with expanding the physical plant of the College had inevitably resulted in relatively minimal improvements in the area of faculty and staff compensation. Since every bit of income from endowment had gone directly to the building program, improvements in other areas had had to come from increased tuition charges, which overall had not come close to keeping pace with inflation during the Cole years.

Almost immediately Park set out to do something about what he clearly regarded as the poor fiscal support given to the faculty by the College in terms of both salaries and benefits. In doing so he was responding both to his own sense of what was needed, and to increasing unrest among the faculty regarding a wide range of issues. With his succession to the presidency the floodgate containing pent-up resentment, particularly among women members of the faculty, built up during the last years of President Cole's administration, burst. Park found himself inundated with requests, some polite, some irate, but all insistent, for overdue salary adjustments and promotions. Although more often than not these individual requests were not successful, or at best resulted in carefully hedged promises of some action after another year or two, they hardly fell on deaf ears.

In the spring of 1929, Park for the first time presented to the trustees a full list of individual faculty compensations. Noting that salaries for full professors at Wheaton ranged from a low of $1800 plus room and board to a high of $3600 plus a house, Park indicated that in order to be competitive with other eastern women's colleges in attracting faculty, the College should be compensating its faculty at a minimum of $3000 for an assistant professor up to a maximum of $6000 for senior full Professors. The long-term results of his comments, however, were minimal; the economic crisis into which the nation plunged in the fall of 1929 obviated the possibility of any major improvement in faculty compensation.[34]

Two instances from this period serve to highlight the problems many faculty had in dealing directly with the President on an individual basis concerning salary issues. In a letter to Dr. Park in which she asked politely if he thought the $1700 plus living that she was receiving was "adequate," Grace Shepard commented that she found it impossible to talk to him directly about this matter. Since "girlhood," she wrote, "I have felt that teaching was in a manner a sacred thing, and that the thought of money should not be associated with it."[35] In expressing this view, Miss Shepard mirrored almost exactly the sentiments that had been expressed by Mary Lyon to the first group of students enrolled at Wheaton Female Seminary ninety years earlier.[36]

The opposite end of the spectrum can be found in the person of Dr. Mathilde Lange, who had come to Wheaton in 1921 as Assistant Professor of Biology. Initially President Cole had offered her the rank of professor, which was standard for all men with a Ph.D., but he had been compelled by the Board of Trustees to reduce the rank, though interestingly, not the salary. Annually Miss Lange lobbied the administration regarding her promotion. In 1924 she was advanced to associate professor, but this only led to greater intensification of her efforts to attain full professorial status. In 1927–28 she applied for and received an unpaid leave of absence. Subsequently, while studying at the Stazione Zoologica in Naples, Italy, she informed Wheaton both of her resignation and that she had applied for a position at Hunter College.[37]

President Park was nothing if not distressed. In Miss Lange he had found strong support for his attempts to change College policies in many areas, as well as an ally within the science departments regarding curricular changes to which his strongest opponents were two male full professors, Glenn Shook and Auguste Pouleur. Distraught over her resignation, Dr. Park cabled to Italy, "Cable before Saturday if any change makes it possible to accept professorship next year."[38] Obviously scenting victory, Miss Lange tersely replied, "Accept Professorship at $250 per month and living," to which Park simply replied "Offer accepted."[39] Perhaps to insure that it was clear who was in the driver's seat on this issue, Dr. Lange wrote a long letter to President Park on April 2, 1928, in which she carefully detailed his acceptance of *her* offer, concluding with the comment, "I am glad to return to Wheaton and look forward to seeing the dear old place again next September."[40]

Park was most successful in improving fringe benefits for the faculty. He made available through the auspices of the College a life insurance plan at low group rates, though the trustees insisted that the premiums be paid entirely by faculty members themselves. Much more willing than President Cole had been to contemplate unpaid leaves of absence, he also successfully persuaded the Board in March, 1928, to implement a plan for paid sabbatical leaves after seven years of service, though the trustees, ever prudent in their fiscal concerns, ruled that normally only one faculty member should be granted a sabbatical in any year.[41] Although faculty on sabbatical were required to vacate College-owned housing, financial compensation during the leave period was based solely on cash salary, with no allowance for the value of the residential compensation they were being required to forfeit for the sabbatical year or term.[42]

But Park's biggest achievement by far in this area was the implementation of the College's first retirement plan, the need for which had long been apparent. In his *President's Report* for 1920–21, President Cole had called for the development of such a plan, but there is no evidence that any action was even considered. The College's custom had generally been to reward long-time employees, both faculty and staff, with a single lump-sum payment of a few hundred dollars when they retired. In 1927, the faculty Academic Council raised the issue of retirement compensation with President Park. Faced with the imminent retirement of former Dean Everett from teaching, Park proposed and the trustees accepted that she be given a small part-time position in student services, which would then allow the College to provide her with a home and $1200 per year to compensate for years of low pay. But Ida Everett's extreme situation served to highlight the need to develop some system to assure that many members of the faculty would not approach retirement totally devoid of any means of fiscal support.[43]

Therefore, at Park's urging the trustees voted in March, 1928, to establish a "contingent fund" equal to 5 percent of the total salaries paid to the faculty "for the purpose of paying pensions to retired members of the faculty."[44] The following March the Board voted another 5 percent to the fund, but in November, 1929, because of Park's insistence that this was not enough, the trustees increased the 1929–30 allocation to 10 percent of the salaries paid to both faculty and administration, and agreed that this policy should continue annually until further notice. They added, however, the stipulation that the cost of funding sabbatical leaves should be taken out of the contingent fund, rather than the annual operating budget.[45]

It turned out that all this was preliminary to a plan developed by Dr. Park and approved by the Board on March 10, 1930. It called for the establishment of a Retirement Allowance Fund into which a faculty member and the College would each annually contribute 5 percent of the faculty member's cash salary. If a faculty member left Wheaton before age sixty, only the amount deposited by the individual, plus earned interest, could be withdrawn from the fund. Retirement between age sixty and the academic year when a faculty member reached the mandatory retirement age of sixty-five, would result in either a lump-sum payment or an annuity equal to the value of the combined faculty/college contributions to the fund, plus interest. It was also stipulated that the retirement allotment must at least equal the salary received by the faculty member in the final year of employment. All continuing faculty were required to join in the fall of 1930 or forever renounce their eligibility, while participation by new members of the teaching staff was mandated as soon as their cash salary reached either $2000 or $1500 plus living. In order to enable the plan to become operational immediately, and to cover those faculty scheduled to retire shortly, the Board voted on June 16, 1930, to place the $14,700 already in the Contingent Fund into the Retirement Allowance Fund in addition to the funds to be collected or reserved starting in the fall of 1930.[46]

Meager as it may seem today, implementation of this plan constituted a major step forward in the area of faculty compensation, and on the whole the faculty apparently recognized it as such. Although the withholding of 5 percent of their salaries undoubtedly caused considerable hardship for many faculty members, there seems to have been a genuine recognition that the President had achieved an important breakthrough in the area of total compensation. This plan, coupled with the new sabbatical leave policy, helped at least partially to assuage continuing faculty disgruntlement over low salaries and long years spent in rank waiting for promotion.

However, unrest on the part of women faculty members was not limited to financial issues. President Park found himself confronted with growing resentment over the requirement that they live in the dormitories. The competitive, sometimes backbiting politics that surrounded the assignment of dormitory suites to faculty, especially the prized attainment of a single rather than double accommodation, was hardly edifying. After fifteen years of living on campus, Agnes Riddell complained, "the disadvantages of 'mass habitation' seem to me to outweigh its advantages."[47] Similarly, a meeting of "campus faculty" (those living in the dormitories) produced a resolution protesting the requirement that faculty eat at tables with students. Although one of Park's first actions as President had been to authorize separate tables from students in the dining room for faculty and administration at breakfast and lunch, women faculty still resented the requirement that they serve as table hostesses at evening dinner.[48]

In both cases there was no administrative movement, at least in part because of strong trustee sentiment that a diminishment of faculty presence in the dormitories and dining halls would undermine the special "home" environment that had been treasured and preserved throughout the nearly full-century of Wheaton's existence. In an effort to create a permanent solution to the dining issue and mindful of views on the Board of Trustees, in April, 1930, the President mandated that faculty living in dormitories serve as table hostesses at four dinners each week. No women's college, he asserted, "has dared to have its students eat in large dining rooms without any adult at any of the tables." To give up this practice would mean that Wheaton would have to incur the expense of hiring hostesses. He also requested resumption of a past custom in which faculty "received students" in their dormitory suites on Sunday evenings, though this was not put in the form of a requirement. Park did express sympathy with a faculty request for a room with a furnished kitchenette to serve as a base of operations for the Faculty Club, a request that would resurface periodically over the decades but with no realized result.[49]

In terms of hiring, retaining, and promoting faculty, President Park took a distinctly different position from his predecessor. President Cole had sought to alter the composition of the faculty by seeking candidates with a Ph.D. and actively recruiting men. However, once at Wheaton the litmus test for faculty survival had focussed exclusively on teaching competence and personal loyalty to the President, and through him to the community at large. Promotion had been achieved primarily on the basis of graduate degrees attained and very occasionally because of longevity of service.

With the advent of Dr. Park's administration, much of this changed. He immediately began using the position of instructor for persons holding only a bachelors degree, who would be retained on a three-year contract and then expected to leave to pursue more advanced graduate work.[50] Though attainment of graduate degrees was generally a prerequisite for promotion, faculty were not encouraged to pursue graduate studies while teaching at Wheaton. When Dorothy Littlefield did succeed in completing work for her Masters degree, President Park rewarded her with a promotion to assistant professor, but with the proviso that she should not immediately continue course work toward the Ph.D., but must devote herself entirely to Wheaton for at least one year.[51]

> What I am trying to avoid is the type of instructor who teaches the necessary courses and drops there all further interest in the college, neither being present at chapel or faculty meetings or meetings of the Faculty club or having very much touch with the students outside of the classroom. It seems to me that the only reason for the existence of a college like Wheaton is that its teaching force can do something more than officiate at the desk in the classroom, and that attendance and participation at other affairs in the college does help in producing a college morale and a genuine spirit which is entirely different from the Rah! Rah! spirit which is coming to be despised.[52]

Promotion to associate professor now more often, though not always, required the faculty member to already hold a Ph.D., while the speed with which one attained that rank or a full professorship came to be influenced heavily by evidence of scholarly activity beyond the classroom. The advancement of Elsie Gulley from Assistant to Associate Professor of History after only two years in rank was a direct reward for the publication of her scholarly monograph on Joseph Chamberlain by the Columbia University Press. Conversely, when pressed by Elizabeth Amen,

Park informed her that promotion to full professor would depend "upon the publication of something valuable."[53]

Almost immediately on taking office, President Park announced to the faculty that since the Academic Council already included the "greater part" of the faculty, he was expanding it to include all teaching members of the staff, who would now be automatically eligible to attend faculty meetings, which would replace the meetings of the Academic Council. This decision was only incorporated into the College Statutes in 1929, when the trustees authorized a revision of the Statutes that replaced all references to the Academic Council with the term "Faculty," and broadened the automatic definition of the faculty to include all those holding positions ranging from instructor to full professor. Included also were the President, Dean, Registrar, and the Secretary to the Board of Admissions, though interestingly the College Librarian, Marian Merrill, was not granted the faculty status that Park had accorded her predecessor, Mary Armstrong. A new Administration Committee, made up of four administrators and five faculty chosen by their peers, was authorized, with the proviso that the faculty might, "when deemed advisable, delegate to it the authority of the Faculty" in the areas of academic policy, curriculum, degree requirements, admissions and academic standing that the Statutes specifically designated to faculty oversight. The President continued, however, to retain the right "to suspend or veto any act of the Faculty when in his judgment it seems expedient to do so."[54]

Major disciplinary measures were to be handled by a newly created committee of the College Government Association, the Judicial Board, to be composed of the President, Dean, one faculty member and two students. The faculty were specifically designated as members of the College Government Association (no longer to be called the Student Government Association), and were required to approve annually the constitution and by-laws of the Association. Though formally approved by the Board of Trustees only in 1929, most of the changes involving the College Government Association had been in effect for some years, and the action of the trustees constituted recognition of changes already implemented rather than authorization of new innovations.[55]

Other than those already mentioned, three members of the faculty during the 1920s deserve a word of comment, each for different reasons. In the spring of 1922, Hiram Tucker, Professor of Music, suffered a stroke and fell at the bottom of the stairs in his son's home. He never recovered, and died the following October. Commencing his teaching at Wheaton Seminary on a part-time basis in 1879–80 while continuing his career as organist for the famed Handel and Haydn Society of Boston, Professor Tucker had joined the faculty full-time in the first year of Wheaton's existence as an accredited college. His forty-three years of continuous service as head of the Music department would remain the standard for teaching longevity at Wheaton until 1994, when it was surpassed by Professor Edwin Briggs of the English department.[56]

A signal honor was accorded the Head of the History and Economics Department, Allen West, when he was designated in the spring of 1925 as one of the first group of scholars to be awarded a Guggenheim fellowship. During his fellowship year away from Wheaton, Dr. West received the offer of an appointment from Princeton University. Perhaps the most interesting aspect of his decision not to return to Wheaton was the reason presented as primary in his letter of resignation to Acting President Smart. Commenting regretfully that Wheaton salaries were not sufficient to allow a private school education for his son and daughter, and stressing the inadequacies of the Norton public school system, West commented that his leaving Wheaton would have been inevitable at some date.[57]

President Smart was more than understanding, noting in his reply to West that his own children's education had been the deciding factor years before when he reluctantly had left a Vermont parish where he had been very happy for one in the fashionable Boston suburb of Newton. Interestingly, West never went to Princeton; instead he received a one-year renewal of his fellowship from the Guggenheim Foundation, and subsequently took a position on the faculty at the University of Cincinnati.[58]

Finally, mention must be made of perhaps the most colorful and ideosyncratic member of the faculty during these transition years. Glenn Shook had come to Wheaton in 1918 as Professor of Physics; in 1927 he also assumed the duties of Director of the Observatory. Fascinated with anything electronic, he had a radio installed in the physics laboratory in 1922. Broadcasts were limited in that era, but almost every evening when he was free, President Cole would join Shook in the laboratory to listen to the speech or concert which was broadcast each night at eight. Clearly not happy about her husband's frequent evening absences, Mrs. Cole nonetheless conceded that "it is good that S.V. has some sort of plaything."[59]

But Professor Shook, who always lectured to his classes in a morning coat and striped trousers, was best known for his invention of what he called his "color organ." "It was a machine," one of his colleagues later recalled, "an amazing jumble. It was run by electricity, but it had prisms and globes full of different colored water and rotating disks with different colors in them. . . . And you let it go and it would project great masses of color on a screen. And as the parts of the machine went around, they'd change and you'd have a glaring burnt red color which changed to bright green. Lines would come across and things would burst out like a flower opening. Oh, an amazing thing! The only thing was he couldn't control it. You couldn't play it. There was no keyboard or anything."[60] Although his invention earned him a feature article in the

Boston Globe, it apparently never became anything more than an item of curiosity and entertainment on the Wheaton campus.[61]

Nowhere in the College administrative structure was there more growth and change during the 1920s than in the area of student government. The development of a student run organization that would implement and enforce regulations governing extracurricular organizations, student life in the dormitories, and academic and social honor codes had begun shortly after Wheaton attained collegiate status. However, its full flowering was only achieved under the watchful eye and obsession for procedure evidenced by Dean Denkinger. Fully committed to the concept of student self-governance, the Dean also believed that students could be entrusted only to administer the "law" rather than create or interpret it. Under her aegis the College Government Association became a complex organization in which each dormitory developed an internal governance structure that in many ways mirrored the larger CGA Board, which was composed of the officers of CGA and the student Head of each residence hall. Infringement of the many rules and "privileges" governing everything from lights out, cooking with alcohol in one's room, and chapel attendance, to male visitors and trips off campus (rules which often varied for each class) was dealt with initially by the CGA dormitory administrations. Serious violations of the social code and any violation of the academic honor code were sent forward to the Judicial Board on which the President, Dean, one faculty member and two students sat.[62]

Wheaton was not unique in terms of the structure of student governance created during the 1920s. Almost all women's colleges, responding to increasing student sophistication, affluence, and demands for independence and freedom, reacted with some limited relaxation of the concept of a semicloistered environment that had dominated until the close of World War I. Most did so not so much by lessening the network of carefully permissive rules and regulations that governed every aspect of student life, as by turning their administration over in some degree to the students themselves. What distinguished Wheaton from other institutions was the fact that the College did not employ professional "heads of houses" as was the case at Smith, Bryn Mawr and the other "seven sisters." Instead, the responsibility was placed in the hands of a senior undergraduate House Chairman, who, aided by appointed student assistants, administered each residence hall.[63]

While women faculty both at Wheaton and elsewhere continued to be required to live in dormitory suites and dine with students, the responsibilities for day-by-day, hour-by-hour residence hall supervision that had been part of the job of nineteenth-century faculty members disappeared at Wheaton as it did on other campuses. Though one member of the resident faculty would be appointed "Head of the House," her duties were limited to signing permission slips for day trips off-campus, dispensing medications prescribed by the infirmary, and providing general support for the undergraduate House Chairman. Thus the role of student self-government at Wheaton, albeit under the watchful eye and minute regulation of Dean Denkinger, assumed a level of importance in the operation of the College that exceeded what could be found at most similar institutions.[64]

Punishments for social code violations for the most part involved various forms of what was known as "campusing." This involved loss of the right to leave the campus grounds for varying lengths of time; in extreme cases it might also include prohibition from attending social events held on campus (later referred to as social probation). Multiple social violations could lead to the case being heard by Judicial Board, with suspension or permanent expulsion the ultimate penalties.[65]

Academic violations were automatically heard by Judicial Board; cases of plagiarism received a variety of punishments, but those involving cheating on examinations were always dealt with by suspension or expulsion, except in the case of first semester freshmen. Examinations were proctored, but faculty members were relieved of part of that duty in 1927, when the policy of hiring seniors to serve as "corridor proctors" during midyear and final examinations went into effect. Upperclass students also served as academic advisers for incoming students, except for "low-grade freshmen," who were assigned a faculty adviser.[66]

Overall, this system seems to have worked well. Only in one instance did a serious challenge occur, but it was one that caused considerable turmoil in all circles, from the Board of Trustees to the College Government Association. Bertha Ludwig had transferred to Wheaton from Mount Holyoke in the beginning of her junior year, ostensibly to be with her sister, who was entering Wheaton as a freshman. A fine student, she evidenced nothing but contempt for the rules and regulations of Wheaton's social governance system. Campused for signing in for a chapel service which she did not attend, she then violated that restriction by going to Boston to attend a concert of the Harvard Glee Club. So frequent were her violations of the social code that the Cabinet of the College Government Association recommended informally to the Dean that she be asked to withdraw at the end of her junior year.

This advice was not followed, and she was allowed to return. Her senior year proved to be a repetition of the previous one. Chapel attendance violations, plus rumored but not proved violations of the ban on smoking, all culminated in May when she and a friend, after attending a movie in Taunton, hitchhiked back to campus rather than waiting for a trolley. Once in Norton they appropriated a car belonging to the father of another friend, took it for a joyride, returned it, and then proceeded to the station to meet the trolley they should have taken home, walking back to campus with the students who had arrived on it from Taunton.

The resultant Judicial Board hearing led to Bertha's expulsion, despite the fact that she was only several weeks away from receiving her degree. It also prompted a suit filed by Mr. Ludwig asking that the degree be awarded, and seeking $25,000 damages. The College was forced to hire a special attorney, and the case was argued in June, 1928, before a Court Master, who ultimately found in favor of Wheaton. Nonetheless the College was required to absorb half the costs of the hearing, a sum not far removed from the cash salary paid to a new faculty member who resided in a residence hall, and more than the amount the Ludwigs had paid for Bertha's tuition, room and board during her two years at Wheaton.

The impact of these events on the campus was considerable. Several students were required either to testify at the hearings or prepare briefs for the College lawyer. The President of the College Government Association was excused from taking the final examination in a course because of the time she had been required to spend on the case. William I. Cole, in a letter to President Park, commented that other colleges would also benefit from this decision, which essentially upheld the right of private educational institutions to govern and administer their own affairs. Indeed, the case did lead to numerous inquiries for information from other colleges who were experiencing similar difficulties.[67]

During the 1920s Wheaton, like most colleges, found itself continually challenged by the changing social mores of the student generation. This was the "jazz age," the era when football, fraternities, and the automobile combined to revolutionize social life, particularly during weekends, on college campuses throughout the nation. Young women reveled in their new-found freedoms, symbolized politically by attainment of the right to vote, and socially by bobbed hair, short skirts, frenetic dancing and smoking in public. Louise Barr Mackenzie (W1930), editor of the campus newspaper and subsequently a long-time member of the English department, recalled later that a few students would occasionally sneak men into their rooms, and that many took walks in the woods in order to smoke. She also remembered with some relish feeling "so wicked" when she and others accompanied their dates to speakeasies (this was the prohibition era), where admittance was gained only through knowledge of a password.[68]

"As men came on campus to dances or took women away in their automobiles, the all-female world of the women's college dissolved," writes historian Helen Lefkowitz Horowitz. "Students turned the energy that had once gone inward into the college community—into college organizations, teas, and athletics—outward toward men. Female collegians

Student room in Stanton dormitory, 1927. The existence of only one overhead electrical outlet led to creative use of extension cords.

did not cease to have friends or to run for student government, but their sense of the location of college's central drama shifted."[69] The inward focus on the campus community, with its emphasis on academic achievement, spiritual growth, and moral and physical development, which had characterized both the Seminary and early College years at Wheaton, found itself challenged on all fronts.

For those who administered and taught, adaptation did not always come easily. Presidents Cole, Smart, and Park were, after all, members of the clergy. The Board of Trustees was comprised of businessmen, clergy and Wheaton alumnae, all educated and trained in the world of the late nineteenth century. The formative years for all but the youngest of the faculty had also occurred prior to the watershed period of the Great War. The result was that Wheaton, like most colleges for women, fought what might be described as a "rearguard action," retreating both slowly and reluctantly in the face of persistent efforts by students to achieve what they regarded as their rightful "freedoms."[70]

The conflict played itself out in two separate but intertwined arenas— the structure of campus life in Norton on the one hand, and on the other the ever-increasing determination of students to seek their weekend social life elsewhere, for the most part at the many colleges for men located throughout New England. Evidence that the problem of weekend absenteeism was becoming a concern can be found in the somewhat plaintive plea in the 1924 *College Handbook*: "Week-ends spent at college add fifty per cent to your college life. We have good times—stay and enjoy them!"[71]

Until 1926, when J. Edgar Park assumed the presidency, the College in general dug in its heels, and moved only slowly to adjust. Park, with daughters of his own, was much more understanding of the outlook of the young women of the 1920s. The result was that beginning in 1926 considerable easing of traditional taboos was gradually achieved. Nonetheless, in most cases as old walls crumbled new ones were built. Rules regarding absences from campus, "motoring," male visitors, or card playing and dancing might indeed be considerably liberalized, but once that was done an equally prickly new hedgerow of rules, procedures, forms, and penalties was created to ensure that in most respects the College still retained control over almost every aspect of student behavior on campus. Students still were required to wear a long dress to Wednesday night dinners, or to any evening lecture or concert. Seniors wore their caps and gowns to all classes, and all students customarily stood when a professor entered the classroom.[72] Moreover, the College, at least in theory, knew the whereabouts of students in considerable detail any time they set foot beyond the confines of Howard, East Main and Pine streets.

This was particularly true as long as Emma Denkinger remained as Dean. With her departure and the arrival of Miriam Carpenter, a greater degree of flexibility and adaptation began to infuse, rather than replace, the web of rules and regulations that continued to dominate every moment of a student's existence. Today one can only marvel at a system which still required in 1929 that each student note on a card reserved for that purpose which days she had bathed, and which created a carefully delineated set of regulations regarding the use of napkins in the dining rooms.[73]

Nonetheless, the more liberal attitudes of the Park administration soon became apparent. Park regarded the automobile and the lifestyle it created as something to be accepted. Not only did his speech admonishing mothers to stop worrying about the dangers of the combination of men and automobiles receive national attention, but Wheaton adopted policies relating to cars that were much more permissive than those at most women's colleges. Up until 1928, riding alone with a male was prohibited, but parties of four were allowed, with only signout rules and evening return hours serving as a control mechanism. Subsequently these regulations were relaxed considerably for seniors, and to a lesser degree for underclasswomen. As early as 1926, seniors were permitted to have cars on campus, and by the opening of the next decade this privilege could be extended by special permission to students in lower classes.[74]

Equally revolutionary was Park's attitude toward the presence of young men on campus. "Every effort is being made under this administration," Park reported to the trustees in 1930, "to welcome young male visitors to the college so that the weekend dances and parties of students are looked upon as a real part of education without being definitely required."[75]

Even in the area of smoking some limited accommodation was ultimately achieved. On this issue Wheaton's administration throughout the decade had remained adamant. Smoking by Wheaton students anywhere, even during vacations, was an offense which theoretically could lead to suspension or even permanent expulsion. In actual fact, such punishments were enforced only on students who smoked during the academic year while they were resident on campus, or on weekend or day trips away from Norton. Noting in February, 1928, that Wheaton was indeed different from other colleges in its total prohibition of smoking, President Park commented that in his view it was not a moral issue; rather, it was physically bad, and better postponed "until people are self-supporting."[76]

One year later, however, the pressure for accommodation had become overwhelming. On April 4, 1929, Park received permission from the Board of Trustees to limit the prohibition on smoking to those situations in which the student was "under the jurisdiction of the college." This was defined as when students were on campus, in Norton or towns immediately adjacent to Norton, or "in a public conveyance coming from or going to the college." Thus, former restrictions on smoking while in Boston or Providence on day trips or on weekends no longer applied. Noting also that it was impossible to control the situation within a student's home, especially if her mother smoked, Park nonetheless supported the continued, though more localized restriction. "I think the longer we can postpone the present tendency to fasten the habit of smoking upon every student at Wheaton," he told the trustees, "the better for the health of the students." In taking this position the President was indeed ahead of his time, for in the 1920s and 1930s there was, at least in the United States, no public or medical objection to smoking on health grounds.[77]

Aside from trying to create an atmosphere that would attract young men to the campus on weekends, the growing problem of Wheaton becoming what in later generations would be known as a "suitcase college" generated two specific responses. Beginning in 1925, the College published a list of "approved houses" in Boston and Cambridge, where students, with the prior approval of both the College and their parents, could spend the night.[78] Secondly, faced with growing problems of low student attendance, Wheaton discontinued both Monday and Saturday chapel services, and lifted the requirement for attendance at Sunday evening vespers. Students were still required to attend four chapel services and the regular Sunday morning church service each week. Despite this reduced requirement and the right of each student to miss four chapel and three church services each semester, attendance at these functions remained problematic in many instances, as did issues relating to noise and tardiness on the part of those who were present.[79]

At the heart of the successful administration of the many complex rules and regulations was the Honor System. Begun on a trial basis in Cragin dormitory as a fairly modest and purely social honor code in January, 1921, its initial success led to campus-wide implementation the following December. In subsequent years however, the system fell into disrepute, apparently because students did not take seriously what they regarded as minor violations involving matters such as lights-out regulations, chapel attendance, and rules governing the use of reserved-book reading in the Library. In addition, students proved particularly reluctant to comply with the requirement that they report not only their own violations but those of others. In the fall of 1926 the whole system was abandoned, and a total reexamination of an honor system was undertaken by the College Government Association.[80]

The result was the formulation of the Wheaton College Citizenship Code, which was adopted by the College community in the spring of 1927, and went into effect the following fall with admirable results. Extending the honor system to include academic as well as nonacademic matters, the code specified that it was "the duty of every Wheaton citizen to report herself to the proper authorities in case of personal violation."[81] Responsibility for the behavior of others was nowhere mentioned, though apparently officers in the Student Government were still expected to report violations by others if they observed or heard about them.

Perhaps because it included academic honesty as well as reponsibility in conforming to the social order, perhaps because it did not require students to report others—for whatever reasons the new Citizenship Code proved, at least in the eyes of the Dean, to be a success. "It has worked admirably during 1927–1928," Dean Denkinger noted.[82] The Code would remain unchanged as the basis of the College Government's honor system for the next two decades.

One of the less pleasant practices that appeared in the 1920s was an elaborate system of "hazing" incoming freshmen. Initially involving relatively innocuous tasks and the wearing of name-signs and other specified apparel, the process evolved into a protracted period of several weeks culminating in a climactic Halloween party at which the first-year students were "initiated" by the sophomores. Blindfolded and led through a chamber of horrors, the freshmen were subjected to taunts and pranks of various sorts, resulting all too often, according to Dean Denkinger, in "accidents and unpleasantries." In an effort to curb these excesses, the faculty Academic Council voted in March, 1926, to discontinue the Halloween Party entirely, and later approved a plan to limit all special freshman obligations to a single week designated specifically for that purpose.[83]

Two new practices that would remain a permanent part of Wheaton's traditions were firmly established during the 1920s. The right of seniors alone to sit on the steps of the Library commenced in 1923, one year after the new Library opened. It appears that the annual senior class tree planting began in 1918; by 1925 it was firmly enough established to be classified as a "Wheaton tradition."[84] Other annual events such as the May Day Pageant, which attracted a large audience from Norton and surrounding communities, and the student-written and directed variety show "Vaudeville," continued to flourish and prosper.[85]

One major tragedy shook the campus in 1929. On March 2, two freshmen members of the Wheaton delegation to a YWCA conference at Poland Springs, Maine, were killed in a bobsledding accident. In a letter to trustee Annie Kilham, President Park observed that the mishap did not seem to have been avoidable. The rest of the Wheaton delegation, he commented, "acted so heroically as to have done honor to the college."[86]

During the second and third decades of the twentieth century, participation by women in both individual and team athletic endeavors in-

A popular Wheaton custom in the 1920s was singing college and class songs in the Dimple, here led by Iris Entwistle (W1925).

creased dramatically throughout the nation. Activities sponsored by the YWCA and numerous independent clubs provided rapidly expanding opportunities for participation in a wide variety of activities at all skill levels. Wheaton, which in 1844 had been the first institution of higher learning in America to build a free-standing gymnasium for its students, had always been and now remained in the forefront of this development. Not only was there a substantial physical education requirement that students had to meet in all four years of their college experience, but an extensive intramural program of competition based on a system of class teams became a central focus of College life during the 1920s.

Individual students were also encouraged to test their skills in national events; perhaps the most noteworthy being the success of Lorna Noyes, who in 1924 single-handedly won for Wheaton the first Women's College Competition at Lake Placid by placing first in the down-hill ski race and second in skating. Students on occasion were chosen to participate on all-Boston or all-Providence teams; for three consecutive years between 1927 and 1929 three Wheaton students were selected for the all-Boston field hockey team, while in 1936 three Wheaton players were members of an all-Providence team that played a game against the Irish Nationals.[87]

By 1929, it was possible to participate in club activities or interclass competition in ten different athletic activities at Wheaton, ranging from hiking and archery to soccer and baseball. Dancing, tennis, golf and fencing were also available through the physical education program. Participation in most of these activities could lead to an accumulation of "points" resulting in the awarding of a Wheaton "W." The College also took part in intercollegiate "play" days. These were gatherings advocated by the Women's Division of the National Amateur Athletic Federation. In one held in 1929 five colleges sent delegations to Wellesley, where lots were drawn to create mixed teams which played against each other in events, none of which could last more than a half-hour. The purpose of these games was to enhance sportsmanship, deemphasize competition, and remove any sense of representing one's own college. Prizes by definition were to have no intrinsic value, and thus gumdrops were awarded for outstanding performances.[88]

Neither these "game days" or alternative "sports days," at which athletes played as a team representing their college for short periods against a number of opponents rather than a full game against one, proved appealing to Wheaton participants. Although Wheaton participated in a number of these events and even hosted one, they were never popular. "We tried one or two . . . but both students and staff did not enjoy them much," commented Miriam Faries, who headed the Department of Physical Education from 1933 to 1938.[89] In retrospect the reason seems obvious. Wheaton, which had begun fielding varsity teams almost as soon as it became a four-year college in 1912, was one of only a handful of colleges that continued to participate in and strongly advocate traditional intercollegiate competition at the varsity level in the 1920s.

President Cole clearly regarded intercollegiate varsity competition as a means of cementing Wheaton's new status as a full-fledged college, and both he and his wife reveled in the success of Wheaton teams. Time and again Helen Wieand Cole felt compelled to comment on Wheaton's triumphs on the playing field in letters to her family. In particular she exulted over Wheaton's victory in field hockey on the day Ada Comstock was inaugurated as Radcliffe's president. "We won, as we always do over Radcliffe, 4–2," she wrote to her sister, "Great publicity for us, since there were representatives from all the colleges there."[90]

In 1924, Wheaton fielded varsity teams in field hockey, basketball and tennis. Riding meets with the House in the Pines, the college preparatory school located in Norton, which possessed its own stables and riding oval, commenced in 1925. By 1930, swimming had been added, though meets had to be held at other institutions due to the small size of the Wheaton pool.[91]

Opponents occasionally included YWCA and club teams, but the core of the varsity schedules was provided by Radcliffe, Jackson and Pembroke, the last two the women's colleges affiliated with Tufts and Brown Universities. Occasionally, games were also scheduled with the Sargent School of Physical Education in Boston. These colleges, along with Wheaton, continued throughout the 1920s to defy a growing national movement aimed at discontinuing intercollegiate competition for women. A study conducted in 1923 indicated that of fifty colleges surveyed, only six had varsity sports for women; in 1930 it was eleven out of ninety-eight.[92]

The growing hostility to intercollegiate competition for women was justified both on the grounds that it placed too much stress on the fragile female nervous system, and by the argument that intense competition at the varsity level might all too easily "jar women's pelvic organs and harm their reproductive abilities."[93] Both the Women's Division of the

Wheaton College Riding Team, 1929.

NAAF and the American Physical Education Association basically accepted the popular belief that women were "innately weaker both physically and emotionally than men."[94] Therefore, emphasis on sportsmanship, physical fitness, modest skills attainment, and participation by many rather than a highly skilled few seemed to these organizations the path that women's athletics should follow. The "play day," in which college delegations drawn from all skill levels participated, was seen as the appropriate form of "extramural" competition. To symbolize this point of view the Women's Division of the NAAF petitioned the International Olympic Committee in 1930 to remove women's events from the 1932 Games.[95]

In the face of this preponderance of sentiment, Wheaton, Jackson, Pembroke and Tufts in 1931 formalized the unofficial grouping that had been formed during the 1920s. "The League," as it would unglamourously come to be known, continued to provide the backbone for maintaining the intercollegiate competition that had been developed during the 1920s and for adding new sports in the 1930s.[96]

Thus, while Wheaton throughout the 1920s and into the 1930s required a full four-year physical education program of all its students, and placed great emphasis on intramural competition through the aegis of class teams, it also retained its commitment to the value of intercollegiate competition, which would allow its best athletes to test their skills against the best from other institutions. Bolstered by the fact that there were several other like-minded colleges nearby, the members of "The League" continued on their own way, not unmindful of, but clearly in disagreement with the philosophies being espoused by the national organizations which sought to deemphasize and diminish organized athletic competition among women.

NOTES: CHAPTER 12

1. Provost/Registrar: Student Enrollment Statistics.

2. Lists of approved, or "accredited" schools were compiled by such organizations as the New England College Entrance Examination Board, the North Central Association of Schools and Colleges, or the Regents of the State of New York. *Wheaton College Bulletin: Catalogue and Announcements,* 1920–21, p. 48. For a general account of the development of the certificate system, see H. Wechsler, *The Qualified Student: A History of Selective College Admission in America* (New York: Wiley, 1977), pp. 40–61.

3. See Wechsler, *Qualified Student,* pp. 97–105, 245–47.

4. Trustees Minutes: 6/18/27; 3/12/28; 11/26/28.

5. Staff: Young: Young to Smart, 7/17/25; 7/31/25; Faculty: E. White: White to Park, 1/26/28; Trustees Minutes: 11/15/26; 3/12/28; Provost/Registrar: Student Enrollment Statistics; Dean's Office, Admissions: Admissions Office report, 1928–29; "Summary of Changes in Wheaton's Admission Policy, January, 1927 to January, 1932"; Faculty Meeting Minutes: 11/18/26; 9/21/27.

6. Trustees Minutes: 11/26/28; Dean's Office, Admissions: "Summary of Changes in Wheaton's Admissions Policy, January, 1927–January, 1932."

7. Admissions acceptance in the 1920s and 1930s was on a rolling basis; applicants were supposed to indicate their first-choice college on the admissions application. Trustees: W. I. Cole #2: Park to Cole, 6/25/28; Trustees Minutes: 11/26/28; Dean's Office, Admissions: Annual Reports, 1929–30, 1931–32; "Summary of Changes in Wheaton's Admissions Policy, January, 1927–January, 1932"; Applicants, 1928–33.

8. Trustees Minutes: 6/18/27; 11/28/29; Trustees: R. Smith #4: Park to Smith, 9/22/27; Crapo #2: Park to Crapo, 3/14/30.

9. Faculty: E. White: Memorandum for Park, n.d. 1929; White to Park, 4/5,6/29.

10. Dean's Office, Admissions: "Summary of Changes in Wheaton's Admission Policy, January, 1927–January, 1932."

11. Trustees 1834–1910: Curtis #2: SVC to Curtis, 3/30/18; Hervey #2: SVC to Hervey, 5/21/18; Trustees Minutes: 6/17/23; HWC, Letters to Family: to Sister, 6/15,21/23.

12. See chs. 6, 9; Trustees: K. U. Clark: SVC to Clark, 2/7/13.

13. Trustees: K. U. Clark: SVC to Clark, 2/27/13. Professor Holcombe Austin recalled that in the 1940s Dr. Park was fond of saying, as a joke, that he had written to the President of "the other Wheaton" to suggest that if it would change its name to "Wheaton Christian College, we'd be willing to call ours "Wheaton Pagan College." Oral History Project: H. Austin interview, 1983.

14. Trustees: Kilham #2: Park to Kilham, 3/9/29; Trustees Minutes: 11/15/27; 6/18/28; 11/26/28; Faculty Meeting Minutes: 9/21/27.

15. Faculty: Denkinger: R. Smith to Park, 12/4/28.

16. Trustees Minutes: 3/10/30.

17. Faculty: Meredith: Denkinger to Park, 7/8/27; Wallis: Park memorandum, 9/26/29.

18. Trustees Minutes: 11/26/28; 4/4/29; Trustees: Meadows #12: Meadows to Park, 2/2/29; Faculty: Denkinger: R. Smith to Park, 12/4/28. The possibility of changing the College's name resurfaced briefly again in 1944, when President Park, noting that the Illinois Wheaton had grown to 1200 students, brought the matter before the Faculty Curriculum Committee, commenting that the conflict in names was likely to become "even more embarassing" in the future. Although some time was spent discussing possible alternatives, there was little enthusiasm for a change, and no further action was taken. Faculty Committees: Curriculum Committee Minutes: 2/23/44; 3/31/44.

19. Trustees Minutes: 6/16/24; Faculty: Amen: Amen to SVC, 4/12/25; President's Secretary to Washburn, 4/27/25; HWC to Amen, 5/7/25; Dean's Office, Denkinger: "History and Procedure," vol. 6: Standards (Honors); vol. 3: English, poor.

20. This was increased to thirty-six credit hours beginning with the Class of 1931.

21. Academic Council Minutes: 4/24/22; Wheaton College Handbook: *Legislation and Practice, 1923*, pp. 3, 5.

22. According to Louise Barr MacKenzie (W1930), an unauthorized class absence resulted in a loss of two points in the grade for the course, which became a deduction of four points for an immediate pre or postvacation absence. Oral History Project: L. MacKenzie interview, 1983. See also *The College Handbook*, 1929–30, pp. 52–53, 92–95.

23. Smart/Park: Smart: Park to Smart, 5/2/27.

24. Trustees Minutes: 6/18/27.

25. Faculty: Otis: Park to Otis, 11/10/27; see also Webster: Park to Webster, 11/10/27; Shepard, "Reference History," p. 375.

26. Trustees Minutes: 3/22/27; Faculty: Riddell: Park to Riddell, 3/22/27; also pas-

sim; Smart/Park: Smart: Park to Smart, 9/22/27; *Wheaton College Bulletin: Catalogue and Announcements*, 1928–29, p. 92; see also Dean's Office, Denkinger: "History and Procedure," vol. 3: French House.

27. Dean's Office, Denkinger: "History and Procedure," vol. 3: Group System; Dean's List; Trustees Minutes: 3/12/28; Faculty: Denkinger: Dean's list provisions, n.d.; Memorandum by Park, 11/8/28; Shepard, "Reference History," p. 375; General Files: Class of 1929: "Majors and Minors," April, 1928; Faculty Meeting Minutes, 2/14/28; 2/23/28; 9/24/31.

28. Faculty: Work: Park to Work, 11/12/27; see also Park memorandum, 11/9/27.

29. Faculty: King: *Wheaton News* clipping, 12/14/29; King to Park, 4/19/30; Faculty Meeting Minutes: 1/9/30.

30. Trustees Minutes: 3/10/30. The ending of the Latin entrance requirement was prompted by a letter from the Midwest Secondary Schools Principals Association, saying that many of their best students did not take Latin, and that in fact many schools in their area did not even offer it.

31. Faculty: Denkinger: Denkinger to Park, 3/5/27.

32. Trustees Minutes: 6/17/29; Faculty Meeting Minutes: 6/15/29; Oral History Project: L. B. MacKenzie interview, 1983. Mrs. MacKenzie commented in 1983 that as a result of this project many faculty became very angry with her, and she learned that she had to be careful in her relations with Dr. Park. "He could put you on the spot and slam the door."

33. Faculty Meeting Minutes: 9/21/27.

34. The lowest salaries for full-time teaching faculty were $1400 cash or $1000 plus room and board. One assistant professor, holding a Ph.D. degree, received $1600 plus "living." Trustees Minutes: 4/4/29. For examples of faculty concerns regarding salaries, see Faculty: Riddell: Riddell to Park, 12/5/27; Shepard: Shepard to Park, 2/6/28.

35. Faculty: Shepard: Shepard to Park, 2/6/28.

36. See ch. 2.

37. Faculty: Lange: Park to Lange, 2/25/28; Lange to Park, 3/13/28.

38. Ibid.: Park to Lange, 3/22/28.

39. Ibid.: Lange to Park, 3/22/28; Park to Lange, 3/23/28.

40. Ibid.: Lange to Park, 4/2/28. Professor Lange was also quietly famous for giving election eve parties in her dormitory apartment at which she served wine, which was of course totally against the rules. Oral History Project: E. J. Knapton interview, 1983. For another example of faculty using the offer of a position elsewhere as leverage to obtain better pay and conditions, see Faculty: Amen: correspondence with Park, 1927.

41. Faculty Meeting Minutes: 1/10/27; 11/20/28; Trustees Minutes: 11/15/27; 6/16/30; Trustees: Soliday: Soliday to Park, 10/19/27. One of Park's first acts was to by-pass the one-semester sabbatical leave policy by awarding the senior member of the teaching faculty, Walter McIntire, a year's leave at full pay, on the grounds that he had completed fourteen years of teaching, almost all of them with the highest student load of any member of the faculty. Trustees Minutes: 3/12/28; Faculty: McIntire: passim.

42. Faculty: Riddell: Park to Riddell, 6/6/29; Riddell to Park, 6/10/29. Park himself was granted a sabbatical leave by the Board of Trustees in the fall semester of 1937.

43. SVC, *President's Report, 1921–1922*, p. 56; Dean's Office, Denkinger: "History and Procedure," vol. 5: Pensions of the Faculty; Trustees Minutes, 11/15/27; 3/12/28. Miss Everett served as Head of Holmes Cottage and Secretary to the Committee on Heads of Houses, was in charge of the after-dinner Sunday coffee for faculty, and was also given the title of Hostess at Large, with the reponsibility for entertaining alumnae and other guests of the College whenever needed. See Faculty: Everett: Carpenter to Everett, Sept. 1929.

44. Trustees Minutes: 3/12/28.

45. Ibid.: 3/4/29; 11/18/29.

46. Twenty-seven members of the faculty opted to participate in the plan; four declined. Trustees Minutes: 3/10/30; 6/16/30; 11/13/30. Trustees: Mirick: Mirick to Park, 3/27/30; Faculty Meeting Minutes: 4/4/30; 9/18/30; 11/17/30.

47. Faculty: Riddell: Riddell to Park, 12/5/27.

48. Ibid.: Work: Work to Park, 3/15/30; Park to Work, 3/19/30; Work to Park, 4/8/30; Lange: S. B. Young to Park, 7/2/29; Amen: Amen to Smart, 8/10/26; Smart to Amen, 8/12/26; Spalckhover: Park memorandum, 3/27/29; Spalckhover to Park, 5/23/30; Staff: Lincoln: Park to Lincoln, 5/9/30.

49. Faculty: Tenney: Tenney to Park, 6/5/27; Park to Tenney, 6/7/27; Academic Council Minutes: 11/8/26; Faculty Meeting Minutes: 4/4/30.

50. Faculty: Louise Bannister Merk: Park to Bannister, 2/4/30; see also Parker: Park memorandum, 2/14/36; Trustees Minutes: 3/16/36.

51. Faculty: Littlefield #3: Park memorandum, 3/13/29.

52. Ibid.: Littlefield #3: Park to Littlefield, 6/6/29.

53. Ibid.: Amen: Park memorandum, 2/27/29; Gulley: 1915–30, passim.

54. Trustees Minutes: 6/17/29; Academic Council Minutes: 11/8/26.

55. For example, the change from a "Student Government Association" to the more inclusive "College Government Association" was actually implemented in May, 1922. See Dean's Office, Denkinger: "History and Procedure," vol. 5: Mass and Community Meetings, 5/29/22; Trustees Minutes: 6/17/29.

56. Trustees, 1834–1910: Hervey: SVC to Hervey, 4/28/22; HWC, Letters to Family: to Sister, 10/8/22; Trustees Minutes: 11/21/22. Professor Briggs retired in 1997 after forty-seven years of teaching at Wheaton.

57. Trustees Minutes: 6/15/25; Faculty: West: West to Smart, 2/7/26.

58. Faculty: West: Smart to West, 2/25/26; and passim.

59. HWC, Letters to Family: to Sister, 7/4/22.

60. Oral History Project: E. J. Knapton interview, 5/13/83.

61. Faculty: Shook: *Boston Globe,* 8/16/25.

62. For examples of the myriad minor rules and regulations, as well as how specific cases of a more serious nature were handled during both the Kerr and Denkinger deanships, see Dean's Office, Denkinger: "History and Procedure"; and "Study of College Government."

63. Horowitz, *Alma Mater*, p. 185.

64. It was during this period that the job of "bellhopping," shared by all residents of each dormitory, came into existence. The duties included answering the door and the main dormitory phone, seating guests in the parlor, turning on lights, and handling the book that students had to sign both when they left and when they returned to campus. Dean's Office, Denkinger: CGA Committee of Heads of Houses, 1925–28.

65. Ibid.: "History and Procedure," vol. 1: Campusing; Judicial Committee.

66. Ibid.: Judicial Committee; Cheating; vol. 3: Faculty Advisors; vol. 4: Honor System; vol. 5: Proctors for Exams; also Committee on Dishonesty; Faculty: Denkinger: Park to Denkinger, 6/1/27.

67. I am greatly indebted to my student assistant Rachael Class-Giguere (W1991), who researched the considerable material relating to the Ludwig case and prepared the account on which I have relied. See General Files: Class of 1928: Ludwig vs. Wheaton; also Trustees: W. I. Cole #2: Park to Cole, 7/10/28; Cole to Park, 9/26/28; R. Smith #4: Park to Smith, 6/28/28; Page #3: Park to Page, 6/29/28; Trustees Minutes: 11/26/28; Dean's Office, Denkinger: "History and Procedure," vol. 1: Judicial committee; vol 2: Commencement Degrees.

68. Oral History Project: L. B. MacKenzie interview, 1983.

69. Horowitz, *Alma Mater*, p. 284.

70. For an excellent general discussion of college life at the "seven sisters" during the interwar period, see ibid., ch. 17. See also Horowitz' broader investigation of student life at both single-sex and coed colleges and universities in *Campus Life*.

71. Wheaton College Handbook: *Wheaton College Handbook, 1924*, p. 14.

72. Oral History Project: H. Harris (W1931) interview, 1983.

73. General Files: Class of 1929: "Bath Report"; Dean's Office, Denkinger: "Study of College Government," #5: Napkins.

74. Dean's Office, Denkinger: "History and Procedure," vol. 1: Automobiles; vol. 5: Motoring; Motoring Slips; vol. 6: Sunday Motoring; Wheaton College Handbook: *Wheaton College Handbook*, 1927–28 through 1930–31: College Government Association, "Motoring"; Faculty: Carpenter: Letter to Wheaton Parents, 9/1/30.

75. Trustees Minutes: 3/10/30. Not only were young men welcomed on the weekends, but visiting hours in the parlors were extended on weekday evenings to 9:45 pm. Dean's Office, Denkinger: "Study of College Government," #1: Accomplishments, 1925–26; #4: Men Callers.

76. Faculty: Markey: Park to Markey, 2/15/28; Dean's Office, Denkinger: "History and Procedure," vol. 6: Smoking; "Study of College Government," #6: Smoking.

77. Trustees Minutes: 4/4/29; see also Faculty: Everett: Everett to Park, 5/16/29; Park to Everett, 5/18/29.

78. Dean's Office, Denkinger: "History and Procedure," vol. 1: Approved Houses; Wheaton College Handbook: *Wheaton College Handbook*, 1929–30, p. 147.

79. Trustees Minutes: 6/17/29; Dean's Office, Denkinger: "History and Procedure," vol. 1: Chapel; Chapel Attendance; "Study of College Government," #2: Chapel attendance; Chapel, Noise in; Chapel Services; Chapel, Signing up ahead.

80. Dean's Office, Denkinger: "History and Procedure," vol. 4: Honor System; "Study of College Government," #3: Honor System, Non-Academic.

81. Wheaton College Handbook: *Wheaton College Handbook*, 1927–28, p. 19.

82. Dean's Office, Denkinger: "History and Procedure," vol. 4: Honor System.

83. Wheaton College Handbook: *Wheaton College Handbook*, 1925, p. 14; Dean's Office, Denkinger: "History and Procedure," vol. 4: Hallowe'en Party.

84. Dean's Office, Denkinger: "Study of College Government," #6: Senior Steps; *Wheaton Traditions*, pp. 14–16; *Wheaton Record*, 5:5 (June, 1918), p. 32.

85. Trustees Minutes: 6/16/30.

86. Trustees: Kilham #2: Park to Kilham 3/9/29; Trustees Minutes: 4/4/29; General Files: Class of 1929: Clippings.

87. Norton, "Physical Education and Athletics, 1912–1941," pp. 17, 19.

88. Ibid., pp. 8, 13, 24; For the origin of the "play day" concept, see S. Orcutt, "The Advancement of Physical Education for Women and Girls of the United States During the 1920's," Wheaton Honors Thesis #594, pp. 51–53. See also the discussion of "play" and "sports" days in S. K. Cahn, *Coming on Strong: Gender and Sexuality in Twentieth-Century Women's Sport* (New York: Free Press, 1994), p. 66.

89. Norton, "Physical Education and Athletics, 1912–1941," p. 24.

90. HWC, Letters to Family: to Sister, 10/21/23.

91. Wheaton College Handbook: *Wheaton College Handbook*, 1924, p. 19; 1930–31, pp. 99–100; Norton, "Physical Education and Athletics, 1912–1941," p. 17.

92. Norton, "Physical Education and Athletics, 1912–1941", pp. 16–18, 23.

93. Orcutt, "Physical Education for Women," p. 32.

94. Ibid., p. 59; Norton, "Physical Education and Athletics, 1912–1941," p. 22; Cahn, *Coming on Strong*, pp. 62–64.

95. Guttmann, *From Ritual to Record, the Nature of Modern Sports* (New York: Columbia University Press, 1978), p. 34.

96. Norton, "Physical Education and Athletics, 1912–1941," p. 17.

13

Surviving the Great Depression:
Admissions; the Faculty; the Curriculum
1930–1941

IN JUNE, 1932, J. Edgar Park prepared his first formal report to the Board of Trustees. In it he sought to summarize the first six years of his administration. "A college," he wrote, "is a place where eager and inquisitive students, graduating from the irresponsibility of childhood, are inspired by the enthusiasm of learned teachers to delight in the inherited wisdom of the race and to carry on its great traditions of living. The aim of a college is to gather together such a faculty and such a student body."[1]

In his report Park took particular pride in the growth and development of the faculty and the improvement in student quality that had been achieved under his leadership. Noting that by 1931, the College had completely recovered from the severe drop in applications emanating from the 1927 decision to admit students only by examination, Park commented that in 1930 Wheaton had been one of the "ten colleges receiving the largest number of students by the 'New Plan' of the College Entrance Examination Board."[2] As evidence of the improved quality of the Wheaton student body, Park reported that in recent years eighty-seven Wheaton graduates had been awarded advanced degrees from twenty-two colleges and universities nationwide, and thirty-two more had completed certification requirements in such fields as library science, education, music, and social work. Finally he pointed to the seal of approval received during the 1931–32 academic year from the National Council of Phi Beta Kappa, which had sanctioned the inauguration of a Wheaton chapter of the prestigious national honor society.[3]

While the size of the student body was in fact slightly smaller than when he had assumed office, Park reported that the size of the faculty had grown from thirty-six in 1926 to sixty in 1932, constituting forty-six women and fourteen men.[4] He also pointed with pride to the great reduction in teaching load resulting from this increase, plus improvements such as the retirement plan, sabbatical leave policy, partial payment of transportation costs to professional meetings, better housing conditions, and modest increases in salaries. While noting that there was "still much to be done to make the life of the faculty members more normal and pleasant and to save them from unnecessary drudgery and standardization," he happily pointed out that "endless hours formerly spent at faculty and committee meetings have been greatly reduced." Commenting that the small college "demands perhaps more of its teaching body than the large university," Park warned that "the rights of the scholar to some solitude, some home life, some escape from institutional routine must also be safeguarded," undoubtedly a guarded reference to the growing displeasure of single women faculty members with the requirement that they live and eat with the students.[5]

The President particularly emphasized the degree to which College policies governing student academic, social and dormitory life had been altered. "Supervision, check and compulsion have been largely replaced by a clear understanding that the responsibility for organizing her own life aright and getting something worth while from college rests largely upon the student herself."[6] Changes ranged from the abolition of formal class attendance requirements and institution of departmental honors programs to the relaxation of both dormitory and motoring regulations. The aim, Park stated, was to encourage student academic initiative, while at the same time allowing in all areas "as much freedom as possible while safeguarding the health and well-being of all."[7] "With the co-operation of Dean Carpenter, administration, faculty and students are all working together with a greater sense of unity," Park wrote. "The idea of necessarily antagonistic opposing interests is disappearing and problems are more and more being worked out together."[8]

All in all, President Park's optimistic portrayal of the state of the College was undoubtedly justified. Financially stable, if not secure, Wheaton seemed to be holding firm in terms of number of applicants despite the economic crisis which had descended upon the nation in the last months of 1929. An eight to one student/faculty ratio, improved faculty salaries and benefits, a stabilized administrative staff willing to accept rather than combat innovation in both academic and social spheres—all these seemed to bode well for Wheaton's future.

Yet behind the scenes the President also made it abundantly clear to the trustees that financial pressures, both internal and external, posed enormous threats to the continued growth and possibly the very existence of the College. Two years earlier he had complained that "it is more and more impossible to keep any professor of real worth at the college because the other colleges are of course able to pay so much more than we are."[9] At the March, 1931, Board of Trustees meeting, Park commented that the greatest contributor to Wheaton's ability to operate in "the black" for that fiscal year was the faculty, "who serve for smaller salaries and with fewer conveniences than elsewhere."[10] He noted that in order to recruit new faculty it was now necessary to pay larger entry-level salaries than had been Wheaton's custom.

Secondly, Wheaton was faced with the absolute necessity of replacing Metcalf Hall, the rambling wooden structure dating back in some parts to 1836. Housing students, administrative offices, the bookstore, and the post office, the building with its several additions was desperately in need of extensive modernization and repair, which promised to be so expensive as to render it an unwise investment of capital. The alternative was construction of at least two dormitories and a separate administration building, none of which would lead to additional revenues for the College, since they would merely be replacing old structures, rather than adding to existing capacity.[11]

Thirdly, there was the great unknown factor—the long term impact of the economic crisis that was gripping the nation. By the spring of 1932, America was in the depths of the Great Depression, facing presidential elections in November without any sense of economic change or relief in sight. Despite the fact that admissions applications had actually increased for the past three years, it was obvious that in the long run the College could not expect to escape from the impact of an economic crisis the length and severity of which no one could forecast.

In retrospect, however, the decade of the 1930s seems to have been surprisingly tranquil at Wheaton. Short-term problems were dealt with successfully, though not always painlessly. Long-term difficulties,

Flanked by Buildings and Grounds Superintendent Arthur Cutler and two fashionably fur-clad students, President Park gleefully assumed the controls of a steamshovel at the groundbreaking ceremonies for Kilham dormitory in 1932.

mainly fiscal, were accommodated if not conquered. The economic waves of the Great Depression created anxiety at times, but overall were ridden out without major seasickness. Compared with the two previous decades of its existence as a college, the years ending with the United States' entry into World War II appear to have been far less turbulent internally. The sense of "hunkering down" to ride out a storm seems pervasive—first in terms of the economic crisis, and then, as the decade progressed, in the face of growing anxiety and pessimism over war clouds developing, first in Asia and Europe, and finally over the United States itself.

Overshadowing all else during the 1930s was the national, indeed world, economic depression, which had begun with the American stock market crash in October, 1929, and escalated into the most severe global economic crisis the world had experienced since the advent of the industrial revolution. In retrospect, what is most surprising is the relatively minimal effect the Great Depression had upon Wheaton, or for that matter on American institutions of higher learning in general. Enrollment remained remarkably steady, though pressure from students for financial aid and competition among colleges for qualified applicants who could pay became increasingly intense.

At Wheaton the impact of the Great Depression was felt in a number of ways, some more subtle than others. The first overt sign was the decision taken by the Board of Trustees in March, 1931, not to approve a proposed increase in the comprehensive fee from $850 to $900. The general consensus was that although parents would probably accept it without complaint, nonetheless, given "the present depression" it was probably not a good time to implement an increase in charges. It turned out that the times remained bad, and it was not until 1938–39 that fees were increased from $850 to $1000, and then only for incoming students.[12]

Perhaps the greatest concerns brought on by the national economic crisis lay in the areas of admission, retention, and the payment of fees. In all of these it turned out that apprehension far exceeded reality. In March, 1932, President Park commented with some surprise to the Board of Trustees:

> We had anticipated considerable loss due to the financial depression from students who might be unable to pay promptly or to pay at all. So far the total extensions of payment granted to students whose parents are in financial difficulties is only $200 in excess of extensions in force on the same date in 1931. Outstanding to this date there is about $1752, and on this amount regular payments have been made on all except $423.[13]

Two years later Park could report that although the total overdue amount on bills due January 1 was $5000 as compared to $3500 the year before, "all of this with the exception of about $600, which seems doubtful, is in process of being paid."[14]

What did increase dramatically was the need for additional funds for scholarships and student loans. In 1931–32 an Emergency Scholarship Fund was created to which, as a result of appeals to all constituencies of the Wheaton community, donations of $9366 were contributed over the next two years. Since endowment funds specifically allocated for scholarships generated just $1637 in 1932–33, and regional Alumnae Club Scholarships only totalled $2235, it became obvious that the College needed to supplement these funds by allocating moneys from current revenue. Official authorization for such action was voted by the trustees in March, 1933, the aim being "to expend such a sum as will ensure as full an enrollment as possible without net loss to the college."[15] Such action seemed far wiser than reducing the overall comprehensive fee, since the vast majority of students would still be paying the full bill.[16]

This policy continued in effect from that time forward. Although the College would never again limit its scholarship and loan awards to the revenue generated by gifts and endowment funds specified for that purpose, the amount of "current revenue" needed annually fluctuated considerably over the next several decades, before starting to rise steadily in the last third of the twentieth century. In fact, for the Wheaton administration the surest indication that the "depression" might be a thing of the past was the knowledge that in 1936–37 the College was able to reduce the draw on current funds for scholarship and loan purposes by 29.5 percent, and to discontinue entirely giving loans to entering students.[17]

It was also during this period that the trustees formally authorized a practice that had in fact been customary for years. Although the Seminary and College had always allowed students from Norton to attend at half-tuition, this had never been approved formally by the Board. The only reservation was that the family had to have lived in the town for three years prior to the student's enrollment. A single half-tuition scholarship was approved for a resident of each of the towns contiguous to Norton, while full tuition remission was granted for daughters of members of the faculty and administration, but only if the family lived within the confines of Norton. The College also agreed to a reciprocal tuition exchange plan for faculty children with Middlebury College, and a student from Middlebury very soon used that option to attend Wheaton. Only in the early 1950s did the daughter of a Wheaton faculty member take advantage of the resultant exchange "slot" that was created.[18]

Without a doubt, admissions issues proved more sensitive than any other to the economic crisis of the 1930s. But the impact was similar to a bomb with a delayed time fuse. The immediate expectation had been that the stock market crash in October, 1929, would result in a sharp decline in applications and far greater difficulty in securing the number of freshmen desired. Instead applications increased until 1932 and enrollment held steady through 1932–33. In his report to the Board of Trustees in March, 1932, Park sought to explain this phenomenon by advancing the hypothesis that parents were choosing less expensive colleges like Wheaton over those that charged more, thus compensating in terms of admission applications for those families who could no longer afford college at all. Equally striking was the steady increase in the number of Wheaton students who petitioned for acceptance of courses taken in summer school. This was attributed by the Director of Admission to the fact that families could no longer afford to take vacations and thus needed something for their college-age daughters to do during the summer months.[19]

However, when the admissions "time bomb" finally exploded, it did so with considerable force. Total applications in 1933 were 203, down from 251 in 1932 and 312 in 1931. The entering class numbered only 122, which with the exception of 1928, the year after termination of admittance by certification, was the smallest class since 1920. The following year only 190 applications were received. To achieve an entering class of 127 the College had to expand a policy begun in 1931, in which students whose grades on one or more of the College Board examinations were "alarmingly low" were offered admission, but with a formal warning to their parents that "their daughter might prove unequal to college work."[20] Since more than half of those admitted with these warnings did well enough to avoid academic probation the judgment was that this practice was justified, "provided that the total number of applicants is such that the admission of these students does not mean the rejection of better candidates."[21] Only in 1936–37 did an increased number of applicants permit the discontinuance of this strategem.[22]

To enhance further the College's appeal, the faculty in November, 1933, approved the abandonment of Wheaton's rigid fifteen-unit requirement for admissions and replaced it with a statement emphasizing that the college made "no rigid prescription as to the content of the secondary school course or the accumulation of a specific number of entrance requirements."[23] Instead emphasis would be placed on the general adequacy of preparation and the overall quality of the applicant's work. In addition, in March, 1934, the faculty approved Wheaton's participation in what was known as the "upper seventh plan." Adopted the previous year by Bryn Mawr, Mount Holyoke, Smith, Vassar, and Wellesley, it stated that any student ranking in the highest seventh of her class during her last two years of preparatory work would be exempted, upon recommendation of her principal or headmistress, from taking CEEB examinations in specific subjects, though she would be required to complete the general Scholastic Aptitude Test.[24]

By September, 1936, it was clear that the worst of the crisis was over.

Applications had increased to 268, the entering class numbered 163, the practice of admitting students with formal warnings had been ended, no loans were being given to entering freshmen, and the number of competitive scholarships for entering students had been reduced from fourteen to five. The next year the College opened with six more students than it had rooms for, and temporary housing had to be arranged. By the fall of 1938, applications had climbed to 307, and despite the first increase in the comprehensive fee in more than a decade, the admissions office had little difficulty filling the freshman class. The next year an entering class of 157 was drawn from a record applicant pool of 349 applicants, and the following March the trustees happily voted to discontinue one of the admissions plans that it was felt had brought in some of the weakest students. It was evident that the College had weathered the storm with comparative ease, if not without great anxiety.[25]

Wheaton's experience was not unique, and for the most part mirrored that of other women's colleges, in fact of private colleges in general. Similar to Wheaton, during the mid-1930s many institutions were reduced to what came to be known as the "warm body" policy—admitting even the most minimally qualified if they could pay their way. Scholarships in turn became highly sought after, and were used to attract candi-

In a tradition long since forgotten, members of the graduating class washed the "senior steps" of the library prior to the May Day celebration in 1931.

dates with superior academic qualifications. Wheaton was able to compensate in part for its lack of scholarship and loan funds by the fact that it had long since built into its budget many student self-help jobs ranging from housecleaning and waitressing to clerking in the library and assisting with the physical education program, duties traditionally performed by hired employees at other institutions.[26]

Overall there was also the fact that the very paucity of employment opportunities led those parents who could afford a college education for their children to turn in that direction, both as a means of preventing unemployed idleness at home, and as a way of better qualifying their children for a chance at the few job openings that were available during the depression era. Nonetheless, it must be noted that of the 197 applicants for the entering class in the fall of 1935, only 21 were deemed academically ineligible. On the surface it would seem that at Wheaton, and many colleges similar to it, any pretense of maintaining selectivity among qualified candidates had to be totally set aside during the first half of the 1930s.[27]

But was that in fact the case? It turns out that it was not. Hard evidence on this issue is difficult to obtain, for it is a story no educational institution is proud to have as part of its history. Only recently has documented proof begun to be added to the wealth of anecdotal information that has been available for years. The "problem," as it was called at that time, was the growing number of highly qualified Jewish applicants seeking admission to private colleges, particularly in the Northeast. Worried that too high a percentage of Jewish students would lead gentile families to turn elsewhere for their children's education, and concerned that a reputation as a place where Jews were easily admitted would only encourage greater numbers of Jewish applicants, most of the private colleges quietly began imposing restrictions on the number of Jewish students who could be accepted. These quotas were intended to keep the total number of "Hebrews," as they were generally referred to, within the student body at 10 percent or lower.

> Not only did Columbia, Harvard, Yale, Princeton, Dartmouth and Amherst, for example, aim to restrict access of Jewish students, but comparable women's colleges harbored similar inclinations. Privately administrators referred to the "Jewish problem," by which they meant the large number of qualified women (as well as men) applicants in this group. Each college's admissions policy was made arbitrarily, based on the availability of other applicants. In 1937 five eastern women's colleges [Mount Holyoke, Wellesley, Vassar, Smith, and Radcliffe] exchanged information on their admission policies. . . . Nevertheless, despite tacit or overt restrictions, the numbers of Jewish women rose at all types of colleges.[28]

Wheaton was no exception in terms of implementing such policies. The number of Jewish students began to be a matter of concern at approximately the same time the economic crises leading to the Great Depression began to develop. Wheaton had always had a few Jews among its students, perhaps the most notable being Catherine Filene, who had been the driving force in organizing the first intercollegiate Women's Vocational Conference, held at Wheaton in 1917. President Cole had worried extensively about presenting the 1918 commencement baccalaureate service in a manner that would not offend the Filene family, which had already evidenced willingness to serve as financial benefactors to the institution. But the number of Jewish applicants had remained so small that the issue of numbers had never been something to draw official concern. In fact, though records were kept throughout the 1920s of the religious persuasion of all applicants, it is impossible to discern evidence of a concerted policy of discrimination against any group.[29]

Data concerning the total number of Jewish students at Wheaton was first compiled in 1929–30, when Jews were recorded as comprising 6 percent of the student body. In 1932, when the admission of fifteen Jewish students pushed the College total to thirty-five (7.5 percent), the Secretary to the Board of Admissions, Edith White, felt compelled to write to President Park, "I am sorry we had to relax a bit this year. I should like to see the figures kept down to 6%."[30]

Even more concern was expressed by Miss White in her annual report for 1933–34. This time the issue was scholarships. In an effort to recruit students from the Midwest, the College had for several years designated two $100 scholarships exclusively for students from that area. Suggesting that Wheaton might want to consider terminating these restricted awards, Miss White wrote:

> The number of students earning College Board Grades sufficiently high to entitle them to the Western Awards has been disappointingly small. The Board has also been somewhat embarrassed by the fact that in most cases the candidates making outstanding records have been of the Jewish faith. For example, awards have been made twice to Jewish candidates from Cincinnati and since we are particularly anxious to attract Gentile candidates from Cincinnati it is doubtful whether we wish to continue granting awards which give publicity to the number of Jewish students coming to Wheaton from that city. Two [western] awards were made in 1931, one in 1932 and two in 1933. Four of the five students receiving these awards were Jewish.[31]

How seriously the College regarded this issue became clear in November, 1934. In his written report to the Board of Trustees, President Park commented on the small size of the incoming freshman class. Coupled with the larger percentage of upperclass students who had been forced to withdraw for financial reasons, the size of the student body had been reduced by twenty-three students over the previous year, resulting in a decrease in income of nearly $14,000.

It would have been possible to fill most of all these vacancies by taking a much larger contingent of students of the Jewish race than usual. I thought it was better that we should have some vacant rooms and lose a little income rather than let this situation get out of hand. The applications for the next year show an even greater number of Jewish applicants. Our policy at this time is to try and keep the quota down below 10%.[32]

The following July, in a letter discussing upperclass retention, Park reported to Dean Carpenter, "Several of those belonging to a race unmentionable to Hitler have dropped out, so that we should be below our quota in that respect this year."[33]

Concern regarding the percentage of Jewish students at Wheaton came from many sources. In November, 1936, the new Secretary to the Board of Admissions, Barbara Ziegler, reported that "the number [of Jews] on campus and applying for admission during the year 1935–1936, called forth considerable comment particularly from the alumnae. For this reason it seemed wise to the Secretary to recommend to the Board of Admission in July, 1936, that only twelve 'new' Hebrews be admitted although there were sixty on the roll, and one of the largest classes in the history of the college was graduating."[34] By thus limiting the number of new students the overall percentage of Jewish students on campus was reduced from 9.5 percent to 8 percent.

In addition, Miss Ziegler reported, the Director of the Women's College Information Bureau in Chicago had "warned particularly against allowing Wheaton to become known in Chicago as a haven for Jewish students." "The best representatives of the race themselves wish to have the number limited," Miss Ziegler averred. "It is a very real problem to deal with for there are many more individuals acceptable academically and socially than it is wise to admit, and because they are barred from so many places they are likely to bring every kind of pressure possible to bear to the administration. . . ."[35]

The message the College was trying to convey got through. The following year Miss Ziegler was able to report that the policy of limiting the number of Jewish students admitted had resulted in a substantial reduction in Jewish applications, "and we were able to accept all the representatives of the group who had met the competitive requirements without discrimination because of race."[36] It is interesting to note that the College also adopted a policy of choosing "representatives of this group from the west and south, rather than from New York or Boston."[37] Experience, Miss Ziegler suggested, had shown that those from eastern urban settings were "less likely to adjust to life at Wheaton than any other particular group of students, and therefore are not likely candidates."[38]

Nonetheless the College continued to monitor the situation closely. "We again definitely limited the number of Jewish students admitted in order that the total number in the college should keep well under ten percent," reported Miss Ziegler in November, 1938.[39] This was the last time that mention of this issue appeared in the annual admissions reports to the President, though the office continued to keep a careful tally of both the number of Jews applying and those accepted well into the 1940s.[40]

Quotas relating to Jews were not limited to students. The number of Jewish faculty at Wheaton was carefully monitored. In April, 1939, Hedda Korsch, Head of the German Department, requested the addition of a third person to the department, suggesting a candidate who happened to be Jewish. Park's reply, as communicated to Mrs. Korsch through his secretary, revealed an attitude and policy similar to that found on many college campuses.

> Dr. Park says that we aren't in a position yet to know if there will be a need for a third person in the Department, but it is quite unlikely that if there is to be another it would be a Jew. There are two already on the faculty with the possibility of a third coming into the Department of Psychology as a [temporary] refugee scholar, which number at the present time Dr. Park thinks is about all that a college of our size should have. So he advises you to reply to Professor Weigand's letter in a discouraging vein.[41]

In contrast to policies designed to limit the number of Jewish students attending Wheaton, the question of admitting African-American students did not even arise. Only one African-American student attended Wheaton in the interwar years, and then only for one year (1919–20) before transferring to Radcliffe. Other than this one instance, it appears that the College neither sought nor received applications from African-American students, and there is no record of any discussion regarding the admission of African-Americans during the interwar period. However, the wartime and immediate postwar discussions preceding the decision to admit Wheaton's first African-American students in 1946 suggest that any such applications in the 1920s or 1930s would not have been regarded favorably.[42]

One of the first changes initiated by Admissions Secretary Edith White was to delete the requirement that students submit a picture of themselves with their first admissions application, which was often filed several years before the student would actually matriculate. The one major drawback Miss White recognized to deleting this requirement was that these photographs "might indicate the race of the applicant in cases where the student failed to be entirely frank. I can imagine, however, that there might be doubtful cases where I should be hesitant to make a decision as to traces of colored blood or Hebraic ancestry on the basis of a photograph."[43]

Paralleling the freeze implemented on the comprehensive fee during most of the 1930s, a long-term moratorium also was placed on faculty salary increases. In April, 1931, when President Park notified Associate Professor Marguerite Metivier of a raise in salary from $2000 to $2100 (plus living), he commented, "this salary will probably be the maximum at the present time and is that which will be paid for the next few years."[44] During the next decade, the salary budget remained basically static. In 1940–41, the cash salary of the two professors at the top of the scale, Ralph Boas and Walter McIntire was the same as it had been in 1932–33. Professor of Economics Henrietta Jennings wrote plaintively to Park in 1940, "Last year you said I could expect an increase in salary this coming year. I am at the same salary as when I came here nine years ago."[45] Although Park had not originally scheduled her for an increase, she ultimately was rewarded with a $200 raise to $2800 plus room and board.[46]

In the five years between 1932–33 and 1937–38, the total "cost of instruction" (i.e., salaries), exclusive of the value of housing accommodations or room and board in the dormitories, increased by only $9,012 to $151,254, and even this modest addition primarily reflected an increase in the number of teaching faculty and assistants from fifty-six to sixty-three. Nonetheless, an evaluation of Wheaton's salaries in each rank, including the estimated cost of room and board, or a house, indicates that the College rated quite satisfactorily when compared to a study of faculty compensation in thirty-eight private women's colleges published by the federal government.[47]

Wheaton was unusual in the fact that, unlike what occurred at many colleges, faculty were not forced to take a salary cut during the depression years.[48] This is not to say that other types of reductions did not take place. Paid sabbaticals already awarded to Pearl Wallis and Eunice Work for the spring of 1933 and 1933–34 respectively were summarily "postponed." When such leaves were finally resumed in 1935–36 it was with the proviso that the cost of needed teaching replacements should be born by the recipient of the leave, rather than by the College.[49] Regular sabbatical leaves, limited to two per year, were only reinstituted in 1937–38. Katherine Burton, at the insistence of Park, took a one-year unpaid leave of absence in 1935–36 which she could ill-afford—the College agreeing only to contribute both hers and its share to her account in the Retirement Fund. As Miss Burton subsequently pointed out, the result was that over the course of the depression years she did in fact suffer a nonvoluntary reduction in income.[50]

In general, there seems to have been acceptance on the part of the faculty regarding the virtual freeze placed on salaries. Only when the College, after nearly a decade of holding the line on the comprehensive fee, increased it by $150 in 1938–39, did faculty start agitating seriously for increases in pay. But that did not prevent considerable unhappiness about salaries from another perspective. The almost total hold on pay increases imposed by the Great Depression also perpetuated the glaring salary inequities that had developed during the 1920s and early 1930s, inequities that for the most part were gender based. These inequities were, of course, partly created by the realities of the marketplace. But President Park also believed that it was very important for students to see the examples of family life provided by male members of the faculty living with their families in the houses adjacent to the campus. Moreover, Park's attitude, also held by his predecessor and successor, was that male members of the faculty should by rights be paid at a different rate from women, since they all had families to support. Though from the perspective of later decades this reasoning must be regarded as totally without merit, the fact at least was true, since Wheaton's faculty as a matter of policy did not include single men.[51]

Moreover, even within each gender group there were glaring inequities. The lowest paid male full professor (with Ph.D.) in 1939–40 received the same salary and housing arrangements as two of the men assistant professors. The highest paid woman assistant professor (without Ph.D.) received the same cash salary as four female full professors and $400 more than another, all of whom held doctorates, though the senior women also received room and board during the academic year. Even more glaring, of course, were the inequities between the genders. The cash salary received by two male assistant professors in 1937–38 was higher than that paid to any of the forty-four women holding the ranks of instructor to professor. In 1940–41, out of fourteen men on the faculty, ten were among the top twelve teaching faculty in terms of cash salary. All also received a house or apartment "rent free."[52]

The discontent aroused by these discrepancies led the Wheaton Chapter of the American Association of University Professors to undertake in October, 1936, an investigation of salary scales at other colleges in New England and upstate New York, with a view toward gaining one at Wheaton. Founded in May, 1933, the fledgling chapter up until this point had engaged in no concrete projects aimed at creating change on the campus. However, as a result of the study undertaken by two assistant professors, E. J. Knapton and Paul Cressey, the chapter voted in March, 1937, to send a letter to the Board of Trustees through the President, requesting the creation of a standardized salary scale. The trustees in turn voted to take the matter under consideration.[53]

However, when Knapton and Cressey met with President Park on behalf of AAUP to discuss the issue, it quickly became clear to them that Park was not enamored with the proposal. Some trustees liked the idea because it seemed a "clear-cut business practice," Park reported, but he favored a more individualistic and flexible method of dealing with salaries. "The building up of a faculty required considerable freedom of bargaining on the part of the president." Moreover, Park told them, a number of faculty had recently requested a promotion, but "not necessarily a rise in salary," which would of course be impossible if rank were rigidly tied to monetary compensation.[54]

Park was even more explicit in his comments to the Board of Trustees. While expressing sympathy in principle for the idea of a salary scale, he indicated that the time was not right for one at Wheaton. Perhaps, he said, when older faculty hired when Wheaton was making the transition from Seminary to College were gone some sort of scale could be implemented. However, the President must always have the right to pay some faculty members more than others if their value to the College was clearly greater. Somewhat later he commented to Esther Seaver in the Art Department that a salary scale would make it impossible for the President to offer special inducements to keep "particularly brilliant professors."[55] Whatever the validity of this last point, Park's comment regarding faculty from the transition era was clearly far-fetched, since in 1936–37 only four faculty remained from the teaching staff in 1919–20, which was already eight years after Wheaton had become a College. Of those four, Walter MacIntire was one of the two highest-paid members of the faculty.[56]

The end result was that the Trustees never took any action, and no salary scale was ever seriously contemplated. The President continued to deal with faculty unrest on an individual basis, uniformly refusing initial requests, but often holding out the possibility of either advancement in rank or a possible salary adjustment in some future year as a pacifying inducement to accept the current status quo. In a letter to Eunice Work, who was away on sabbatical, Park enclosed her contract and salary figures for the next year. "I am going through the awful experience of interviewing all the faculty now," he wrote, "and explaining to them why they are not receiving incomes commensurate with their services. It is a great pleasure not to have to see you but be able to do it by correspondence."[57] The result was that as the College entered what turned out to be the final year prior to America's involvement in World War II, the pattern of salary inequities remained essentially the same as it had been throughout the preceding decade, and indeed throughout Wheaton's years as a four-year college.[58]

If efforts by AAUP to generate a salary scale proved nonproductive, the organization had better success with another project. One of its major concerns, though this was not communicated for some time to the Board of Trustees or the President, was gaining effective faculty consultation regarding the appointment of future presidents. "Our present administration might be described as 'benevolent'," commented Sociology Assistant Professor Elizabeth Nottingham in a letter seeking advice from the national headquarters of AAUP, "but the chapter is concerned with security for the future."[59] Therefore, in March, 1938, the chapter sent a letter to the Board of Trustees through President Park requesting that some form of direct communication between the faculty and the trustees be established. In presenting the letter to the Board, Park expressed some limited sympathy with the concept, noting, however, that the by-laws as constituted only provided for indirect communication through the President. He suggested that it might be a good idea to make it possible for a trustee committee to meet with either a faculty or student committee "in cases of special problems or emergencies." Noting that he did not believe such meetings should be a regular occurrence, he commented that "whether the machinery were used much or not, the very fact that such existed would deliver weary souls on the faculty from a sense of degradation."[60] After much discussion the trustees agreed that some such mechanism would be appropriate, but voiced strong opposition to the possibility of any future suggestion that a faculty member should sit as a member of the Board.[61]

The wheels of progress ground slowly, and it was not until June, 1941, that the Faculty Committee on Conference with the Trustees was constituted and the Trustee Committee on Administration designated as the group with whom it should meet. And it would be two more years before such a meeting actually occurred. The glacial pace of these developments may have been due, at least in part, to Park's personal antipathy to direct faculty/trustee contact, a view he expressed privately to trustee Richard Chapman.[62]

One commonly implemented employment policy brought on by the Great Depression seems to have had no impact on Wheaton. The concept that married women should not hold a job if their husbands were gainfully employed was widely in force. The Federal government prohibited both husband and wife from holding jobs with government agencies, and many states and municipalities followed suit. Marjorie Hill Ford, who would later serve for many years as Director of the Wheaton College Nursery School, was summarily dismissed from her teaching position in the Providence, Rhode Island, school system as soon as she got married, on the grounds that teaching positions had to be reserved for women who had no other means of support.[63]

Although Park was not above using this reason as the excuse for terminating a library staff member whose work had been deemed unsatisfactory, Wheaton during this period employed several husband/wife teams, the most notable being Ralph and Louise Boas in the English Department.[64] Several other men and women members of the faculty were employed without regard to the work status of their spouses. In response to a letter from Zoology Instructor Elsie Laity in the summer of 1938, anxiously inquiring if her recent marriage to a Dr. McFarland would affect her relations with Wheaton, Park replied in the negative. "The political agitation at present so active in Massachusetts for preventing married women from occupying gainful positions," he wrote, "has not yet gone so far as to prevent you from continuing your connection with Wheaton next year."[65]

On issues other than salaries, a tug-of-war of sorts developed between the faculty and administration as the Depression years progressed. Some matters affected the faculty as a whole; others were of specific concern to those women faculty required to live in the dormitories and take their meals in the College dining halls.

With the exception of an occasional married female faculty member, commuting to work by full-time faculty was severely frowned upon. In fact, living in Norton was made a condition of being offered a job in the first place for some, and of keeping it for others. "When I was negotiating for my position I had asked the President what financial adjustment he would make if I chose to continue living in Cambridge and commute by car or train three days a week for my teaching," E. J. Knapton, a male member of the faculty, wrote in his memoirs. "I was informed that under such circumstances someone else among the numerous candidates would be offered the post."[66]

More than any other issue, Wheaton's housing policies engendered

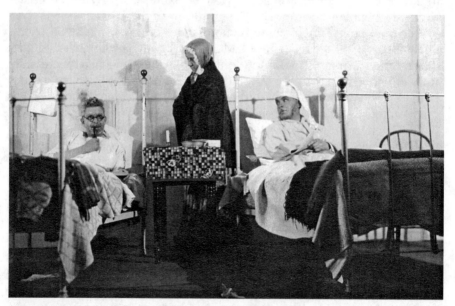

An annual tradition in the 1930s, the purpose of which was to raise funds for construction of the Student Alumnae Building, was an evening of entertainment provided by the faculty. In this 1933 skit, "Nurse" Alice Mifflin (Nursery School staff) had to deal with patients J. Edgar Park (President) and E. J. (Jack) Knapton (History).

real hostility and bitterness among women faculty. In his report to the Board of Trustees in March, 1931, President Park commented that his goal was "to give every married man a comfortable house and every unmarried woman a place to live which will be more than a room and a share of a bathroom way down the corridor." "We have a long way to go," he added.[67]

Although by this time the increased number of faculty precluded requiring all women to live in the dormitories, stipulations regarding residence in Norton in College-owned housing remained. In the spring of 1938 twenty-nine women still lived in student dormitories, while eight more inhabited Holmes Cottage, which was outfitted essentially as a boardinghouse in which bathrooms were shared by several residents, and meals were still taken in the College dining halls.[68] In one case, when a female faculty member's husband lived well beyond commuting or even weekend visiting distance, she was required to rent lodgings at her own expense in Norton, since there was no available space in Holmes Cottage. Although it was clear that her husband would not be able to visit her in Norton, the College held to its firm policy that no married person could live in the dormitories.[69]

Suggestions by both men and women faculty that they might move out of College-owned housing were systematically responded to with the observation that individuals were free to do as they liked, but that no cash adjustment to their salary reflecting such a change could be made. Faculty members did not pay rent, Park insisted, housing was just a nonmonetary part of their compensation. This distinction was important, for if cash were paid in salary and then returned or deducted as rent, faculty would have to pay state and federal income taxes on the sums involved, and the College would have to pay real estate taxes on the rental properties to the town of Norton. Moreover, Park insisted, a faculty member's contract was for salary and housing, and since Wheaton had invested in the real estate necessary to provide this, it could not pay additional amounts to those who chose not to accept the College's accommodations while those quarters in turn stood vacant.[70]

In one instance this controversy resulted in what can best be described as a Mexican standoff. In the spring of 1940, Economics Professor Henrietta Jennings informed Dr. Park that she wished to move out of her suite in Everett Hall in order to live with her good friend and recently retired member of the faculty, Caro Lynn. She asked that either a College house be made available for her, or that the College add $450 to her salary if she and Miss Lynn rented a house not owned by Wheaton. Park refused, giving his standard economic reasons, and noting that there were six or seven applications ahead of hers for admission to College houses and apartments. Miss Jennings, however, proceeded to rent a house on Mansfield Avenue, and informed Dr. Park that since the suite in Everett was still part of her salary she would retain it. She would be happy to allow Wheaton to use these rooms as soon as it agreed to compensate her $450 per year for their use. To emphasize that she meant business she had the locks changed on her Everett accommodations.

This standoff continued for two years. In January, 1942, Professor Jennings volunteered to rent her apartment to retired Botanist Mabel Rice, who had been recruited in December to fill in for a faculty member who had resigned as of the end of the first semester in order to be married. The arrangements were made directly between Miss Jennings and Miss Rice, with the College playing no role in the negotiations. Ultimately, in the fall of 1942, as part of a private "gentlemen's (or ladies') agreement," Miss Jennings granted the College the use of the Everett suite. In return Park agreed that she had the right to a room whenever she wanted one, and that she could eat whenever she wished in the College dining room at no charge. But officially, no compensation in salary per se was approved.[71]

Park's stubbornness on this issue was not entirely self-imposed. He had to contend with strong sentiment among the trustees that ending the traditional living and eating requirements would destroy the very basis upon which good faculty-student relations were built. To have all faculty living outside the dormitories would not only necessitate the hiring of professional dormitory administrators, but it would also turn the college experience into one similar to public high school, where contact with one's teachers was limited almost exclusively to the classroom. Such a situation, it was thought, would destroy the "family" atmosphere at Wheaton, and undermine "the idea that it is a residential college where the scholars of two generations live with one another."[72]

Nowhere was the Board's position made more clearly regarding this situation than in its response to a formal vote taken by the entire faculty urging termination of the requirement that women faculty serve as formal hostesses at tables in the dining room four nights a week. Responding that it was their decision that the practice should be continued, the trustees' letter to the faculty took a distinctly admonishing tone.

> In the largest possible way social relationships between faculty and students should be cultivated. One of the chief justifications for the existence of a small college like Wheaton is that it affords opportunities for bringing together faculty and students outside the classroom. A friendly relationship of faculty and students at mealtime is one of the best of such opportunities, and it incidentally is the best means of breaking up the cliques of students who always eat together whenever there is no formal arrangement. The trustees feel sure that the faculty will cooperate with them in carrying on the gracious traditions of our past.[73]

Given the composition of the Board, which was made up of relatively senior businessmen, clergy and alumnae, the desire to cling to those practices seen as defining the best of Wheaton's past is understandable.

President Park himself was clearly sympathetic with this point of view. Yet he was also very much aware that times were changing. Time and again throughout the years he commented on the problems inherent in the College's policy regarding dormitory living for unmarried women faculty. The message was always the same. More faculty housing was needed, especially some means of accommodating women who would like to keep a dog or "live where it would be possible easily to entertain gentlemen friends without resorting to public parlors for the purpose." Reporting that Wheaton was almost alone among colleges in requiring faculty to eat with the students, Park noted: "One can see how the members of our faculty, associating with the faculty of other colleges and visiting them, find the freedom of the life in these other colleges attractive."[74] In bringing the standoff with Miss Jennings to the Board's attention Park commented: "This example will show the keenness of feeling engendered. The fact probably is that the type of person envisaged by the builders of the college does not exist to any great extent today and that most unmarried women resent having to spend about nine months of the year in suites of rooms in college dormitories."[75]

In 1938, the first small steps were taken to deal with the issue of separate housing for women faculty. The Board of Trustees authorized the building of two small houses specifically for that purpose. Two faculty members, Mary Winslow and Eunice Work, agreed to contribute $500 and $200 respectively toward the cost of building them, and in return were granted the privilege of being the first occupants. It was hoped, Park commented, that houses of this sort "might solve some of the dissatisfaction which middle-aged unmarried members of the faculty feel living in dormitories."[76]

The estimates were that the cost of constructing the two units would not exceed $5000. Actually the cost of the two, placed in back of Barrows House on what was known as College Green, was more than twice that amount. This in turn called forth severe criticism from the College auditors, and undoubtedly had much to do with the fact that contemplated additional units never materialized. It would be another decade before further housing for women faculty and staff was built.[77]

Another matter of growing concern for members of the faculty was the lack of any group health insurance plan. The College protected itself from extended disability or illness by covering half of the cost of hiring a substitute for one month only, the other half to be born by the faculty member. This applied only to faculty who had been employed for a minimum of five years. Salaries for substitutes needed beyond the one-month period were deducted fully from the pay check of the absent faculty member. The same policy applied to faculty who were required to leave campus temporarily to care for an ill family member.[78]

In June, 1938, fifty-two faculty and staff plus fourteen family members enrolled in a hospitalization plan offered by the Associated Hospital

Services. Providing three weeks of semi-private room accommodations, routine laboratory work, operating room costs and general nursing services, the cost was $10 per month for an individual and $24 for a family. Although the College gave its blessing to the formation of the policy group, the charges were borne entirely by the subscribers.[79]

There was one final issue that time and again presented itself to President Park in terms of administrative policies vis-à-vis the faculty. This involved age of retirement and the provisions of the retirement plan. On at least five separate occasions during the 1930s, Park found himself faced with requests from faculty that they be allowed to teach beyond the College's mandatory retirement age of 65. Park strongly resisted these requests, and though he dutifully reported each one to the Board of Trustees, he urged the Board to adhere to its policy, which had gone into effect with the establishment of the Retiring Allowance Fund in 1930. Acknowledging to Religion Professor Henry Waring that most men's colleges did not mandate retirement until age seventy, Park asserted that "it had been found that a woman becomes rusty as a teacher about 5 years earlier than a man and therefore in the women's colleges it was customary to have the retirement 5 years before that in a men's college."[80] To the trustees, however, Park told a different story. Urging them to uphold the standard, he remarked that Waring's increasing deafness and dogmatism made him "less and less valuable" as a teacher.[81]

In 1939, at President Park's suggestion, the Board began the practice of voting retiring members of the faculty the title of professor emerita. Prior to that date only former Dean and Professor of English Ida Everett had been accorded that honor. Commenting that he thought the honor had "some value for its recipients," Park also noted shrewdly that it was totally an "honorary position without salary."[82]

The Retiring Allowance Fund itself proved less and less satisfactory to President Park. In 1934, the Federal Government began taxing lump sum payments made at retirement as part of that year's current income, thus advancing recipients into higher tax brackets for that year. In an effort to mitigate this penalty the College in 1936 began dividing the payment in two, with payments in July and the following January, in order that they might be counted in separate tax years. President Park also commented to the faculty that the trustees hoped at some time to transfer the Retiring Allowance Fund into a new nonprofit retirement program known as the Teachers Insurance and Annuity Association (TIAA), which was sponsored by the Carnegie Corporation.[83]

While the President may have talked about this in 1936 with individual trustees or the Trustee Finance Committee, it was only in June, 1938, that he raised the issue with the full Board. Noting that the Retiring Allowance Fund rarely returned to the retiring faculty member a sum much greater than the guaranteed minimum of one year's full salary, Park urged the trustees to look toward developing either a true pension system of Wheaton's own or joining the system offered by TIAA.[84] The Board agreed and over the next two years a careful study was made of a number of pension plans. On June 8, 1940, a tentative decision to join TIAA was arrived at, which was formally confirmed the following November. Faculty members who belonged to the Retiring Allowance Fund were given the option of remaining with that plan. Those who wished to shift to TIAA were allowed to transfer to the new plan the sum of money, plus accrued interest, that they had contributed to the original fund. But they were required to forfeit the sum the College had deposited in their names in the Retiring Allowance Fund.[85]

This last provision provoked, as one might have expected, considerable negative reaction from the faculty. The Wheaton Chapter of AAUP sought outside legal opinion, which, to the members' great disappointment, upheld the College's right to withhold the funds. The College's justification was that under the old plan those who left Wheaton's employ before formal retirement could take with them only their own contributions. Since faculty members had the right to choose whether to switch to the new plan, the same provisions applied. In fact, it was argued, under the TIAA plan the cost to the College ultimately would be considerably more, since the 5 percent matching contributions made by Wheaton to TIAA would never be returned, regardless of whether or not the faculty member remained at the College until retirement.[86]

Despite their unhappiness with this provision, twenty-eight of the forty-eight members of the old plan opted to make the shift, effective January 1, 1941. Of those who chose to remain with the College's own plan, ten were nearing retirement; others "professed to have more faith in the financial security of Wheaton College than they do in that of any insurance company."[87] The Board, meanwhile, voted to use the College reserves credited in the old fund to those who had changed plans as the source for the new mandated 5 percent College contributions to TIAA over the next several years.[88]

All of this was well and good for faculty members and administrative officers. But no fund for the retirement of other College staff existed. While the President did not recommend the creation of any systematic retirement scheme for these employees, he did gain the approval of the Board in March, 1941, for creation of a permanent Contingent Fund into which a sum equal to 5 percent of the staff payroll would be put each year. From it sums could be drawn as needed, and as seemed best in individual cases, in order to provide appropriate bonuses for retiring long-term staff members.[89]

One other general issue proved to be of some concern to both administration and faculty in the 1930s. In response to the national "red scare" prompted by the increased political appeal of socialism and communism during the Great Depression, in 1935 the Commonwealth of Massachusetts passed a law requiring all teachers to take an oath of allegiance to the federal and state constitutions. President Park joined with other Massachusetts college and university presidents in publicly opposing this legislation. One member of the faculty, Henrietta Jennings, initially refused to comply on the grounds that the Commonwealth had no authority to impose conditions on private institutions. However, she indicated that if the College itself made taking the oath a condition of employment she would do so. The Student Council drafted and signed a petition protesting the Teachers Oath Bill, and in March, 1936, the Wheaton AAUP chapter passed a formal resolution in support of state-wide efforts to repeal it. Nonetheless, the law remained in place, and for more than three decades new faculty were required to take this oath as a condition of employment.[90]

Tenure as a concept relating to academic freedom and faculty security did not have any official status at Wheaton during this period. This does not mean that the matter was not discussed, or that a form of de facto tenure did not exist. In 1936, Wheaton's AAUP chapter undertook a study of tenure practices and salary scales at other institutions, but no communication regarding tenure was ever initiated with the President or the Board of Trustees. However, in December, 1940, Park felt able to say in a "To Whom It May Concern" letter that Louise Boas had "the maximum security of tenure."[91] With or without formal tenure status, it is evident that faculty who had served for a number of years, particularly those with the rank of full professor, were regarded as permanent, long-term employees whose connection with Wheaton would end only with their retirement.

Perhaps the best example of this was Glenn Shook, Professor of Physics since 1918, to whom Park bluntly posited in 1935 that Shook had

Carrying the traditional daisy chain, seniors took part in Class Day ceremonies on the steps of the library in 1932.

lost interest in teaching, and "did not really in his heart believe that women could learn physics." The result, Park maintained, was that the department "was entirely out of date." Park suggested Shook resign, and that he apply for a sabbatical during which he could seek another position. However, Park also commented that he was not going to "force any resignation," because "I felt that the college owed something to him for all his years of faithful service."[92]

Shook courteously but bitterly agreed; he applied for and received the sabbatical, and promised to look for a new position. Ultimately, however, his resignation was not insisted on; he returned to Wheaton, where he remained in the Physics department for another decade. Clearly, an unwritten recognition of de facto tenure on Park's part contributed greatly to Shook's survival.[93]

Nonetheless, lack of any formal restrictions on presidential power left Park free to deal individually with each faculty member as he saw fit. Serious complaints about teaching inevitably led to a summons to the President's office. The fact that each person's salary was negotiated individually with the President allowed Park to use this as a weapon, and he was not loath to inform someone that substandard performance was the reason for failure to receive any upward adjustment in salary.

For Park teaching performance was the sine qua non, and demonstrated excellence in this area was the surest way to gain promotion. From those who excelled as teachers no demands in the way of research or scholarship were made. In truly exceptional cases Park was even willing to waive the normal requirement that faculty members should attain the Ph.D. degree. For others, Park was equally blunt in asserting that a Ph.D. was in itself not enough; promotion would be dependent on their ability to achieve some level of scholarly publication. Success as a department head, or substantial contributions to the "life" of the College also were considered important.[94]

Since the College Statutes stated that the President at his discretion could award three-year contracts to those holding professorial rank at any level, Park from time to time withheld this security, replacing it with a letter saying that no contract of any length would be issued, thus leaving both sides free to act as they wished, the only proviso being that six months notice of termination must be given by either side. While he was generally reluctant to terminate abruptly the employment of those who had received one or more contract renewals, he did on occasion suggest resignation to persons whose service was of long standing, but whom he felt were no longer performing well. As an additional incentive to encourage individuals to seek another position, raises were at times withheld for a number of years in succession. In one instance, Park was adamant in his insistence that one long-time department head step down from that position, despite her assertion that she could not hold her head up if she lost the position and would leave Wheaton rather than allow someone else to head the department in which she served. Yet in every case involving senior faculty, the issue was never one of personal loyalty to him, as it often had been for President Cole. Rather it was always in response to serious and continued complaints from other faculty members regarding teaching incompetence or unwillingness to work cooperatively with colleagues. In all cases involving termination of persons with lengthy service, Park sought and obtained the agreement of the Board of Trustees, which often approved (usually at Park's suggestion) some sort of modest severance package.[95]

Only once did Park's efforts to handle these matters quietly and away from public scrutiny fail. In November, 1931, as a result of ongoing conflicts between a long-time member of the Chemistry Department, Auguste Pouleur, and a recently appointed assistant professor, Mildred Evans, Park became convinced that Pouleur's employment should be terminated. The gist of the problem was that Pouleur, who had come to Wheaton in 1918, apparently was a competent teacher of elementary chemistry courses, but was not knowlegeable concerning the theoretical and advanced levels needed for the full major in chemistry. This in itself would not have constituted a problem if Pouleur had been able to tolerate the appointment of a second person in chemistry. However, he clearly regarded any other person, particularly one with a Ph.D., as a personal threat to his position and authority, and having earlier forced (unwarrantedly in Park's opinion) the resignation of a junior male colleague, he was now intent upon doing the same with Miss Evans. With the approval of the Board of Trustees, Park set out to obtain Pouleur's resignation, prepared to offer a series of financial inducements, including a paid sabbatical leave, in order peacefully to achieve his aim.

Instead, Professor Pouleur resisted in every conceivable fashion. He repeatedly maligned both Dr. Evans and President Park in front of his classes, telling students who worked as assistants for Miss Evans that they would flunk his courses, and stating publicly to one class that Park was "the worst liar of anybody at the college."[96] Pouleur also contacted several members of the Board of Trustees directly, and solicited the aid of the national AAUP, which asked John Maguire of the Harvard Law School to investigate the case. After a preliminary investigation, Maguire sided completely with the College, but suggested that in order to create the best subsequent legal position for itself the Board of Trustees should grant Pouleur a hearing. Maguire then proceeded to outline to Park how the hearing should be conducted in order to make the best case for Wheaton, surely a remarkable action for a representative of AAUP to undertake.

The hearing was held; the Board upheld the termination; and despite his continued public resistance, Pouleur's teaching career at Wheaton ended in June, 1932. However, he refused to vacate his College-owned house, leaving finally only in late September, 1932, under the duress of a court writ obtained by the College. Eventually he moved to California, where ten years later he unsuccessfully tried to claim that Wheaton owed him salary for two sabbaticals, since he had taught without one at Wheaton for fourteen years.[97]

The saga of this struggle, followed avidly by faculty, staff, and students alike, constituted a considerable embarrassment for President Park and for the College in the wider academic community. Yet the termination of Auguste Pouleur (and also in a sense the unsuccessful subsequent effort to bring about the resignation of Glenn Shook) signalled President Park's determination to upgrade the quality of the science offerings and the science faculty, as well as the end of the preference for men in senior faculty positions which had been so dominant during President Cole's administration. Leadership in the science departments passed into the capable hands of Mathilde Lange and Mildred Evans, where it remained for many years.

Since there was no Provost or Academic Dean in the more modern sense of that office, anything relating to academic or faculty business passed directly through President Park's hands. He reviewed all book orders for the Library. All repairs or renovations to faculty houses needed his approval, even the replacement of a five square foot piece of linoleum in the kitchen of one apartment. Complaints regarding the quality and type of food served in the dining halls, abuse of the College linen service, or the delivery schedule for packages received by the College post office passed across his desk and required his attention. All of this served to perpetuate the direct, paternalistic control exercised by President Park over all aspects of Wheaton's operation as well as, directly or indirectly, over all who were members of the College community.[98]

Although he is described as remaining distant from most faculty, Park, as is the case for most administrators, did have special confidants, both male and female, on whose counsel he particularly relied. But there was an additional aspect of Park's administration that was particularly problematic to many. This was the so-called "Conversation Club" organized by President Park, which met once a month in the evening at his home. Open only by invitation to some, but not all, male members of the faculty, it also included Norton Superintendent of Schools and occasional part-time faculty member, L. G. Nourse. A paper or presentation would be given followed by discussion which often drifted to more general issues affecting the College, Norton community, and world. What also made this group particularly convivial is revealed in a letter sent to Park by former head of the German Department Otto Springer, who left Wheaton in 1936 to become Chairman of the German Department at the University of Kansas. "I have already given up hope," Springer wrote, "of ever establishing here anything that may even remind me of Wheaton's masculine Beer-Club."[99] In later years William Hunt, on leave from

Wheaton while stationed with the Navy in Newport, Rhode Island, would make a special effort to return for the meetings of the "Conversation Club."[100]

For both faculty and administration, the location of the College in a small, basically rural, working-class town, plus the economic exigencies caused by the Great Depression, meant that the College community became, both socially and professionally, very tightly knit, one could almost say "in-bred." Katherine Burton, a member of the English department, described the Wheaton of that era as "a very informal, monastic kind of place."[101] In terms of daily existence during the academic year its members were both isolated and insulated from the outside world. Women faculty in particular sought to escape their sense of confinement in the dormitories by meeting daily to play bridge. A group of fifteen faculty each purchased one book a year and then circulated the books to be read and discussed by all. Those faculty with houses or access to kitchen facilities entertained each other regularly at small dinner parties on weekends.[102]

One unfortunate result of this parochialism was that tensions over small matters could attain a level of intensity far beyond what might normally have been expected. For faculty this was exacerbated by an open, though always civilized, rivalry and power struggle between Dean Miriam Carpenter and long-time Registrar of the College Sarah Belle Young, which at times created situations that led faculty to feel somewhat trapped between the two. Park was not unaware of the situation, and in particular of what one faculty member described as Miss Young's "jealousy" over what she perceived as Dean Carpenter's favored position vis-à-vis the President. Nonetheless, Dr. Park clearly respected Miss Young and the competent manner in which she accomplished the many scheduling and record keeping duties of the Registrar's Office. In fact, he went out of his way privately to advise new members of the faculty to be sure to get and stay on the good side of Miss Young. "You will come to realize that Sarah Belle is the bulldog of the campus," he told new Philosophy Instructor Holcombe Austin. "She guards things, guards things if necessary with a growl, and she doesn't need to bark, a growl is enough."[103]

During the 1930s, many faculty were appointed who would have long and illustrious careers at Wheaton and leave an indelible mark upon the institution. In particular Ralph Boas, Jane Chidsey, Paul Cressey, Mildred Evans, Henrietta Jennings, E. J. (Jack) Knapton, Louise Barr MacKenzie, Maud Marshall, and Esther Seaver come to mind. But perhaps none had as immediate an impact as Carl Garabedian. Having received an undergraduate chemical engineering degree from Tufts University, he subsequently obtained his Ph.D. in mathematics from Harvard University, and his academic appointment at Wheaton in the spring of 1936 was in that department. But his great love was choral music, and his

Sarah Belle Young,
Registrar, 1909-1946.

teaching load in the Mathematics department was soon reduced so that he could take on the duties of College Organist and Choir Director. He approached these tasks with the precision and discipline of a mathematician and the firey commitment of someone who believed all else should take second place to the performance of classical choral music. Within a few years he established the tradition that no lectures or special events could take place on Monday night in order that nothing should compete with his Choir and Glee Club rehearsals. In turn, the level of performance demanded of and returned by his students quickly propelled Wheaton's choral organizations into the forefront of those found among New England colleges. But the impact that his single-minded devotion had upon the campus was perhaps best described by President Park in a letter he wrote to Ralph Boas, who was on sabbatical leave in Switzerland in the spring of 1939.

> Mr. Garabedian is going to have a concert. Everybody on the campus has already put in their hours of forced labor upon it, and it is interesting from the window of my office to see him appearing at the edge of the campus and every person previously in sight immediately disappearing— although they all have the best of good will for him in his enterprise.[104]

In the first years of his administration President Park had very quickly brought Wheaton into line with other liberal arts colleges for women in

terms of admissions by examination rather than certification, and by replacing the old four-year "group" programs with a set of general education requirements followed by departmental major and minor
concentrations. Having achieved this major restructuring of the academic program, President Park was content during the 1930s to tinker
peripherally with the curriculum, occasionally proposing or supporting
a new initiative, and more wistfully than assertively suggesting that
courses and departments be structured along interdisciplinary lines. The
financial constraints imposed by the economic crisis of the 1930s also
were undoubtedly a limiting factor in terms of curricular expansion. The
result was that in the academic arena, as in most others, one again has
the sense of an institution seeking to survive and preserve what it had,
rather that looking toward major change or curricular reformulation.

Nonetheless, it is interesting to note the implementation of some new
elements that would become permanent fixtures at Wheaton. In June,
1934, Wheaton conferred its first earned Master of Arts degree upon
Laura Povey (W1930), who taught Classics at Norton High School. Although in its original charter as a college Wheaton had received authorization from the Commonwealth of Massachusetts to award Masters
degrees, only in 1930 did the faculty approve a set of general requirements for attaining that degree. Never was there any intention to establish a regular graduate program of study. In succeeding years the very
occasional graduate degree candidate's course of study would always be
individually crafted by the sponsoring academic department and specifically approved by a subsequent vote of the faculty.[105]

In 1931, Wheaton was one of thirty-one colleges that sent delegations
to a model League of Nations Assembly held at Wellesley College, with
Wheaton representing South Africa. Nearly seventy years later the College still participated in the Model United Nations sessions that had become the successor to the original mock League of Nations forum.[106]
Similarly, the tutorial program headed by Professor Katherine Burton,
sponsored by the English Department to help students who were having
trouble writing papers in courses across the curriculum, presaged the extensive support programs provided in later decades by the department.[107]

Chemistry Professor Mildred Evans experimented successfully with a
policy of unscheduled laboratory assignments for upperclass students,
who were free to do the work whenever they pleased—very similar, she
maintained, to reading assigned to be done in the Library in other
courses. Other departments tried out three or four-day "reading periods"
in their courses. Park also expressed considerable interest in a proposal
made to him privately by English Professor Ralph Boas that courses be
offered that "dwell particularly on the problems from the women's point
of view—e.g., in literature, physiology, art, etc. etc.," though nothing
concrete ever resulted from this idea.[108]

Throughout the latter 1930s and into the 1940s, Dr. Park continually urged the faculty to take a more interdisciplinary approach to both the organization of the faculty and the structure of courses. To this end in July, 1937, he authorized an experimental year-long course, entitled Elements of Composition, without seeking approval from the Faculty Curriculum Committee (which he thought might be difficult to obtain). Regarding his decision to circumvent the Curriculum Committee, Park wrote to the Registrar: "It is the nature of the case that one has to try a thing out before you can make any real judgment upon it, and the average college faculty cannot approve a thing before it has been tried and it cannot be tried out until it has been approved."[109]

The course involved members of the Art, English and Music departments, and was offered to a very few handpicked entering students. It was allowed to take the place of required freshman English composition and the Art department's introductory course dealing with the Theory of Representation and Pictorial Design. Although the course was deemed successful and became a fixture in the curriculum, detractors among the faculty regarded its content as a dilution of the standard introductory offerings of the disciplines, and they decried the "underhanded" way in which it had been implemented. More importantly, there is no evidence that this example resulted, as Park had hoped it would, in the creation and implementation of other interdisciplinary courses.[110]

As Wheaton entered the decade of the 1940s, Park began to articulate his desire for curricular change ever more forcefully. Believing that it was necessary to get away from a rigid structure centered on quizzes, exams and grades, he argued strongly to the faculty that it was necessary to give students more freedom to pace themselves, even if it meant that the weaker ones "would hang themselves as a result."[111] In the fall of 1941, seeking to create a freshman curriculum that would emphasize methods and approaches to knowledge in various areas presented from an interdisciplinary perspective, he commented in faculty meeting:

> Our custom here at Wheaton is to have discussion of ways of improving our educational system in the faculty, then to appoint committees to report on the matters raised. These committees have many meetings, do a great deal of work, report back to the faculty that there does not seem to be anything to be done, and the order for the day is retreat in good order to previously occupied positions. . . .
>
> It would be better that Wheaton should go down with its experimental flag flying than rot to death in departmental port because it was afraid to go to sea. In other words, I think we could improve our freshman year.[112]

The President also toyed with the idea of dividing the faculty into four broad divisions, suggested that Chemistry and Physics combine to create a Department of Physical Science, and approved the creation of a major in Philosophy and Religion. He urged disciplines such as History and English, or Economics, Sociology and Government to try in their courses to interconnect with one another, rather than teaching in a manner that resulted in students being "dosed with mere unconnected fragments of knowledge."[113] He also suggested that juniors and seniors be allowed to take four rather than five courses, so they could spend more time reading and studying in depth.[114] While his comments triggered a lengthy and, according to Park, healthy debate among the faculty, the results per se were minimal. The President's comments to the Board of Trustees indicate the high level of his personal frustration regarding this issue.

> It is very hard to move a faculty because each one of them is in a little pen of specialized knowledge and has a sense of the necessity for some security of tenure in that enclosure. But we have had most interesting discussions in the faculty. The results have been meager because while the process of educating a student is complicated, that of educating a member of the faculty is almost impossible.[115]

Nonetheless, three major changes in the academic area did occur. The first was the introduction in 1936 of Latin Honors, awarded at graduation. Up to that point honors had been awarded only for work in a department, not on the basis of overall academic performance. While the first *cum laude* and *magna cum laude* awards were made in 1936, it was only in 1938 that the college graduated its first three students *summa cum laude*.[116]

In 1937–38, following the earlier lead of the English Department, other departments began requiring senior majors to take and pass a set of general examinations during the spring of their senior year in order to graduate. Not all departments were enthusiatic about this development— the longest holdout was Mathematics, but under rather forceful pressure from the President the department agreed in early 1939 that it would participate.[117]

The third major change was the introduction in the fall of 1940 of the Wheaton Scholars Program, designed to establish formally the process by which students could graduate with Departmental Honors. Wheaton Scholars were selected in the middle of their junior year and were given unique pins to place on the robes that seniors wore to special academic events during their senior year. All were required to complete a senior thesis and stand a special examination which would include one faculty member from outside their own department. Students who failed to attain a high enough grade to graduate with Departmental Honors still received course credit for their work. The program was immediately successful; it continued unchanged for more than twenty years, and remained in basically the same form, though without the Wheaton Scholar designation, as the twentieth century came to a close.[118]

∞

In 1935, poet Robert Frost (here with President Park) delivered the address at the annual Founders Day ceremony.

On no problem was greater time spent in committees, general discussion, and faculty meeting debate during the 1930s than the steadily increasing amount of class cutting by students. In 1931, in response to the President's request that an effort be made to move away from emphasis on exams, grades, rules, and regulations toward greater development of academic concerns and student reponsibility, the faculty voted a substantial liberalization of attendance policies in several areas. While the regulations requiring attendance at classes immediately before and after vacations were made more stringent, attendance requirements for classes at all other times were abolished. The number of weekends that members of each class year could spend away from campus was greatly liberalized; students on Dean's List were given unlimited weekend privileges, as well as the right to absent themselves from announced quizzes in courses, should they so desire. Concomitant with this came the revocation of the provision that unauthorized class absences would result in an automatic reduction in the final course grade by the Registrar.[119]

Within two years, class cutting was back before the faculty, where it remained a dominant topic of concern up until America's entry into World War II. In November, 1933, the faculty debated at great length the high level of cutting that occurred on football weekends. Convinced that it was impossible to find an academic schedule that would totally eliminate Saturday classes, the faculty considered, but ultimately rejected, the suggestion that classes might be suspended on "major" football Saturdays.[120]

President Park's position was to suggest that since class attendance was voluntary, it was incumbent on the faculty to design lectures and class activities that contained material students could not get from the assigned reading. Faculty response, articulated in a lengthy discussion in September, 1935, was that it was not enough to structure courses in this way—the crux of the issue was convincing students that they needed to attend class in order to perform decently in a course, that reliance on reading assignments or someone else's class notes would not suffice. On only one matter was the faculty agreed—that it would violate the whole spirit they were trying to inculcate among students if individual faculty resorted to penalizing students for absences in their classes.

In 1936, a special ad hoc "Cutting Committee" reported at length to the faculty regarding class absences at different times and on different days, as well as the frequency of cutting on the part of students with good as opposed to poor academic averages. While the committee's recommendation that the problem was not serious enough to warrant major changes in class schedules was upheld, two years later the faculty voted to reexamine the issue. In the fall of 1938, the Chair of the new committee, Economist Henrietta Jennings, reported that it appeared that freshmen and sophomores were much more likely to take weekends that ran from Thursday to Monday or Tuesday than were upperclass students. Even more serious was the increased cutting of classes by students when they were not away from campus.[121]

In January, 1939, the faculty was finally moved to take at least limited action. Convinced by the data that there was indeed a correlation between class attendance and class standing, it was voted that those on academic probation should have their class cutting privileges rescinded. Strangely, up until that time academic probation had carried with it severe restrictions on participation in extracurricular activities, but no limitations on the right to miss class. Even more shocking to the faculty was a report from the committee that it had conducted a group meeting with fifteen students who were among the heaviest class cutters, but who had managed to attain grades sufficient to keep them off academic probation.

> The meeting was illuminating. The most vocal of these students were quite frank in declaring that they had come to college quite as much for social as for intellectual reasons and that Wheaton is the base for an education which is pursued elsewhere and centers chiefly about men. They con-

sider that their various fees and the requirement of certain minimum grades constitute a high price which they pay for this privilege, and that as long as the payment is made the Faculty should not question their cutting as frequently as they want to, or feel any sense of responsibility for them.[122]

The committee, positing that such students constituted "an undesirable element in a college community," recommended and received the support of the faculty for the creation of a "Committee on Class Attendance," which would be empowered to receive reports from faculty members regarding students whose cutting practices seemed "to be impairing either their own work or the efficiency of class instruction." If a student failed to accept the admonishment of the committee, or a subsequent requirement to attend classes, the committee could recommend to the whole faculty that she be asked to withdraw on the grounds that she was "not in sympathy with the educational aims of the College," even though her grade point average in itself did not merit such action.[123] In an effort to inculcate in incoming freshmen a greater sense of academic responsibility the faculty also voted, in May of 1939, to create a "non-compulsory" (for faculty) system of freshman faculty advisers.[124]

There matters rested until travel restrictions and the national sense of greater work responsibility imposed by America's entry into World War II combined to create a different atmosphere on the Wheaton campus when the College reconvened following the Christmas vacation in January, 1942.

NOTES: CHAPTER 13

1. Wheaton College, *Report of the President of Wheaton College, June 22, 1932,* p. 1.

2. Ibid., pp. 5–6.

3. Wheaton's application for membership in Phi Beta Kappa had been held up by the small number of volumes in the Wheaton Library, a fact that Park used successfully in November, 1929, to persuade the Board of Trustees to authorize a substantial increase in the Library book budget. The Wheaton chapter was formally inaugurated on March 18, 1932. Ibid., p. 11; Trustees Minutes: 11/18/29; 3/6/31; 11/19/31; Trustees: R. Smith: Park to Smith 11/12/30; Faculty: Shepard: Park to Shepard, 9/11/31.

4. These figures included both teaching faculty and administrators such as the President, Dean, and Registrar.

5. Wheaton College, *President's Report, 1932*, pp. 2–5.

6. Ibid., p. 10.

7. Ibid.

8. Ibid., p. 8.

9. Trustees Minutes: 6/25/29.

10. Ibid.: 3/6/31.

11. Ibid.; see also 4/4/29; President's Reports to Trustees: 6/15/31; Trustees, Gen-

eral Information: Miscellaneous, 1925–45: Report on Condition of Metcalf Hall, by Park to Channing Cox, 6/27/31.

12. In 1927–28 and again in 1938–39 the College allowed those who had been enrolled the previous year to continue until they graduated at the rate in effect before the increase. Trustees Minutes: 3/6/31; Faculty Meeting Minutes: 9/22/38; *Wheaton College Bulletin: Catalogue and Announcements, 1927–28; Wheaton College Bulletin: Catalogue,* 1938–39.

13. Trustees Minutes: 3/10/32.

14. Ibid.: 3/5/34.

15. Ibid.: 3/13/33; 11/16/33; see also President's Reports to Trustees: 11/21/32.

16. Trustees Minutes: 6/20/32; 6/19/33; Trustees: R. Smith #2: Scholarship Committee to Friends of Wheaton College, 5/3/34.

17. Trustees Minutes: 11/17/36; Dean's Office, Admissions: Annual Reports, 1928–61: Report for 1936–37. Park later referred to 1934–35 as "our real depression year." Faculty Meeting Minutes: 9/19/35. It is interesting to note that beginning in 1936–37, the President on several occasions referred to the depression in the past tense. See for example Trustees: Meadows: Park to Meadows, 1/18/37. Equally enlightening is the fact that both Park and the Board of Trustees were confident that the College was doing well enough for Park to take an authorized sabbatical leave during the fall semester of 1937. The administration of the College was left in the hands of a committee made up of trustees Herbert Plimpton and William Chase, Dean Carpenter, Miss Young (Registrar), and Professors MacIntire and Boas. Faculty Meeting Minutes: 5/20/37; Trustees Minutes: 3/22/37.

18. Trustees Minutes: 3/13/33; 3/11/35; 11/7/38. The student who attended Middlebury in the 1950s was Rosemary Knapton, daughter of History Professor E. J. Knapton.

19. Ibid.: 3/10/32; Dean's Office, Admissions: Annual Reports, 1928–61: White to Park, 11/10/33.

20. Dean's Office, Admissions: Annual Reports, 1928–61: Annual Report, 1931–32, p. 1.

21. Ibid.: Annual Report, 1932–33, p. 3.

22. Ibid.: Annual Reports, 1933–34; 1934–36; 1936–37; Trustees Minutes: 6/19/33. Regular admissions decisions were made by the Board of Admission early in July. Subsequent admissions were drawn from a short waiting list and from late admissions applications. Ideally they replaced those who declined admission and also matched any late upperclass student withdrawals.

23. Faculty Meeting Minutes: 11/17/33; *Wheaton College Bulletin: Catalogue,* 1934–35, p. 24; Staff: E. White: White to Park, 11/29/33.

24. Faculty Meeting Minutes: 4/24/33; 3/8/34; Staff: E. White: Memorandum for Dr. Park for Faculty Meeting, March 8, 1934.

25. Trustees Minutes: 11/7/38; 3/20/39; Dean's Office, Admissions: Annual Reports, 1928–61: Annual Report, November, 1939, p. 6; Faculty Meeting Minutes: 3/10/39.

26. Barbara Ziegler, who became Secretary of the Board of Admissions when Edith White died in 1935, commented that during the Great Depression Wheaton, and many other colleges, looked for "students that breathed." Oral History Project: B. Ziegler interview, 1983.

27. Trustees Minutes: 11/22/35.

28. Solomon, *Educated Women,* p. 143–44. See also Horowitz, *Alma Mater,* pp. 258–259; Horowitz, *Campus Life,* pp. 105–6; W. H. McNeill, *Hutchins' University: A Memoir of the University of Chicago, 1929–1950* (Chicago: University of Chicago Press, 1989), p. 174, n. 14; Wechsler, *Qualified Student,* pp. 131–85; M. G. Synott, *The Half-Opened Door: Discrimination and Admissions at Harvard, Yale, and*

Princeton, 1900–1970 (Westport, CT: Greenwood Press, 1979); S. M. Lipset and D. Riesman, *Education and Politics at Harvard* (New York: McGraw Hill, 1975), pp. 145–50; D. A. Oren, *Joining the Club: A History of Jews and Yale* (New Haven: Yale University Press, 1985); J. O. Freedman, "Ghosts of the Past: Anti-Semitism at Elite Colleges," *The Chronicle Review: Chronicle of Higher Education*, 47:14 (December 1, 2000), pp. B7–B10.

29. Dean's Office, Admissions: Applicants, 1927–31; HWC, Letters to Family: to Family, 6/9/18.

30. Staff: E. White: White to Park, n.d., "Hebrew Statistics, 1928–32."

31. Deans Office, Admissions: Annual Reports 1928–61: Annual Report, 1933–34, p. 5.

32. Trustees Minutes: 11/19/34.

33. Faculty: Carpenter: Park to Carpenter, 7/31/35.

34. Dean's Office, Admissions: Annual Reports, 1928–61: Report for 1934–36, pp. 2–3.

35. Ibid.: p. 3.

36. Ibid.: Annual Report, 1936–37, p. 5.

37. Ibid.

38. Ibid.: Report for 1934–36, p. 3.

39. Ibid.: Report Ending November, 1938, p. 4.

40. Dean's Office, Admissions: Minutes of Board of Admissions, 3/11/42; Admissions Statistics, 1941–48: "Hebrew Students, 1927–43." The total percentage of Jewish students on campus in any of these years ranged from 6 to 9.75 percent. The greatest number entering in any year was fourteen, plus a transfer student, in 1943.

41. Faculty: Korsch: Remick to Korsch, 4/7/39. See Oren's discussion of Jews on the faculty at Yale in the interwar period, in *Joining the Club*, ch. 6; also Synnott re Harvard in *Half-Opened Door*, p. 201; and Freedman re Dartmouth and others in "Ghosts of the Past," pp. B7–B10. Erich Goldmeier, a refugee scholar, did serve one year as a Research Associate in Psychology at Wheaton. His salary of $100 per month was paid through Wheaton by the Associated Jewish Philanthropies, while the College provided laboratory space and use of the College Library. Employment of this nature allowed Dr. Goldmeier to bring his wife from Europe, since he could certify to American immigration officials that he was gainfully employed and therefore she would not become an "object of charity." Faculty: Goldmeier: Park memorandum, 4/4/39; Trustees Minutes: 6/10/39.

42. The student who attended Wheaton for one year was Elizabeth Baker Lewis from Cambridge, Massachusetts. Miss Lewis graduated from Radcliffe in 1924, earned an M.A. degree in 1925, and died less than a year later in March, 1926. For African-American student admissions issues during the Seminary period, see ch. 7, and 7, n. 12. The post WWII decision to begin admitting African-American students is discussed in ch. 18.

43. Staff: E. White: White to Park, 12/21/26.

44. Faculty: Metivier: Park to Metivier, 4/10/31.

45. Ibid.: H. Jennings: Jennings to Park, 4/10/40.

46. Ibid.: Park to Jennings, 4/17/40.

47. These figures include the salaries of the Dean, Registrar, Director of the Nursery School, and Secretary to the Board of Admissions, but not of the President or College Librarian. Trustees Minutes: 3/20/39; Cash Disbursement Sheets: 7/1/38–6/30/41; *Wheaton College Bulletin: Catalogue, 1932–33; 1937–38; Wheaton College, The President's Report, The Treasurer's Report to the Board of Trustees, 1939*. Room and board for accommodations in the dormitories were scaled from $476 to $545. The rental value of houses, which were reserved for male faculty members, ranged from $500 to $600. The total estimated value of noncash payments to faculty was $40,500.

For the comparison data with other institutions, see Trustees Minutes: 3/21/38. Tables listing individual faculty salaries and housing arrangements between 1930–31 and 1940–4l are attached to the following Trustees Minutes: 6/15/31; 3/10/32; 3/5/34; 6/17/35; 3/16/36; 3/21/38; 3/20/39; 3/18/40.

48. Well aware of what had occurred elsewhere, the faculty in June, 1933, passed a resolution thanking the President and the Board of Trustees for keeping the salary scale and the size of the faculty intact. Faculty Meeting Minutes: 6/13/33.

49. Faculty Meeting Minutes: 9/22/32; Trustees Minutes: 6/20/32; 11/21/32; 3/11/35; 11/22/35; Faculty: Work: President's secretary to Bursar, 1/13/36.

50. Park told the Board of Trustees that Miss Burton had asked for a leave of absence in order to study abroad, which Miss Burton in later years always denied. Trustees Minutes: 3/11/35. Oral History Project: K. Burton interview, 5/19/83; K. Burton, interview with author, 1984. See also, Faculty: Burton: Burton to Park, 10/16/33; and passim.

51. Oral History Project: R. Chapman interview, 6/13/83. Barbara Ziegler, Wheaton's Admissions Director, was of the opinion that Park gave her a very low salary because he was aware that she came from a family which "had means." Ibid.: B. Ziegler interview, 1983; see also D. Littlefield interview, 1983; M. Hidy interview, 1985; Faculty Meeting Minutes: 9/22/38.

52. Trustees Minutes: 3/21/38; 3/20/39; 3/18/40.

53. AAUP: Foundation of Wheaton Chapter, 1932–33; Minutes, 1933–56: 5/8/33; 10/27/36; 2/18/37; Faculty Salary Scale, 1935–59: passim; Trustees Minutes: 3/22/37.

54. AAUP: Faculty Salary Scale, 1935–59: Knapton to Shepard, 3/22/37. President Park is reported to have viewed the Wheaton AAUP chapter "with a mixture of friendliness, mused tolerance, and great caution." Yet he apparently came in time to regard the AAUP executive committee as a sort of regular faculty committee. Oral History Project: H. Austin interview, 1983.

55. Faculty: Seaver: Park memorandum, 2/25/38.

56. Trustees Minutes: 3/22/37.

57. Faculty: Work: Park to Work, 2/5/36.

58. For example, two individuals, both hired at the rank of instructor beginning in September, 1941: the woman, with a Ph.D. and three years' experience received $1200 plus dormitory room and board; the man, without a Ph.D. and having one year's teaching experience, received $2000 plus a house. Trustees Minutes: 11/3/41. See also Faculty: Van Ingen: Park memorandum, Spring, 1938; K. Neilson: Park to Neilson, 4/6/40; Evans: Park memorandum, 1/30/35; Littlefield: Park memorandum, 3/20/40; Cressey: Park memorandum, 2/16/38.

59. AAUP: Correspondence, 1935–50: Nottingham to Himstead, 2/1/40.

60. Trustees Minutes: 3/21/38.

61. Ibid.: 11/7/38; 3/20/39; 6/10/39.

62. Ibid.: 6/14/41; 5/30/43; 11/8/43; Faculty Meeting Minutes: 5/12/41; 6/13/41; Oral History Project: R. Chapman interview, 6/18/83; see also Trustees, General Information: Miscellaneous 1925–45: Correspondence, 1941–43, re Faculty Committee for Consultation with the Trustees.

63. M. H. Ford, interview with author, October, 1987. Hilda Harris (W1931) asserted that she was denied a job paying $900.00 a year at Brown University following her graduation on the grounds that her family was well enough off to support her. Oral History Project: H. Harris interview, 1983.

64. Faculty: Penniman: Park memoranda, 4/24/34; 5/2/34; see also W. H. Chafe, *The Paradox of Change: American Women in the 20th Century* (New York: Oxford University Press, 1991), pp. 115–16.

65. Faculty: McFarland: McFarland to Park, 7/14/38; Park to McFarland, 7/20/38.

66. Knapton, *Small Figure,* p. 162.

67. Trustees Minutes: 3/6/3l.

68. Faculty: Marshall: Marshall to Park, 3/25/38; Randall: Park to Randall, 2/18/30; and Park memorandum, 6/17/32.

69. Ibid.: Appel: Park to Appel, 5/25/35.

70. Ibid.: Sharp: Sharp to Park, 5/29/41; Park to Sharp, 5/31/4l; W. Nickerson: Park to Nickerson, 4/16/42; Metivier: Metivier to Park, 12/16/3l; Park to Metivier, 12/17/31; H. Jennings: Jennings to Park, 2/18/34; Park to Jennings, 3/1/34; Riddell: Riddell to Park, 7/8/34; Park to Riddell, 7/13/34; Seaver: Park to Seaver, 11/10/32; Evans: Evans to Park, 11/20/33; Marshall: Marshall to Park, 3/25/38; Park to Marshall, 6/4/38.

71. Trustees Minutes: 6/8/40; Faculty: H. Jennings: 4/17/40–9/8/43, passim; Rice: Remick to Rice, 12/13/41; Remick memorandum, 1/20/42.

72. Faculty: Metivier: Park to Metivier, 12/17/31; Marshall: Park to Marshall, 6/4/38; Trustees Minutes: 3/5/34; 3/16/36; 6/8/40.

73. Trustee Minutes: 11/19/34; see also Faculty Meeting Minutes: 11/13/34; 3/7/35; Faculty: Evans: Park memorandum, 5/3/33; Lynn: Lynn to Park, 5/7/36; 5/14/36; H. Jennings: Park memorandum, 5/16/36.

74. Trustees Minutes: 3/22/37.

75. Ibid.: 6/8/40.

76. Ibid.: 6/18/38; Faculty Meeting Minutes: 9/22/38.

77. Trustees Minutes: 6/18/38; 11/27/39; Faculty: Winslow: Remick to Dunkle, 1/18/39; Wheaton College Financial Reports: Audit Report, 6/30/39, p. 8.

78. Faculty: Gulley: Park to Gulley, 10/23/35; Carpenter to Gulley, 10/20/37; Hubbard: Park to Hubbard, 4/27/39. There was some discussion regarding a group disability insurance program for which faculty would be responsible for the premiums, but when only twenty of forty-nine faculty indicated interest, the matter was abandoned. Faculty Meeting Minutes: 11/27/33.

79. Trustees Minutes: 3/21/38; 6/18/38; Faculty Meeting Minutes: 5/18/38; 9/22/38.

80. Faculty: Waring: Park memorandum, 11/7/35.

81. Trustees Minutes: 11/22/35; see also 11/1/37; 11/7/38; 3/10/41; Faculty: Lynn: Meadows to Lynn, 12/30/37; Riddell: Riddell to Park, 11/1/38; Park to Riddell, 11/7/38; Rice: Park to Rice, 3/11/41.

82. Trustees Minutes: 6/10/39; 3/18/40. Ida Everett held this title from her retirement in 1928 until her death in 1934.

83. Faculty Meeting Minutes: 9/24/36; 11/30/36.

84. Walter McIntire, for years one of the two highest paid members of the Wheaton faculty, retired in June, 1941, with a lump sum payment that exceeded his $4000 cash salary by only $1536. Trustees Minutes: 11/3/41.

85. Trustees Minutes: 6/18/38; 6/8/40; 11/25/40; "The New Retiring Allowance Fund," attached to Minutes of 11/25/40; Faculty Meeting Minutes: 6/7/40; 9/25/40.

86. AAUP: Correspondence 1935–50: Thayer to Knapton, 12/16/40; Trustees Minutes: 6/8/40; Faculty: Cressey: Cressey to Park, 12/24/40; Park to Cressey, and general memorandum to faculty, 1/3/4l; Cressey to Park, 1/6/41.

87. Trustees Minutes: 3/10/41; see also Faculty: Burton: Burton to Carpenter, 12/17/40.

88. Trustees Minutes: 3/10/41.

89. Ibid.

90. Faculty Meeting Minutes: 6/11/35; 9/19/35; Faculty: H. Jennings: Jennings to Park, 12/1/35; Garabedian: Park to Garabedian, 2/5/36; General Files: Class of 1935–1936; AAUP: Minutes, 1933–66: 3/17/36; *Wheaton News,* 4/13/35.

91. Faculty: L. Boas, private: Park letter, 12/10/40; see also AAUP: Minutes, 1933–56: 10/27/36.

92. Faculty: Shook: Park memorandum of interview with Shook, 11/15/35.

93. Ibid.: Shook: 1933 ff.

94. Oral History Project: L. B. MacKenzie interview, 3/25/83; K. Burton interview, 5/19/83; Faculty: Burton: Burton to Park, 10/16/33; Cressey: Park memorandum, 2/16/38.

95. Trustees Minutes: 11/19/31; 2/13/32; 6/20/32; 11/21/32; 11/22/35; 6/14/41; 3/6/44; Faculty: Shepard: Park memorandum, 10/10/33; Pouleur: Park to Chamberlain, 12/21/31; Park to Soliday, 1/16/32; Hubbard: Woodbridge to Park, 5/22/33; Park to Hubbard, 6/28/34; Hubbard to Park, 7/3/34; Park memorandum, 9/18/34; Shook: 1933–37, passim; Amen: 1937–40, passim.

96. Faculty: Pouleur: Memorandum by Park for Soliday, 6/4/32.

97. Ibid.: Pouleur: 1931–41, passim; see also Jennings, *Chemistry at Wheaton,* ch. 4.

98. Faculty: Knapton: Knapton to Park, 2/16/33; Park to Knapton, 2/18/33; Metivier: Metivier to Park, 4/22/33; Park to Metivier, 4/27/33; Seaver: Lincoln to Park, 10/14/38, and Park memorandum; Staff: S. B. Young: Young to Park, 7/6/37; Park to Young, 7/7/37.

99. Faculty: O. Springer: Springer to Park, 9/23/36; see also Anni Springer: Springer to Park, 9/22/36, in which she comments that Otto missed "the fun of the beer club."

100. Oral History Project: E. J. Knapton interview, 5/13/83; H. Austin interview, 1983; Faculty: Hunt: Park to McConaughy, 2/17/39; Hunt to Park, 1/10/42.

101. Oral History Project: K. Burton interview, 1983.

102. Ibid.: M. Hidy interview, 1985; K. Burton interview, 1983.

103. Ibid.: H. Austin interview, 1983; see also interviews with E. J. Knapton, K. Burton, D. Littlefield and L. B. MacKenzie.

104. Faculty: R. Boas: Park to Boas, 5/5/39.

105. Faculty Meeting Minutes: 11/17/30; Trustees Minutes: 11/21/32; 6/18/34.

106. Faculty: L. Bannister Merk: Program, Model League of Nations Assembly, 1931.

107. Ibid.: R. Boas: Notices to Faculty Regarding Tutorial Program, 1931-32, and 1940; Burton: material regarding tutorial program, 1932 ff.

108. Ibid.: Evans: Evans to Park, 12/16/38; McIntire: Park memorandum, 1/21/37; Work: Work to Park, 11/30/38; R. Boas: Park memorandum, 2/7/34; Jennings, *Chemistry at Wheaton,* pp. 53–55.

109. Staff: S. B. Young: Park to Young, 7/26/37. See also *Wheaton College Bulletin: Catalogue,* 1938 ff.; Faculty Meeting Minutes: 10/12/38; 11/9/38; 12/7/38; 10/21/40.

110. Faculty: Seaver: Seaver to Park, 11/30/38.

111. Faculty Meeting Minutes: 9/25/40; see also Park's comments in the faculty meeting of 9/22/38.

112. Ibid.: 10/21/41.

113. Trustees Minutes: 11/3/41.

114. Faculty Meeting Minutes: 9/22/38. See also Faculty: Evans: Park memorandum, 11/23/40; R. Boas: Park memorandum, 5/1/40; Work: Work to Park, 10/23/40; Park to Work, 10/24/40.

115. Trustees Minutes: 11/3/41. Park did have his supporters among the faculty regarding this matter, most notably Mildred Evans, Ralph Boas, Eunice Work, and Esther Seaver.

116. Ibid.: 6/15/36; 6/18/38; Faculty Meeting Minutes: 4/27/36; 5/11/36.

117. Faculty Meeting Minutes: 9/22/38; 10/12/38; 12/7/38; Faculty: Watt: President's secretary to Watt, 2/2/39; President's secretary to S. B. Young, 2/6/39. Psychology was also very reluctant to conform. See Faculty: Amen: Amen to Park, 11/30/38; Young to Park, 12/9/38; Park to Amen, 12/13/38.

118. Faculty Meeting Minutes: 1/15/40; 5/9/40.
119. Ibid.: 5/13/31; 9/24/31.
120. Ibid.: 11/27/33.
121. Ibid.: 4/27/36; 6/17/38; 10/12/38.
122. Ibid.: 1/5/39.
123. Ibid.
124. Ibid.: 5/11/39.

14

Surviving the Great Depression: Campus Finances, Construction, and Student Life; Other Constituencies, 1930–1941

FINANCIALLY, WHEATON WEATHERED the economic crisis of the 1930s surprisingly well. Once the drop in admissions applications and enrollment experienced in the early years of the decade had passed, the College began, more often than not, to show a surplus on its books. This disturbed a number of the trustees considerably, in part because they were apprehensive that a published surplus would make the faculty restless in regard to salaries, but even more so because they believed that in actuality the surplus was not real. Wheaton had long followed a practice of lumping together all annual income, whether from endowment, gifts, tuition, room and board rates, or special fees, and then using this sum as the amount against which the cost of current operations could be charged. The income generated from funds received from the rental, and subsequently the sale of the Winter Street property, had by vote of the Board of Trustees been reserved for new building projects.

But nowhere was any provision made for facilities depreciation, and the accumulation of funds needed for replacing, repairing or improving the existing physical plant. Pointing to the fact that Mount Holyoke and other institutions regularly charged a sum approximating 5 percent of plant value to a deferred maintenance account, Trustee John Cobb as early as 1928 had urged that Wheaton do the same, insisting that this should be accounted for separately from current operating expenses. Once this was done, Cobb maintained, the fact that in reality the College was not accumulating meaningful surpluses would become apparent.[1]

During the worst years of the Great Depression this issue became moot, since every dollar of available revenue from fees and the regular endowment was needed for operational purposes. Finally, in 1939, the trustees decided to investigate establishing a "plant depreciation" fund. However, it was not until the end of the academic year 1943–44, that the Board formally voted to establish a deferred maintenance account, and even then funded it with a lump sum of $50,000 rather than tieing it to a percentage of total plant value, or an estimate of the real cost of deferred maintenance needs.[2]

If the College managed to maintain a balance in the "black" and even to fund new construction during the 1930s, it did so only at the price of restricting almost totally the growth of the endowment. All gifts, unless specified for endowment purposes, were used to fund current operations. All income generated by the endowment went either into current operating expenses, or if it came from the Winter Street account, into new construction projects. This was nothing new. Wheaton had operated in this manner ever since Mrs. Wheaton's death in 1905. The result was that an endowment valued at $1,074,000 in 1928 had increased only to $1,187,000 by June, 1941.

One would normally be tempted to attribute much of this nongrowth to the economic vicissitudes of the Great Depression. However, one of the fortunate aspects of the very conservative nature of Wheaton's investments was that it prevented the College from major losses during the economic crisis. In fact, the low point in endowment value during the Depression years, reported in June, 1932, was still $6000 greater than the value of the endowment in 1928. Rather, the explanation for the lack of growth in the endowment really derives from the fact that all nonrestricted income from any source was used for operating expenses or plant expansion. While such a policy kept the College out of debt, it also starved the endowment in terms of ploughing back investment income or adding new moneys in order to increase the base size of the permanent fund.[3]

Although the early years of President Park's administration coincided with the first hiatus in building construction that Wheaton had experienced since the turn of the century, the pause turned out to be short-lived. Beginning in 1931, the College embarked on a new building program that continued for a decade, concluding just in time to escape the building restrictions and supply shortages brought on by the United States' entry into World War II in December, 1941. The fact that several major projects were undertaken during years when privately financed construction of almost any type had all but disappeared made it possible for Wheaton to achieve spectacular results at relatively modest cost. It also bears witness to the insistence of Dr. Park that, no matter what, additional facilities were needed in order for Wheaton to remain competitive in attracting its share of the smaller number of students attending college during these years of economic crisis.

In 1932–33, two new residence halls were constructed on the former site of the rambling wooden dormitory known as Old Metcalf, parts of which had served the Seminary and College for nearly a century. Renamed for former principal Caroline Metcalf, and for Seminary alumna and long-time trustee Annie Kilham (WS1870), the two dormitories were connected at one end by a series of parlors, thus forming a court-yard in which stood a statue of the Greek goddess of youth, Hebe, given to the Seminary years earlier by Mrs. Wheaton. While Mrs. Metcalf was long since deceased and therefore could not comment on the use of her name, Miss Kilham initially objected to having a dormitory named for her, maintaining that the students would call it "Kill 'em all."[4]

In 1934, a separate administration building was erected to house the offices that had also been part of Old Metcalf. "I especially remember," President Park wrote years later, "how the architects had it all designed to be along the main street, and how I got them to turn it round at right angles to the street."[5] Subsequently, the Board authorized the construc-tion of a nursery "laboratory" school for the Psychology and Education department, and a new state-of-the-art swimming pool. A large mainte-nance building providing facilities for the college carpenters, electri-cians and plumbers, along with set design space for theatre productions, was also built, using lumber cut from the trees lost by the College in the 1938 hurricane. In June, 1940, the long-awaited Student Alumnae Building was dedicated, and the next year new wings on both the Sci-ence Building and the Library were completed, just before federal war-time restrictions on new construction went into effect.[6]

In addition, the first classroom building at Wheaton, erected in 1834 and most recently used as the College bookstore and post office, was moved to Howard Street, where the first floor served for the next eight years as a student "social room," while the second floor became a fac-ulty residence. A barn on Taunton Avenue was remodeled to serve as a "Little Theatre" for drama productions, and the Doll's House was con-verted from administrative offices into classroom space. Many smaller improvements were also made, ranging from soundproofing the ceilings in the dining halls to installing sprinkler systems, heat regulating ther-mostats, and time clocks in all the dormitories, the Gymnasium, Mary

Kilham and Metcalf dormitories, joined by Hebe Parlors, were built on the site of Old Metcalf in 1932.

Lyon, and Emerson Dining Hall. New greenhouses were erected next to Mary Lyon and in the President's garden. In 1935 a "Greek temple," constructed out of columns rescued from Old Metcalf, was built on the banks of Peacock Pond. The old coal hole next to the former power house (now Doll's House) was roofed over, and flooring, heat, and lighting were installed. Christened "The Cage," it was used for extra gymnasium space. Walks and drives were paved with asphalt, two tennis courts were built, a new well was sunk, a botannical garden was created on two sides of the Library, and stone steps between the Library and Doll's House were constructed in honor of the College's long-time botanist, Mabel Rice.[7]

Occasionally, small gifts from alumnae for a project were received, a case in point being a birdfeeder in the form of a miniature Chinese pagoda designed by Ralph Adams Cram, which was donated, along with a memorial bench, in 1937 by the Class of 1901 to honor former Seminary science instructor Clara Pike.[8] But all the major construction or renovation projects, with two exceptions, were paid for out of surpluses in current income achieved by lumping all revenue sources together, by managing to keep all available "beds" filled, and by using every bit of income generated by endowment investment. This included the interest payments by the Stowell Company in Boston on the mortgage resulting from its purchase of the Winter Street property, a mortgage whose interest rate had to be negotiated downward from 5 percent to 4.5 percent in 1937, and which was paid off in the spring of 1941.[9]

The College also took advantage of the fact that several pieces of property adjoining that already held by Wheaton came onto the market, including land with a cabin that bordered on the Norton Reservoir, plus a small island in the reservoir itself. The exigencies of the economic crisis of the 1930s made these properties a bargain, and President Park was clearly glad to be able to expand the College's real estate holdings.[10]

In undertaking all these projects, the College was able to obtain an enormous return for the amount of money spent. Perhaps nothing better summarizes the tenor of the times than a letter sent to Dr. Park from the architectural firm of Cram and Ferguson in November, 1932.

> It is with most unusual satisfaction that we acknowledge your telephone call of yesterday afternoon, authorizing us to proceed with the working drawings and specifications for the Administration building. They are already underway.
>
> Whereas, normally we would be receiving orders of this nature every few days, it has been months now since we have developed new business of any kind. It is such an occasion that we are holding a little celebration in the office today. We can assure you that it is of very major importance to us and our employees to receive this commission at the present time. It will mean employment for several men for some weeks who would otherwise be without work.
>
> Will you kindly convey this word of appreciation to your Trustees?[11]

Freshmen members of the class of 1937, wearing their required identification signs, admire the statue of Hebe which was moved from its old location outside Mary Lyon Hall to the courtyard between Kilham and Metcalf dormitories.

Despite this expression of good will, the 1930s witnessed the deterioration and ultimate termination of the special arrangement that had existed between Wheaton and Cram and Ferguson since the late nineteenth century, when President Cole and Ralph Adams Cram had sketched out the basic design of a rectangular central court around which the buildings for a college campus would be erected. Cram's firm, one of the most noted in the Northeast, had been designated supervising architect for the campus as a whole in 1907. Between 1900 and 1936 Cram and Ferguson designed twelve buildings and one major addition for Wheaton, the last of which were the Administration Building and the new 12 by 20 yard swimming pool.[12]

But even as these buildings were being constructed, relations with the architectural firm were deteriorating. The initial source was a long-standing dispute regarding leaks in the roof of Everett dormitory, an ongoing problem ever since the building's completion in 1925. Despite numerous attempts, repairs had been ineffectual, and the College and Cram and Ferguson had become involved in an escalating dispute regarding responsibility and liability for costs associated with the ongoing repair attempts. When the College acceded to Cram and Ferguson's request for payment of half the Administration Building design fee even before the decision to begin actual construction was taken, it attached a condition that Cram and Ferguson guarantee to make Everett leak-free. Four years later the Everett roof was still pourous; Cram and Ferguson attempted to repudiate all further responsibility, only to have the Treasurer of the College, Joseph Soliday, remind them of the firm's earlier guarantee.[13]

But the final straw leading to a full break with the architectural firm came as a result of the twists and turns involved in bringing to fruition the long-desired erection of a Student Alumnae Building (SAB), which would house both the Alumnae Association offices and serve as a student union. From the time President Park arrived at Wheaton he had recognized the need for a building which could serve as a center for the College Government Association, the many other student extracurricular organizations, and the Alumnae Association, as well as provide space other than the Gymnasium for college dances and other major social events. "I am anxious," he wrote in 1931, "that before the habit of rushing away from college at every pretext is established at Wheaton we do as much as we can to make the college itself a homelike place for the students."[14] To this end donations were solicited for years from alumnae, students ran a variety of fund-raising events, and the Board of Trustees voted that profits from the College bookstore should be placed in the SAB fund.[15]

However, plans to build SAB soon became embroiled in another controversy. In a report submitted to the trustees in 1931, President Park indicated that following closely on the heels of new dormitories and SAB was a need for adequate facilities for the Art and Music departments. The result was that in 1932, Cram and Ferguson was authorized to draft preliminary plans for both a fine arts center and a student alumnae building. Throughout the early 1930s planning continued, with the slowly growing SAB fund created by small student and alumnae gifts on the one hand, and a $50,000 pledge in honor of his mother from trustee Herbert Plimpton to be used for an Art Center on the other, each fueling hopes that both buildings might some day become a reality.[16]

By 1937, however, the planning processes had completely stalled. It was obvious that the College's chances of funding both buildings from outside sources was highly unlikely. Moreover, there was growing dissatisfaction with the plans for both buildings drawn up by Cram and Ferguson. Clinging to the traditional Georgian style which had been used for all the major campus buildings, the architectural firm's plans came up against the indomitable will and Modernist outlook of the Head of the Art Department, Esther Seaver, who maintained that Cram and Ferguson's designs paid little attention to interior use of space, caring mainly for creating a stately and impressive exterior image. Not only did the firm's plan for an Art Center fail to satisfy the needs of her department, she maintained, but the buildings themselves would be unnecessarily expensive to construct.

Dr. Seaver's alternative idea was ingenious. She proposed a national architectural competition for an Art Center design, with a cash prize that would become part of the architect's fee if a Center were actually built.[17] The terms of the contest would require that all submitted designs be "according to the modern plan of functional architecture."[18] Such a competition, Miss Seaver argued, would bring Wheaton to the attention of those interested in art and architecture throughout the country. It would provide invaluable publicity for the College; moreover, a successful and highly publicized competition might well serve as the catalyst to attract the outside funds needed to construct the Art Center.[19]

Park was skeptical, but the trustees were not, and on June 19, 1937, they approved the national competition, which would be judged by an independent board of qualified jurors.[20] Ultimately an expenditure of $4700 was authorized, with $1000 of that to be held in escrow as the prize for the winning design. Writing to trustee Robert Smith in January, 1938, Park's scepticism clearly showed. "I have just seen the proofs of the article in *Architectural Forum* about to appear. It certainly gives Wheaton a great deal of publicity, although it sometimes seems to me like the attempt made by the Lord in the beginning of Genesis, which in that case it is true was successful, namely that of making all things out of nothing."[21] Of course, Park admitted, the cost of funding the competition would be worth it "if there is a chance of raising money for this art centre. The miracle may occur and heaven may send a life belt. . . . I am embarrassed and hope to be still further embarrassed, as all unbelievers in the miraculous are when the miracle occurs."[22] In a subsequent letter he commented to Smith that the whole business seemed to him "to be largely in the nature of a gamble," and complained that the art center competition had "swept away" the possibility of building SAB and a modest building for the art department.[23]

The competition, cosponsored by the Museum of Modern Art in New York and *Architectural Forum*, received formal sanction from the American Institute of Architects. It proved to be a resounding success; 253 entries from 243 firms were received by the midnight deadline on May 24, 1938. Although, interestingly enough, the prospectus did not specify that the design should be Modernist, statements by Esther Seaver and others had made it clear that this was what would be looked for by the jury.[24] On June 9, the panel awarded first prize to two relatively unknown architects, Caleb Hornbostel and Richard Bennett. The runner-up was the internationally recognized pair of architects, Walter Gropius and Marcel Breuer. Modernist in concept, it was clear that the winning design, if brought to building fruition, would provide a major breakthough for new forms of architecture on college campuses nationwide, not just at Wheaton. In fact the competition itself represented "the first instance of an American college actively seeking a Modernist building."[25]

Professor Seaver was ecstatic; President Park was not, though his objections were not to the Modernist design. The plans for the new Art Center presupposed the availability of nearly $1,000,000, half to cover the cost of construction and the rest to endow the Center's continuing maintenance costs. Nothing approaching such a sum was available, nor was there any indication that such amounts might appear in the foreseeable future. Park therefore proposed that construction of the Art Center be postponed indefinitely, and to this end he persuaded Mr. Plimpton to allow the $50,000 he had pledged for that building to be transferred to the fund already accumulated for the proposed Student Alumnae Building. This sum, together with an additional pledge of $20,000 from trustee Henry Crapo, would allow the erection of SAB without exercising any draw upon regular endowment income. Park further suggested that the winning architects in the Art Center competition be retained to design the new Student Alumnae Building—thereby providing them with a project that would in part compensate for the fact that the center itself was unlikely to be constructed in the near future.[26]

All of this was accepted enthusiastically by the Board of Trustees and very reluctantly by Miss Seaver, with the result that not only SAB, but the new additions to the Science Building and the Library were designed by Messrs. Hornbostel and Bennett. This in turn led to a demand from Cram and Ferguson that they be compensated for the preliminary design work they had done on both the Art Center and SAB, a claim that the College contested vigorously in terms of amount if not legitimacy, and which, though ultimately settled out of court, led to a final and permanent break with the firm that had served so long and well as Wheaton's supervising architect.[27]

The Student Alumnae Building, which was dedicated in the spring of 1940, represented a breakthrough in terms of modern architecture on traditional American college campuses.[28] Utilizing traditional brick construction in order to harmonize with the rest of the campus, the design itself was uncompromisingly modern, emphasizing clean straight lines and an angled form, designed to fit harmoniously with the terrain which sloped downhill from the main campus toward the recently constructed Peacock Pond. In time the building would become recognized nationally as the first, and very successful, attempt to incorporate modern architectural forms on a campus dominated by traditional Georgian style architecture. Even Professor Seaver was pleased, commenting on "the directness and honesty of the solution and its usefulness in helping students to understand the underlying principles of genuine American as well as modern architecture."[29] Of course, the issue of the Art Center itself remained, but the outbreak of war made it obvious that any decision on that matter would have to wait for more propitious times.

The construction of SAB also triggered a major personnel change, the need for which had been apparent to Dr. Park and many others for some time. Arthur Cutler, who had served as Business Manager during the last years of President Cole's administration, and as Manager of Buildings and Grounds under President Park, had in recent years come under criticism both for increasing coarseness of language, and for his unwillingness to undertake new projects or to adapt to newer forms of technology. The culminating issue came in the spring of 1940, when it was discovered that Cutler was "purposely sabotaging" the newly installed Minneapolis/Honeywell heat control system, turning the heat off in some buildings, and by-passing thermostats in others. Whereas only 2 to 2.5 pounds of steam pressure ideally should have been necessary to operate the system, Cutler was forcing 5 to 10 pounds through the pipes to compensate for the fact that he had never had the radiators cleaned so they could function efficiently. Just as it became clear to the President that it was necessary to terminate Cutler, even though it would be hard to "pry him loose," an ideal replacement appeared on the scene in the person of Irving Fillmore, the foreman in charge of constructing SAB, who

The Modernist design of the Student Alumnae Building (1940) presented a striking contrast to the traditional Georgian architecture of the rest of the Wheaton campus.

quickly impressed the administration with his energy, knowledge and cooperative personality. On June 8, 1940, the trustees approved the forced "retirement" of Cutler and his replacement by Fillmore, who would remain as Head of Buildings and Grounds for twenty-four years. Everyone was much happier now, Park reported to the Board of Trustees. "The waste of time and energy which was necessary to persuade Mr. Cutler to operate at all is no longer required."[30]

One other college-owned building deserves brief mention. The former home of Judge Laban Wheaton, located adjacent to the campus in Norton Center, had long served as an inn whose main source of revenue had been students, parents and others whose business related to Wheaton Seminary and College. The Wheaton Inn also possessed a long row of automobile garages, which were rented out, primarily to students who brought cars to campus. For a brief time during the latter nineteenth century the Inn had been privately owned. However, problems related to the selling of alcohol had led the College to repurchase it shortly after the turn of the century. Subsequently the Inn had been leased to a number of persons, who had operated it with mixed success.

The advent of the economic depression had a very negative effect on the ability of the Wheaton Inn to operate at a profit. Having fallen considerably in arrears in her rent, one operator, Florence Churchill, closed her bank accounts, packed up her belongings on June 1, 1931, and without warning either to the College or the guests at the Inn, vanished suddenly into the night, leaving the College facing its graduation ceremonies with an inn with no operator and limited furnishings.[31]

Subsequent operators continued to fall behind in the rent, so much so that Wheaton quietly agreed to accept whatever could be paid, although the formal amount owed was never decreased. Discussing the matter with the trustees, President Park noted that "much of her [the inn operator, Mrs. Guiler's] income came from the renting of garages, and quite a number of them are vacant owing to the fact that students are financially not able to operate cars."[32] In 1939, summarizing the cost of the Wheaton Inn for the trustees, Park noted that while Wheaton received $1350 in rent from the inn operator and $350 from the phone company which had its local offices there, the annual tax bill was $414, and the College had spent $10,000 over the last ten years on repairs to the property. The result, Park went on, was "that it is not a very money-making affair, but it is to the advantage of the college to have a Inn like this in the vicinity."[33]

By 1927, the duties of the Appointment Bureau, which provided job placement services both to undergraduates and graduates, had been integrated into the office of the Alumnae Secretary. This system continued relatively unchanged throughout the 1930s. Only with the opening of the new Student Alumnae Building in 1940 did the two again become separate entities. By 1937, the salary of the Alumnae Secretary, which initially had been paid entirely by the Alumnae Association, was funded primarily out of College resources. The Association itself continued to operate on a relatively low-key basis, concentrating its efforts on the publication of the *Wheaton Alumnae Quarterly*, providing a link to the campus for the various regional Wheaton Clubs, and serving as on-campus liaison with alumnae for planning and implementing class reunions and in developing plans for the College's centennial celebration in 1935. But one aspect that would normally be expected of such an organization—annual fund-raising—was noticeably absent during the 1920s and early 1930s from the Association's agenda. Aside from occasional contributions from the clubs for scholarships and to the fund to build the proposed Student Alumnae Building, gifts from alumnae were rarely received, nor were they systematically sought.[34]

Much of this was clearly a backlash from the unsuccessful attempt to raise funds through a capital campaign in the early 1920s. The scars from that failure were very slow to heal. Secondly, the dichotomy that existed between those in the Alumnae Association who had attended Wheaton Seminary and the more recent graduates of the College did not help strengthen the Association internally. Trustee Frances Vose Emerson (W1872) suggested that a misperception that Wheaton did not need money because of the largesse of the Wheaton family might also be a factor in explaining the lack of fiscal support from alumnae. Finally, the general economic crisis that began in 1929 certainly exacerbated the situation when it came to encouraging alumnae giving.[35]

In 1935, however, motivated especially by the need to raise funds for building purposes, the College and the Association agreed that an annual alumnae fund drive should be instituted by the Association, the proceeds from which would be designated toward construction of the long-awaited Student Alumnae Building. The quid pro quo, however, was a Presidential promise that except in the case of some special emergency, a successful annual fund drive would free alumnae from "additional appeals from the college and the Alumnae Association."[36]

The results were moderately successful—in June, 1939, as construction of SAB was beginning, the Alumnae Association was able to turn $37,019 over to the College. The effort, however, proved to be unsustainable. Though many Wheaton Clubs continued the old policy of raising money and donating it directly to the College for specific purposes, most usually regional scholarships, the Alumnae Association's next contribution occurred only in June, 1943, when $1000 was given to the general Scholarship Fund.[37]

∞

Traditional Junior-Freshman "Bacon Bat," Fall, 1938.

The basic stability and continuity that characterized the College's internal administration during the 1930s extended as well to the Board of Trustees. Aside from the resignation of Joseph Soliday as Treasurer and the election of William Chase to succeed him, the only major change within the Board was the decision, taken in 1931, to include among its members a representative of the Alumnae Association, who would serve a limited five-year term. While women had been elected as regular members since 1896, the concept of a rotating alumnae seat on the Board of Trustees, though hardly unique in terms of other colleges, was new to Wheaton. To fill this new position the Association chose Seminary alumna Mary Woolley (WS1884), President of Mount Holyoke College; she was succeeded in 1936 by an alumna of the College, Lovis Sawyer Nichols (W1925). It was also in 1936 that Helen Wieand Cole assumed the "Cole" seat on the Board, which had become vacant with the death of President Cole's brother William. Finally, in the spring of 1941, the Board began a new tradition when it voted the title of Trustee Emeritus [*sic*.] to Frances Vose Emerson (WS1872), daughter of the third Principal of Wheaton Female Seminary and member of the the Board of Trustees since 1922.

Despite the fact that a number of women served as trustees, it appears that the male Board members never took them very seriously. Commenting on the qualifications of one alumna for a regular seat on the Board, President Park wrote to Trustee John Clark, "Most important from the point of view of Dr. Page and Mr. Plimpton, she is easy to look at."[38] Trustee Richard Chapman would comment much later that President Park's attitude toward the women on the Board was "courteous but condescending," and ascribed to him by inference "anti-women prejudices" absent in his successor, A. Howard Meneely.[39]

During the 1930s, two unusual special events had an enormous impact on the Wheaton campus. One was recognized and planned for; the other took not only Wheaton, but all of New England by surprise. The first was the celebration of Wheaton's Centennial in June, 1935; the second was the great hurricane of September, 1938.

Planning for the Centennial observances had begun as early as 1927, when Professor of English Grace Shepard proposed that she write a history of Wheaton to be ready at the time of the Centennial. The Alumnae Association agreed to fund its publication, with the hope of recouping the costs through sales. President Park, however, apparently dubious as to whether Miss Shepard possessed the necessary literary skills to create a readable history, sought, as he admitted privately, to "sidetrack" the proposal. He therefore recommended to the Board of Trustees that they appropriate $100 in expenses to allow Miss Shepard to assemble a large "manuscript history of the college . . . containing full data about everything she can discover."[40] And that is exactly what Miss Shepard eventually did.

The resulting volume, produced in typescript, was bound and deposited in the College Archives, where it became an invaluable resource tool for those who subsequently sought information about Wheaton's early history. The trustees subsequently voted a $250 stipend to Miss Shepard for her work, but Park steadfastly resisted alumnae pressure to have the volume published and widely distributed, commenting that while Miss Shepard's work was an extremely useful "source book of data," a published history would "need to be something shorter prepared by some one who has a particular gift for that kind of thing."[41] To this end the President turned to Louise Boas of the English department to prepare a brief volume examining the growth of higher education for women over the preceding one hundred years, with the supposition that Wheaton would play a prominent role in the more general account. The result was *Woman's Education Begins: the Rise of Women's Colleges*, which Wheaton published under its own imprint in 1935.[42]

Park's initial approach to the Centennial celebration was as a potential fund-raising tool. Discussing the Centennial with the Board of Trustees in June, 1929, Park lamented that Wheaton was the only college in New England which had not received large gifts in the past twenty-five years. Complaining that he found it impossible "to keep any professor of real worth . . . because other colleges are of course able to pay so much more than we are," he went on to state that Wheaton must obtain enough resources to retain its best teachers and also "provide a first-rate accommodation for its students in such a matter as a swimming pool as well as instruction." If these things proved to be impossible "there are grave doubts whether it can continue to operate as a first-class college."[43]

Despite these desperate needs, the very fact that fund-raising historically had been so problematical led to a general reluctance to connect the Centennial celebration with any sort of special, formal, fund-raising effort. Instead it was decided that while alumnae would be asked to contribute to the fund for a student alumnae building, no formal capital campaign would be undertaken. The celebration was to be simple and modest, both in terms of the festivities and of the cost involved. Central to the planning was a decision that the theme should be a century of development in the higher education of women in general, rather than an exclusive focus on Wheaton in particular. Thus, while the exhibits that were prepared for display in various College buildings dealt with Wheaton life and students, both past and present, the College-wide festivities that encompassed the three days of Commencement activities in June, 1935, focused on the history of "women's emancipation over one hundred years." Six pantomimes, interspersed with six short "plays" written and directed by Assistant Professor of Spoken English Ellen Ballou, were designed to represent "six decades of the history of Wheaton students intertwined with national women's history."[44]

On the day of the festivities the College hosted 800 alumnae, students, and faculty for lunch, while the audience for the pageant itself was estimated at 4000. Over 350 students participated in or worked in some capacity on the various presentations. Although the performances were interrupted by a severe thunder shower, the pageant was eventually able to resume. Writing to trustee Robert Smith, President Park commented: "The thunder shower which seemed about to destroy the entire pageant proved in the end rather an advantage than otherwise, as it brought out the morale both of actors and audience to such a remarkable degree."[45]

But in the long run, the most important feature of the Wheaton Centennial turned out to be musical. To commemorate the event President Park teamed with Professor of Music Herbert Jenny to compose the Wheaton Hymn, which would be sung at opening and honors convocations, commencements, and other less formal occasions from that day forward. In time it became the one song that countless generations of Wheaton students, faculty, and alumnae identified as capturing the essence of both Wheaton's past and vision of the future—the message,

Costumed members of the senior class rode in Eliza Baylies Wheaton's own buggy, restored for the Centennial Celebration in 1935.

particularly in two of its stanzas, still fresh and powerful sixty-five years later as Wheaton prepared to enter a new millenium.

> They builded better than they knew;
> They trusted where they could not see;
> They heard the sound of voices new,
> Singing of all the years to be;
> And for both man and womankind
> An inner temple of the mind.
>
> A hundred years pass like a dream,
> Yet early founders still are we,
> Whose works are greater than they seem,
> Because of what we yet shall be
> In the bright noon of other days,
> Mid other men and other ways.[46]

The other event which substantially affected the Wheaton campus, came figuratively, if not literally, out of nowhere. No one in New England was prepared for the ravages visited by the great hurricane of 1938, which hit on September 21 without advance warning. Even sixty years later the storm was described as one of the most severe ever to strike the region; more than five hundred persons lost their lives, and the general devastation was enormous. Fortunately, the campus buildings on the whole emerged relatively unscathed, suffering approximately $6000 in damages involving the roof tree of the chapel, a cornice of Larcom dormitory, the water standpipe, and replacement of missing roof slates on almost all buildings. But the grounds, particularly the pine woods in back of the Library, were devastated. "Our College Pines is just a mess of matchwood," Park reported. "Hardly three out of hundreds seem to have stood."[47] For the next two years the College systematically harvested the trees and had them sawed into lumber, which was sold publicly at the rate of $8.00 per thousand board feet, only 8 percent of what the going price had been prior to the hurricane. Some of the lumber was also used to construct the new maintenance building and set-design studio located on the edge of campus behind SAB.[48]

Fortunately for the College, just a few weeks prior to the hurricane a decision that had caused much *Sturm und Drang* within the Wheaton community had been resolved. For nearly two years not only the administration, but the campus as a whole had debated whether the college horses should be retired and replaced by a modern tractor. The discussion was intense and apparently rather emotional, with the pros and cons, at least in the minds of those involved, about evenly matched. However, during the summer of 1938 the issue had resolved itself when the last, quite elderly College-owned horse died, thus smoothing the path for the purchase of a new Ford tractor, a development that Trustee Henry Crapo privately described as "a lamentable submission to the mechanistic . . . tendency which appears to be affecting even seats of learning."[49] The tractor, however, proved invaluable in facilitating the cleanup after the hurricane, demonstrating that despite its large initial purchase cost, the greater efficiencies afforded by this triumph of modern technology could not be refuted.[50]

During the 1930s, life on campus did not seem as turbulent as it had during the previous ten years. The "roaring twenties" were replaced by the "depression decade," and although Wheaton was not severely affected by the national economic downturn, one senses that there was greater student seriousness of purpose and concern for what lay in store for them upon graduation. The scrapbooks chronicling their college years that they kept are filled with copies of letters asking for jobs, both during the summers and following graduation. A constant theme, which made its way into the pages of the *Wheaton News*, was the issue of whether it was possible to be married and have a career at the same time. Concern with national political issues increased enormously; a student poll conducted on the eve of the 1932 presidential elections placed Republican Herbert Hoover first, while second place was accorded to the

Socialist Party candidate, Norman Thomas. In 1940, the campus over-whelmingly favored Wendell Wilkie.[51]

Developments in Europe, particularly the growth of Nazism in Ger-many, prompted greater concern with world affairs, which in turn gener-ated increased anxiety about war and concomitant support for antiwar peace movements. As part of a national movement limited to persons between the ages of eighteen and thirty-six, Wheaton students formed a chapter of the "Veterans of Future Wars," whose purpose was to "ridi-cule national policies, make a wholesale mockery of many governmental platforms."[52] A student peace rally was held on campus in conjunction with those held at other colleges across the nation. In 1939, President Park reported to the trustees that students had raised $500 to fund half the tuition cost for a refugee student; he had agreed that the College would put up the other half.[53]

One of President Park's major reasons for pushing so hard for the con-struction of SAB had been his hope that it would serve to make Wheaton more attractive to students on the weekends, and that special events and dances in the new facility would slow down the weekend exodus that was becoming pandemic on all women's college campuses.[54] However, since SAB was only completed shortly before the outbreak of war, there was no great opportunity to test fully the degree to which it might be effective in this regard. Throughout the 1930s students ever more in-creasingly found their social life beyond the Wheaton campus, particu-larly at weekend events held on the campuses and in the fraternities of New England's many all-male colleges and universities. Seniors and

Seniors waiting to be admitted to the Class Day Banquet in Emerson Dining Hall. Commencement, 1932.

those on Dean's List were permitted to have cars; sophomores and juniors could bring them on campus for a total of fourteen days during the
academic year. However, the greater freedom provided by the automobile was not without its price. In October, 1936, five students returning
from visiting the Boston Art Museum and attending a symphony concert
were involved in an accident that left one student dead and three seriously injured.[55]

Pressure to do away with required attendance at weekend events at
Wheaton increased steadily. Founders Day ceremonies, traditionally a
full-day affair, were reduced to a single speaker in a chapel service on
Saturday morning. Student requests to abolish required attendance at
Sunday church services became ever more insistant. Although the President, with the support of the Trustees, sturdily resisted these efforts,
Park readily acknowledged to the Board that unless the attendance requirement was kept, church services would have to be given up. Voluntary attendance would be so low that it would be impossible to justify
bringing to campus the guest preachers who traditionally had conducted
Sunday services ever since the Chapel had been built.[56]

President Park also found himself under increasing pressure from various outside religious organizations to allow the establishment of chapters of sectarian youth organizations on campus. He assiduously resisted

Members of the Aviation Club, 1935.

attempts by various religious groups, Protestant, Catholic and Jewish, to obtain lists of students belonging to their particular faith. Equally, he denied all requests from religious organizations to hold meetings or services on campus that would be open only to members of that sect. Any speaker or organization was welcome, Park maintained, as long as the event they sponsored was open to all members of the College community. Writing to Rev. Hazel Rogers Gredler (W1919), who was pastor of the Unitarian church in Norton, Park commented:

> We feel that a great part of the fine atmosphere at the college is due to the fact that we do not allow this break up into sectarian groups. We hold to the position that a Roman Catholic speaker or a Jewish speaker is welcome provided that everyone in the college is invited to the meeting. . . . This position is, however, I know too liberal a one for certain denominational headquarters, and we have some very acid letters from quite a number of denominational secretaries about it. But I find that this liberal point of view has the backing of all who know the college well.[57]

Another on-going issue was the ever-present agitation from students to allow smoking on campus. Although the rules forbidding smoking by students on vacations and away from the campus and town of Norton had been repealed in 1929, overwhelming student pressure prompted a revisitation of the issue in 1932. Central to this was the circumstance that more and more students were being brought before the College Government Judicial Board for on-campus smoking violations. The suspension of the daughter of an editor of the *New York Times*, plus the apprehension the following year of nine students in a single incident brought matters to a head. Having gotten faculty approval to convene a special student/faculty committee to review the issue, Park brought the matter to the Board of Trustees in March, 1932. Categorizing smoking as an "insignificant but irritating question," Park reported that "while practically none of the members of the administration of the college feel that smoking adds anything to the college life, yet one has to live in a world which is determined largely by such conventions."[58]

Reluctantly the Board agreed to "some amelioration of the present smoking situation," and authorized the President to act on the matter as he saw fit. With this authorization in hand, Dr. Park convened a special meeting of the faculty, at which, over the tearful objection of a number of senior women, led by Grace Shepard, he convinced the faculty that new regulations were called for. A social room in the basement of the Science Building was opened to smoking, and students were granted permission to smoke in the tea houses in the neighborhood of the College. Otherwise, with the exception of hours during and immediately after College dances, smoking was still prohibited on campus and in the stores and streets of Norton contiguous to the campus.[59]

As the decade progressed more and more places on campus were gradually legalized for smoking. This included the first floor social room in the old Seminary classroom building, which had been moved across Howard Street when Old Metcalf had been demolished. Distressed that the whole building had become known on campus as the "Smoking Room," President Park formally christened it "The Sem" and insisted that it be so referred to in all College announcements and publications. The roofs of the administration building and the swimming pool, additional "social rooms," and finally the entire Student Alumnae Building when it was opened in 1940 were declared smoking areas. However, the opening of "smokers" in dormitories was still several years away. In 1940, again over the objections of senior faculty, smoking was authorized in the dining halls on Friday night. Smoking on the streets and in the stores of Norton continued to be prohibited.[60]

For some, though certainly not all students, perhaps the greatest change in student life in the decade leading up to the outbreak of war came in the area of intercollegiate athletics. For most of the decade Wheaton continued to buck the national trend moving away from intercollegiate competition for women. Regular competition within "The League" with Jackson, Pembroke and Radcliffe was maintained. Varsity teams in track, baseball, fencing and lacrosse were discontinued, but badminton, golf, and for a short period of time, soccer, were added. In 1940–41 Wheaton still participated in intercollegiate competition in seven sports.

Nonetheless, pressure to abandon varsity competition in favor of informal "games" days with other colleges continued to increase. In 1940–41 only one away game in each sport was scheduled, officially because of the increasing cost of team transportation, though it is hard to understand how the substitution of more "sports days" with other colleges effectively addressed the transportation cost factor.

Then, in the second semester of 1940–41, the Athletics Association voted to terminate all intercollegiate varsity competition. The final impetus for this change came from the Federal Government. Although the United States was not yet involved in the wars which had already engulfed most of Europe and much of Asia, most Americans anticipated that eventually the country would be drawn into the fray. In the spring of 1941, Economics Professor Henrietta Jennings represented the College at a conference in Washington where, she reported, "the suggestion was made that in grave times such as these it is far wiser to devote as much time as possible to training well a large group rather than a highly-trained but small one."[61]

After nearly thirty years of intercollegiate competition, Wheaton dropped the program in 1941, officially because of defense and wartime needs. Whether purposely or not, this brought the College into line with

Intramural Track and Field Meet, 1931.

the policies of the national women's sports organizations which maintained that strenuous competition was not good for young women, that their nervous systems were too fragile for such stress.[62]

In retrospect, it seems likely that a major staff change within the Physical Education department may have had more to do with this sea change in policy than any of the considerations used publicly to justify it. In the spring of 1938, Miriam Faries, Head of the Physical Education Department, and a devoted protegee of Dr. Park's, requested permission to take an unpaid leave of absence in order to pursue further graduate study at Columbia University.[63] Park, whose support of her work in the department was so strong that he had elevated her and other department members to faculty status in the mid-1930s, reluctantly agreed, not because he disapproved of what she was planning to do, but because he feared she would choose not to return to Wheaton. In February, 1939, Park's fears were realized, for despite his best efforts to bring her back to Norton, Miss Faries resigned.[64]

With her departure, Wheaton lost a staunch advocate of the benefits of intercollegiate competition. Miss Faries successor, Marna Brady, in 1941 was elected Secretary-Treasurer of the Eastern Directors of Physical Education for College Women, an organization which espoused the view that women should avoid strenuous, intense, physical competition. It seems likely that under Miss Brady's leadership, the Physical Education department at Wheaton was more than willing to acquiesce to the changes that were suggested from Federal sources in the spring of 1941.[65]

It was also during the "depression years" that two groups were formed which would go on to have a permanent presence on the Wheaton campus. In 1933, the Wheaton Dance Company was first organized, and in

1935–36, when it presented its first independent recital, it was recognized formally as a separate campus organization. Similarly, in 1941 the synchonized swimming group "Tritons" became one of the first such clubs in the country to be organized at the collegiate level. Both groups remained under the general supervision of the Physical Education department.[66]

During the "depression era," relations between Wheaton and the town of Norton remained outwardly cordial, but in fact were quite strained. Central to all other matters was the issue of taxes, which had contributed to the creation of so much town-gown ill will during the first years of Wheaton's existence as a college. In 1940, Wheaton's buildings and real estate in Norton were estimated at more than $2,000,000 in value by the College in the annual report it was required by law to file with the Town Board of Assessors. This was a sum greater than the total value of taxable real estate in the town as a whole. However, Wheaton only paid $600 in taxes on property assessed at less than $18,000, primarily the Wheaton Inn and a couple of vacant lots that were separate from the main body of the College's real estate.[67]

For the fewer than three thousand residents of the farming and working class community in which the College existed this exemption from taxation, however legal, was a constant source of irritation. So great was the community's frustration over this issue that Norton's representative

The "new pool," constructed in 1936, became the site of elaborate annual performances by the Tritons Sychronized Swimming Club.

to the General Court, Elmer Lane, filed a bill in 1932 specifying that "no real estate acquired after the passage of this act by any educational corporation shall be exempt from taxation."[68] The proposition was shortlived. Opposition from private educational institutions across the state was expressed strongly at the committee hearing on the bill, and it died without reaching the floor of the House for a vote.

The town's frustration regarding the tax issue was further exacerbated in the mid-1930s when the House in the Pines School, which had been paying taxes in excess of $3500, incorporated itself as a nonprofit institution, meaning that its land and buildings were also lost as sources of tax revenue for the town. "This has added a great deal to the bitterness of the feelings in the town," Park commented to the Board of Trustees in March, 1937.[69]

Repeated attempts by Norton to obtain more tax revenue from the College also led to a series of unpleasant discussions between College officials and members of the faculty who lived in College housing— especially the women faculty who lived in dormitories—and even occasionally with students and their parents. In a letter explaining why a mother whose daughter was attending Wheaton could not eat in the College dining hall as a paying guest, Dr. Park wrote:

> One of the questions which has arisen both here and at South Hadley [Mount Holyoke] is as to whether the college dining room can without being taxed entertain guests and relatives of students. The best legal opinion is that it cannot and that we shall have to choose between paying taxes on the college property or not competing with local inns and tea houses. We have promised the authorities in Norton that we will not run into this competition with them and entertain guests of students in our tax-free property. For this reason the entertainment of paying guests in professors' houses owned by the college has also been prohibited.[70]

The basic guideline of Massachusetts municipal tax law was that any property not used for educational purposes, or which generated separate business income, could become liable for municipal taxes. Therefore the College maintained that faculty, whether residing in dormitories or college-owned houses, paid no rent—rather their accommodations were a noncash part of their general employment contract. This also benefitted the faculty, since federal and state law required payment of income taxes only on monetary forms of compensation.[71]

However, for those living in dormitories and College-owned housing this decision produced a particular hardship. President Park was faced repeatedly with requests by faculty that they be allowed to have family relatives, usually an elderly mother or aunt, visit them in their accommodations for extended periods of time. These requests were regularly refused on the grounds that it was necessary to impose a two-week limit per year on any such visits in order to avoid taxation problems with Norton officials. Time and again Park cited his "agreement" with the town that the dormitories and College-owned apartments and houses would not be used for housing relatives of faculty. To go beyond the two-week limit would "simply mean that the old tax question will be revived here, which will cost the college many hundreds of dollars a year."[72] Town officials, Park maintained, were adamant that as a tax-free institution Wheaton must give to private establishments the business of feeding and lodging all those who were not studying or teaching at the College. For the same reasons, faculty residing in houses could not under any circumstances rent out an extra room to a guest or boarder.[73]

Only once did President Park indicate his willingness to deviate from this policy. In May, 1940, Chemistry Assistant Professor Maud Marshall, who was being allowed to stay in a College-owned apartment during the summer in order to continue research work in her laboratory, asked if her mother could move in with her for the summer months. In his reply Park denied the request, citing all the established tax reasons and noting his many refusals of other similar petitions. Having done this, he added an interesting final paragraph:

> The only way out of it I can see is for you to invite your mother to stay with you for two weeks, and tell everybody, ourselves included, that she is just staying two weeks. If you happen to lose count I doubt if we will be able to check up on you.[74]

Privately, the President was not reluctant to state his view that "the town of Norton is of absolutely no help to the college." Noting that with perhaps a couple of exceptions, "practically everybody else has very, very slender means," Park commented that as a result no one was interested in developing real estate in the area which might serve to attract the kind of people that Smith and Wellesley had living near their institutions—people who understood the nature and purpose of the colleges and supported their endeavors.[75]

Town-gown acrimony would have been even greater had the public been fully aware of private conversations that took place sporadically from 1927 to 1940 between President Park, the Massachusetts Federation of Churches, and the Massachusetts Congregational Conference. Both the Unitarian Church and the Trinitarian Congregational Church, located at opposing corners of the College campus, had fallen on hard times in terms of declining membership. The Unitarian congregation, however, was regarded as the stronger of the two; the church could also boast a reasonable endowment, which provided it with some level of financial stability. The Trinitarian Church, which had been founded through the leadership of the Wheaton family, had not, in President Park's opinion, been able "to support itself in a respectable kind of way" ever since the College Chapel had been built and the church had lost the traditional pew rental revenue from both the College and the House in the Pines school.[76]

The solution seemed obvious, at least to the Massachusetts Federation. The two churches should reunite (they had split in 1832), and the Trinitarian Church should be sold, since the Unitarian was both better endowed and in better condition. Both Presidents Cole and Park also admitted privately that either the College or the House in the Pines School would be delighted to be able to acquire the Trinitarian property. In a 1929 letter to the President of the Massachusetts Congregational Conference, Frederick Page (also a Wheaton Trustee), President Park noted that the pulpits of both churches stood empty, that both groups were very "moribund," and that the sorry sight of these two institutions was "enough to give young people a turn against the church altogether."[77]

Apparently the idea of possible reunification was discussed with enough people that the local Attleboro newspaper got wind of it and published a story suggesting that such a step was imminent. The reaction of both President Park and the regional confederations was to drop the issue immediately. In October, 1936, when President Park agreed to serve as an intermediary to arrange union services during the winter months for the two churches, the Massachusetts Congregational Conference again expressed interest in pushing for a permanent union, but by this time the President would have no part of it, and strongly advised against raising the issue in any form.[78]

Despite his private, clandestine activities relating to the affairs of these two churches, there is considerable evidence that President Park did everything that he regarded as being within his power to improve relations with the local community. He readily accepted an honorary membership in the Norton Board of Trade, and used this association with the businessmen of the town to point out repeatedly the amount of business brought to them by Wheaton students and faculty. Emphasizing that nearly 70 percent of the domestic and maintenance staff at the College lived in Norton, he consistently noted that despite most of its property being tax-exempt, the College was still the third or fourth largest taxpayer in the town. The College also continued its long-standing practice of granting partial tuition scholarships to daughters of families residing in Norton. In 1937, after lengthy discussions with Fire Chief Harold Wetherell, Park commited $500 from the College toward the $1,400 cost of a new fire truck for the town.[79]

The trustees also approved a proposed property swap with the town by which the College would receive the Town Hall property on Taunton Avenue in exchange for a large piece of land on West Main Street on which Norton, with substantial assistance from the federal government, would build municipal offices and a new high school. However, this agreement came to naught when three successive Town Meetings in

1937 and 1938 refused to fund the town's share of the building project. Subsequently, the College agreed in 1941 to a $10 per year twenty-five-year lease of a small parcel of land on West Main Street to the American Legion, upon which the organization built a new Post.[80]

In early 1939, a new crisis suddenly appeared. Meeting in closed session, the Board of Selectmen voted on February 11 to grant a license to the Readville Racing Association to build and operate a dog track on property located off Route 123 in the Chartley area of Norton. Reaction within the town was instantaneous, intense, and very divided. A coalition of owners and operators of the major businesses in Norton, led by John Bannon, President of the Defiance Bleachery, was joined by the pastors of the four churches in Norton, the administrations of Wheaton and House in the Pines, and the Mayor of Attleboro in vehement and vocal opposition. Support for the proposal came from many within town government and from a group of small-property owners. As Park reported to the Board of Trustees, the citizens of the town were very divided, "some feeling that the track would be a legitimate source of revenue for a town that needs the money, others believing that it would ruin the residential college community irreparably."[81]

Since the actual racing dates had to be approved by the State Racing Commission, a public hearing was held by the Commission in Norton on March 6, at which President Park led the voices in opposition to the track. The proponents, headed by the Chair of the Norton Board of Selectmen, Vinton Reynolds, argued that the tax revenue generated by the track was essential chiefly because the College, which was far and away the largest property holder in the town, was tax exempt. However, the strength of the opposition prevailed, the Commission refused to assign dates for a race meeting, and a subsequent Town Meeting voted 260 to 80 against pursuing the matter in the future.[82]

Nonetheless, the gulf between College and Norton officials widened and hardened perceptibly as a result of the dog track affair. "The public discussions," Park wrote to Ralph Boas, who was on sabbatical leave, "were made the occasion for a lot of diatribes against the college, and the town is retaliating at the present time by leaving Howard Street and a part of Main Street that runs past the college full of deep crater holes, on the general understanding that they do not have money enough to fix these particular roads."[83]

In fact the issue of repairs to Howard Street became a major issue between the College and the town in the final months before the outbreak of war. East Main Street was a state highway, but Howard Street was regarded by town officials as an accepted Norton public way. Strapped for money, the view of the Board of Selectmen was that wear and tear on Howard Street was due almost exclusively to College-generated traffic, and that rain drainage from the roofs of the various dormitories, especially Everett Hall, also contributed greatly to the deterioration of the road. They repeatedly requested that the College undertake the resurfacing of the street. The Selectmen did suggest that they were willing to seek a Federal WPA grant which would cover 75 percent of the cost of reconstructing Howard Street if the College were willing to cover the town's share of the project.

Wheaton, however, was reluctant to agree to these proposals, first because there was concern as to whether maintenance of public roads was something the College could legally do under the terms of the Wheaton family endowment. "The Wheaton heirs do still exist," Park noted to the Board of Trustees, "and one at least of them is unfriendly to the college and might well be informed of such action as violating the terms of the trust."[84] Secondly, both Park and the Board were concerned about setting a precedent regarding College funding of municipal expenses, fearing that in hard economic times Wheaton would be "called upon gradually to provide for more and more of the expenses of the town."[85] "Since I opposed the coming of the dog track to Norton there have been signs that an attempt has been made to get back at the college in every way and I have had a number of callers about similar projects," Park wrote to Trustee Joseph Soliday.[86] Noting that the Board of Selectmen was pushing Wheaton "to shoulder the expenses of certain improvements in the town" which the College Charter would not allow, Park admitted that the feeling toward the College in the town "is presently not very happy."[87]

For a time, the possibility of the College taking possession of Howard Street from the town was considered, but since two parcels of land bordering the street were not owned by Wheaton, this solution was deemed unworkable. The issue of Howard Street's maintenance and repair would remain an irritant in terms of the College's relations with Norton town officials for years to come.[88]

NOTES: CHAPTER 14

1. Trustees: Cobb: Cobb to Park, 10/8/28; Soliday #4: Park to Soliday, 6/21/28.
2. Trustees Minutes: 11/16/33; 11/27/39; 11/3/41; Trustees: Cobb: Cobb to Park, 6/15/32; Chase #2: Park to Chase, 11/13/39; Chase to Park, 11/15/39; Chase #3: Park to Chase, 10/3/41; Oral History Project: R. Chapman interview, 1983.
3. Wheaton College Financial Reports, 6/30/28–6/30/41; Trustees Minutes: 3/10/41; Trustees: Soliday #3: Comparative Balance Sheet, 1935–36, 9/1/36.
4. Trustees: Chapman: Meneely to Chapman, 10/5/54.
5. Ibid.: quoted by Meneely in letter to Chapman, 10/5/54. From 1932, when Old Metcalf was demolished, until the new Administration Building was opened in 1934, the administrative offices were located in Doll's House.
6. The year built and the cost of construction of each facility were as follows: Kilham dormitory (1932), Metcalf dormitory (1932–33), and Hebe parlors, $280,000; Administration Building (1934—in 1954 named Park Hall), $177,000; Nursery school (1931), $10,400; New swimming pool (1936—including showers and dressing

room for men, 1937), $50,000; Maintenance Building (1939), $5725; Student Alumnae Building (SAB) (1939–40), $149,291; New Science Building wing (1941), $54,795; New Library addition (including a $30,000 gift from the Paul Wilde Jackson Fund—1941), $41,360.

7. Trustees Minutes: 11/13/30; 6/19/33; 6/18/34; 3/11/35; 11/17/36; 11/1/37; 6/10/39; 11/27/39; 11/25/40; 3/10/41; 6/14/41; Faculty: Ballou: Ballou to Park, 9/12/32; Park to Ballou, 9/13/32; Rice: Park memorandum, 2/7/36; Park to Rice, 2/25/43.

8. Trustees Minutes: 3/22/37; Professor Lange and the whole Biology Department took an extreme dislike to this feeder. "It makes my blood pressure rise a little whenever I pass it," Lange wrote Park, who replied that he would favor selling it unless there was some chance the College could successfuly sue Cram and Ferguson "for putting something like that up." Faculty: Lange: Lange to Park, 9/29/40; Park to Lange, 9/30/40.

9. Trustees Minutes: 3/13/33; 11/22/35; 3/22/37; 3/18/40.

10. Ibid.: 6/15/31; 6/18/34; 11/22/35; 3/18/40; Faculty: Faries: Park to Faries, 7/9/37; Faries to Park, 7/14/37; Park to Faries, 7/15/37; Faries to Remick, 7/20/37.

11. Buildings: Park Hall #2, 1926–35: Godfrey to Park, 11/22/32.

12. See ch. 6; Trustees Minutes: 6/15/36.

13. Trustees Minutes: 3/5/34; 3/16/36; 3/22/37.

14. Trustees: Crapo #2: Park to Crapo, 8/28/31.

15. Trustees Minutes: 11/1/37.

16. Ibid.: 11/17/36; *Wheaton News*, 11/23/29. Priscilla Guild Lewis (Plimpton) attended Wheaton Seminary in 1836–37.

17. For a detailed account of the Art Center competition, pictures of the award-winning designs and related issues, see T. J. McCormick, "Wheaton College: Competition for an Art Center, February 1938-June 1938," in *Modernism in America 1937–1942: A Catalog and Exhibition of Four Architectural Competitions*, ed. J. D. Kornwolf (Williamsburg, VA: Joseph and Margaret Muscarelle Museum of Art, 1985), pp. 22–67. I am indebted to Rachael Class-Giguere (W1991), who reviewed much of the material relating to the 1938 Art Center competition while working as my research assistant during the summer of 1990.

18. Trustees Minutes: 3/22/37.

19. Although it was always referred to as an Art Center, from the beginning the building was conceived as a structure that would meet the needs of Art, Music, and Drama at the College.

20. Trustees Minutes: 6/19/37.

21. Trustees: R. Smith #1: Park to Smith, 1/27/38.

22. Ibid.: 2/25/38.

23. Ibid.: 3/23/38, see also Soliday #3: Park to Soliday, 3/4/38; Trustees Minutes: 11/7/38.

24. McCormick, "Wheaton College: Competition," in Kornwolf, *Modernism in America*, pp. 28–29. The jury of seven included Professor Seaver as Wheaton's formal representative.

25. J. D Kornwolf, "Introduction: The Competitions, the Thirties, and Architectural Issues related to Them, Then and Now," in *Modernism in America*, p. 3. Also McCormick, "Wheaton College: Competition," in Ibid.: pp 28–33. Pictures of the winning design and of nine other highly-rated designs are reproduced on pp. 41–67; see also *Wheaton News*, 2/2/46; Buildings: Art Center Controversy 1945–46: published contest announcement, *"A Competition to Select an Architect for a Proposed Art Center for Wheaton College."*

26. Trustees Minutes: 3/21/38; 11/7/38; 3/20/39; 6/10/39.

27. Trustees: Chase #2: Park to Chase, 10/8/38; R. Smith #1: Park to Smith, 10/31/38; J. Clark #2: Park to Clark, 2/4/39; Trustees Minutes: 11/7/38; 3/20/39; 11/27/39; 6/14/41.

28. General Files: Class of 1939; Class of 1940: Clippings, 1939–40.

29. McCormick, "Wheaton College: Competition," in Kornwolf, *Modernism in America*, p. 36.

30. Trustees Minutes: 11/25/40; see also 3/18/40; 6/8/40; Staff: Cutler: Lincoln to Park, 2/27/33; Park to Cutler, 6/11/40; Trustees: Meadows #11: Park to Meadows, 3/19/40.

31. Trustees Minutes: 6/15/31.

32. Ibid.: 3/13/33.

33. Ibid.: 11/27/39.

34. Alumnae Association 48: Agreements with College, 1912–69; Staff: Ridlon: Park to Fenstermacher, 3/22/37; Fenstermacher to Park, 3/29/37; *Nike*, 1931; 1934; Trustees Minutes: 6/19/37. The practice of having a College-sponsored alumnae luncheon at Commencement began in 1940. See Trustees Minutes: 3/10/41.

35. Alfred Emerson Family: F. V. Emerson correspondence, 1923–30: Emerson to Park, 5/16/27; Trustees Minutes: 6/17/29.

36. Trustees Minutes: 3/21/38.

37. Alumnae Association 48: Agreements with College, 1912–69; Wheaton College Financial Reports, 6/30/39, Schedule C-1—6/30/43, Schedule C-1; Oral History Project: R. Chapman interview, 1983.

38. Trustees: J. K. Clark #3: 11/10/41.

39. Oral History Project: R. Chapman interview, 1983. See also, Trustee Minutes: 11/19/31; 11/21/32; 11/17/36; 6/19/37; Alfred Emerson Family: F. V. Emerson correspondence, 1931–51: Letter of resignation, 3/5/41; Park to Emerson, 3/6/41.

40. Smart/Park: Smart: Park to Smart, 10/21/27; Trustees Minutes: 6/18/27; 11/15/27.

41. Faculty: Shepard: Park to California Alumnae Club, 6/1/31.

42. Ibid.: California Alumnae Club to Park, 5/25/31; Park to California Alumnae Club, 6/1/31; Park to Shepard, 9/30/31; Trustees Minutes: 11/13/30; 3/6/31; 11/21/32; 3/11/35.

43. Trustees Minutes: 6/17/29; see also 11/26/28.

44. I am indebted to Megan E. McKeown-Folker (W1989), who served as my research assistant in 1988, and prepared an essay, "The Wheaton Centennial Celebration of 1935," now on file in the Wheaton College Archives, from which much of the material in this account is drawn. See pp. 4–8. See also Faculty Meeting Minutes: 11/13/34; 4/17/35. Extensive materials relating to the Centennial celebration, including the original directions for the pantomimes and the manuscript of the plays, can be found in Anniversaries: Centennial Celebration, 1935.

45. Trustees: R. Smith #2: Park to Smith, 6/18/35; Wheaton Histories, Seminary: Reminiscence: Article by Lois Perry. Altogether, the College spent $4,012.99 on the celebration. This included $250 paid to the Leroy Anderson Orchestra, which was retained to play during the pageant. Anniversaries: McKeown-Folker, "Centennial Celebration," p.10.

46. H. Jenny and J. E. Park, "Wheaton Hymn."

47. Trustees: Chase #2: Park to Chase, 9/24/38.

48. Trustees Minutes: 11/7/38; 3/20/39; 6/10/39; 11/25/40; Smart/Park: Park Chapel Talks: 9/21/39; *Wheaton News*, 10/1/38.

49. Trustees: Crapo #2: Crapo to Park, 9/20/38.

50. Trustees Minutes: 3/21/38; 6/18/38; 11/7/38; Staff: S. B. Young: Park to Young, 7/8/38.

51. *Wheaton News*, 10/29/32; 11/5/32; 11/12/32; 10/24/36; 10/19/40; 4/26/41.

52. Ibid.: 4/11/36.

53. Ibid.: 11/14/31; 4/25/36; 10/24/36; 1/15/38; Trustees Minutes: 3/20/39.

54. In his formal six-year report to the Board of Trustees in 1939, President Park

commented sardonically that "weekends rapidly approach a point where they will both begin and end on Wednesday." Wheaton College, *The President's Report, 1939,* p. 9.

55. Trustees Minutes: 11/17/36; President's Reports to Trustees: 11/17/36. The student who died, Elizabeth Shippee, a member of the class of 1937 and a young poet of exceptional promise, was subsequently memorialized by her family through the endowment of an art collection for student rental and an annual lecture at the College on art or art history. In 2000, some of her poetry was arranged for choral and instrumental music by Wheaton Choral Director Tim Harbold. See also Ibid.: 3/5/34; Wheaton College Handbook, *Wheaton Handbook,* 1930–41, passim; Faculty: L. Boas: Boas to Park, 1939.

56. Trustees Minutes: 6/20/32; 11/19/34; Faculty: Work: Work to Park, 7/12/34.

57. Town of Norton: Churches, 1917–42: Park to Gredler, 10/5/39; see also President's Office: Wheaton College Practices (Regulations) 1937–45: passim. The College also refused to send campus directories to any firm or person whose request was deemed to have an ultimate commercial intent.

58. Faculty Meeting Minutes: 3/5/32; Trustees Minutes: 3/10/32.

59. Trustees Minutes: 3/10/32; 6/20/32; Faculty Meeting Minutes: 3/21/32; Oral History Project: E. J. Knapton interview, 1983; K. Burton interview, 1983; Wheaton College Handbook: *Wheaton Handbook, 1932–33.*

60. Faculty Meeting Minutes: 5/20/37; 5/9/40; *Wheaton News,* 1/14/39; Oral History Project: K. Burton interview, 1983; Wheaton College Handbook: *Wheaton Handbook,* 1932–46, passim.

61. N. Norton, "Physical Education and Athletics at Wheaton, 1912–1941," p. 25.

62. N. Norton, "Physical Education and Athletics at Wheaton, The Christine White Years, 1941–1969," p. 1.

63. Signing herself, "cordially, gratefully, affectionately yours," Miriam Faries wrote in her letter of goodbye to the President, "A student the other day in speaking of you said, 'He could make me do anything!' I am not sure that I can go that far, but I do know that you have been a much greater stimulus to me than you dream of." Faculty: Faries: Faries to Park, 6/23/38.

64. Ibid.: letters between Park and Faries, January, 1938-March 1939.

65. Faculty: Brady: passim.

66. Norton, "Physical Education and Athletics, 1912–41," p. 7.

67. For example, in 1939 the college paid $602.85 on property assessed at $17,729.41. Trustees Minutes: 11/27/39; see also Bursar's Office Correspondence, 1889–1940: #57, Norton-Taxes, "Report to Norton Board of Assessors," 1930, 1940; #58, Norton–General: Dunkle to Smith, 11/24/36; Town of Norton: Annual Report of the Town of Norton, 1940, p. 83.

68. Trustees: Soliday #3: Park to Soliday, 2/16/32.

69. Trustees Minutes: 3/22/37. Joseph Yelle, who became Norton's Postmaster, Selectman, and long-time Town Moderator, commented in 1983 that during the 1930s candidates for public office in Norton often ran on an anti-Wheaton platform. Oral History Project: J. Yelle interview, 1983.

70. Faculty: Landau: Park to Landau, 12/16/30; see also Trustees Minutes: 5/31/42.

71. Students could entertain guests from other recognized colleges in the dining rooms. Alumnae were permitted to eat in the dining rooms and stay in the dormitories free of charge. Other friends and families could stay in the dormitories, at a cost of 75 cents per night, but only if no other accommodations in the vicinity were available. See Faculty: Shepard: Shepard to Park, 4/8/31; Park to Shepard, 4/10/31; 4/22/31; Marshall: Park to Marshall, 6/4/38; President's Office: Dorms and Policies: President Park Practices, 1931–37.

72. Faculty: Lange: Park to Lange, 10/10/31.

73. Ibid.; see also Korsch: Park to Korsch, 4/21/36; Rice: Park to Rice, 6/18/41; Faculty Meeting Minutes: 11/21/29; 9/18/30; 5/13/31.

74. Ibid.: Marshall: Park to Marshall, 5/22/40. Marshall and her colleague, Dorothy Thompson, had been funded by a U.S. Public Health Service grant to try to synthesize a drug to replace quinine. Marshall to Park, 8/25/40; Park to Marshall, 8/29/40.

75. Trustees: Mirick: Park to Mirick, 6/20/30.

76. Town of Norton: Churches: Park to Merrill, 1/16/40. Ironically, by the year 2000 the Unitarian Church as an active congregation had almost ceased to exist, while the Trinitarian Church had become a thriving, vibrant church community.

77. Trustees: Page #3: Park to Page, 9/13/29; see also Page to Park, 9/16/29; Town of Norton: Churches: Page to Park, 5/4/27. Writing to President Meneely two decades later, Dr. Park commented, "You should unite the two churches in Norton and turn the Congregational church into a big faculty hotel! I tried to do so but failed, but the cemetery has received most of the then objectors since." Smart/Park: Park correspondence: Park to Meneely, 5/20/48. For a discussion of the 1832 separation of the two churches, see ch. 1.

78. Town of Norton: Churches: 1927–40, passim; Faculty: Sprague: Park memorandum, 10/7/36.

79. Town of Norton: Norton Miscellaneous, 1928–40: Alexander to Park, 12/28/26; Park to Alexander, 12/29/26; Dunkle to Park, 11/26/29; Park to Reynolds, 11/4/36; Memoranda and letters relating to Fire Truck Purchase, 1936–37; Employees in Domestic and Maintenance Dept, 3/16/39; Faculty Meeting Minutes: 9/24/41.

80. Town of Norton: American Legion, Trustees Minutes: 3/22/37; 6/19/37; 11/1/37; 11/7/38; 6/8/40; 11/25/40; 6/14/41; Trustees: R. Smith: Park to Smith, 5/7/37; Faculty: E. White: Park to White, 9/12/30. In 1966, the College decided not to renew the American Legion lease and the building was moved by the Legion to a new site on East Main street.

81. Trustees Minutes: 3/30/39.

82. Town of Norton: Norton Miscellaneous, 1928–40: Collected clippings and letters relating to Dog Track, 1939. See also Trustees Minutes: 3/30/39; Trustees: Chase: Park to Chase, 3/11/39. The bitterness engendered in some by this experience lasted for many years. When the author first began attending Norton Town Meetings in the early 1960s, one could still hear on occasion the opinion expressed that the lack of a strong tax base in the town was the fault of the College, both in terms of its tax exempt status and because Wheaton also was to blame for the race track not having been built. See also Oral History Project: J. Yelle interview, 1983.

83. Faculty: R. Boas: Park to Boas, 3/22/39.

84. Town of Norton: Norton, Miscellaneous, 1928–40: Park to Board of Trustees, 3/18/40.

85. Ibid.

86. Ibid.: Park to Soliday, 4/14/39.

87. Town of Norton: Churches: Park to Merrill, 3/15/40. So negative was Park's attitude toward the town, that in 1942 he consulted legal counsel to find out if the College could possibly stop making the annual $200 payments to the Norton Public Library that Mrs. Wheaton had mandated in her will. Unfortunately, Park reported to the Board of Trustees, the answer was no. Trustees Minutes: 5/31/42.

88. Town of Norton: Norton Miscellaneous, 1928–40: Park to Reynolds, 3/20/40; 12/4/40.

15
The War Years, 1940–1944

THE OUTBREAK OF WAR in Europe in August, 1939, caught several members of the Wheaton faculty in Europe. All managed to return safely. A member of the Psychology Department, Maria Rickers-Ovsiankina had been in Germany arranging passage for her mother out of Germany via Manchukuo. Originally scheduled to return on a German liner, she was able to rebook on a Dutch ship, whose neutral status was respected by a German submarine which "saluted" the Dutch vessel in the English Channel. Three students, from France, Argentina, and Canada, withdrew from the College because "their parents felt it unwise for them to leave home."[1]

Hostility toward Germany within the Wheaton community was such that President Park felt compelled to advise Professor of German Hedda Korsch that if she decided to continue her annual tradition of a German Christmas party she should "do it as quietly as possible and not invite many outsiders to it."[2] Nonetheless, real commitment to the anti-German cause was not apparent on the Wheaton campus until the College reconvened in September, 1940. This intensified animosity was undoubtedly triggered by the fall of France in May, 1940, and the raging air "Battle of Britain," which reached its peak during the late summer and fall of 1940. The new atmosphere on campus unquestionably reflected heightened anxiety about the course of the war, and a general willingness to become involved in both defense preparedness and war relief activities. The possibility of a German invasion of Great Britain was clearly seen as a threat to United States security, and in the fall of 1940 the campus sprang to action under the leadership of a newly created faculty/student Committee on National Defense and War Relief, chaired by E. J. Knapton of the History Department.[3]

Through the auspices of this committee a series of lectures and symposia were conducted, which were open to residents of Norton as well as members of the Wheaton community. Topics included the possibility of American involvement in both the European and Pacific conflicts, the likely social, economic and political impact of such involvement at home, and finally a discussion of what could be done in Norton. Faculty also participated in similar lecture/discussion series held in Attleboro

363

and other communities. More broadly, the committee became a charter member of a Harvard based group called American Defense, New England College and University Groups, which sought to coordinate activities and communicate information about work being done on various New England campuses. The committee also established relations with the Norton Chapter of the American Red Cross as well as the fledgling civil defense structure being established in the town.[4]

On campus, student and faculty fund-raising drives, plus donated receipts from concerts, plays, "white elephant" sales and other student-run activities, netted well over $4000. This was distributed mainly to British War Relief, including a $1750 "rolling kitchen" on which a plaque was placed bearing the College's name. Smaller contributions were made to a wide range of groups, including the American Red Cross, Finnish War Relief, Save the Children Foundation, and the American Friends of France. A sewing center was set up in the former social room in The Sem, which was devoted to making children's clothes and sewing bandages. Students were also provided with wool with which they could knit items to be sent to war relief, and the click of needles became pandemic on campus, not only in dormitory rooms and social facilities, but in the classroom as well. Knitting during Chapel services was specifically forbidden by vote of the faculty in November, 1940.[5]

President Park initially expressed to several people a very dark, depressed view of the future. In June, 1940, he wrote to Librarian Marian Merrill, "By the end of that time [1940–41 academic year] there will probably be no Europe, very little America, and just a memory of Wheaton College, so that we can look back upon it, glad that we were able to carry on as well as we can."[6] However, by 1942 his outlook was considerably more positive. "As Wheaton has lived through the Civil War and World War #1," he wrote to trustee Joseph Soliday, "it will probably weather this one also. In many ways with our modest overhead we are in a more ship-shape position to weather the storm than most larger institutions."[7]

In June, 1940, the Board of Trustees, at the request of a faculty member, voted that any member of the teaching staff who was called to military service should be considered as being on leave of absence. In December, 1940, forty-seven faculty members signed a letter to President Roosevelt urging that "all appropriate measures be taken to advance the defense program and increase the production of vital supplies. We urge that, in pursuance of our accepted policy of nonbelligerent aid to Britain, all possible steps be taken to insure successful British air and naval resistance."[8]

By the summer of 1941, intensification of industrial defense efforts, the call-up of those in the military reserves, and the initiation of the draft for military service all began to pose staffing problems for the College. William Hunt and Ralph Hidy both left the faculty for naval duty, while

Ellen Ballou departed to join her naval officer husband at his base. The President's initial reaction to this loss of teaching staff, and the anticipated removal of more, was to rescind in September a policy change announced the previous May establishing three-year rotating department chairmanships in academic departments with more than two persons. This was necessary, he told the faculty, because of the many temporary changes in staffing that would undoubtedly be necessitated by the war effort.[9] In his reports to the Board of Trustees, Park commented that the College was also losing both domestic and maintenance employees to military service or better paying jobs. Particularly problematic, Park noted, was the fact that Wheaton was not allowed to be part of the Federal Social Security system. As a result, people who already held Social Security cards were reluctant to take jobs at the College.[10]

The news of the Japanese attack on Pearl Harbor reached Wheaton during the afternoon of December 7, 1941, as many students and faculty turned on their radios to listen to the regular Sunday afternoon concert of the New York Philharmonic Symphony Orchestra. Reaction on campus was one neither of hysteria or panic; rather, according to the *Wheaton News*, the "news that the country is at last actively engaged in war," was taken by all "with great calmness."[11] At the first Chapel service following the outbreak of war, the atmosphere was described as one of "sadness and sobriety."[12]

The outbreak of hostilities directly involving the United States resulted in an immediate intensification of the various war-relief activities already in place. The College annually raised between four and five thousand dollars, an amount which, coming from an institution of such small size, generated quite a bit of favorable publicity for Wheaton. The money went primarily to the American Red Cross and the British War Relief Society, but Russian and Chinese relief agencies also regularly received donations.[13]

Initially, coordination of these efforts remained under the Committee on National Defense and War Relief that had been organized in 1940, and whose subcommittees were chaired by members of the faculty. However, in May, 1942, this committee was abolished and oversight of all war-related activities was placed in the hands of the College's Administration Committee, which was authorized to create six subcommittees, each chaired by a faculty member, to administer various functions. One year later a further reorganization resulted in many of the on-campus activities not related to security and defense issues being placed completely in student hands. A Student War Activities Board (always referred to as SWAB) organized blood, book, and war bond drives. It also coordinated the knitting and sewing programs, as well as volunteer work folding surgical dressings in The Sem. Newspapers and tin cans were collected for the war effort, along with magazines which were forwarded weekly to Camp Miles Standish, an army embarkation base located on the Norton-Taunton line.[14]

Each student was asked to volunteer four hours each month to one of the many war-related activities, or to kitchen, domestic, or farm labor duties necessitated by the shortage of grounds and domestic employees at the College. A number of students obtained paying jobs clerking at the post exchange at Camp Miles Standish, or volunteered for regional farm work organized by the Bristol County Commissioner of Agriculture. They served as nurses aides at hospitals in Attleboro and at Camp Miles Standish, plucked turkeys each fall at the State Agricultural School in neighboring Dighton, and took noncredit evening courses on-campus in home nursing and typing. Student groups conveyed presents to wounded sailors at a naval hospital, and the cast of Vaudeville entertained at both Camp Miles Standish and Camp Edwards.[15]

Many students also enrolled in special courses for credit instituted by the College in response to general requests made by leaders of business and industry to American colleges. Subjects included the use of commercial art forms in preparing propaganda and advertising materials, mechanical drawing, practical bacteriology, and industrial analytical methods, all designed to make Wheaton women more prepared for the many summer and post-graduate jobs available in the burgeoning industry of wartime America. In 1943, the College also joined a consortium of women's colleges in a scholarship program, sponsored by the Vought

Charlotte Covell (W1943), a member of the war-time Messenger Service.

Sikorsky Co. in Connecticut, that would allow students to take aeronautical engineering at New York University during their senior year and still obtain a B.A. upon completion of the program.[16]

Perhaps the most interesting noncredit course was one promulgated by the United States Navy. During 1942–43, a few seniors were quietly selected under the strictest secrecy to undertake training sessions in cryptography twice a week in the evening in Mary Lyon. Recruited by History Professor Ralph Hidy, who had been on active naval duty since 1941, both they and their families were subjected to intensive security clearance reviews by federal agents. Sworn not to reveal the nature of their course work to anyone, the students were trained by Navy personnel in techniques for breaking secret codes used by the Germans. Upon graduation in June, 1943, eight members of the course were offered civilian appointments in the Navy for confidential work. It appears that several accepted.[17]

By far the greatest impact of the war on campus resulted, however, from the fact that in the spring of 1942 the town of Norton was officially declared to be a "theatre of war." The reasons for this seemingly strange action stemmed from a federal government decision to build a large army base on land located in the southeastern section of Norton and the northern portion of Taunton. Named for the famous Pilgrim leader Miles Standish, the camp was intended to serve as the embarkation point for troops destined for the European theatre of war. With a permanent staff of two thousand military personnel, the camp was designed to hold an additional twenty to thirty thousand soldiers, most of whom would only be in camp for thirty-six to forty-eight hours before being shuttled onto ships loading in ports from Buzzards Bay to Boston. Convoys would then form within the protection of Cape Cod Bay, from which they would proceed with destroyer and submarine chaser escort to Great Britain.[18]

By the end of 1942 the camp was in full operation. Trains moved on tight schedules day and night through Norton and Taunton. Only permanently stationed personnel were allowed leaves from the base. However, one Norton resident, in transit to Europe from basic training in the South and frustrated by his inability to obtain a pass to visit his nearby home, managed to slip off base one evening, returning the next morning by walking unchallenged through the main gate.[19] By the end of the war, Camp Miles Standish had become the embarkation point for the vast majority of US soldiers sent to Europe. It also served as a containment center for Italian prisoners of war brought back to the United States in what otherwise would have been empty transports, and who were subsequently shipped to rural areas throughout the country where they were required to perform much needed agricultural labor.

In addition to Camp Miles Standish, the small municipal airport in Mansfield was converted into a satellite training field for naval aviators officially stationed at Squantum Naval Air Station in Quincy, Massachusetts. These pilots apparently delighted in showing off their skills, often buzzing the campus at low levels to observe sunbathers on the roof of the gymnasium and women in short skirts on the tennis courts. While a call to the Commander of the base brought a halt to the most egregious behavior, the campus remained a very real attraction for these pilots throughout the duration of the war. "We had to report one man, giving the number of his plane, who was really dangerously near buildings," Park reported to the trustees, "and when Lieutenant Becker called him in and asked, 'What were you doing on Saturday afternoon?,' he said, 'Sir, I could not resist all those pretty girls on the tennis courts.' "[20]

To add to the College's concern, federal officials inspected the campus because of its potential to serve as a hospital site if a "major disaster" were to occur at Camp Miles Standish, or for that matter in Boston or Providence. Aware that both men's and women's liberal arts colleges were being asked to accommodate special training units for officer candidates, Park also informed the trustees in November, 1942, that he anticipated the distinct possibility that Wheaton might be asked to house and train women for war service.[21]

The result of Norton's designation as a war zone, President Park reported to the faculty on March 25, 1942, was that Wheaton needed to embark immediately on a program to prepare the campus for the possibility of air bomber attacks. Procedures for evacuation of all buildings, and for instituting "blackouts" at night were to be developed immediately. Students and faculty must be trained in first aid, fire combat, auto driving and mechanics. It was distinctly possible, Park reported, that the College might need to lessen its academic demands slightly.[22]

Immediately the campus swung into action. Well over half the faculty, students, and staff completed training courses in first aid; nearly ninety also took the air raid warden's training course, while a fair number of students immersed themselves in the basics of auto mechanics. Four faculty were designated, along with Supervisor of Buildings and Grounds Irving Fillmore, as Head Air Raid Wardens. Air raid procedures for each dormitory were established, and each had its own faculty and student wardens, fire fighting crew, and first aid corps replete with trained stretcher crews. A central first aid station was set up in the Gymnasium, and a motor corps of six cars, each with two student drivers, was established. A number of faculty took an intensive course in how to treat victims of a poison gas attack. Five members of the faculty and staff became commissioned officers in the Massachusett's Women's Defense Corps, while four more achieved noncommissioned officer status. Several women faculty later recalled none too fondly their experiences participating in required military drill sessions in Attleboro and in Wheaton's own gymnasium.[23]

Local civil defense wardens regularly patrolled the streets of Norton at night, and a Civil Defense Communications Center linked to half a dozen telephones throughout the town of Norton was established in the basement of the Norton Public Library. It was staffed by volunteers from both the College and town twenty-four hours a day for more than two years. Blackout and air raid drills for the town and College were conducted frequently. On campus, blackout screens were made for stairwells and corridor windows, and for all rooms where people were required to congregate during an "air raid." Evacuation procedures for the Library and all classroom buildings were established. The College purchased three hundred feet of fire hose along with a fog nozzle and four pump-type fire extinguishers, and male faculty members were trained in the use of this equipment. A special hut opposite the Chapel was built to house the hose. Boxes of sand to help extinguish possible blazes were placed in the upper stairwells of all buildings.[24]

Although student participation was technically voluntary, President Park reported that peer pressure forced most students to take at least one of the various war courses offered. Inevitably, some students came to regard these courses as "work," perceiving no differentiation between them and their regular academic courses. The result, as President Park noted to the trustees, was that there developed on campus some agitation for overall adjustments that would allow the students more time for "relaxation and fun."[25]

Lieutenant (later Captain) Louise Perry (W1923), Manager of the College Bookstore and a member of the Massachusett's Women's Defense Corps, explained incendiary bombs to Dorothy Reed (W1943) during a course on Civilian Defense.

Report Center Group, 1942. Members of the Wheaton community took regular shifts
manning the phones at the Norton Civil Defense Communication Center. <u>Front row</u>:
Henrietta Jennings, *Economics*; Jane Chidsey, *Biology*; Caro Lynn, *Classics*; Jocelyn
Knapton, wife of E. J. Knapton; <u>Back Row</u>: Ernest J. Knapton, *History*; Paul
Sprague, *Religion*; Walter Shipley, *Psychology*; Holcombe Austin, *Philosophy*.

    As the war progressed, all these activities in time became part of the
campus routine. One of the greatest changes in student life was the decision to abandon, because of the labor shortage, Wheaton's time-honored
tradition of allowing students to move on the basis of seniority to a new
room or dormitory each year. Chaperoned groups of students attended
social functions at Camp Miles Standish, and faculty often did volunteer
work there. Some attempts were made to entertain soldiers from the
camps at events on campus, none of them apparently very successful,
but the College did provide needed instruction in Spanish for the permanent officers at the base. Overall, relations between Wheaton and the two
nearby military bases remained cordial. When asked by the Chairman of
the Norton Board of Selectmen if the camps posed any problems for the
College, Park replied in the negative, adding gratuitously that the only
real problem Wheaton had was with "the boys and young men of the
civilian population who haunt parts of the campus and roads near the
campus and annoy our students and faculty."[26] Nonetheless, because of
its proximity to Miles Standish, the Administration Committee approved

an "emergency war measure" in April, 1944, declaring the city of Taunton "out of bounds" after 6 P.M. for students "without a chaperone or escort to and from the college."[27]

The ability of students and faculty to leave campus was sharply curtailed by gasoline rationing and urgent requests from authorities that long distance travel on trains and busses unrelated to the war effort be restricted. This last particularly affected several aspects of the College calendar. The Christmas vacation in 1942 was extended nine days at government request in order to ease the travel rush right at the holidays. A shortening of both spring vacation and the final examination period allowed Commencement to be held at the end of May in 1942—the aim being to allow students to take summer courses elsewhere more easily or to have more time available for summer employment opportunities. In 1943 and 1944, again at the request of the Department of Transportation, spring vacation was cancelled completely, which resulted inevitably in an increase in class cutting during the final weeks of the semester. In March, 1945, a one-week vacation was reinstituted, but students were asked to pledge that they would travel no more than fifty miles from campus, a promise that a relieved President Park reported was apparently violated by only one student. Concomitantly, however, in an effort to make weekend access to Boston easier, the faculty in December, 1943, moved the starting time for Saturday classes from 8:30 to 8:00 A.M., so that students could catch the 12:34 train from Mansfield without cutting their final morning class.[28]

Despite its relative isolation, the campus was not immune from the general pressures of wartime America. Regulations limiting the amount of academic credit transferable from summer school were relaxed in order to permit students to accelerate the completion of their degree work. The College routinely approved requests for deferred midyear or final examinations so that students could be with husbands or fiancés who were on leave from military duty. Faculty members later recalled numerous experiences of counselling and comforting students who came to them, or who could be heard crying at night as they sought to deal with fears for the safety of brothers and boyfriends in military service. The whole campus was devastated by news of the death in action in 1943 of Paul Fillmore, son of Buildings and Grounds Supervisor Irving Fillmore.[29]

The number of marriages, both student and faculty, increased enormously, and the College routinely allowed those who were married to continue living in the dormitories, although without spousal overnight visitation rights. Married seniors were also allowed to take their senior year elsewhere, if necessary, and still receive a Wheaton degree. One of the highlights of the 1943 fall semester was the marriage in the Chapel of the College Government Association President, Cameron Biggers, to Naval Air Force Lieutenant Hugh Wagner. The wedding was attended, in

President Park's words, "by the whole college" and was followed by a small reception hosted by the President in his home. Park's personal views were perhaps best reflected in a letter he wrote to trustee Joseph Soliday, in which he noted that "a great many college girls seem to have the very common sense idea that the best service they can render to their nation is to go ahead and get married."[30]

Students and faculty who resided in the dormitories were required to turn in their food ration books, and the College established a special Ration Bank Account with State Street Bank in Boston. This enabled the College to purchase rationed goods, and Wheaton's Director of the Domestic Department, Edith Lincoln, traveled regularly to Boston's Fanieul Hall market district to work miracles in obtaining scarce items for the College dining halls. Testimonial after testimonial exist lauding the incredible achievements of Miss Lincoln and her staff in presenting meals far beyond what could legitimately have been expected. The College dutifully, along with the rest of the nation, observed "Meatless Tuesdays," but the number of times that steaks and lamb roasts appeared on the table never ceased to amaze the thankful consumers.[31]

Part of what made this possible was the fact that the College was minimally dependent on outside purchasing for garden produce. The College farm, which for decades had served as a source for potatoes, cabbages, onions and turnips, was now greatly expanded. Students and faculty volunteered to assist with the planting and harvesting, and two faculty members, Katherine Burton and Grazia Avitabile, agreed to remain in Norton and work on the farm full-time one summer in return for room and board. However, despite the enormous amount of fresh produce grown for College consumption, the College auditors reported in October, 1944, that fiscally the farm was operating at a net loss. They recommended that once the war ended and normal supply channels resumed the farm operation should be terminated, a recommendation that newly inaugurated President A. Howard Meneely indicated he was inclined to support.[32]

In addition to the main farm, the College also made a small portion of land available for subdivision among resident faculty who wished to grow vegetables for personal use in what were known at the time as "Victory Gardens." These gardens came often to reflect not only the eating tastes but on occasion the personalities of the cultivators themselves. In particular the garden of Mathematics Professor and Choir Director Carl Garabedian stood out. Totally obsessed by a passion for structure and precision, Garabedian could be found in the spring on his hands and knees measuring with a ruler the appropriate distance between rows and even between individual seeds and seedlings within rows. As his crops approached the time for harvesting, Garabedian apparently went through a personal crisis, finding it very distressing to pull some carrots or harvest one or two heads of lettuce from a row because doing so destroyed the precision and symmetry of the garden he had created.[33]

On campus, the war years brought one major change that impacted enormously upon faculty and students alike. In October, 1942, President Park agreed to allow faculty residing in dormitories the privilege of smoking in their rooms. Less than a month later it was decided that students visiting faculty in their apartments or houses could smoke if invited to do so by their hostess. However, it was not until January, 1944, that a student committee was created to investigate the possibility of using basement rooms in dormitories as "smokers," a policy that was finally approved by the administration in March. The maintenance department installed lighting and fans, students both donated and raised money for furniture, and in April the first four dormitory smokers were opened with considerable fanfare.[34]

Other than the implementation of both credit and noncredit courses designed to facilitate organized war activities on campus or better prepare students for summer and postgraduate employment in a wartime economy, there was relatively little curricular change or innovation at

Professor of History "Jack" Knapton and his family in their Victory Garden.

Wheaton during the war years. With a number of faculty away serving in military or government service, and others engaged in part-time war-related work or research on campus or in the local area, it became difficult to undertake and maintain any long-term new curricular programs. This is not to say there were no new initiatives—there were several—but the only one that survived the war itself and became a permanent part of the postwar academic structure was the the study of Russian. First offered in 1942–43 by German Professor Hedda Korsch, the program blossomed with the hiring of Nicholas Vakar in 1944, who over the next two and one-half decades developed a program in Russian language, literature and civilization that took its place as a permanent part of the College's modern language offerings. Conversely, the study of Portuguese, also instituted in 1942–43, never progressed beyond two years of language instruction, and was withdrawn from the curriculum at the end of the 1952–53 academic year.[35]

Two other programs, both experimental and interdepartmental in nature, were tried and ultimately abandoned during the war years. President Park had long advocated the development of courses and programs that bridged traditional academic disciplinary fields, and had ruefully lamented the footdragging tendencies of the faculty in his comments at meetings of the Board of Trustees. The one success that had been achieved in that area was the Elements of Composition in the Arts course which Park had authorized without formal faculty approval in 1937, and which remained a part of the Wheaton curriculum until the end of the war.[36]

Building on that success, in the fall of 1940 the President urged the faculty to develop what he initially proposed as a four-year program in the social sciences, and in literature and the arts. Two groups of 15–20 students would take as part of their work an independent program of study under the supervision of one faculty member; all normal distribution and major requirements would be waived. The response was less than enthusiastic. In discussing these issues with the faculty, Dr. Park commented ruefully to the Board of Trustees in November, 1941, "the net result frequently is that they approve of my suggestions in principle, but they cannot see any practical way of carrying them out."[37]

Nonetheless, a reluctant faculty ultimately authorized the implementation of a one-semester pilot program in the literature and arts field only, and ten students were selected from among the freshmen who applied toward the end of their first semester in the fall of 1941. During the second semester each student was assigned to an adviser who supervised her independent work. Occasional group meetings were also held, in order to encourage discussion and debate among the participants.[38]

The experiment proved to be both a success in terms of the students involved, and an enormous addition to the workload of the individual faculty members charged with supervising the independent studies programs. In a report to the faculty the following fall, the chair of the committee in charge of the program, English Professor Ralph Boas, recommended that because of the academic and nonacademic demands of the many new wartime programs, plus the amount of time required for supervising the work of one individual, the program be "temporarily" suspended. The faculty concurred.[39]

Much more successful was the Wartime Studies Program inaugurated in the fall of 1943. Designed to help prepare a selected group of students for postwar jobs either in government service or the world of science and technology, the program was structured to allow early intensive training in either economics or the sciences. Participants also met regularly with faculty in discussion groups focussing either on "Science and its Influence on Human Affairs," or "Problems of Peace," both seeking an interdisciplinary exposure to problems and issues likely to be faced in the postwar world. A special section of History 1 (Modern European History) was created for those in the program, designed to provide "the background necessary for an understanding of the political situation in the world today." Ten $400 scholarships were authorized to help recruit entering freshmen into the program, which lasted two years, after which students entered into the regular major curriculum in the area of their choice.[40]

Directed by economist Henrietta Jennings and Philosophy Instructor Holcombe Austin, the program proved to be quite successful, though short-lived. Groups of entering students were admitted as Wartime Studies Scholars in both 1943 and 1944, after which, as it became apparent the war was drawing to a close, the program was discontinued at the suggestion of Wheaton's new president, A. Howard Meneely, and the scholarships made available to the student body as as whole.[41]

One other academic, though noncurricular, wartime innovation deserves mention. In the final year of the war a semimonthly series of current events programs on Friday afternoons was organized by Professors Knapton and Cressey. These sessions, involving both presentations and discussion, were led by one or another member of the faculty. They proved to be extremely popular, and remained a regular part of Wheaton's extracurricular academic programming for more than a decade.[42]

World War II also saw the complete demise of the College's participation in intercollegiate athletics. Gasoline rationing and the enormous expansion of war-related activities on campus both contributed to put the final terminating stamp on a program that Wheaton had supported from the time it had become a college until 1941. This change also brought Wheaton into line with the philosophy prevailing at schools of physical education, which taught their students that strenuous competition placed far too much stress on the nervous systems of young women.[43] This point of view was accepted by Marna Brady, who had replaced Miriam Faries as head of the Physical Education Department in 1939. It became the official policy of the Wheaton Department of Physical Education with the advent of Christine White as Department Head in 1943, and continued to prevail as the Department's guiding operational philosophy for nearly two decades.[44]

But the demise of intercollegiate competition did not mean that physical fitness was regarded as an unimportant aspect of student life on the Wheaton campus. Completion of the physical education requirement remained a stipulation for graduation, and the requirement was expanded as a "temporary war measure" to include two hours a week of physical conditioning for all seniors who did not participate in class sports. The campus intramural program included a host of team activities, and the fact that students often competed very strenuously in them did not seem to be regarded as threatening to the female constitution in the manner ascribed to intercollegiate competition.[45]

Unlike men's or coed colleges, colleges for women did not suffer dramatically from a decline in admissions applications during the war. Studies of this phenomenon have of course pointed to the absence of a military draft for women, but there are indications that the increase in both number and quality of the applications experienced during the war can be attributed to a number of other factors as well.

The war brought the economic unemployment of the great depression era to an end. Jobs, and the money that went with them, were readily available. At the same time food rationing, a general shortage of consumer goods, and the bans on new housing construction and the manufacture of automobiles for civilian purchase left comparatively little on which to spend new-found income. Sons were going into military service; money was available for the education of daughters. Secondly, the dearth of undergraduate males on coed campuses, and the decimation due to military service of many male-dominated faculties at those institutions, led many women who would normally have gravitated to coed colleges to turn to women's colleges. There the predominantly female teaching staff remained relatively intact, as did the quality and breadth of the academic programs offered.[46]

Wheaton was not immune from these positive developments. In May of 1942, Dr. Park reported to the trustees that the College had the greatest number of applicants in its history. Moreover, the number of applicants with general SAT board scores over 650 had more than doubled. Despite an early slump in applications the following year, when classes started in the fall of 1943, six entering students had to be housed temporarily in College guest rooms. Wheaton's recruitment literature emphasized the importance of a college education in order to prepare women for the many jobs that would become available in the postwar reconstruction period. In 1944, and again in 1945, the number of applications greatly exceeded anything ever experienced before. Moreover, unlike admissions in the latter part of the twentieth century, the rate of enrollment of accepted students was remarkably high. Nearly 500 students applied for admission in the fall of 1945. Of those, the Admissions Office accepted 178 in order to fill a class target of 135–140. In doing so, President Meneely reported, "we did not take religious affiliation into consideration in selecting our freshman class," meaning, of course, that Jewish candidates for the first time in nearly two decades were not subject to a specific numbers limitation.[47] The College's problem, President Meneely happily reported to the Board of Trustees in March, 1945, was not in getting good students, it was in attracting "first-rate" ones.[48]

Part of this upturn in admissions may also have been due to Wheaton's growing acceptance in the upper echelon of women's higher education. In March, 1942, Dr. Park reported to the trustees that nine women's colleges, the "Seven Sisters" plus Wheaton and Wells, had jointly sent out a notice stating that they would no longer require entering students to take SAT subject examinations, and instead would require only the general SAT achievement tests.

> This is almost the first time that the big seven colleges have recognized the existence of Wells and Wheaton. The seven colleges for women when this organization was started seemed to be in some doubt as to whether Wheaton and Wells, owing to their smaller size, would be able to survive, and so did not include them in their number. Since then public opinion has changed considerably and the smaller college might be said to be in a much better position than some of its larger competitors.[49]

With all dormitories filled to capacity, plus government mandated price and wage increase restrictions, Wheaton was able during the war years to remain debt free, operate annually in the black, and increase considerably the amount of money available for scholarships. Over the years it even amassed a surplus of more than $100,000, which was designated as a fund to be used for maintenance projects deferred because of the wartime lack of labor and materials. The dedication of the new wings to the Science Building and the Library in January, 1942, marked the end of any building project, other than a new water tank, until well after the conclusion of hostilities. The College did purchase two houses on Howard Street, and also authorized a complete survey map of its real estate holdings, since, as Park told the Board of Trustees, "there is really nobody who knows exactly where college land ends or begins."[50]

Wheaton also turned out to be fortunate that, unlike many institutions in the area, it had never converted its heating system to the use of oil. Although coal was in constant short supply during the war, the College never experienced the heating crises or coal shortages that had plagued it during World War I. In fact in January, 1943, President Park gloated mildly to trustee Sylvia Meadows that Wheaton remained open for business, while Wellesley had been forced to close until March because of the unavailability of heating oil. However, in an effort both to upgrade service and conserve coal, the Trustees did instruct the President in May, 1943, to discontinue use of the College's electric plant, and contract instead with New England Power Company for all its power needs.[51]

Until his retirement in 1944, President Park was able to retain all but one of the key members of his administrative staff. Only the departure of Admissions Director Barbara Ziegler for Naval duty in September, 1942, marred the stability of the adminstrative and support services team in place when the war broke out. In one instance, that of long-time Bursar Mabel Dunkle, Park did make a determined effort for more than a year to force her resignation, on the grounds that she could not work with other people, and that additional staff appointed to her office were constantly resigning in protest over her treatment of them. Initially Miss Dunkle verbally agreed to resign, but soon changed her mind. Protected by a contract that ran through June, 1945 (and the President's unwillingness to fire a long-time employee), she refused to resign in writing, rode out the storm, and ultimately survived in her position until 1953.[52]

Perhaps the largest on-going set of problems President Park had to face between 1941 and the end of his term in office in July, 1944, had to do with the faculty. Restless after years of fiscal stringency imposed by the economic depression, the faculty grew increasingly peckish as they tried to cope with all of the new demands placed on their time by war-related activities, even as they continued to teach the same, and in some cases increased, course loads. Positions elsewhere, both civilian and military, appeared tantalizingly enticing to many, as did the larger salaries that often went with them. Federal restrictions on increases in wages posed ever-increasing hardships as living costs increased in response to the inflationary pressures of a wartime, full employment economy. Restrictions imposed by gasoline rationing and a general ban on overnight rail travel helped turn the Wheaton community even more in on itself, making issues relating to salaries and promotion even more acrimonious than might otherwise have been the case.[53]

Overall, seven members of the faculty, including two in Physical Education, were granted indefinite leaves of absence in order to enter military service. Of these, four—Ralph Hidy, Walter Nickerson, Robert Sharp, and Eunice Work—returned to Wheaton at the end of the war, but Professor Hidy left shortly thereafter to accept a position at the Business History Foundation, while Nickerson departed for Rutgers University in 1949. In addition, leaves were granted for civilian work with the French

Committee of National Liberation, the Office of Strategic Services (OSS), the Stanford Far East Area and Language School, and in one case to enable a member of the English Department to be with her husband who had been stationed in another part of the country. Two additional members of the Physical Education staff left without a leave of absence to take positions with the American Red Cross overseas.[54]

But this was only part of the problem. In May of 1942, the President commented wryly in a faculty meeting that he had already received nine resignations for the upcoming academic year, a number due to wartime marriage plans.[55] People were also leaving for better paying jobs, he told the trustees. "War conditions offer many opportunities not available to women in peace time."[56] One year later he commented that he was "at wit's end how to get science instructors."[57]

The President was not above some fairly severe arm-twisting in encouraging faculty to remain in Norton. In April, 1943, he successfully persuaded Elizabeth MacLeod of the music department to turn down a Radcliffe Fellowship she had been awarded for graduate work toward a Ph.D. by offering her a promotion to assistant professor after one more year. "I was largely influenced by your discussion with me in March,"

Shown here in the uniforms of the Masachusetts Women's Defense Corps, Physical Education Professors Marna Brady and Dorothy Mott trained the student first aid corps at Wheaton in 1942-1943. Subsequently both were granted leaves of absence in order to enter military service.

she wrote the president, "in which you felt it unnecessary and rather inadvisable for one to start working for a Ph.D. at this point."[58] Park also convinced Dorothy Littlefield, who was a member of the French Department and Dean of Freshman, to turn down outside opportunities. "The war will last four to six years, but education will go on forever," he told her. "Please stay."[59]

When historian E. J. Knapton approached President Park concerning the possibility of his obtaining a leave of absence to work for the Board of Economic Warfare in Washington, Park (despite having received Board of Trustees approval for a one-year leave) told him bluntly that since this would be civilian rather than military service, he would have to resign his position at Wheaton, with no guarantee that there would be a place for him when the war was over. Only much later did Professor Knapton discover that Park's action had been illegal.[60]

Even more irritating to Park was the fact that some of the faculty and staff began using possible offers elsewhere to pressure for improvements in their situation at Wheaton. "We are still having great difficulty," he wrote to trustee J. K. Clark in April, 1943, "as everybody on the campus here—well, perhaps not everybody, but fifty percent, are anxious to make something out of the war, and the continual holdups for increases are very trying."[61] People were getting offers with only a few days to respond, he reported to Sylvia Meadows. The result was that he often had to act unilaterally, without consulting the Trustee Administration Committee as he was supposed to. Younger faculty were continually asking for salary increases, while the older ones sought adjustments to match the increased cost of living, "but I feel, especially for those living at the college, this is not nearly so necessary in their case."[62] Some would get raises, he went on, others would then inevitably feel poorly treated. Noting that he had had to offer increases to all the members of the Chemistry department in order to retain their services, he admitted that he could see why others "may feel unfairly dealt with."[63]

Adding to issues concerning financial compensation was the fact that while negotiations regarding individual contracts were allowed, federal wartime regulations prohibited any general increase in wages and salaries. However, with the blessing of the College accountants, the Board of Trustees authorized for three years running an end-of-year bonus of $100 for every full-time faculty member, and a sum equal to 5 percent of annual salary earned to all staff personnel. The first announcement of this policy in faculty meeting, Park reported, "was received in stunned silence, none of them ever having had such an experience before and unable to realize it until well into the night, when they woke up smiling."[64] Even more important was the fact that the staff bonus "enabled us to keep the men who were wobbling" on the buildings and grounds crew.[65]

Throughout the years between 1941 and 1944, President Park was besieged by requests for promotion and salary increases, almost exclusively from women faculty members. In some cases promotions were requested as a reward in lieu of forbidden salary increases, in others due to length of service, or as a matter of equity. Claims of this sort never failed to irritate Dr. Park. In March, 1942, he stated to the trustees his belief that it was highly laudable that "the general seniority principle adopted in so many of the other colleges by which an individual receives maximum salary automatically even although not at all as valuable to the institution as other members of the department has never won a place at Wheaton. The seniority principle . . . is in my opinion a cause of a great deal of the dullness of the classroom in American colleges."[66] Writing to the Head of the Art Department, Esther Seaver, Park was even more explicit.

> This promotion by seniority will lead any army into defeat and will make a dead place of any college. . . . The idea that everybody who is doing satisfactory work ought to be promoted and given a raise of salary year by year until she becomes a full professor would lead to an intolerable situation and would produce mediocrity, as all the better people would be called away before the entire rank and file mass slowly moved upward.[67]

It was absolutely necessary, Park maintained, that the President have the right to "keep good people offered positions elsewhere by raising salaries of such people."[68] He also was careful to point out to the trustees that in several cases, as authorized by the Board, he had failed to grant raises for a number of years in order to provide additional incentive to leave for persons whom he had advised to seek jobs elsewhere.[69]

As a result of following this general dictum, Park's decision in February, 1942, to promote one of two assistant professors in the Art department to associate professor touched off a series of meetings, irate but polite letters, and threats of resignation from not only the two young women involved, but also Esther Seaver herself, who came to believe that Park had insulted her own professional capabilities in one of the letters dealing with this issue. Within a year both of the younger professors had resigned, while what Park always referred to as the "misunderstanding" with Professor Seaver remained buried but unresolved.[70]

Even more bitter was the President's confrontation with psychologist Maria Rickers-Ovsiankina. Having signed in February, 1942, a two year-contract renewal with promise of promotion to associate professor at the end of the contract term, Dr. Rickers approached Park at the end of May with the news that she had been offered an associate professorship and more money at a mid-western college. In light of this offer, she requested that the President reconsider his decision to withold her promotion for two years. His reply was vintage J. Edgar Park.

> Your fitting fate would be to be allowed to go to this place in the middle west and enjoy there the honors of an associate professorship, and even of

a professorship, for as the old proverb says, "It is better to be an assistant professor at Wheaton, Massachusetts, than to be a fool professor in the Mississippi Valley." But I should say that you win and there is no use protesting when one is licked. It is so late in the day and times are so critical that there is nothing for me to do but say I should be glad to change the word "Assistant" on your contract to read "Associate" if you would bring your contract in to the office.

In spite of the hard feelings implied in the above, we really do appreciate what you have done for Wheaton and the prestige your work brings to the college.[71]

Having turned down several other requests for promotion that spring, and created a major flap within the Art department because of the one he had granted, President Park was understandably not happy at having his hand forced in this way, nor at the subsequent rumors on campus that he had been successfully "held-up." Thus when Miss Rickers approached him again in June saying that MacMurray College had increased the salary offer to the point where she felt her family obligations could not allow her to refuse, President Park dug in his heels. Firing off an irate letter to the President of MacMurray, he implied that he was not prepared to allow a resignation coming so long after the end of the college year and so far after the notification standards established by the national AAUP in its new guidelines involving the principles of academic tenure. The reply from the President of MacMurray, while denying that any specific new offer had been made, suggested that it was unwise for any president to try to hold an unhappy professor against his or her will, especially if the new opportunity provided a real chance for professional advancement. Nonetheless, Dr. Park remained adamant and made it clear to Miss Rickers that while he would be willing to release her after one year of her new two year contract, he was prepared to take legal action if she persisted in attempting to violate AAUP standards by resigning at that time. In the face of this opposition, Dr. Rickers capitulated and returned unhappily to Wheaton in September, 1942, where, despite a bitter contretemps with President Park in March, 1944 over the terms of a new contract, she remained until 1950.[72]

Interestingly, a year later Katharine Neilson, whose promotion the year before to associate professor had created such turmoil in the Art department, requested permission to resign in August to take on the position of Curator of Education at the Buffalo Museum of Art. Instead of resisting, President Park, though citing the AAUP notification standards, readily agreed, on condition that a suitable replacement could be found. Despite the fact that College was due to open in less than a month, two good candidates were quickly identified, one was hired, and Dr. Park happily wired the news to Dr. Neilson on September 9, adding at the end, "Godspeed to you."[73]

In retrospect, the most fascinating element in these stories was Dr.

Park's repeated use of the 1940 *Statement of Principles on Academic Freedom and Tenure*, which had been issued jointly by the American Association of University Professors and the Association of American Colleges and Universities. Despite the fact that a form of de facto tenure had clearly existed at Wheaton for some time, as evidenced by the ability of Glenn Shook to resist Dr. Park's strong suggestions that he resign, and the President's willingness to state in a letter that Louise Boas had "the maximum security of tenure," Wheaton's Board of Trustees had never endorsed the concept of tenure, or put into effect any systematic plan authorizing the granting of that status to senior faculty.[74]

Nonetheless, it is evident that President Park welcomed the publication of the new joint statement on tenure, and immediately began to refer to it in his discussions with faculty. The fact that Wheaton had never formally accepted the concept of tenure did not seem to concern him. He clearly regarded the statement's specifications concerning the timing of intent-to-resign notification as totally applicable when he accused Maria Rickers of failing to play by "the rules of the game," noting that her proposed action was "contrary to the standards on academic tenure adopted by both the American Association of University Professors and the Association of American Colleges."[75]

However, in early 1944 the issue of tenure was placed squarely before the President and the Board of Trustees. Walter Shipley, who had been hired in 1941 as a wartime replacement for William Hunt in psychology, came to the President with two offers in hand from other institutions, both of them with tenure. Since Hunt was eligible to return to Wheaton after the war, Dr. Park took the matter to the Board of Trustees. Commenting that Shipley had proven himself to be a highly valuable member of the faculty, Park recommended that he be kept, regardless of whether or not Hunt returned. But Professor Shipley had made it clear that he was not prepared to stay without a written guarantee of tenure. Following the President's lead, the Board voted formally to "grant tenure to Professor Shipley," though they were careful to insert into the minutes a statement that "this vote is not to be taken as the usual procedure, but each case is to be taken upon its own individual merit."[76] The result was that Professor Shipley was sent a letter on March 14, 1944, awarding him "full tenure as associate professor."[77]

Issues related to the concept of tenure were also generated by a very different sequence of events. Clifford Hubbard had been Professor of History and Political Science since 1926, and had been Head of the department bearing the same name for many years. Productive as a publishing scholar in his first years at Wheaton, he became increasingly active in local politics and town government during the 1930s. He also received a Governor's appointment to the Board of Trustees of Massachusetts State College at Amherst (today the University of Massachusetts, Amherst), and served on a state commission to examine teacher

certification requirements and the training of teachers at the Massachusetts colleges of education.

However, his teaching preparation and classroom presentation apparently suffered as he became more and more involved in matters outside
the College. As early as 1934, President Park felt compelled to write to
Professor Hubbard regarding student indignation about the courses offered in political science. In 1941, faced with escalating student and
alumnae protest concerning his classroom manner and lack of preparation, Park again wrote to Hubbard, detailing the nature of the critical
comments he had received.[78]

One year later Dr. Park found himself having to deal with a palace
revolution. Two younger members of the department, Ralph Hidy and
Jack Knapton, both of whom the President regarded as among the very
best instructors at the College, met with Park and informed him that they
did not feel they could continue at Wheaton if Hubbard remained Head
of the Department, "as they were so humiliated by his exhibition of himself both before students and at professional conferences."[79] "Feeling
that there was a good deal of force in Mr. Knapton's position," Park
later wrote, "I did appoint him head of the department in place of Dr.
Hubbard."[80]

Professor Hubbard apparently accepted this change with relative good
grace. However, in subsequent years his teaching did not improve, and
in January, 1944, the President of the Student Government and Chair of
the Student Curriculum Committee, Cameron Biggers Wagner, came to
the President Park with a student petition asking for Dr. Hubbard's retirement. Well aware of the long-term nature of the problem, and having
assured himself that the rest of the History and Political Science department were equally distressed about the courses being offered by Hubbard, Dr. Park decided to move forward. "He has become objectionable
as a lecturer owing to extreme pomposity of manner united with paucity
of material," Park wrote in a confidential memo prepared for a Board of
Trustees meeting in March, 1944.[81] Park therefore suggested that a financial settlement be offered to Dr. Hubbard in an effort to secure his
immediate retirement, rather than waiting for him to reach mandatory
retirement age in 1949.[82]

With the approval of the trustees, negotiations were begun, and on
March 31, Professor Hubbard wrote to the President indicating his acceptance of the terms proposed, and concluding, "I intend to submit my
resignation as Professor of History and Political Science effective as of
June 30, 1944."[83] And indeed on May 1 such a letter was received; the
final settlement was approved by the Board the following day.[84]

Undoubtedly President Park thought the matter was over and done
with, but he soon learned this was not the case. It turned out that at the
end of April, Dr. Hubbard had written to both the national AAUP and
the Wheaton chapter, alleging that he had in effect been fired, and seek-

ing AAUP intervention on his behalf. On May 11, the President received a communication from Robert Ludlum, Associate Secretary of the national AAUP, alleging that no hearing had been held prior to termination, and asking that Hubbard be continued in his position until all the facts were established. He requested that the College respond with its "side of the issue" in detail, including why it had asked for Hubbard's resignation.[85]

Unwilling to comply, the Board of Trustees instructed Park simply to respond that the matter was not an issue of termination. Rather, Dr. Hubbard had merely been offered a chance to retire early, which he had chosen of his own free will to accept. "We do not think of any additional facts which would clarify the situation," Park wrote, "except to assure you that the president and trustees have adhered scrupulously to the rules of tenure laid down by the AAUP and the Association of American Colleges during the present administration."[86] However, he failed to add that Wheaton had not yet officially accepted the concept or practice of tenure outlined in the referred-to rules.

While it is true that Park's discussions with Dr. Hubbard were always framed within the terminology of an early retirement offer, there is abundant evidence that both the President and the Board of Trustees were prepared ultimately to take whatever action was necessary in order to gain the desired result. Central to their concern was the fact that Dr. Park was due to leave office on July 31, 1944, and there was a definite determination that resolution of this messy matter should not be left for an incoming president. In time the national AAUP let the matter die down, while the brunt of the local chapter's inquiry had to be borne by Professor Knapton, who, as Head of the Department, was asked to respond to questions posed by the Wheaton chapter's executive committee. Nonetheless, the remaining sense of AAUP involvement, at both the national and local level, is of a distinctly pro forma investigation. On the Wheaton campus there was a general, though not universal, feeling of relief that a matter desperately in need of resolution had been taken care of.[87]

Aware that the broader issue of tenure had not been dealt with, the trustees asked President Park shortly before he left office to prepare a statement for them concerning that subject. In his report, dated June 1, 1944, President Park commented negatively regarding the timing of three summer faculty resignations that had occurred during his term in office, and also implied that he had doubts as to whether AAUP principles regarding tenure were really suited for a small college. Noting that Article C specified that termination of a permanent or long-term appointment required action by both a faculty committee and the governing board of the College, and also undoubtedly with the recent Hubbard "retirement" in mind, he observed: "My experience leads me to believe that in the intimacy of a small residential college for women it would be wholly impossible under almost any circumstances to get a group of colleagues to accept this responsibility."[88] Regarding the existing situation at Wheaton, Park commented:

> At the present time our bylaws state, "Any professor may be appointed for a term not exceeding three years and shall be eligible for reelection." My understanding of that clause has been that this defines the status in case of legal proceedings, but that the trustees as a whole have accepted the general principle that there is tenure beyond these three years at least in the case of full professors and associate professors.[89]

This informal concept of de facto tenure was exemplified by President Park in one of his final acts in office. Carolyn Clewes, who like Walter Shipley had come to Wheaton in 1941 as a temporary wartime replacement, in her case for Ralph Hidy, was awarded a promotion to assistant professor and a new contract, which, in Park's words, "carries tenure as a member of the faculty here and not merely a substitute. We look forward to having you with us for years."[90]

There matters rested. Only under the administration of A. Howard Meneely, who assumed the presidency on August 1, 1944, would the formal acceptance of the principle of tenure at Wheaton finally be achieved.[91]

One aspect of faculty professional activity was negatively impacted by the time and energy demanded of them for campus war-related activities. While the College had never placed a high premium on faculty scholarship in terms of research and publication, a surprising number of faculty had been steadily though modestly active in that area. Although promotion had never been denied to good teachers who failed to publish, from time to time failure to engage in this activity had been used by the President to deny advancement to full professor to those whose classroom performance he regarded as mediocre.[92] But except for several faculty members who were retained by federal agencies to conduct research on campus, it is apparent that even the relatively modest level of scholarly activity normally conducted by Wheaton faculty was greatly reduced as a result of wartime pressures.[93]

According to English Professor Katherine Burton, both President Park and his successor, A. Howard Meneely, placed "great" emphasis on teaching, but not on scholarship. Muriel Hidy, while agreeing that there was no pressure for publication, commented that it was encouraged, but there was just not much time for research activities. E. J. Knapton, however, maintained that there was little incentive to engage in research during the 1930s. Faculty were not asked about it by the administration, nor were secretarial services provided to help with the preparation of manuscripts. The publication of his first book in 1939, he stated, received no recognition from the College. On the other hand, when Walter Nicker-

In 1944, members of the Wheaton faculty auctioned off their services as waitresses at student tables as part of a drive to raise money for War Bonds. Front Row: Elizabeth Miller, *French*; Barbara Bradshaw, *Physical Education*; Jean Sudrann, *English*. Back Row: Rita Benson, *Physical Education*; Emeline Hall, *Classics*; Lena Mandell, *Romance Languages*.

son, serving in the Army during the war, wrote Dr. Park requesting a promotion in absentia from instructor to assistant professor because of the recent publication of his book, the President readily assented.[94]

The most important on-campus war research was that conducted by psychologist Walter Shipley in connection with a major grant received by Brown University from the federal government. Retained to work one-quarter time during the academic year and full-time during the summer, half of Shipley's regular salary as well as the full salary of two assistants was paid by the grant, while the College provided free work space and furniture in the basement of the Chapel. Biologist Anna Faull also received government support for conducting tests to see if seeds of plants producing rubber or oil in other countries could be induced to grow in New England.[95]

A number of faculty also were hired, with the College's blessing, to engage in part-time work in neighboring industries or at other academic institutions. Chemist Mildred Evans was employed to do confidential research for the National Defense Research Council at the Kendall Company in Walpole during the summer of 1943, at a salary twice the monthly rate of her Wheaton pay. Her colleague, Maud Marshall, spent the same summer teaching chemistry to Navy students at Amherst College. Denied the opportunity to take a civilian position in Washington, E. J. Knapton began working full-time during the summers and three afternoons a week during the academic year for Spencer Thermostat in Attleboro.[96]

"I have two pieces of good news for you today," President Park announced to the faculty on November 17, 1943. The first was that the end-of-year $100 bonus for all full-time faculty that had been awarded the previous year would again be granted that December.

> The second piece of good news which I have for you is even better than this. I have always held that there were three general principles about resignations: (1) resign too soon, do not wait for a good reason; (2) resign when sane, do not wait until you have lost your mind and consider yourself indispensable; (3) resign before the young person destined to take your place is too old to enjoy it.
>
> In obedience to these principles, more than a year ago I indicated to the trustees my intention of resigning under the age limitation on Commencement, 1944, and told them that my resignation was in their hands at any time. The trustees immediately entered upon an intense and strenuous period of inactivity with respect to this statement. As a result, before the trustee meeting in March, 1943, I sent them each a written resignation. I have not been able in three trustee meetings that have taken place since they received that resignation to get them to accept it, but we have got to the point at least where they have appointed a committee of trustees . . . to take up the question of finding a new president. . . .
>
> I suppose I ought at this time to give you a review of the accomplishments of the eighteen college years which have elapsed since I came here, but you will be glad to know I am going to spare you this recital. And in return I hope that you will all forget for the time being the negative side of the picture, which is almost as well known to me as to you. Needless to say, however, I feel the greatest gratitude to the faculty for the years of our common work together, and fatuously enough do not feel altogether ashamed of the result as it is seen in the college today. I know Wheaton will rise to further heights of distinction under my successor who will be, as is fitting, a younger and more conservative man.[97]

In his formal letter of resignation to the Board, President Park emphasized that over the years he had refused to grant all faculty requests for exemptions to the mandatory sixty-five retirement age, which had been instituted in 1930 when the College first established the Retiring Allowance Fund. Thus it was totally appropriate that the same rule should apply to him. "After sixty-five, college presidents as a class are apt to

Aerial view of the campus and Norton Center, circa 1946. The Power Plant, Carpenter Shop and SAB are in the foreground.

attain an unshared conviction of their own indispensibility," he commented. "My only suggestion is that in making arrangements for the choice of a successor, the trustees might find it helpful to cooperate with a committee which the faculty appointed some time ago to confer with the trustees on matters of common interest."[98]

The response of the trustees was to appoint a three-member committee headed by John K. Clark to discuss retirement benefits for Dr. Park, and to constitute a search committee for a new president. However, during the spring, summer, and fall of 1943, nothing much was done to further this process. In part this was due to the fervent hope of the majority of the Board, expressed both individually and in collective resolutions, that President Park would reconsider. The point was made repeatedly that under the Statutes of the College the mandatory retirement age did not apply. The President served at the pleasure of the Board, and the Board's pleasure was that he should remain in office. Part of the delay, however, was also due to the "leisurely approach" taken toward the search process by Mr. Clark, which according to another member of the selection committee, Richard Chapman, would have taken two years at the pace that Clark was willing to proceed.[99]

Finally, on November 8, President Park forced the Board's hand. Although recognizing that he was not required to do so, he reaffirmed his determination to hold himself to the retirement age provisions of the Retiring Allowance Fund. He indicated that he wanted permission to tell the faculty at its next meeting, and reiterated his desire that the name of his successor be announced at the June, 1944, Commencement ceremonies. He also asked for and received permission to have the faculty approve the selection of two members of the Committee on Consultation with the Trustees, Ralph Boas and Muriel Hidy, to serve in an advisory capacity to the Trustee Selection Committee.[100]

Park subsequently became quite miffed when Clark sent the letter requesting that the faculty appoint these two members directly to Boas, rather than to Park, who had planned to give it to Boas just before the faculty meeting. Clark's action meant that Professor Boas was tipped off to the announcement several days in advance, with the result that Park felt compelled to give advanced warning to his officers. "Mr. Clark operated on an independent line, balling up things rather badly here," Park wrote to trustee Sylvia Meadows.[101] And in a letter to Clark, he peevishly commented, "And while I had been looking forward for years to the pleasure of announcing my resignation on time to the unsuspecting faculty, I came to the conclusion when that was denied to me that it was a kiddish expectation, not worthy the dignity of a college president."[102]

It was only with the public announcement of Park's resignation that the search process began in earnest. The addition of College Treasurer and trustee William Chase to the selection committee did much to accelerate the process. But the trustees made one final futile attempt to get Park to change his mind. At a faculty meeting on December 1, Ralph Boas reported that the Board wished the faculty to vote a resolution urging the President to stay on another year, a motion that the faculty dutifully endorsed.[103]

The extensive press coverage of Dr. Park's resignation led to the receipt of many unsolicited applications for the presidency. This was a day and age when searches of this nature were generally conducted privately, quietly, and very clandestinely, with nominations obtained and inquiries undertaken via what would later become known as the "old boy network." "I really think it would have been much wiser," Park wrote to Chapman, "for the trustees to have announced the appointment of Dr. J. B. van Stoozen as my successor. That would have eliminated the applications and given the trustees time to look around before the public found there was no such person of that name."[104]

There is very little information regarding the actual course of the presidential search. What is known is that from the beginning the Board was determined that the next president should be an academic by profession. Although other women's colleges had women as presidents, no consideration to female candidates was given. By April a number of persons had been interviewed. The Chair of the Search Committee, J. K. Clark, wrote to President Park on April 11, complaining mildly about the fact that he had been on the road for four days over the Easter weekend interviewing candidates. He also reported that a first choice had emerged, a Harvard professor by the name of Finley. Clark had already interviewed him; Chapman and Chase would see him shortly.[105]

It was sometime shortly thereafter that a new candidate appeared on the scene. Although it is not clear how A. Howard Meneely first came to the attention of the selection committee, E. J. Knapton recalled in his memoirs that he had met the Dartmouth history professor briefly at the home of Jack's good friend, Dartmouth historian Arthur Wilson. Wilson "spoke highly of his abilities," Professor Knapton stated. "I mentioned his name as a possibility to the search committee, of which I was not a member, but otherwise had nothing to do with his appointment."[106]

Be that as it may, by the end of April Howard Meneely had clearly become the candidate of choice. In a letter to President Park, which indicates that Park was very much aware of the progress of the search, William Chase commented that a letter received from Meneely had "the right tone," to which Park replied that it was indeed a "very nice letter." In the same letter Park reiterated his desire that the Board accept his resignation as of May 31, but indicated his willingness to stay on until the arrival of a new President in August, or even "in a pinch" until the beginning of the second semester if that were needed.[107]

No such heroic measures were required. On May 2, 1944, the Board met in special session and unanimously approved an offer to Professor Meneely, with an annual salary of $10,000 plus $300 for moving expenses, and of course free living accommodations in the former home of Eliza Baylies Wheaton, now reserved for occupancy by the President of the College. Two days later Meneely accepted, and President Park was authorized by the Board to make the formal announcement at the regular Chapel service on May 5. It was agreed that the new president would assume his duties on August 1.[108]

During the course of the presidential search, a long-submerged trustee concern suddenly surfaced. Since 1908, the President of the Seminary or College had also served as Chairman of the Board of Trustees. This was mainly because at the time he had been chosen to head the Seminary, President Cole was already serving as Secretary of the Board of Trustees. He had therefore continued to serve on the Board in an appointed, rather than ex officio, capacity. In 1908, the trustees had elected him Chairman, and when Dr. Park succeeded Cole as President, he automatically also assumed the chairmanship of the Board. In fact, the College Statutes, drawn up well after Cole had assumed the chairmanship of the Board, specified that the President would hold a regular seat on the Board and serve as its chairman.

However, a number of trustees, led by Mr. Clark, had come to the conclusion that this was not a practice they wished to continue, and the advent of a new president seemed the appropriate time to make a change. Therefore, Clark proposed in February that the position of President be designated ex officio on the Board of Trustees, and that the linkage between the presidency and the chairmanship be dissolved. The trustees believed, Richard Chapman later commented, that the Board should have its own Chair. It was necessary that the Board be an independent body to which the President, though an ex officio member, reported, rather than his being in a position to direct its actions.[109]

To that end, on March 6, 1944, the trustees voted to amend the Statutes, separating the two offices and making the President's position on the Board ex officio. Not wishing to change the status of President Park, the Board immediately elected him to the chairmanship. However, on July 21, eleven days before his term of office was to expire, Park resigned from the Board at a special meeting of the trustees, and Joseph Soliday was elected as Chair. Writing to President-elect Meneely two days later, J. K. Clark informed him of the change and explained the Board's position.

> Hitherto the President has been the Board of Trustees, and we have been merely his counsellors, for the most part. As time went on and more and more of the Board was composed of those who were juniors in the service, this development became so noticeable that it created an undercurrent of mild resentment. This resulted in a change in our By-Laws, whereby we created the office of Chairman of the Board of Trustees and, as you may already have heard, Mr. Soliday was elected to that office. . . . I know that most of my fellow Trustees . . . look forward to the new arrangement with keen anticipation.[110]

During the last months of his administration, President Park consciously set out to redress some of the inadequacies and inequities in the faculty salary structure that had come into existence during the war years. Several faculty received unexpected promotions. Writing to

French Professor Dorothy Littlefield on March 21, he proffered a new three year contract with spelled out increases in each year, far different from the traditional Wheaton practice of awarding increases only in the first year of a contract. This was done, Park assured Miss Littlefield, "anticipating the well-known parsimony of Van Stoozen," in order that the contract would be "on file to bind him."[111]

In his final reports to the Board of Trustees, President Park wrote with pride concerning the growth and development of the College under his administration. Yet at the same time, two specific areas of regret were clearly apparent. The first was his inability to persuade the faculty to be even more innovative than it had been in terms of curriculum development. In particular, he argued strongly, it was necessary for Wheaton to try to incorporate and combine experiential learning with the theoretical and abstract knowledge emphasized in the traditional classroom. Wheaton, he maintained:

> should still be loyal to the liberal arts tradition but should provide for students more and more opportunities during the process of learning of trying out their theoretical knowledge in practice. . . . In women's education especially this sharp division between theoretical and practical must be broken down in the future more and more, and I think it can be done without sacrificing any of the valuable disciplines of the liberal arts education. . . . The present method is logical and neat, but it is not pedagogical or sound, It is not the natural way for people to learn.[112]

Secondly, Park expressed strongly his regret that he had not been able "before leaving Wheaton to have an adequate system of faculty housing established in Norton."[113] Here he was reiterating a position he had taken time and again before the trustees. Noting that the College had built two small houses on College Green in 1938, he lamented that his desire to add to that number as the years went by had proved impossible due to the war. Solving this problem, he stated, would contribute greatly to diminishing faculty unrest. "I am convinced," he wrote in his final published report, "that the average unmarried woman in college teaching should not be asked to live in a dormitory with students indefinitely. There comes a time in her life when she wants a home of her own where she can keep a dog, prepare her own meals at times and entertain friends, and there is something inhuman in denying it."[114]

"I wish to express my gratitude to all Wheaton," President Park wrote on July 31, 1944, his last day in office, "I have received much kindness from everybody. Seldom is a human relation entered into, continued, and terminated with such good will."[115]

NOTES: CHAPTER 15

1. Faculty: Korsch: Korsch to Remick, 9/12/39; H. Jennings: Jennings to Park, 9/5/39.

2. Ibid.: Korsch: Park memorandum, 11/7/39.

3. Faculty Meeting Minutes: 9/25/40.

4. Wheaton Histories, Wheaton in World Wars I and II: Defense and War Relief Committee, 1940–41: Minutes and Reports; American Defense, Harvard Group, 1940–41; World War II, 1940: Knapton to Park, 10/12/40; Park to Knapton, 10/15/40.

5. Trustees Minutes: 11/25/40; 3/10/41; Wheaton Histories, Wheaton in World Wars I and II: National Defense and War Relief Finance Committee, 1940–43; Faculty Meeting Minutes: 11/21/40. The custom of student knitting would continue into the latter 1950s, with boyfriends replacing relief agencies as the beneficiaries of this activity!

6. Faculty: Merrill: Park to Merrill, 6/18/40. See also Oral History Project: H. Austin interview, 1983.

7. Trustees: Soliday #2: Park to Soliday, 3/2/42.

8. Wheaton Histories, Wheaton in World Wars I and II: American Defense, Harvard Group, 1940–41: Letter to President of the United States, 12/19/40; Trustees Minutes: 6/8/40.

9. Faculty Meeting Minutes: 5/12/41; 9/24/41. Hunt and Hidy were "temporarily" replaced by Walter Shipley and Carolyn Clewes, both of whom eventually remained at Wheaton for many years.

10. Trustees Minutes: 6/14/41; 11/3/41; see also 5/31/42; 11/9/42; Faculty Meeting Minutes: 9/23/42; Faculty: Hunt: Park memorandum, 1/13/41; Park to Hunt, 5/13/41; Wheaton Histories, Wheaton in World Wars I and II: American Defense, Harvard Group 1940–41: Knapton to H. Schwarz, 8/20/41.

11. *Wheaton News*, 12/13/41.

12. Ibid.

13. Wheaton Histories, Wheaton in World Wars I and II: National Defense and War Relief Finance Committee, 1940–43.

14. Ibid.: National Defense and War Relief Finance Committee, 1940–43: Suggested Reorganization of Wheaton College War Activities; Faculty Committees: Administration Committee Minutes: 5/21/42; 10/12/42; 4/20/43; Faculty Meeting Minutes: 5/6/42; 5/28/43; Student Groups and Activities: Student War Activities Board: SWAB Minutes, 1943–45, passim.

15. Student Groups and Activities: Student War Activities Board: SWAB Minutes, 1943–45, passim; *Wheaton News*, 3/14/42; 10/24/42; 11/7/42; 1/23/43; 10/2/43; Trustees Minutes: 11/9/42; *Nike*, 1943; Faculty Meeting Minutes: 9/23/42; 5/28/43; Faculty Committees: Administration Committee Minutes, 1/25/43.

16. *Wheaton College Bulletin: Catalogue,* 1943–44; Faculty Meeting Minutes: 5/28/43; *Wheaton News*, 1/23/43; Faculty Committees: Administration Committee Minutes, 1/18/43; Curriculum Committee Minutes, 1/15/43; Trustees Minutes: 11/9/42; Faculty: Evans: Report of meetings with industrial representatives in Boston, May, 1942; Report of Trip to Industrial Plants, December, 1942; see also Jennings, *Chemistry at Wheaton*, ch. 6. Sikorsky was recognized as the leading developer of combat helicopters. A graduating senior in the class of 1943 was immediately accepted into the engineering program.

17. Trustees Minutes: 11/9/42; 5/30/43; Wheaton Histories, Wheaton in World Wars I and II: WWII–1943: Letter, M. Casey to P. Helmreich, 2/19/98, regarding interview with Dorothy Williams (W1943).

18. Trustees Minutes: 9/23/42; 11/9/42.

19. George Yelle, interview with author, 2/15/2000. The soldier was George Charette.

20. Trustees Minutes: 11/9/42.

21. Ibid. Both Mount Holyoke and Smith hosted training schools for US Navy WAVE units during WW II. See Staff: Ziegler: fall, 1942, passim.

22. Faculty Meeting Minutes: 3/25/42.

23. Trustees Minutes: 3/16/42; Oral History Project: L. Mandell interview, 1983; D. Littlefield interview, 1983; E. J. Knapton interview, 1983. Bookstore Manager Louise Perry became a Captain in the Women's Defense Corps. In 1944 she was authorized by the FBI to obtain information from the College regarding all faculty who had family members living outside the United States. See Staff: Perry.

24. Trustees Minutes: 3/16/42; Faculty Meeting Minutes: 9/22/43; Oral History Project: E. J. Knapton interview, 1983; Knapton, *Small Figure*, p. 189; Wheaton Histories, Wheaton in World Wars I and II: 1940–43: passim; see also National Defense and War Relief Finance Committee, 1940–43.

25. Trustees Minutes: 9/23/42.

26. Town of Norton: Miscellaneous, 1940–60: Reynolds to Park, 4/20/43; Park to Reynolds, 4/23/43.

27. Faculty Committees: Administration Committee Minutes, 4/19/44; see also Trustees Minutes: 5/30/43; Faculty: Riddell: Remick to Riddell, 6/9/43; Oral History Project: L. Mandell interview, 1983; K. Burton interview, 1983; J. Chidsey interview, 1983.

28. Trustees Minutes: 3/16/42; 11/9/42; Faculty Meeting Minutes: 1/20/42; 9/22/43; 12/1/43; 9/20/44; 11/20/44; 2/6/45; 4/19/45; President's Reports to Trustees: 3/25/45, pt 2; Faculty: Cressey: Park to Cressey, 3/28/44; Rice: Remick to Rice, 2/22/43; *Wheaton News*, 10/31/42; 12/4/43; Faculty Committees: Curriculum Committee Minutes, 11/23/44; Administration Committee Minutes, 10/26/42; 11/16/42; 11/17/44.

29. Staff: Fillmore: notification of son's death, 11/4/43; *Wheaton News,* 11/6/43; Trustees Minutes: 11/8/43. The Norton Veterans of Foreign Wars Post is named for Paul Fillmore and Donald Nason, both of them Norton residents who died in combat during WWII. See also Faculty Meeting Minutes: 3/25/42; 12/1/43; Faculty Committees: Administration Committee Minutes: 4/20/43; 1/25/44; 5/19/44; 4/16/45; 6/1/45; Oral History Project: L. Mandell interview, 1983; M. Hidy interview, 1985; B. Jennings interview, 1983; Ruth Goold (W1953), interview with author, 11/20/2001.

30. Trustees: Soliday #2: Park to Soliday, 3/2/42; Faculty: Cressey: Park to Cressey, 11/6/43; Hunt: Park to Mrs. Hunt, 1/12/42; Riddell: Remick to Riddell, 6/9/43; Trustees Minutes: 5/31/42; 3/8/43; Faculty Meeting Minutes: 3/25/42; *Wheaton News*, 10/10/42; 11/6/43.

31. Trustees Minutes: 11/9/42; 3/8/43; 5/30/43; Trustees: Meadows #10: Remick to Meadows, 2/17/43; Wheaton Histories, Wheaton in World Wars I and II: 1943–45: College ration and food purchase ledgers; Wheaton College, *President's Report to the Board of Trustees, 1944*, p. 12; Oral History Project: K. Burton interview, 1983; D. Littlefield interview, 1983.

32. Trustees Minutes: 11/9/42; 5/30/43; President's Reports to Trustees: 10/14/44; Wheaton College Financial Reports: Audit Report, 6/30/44; Faculty Meeting Minutes: 9/22/43; Faculty: Riddell: Remick to Riddell, 6/9/43; *Wheaton News*, 10/2/43. In 1943 the farm grew all the vegetables consumed by the twenty persons eating in the College dining hall during the summer, as well as 6000 seedlings sold at cost to people in the Norton community. In addition, it harvested large quantities of grapes and apples, along with fresh salad and green produce consumed during the first months of the fall semester. Finally, the farm produced for consumption throughout the academic year: 1000 bushels potatoes, 160 bushels carrots, 75 bushels onions, 1500 lbs. squash, 1460 heads cauliflower, 232 lbs. dried soybeans, 950 heads cabbage, 1200 lbs. yellow turnips, 600 bunches celery, 500 lbs. parsnips. These items were stored in an underground cold storage cellar built into the slope on the south side of SAB. Trustees Minutes: 11/8/43.

33. Ethelind Austin, interview with author, 2/9/2000.

34. Faculty Meeting Minutes: 9/23/42; *Wheaton News*, 10/17/42; 11/7/42; 2/12/44; 3/11/44; 3/18/44; 3/25/44; 4/8/44.

35. Faculty Meeting Minutes: 5/6/42; 5/31/42; Faculty: Korsch: Park to Korsch, 3/11/42; 4/24/42; 3/17/43; 8/13/43, 11/10/43; Faculty Committees: Curriculum Committee Minutes: 9/28/44.

36. See ch. 13; also Faculty Meeting Minutes: 10/21/40.

37. Trustees Minutes: 11/3/41.

38. Faculty Committees: Curriculum Committee Minutes, 10/9/40.

39. Faculty Meeting Minutes: 10/20/40; 5/12/41; 3/16/42; 9/23/42; 12/10/42.

40. Trustees Minutes: 3/8/43; *Wheaton College Bulletin: Catalogue,* 1944–45, pp. 35–36.

41. Faculty Meeting Minutes: 2/8/43; 9/22/43; 9/20/44; Faculty Committees: Curriculum Committee Minutes, 10/20/43; Faculty: Evans: Report of Trip to Industrial Plants, December, 1942; Lange: Meneely to Lange, 9/19/44; President's Reports to Trustees: 10/14/44; Oral History Project: H. Austin interview, 1983. Of the students who participated in the Wartime Studies Program, the person later most widely renowned was Dr. Mary Ellen Avery (W1948), who became Physician-in-Chief and Head of Pediatrics at Children's Hospital Medical Center in Boston, the first woman to head a department at Harvard Medical School. She also was a long-time member of Wheaton's Board of Trustees.

42. Faculty: Cressey: Meneely to Cressey, 3/24/45; President's Reports to Trustees: 6/3/45.

43. See ch. 14.

44. Norton, "Physical Education and Athletics, 1941–69," p. 1.

45. Ibid., p. 4; Faculty Committees: Curriculum Committee Minutes, 12/9/42.

46. Kendall, *Peculiar Institutions,* ch. 19. See also Trustees Minutes: 3/16/42. One example of the war's impact on a New England men's college will suffice. In 1943–44, Bowdoin College's civilian enrollment shrank to 152. The college, like many others in New England, survived because of the presence on campus of military training units, in Bowdoin's case an Army Air Force meteorology unit and a Naval radar school. Charles C. Calhoun, *A Small College in Maine: Two Hundred Years of Bowdoin* (Brunswick, ME: Bowdoin College, 1993), p. 221.

47. President's Reports to Trustees: 11/3/45.

48. Ibid.: 10/14/44; 3/23/45; 6/3/45; Trustees Minutes: 5/31/42; 5/30/43; 3/6/44; 5/28/44; Wheaton Histories, WWI and II: World War II, 1943–45; Faculty: McIntire: Park to McIntire, 9/28/43. The last mention of Jewish candidates per se appears in the minutes of the Board of Admission for 1943. However, separate lists of Jewish applicants, euphemistically called "other" after 1943, were maintained through 1946, disappearing only in the 1947 admissions records pertaining to the Class of 1951. Applicants in the 1940s were asked to designate on their application forms whether Wheaton was their first choice and if they had registered at any other college. The College also was notified by the CEEB whether the person taking the SAT achievement test had designated Wheaton as her first choice. Dean's Office, Admissions: Admissions Committee Minutes and yearly admission files, 1941–47; Class statistics: Classes of 1944–51; Wheaton Alumnae/i in Office: Microfilm Records, 1940, 1946.

49. Trustees Minutes: 3/16/42. A conference of representatives of the nine colleges was held in 1942 and again in 1943. Dean's Office, Admissions: Admissions Board Minutes: 1/8/42; 3/19/43.

50. Trustees Minutes: 5/2/44; see also 3/16/42; 5/31/42; 11/8/43; 9/19/45; *Wheaton News,* 1/17/42; Faculty Meeting Minutes: 9/22/43. Nearly $22,000 was used for scholarships in 1944–45, an unheard of amount in terms of Wheaton's past history. President's Reports to Trustees: 6/3/45.

51. Trustees Minutes: 5/31/42; 5/30/43; 5/2/44; Trustees: Meadows #10: Park to Meadows, 1/25/43.

52. Staff: Dunkle: July, 1942–November, 1943. Unlike faculty who went into military service, Ms. Ziegler was granted only a one-year leave of absence, after which President Park hired Virginia Townsend to take over permanently the position of Admissions Director. Staff: Townsend: Park to Townsend, 6/21/43.

53. For an example of voluntary assumption of increased teaching loads, see Faculty: R. Boas: Park memorandum, 3/24/42. It states that Boas reported to Park that the English Department had voted to seek no new appointments, and that normal resignations would not be filled. Instead the Department as a whole would take on the extra teaching burden.

54. Trustees Minutes: 5/30/43; Faculty Meeting Minutes: 5/28/43; 9/22/43; 9/20/44; Faculty: Ballou: Park to Ballou, 1/18/43; Ballou to Park, 1/28/43; Cressey: 1943–44, passim; W. Nickerson: correspondence, 1945–49: passim. Marna Brady, William Hunt, and Dorothy Mott chose not to return to Wheaton upon conclusion of their military service. Ellen Ballou's leave was terminated by President Park on the grounds that her husband was unlikely to be located near enough to the College in the postwar world for her to resume her duties in the Drama department. Leonard Hill, part-time College Physician, was also granted an indefinite leave, and returned to the College from naval duty in 1947. Barbara Ziegler, former Admissions Director, was granted only a one-year leave, and therefore could not claim a right to return at the end of the war. Ultimately she was rehired in 1951 to reassume her former position.

55. Faculty Meeting Minutes: 5/29/42.

56. Trustees Minutes: 5/31/42.

57. Trustees: J. K. Clark #4: Park to Clark, 5/11/43.

58. Faculty: MacLeod: MacLeod to Park, 4/22/43; Park to MacLeod, 11/11/43.

59. Oral History Project: D. Littlefield interview, 1983.

60. Knapton, *Small Figure*, pp. 189–90; Oral History Project: E. J. Knapton interview, 1983; Trustees Minutes: 5/30/43.

61. Trustees: J. K. Clark #4: Park to Clark, 4/17/43.

62. Ibid.: Meadows #10: Park to Meadows, 3/26/43.

63. Ibid.; See also Trustees Minutes: 5/31/42; 3/8/43; Faculty: Evans: Park Memorandum, 2/19/42; Park to Evans, 3/15/43; Marshall: Park to Marshall, 3/11/43.

64. Trustees: Chase #3: Park to Chase, 9/24/42.

65. Ibid.; see also Trustees Minutes: 11/9/42; 3/8/43; 11/8/43; Faculty Meeting Minutes: 9/23/42; 11/17/43; 11/20/44; President's Reports to Trustees: 3/23/45. The annual cost of the bonuses to the College was estimated in the vicinity of $12,000.

66. Trustees Minutes: 3/16/42.

67. Faculty: Seaver: Park to Seaver, 3/6/42.

68. Confidential Report on Faculty Salaries, November, 1943, appended to Trustees Minutes: 3/6/44.

69. Ibid.

70. Faculty: K. Neilson: Park memoranda, 2/12/42; 3/31/42; Neilson to Park, and his reply, 4/15/42; "Account of Adventures in the Art Department, spring of 1942"— Park Memorandum, 4/15/42; Seaver: Seaver, Randall, and Neilson to Park, 3/5/42; Miscellaneous correspondence between Park and Seaver, 2/2/42—4/15/42.

71. Faculty: Rickers: Park to Rickers, 5/28/42.

72. Ibid.: Rickers: 2/18/42–7/21/42; Park memoranda, 4/4/44; 4/6/44; Marshall: Marshall to Park, 3/9/42; Park to Marshall, 3/11/42; L. Boas: Boas to Park, 2/5/42; Park to Boas, 2/6/42; Mandell: Park memorandum, 2/4/42.

73. Ibid.: K. Neilson: Neilson to Park, 8/19/43; Park to Remick, 8/23/43; Neilson to Park, 8/27/43; Park to Neilson, 9/9/43; Seaver: Remick to Seaver, 8/24/43; Seaver to Remick, 8/27/43; Seaver to Park, 8/28/43; Van Ingen (Elarth): 1942–1946, passim.

74. See ch. 13.

75. Faculty: Rickers: Park to Rickers, 6/26/42; 7/7/42.

76. Trustees Minutes: 3/6/44.

77. Faculty: Shipley: Park to Shipley, 3/14/44.

78. Ibid.: Hubbard: Park to Hubbard, 6/28/34; 9/11/41.

79. Ibid.: Park memorandum, 3/31/44.

80. Ibid.; see also Park to Hubbard, 2/4/42; Trustees Minutes: 3/16/42.

81. President's Reports to Trustees: 3/6/44.

82. Trustees Minutes: 3/6/44; Faculty: Hubbard: Student Petition re Hubbard, 1/22/44; Park Memorandum of meeting with Gulley and Knapton, 3/31/44.

83. Faculty: Hubbard: Hubbard to Board of Trustees, 3/31/44.

84. Ibid.: Board of Trustees to Hubbard, 3/10/44; Trustee Finance Committee Approval of Settlement, 3/20/44; Trustees Minutes: 5/2/44; Trustees: Meadows #10: Park to Meadows, 5/9/44.

85. Faculty: Hubbard: Hubbard to Marshall, 4/30/44; Ludlum to Park, 5/11/44.

86. Ibid.: Park to Ludlum, 7/20/44; see also Park to Ludlum, 5/18/44; Trustee Minutes: 5/28/44; 7/21/44.

87. Faculty: Hubbard: Knapton to Boas, 5/28/44.

88. "Statement on the Question of Tenure," 6/1/44, appended to Trustees Minutes: 5/28/44.

89. Ibid.

90. Faculty: Clewes: Park to Clewes, 4/7/44; see also Gulley to Park, 3/10/43; Park memorandum, 3/17/44.

91. See ch. 9.

92. See chs. 4, 5.

93. A crude statistical survey indicates that between 1926 and 1932, 13 of approximately 50 faculty published at least one scholarly book or article. For the period 1932 to 1939, the numbers were 34 out of 57, while between 1939 and 1944 only 16 out of a faculty averaging 68 in size published a professionally related book or article. Wheaton College, *Report of the President*, 1932, *President's Report* 1939, 1944.

94. Oral History Project: K. Burton interview, 1983; E. J. Knapton interview, 1983; M. Hidy interview, 1985; Faculty: W. Nickerson: Park memorandum, 4/14/44.

95. Faculty: Shipley: Park memoranda, 9/9/42; 9/22/43; Park to Shipley, 11/2/42. Trustees Minutes: 11/9/42; Faculty Meeting Minutes: 9/23/42.

96. Jennings, *Chemistry at Wheaton*, p. 68; Faculty: Evans: Park memorandum, 7/43; Marshall: Marshall to Remick, 6/10/43; E. J. Knapton: Correspondence between Park and Spencer Thermostat, 7/14/43; 7/16/43; 7/20/43; Knapton, *Small Figure*, pp. 190–91; Oral History Project: E. J. Knapton interview, 1983. Spencer Thermostat subsequently became part of Texas Instruments.

97. Faculty Meeting Minutes: 11/17/43.

98. Smart/Park: Park correspondence: Park to Trustees, 2/20/43. Aside from President Park's statement to the faculty on November 17, 1943, that he had indicated his plans to retire verbally to the Board of Trustees "more than a year ago," there is nothing on record to indicate any mention of this matter prior to the submission of his formal letter of resignation on February 20, 1943.

99. Trustees Minutes: 3/8/43; Trustees: J. K. Clark #3: Clark to Park, 3/6/43; 3/12/43; Meadows #10: Park to Meadows, 3/26/43; Oral History Project: R. Chapman interview, 1983. The third member of the selection committee was alumnae trustee Josephine Dawson (W1926).

100. President's Reports to Trustees: 11/8/43; see also Trustees Minutes: 11/8/43; Trustees: J. K. Clark #4: Park to Boas, 11/15/43; Chapman, #1: Park to Chapman, 1/11/44.

101. Trustees: Meadows #10: Park to Meadows, 11/24/43.

102. Ibid.: J. K. Clark #4: 11/19/43; see also Park to Clark, 11/9/43; Clark to Boas, 11/13/43; Park to Clark, 11/15/43.

103. Faculty Meeting Minutes: 12/1/43. At Dr. Park's final Commencement ceremony on May 28, 1944, in a move designed both to please the President and to say thank you for years of unpaid service to the College, the Board of Trustees awarded an honorary Doctor of Humane Letters degree to Dr. Park's wife, Grace Burtt Park. Trustees Minutes: 5/2/44.

104. Trustees: Chapman #1: Park to Chapman, 11/19/43. See also *Wheaton News*, 11/20/43.

105. Trustees: J. K. Clark #5: Clark to Park, 4/11/44.

106. Knapton, *Small Figure*, p. 198; see also Oral History Project: E. J. Knapton interview, 1983.

107. Trustees: Chase #3: Chase to Park, 4/26/44; Park to Chase, 4/27/44.

108. Trustees Minutes: 5/2/44; Trustees: J. K. Clark #5: Park to Clark, 5/4/44; 5/18/44; Chase #3: Chase to Park, 5/29/44; Faculty Meeting Minutes: 5/26/44; *Wheaton News*, 5/13/44. At its meeting on May 28, the Board voted an additional allowance of $1500 to the Meneelys to enable them to buy new furnishings for the President's House. Trustees Minutes: 5/28/44.

109. Trustees: Chase #3: Park to Chase, 2/10/44; Oral History Project: R. Chapman interview, 1983; M. Reynolds interview, 1984.

110. Trustees: J. K. Clark #5: Clark to Meneely, 7/24/44; see also Trustees Minutes: 3/6/44; 7/21/44.

111. Faculty: Littlefield: Park to Littlefield, 3/21/44; Oral History Project: D. Littlefield interview, 1983; J. Chidsey interview, 1983.

112. Wheaton College, *The President's Report, 1944,* pp. 15–16.

113. Ibid.: p. 18.

114. Ibid.; see also Trustees Minutes: 3/6/44, Confidential Report on Faculty Salaries, November, 1943; President's Report Mailed in Advance of Meeting, February, 1944.

115. Wheaton College, *The President's Report, 1944*, p. 18.

16

Riding Out the Storm: The Great Art Center Controversy, 1944–1946

The transition from seminary to college occurred only thirty-two years ago, managed under the skillful hand of Dr. Samuel Valentine Cole. Since then . . . Wheaton college has weathered the shocks of war, flamboyant prosperity and grinding depression, and today takes rank among the best of our women's colleges. It has resisted the modern cult of bigness, the lure of headlines, the lust for novelty. It has preserved its character, cherishing its old ideals while embracing new ideas of demonstrated worth. It has sought to foster in its students that richness of life which springs from integrity of character and soundness of learning.[1]

So SPOKE ALEXANDER HOWARD MENEELY in his address on the occasion of his inauguration as Wheaton's third president on October 14, 1944. Paying tribute to those who had come before him, and to the timeless utility of "liberal studies, taught in a liberal spirit," President Meneely went on to posit that for women in the coming postwar world the need for a "well-rounded general education" would be greater than ever.

At the outset may I hazard the assumption that the aims and the work of a woman's college today do not materially differ, save in particulars, from those of the men's colleges. The day has long since passed, if it ever existed, when women were exposed to education to enhance their prospects of a good marriage. The modern woman, while happily not indifferent to that ancient and honorable estate, expects to be an active force in the shaping of society. No field or endeavor is alien to her influence. No avenue to a career is any longer completely barred to her. Her service to the public welfare has become indispensable in war as well as in the happier times of peace. Women's education must be shaped accordingly.[2]

Enlightened words, spoken in honest anticipation of the brave new world that everyone assumed would emerge before too long from the turmoil and chaos of global military conflict. And indeed, the seventeen years of the Meneely administration almost exactly encompassed what historians today see as the period of postwar economic and social recovery, a recovery highlighted by a return, at least in America and Western Europe, to a level of economic prosperity unknown since the 1920s.

400

Moreover, the upward economic and social mobility engendered by the industrial and commercial expansion of the 1950s opened the doors to higher education and career prospects for large segments of society for whom those avenues had been effectively closed in the previous decades. All of this was tempered in turn by the anxieties created by the advent of the atomic age of military weaponry, coupled with the political, economic, military and ideological bipolarization of the globe into two conflicting and contesting spheres, one led by those in power in Washington, D.C., the other by their counterparts in Moscow.

Notwithstanding President Meneely's tentative, and perhaps unconscious, inaugural delineation of a new "feminist" vision, for most women in America these years turned out to be more reversionary than visionary. The return of millions of service personnel, most of them men, led to the rapid reduction of positions available for women in the workforce. There was a deep desire on the part of members of both genders to put the war era behind them and return to a "normal" existence as quickly as possible. This was broadly defined as marriage, family, and home, with men engaged in the traditional role of breadwinners and the concomitant reversion of women to the equally traditional functions of homemakers and child rearers.

For thousands of returning military veterans, these goals were furthered by the availability of money for both educational and housing assistance provided under the auspices of special federal legislation authorizing these veterans' benefits. This support also made it easier for veterans to marry and start families while still in the process of completing their education, and long before they had attained the income level normally needed for such a course of action. Women assisted in this process by working at what both spouses viewed as temporary jobs, which would last only until such time as both could revert to the traditional gender roles of breadwinner and homemaker.[3]

Not only was this pattern established by returning veterans and the wives, fiancées and girlfriends they came back to—it also was adopted by the generation of young men and women who came of age in these early postwar years. Those who did not go on to college routinely married within a year or two of graduating from high school, or as soon as the young men completed their military draft service. Men who did attend college more often than not married immediately upon graduation, or shortly thereafter, often to younger women who left college in order to get on with the primary life role they saw for themselves. This usually meant working for pay while husbands completed their professional training, and then assuming the lifetime role of mothers and homemakers. They would also become active participants in voluntary charitable and community programs on behalf of a family unit whose male adult member was far too busy earning the family income to engage in such activities. Therefore, most young women tended to think of paid work outside the home in terms of a job, not a career, regarding it as temporarily necessary in order to support themselves until the "right man" came along, or until that right man, already found, had gotten himself launched on his own permanent professional career.[4]

For Wheaton, these factors impacted on the College in different ways at different times. Applications for admission increased dramatically in the first years after the war, only to be followed by a sharp downturn as the decade came to an end and a new one began. Increasing economic prosperity again brought a rising tide of applications in the mid 1950s, yet at the same time the number of entering students who stayed until graduation declined substantially. Efforts to persuade young women to think in terms of career options and preparation more often than not fell on unlistening or uncomprehending ears. Lamenting that she tried time and again to make students understand what it would be like to be thirty-five years old, Academic Dean Elizabeth May commented later: "It was as though we were projecting TV with color and their receivers were all black and white; they couldn't understand what their lives would be like, that this was something very important."[5]

Thus, a redefining of appropriate and legitimate roles for women in the economic and social world of the late 1940s and 1950s did not take place, nor did most women seek to alter those that existed. In 1955, two-time Democratic presidential candidate Adlai Stevenson found it totally appropriate to urge the graduating class at Smith College to use their Smith education to become the most supportive wives and nurturing mothers possible in their subsequent careers as homemakers for the professional and business leaders of the free world. Not all the graduates received this message kindly, but overall Stevenson's comments may be taken as accurately reflecting the stereotypical images of gender roles prevalent in the 1950s, and the general, if not unanimous, acceptance of these concepts by generations young and old.[6]

The man chosen to lead Wheaton out of the war years and into the postwar era was not at all similar in personality or administrative style to his ebullient, witty, autocratic predecessor. A historian by profession, Howard Meneely came to Wheaton from the Dartmouth history department, and he remained throughout his term as President an academic at heart, evincing minimal interest in financial matters or fund-raising, and even less in issues relating to public relations.[7] Described by many as quiet, decent, and somewhat self-effacing, he operated in a consultative manner with faculty and the Board of Trustees that was far removed from the methods used by President Park in dealing with both groups. Formal and reserved in his administrative style, he maintained thoughout his tenure an open door policy which made him extremely accessible to any and all who wished to consult him on matters large and small. "I am a Serious Fellow," he once commented, and certainly there was little of the effervescence and wit that had characterized his predecessor.[8]

Not that President Meneely lacked a sense of humor. According to witnesses, his prepared set-piece commentaries at the annual Christmas banquet were often hilarious in their characterizations and presentation. Writing to new Academic Dean Elizabeth May in March, 1950, the President noted that previous Deans traditionally had gone to the Mansfield train station at noon to see students off on the day spring break began. Since Dean May was going to be away from Norton, he indicated that he would do the honors instead. "I do not expect to kiss all five hundred goodbye," he wrote, "but I am quite willing to take on those who make a bid at a farewell gesture."[9]

The few members of the staff or faculty who got to know Howard Meneely socially found him much more relaxed and voluble in small group settings. Insisting on the use of Mr., Mrs., or Miss at all times in his office, he was equally determined that in his home his secretary, Marjorie Person Ford, should call him Howard, telling her when she forgot that what she needed was another manhattan. The Meneelys developed a close friendship with the College Physician, Ronald Duffield and his wife, and also with Llewellyn Jennings, a local accountant, and his wife Bojan, who was an assistant professor in the Chemistry department; the six of them often got together for dinner at each other's homes. But above all, Howard Meneely was very much a private individual, and this was enhanced by the similar outlook of his wife, whose poor health and disinclination to entertain meant that the President's house was only rarely used for College functions or entertainment. "When President Meneely came home from his office they would turn out the porch light and pull the shades—and that was that!" commented E. J. Knapton.[10]

Alexander Howard Meneely,
President, 1944-1961.

Nor did the new President develop, as had his predecessor, a coterie of faculty upon whom he particularly relied for advice and guidance. Unlike Dr. Park, who was away from campus often on various speaking engagements, President Meneely rarely left Norton during the academic year. "The sense of his presence on campus was <u>very</u> great," commented Philosophy Professor Holcombe Austin, who noted that Meneely was renowned for "forever going into buildings in the evening to turn off the lights."[11] Not possessing the social skills of Dr. Park, he made up for it in his conscientious and evenhanded approach to College affairs and to its personnel, and by being a good listener to the concerns of all who came to his office. Like his predecessors, President Meneely continued to be involved in the most minute affairs of the College, ranging from requests for lawn seeding and bathroom renovations to authorizing a $100 increase in a departmental library budget. In 1950, distressed over escalating prices, he decided to go to Boston himself and personally purchase furniture needed by the College.[12]

Without question the new President lacked the personal charisma and charm that his predecessor had used to such good effect in his one-on-one meetings with faculty members. Contrasting the methods and styles of Drs. Park and Meneely, English Professor Katherine Burton later commented that when President Park got two requests from faculty members he would say, "well, maybe" in a manner that would lead both petitioners to think "yes." Later one would get what was asked for and be grateful, and the other would call him a liar. In contrast, President Meneely would say "well, maybe" in a way that would lead both persons who had asked to think "no." Later one would be granted the request, but not feel grateful because of having had to "battle" the President to get it, and the other would just feel bitter. Park, she commented, would say "Where's your sense of humor?" and you had to laugh as you gave in. Meneely would say "Where's your sense of responsibility?," which made you feel guilty even as you conceded the issue.[13]

Described by Board Chairman Richard Chapman as "Scotch, conservative and cautious by nature," the President's great strength was that coming from an academic background he understood the academic world, and in particular the faculty who inhabited it, as had neither of the previous two Presidents.[14] Characterized as forceful in his leadership, he also was willing to delegate authority to his senior administrators and to back them to the hilt, even when their decisions might well be ones for which he did not particularly care. Sometimes, Academic Dean Elizabeth May recalled, when he did not think a particular course of action she was recommending was a good idea, he would say, "You go ahead and do it and don't let me know about it."[15] Believing in making haste slowly, he was willing to allow the faculty in its deliberations both greater power and time to institute change. He also proved to be very sensitive to issues involving faculty compensation, benefits, and the living and boarding requirements imposed on most of the single women members of the teaching staff.[16]

In the same manner, Dr. Meneely gracefully accepted the new restrictions on presidential power imposed by the Board of Trustees as he entered into office. Mindful of the serious unrest on the Board over the autocratic manner in which President Park had operated in relation to the trustees, he expressed himself as thoroughly comfortable with the fact that the chairmanship of the Board was no longer held by the President. His presentations to the Board were always couched in consultative terms, rather than as a prescribed plan of action which the Board was expected dutifully to approve. As a result the Board of Trustees, which was expanded from fifteen to twenty members in 1947, and from 1949 on included two, rather than one, elected alumnae trustees, played a much more important role in policy formulation than it had under Dr. Park. In fact, in at least two major instances—ending required attendance at Sunday church services and expanding the size of the College—the Board was the initiator of new and controversial courses of action.[17]

The first year of the Meneely administration proved to be a classic example of what is referred to in the world of academia as a "honeymoon" period, often granted, consciously or unconsciously, by faculty and students to a new President or Academic Dean during his or her first year in office. During this time the new administrator is reluctant to introduce new initiatives until he has had time to learn a good deal more about the inner workings of his new institution than he knew when he arrived. The faculty and staff, relieved to be free of whatever personality and methodological irritants of the previous administration had particularly annoyed them, approaches the new leadership with considerable good-will and the hope that issues ignored, or at least not dealt with, by the old administration will now receive a more sympathetic hearing, and even perhaps some resultant positive action.

For such a period of relative calm to occur, the times also must be propitious. External and internal pressures on the institution need to be relatively minimal, or at least not loom as crises demanding immediate attention. Such was the case in 1944 when Howard Meneely assumed office. Anxiety as to the eventual outcome of the war had all but disappeared, though the personal emotional trauma created by events of the times of course remained severe. The pattern of wartime existence on the Wheaton campus had long since become well established and required no change or alteration. Moreover, on-going wartime restrictions and regulations precluded, as everyone recognized, addressing many issues involving staffing, wages, building construction, and a host of other matters with any but the most stop-gap measures. Until the war ended everything had, for the most part, to be "put on hold." Thus in many respects the academic year 1944–45 proved to be an ideal time for the College and its new administration to get to know one another.

There was, however, one new initiative undertaken by the President during his first year in office. Almost immediately President Meneely set out to address a set of issues that had increasingly concerned the faculty during the last years of the previous administration. Under President Park, faculty committees had been completely dominated by the President. With the exception of the Administration Committee, which dealt with student academic issues, and the newly created Committee on Conference with the Trustees, Dr. Park had appointed the members of all faculty committees. He also had sat as a member on all of them, controlled the agenda, and most often served as the chair. President Meneely, coming directly from the faculty at Dartmouth where he had played a major role in a reorganization of faculty governance, wasted little time in setting out to overhaul the committee system at Wheaton. In November, 1944, he asked the faculty to create a special "Committee on Committees" to consult with the President regarding committee reform. The following January, Dr. Meneely presented his suggestions to that committee, which accepted them with minimal change, and after lengthy discussions in full faculty meetings and some minor fine tuning, the new system was voted in at the faculty meeting in October, 1945.[18]

Remarking that in his experience, when a "new administrator comes in, he continues to live at the institution where he was before that," Professor Holcombe Austin noted, "so we got a Dartmouth set-up here, which I think worked pretty well."[19] Eight committees with duties involving the academic curriculum, admissions, scholarships, student academic affairs, the library, academic calendar and catalogue, public events, and student health were empowered to implement existing faculty legislation. They were also authorized to draft and bring to the faculty for action any new policy initiatives deemed necessary. In addition, the duties of the Committee on Conference with the Trustees were expanded to include, at the President's request, serving as an Advisory Committee to the President concerning all general matters on which he wished to consult.[20]

Members of these committees were to be selected either by direct faculty preferential ballot, or by a new standing committee, the Committee on Committees, which would submit a list of its nominees to the President for his review and final approval. However, the three members of this committee were to be appointed by the President, rather than elected by the faculty. In retaining this authority, President Meneely commented privately, "I thought it inexpedient for a new president to depart much further from existing practice than is provided in the proposal. Moreover, I have thought that the trustees might not want me to at this early stage in my administration."[21]

In assessing this matter, the President proved to be an astute appraiser of trustee and faculty sentiment. Ten years later in 1955, the faculty, with the President's blessing, did vote to elect the members of the Committee on Committees. However, apprehensive about the politicking that might go on, the faculty overwhelmingly rejected the opportunity to nominate the slate of candidates for that committee through use of a preferential ballot, preferring to allow the President to nominate two persons for each vacancy.[22]

This restructuring of the committee system, and the accompanying re-definition of various committee duties and responsibilities, constituted a permanent transition from the fundamentally paternalistic and autocratic method of academic governance that had characterized the administrations of Presidents Cole and Park. From 1945 on, the internal administration of much of the routine academic business of the College, as well as development and control of policies involving the curriculum and most academic activities, became the purview of the faculty. The result was that delineation and oversight of academic, admissions, health, and library matters subsequently involved much more of a collaborative effort between administration and faculty than had been the case in prior years.

"I favor faculty participation since it is in line with the common practice in the colleges," President Meneely stated when he presented these changes to the Board of Trustees for their approval. "I am inclined to think it desirable for the Faculty to have responsibility in such matters." Noting that since "the Statutes authorize the President 'to suspend or veto any act of the Faculty when, in his judgment, it seems expedient to do so'," he sought to alleviate the Board's concerns by maintaining that this provision afforded "ample protection in the event that the Faculty should act in a way contrary to the best interests of the college."[23] Nine years later he commented: "Faculty should be accorded the privilege of choosing committee members in whatever manner they prefer."[24]

This revision of the committee structure and the enhanced role it gave to the faculty in formulating academic policy, advising the President on administrative affairs, and administering student academic affairs did much to assuage dissatisfaction with what many faculty had perceived as increasingly high-handed administrative behavior by President Park in his final years. Decades later faculty who were present in 1944–45 would assess the voluntary granting to the faculty of vastly increased influence and authority in matters of curriculum and academic policy as the single greatest contribution of the Meneely presidency. Certainly it created among many on the teaching staff a reservoir of good will which the President found he sorely needed when a crisis of major proportions exploded on campus in the early months of 1946, a crisis so severe that it created bitter divisions within the faculty, student and alumnae bodies, and according to some accounts, came close to leading to a Presidential resignation.[25]

The issue was hardly new, in fact its origins went well back into the prewar period. The long-standing need for an Art Center, which would include facilities for the art and music departments along with the extra-curricular drama program, had been the focus of a national design competition in 1938 that had brought Wheaton enormous amounts of favorable publicity in architectural circles. Now, with the war concluded, questions regarding the design and future construction of the Art Center reappeared as issues of concern and controversy.[26]

In 1939, the Board of Trustees had requested the winner of the competition, the firm of Hornbostel and Bennett, to submit new severely scaled-down plans for an arts complex, preferably one that could be built in stages. This was done, and in March, 1940, President Park recommended positively to the Board of Trustees that Wheaton proceed with the central and most important of the three sections. This recommendation was initially approved by the trustees, but in June, 1940, the vote was rescinded on the grounds that a declining stock market had so lessened the value of stocks scheduled to be sold to fund the construction that it was inappropriate for the College to take the "considerable loss" a stock sale at that time would produce. However, in November, 1940, the Board did authorize the future commitment of $50,000 in College funds toward the Art Center if that sum were matched by new contributions from outside.[27]

Subsequently, of course, the advent of war made any new construction impossible, nor were funds in fact raised or set aside for that eventual purpose. However, despite the lack of progress in building the Art Center, the fact that the prize-winning architects had been retained to design and supervise the construction of the highly successful Modernist Student Alumnae Building, plus Modernist wings to the Science Building and the Library, served to cement Wheaton's position as the pioneering leader for the Modernist movement in its attempts to penetrate traditional architectural styles found on American college and university campuses.

Thus as the end of the war approached, and with it the anticipated lifting of restrictions on domestic building projects, it was natural that proponents of the new Art Center should begin to hope that the long-delayed construction might begin in the reasonably near future. In April, 1945, in an open meeting for all interested Wheaton students, the Head of the Art Department, Esther Seaver, described the proposed structure in detail, commenting that "Wheaton committed itself to a modern American tradition rather that a European abstract style when it chose the plans of Hornbostel and Bennett." The Art Center, she went on "will fit into the dream castle of the Wheaton of tomorrow."[28]

Architects Richard Bennett and Caleb Hornbostel display their winning design in the 1938 Art Center Competition.

President Meneely was not unsympathetic. "Our Departments of Art and Music have been doing superior work with their present limited facilities," he reported to the Board of Trustees in June, 1945. "There is reason to believe that they and our drama staff could do much better if there were an Art Center." The problem was that the College, though emerging from the war years financially stable, had no appreciable funds held specifically in reserve for constructing this building. "I sincerely hope," the President went on, "that ways and means may be found within the next few years to bring this enterprise to realization."[29]

However, when hostilities ceased in the summer of 1945, the College also found itself faced with a list of accumulated projects and fiscal demands that in the eyes of many, including the new President, seemed of more immediate importance. These included refurbishing and increasing the bathroom facilities in several dormitories, providing off-campus residential quarters for single women faculty, and the erection of a new classroom building and an infirmary.

On top of this President Meneely, an academic himself, was acutely aware of the pressing need to improve faculty salaries and benefits in order to attract and retain faculty. In fact, faculty compensation proved to be perhaps the most critical issue facing Wheaton in the immediate postwar years. The College was challenged not only by a national inflationary tide, but also by the increased competition for faculty coming from men's and coed institutions, most of which sought additional teaching staff as they struggled to accommodate the thousands of returning veterans who, financed by the G.I. Bill, swelled undergraduate enrollment in the years following the war.

Thus, when President Meneely began discussing refurbishing and construction projects with the Board of Trustees in the fall of 1945, the Art Center was not even part of their considered agenda. But what *was* needed, President Meneely believed strongly, was some long range planning regarding the development of the campus, especially in terms of the location of faculty housing, an infirmary, and a new classroom building. To that end he suggested to the Board that it was time to engage a new "college architect," who could serve in the same capacity that Cram and Ferguson had in the major development of the campus during the first three and one-half decades of the century. The trustees agreed; moreover they also subscribed to Meneely's suggestion that it was important that someone be found who would plan future development in accordance with "the prevailing architecture" found on the Wheaton campus.[30]

The President's preference, by his own admission, was for the Georgian style architecture used by Cram and Ferguson in their development of the Wheaton campus. Thus it was hardly surprising that in December, 1945, the President and the Grounds and Building Committee of the Board of Trustees chose the Boston firm of Perry, Shaw & Hepburn, renowned for its work in designing the colonial restoration of Williamsburg, Virginia, to be the official College Architects.[31]

It turned out that exactly what this title meant was something on which the President and the Chairman of the Board of Trustees, Joseph Soliday differed. The President assumed that it implied that "all future construction would be in the colonial style, [and] that Perry, Shaw & Hepburn would do the work."[32] The Chair of the Board, however, subsequently indicated that it was his understanding that the College Architects would render advice as to long-range planning for campus development and on the location of proposed buildings, but would be retained in terms of actual design and construction of any given building only by an express vote of the Board. Despite this difference of opinion, which subsequently turned out to be a critical one, there is abundant evidence that, as Dr. Meneely stated in a letter to President Park, the Board and the President concurred that in planning future construction "the general sentiment was in favor of adhering to the prevailing architectural style rather than going forward with a strictly contemporary type of architecture."[33]

At the trustees' meeting on November 3, 1945, the President asked for and received permission, after consultation with the Grounds and Building Committee, to obtain "preliminary plans for such projects as in their opinion should be undertaken without delay."[34] Though the Art Center was briefly discussed, it was not included in this list, and no action relative to it was taken. Immediately following the appointment of Perry, Shaw & Hepburn, the firm was assigned the task of designing housing units for single faculty to be located on a plot of land on Howard Street next to the old infirmary and more or less across from the Everett Hall complex.[35]

But the Board's affirmation that future construction should adhere to the "prevailing style of architecture at Wheaton," and the subsequent retention of a firm known for its Georgian colonial restoration projects, immediately aroused great concern among those who had long promoted a transition to Modernist construction on the campus. Chief among these was Esther Seaver, Head of the Art Department, whose brainchild the 1938 competition had been, and who had served as Wheaton's representative on the jury that selected the winning architects. Energetic, forceful, a master teacher and a productive scholar, Dr. Seaver had proved over the years to be a dominant force on campus, and often a thorn in the side of the President. Possessing independent financial resources, she rented an apartment in Cambridge to which she could flee from her required Wheaton lodgings on weekends and vacations. She had repeatedly irritated Dr. Park by ordering Art Department supplies direct from the supplier without receiving business office approval or using the College invoice forms. Often she would pay for supplies herself and then bill the College for reimbursement, paying little or no attention to authorized spending levels in the departmental budget. She had not hesitated to use the threat of personal resignation in a confrontation with President Park in 1942 over his failure to promote a member of the Art Department, and she apparently was quick to perceive a personal slight in a comment or letter where none was intended.[36]

Having got wind of the developing situation, Miss Seaver was already primed for a fight well before the November trustees' meeting and the decision to retain Perry, Hepburn & Shaw. Meeting with trustee Harriet Hughes in New York prior to the Board meeting, Professor Seaver told Miss Hughes that she would probably resign if the College "went Georgian."[37] And indeed she was as good as her word. On January 1, 1946, she submitted a letter of resignation to President Meneely, couched in cordial terms, but making unmistakably clear her reasons for doing so.

> First, I believe Wheaton's recent architectural decision is a distinct break of faith with the various institutions and individuals involved in the Art Center Competition. As one of the sponsors of that Competition who is still loyal to the principles involved I cannot remain at Wheaton and thus appear to give tacit approval to this change. As I understand this the selection of a college architect for all future works will preclude carrying out

Esther Seaver, Professor of Art,
1931-1946.

the terms of the Art Center competition that stated the winner of the competition would be the architect when and if the building were built. Parenthetically, I could not even be interested in an Art Center built in the traditional styles.

My second reason for wishing to be released from my contract at the end of the year is that I could not continue to serve loyally an administration and Board of Trustees, who in the field of architecture, choose to relinquish the place of leadership that Wheaton has enjoyed in recent years. To move into the future walking backwards does not in any way fit into my educational philosophy and it would be impossible for me to serve with the same enthusiasm and energy that I have tried to give all my work at Wheaton during the past sixteeen years.[38]

In his reponse the President indicated that because of past conversations he was not "completely surprised" at Seaver's decision, but viewed it with "acute disappointment." "I need hardly say that I understand and respect your decision since I realize how honestly and sincerely you are committed to the merits of contemporary architecture. . . . I cling to the hope that you will change your mind, although your letter gives me no ground for such a hope."[39]

This response in many ways confirmed that, at least as far as the President's views were concerned, Miss Seaver's assumption that the door to construction of a Modernist Art Center had been closed was indeed accurate. But the fight was only beginning. Miss Seaver lost no time in notifying alumnae and friends in the architectural world of what had taken place. Nor was she loath, upon returning to Norton after the Christmas recess, to discuss the matter clandestinely but widely with colleagues and a few students.

However, it was only when a lengthy telegram to the *Wheaton News* from an architect and alumna, Margaret King Hunter (W1941), was published within a highlighted black border on the front page of the *News* on January 12, 1946, that the "Art Center Controversy," as it later came to be called, began to escalate out of control. Charging that "Wheaton is about to abandon the winning design for the art center and quietly substitute for it a Georgian building," Mrs. Hunter expressed surprise "that the college would consider violation of a professional code of ethics in this substitution, and that it is willing to destroy the validity of such a well established procedure as a national competition." All great architecture, she went on "is a reflection of the life and techniques of its time and its freedom from the decadence of copy-book clichés which do not represent the thought and abilities of living people." The College's physical structure "should reflect the fact that the college is fitting young women to play a vital role in contemporary life." Asserting her pride in what Wheaton had done in building SAB, Mrs. Hunter decried the fact that with this decision Wheaton faced losing its well-earned leadership position. In conclusion she urged students and alumnae to protest strongly to the administration and to do it immediately. In an accompanying editorial, the editors of *News* attested that they had checked into the matter, and found that Mrs. Hunter's account "expresses the truth of the matter pretty clearly."[40]

Many alumnae and parents subscribed to the *News*, and over the next several weeks letters from both constituencies poured in, sent to the President and also on occasion directly to the Chair of the Board of Trustees, Joseph Soliday. Most were strongly and politely worded, a few were vituperative and occasionally sarcastic. Only two or three supported the purported return to Georgian style buildings. In a letter sent both to the President and to the *News*, which published it, Janet Hoffman Shands (W1937) and her husband argued that one of the major lessons of the war was that "if we do not loosen the dead hand of tradition, we are lost."

> Ideas do not occur alone and unrelated. It is almost inevitable that one who rejects a new idea in building, or in science, literature, art, or history because it is new will also reject a new idea in human relationships simply because of its novelty. . . .
> If Wheaton must build a palace fit for the transplanted, dull-witted princes of an unimportant, mid-European principality, is it not an anachronism to light it with electricity? Is it not incongruous to install plumbing? And finally, should not the instructors, to be in tune with their surroundings, address their classes clad in knee pants and topped with powdered wigs?[41]

But reaction from Wheaton's external constituency was nothing compared to the indignation Mrs. Hunter's telegram created within the undergraduate student body. The College Government Association scheduled a mass meeting for February 14, and invited Mrs. Hunter to come to campus to address the gathering. Attendance at mass meetings was mandatory for students, voluntary for faculty, and Plimpton Hall was filled to overflowing when the meeting convened that evening. Mrs. Hunter's address mainly reiterated the contents of her original communication. Quoting *Time* magazine's January, 1938, comment that "the Wheaton College project has been called the most important competition in the U.S. since the world-wide competition for the Chicago Tribune Tower in 1922," she asserted: "Modern architecture is a basic ideal, not a face you put on a building. Nor is it a so-called 'functional plan' with a traditional face. No plan can possibly be functional when dictated by a traditional exterior."[42]

Following Mrs. Hunter's comments, President Meneely walked from the back of the room to the podium and read a prepared statement. Decrying Mrs. Hunter's failure to request information either from him or the Board of Trustees before telegraphing to the *News*, he lashed out at the sensationalism of the newspaper's black-bordered front page display of the telegram, characterizing it as "a gross violation of the ethical principles that should characterize journalism." Stating that he had become "increasingly concerned over the hysteria which has come to characterize this campus," he labelled the methods used by those who were agitating as "very much the same kind of tactics which have been used with devastating effect from time to time all over the world in the last twenty years with such tragic consequences to mankind." At a time when the campus was approaching final exams, he maintained, such turmoil could not but have a highly negative effect.[43]

The President went on to explain and defend the Board of Trustees' right to decide to engage a consulting architect and to choose what firm that should be. Maintaining that neither he nor the Board owed any explanation for actions that were exclusively theirs to take, he nonetheless detailed the process by which the trustees had reached their conclusion, and reasserted and defended the Board's decision to adhere to "the prevailing architecture of the campus" in future building construction.

> There was nothing sly or underhanded in any of the decisions reached, and I repudiate utterly any insinuation to the contrary. At every step the Board of Trustees was acting within its authority and in accordance with its statutory responsibility. The members of the Board of Trustees are men and women of high character, of honor, and of integrity, and I do not need to defend the honor or the good faith of the Board of Trustees, collectively or individually. . . . They do not need to be instructed in the matter of ethics or morals by any alumna or by any undergraduate of Wheaton College.
>
> As for my own course in this matter, I defy anybody to prove that there has been anything dishonest or any lack of candor in anything which I have done. I repeat that I regret the necessity of my presence at this meet-

ing. I deplore the way in which a small body of reckless and irresponsible students have persisted in upsetting the life of this college community. I think the time has come for you undergraduates to rise up and demand a cessation of this perpetual agitation. Your own welfare is being impaired, and so too, in my judgment, is the welfare of this college.[44]

With that the President left the platform and strode from the room. "It was the most dramatic moment I experienced in all my years at Wheaton," Professor Holcombe Austin later recalled. Describing the President as "literally white with anger," Austin remembered vividly the high level of tension within the room.[45] "We felt the administration and the trustees had betrayed us," commented Mary Ellen Avery (W1948). "We didn't believe their explanations."[46]

The final speaker was a member of the class of 1946, Mary Tousey, who cited the students' pride in the Modernist form of SAB and the Library and Science Center wings. Quoting from a 1944 book, *Built in the USA*, which had been published by the Museum of Modern Art, she noted its assertion that the 1938 competition constituted "perhaps the first time that an American college was willing or, indeed, eager to have a building of non-traditional design." She presented a resolution that was overwhelmingly endorsed, asking the Board of Trustees to "reconsider the implications of changing Wheaton's architectural policies." However, it was decided that the final wording and content of the resolution should be referred to a student-faculty coordinating committee that had just been authorized a few days earlier, and that the matter should be brought back to the student body for ultimate approval after final examinations, when the college reconvened for the second semester.[47]

In the weeks that followed, the drumbeats of contention and discord only grew louder. The text of the speeches by Mrs. Hunter and Miss Tousey were published in the *News*, but the President refused to give similar permission, which irritated many of those who subscribed to the paper, or to whom copies of the issue containing the account of the January 14 meeting were sent. Alerted by Esther Seaver and her supporters, both the Curator and the Director of Research on Painting and Sculpture at the Museum of Modern Art in New York, which had cosponsored the original competition, wrote letters protesting Wheaton's decision to abandon modern architecture, and asserting that the terms of the competition required that the Center, if built, be designed and supervised by the winning architects. Letters supporting the Modernist cause were received from scholars and famous architects such as Walter Gropius, William Wurster, and President Meneely's former Dartmouth colleague, Hugh Morrison. A highly critical article appeared in the February, 1946, issue of *Architectural Forum*.[48]

The Wheaton Art Club invited a member of the faculty at the School of Design at Harvard, along with a former Curator of the Museum of

Model of the proposed Fine Arts Center, designed by the firm of Hornbostel and Bennett.

Modern Art who was teaching at Wellesley, to come to campus to discuss the issue. Before a packed house, John McAndrew, who also had served as chair of the jury in the 1938 competition, responded to a question asking him to compare and contrast Modernist and Georgian architecture by stating succinctly: "One's alive and the other's dead!"[49] Raising the moral, if not legal, issue of commitments made at the time of the Arts Center competition, Harvard Professor Hugh Stubbins asserted that modern architecture was the "only living architecture," and insisted that the students must let the administration know in no uncertain terms in what kind of buildings they wanted to spend their time.[50]

Meanwhile, unknown to most, a new complication had also appeared. Toward the end of January, President Meneely received a letter signed by both Caleb Hornbostel and Richard Bennett indicating that they believed they had a rightful claim to be the architects for any future Art Center that Wheaton chose to build. This assertion took President Meneely by surprise, for he thought he had received assurances in the fall of 1945 that all such claims had been waived by the architects. There is considerable evidence to indicate that he had good reason to believe this was the case.[51]

On August 30, 1945, Caleb Hornbostel had written to the President inquiring if he might meet with Dr. Meneely to discuss the possibility that he and his wife, who had formed their own business, might serve in the position of College Architect. Subsequently, Mr. Hornbostel came to Wheaton and met with the President on October 19. In his memorandum concerning the meeting, Meneely mentioned that he had told Hornbostel of the trustees' sentiment in favor of Georgian architecture, while Hornbostel in turn indicated his interest in becoming College Architect only if the Board wished future work to be done in Modernist style. "He does not regard his firm as having a special claim upon us concerning the Art Center," Mr. Meneely went on, "since his partnership with Mr. Bennett is dissolved."[52]

This conclusion seemed to be confirmed on October 24, when Hornbostel wrote to Meneely: "As I explained to you, there never was any definite arrangement made between Wheaton college and the firm of Hornbostel and Bennett."[53] However, in a second letter, written on the same day, Mr. Hornbostel stated, "Since I represent the former firm of Hornbostel and Bennett, if Wheaton College does make the above change in policy [reversion to past architectural style] I will accept any simple arrangement that can be made concerning the Competitions, the future Art Center, and Hornbostel and Bennett."[54]

In December and early January the President wrote to both Hornbostel and Bennett (who was now teaching at Yale) indicating the Board's decision to adhere to Georgian style, and the retention of Perry, Shaw & Hepburn as College architects. In his letter to Hornbostel, President Meneely indicated that because the prize money had been paid, he and the Board regarded all obligations to the firm as having been met, since there was not any likelihood that the Art Center would be built in the near future. "If you believe I am in error," he continued, "I assume that you will write me further."[55]

It was in response to that communication that five weeks later, at the height of the public controversy, the letter indicating the architects' continued claim was received. In their private discussions, it was clear that both the President and the Board believed that not only the payment of the prize, but the commissions for SAB and the two building wings that had been given to Hornbostel and Bennett more than fulfilled any real or moral obligation the College had incurred as a result of the 1938 competition. It was also patently untrue that the original contract had called for the erection of three buildings plus the Art Center, an assertion Mrs. Hunter had made in her telegram to the *Wheaton News*. In the Board's eyes it seemed legitimate to contend that the College had no further obligation to a firm which in fact no longer existed.[56]

Nonetheless, it is also evident that as early as the end of November, 1945, President Meneely was beginning to have personal reservations regarding the extent of the College's legal obligations to Hornbostel and Bennett. In a letter to Dr. Park, he noted that in 1938 President Park had told the trustees that the College had given Hornbostel and Bennett a firm commitment for the Art Center contract if the building were ever constructed. "I wonder if you would be willing to give me your impression as to what, if any, claims Mr. Hornbostel has upon the college. I judge he expects some financial settlement to be made with him."[57]

Meanwhile, in an effort to stem the rising furor, Board Chairman Joseph Soliday, after consulting an informal gathering of Boston area trustees, sent a brief communication to the *Wheaton News* which was published on February 9. In it he stated that while it was indeed true that the college had retained an architectural firm to develop plans for other projects, no decision had been taken at any time by the Board regarding the type of architecture of the proposed Art Center—for the construction of which, he also noted, no funds of any consequence currently existed.[58]

The President was also authorized by the trustees to meet with faculty and students to discuss the issue. In a meeting with the faculty on February 11, he candidly admitted that he had "wrongly assumed that the Art Center would be in the prevailing style." Detailing his correspondence with Caleb Hornbostel, he stated that he should have sought a clarification of Mr. Hornbostel's statement that he would accept "any simple arrangement." Emphasizing that the Board of Trustees had in fact made no decision relative to an Art Center, Dr. Meneely indicated that from the Board's perspective the issue was moot since there were no funds available for its construction. However, "if someone should give enough money for an Art Center in the modern style, he would certainly recommend to the Trustees its acceptance."[59]

On February 20, the President again faced the student body, this time not only to read a prepared statement, but also to answer questions. In a descriptive account of this meeting, which Meneely subsequently prepared and released to the *News* for publication, it is indicated that he discussed the residential and infirmary building plans which had been authorized, emphasized that no action had been taken by the trustees regarding an Art Center, and expressed his desire to apologize for his erroneous assumption that the new architect would draw the plans for such a building. Nothing had been done, he reiterated—the matter of an Art Center still stood exactly as it had upon completion of the competition seven years earlier.[60]

From the President's perspective these meetings went well. He was particularly heartened by a letter signed by 232 students which was published subsequently in the *News*. Thanking him for appearing before them, they wrote: "You have been extremely patient and we would like to thank you for all that you have done for us since your arrival at Wheaton last year. We feel that we are not alone in our gratitude."[61] Nonetheless, as the President noted in a letter to Trustee J. K. Clark, "there still remains a small, disaffected minority of undergraduates."[62] The whole process, he commented to Sylvia Meadows had been "a very unpleasant experience. . . . Certainly a vociferous and impetuous minority can do a great deal in a short time to disrupt the life of the community."[63] "I am thoroughly fed up with them," he wrote to Harriet Hughes. "Between you and me I think Miss Seaver has been more active behind the scenes than she cares to admit."[64] In March he added, "It will be a great relief to have the present student agitators graduate in June. I only wish that a couple of the members of the Faculty were going out with them. It would be a boon to Wheaton College."[65]

And indeed, to the disaffected student group the President could rightly add Esther Seaver and her coterie of faculty and alumnae supporters. Noting with pleasure the statement that nothing had been decided about an Art Center, they continued to press for a specific Board decision as to the architectural style in which it would ultimately be built. To this was added the force of a letter unanimously endorsed by another mass meeting of the student body on March 7. This letter, drawn up by the Faculty/Student Coordinating Committee to which the original February 12 resolution had been referred, was clear as to its point, though much less demanding than the original. Addressed to the President, rather than the trustees, it expressed the students' pride in SAB and asked that the College's leadership in college architecture be continued in the form of the Art Center, whenever it should be built.[66]

The Board was scheduled to meet on March 16. But before the meeting took place two other bombshells burst, one public, the other behind the scenes. The first concerned the resignation of Esther Seaver. Although submitted on January 1, President Meneely had not accepted it, expressing to Miss Seaver the hope that she would reconsider. This view had subsequently been seconded by the Trustee Administration Committee, which pointed out to her that there was no need to resign, since her resignation had been prompted by the misperception that a decision had been made to construct the Art Center in the Georgian style. Somewhat mollified, Miss Seaver did agree to rethink the matter, but as the second semester progressed, she became more and more insistent that some sort of formal commitment to a Modernist building was required. She continued to talk about her contemplated resignation with students and faculty alike, a fact which greatly displeased the President.[67]

Then on February 16, in an effort to get the news of Professor Seaver's resignation out to alumnae prior to the President's second meeting with the student body, the Editor-in-Chief and the Managing Editor of the *News* released, without Miss Seaver's permission, a story concerning her resignation to the national wire services and *The Boston Herald*. The press release erroneously stated that the President had accepted the resignation in January. An article which subsequently appeared in the *Herald* further garbled the information, making it appear that her resignation was due to the lack of funds available for constructing the Center.[68]

This action prompted Miss Seaver to respond with a statement to the *News*, which was published on February 23:

> In view of the erroneous report published in *The Boston Herald*, I should like to make clear that I did not offer my resignation because of the lack of funds for an Art Center. My resignation was offered primarily because of the vagueness and uncertainty that has arisen with reference to the college's abiding by the terms of the Art Center competition.[69]

For the embattled President, this was the final straw. Until then Esther Seaver's contemplated resignation, although actually well known, had officially remained a private affair between the two. Now the gauntlet had openly been thrown down. With this statement Miss Seaver was effectively publicly confirming her proffered resignation, and giving the reasons for it. Also clearly implied was what needed to be done in order to bring about a reversal of her position. Meneely, however, would not be blackmailed, and on the day her statement in the *News* appeared he wrote Miss Seaver that he was indeed accepting the resignation she had proffered nearly two months earlier. All subsequent pleas from students and faculty that she be allowed to reconsider fell on the deaf ears of a President who was personally relieved to have a person with whom both he and Dr. Park had found it very difficult to deal removed from the Wheaton environment.[70]

The second surprise came from Caleb Hornbostel and Richard Bennett. On February 28 they sent a letter to Joseph Soliday, suggesting that they be invited to meet with the Board at its next meeting. "Many people concerned with Wheaton's building program have had their opinions aired; but up to the present moment all we have been able to do is to prevent publicity which we thought might hurt the school. We have not had the opportunity to clarify our position to you. . . . Our purpose is to render the best possible service to Wheaton."[71]

The suggestion was quickly accepted by both Soliday and the President. A formal invitation was issued and the two architects met with the trustees in an informal session prior to the official Board meeting on March 16. Expecting that the architects would aggressively press their case, the trustees were surprised when it did not turn out that way. Instead, Meneely later suggested to William Chase, it seemed as if they were there mainly to garner more information from the Board. What they received was an assurance that "no action had been taken by the Board of Trustees to change their former status in regard to the Art Center."[72] Asked if they would want to construct the Art Center in strict accordance with the plans developed before the war, the two architects "replied that they would not."[73]

At its meeting that afternoon, the Board reaffirmed its action the previous November regarding building projects other than an Art Center, and also ratified the December selection of Perry, Shaw and Hepburn as College Architects. Ironically, it was at this meeting that preliminary plans for the new faculty housing project were unveiled. They proved to be of handsome brick and stone Georgian design, but with a price tag so high that the Board instructed President Meneely to seek new plans in which the units would be smaller in size and half as costly. Taking cognizance of the continued agitation for a definite commitment regarding the style in which any future Art Center would be built, the trustees also voted to create a special committee to consult as to what, if anything, should be done.[74]

This committee did not wait long to come up with a recommendation. Central to its considerations were conditions stipulated by the American Institute of Architects to which Wheaton had subscribed in order to gain the sanction of that body for the national competition in 1938. Writing to Trustee Sylvia Meadows, who had missed the committee meeting on March 31, President Meneely said that he, Joseph Soliday and Richard Chapman had carefully considered the implications of that document.

> In the light of Document #213 of the American Institute of Architects, it does appear as though we are morally and possibly legally bound to employ Hornbostel and Bennett, and to have the Art Center along modern lines. If this is the case, we might as well concede the fact. Mr. Chapman has agreed to draft a statement for our consideration.[75]

By the end of April a draft statement had been mailed to all trustees, stating that if no objections were received the committee planned to make it public shortly thereafter.[76] And indeed on May 8, the statement was released to the *Wheaton News* which published it under a triumphant banner headline, "MODERN ART CENTER ENDORSED," on May 11. Reiterating the Board's consistent position that no action had ever been taken concerning the status of the Art Center project, "because funds have not been available for the purpose," the announcement went on to say:

> The Board of Trustees cannot speak for future Trustees, but if funds were now in hand or should become available, the present Trustees would expect to proceed with plans for an Art Center of modern design drawn by the winners of the competition in 1938. The College welcomes gifts from any who wish to advance the Art Center, and such gifts may bear the stipulation that they may be applied only to the project as contemplated.[77]

In one short paragraph the trustees succeeded in accomplishing several things. The Board specifically refused to tie the hands of future Boards on the issue of a design for an Arts Center. At the same time the immediate crisis was defused by the formal commitment to "an art center of modern design drawn by the winners of the competition in 1938" were funds currently available, or should they become available in the near future. Finally in this brief statement the trustees issued an obvious challenge to those who had stated in preceding months that once given a formal commitment to build a Modernist structure, they would be able to raise quickly the funds necessary to proceed with its design and construction.

The trustee committee's action, formally ratified by the Board at its June, 1946, meeting, brought this turbulent seven-months confrontation to a conclusion. By the time Wheaton reopened in the fall of 1946, a basic semblance of normalcy had been restored. Both Caleb Hornbostel and Richard Bennett professed themselves satisfied with the result. No substantial amount of money was forthcoming in terms of donations earmarked for an Art Center, and the matter remained dormant for the next thirteen years.[78]

Ironically, one of President Meneely's last acts, shortly before the commencement of his fatal illness in the fall of 1960, was to join with the trustees in approving the building of a Fine Arts Center that would be Modernist in style. Designed by the firm of Rich and Tucker, which had replaced Perry, Shaw and Hepburn as College Architects in 1948, this structure became one of the main buildings in the completely Modernist "lower campus" which was constructed as Wheaton doubled in size between 1957 and 1964.[79]

When news of the impending construction of the Fine Arts Building reached Caleb Hornbostel in 1960, he wrote to President Meneely on behalf of himself and Mr. Bennett expressing the opinion that there remained "not only a moral question but a legal question as to our status in regards to the present contemplated Arts Center."[80] Both the Board and Dr. Meneely were nonplussed, but after consultation with legal counsel, it was determined that indeed an obligation probably did remain, and that the College should contemplate the potential necessity of reaching some sort of financial settlement with Messrs. Hornbostel and Bennett. Nonetheless, the Chair of the Board, Abram Collier, decided that the College should try, as politely as possible, to stonewall and hope that the architects would accept a fait accompli.[81]

To that end Mr. Collier composed a letter that was, as he put it to the President, "designed to make a sale."[82] Sent out under Dr. Meneely's signature, the letter emphasized that both the site and the design for the proposed new building were totally new—"planning for this building is not in any way connected with the art center contemplated by the 1938 competition."[83] Reminding Mr. Hornbostel that the trustees had specifically not bound future Boards in their 1946 statement, it also argued politely but forcefully that the commissions received by Mr. Hornbostel and his partner to design SAB and the Library and Science Building wings had "served to compensate you for whatever moral obligation the

College had by reason of its inability to go ahead with the art center that was originally contemplated."[84]

Nine months later Hornbostel replied, stating simply that he thought it best that both sides should "consider the matter terminated." The tone of the letter, though cordial, exuded a sense of vindication that probably reflected his satisfaction that Wheaton had now completely committed itself to Modernist architectural forms in its major expansion of campus facilities. "As I look back at it," he wrote to President Meneely, "and I think you will agree with me, Mr. Bennett and I were too advanced in our thinking at that time. When we look at what is being built today and what you are building today at Wheaton College, I think you can realize why Mr. Bennett and myself stated we could not design traditional architecture and be honest with ourselves."[85]

"Perhaps," Hornbostel concluded, "one of these days when you are in New York we could have cocktails or supper together as I have always felt that circumstances beyond our control created an impossible situation to which there was no solution except the passing of time."[86] Sadly, the President, now in the final stages of his illness, could not even reply.

The intensity of this emotional and bitter confrontation in 1946 left scars and doubts that were long in healing. Years later, former students who had supported Professor Seaver still could not forgive Howard Meneely. Nor were the divisions created within the faculty easily smoothed over. During the turmoil, a letter supporting Dr. Seaver signed by ten faculty members and addressed to the Chair of the Board of Trustees was printed in the *Wheaton News*, which added considerably to the tensions on campus. Several persons who had joined with Esther Seaver also resigned, either shortly thereafter or within a few years. The President replaced Osborne Earle as Head of the English Department, in part because Earle had been an outspoken supporter of Miss Seaver.[87]

Maintaining that the whole controversy was "absolutely unnecessary," Professor Muriel Hidy commented subsequently that fond as she and her husband were of Esther Seaver, they also were very embarrassed by her actions. Noting that he had strongly supported Dr. Meneely's position that there were many matters needing attention that were of equal or greater importance than the Art Center, E. J. Knapton remarked later that for years after the controversy there were supporters of Esther Seaver, particularly Chemistry Professor Mildred Evans, who would automatically oppose any position taken by him in a faculty meeting.[88]

For most of the faculty the issue was both clarified and simplified when Professor of Economics Henrietta Jennings commented in faculty meeting that since the existing fund for the Art Center was miniscule "we might as well wait to cut each other's throat on what style it was to be in" until a time when it would be possible to envision the actual erection of the Center.[89] Ironically, when that day did arrive thirteen years later, the efficiencies of cost provided by the simplicity of Modernist de-

sign and construction rendered any discussion regarding style moot before it could even commence.

Others have asserted that President Meneely's firm commitment to
maintaining the enrollment at Wheaton at its traditional level of five hundred students, and his later consistent opposition to trustees' expansionist suggestions stemmed in great part from his reluctance, because of
the Art Center controversy, to embark on any major course of building
construction.[90] And indeed, aside from building the eight units of colonial style housing for women faculty known as Shepard Court, a Modernist new infirmary, and a separate dining room for faculty and staff,
no new construction or remodeling projects of any magnitude were undertaken until the Board of Trustees forced the President's hand on the
question of expansion in 1955.

It has also been suggested that President and Mrs. Meneely's reluctance to entertain, or take a real part in the social life of the Wheaton
community, stemmed in part from Mrs. Meneely's bitterness over what
she regarded as the wrongful treatment of her husband by those supporting the Modernist cause. Be that as it may, it also is evident that among
many members of the faculty the President's firm stance in the face of
strident vocal opposition, plus his subsequent ceaseless efforts to improve the financial situation of both faculty and staff, in time created a
strong, broad base of support for his administration that made the post-
1946 years ones of calm and continuity which contrasted greatly with
the firestorm of opposition endured by the new President in his second
year at Wheaton.[91]

Since no potential sources of outside funding for the Art Center had
appeared on the scene, and because the limited fiscal resources available
within the College were desperately needed for other matters, the Art
Center design controversy can indeed be realistically regarded as a non-
issue that created enormous and unnecessary divisions among students,
faculty and alumnae. Yet it is also evident that neither President Meneely
nor the Board of Trustees ever really comprehended or understood the
significance of the 1938 competition to supporters of the Modernist architectural school throughout the United States, a significance that was
greatly intensified by the actual construction of SAB, the first Modernist
building on a traditional college campus. The betrayal that the Modern-
ists, both at Wheaton and elsewhere, felt at the apparent reversion to a
Georgian architectural style by a college they had come to regard as the
pioneer leader of Modernism on college campuses was real and heartfelt.

Nor was the President ever really aware of the degree of pride which
the construction of SAB and the two Modernist wings of the Science
Center and the Library had instilled in the students who attended
Wheaton in the years between 1940 and 1946. Even though the Art Center had not been constructed, Wheaton's national reputation as the first
college or university to erect Modernist structures on a traditional cam-

pus was well known to its students. As a student union, SAB had turned
out to be a remarkable success, both stylistically and functionally, and
students and young alumnae revelled in the unique and special position
the Modernist structure had brought to their small, relatively unknown
college and campus. Moreover, given the fact that the last three prewar
building projects, none of which was related to the Art Center competition, had been constructed in Modernist style, it is easy to understand
why there was an assumption on the part of many students, alumnae,
and some faculty that future new buildings would follow the same form.

In the months that followed the 1946 crisis, one other casualty
emerged. Joseph Soliday, long-time Treasurer of the College, who had
become the first nonpresidential Chair of the Board of Trustees at the
time of Dr. Meneely's appointment to the presidency, had over the years
developed an acquaintance with many members of the Wheaton faculty.
As a result some faculty found they could gain direct, personal access to
Mr. Soliday, and during the first two years of the Meneely administration
did not hesitate to do so. In particular, faculty whose sights were set on
both the immediate construction and Modernist style of the Art Center
by-passed President Meneely and brought complaints and issues directly
to the Board through its Chairman. This even included at one point an
invitation to several trustees to have breakfast with Esther Seaver. Writing about the Art Center controversy years later President Meneely commented, "My own inexperience and ineptitude in handling such matters
contributed to the difficulties, and the Board Chairman's handling of the
overall situation left something to be desired."[92]

The majority on the Board were very much of the opinion that Dr.
Meneely's priorities, which did not include the construction of an Art
Center in the near future, were correct.[93] Moreover, Mr. Soliday soon
came to understand that there was much criticism among the trustees of
his willingness to listen so extensively to individual faculty members.
Having served on the Board for over twenty years, he offered to resign,
and in March, 1947, his resignation was accepted and the Board replaced
him as Chair with Richard Chapman, who immediately refused to accept
letters or calls from or to meet with any individual member of the faculty. Shortly thereafter Mr. Chapman reinstituted President Park's policy
that all communications from the faculty, either individually or collectively, must come through the President to the Board.[94]

With the close of the 1945–46 academic year, the juxtaposition of
"honeymoon" and "crisis" years resolved itself into a more normal, stabilized progression that in many ways reflected both the steady tempera-
ment of the College's President and the times in general. Despite the
global tensions of the Cold War and the conflict in Korea that resulted

from it, the mood of the nation as a whole was one of optimism, tempered by a "don't rock the boat" attitude. A flourishing, though moderately inflationary, economy provided jobs and peacetime economic opportunities far different from what had been experienced in the depression and war years. Professional and economic success, along with a complacent acceptance of existing social and cultural norms, were the watchwords for the rapidly expanding white middle classes of America. Wheaton, like most other private liberal arts colleges, reflected closely the dominant attitudes and standards of that group from which the vast majority of its students were drawn. The relative, though not total, calm at Wheaton of the months and years after June, 1946, appears in retrospect to be an accurate reflection of the larger domestic mood and outlook of the nation as a whole.

Notes: Chapter 16

1. Wheaton College, *Inauguration of Alexander Howard Meneely, Wheaton College, Norton Massachusetts, October 14, 1944,* p. 13.

2. Ibid.: pp. 15–16.

3. Faragher, J. M and Howe, F., eds., *Women and Higher Education in American History: Essays from the Mount Holyoke College Sesquicentennial Symposia* (New York: Norton, 1988), p. 161. See comments by trustee Mary Ellen Avery (W1948) regarding the generally held student view in the late 1940s that it was impossible to combine marriage and a career. She states that over 90 percent of her class were married within two years of graduation from Wheaton. Oral History Project: M. E. Avery interview, 1983. It appears that only two woman veterans, Mary Robinson (W1947), and Beatrice Alperin (W1954), attended Wheaton under the G.I. Bill. President's Reports to Trustees: 11/8/47; Staff: Dunkle: Meneely to Dunkle, 10/20/50; Faculty Meeting Minutes: 9/20/50.

4. See the interesting comments of trustee Dr. Mary Ellen Avery (W1948) on these issues. Oral History Project: M. E. Avery interview, 1983.

5. Oral History Project: E. May interview, 1983. Interestingly, in 1947, Admissions Director Virginia Townsend urged that the College take advantage of the postwar "sellers market" by starting to recruit on the west coast, stating that it would be a good long-term investment, since a small college in the East that was near, but not in, a large city like Boston would be very appealing. The President vetoed the plan, citing budgetary restrictions as the reason. Staff: Townsend: Townsend to Meneely, 9/19/47; Meneely to Townsend, 9/20/48.

6. A. Stevenson, "Commencement Address." 6/6/55. Smith College Archives.

7. Oral History Project: R. Chapman interview, 1983; M. Clemence interview, 1983; M. P. Ford interview, 1983; G. Hood interview, 1983.

8. Meneely: Meneely: Miscellaneous quotations. President Meneely was described by former Dean of Students Leota Colpitts as being very stable and steady— "he never went off half-cocked." Oral History Project: L. Colpitts interview, 1983; see also B. Ziegler interview, 1983.

9. Faculty: May: Meneely to May, 3/30/50.

10. Oral History Project: E. J. Knapton interview, 1983; K. Burton interview, 1983; M. P. Ford interview, 1983; B. H. Jennings interview, 1983.

11. Ibid.: H. Austin interview, 1983.

12. Faculty: Knapton: Knapton to Meneely, 10/5/55; 1/14/56; 9/21/57; Knapton, *Small Figure*, p. 198; Staff: Lincoln: Meneely to Lincoln, 7/27/50.

13. Oral History Project: K. Burton interview, 1983.

14. Ibid.: R. Chapman interview, 1983.

15. Ibid.: E. May interview, 1983.

16. English Professor Louise Barr MacKenzie later commented that President Meneely was able to "hold the college together in a pleasant way." Ibid.: L. B. Mac-Kenzie interview, 1983; see also N. Norton interview, 1983.

17. Trustees Minutes: 6/8/47; 6/12/49; Trustees: J. K. Clark #5: Clark to Meneely, 7/24/44; Shanks #6: Meneely to Shanks, 5/26/47; Chapman #4: Meneely to Chapman, 10/5/49; 11/4/49; Chapman to Meneely, 10/7/49; 11/7/49.

18. The members of this special ad hoc Committee on Committees were Professors Burton, Muriel Hidy, Marshall, Seaver and Shipley. Faculty Meeting Minutes: 11/20/44; 2/6/45; 5/14/45; 10/17/45; Trustees Minutes: 3/23/45.

19. Oral History Project: H. Austin interview, 1983.

20. Trustees Minutes: 3/23/45; Trustees: Soliday #2: Meneely to Soliday, 3/16/45. See also Faculty Meeting Minutes: 5/9/49.

21. Faculty: R. Boas: Meneely to Boas, 4/23/45.

22. Trustees Minutes: 3/27/54; President's Reports to Trustees: 3/27/54; Faculty Meeting Minutes: 1/10/55; 2/14/55. The Committee on Health and the Committee on the Academic Calendar and Catalogue were abolished in 1955, the duties of the latter being incorporated into those of the Administration Committee. Beginning in 1955, the list of persons appointed by the Committee on Committees to committee positions was approved by the faculty rather than the President.

23. Trustees, General Information: Miscellaneous, 1925–45: "Organization of the Faculty at Wheaton College," submitted with cover letter to Trustees, 10/20/45.

24. President's Reports to Trustees: 3/27/54.

25. Oral History Project: H. Austin interview, 1983; E. J. Knapton interview, 1983; Knapton, *Small Figure*, p. 198.

26. See ch. 14. The following account examines the "Art Center Controversy" primarily from the internal perspective of its impact on Wheaton College. For a detailed account of the Art Center Competition, as well as for its significance in terms of the larger world of architectural design, including pictures of the award-winning designs, see McCormick, "Wheaton College: Competition," in James D. Kornwolf, ed., *Modernism in America,* pp. 22–67. I am also indebted to Rachael Class-Giguere (W1991), who reviewed much of the material relating to the Art Center competition and controversy during her work as my research assistant during the summer of 1990.

27. Trustees Minutes: 6/10/39; 3/18/40; 6/8/40; 11/25/40; Faculty: Seaver: Park memorandum, 1/8/40. In all the documents and correspondence concerning this building it is always referred to as an Art Center, though the more exact term would have been Arts Center, since it was planned to include facilities for Art, Music and Drama.

28. *Wheaton News*, 4/28/45.

29. President's Reports to Trustees: 6/3/45.

30. Trustees: Meadows #9: Meneely to Meadows, 6/26/45; Trustees Minutes: 11/3/45; 3/16/46; Buildings: Art Center Controversy, 1945–46: Meneely memorandum of meeting with Hornbostel, 10/19/45; Meneely to Park, 11/24/45; Meneely to Hornbostel, 12/20/45.

31. Buildings: Art Center Controversy, 1951–61: Memorandum, "Art Center Project", A. H. Meneely, 3/23/60.

32. Ibid.

33. Buildings: Art Center Controversy, 1945–46: Meneely to Park, 11/24/45; Meneely to Hornbostel, 12/20/45. See also Trustees: Soliday #1, Soliday to Meneely, 2/25/46; Meneely to Soliday, 2/27/46; Soliday to Meneely, 3/1/46; President's Reports to Trustees: 3/16/46.

34. Trustees Minutes: 11/3/45.

35. Ibid.: Trustees: Meadows #9: Meneely to Meadows, 12/6/45. Preliminary sketches were also authorized for a new infirmary.

36. Faculty: Seaver: Park Memorandum, 5/22/33; Park to Seaver, 5/17/35; 10/2/36; 11/10/36; Seaver to Park, 11/24/36; Park to Briggs, 11/8/40; Oral History Project: L. Mandell interview, 1983.

37. Trustees: Hughes #2: Hughes to Meneely, 1/13/46.

38. Faculty: Seaver: Seaver to Meneely, 1/1/46.

39. Ibid.: Meneely to Seaver, 1/4/46.

40. *Wheaton News*, 1/12/46.

41. Buildings: Art Center Controversy, 1945–46: J. and H. Shands to Meneely, 2/4/46; *Wheaton News*, 2/9/46.

42. *Wheaton News*, 2/2/46.

43. Buildings: Art Center Controversy, 1945–46: "Talk given by Mr. Meneely at Student Mass Meeting on January 14, 1946." For a similar expression of views see, Faculty: H. Jennings: Jennings to Editors of *Wheaton News*, 1/13/46; Meneely to Jennings, 1/14/46.

44. Buildings: Art Center Controversy, 1945–46: "Talk given by Mr. Meneely at Student Mass Meeting on January 14, 1946."

45. Oral History Project: H. Austin interview, 1983.

46. Ibid.: M. E. Avery interview, 1983.

47. *Wheaton News*, 1/12/46; 2/2/46.

48. Buildings: Art Center Controversy, 1945–46: Morrison to Meneely, 1/13/46; Mock to Meneely, 1/28/46; Barr to Meneely, 1/29/46; *Architectural Forum*, February, 1946, pp. 11–12; also May, 1946, pp. 12–13. See also McCormick, "Wheaton College Competition," in Kornwolf, ed., *Modernism in America*, p. 36; *Wheaton News*, 2/2/46; 2/16/46.

49. *Wheaton News*, 2/9/46.

50. Ibid. I am indebted to Professor of Art History Emerita Mary Heuser for making me aware that the Professor McAndrew who spoke at this forum was the same person who had chaired the prewar Art Center Competition jury. Heuser, interview with author, October, 2000.

51. Buildings: Art Center Controversy, 1945–46: Hornbostel to Meneely, 1/25/46; Hornbostel and Bennett to Meneely, 1/25/46. Interestingly, in Miss Seaver's file in the Wheaton Archives there is a copy of a letter obtained by Professor McCormick, dated January 28, 1946, from "Ruth" to Miss Seaver on Hornbostel Company stationary, indicating that "Dick" [Bennett] and "Caleb" [Hornbostel] were very much at odds with one another and that "Caleb" did not look forward at all to working with "Dick" if by any chance the Art Center commission should indeed remain with them. There is no indication that Miss Seaver ever communicated this piece of information to President Meneely.

52. Buildings: Art Center Controversy, 1945–46: Meneely memorandum, 10/19/45.

53. Ibid.: Hornbostel to Meneely, 10/24/45.

54. Ibid.; see also Hornbostel to Meneely, 8/30/45; also Trustees: Soliday #2: Meneely to Soliday, 9/20/45.

55. Buildings: Art Center Controversy, 1945–46: Meneely to Hornbostel, 12/20/45; Meneely to Bennett, 1/4/46; see also Trustees: Hughes #2: Meneely to Hughes, 1/30/46.

56. Trustees: Chase #4: Chase to Meneely, 1/4/46; *Wheaton News*, 1/12/46.

57. Buildings: Art Center Controversy, 1945–46: Meneely to Park, 11/24/45.

58. *Wheaton News*, 2/9/46; Trustees: Soliday #1: Soliday to Meneely, 1/19/46; Meneely to Soliday, 1/30/46; Hughes #2: Meneely to Hughes, 1/30/46; Trustees Minutes: 3/16/46.

59. Faculty Meeting Minutes: 2/11/46. See also Trustees: Meadows #9: Meneely to Meadows, 12/6/45.

60. *Wheaton News*, 2/23/46.

61. Ibid.

62. Trustees: J. K. Clark #7: Meneely to Clark, 2/22/46; also 2/16/46.

63. Ibid.: Meadows #9: Meneely to Meadows, 1/23/46.

64. Ibid.: Hughes #2: Meneely to Hughes, 1/30/46; see also *Wheaton News*, 2/23/46.

65. Ibid.: Meneely to Hughes, 3/20/46.

66. Buildings: Art Center Controversy, 1945–46: Student Body to Meneely, 3/7/46; *Wheaton News*, 2/9/46; 3/9/46; 5/11/46; Oral History Project: H. Austin interview, 1983. The faculty members of the coordinating committee were Henrietta Jennings, Katherine Burton, and Lena Mandell.

67. Trustees: Soliday #1: Meneely to Soliday, 2/16/46; 2/21/46; Hughes #2: Meneely to Hughes, 4/2/46.

68. Buildings: Art Center Controversy, 1945–46: Fox and Johnson to Meneely, 2/20/46, including copy of press release, 2/16/46; Trustees: Hughes #2: Meneely to Hughes, 4/2/46. The *Wheaton News*, 2/23/46, contained a public apology by the editors of *News* for the paper's role in contributing to unwarranted rumors, and for the unauthorized release of material regarding Seaver's resignation.

69. *Wheaton News*, 2/23/46.

70. See Trustees: Soliday #1: Meneely to Soliday, 2/16/46; 2/21/46; Hughes #2: Meneely to Hughes, 4/2/46; 5/15/46; Heath et al to Meneely, 5/11/46; *Wheaton News*, 5/4/46; President's Reports to Trustees: 3/16/46; 6/2/46; Trustees Minutes: 3/16/46; Faculty Meeting Minutes: 5/31/46.

71. Buildings: Art Center Controversy, 1945–46: Hornbostel and Bennett to Soliday, 2/28/46.

72. Trustees Minutes: 3/16/46.

73. Ibid.; see also Trustees: Soliday #1: Soliday to Meneely, 3/3/46; Meneely to Soliday, 3/4/46; Chase #4: Chase to Meneely, 3/18/46; Meneely to Chase, 3/20/46.

74. Trustees Minutes: 3/16/46; President's Reports to Trustees: 3/16/46.

75. Trustees: Meadows #9: Meneely to Meadows, 4/1/46.

76. Buildings: Art Center Controversy, 1945–46: Meneely to Trustees, 4/29/46.

77. *Wheaton News*, 5/11/46.

78. Trustees Minutes: 6/2/46; Buildings: Art Center Controversy, 1945–46: Bennett to Meneely, 5/15/46; President's Reports to Trustees: 6/2/46.

79. Trustees Minutes: 10/24/59; 1/23/60; 3/19/60.

80. Buildings: Art Center Controversy, 1951–61: Hornbostel to McNealy [*sic*], 3/16/60.

81. Ibid.: Crocker to Collier, 5/23/60; Collier to Meneely, 5/24/60; Meneely to Collier, 5/25/60.

82. Ibid.: Collier to Meneely, 6/16/60.

83. Ibid.: Meneely to Hornbostel, 6/22/60.

84. Ibid.

85. Ibid.: Hornbostel to Meneely, 3/16/61.

86. Ibid.

87. For a very cogent argument in support of Miss Seaver's position, see the resignation letter of Wilhelmina van Ingen Elarth. Faculty: Elarth: Elarth to Meneely, 4/4/46. See also Faculty: Earle: Meneely memorandum of conversation with Earle, 5/14/46. Earle subsequently resigned from Wheaton to create and chair the English department at newly established Brandeis University. President's Reports to Trustees: 6/2/46; Trustees: J. K. Clark #7: Meneely to Clark, 5/6/46; *Wheaton News*, 5/4/46.

88. E. J. Knapton, comment to author, ca. 1968. B. H. Jennings confirms Miss

Evans' strong hostility toward the President on the Arts Center issue. Oral History Project: B. H. Jennings interview, 1983; M. Hidy interview, 1985; H. Austin interview, 1983; B. H. Jennings, interview with author, 1999; H. Austin, interview with author, 2000.

89. Oral History Project: K. Burton interview, 1983.

90. Dean Elizabeth May commented that because of the Art Center controversy, President Meneely "was always just up tight about any kind of building." Oral History Project: E. May interview, 1983.

91. Oral History Project: H. Austin interview, 1983.

92. Buildings: Art Center Controversy, 1951–61: Meneely memorandum, "Art Center Project," 3/23/60; Art Center Controversy, 1945–46: Earle et al to Soliday, 5/21/46; Oral History Project: R. Chapman interview, 1983; M. Hidy interview, 1985.

93. For example, writing to the President in May, 1947, Board Chairman Richard Chapman stated that it was the concerted opinion of the trustees that "improvement in the salaries and working conditions of the faculty is the most urgent need of the College, and it represents, morover, a more realizable goal [than the Art Center] under prevailing conditions." Trustees: Chapman #2: Chapman to Meneely, 5/21/47.

94. Oral History Project: R. Chapman interview, 1983; Trustees Minutes, 3/1/47; Trustees: Chapman #2: Chapman to Meneely, 5/21/47.

17
Mending Fences, 1946–1954

THE DECISION BY PRESIDENT PARK to resign at the end of the 1943–44 academic year triggered a similar action on the part of Miriam Carpenter, who had served as Dean since her appointment by Dr. Park in 1929. "It seems to me good form to leave an incoming president free to choose his own dean," she wrote in her letter of resignation to the President.[1] Agreeing, President Park appointed Eleanor Barker, who had served as Dean Carpenter's secretary since 1937, as Acting Dean. Thus one of the earliest decisions President Meneely faced was the necessity of a permanent appointment to that position.[2]

It was not a decision made quickly or easily. In fact it was only in March, 1945, that the new President confirmed to the Board of Trustees his decision to make Miss Barker's appointment a permanent one. The public announcement was greeted with great enthusiasm by the student body. "I think the students would have mobbed me if I had dared to name anyone else to the post," he wrote to Trustee Sylvia Meadows.[3] Moreover, "since the duties of her office to quite a large extent involve ordinary human problems," he wrote to Dr. Park, general reservations he had about her lack of graduate school training and college-level teaching experience were not taken as important limitations.[4]

What lay behind the President's ambivalence was the fact that he envisaged a major change in the administrative structure of the college, one which he discussed in confidence with Miss Barker before recommending her appointment as permanent Dean. At the same trustees meeting in which Dean Barker's appointment was confirmed, President Meneely informed the Board in confidence of his long-term plan to abolish the position of Dean of Freshmen, and to create separate administrative positions of Academic and Social Deans. He had discussed this plan with Miss Barker, he reported, and she had agreed to accept the position of Dean of Students, rather than seek to be named Academic Dean, for which position the President did not believe she had the necessary academic qualifications. However, this was a proposal the President believed he could neither implement nor discuss publicly at that time, as he noted privately in a letter to trustee Ruth McKay.[5]

Perhaps the major reason for President Meneely's reluctance to proceed immediately with his contemplated administrative reorganization was the fact that it would of necessity involve changes in the operation and chain of command of almost all the College's academic and student services. In particular the duties and authority of the Registrar's office and the position of Registrar within the administrative organizational structure would be altered considerably and inevitably reduced in impor- tance. This would mean a direct confrontation with the indomitable Sarah Belle Young, who had held the position of Registrar since 1909. Miss Young's personal, at times overbearing, dominance in many areas of College affairs, and her fierce protective love of the institution had been experienced time and again by members of the administration and faculty. She was scheduled to retire in the summer of 1946. The Presi- dent's decision not to attempt a major administrative reorganization dur- ing her final year or in the immediate years after her retirement was undoubtedly judicious and wise, especially in light of the divisions and tensions created within the Wheaton community by the Art Center con- troversy of 1945–46.

During the 1944–45 academic year the trustees, prompted by inquir- ies from alumnae, initiated a discreet investigation into the retirement assets held by Sarah Belle Young. As a result, when she retired with an honorary Doctor of Letters degree in June, 1946, she also received an additional annual stipend awarded by the trustees to supplement the small annuity that was her due from the retirement fund. Her departure removed the last on-campus link within the Wheaton community to the Seminary era.[6]

Miss Young was replaced by Catherine Noyes, a 1930 graduate of Wheaton, who came to the Registrar's office directly from her most re- cent position as a Lieutenant Commander in the WAVES. Although she had no experience in the area of college records or administration, she proved to be a quick learner and carried on the duties of the office to the complete satisfaction of the President. However, she did not conceal her long-term ambition to undertake a course of graduate study. In fact, after three years she attempted to resign, and was only reluctantly persuaded by President Meneely to stay on for an additional year in order to pro- vide some level of continuity during a time when the College was expe- riencing major changes in its administrative structure.

For in the spring of 1948, President Meneely decided it was time to implement the administrative plan he had held in abeyance for the previ- ous three years. To that end he suggested to the Board of Trustees that they adopt a proposal he had already broached in a joint meeting of the Trustee Administration Committee and the Faculty Committee on Con- ference with the Trustees. This was to engage an outside agency to con- duct "an objective survey of our administrative organization and procedures, staffing problems, course offerings, etc."[7]

The Board agreed with the concept, but instead of hiring a consultant it designated three of its own members as a Trustee Survey Committee and entrusted the task to them.[8] In January, 1949, this committee submitted a report to the Administration and Finance Committees of the Board, which dealt with issues of administrative organization, a faculty salary scale, promotion, tenure, pensions and sick leave. Consideration of issues relating to curricular and other academic matters were postponed for a subsequent report, which ultimately was never written.[9]

First and foremost, the Survey Committee recommended that the separate positions of Academic Dean and Dean of Students be created. While the Dean of Students would essentially perform the same duties as the current Dean, the Academic Dean would take over from the President the basic operational oversight of academic departments, student advising, and all matters of academic discipline. The Academic Dean would also replace the President as chair of the faculty Administration, Scholarships, and Admissions Committees. This recommendation was approved at a joint meeting of the Trustee Administration and Finance Committees on January 22, 1949.[10]

True to his word, President Meneely offered the position of Dean of Students to Eleanor Barker, but after long and hesitant consideration she decided to decline. Thus it was that in the fall of 1949, two individuals new to Wheaton simultaneously assumed administrative oversight of the academic and social functioning of the College. Each would over the years play an enormous role in defining and shaping the future character of the College.[11]

Academic Dean Elizabeth Stoffregen May brought to her position an impressive list of credentials. A graduate of Smith College, Mrs. May had received her Ph.D. from the London School of Economics. She had taught at Goucher College and held positions from 1941 to 1947 as Senior Fiscal Analyst and Principal Fiscal Analyst with the Bureau of the Budget in Washington, D.C. In 1947–48 she and her husband, lawyer Geoffrey May, had served together on the American Mission for Aid to Greece. She arrived in Norton, having turned down a teaching position at Mount Holyoke, from her most recent situation as a consultant for the Committee on Economic Development. Joined by her husband, who had retired after years of government service and teaching law at Johns Hopkins University, the two took up residence in Hollyhock House and soon became an important part of the Wheaton community. Geoffrey May also quickly established ties within the town of Norton. He became close friends with Postmaster Joseph Yelle and his brother Henri, Principal of Norton High School, and he also was instrumental in helping found the Norton chapter of the Lions Club.[12]

Leota Colpitts, who accepted the position of Dean of Students, arrived at Wheaton after five years as Dean of Women at DePauw University. A graduate of Wellesley College, she had accumulated a wide range of teaching and administrative experience at the high school, junior college

Leota C. Colpitts, *Dean of Students*, 1949-1968, and Elizabeth S. May, *Dean of the College* (Academic Dean), 1949-1964; *Acting President*, 1955, 1961-62.

and university levels. Believing that one of the most important functions of her position involved extensive entertaining of students, she insisted, to President Meneely's initial dismay, that she be provided with off-campus accommodations, rather than the dormitory apartment he had planned. In fact, she proposed that she be allowed to buy a house on Mansfield Avenue that was a quarter of a mile from campus so she could bring her mother to live with her. This the President refused to allow, on the grounds that the house was "too far from campus," but he did reluctantly agree to provide an off-campus apartment.[13]

Dean Colpitts proved to be true to her word when it came to entertaining. By December 16 of her first semester at Wheaton, she reported to Dr. Meneely that she had entertained 498 people in her home, 169 at full meals. By the end of the year the total had swelled to over 1000. The expenses for this, the President reported to the Trustees in June, 1950, especially when coupled with the more moderate but steady entertaining being undertaken by Dean May, had "shrunk considerably" his "Contingent Fund." Over the next two decades Dean Colpitts' penchant for annually entertaining the entire student body with homemade cookies and hot chocolate, plus her great love of sheepdogs, of which she owned several, became an indelible part of Wheaton campus lore.[14]

Perhaps the most unusual aspect of Miss Colpitts' role as Dean of Students was that she, rather than Dean May, had the responsibility for presenting recommendations regarding all financial aid and student loans to the faculty committee responsible for making the final awards. This was because students' personal records, other than formal academic transcripts, were housed in her office, and these included all relevant materials regarding financial need.[15]

Both Mrs. May and Miss Colpitts proved to be strong, dynamic leaders. Intensely loyal to President Meneely, they relished the relatively free hand he gave them in administering the duties of their offices. "You always knew where you stood with him," Dean May commented.[16] Taking great care always to present a public united front, they resolved their disagreements privately, generally before discussing the issue with Dr. Meneely in their regular weekly meetings with him. Both saw themselves as more flexible than the President, ready to deal with issues on a case by case basis, rather than relying heavily on precedence or principle. Shortly after their arrival in 1949, each came to the conclusion that Wheaton bore too great a resemblance to a small boarding school, in which students were over-protected and hemmed in by rules and regulations. They decided in concert to loosen things gradually, a little every year. It was, Mrs. May noted, a sort of unformulated "long range plan."[17] Commenting that the way she managed was to stay a little ahead of students' demands, Dean Colpitts later pointed out that if you gave students a little that they did not expect before they requested it, it then became fairly easy to say no in other areas.[18]

For President Meneely, the presence of two strong individuals to oversee the day-to-day academic and social operations of the College was indeed welcome. The new Deans were working well, he noted in December, 1949. "They are very stimulating and agreeable to work with. . . . I am enjoying a peace of mind, the like of which I have not had about college affairs for quite a while."[19]

In 1950, having stayed one year longer than she had wanted, Catherine Noyes resigned from the Registrar's Office in order to pursue research and study in England. Her replacement turned out to be conveniently at hand. Leah Dearden, who had served since 1946 as the secretary in the Registrar's office, assumed the duties of Registrar and Secretary to the Faculty in the fall of 1950. The Registrar's Office itself was placed under the general supervision of the Academic Dean. Granted faculty status, Miss Dearden served as a voting member of the Administration and Admissions Committees, and as nonvoting secretary of the Committee of Instruction.[20]

It was also in 1950 that Barbara Ziegler was reappointed as Admissions Director, a position she had held before leaving for military service in 1942. Thus the years 1949 and 1950 witnessed not only a restructuring of administrative offices and duties but also a total changeover in personnel. However, once in place, no further turnover occurred in these positions during the remaining ten years of the Meneely presidency.

Three other administrative changes also occurred in the early 1950s. For years the Alumnae Secretary on campus had also served as Placement Officer. In 1952, however, it was decided that the duties of the Alumnae Secretary required undivided attention, with the concomitant result that a separate placement office was created and a full-time person hired to staff it. This was very much in keeping with the views of Deans May and Colpitts, who worked jointly to convince the President that the creation of an independant placement office was long overdue.[21]

The second change was one that also had been recommended by the Trustee Survey Committee. It was high time, the Committee stated in 1949, that the College retained a business manager who would oversee the operation of the Bursar's Office, the Domestic and Buildings/Grounds departments, and the College Bookstore. However, it took three years for the President to seek trustee authorization to implement this recommendation. The reasons for the delay lay in the person of the Bursar, Mabel Dunkle, whom President Park had unsuccessfully tried to persuade to resign a decade earlier. Although she would not reach retirement age until 1955, her contract came up for renewal in 1953. With the approval of the Board of Trustees, the President forced an early retirement, albeit with a two-year salary settlement that enabled Miss Dunkle to delay beginning her pension until she reached age sixty-five. Immediately the duties of the Bursar were redefined to exclude oversight of other departments, and Melvin "Don" Sargent, who had been a member of the Economics department for four years, was retained as Comptroller.[22]

It was also in 1953 that, at the urging of both Deans, President Meneely recommended and the Board of Trustees approved the appointment of a resident College Physician, who would rent a Wheaton-owned house and be employed half-time by the College, with the remaining time allowed for development of a private practice. An initial search for a female physician was unsuccessful, and in July, 1954, Dr. Ronald Duffield was appointed, and provided with a rental office for his private practice in the back of the Wheaton Inn. Although other physicians had been retained over the years to come to Norton to hold office hours for students, this change, taken in conjunction with the opening of the new infirmary in April, 1954, constituted a major upgrading of Wheaton's health services.[23]

Perhaps the most serious issue that faced the administration and the trustees during the late 1940s and early 1950s was that of faculty and staff compensation. The matter was not one that involved disagreement in principle. The Board and the President were acutely aware of the need to bring Wheaton's compensation schedules in all areas into line with other institutions, both in terms of adjusting to the rapid inflationary spiral of the postwar years, and also to make it easier to hire and retain faculty and staff. From the beginning of his presidency, Howard Meneely articulated to the Board the need to improve faculty salaries. The loss of several senior faculty to other institutions during the late 1940s served to emphasize this need.[24]

In the spring of 1945, the College was able to end the wartime policy of annual Christmas bonuses, and begin again to grant permanent increases, most often still only when contracts were renewed at the end of their specified two or three-year terms. However, it proved very difficult to deal with both the general increase in the cost of living and the individual salary inequities that had built up during the depression and war years. These were further exacerbated by the fact that new faculty hired in the postwar period often had to be retained at salaries considerably higher than what others with far longer standing in the Wheaton community were receiving. Time and again the President reported growing faculty unrest on this issue to the trustees.[25]

The matter was brought home to the Trustee Administration Committee in November, 1946, when it met with the Faculty Conference Committee and received a "courteous but urgent appeal" for a 25 percent upward revision of all faculty salaries being paid in the current year. In a letter to trustee Carrol Shanks, President Meneely commented that while the amount suggested might be too much, the request itself "was not unreasonable in view of what is being done at other colleges."[26] And indeed the Board did respond by making an upward adjustment at the beginning of the second semester. Fiscally, the College really could not afford it, the President wrote to trustee Herbert Plimpton, but since other colleges were doing the same thing, and the faculty was "undoubtedly hard pressed because of living costs, . . . it seemed advisable to take action."[27]

Despite these efforts, an independent study commissioned as part of the work of the Trustee Survey Committee indicated that while the Consumer Price Index had increased by 74 percent between 1940 and 1948, only three faculty members had received increases in excess of 50 percent during the same period. Although the study was quick to point out that increases overall in the academic world had failed to keep pace with inflation, it noted that in Wheaton's case, because of lower general salaries and greater inequities built into the system prior to 1940, the problem was particularly acute.[28]

Writing to Dr. Meneely in May, 1947, Board Chairman Richard Chapman stated that it was the concerted opinion of the trustees that "improvement in the salaries and working conditions of the faculty is the most urgent need of the College. . . ."[29] The upshot was that the Trustee Survey Committee, in reponse to faculty requests and with presidential acquiescence, recommended the adoption for the first time in Wheaton history of an official set of salary ranges for each academic rank. This was a concept for which the President, with Board permission, quietly had been working to create a base since the end of 1945. The proposed scale was adopted by the Trustee Administration and Finance committees and distributed to the faculty on February 4, 1949. Although it would take several years to adjust all salaries to their proper place within the range, the President stated, all faculty receiving less than the new minimum for their rank would be advanced to that level beginning in the next academic year.[30]

Subsequently, upward adjustments of the scale were voted periodically by the trustees. In 1951, new federal tax guidelines mandated that individuals pay taxes on the value of housing and board stipends, which up until that time had been awarded in lieu of cash salary. From that time on, all salaries, as well as individual and College contributions to the TIAA pension plan, were computed as a base figure from which rent and board charges were subsequently deducted, a step that did much to lessen gender inequities in the salary structure that had long existed at Wheaton. Nonetheless, despite continuous efforts to improve faculty compensation throughout the 1950s, "we found ourselves chasing our own tail," commented Board Chair Richard Chapman. In terms of the general national inflationary growth as well as in comparison to the wages of other institutions, the College gained little, always "playing catch-up ball."[31]

But in many ways, the most serious challenge to the College's employment and wage policies came from a different source. For some time President Meneely had lamented to the Board of Trustees the difficulties in hiring and retaining domestic, grounds, and secretarial staff. "I have my moments," he wrote to Richard Chapman, "when I wonder whether I shouldn't pray for a depression. Ten years ago candidates all along the line were a nickel a dozen."[32] In addition to a 1947 year-end 5 percent bonus for all staff, the President reported to the Board in March, 1948, that maintenance workers had been given an average 12.5 percent raise the previous January, along with time and a half for overtime, a reduction in hours, and five instead of three paid holidays. Nonetheless, he noted, Wheaton's wages were still lower than those paid by business in general, and the lack of eligibility for Social Security hindered hiring and retention enormously.[33]

Three years later the President was stunned when he suddenly was faced by a serious attempt by the Playthings, Novelty and Jewelry Workers Union of the CIO, a dominant force in the economy of neighboring Attleboro, which styled itself as the "Jewelry Capital of America," to unionize the maintenance and domestic workers at the College. The College immediately responded by granting all domestic service employees a 10 percent raise, and revising sick leave and vacation benefits for those in maintenance. Challenging the union's application to the Massachusetts Labor Relations Board for certification to hold an election, the College's lawyers successfully argued that the Labor Relations Board had no jurisdiction over a nonprofit organization. When the union carried its appeal to the Regional and National Labor Relations Boards, the College maintained the same position, adding the argument that Federal regulations applied only to businesses engaged in interstate trade. At all levels the Boards ruled that indeed they had no jurisdiction over nonprofit institutions.[34]

Fortunately for President Meneely and the Board, exactly at this time a change in Federal regulations also provided relief from perhaps the greatest employment obstacle Wheaton had faced in the preceding decade. An amendment to the Federal Social Security Act in 1950 for the first time allowed nonprofit institutions to participate in the old age and survivors portions of the Social Security system. In October, 1950, the Board of Trustees voted to enroll in the program, contingent on two-thirds of the employees voting in favor of such action. College contributions would be in addition to the already established Faculty Retirement Plans, and participation would constitute the first pension plan for non-faculty employees. The response was overwhelmingly favorable, and in January, 1951, the College and its employees began making payments into the program. To ensure that two faculty, Elizabeth Amen and Louise Boas, who were scheduled to retire that June, could be eligible for Social Security payments, the College granted them the right to teach for one more year in order to amass the six quarters necessary to qualify for a pension under the Act. The trustees also agreed to carry William Rogers, a long-time maintenance employee, on full salary for seven months despite his inability to work, so that he could qualify for Social Security benefits.[35]

In terms of the nonteaching staff, the advent of Social Security was particularly welcome to the College administration. Not only did it help greatly in attracting and retaining new workers, it also lessened the pressure on Wheaton to allow its maintenance and domestic workers to continue working well into their seventies. The College had no mandatory retirement policy for nonteaching staff, and because it had no pension plan in place the general tendency was to allow employees to continue long after their effectiveness had declined substantially. Occasionally, small sums were voted to retiring long-time employees from the "Contingent Fund" set up for that purpose. Now the fact that all employees could draw on Social Security, but only after they retired, was seen as a much needed new incentive to encourage voluntary retirement at a reasonable age.[36]

While the decade from 1945 to 1955 witnessed earnest but not particularly successful attempts on the part of the College to deal with inflationary and competitive wage demands, substantial changes and improvements did occur in the area of fringe benefits. Particularly important was the trustees' decision to enter into a group medical and life insurance program for all employees with the Prudential Insurance Co., which went into effect on Christmas Day, 1949.[37] Up until that time Wheaton employees had been eligible to purchase individual medical insurance policies at a group insurance rate from BlueCross/BlueShield, which now withdrew this option from the College. The new policy, for which the College paid all of the employee and 50 percent of additional family medical premiums, included life, accidental death and medical insurance coverage.[38]

For faculty there were additional positive developments. In the early years of his administration, President Meneely several times urged the trustees to consider increasing the College's contribution to the TIAA retirement program from 5 percent to 7 percent of the faculty member's salary. Once the College joined the Social Security program, his advocacy of this increase ceased. However, in 1952, the Board did vote to allow faculty to shift up to 50 percent of their retirement contributions from the standard TIAA annuity account to the newly created College Retirement Equities Fund, also administered by TIAA. The College, it was agreed, would contribute the same percentage to the fund that was elected by the faculty member. Nonetheless, it was clear that a number of the trustees regarded the investment of retirement funds in a common stock mutual fund as potentially very risky. "It was felt," the Trustees Minutes record, "that the faculty should be cautioned as to the limitations of this fund."[39] Slightly over half of those enrolled in the TIAA retirement program elected to divert some funds to CREF.[40]

Although sabbatical leaves, which had been discontinued during the war years, were reinstituted in 1946, no guidelines existed for awarding them, and the financial terms mitigated very strongly against the vast majority of the faculty who lived in college housing. Required to vacate their lodgings while on leave, they received no cash compensation in lieu of the board or housing provisions that had always served as a nonsalary part of their total compensation package. In 1950, however, the trustees responded to several years of discussion with the faculty Committee on Conference with the Trustees by approving a statement prepared by the President which specified that sabbaticals should be seen not only as a reward for past service, but also as an opportunity to engage in research or other intellectual activities that promised to increase the member's "usefulness" upon return to active teaching. Guidelines specifying the length of service necessary in order to apply were also provided. Only a limited number of leaves could be granted (the President privately told the Board it would be the equivalent of three each semester), and the granting of sabbaticals could not be considered an automatic perquisite.

Most importantly, however, the fiscal terms for holding a sabbatical were for the first time specified in writing. Wheaton would continue to follow the general custom of providing full salary for a half year and half-salary for a full year leave. But that figure would now be determined after computing the full value of the compensation normally received by the individual. Faculty could elect to remain in college housing, in which case the value of the housing would be deducted before determining the cash salary amount. Those who vacated their housing and received a cash allowance for it would have to allow the College to rent out their accommodations during the period they were away. Wheaton would also continue its 5 percent contribution to TIAA/CREF while a person was on leave, providing the faculty member volunteered to do likewise.[41]

In an effort to encourage faculty to attend professional meetings, President Meneely asked for and received permission from the Board to establish a Faculty Convention Travel Fund, which was funded initially with a sum of $500. Since the President indicated that he would probably limit any single application to an award of $25, this amount was regarded as more than enough. But the creation of this fund turned out to be the genesis of what would in time become a larger special account designed to help subsidize faculty research and professional travel.[42]

Finally, in 1952 the Board of Trustees voted action on a matter that had been under discussion, both within the Wheaton community and with a number of other college administrations since 1947. In that year the trustees had voted in principle to approve Wheaton's participation in a plan authored by the Dean of Williams College to create a college exchange program for faculty children among a group of nineteen regional undergraduate institutions. Although this proposed program eventually foundered because of issues involving equity in terms of numbers of children participating, the issue of helping faculty provide for the education of their children in the inflationary economy of the postwar era did not subside. Although President Meneely recognized the implied inequity of such a benefit in a college with so many single faculty members, he nonetheless sympathized with the plight of faculty who wished to have their children leave the confines of small-town Norton for their college education, rather than taking advantage, at least for daughters, of the well-established College policy of remitting tuition to all faculty children who attended Wheaton.[43]

Therefore, the President proposed and the Board approved a policy that would allow faculty to receive one-half of the annual tuition at the college their children attended, provided the sum did not exceed $400 per year, which was more than one-half of Wheaton's current $750 tuition. This amount would be granted regardless of any scholarship aid received from the college that the child attended, and would be continued as long as the student maintained scholarship level grades equal to those required at Wheaton. Several years later, in recognition of the general increase in tuition at colleges nationwide, the maximum was increased to $500, where it remained, notwithstanding faculty efforts to have it increased, until the early 1990s.[44]

Despite continued dissatisfaction over the failure of faculty salaries to improve in the face of the nationally escalating cost of living, the reaction of the faculty to these improved benefits and to the administration in general was one of extreme appreciation, an appreciation that on occasion took interesting forms. Having received a grant for 1952–53 to study in California, Biology Professor Jane Chidsey wrote to Dr. Meneely renouncing the half-salary she had been awarded for her sabbatical year. The grateful President responded by volunteering to pay both the College's and Miss Chidsey's share of her TIAA/CREF contribution for the year. Similarly, after having been awarded a sum equal to one-half the annual tuition at Duke University where his daughter was entering in 1954, Professor of Psychology Walter Shipley wrote to the President giving up the award. He had read the provisions for the Wheaton grant more carefully, he noted, and discovered that it was supposed to apply to faculty who "required" financial assistance. Since he and his family did not require such aid, he wrote, he could not in good conscience take the money. Finally, there was the rather bizarre attempt by English professor Katherine Burton to refuse a promotion to full professor on the grounds that she did not have a Ph.D. and therefore did not deserve the rank. Only when President Meneely gently but firmly insisted did Miss Burton acquiesce.[45]

For the faculty, another benefit was also forthcoming, nonmonetary in nature, but long sought after. Although a form of de facto tenure had existed at Wheaton since the mid 1930s, and had been acknowledged as such in a special report by President Park to the Board of Trustees shortly before his retirement, only one faculty member, Walter Shipley, had been officially granted that status by the trustees.[46] In general, College policy had been to regard those with the rank of instructor as having "impermanent status;" promotion from that rank to assistant professor was taken to mean, on the part of both the administration and faculty, that the College's intention was to continue employment on a long-term basis.[47]

Almost immediately upon assuming office, President Meneely was presented with a request from the Executive Committee of AAUP that Wheaton formally accept the 1940 *Statement of Principles on Academic Freedom and Tenure*. Well aware that President Park had at times invoked that document in his wartime conversations with faculty seeking to leave Wheaton for employment elsewhere, Dr. Meneely immediately entered into discussions regarding a draft tenure statement with the newly created Faculty Advisory Committee to the President. However, he was soon advised by trustee Sylvia Meadows that many on the Board believed the policy should be crafted and approved first by the Board of

Trustees, and only then submitted for faculty consideration. Although he noted that at four other women's colleges faculty had taken the initial step, the President nonetheless acquiesced, and discussions within the Advisory Committee on the matter abruptly ceased.[48]

There the matter languished until the report of the Trustee Survey Committee in January, 1949, which recommended that permanent tenure be granted to all those promoted or appointed to the rank of associate professor, and that contracts for persons at the associate and full professor rank should no longer be issued. This recommendation was approved by the joint meeting of the Trustee Administration and Finance Committees on January 22 and announced to the faculty on February 4, to go into effect the following fall.[49]

What remained was the necessity of revising the College Statutes to conform with this policy. This turned out not to be an easy task for the Board, and led to intense discussion and debate among its members. The issues were whether there should be a probationary period for persons whose initial appointment was at the associate or full professor rank, and the extent and nature of possible limitations to be placed on the holding of tenure. While it was quickly decided that new appointees at these upper ranks should be given an initial three-year contract, with renewal carrying tenure, the second issue created strong divisions within the Board, and delayed ratification of an amendment to the Statutes for nearly a year.

All were readily in accord that tenured service could be terminated for "adequate cause," which they privately agreed could be either demonstrated teaching incompetence or proven commitment of an act of moral turpitude. Equally acceptable to all was termination upon attainment of the mandatory retirement age of sixty-five. But when the President raised the question of whether the phrase "necessity for financial retrenchment" should also be included, as was the case in the tenure provisions at some other colleges, a major split occurred within the Board. While Chairman Richard Chapman and the majority of the Board were adamant that some such provision was necessary in order to ensure that the trustees retained total financial control of the College, a minority, led by William Hastings, Ruth McKay and Frances Jordan maintained that to include financial retrenchment as a grounds for removal seemed "to nullify the concept of permanent tenure."[50] Admitting that it was understandable that faculty might be concerned that financial reasons could be used to mask a dismissal involving issues of academic freedom, Chapman nonetheless insisted that some way be found to allay faculty fears and still include a financial exigency clause. The matter was debated without resolution at both the June and November, 1949, Board meetings.[51]

Subsequent to the latter meeting, Mr. Chapman appointed a subcommittee made up of the President and one proponent of each position.

"All that I expect," he wrote Dr. Meneely, "is a concisely worded statement completely satisfactory to both sides of the issues."[52] He would
need "this masterpiece" in approximately a month, Chapman noted,
commenting that if the subcommittee could not agree, there was little
hope that the full Board would be able to. Responding rather ruefully
that he had been "left on the hot seat,"[53] the President nonetheless was
able to broker an acceptable compromise, which allowed tenure termination "under extraordinary circumstances because of financial exigencies
which are clearly established."[54] Any person involved in a tenure abro-
gation proceeding would be entitled to a hearing before a committee of
trustees, with the final decision always to rest with the full Board. This
statement was accepted by the Board on January 28, 1950, almost exactly a year after the initial approval of tenure and five months after the
implementation of the policy for eligible members of the Wheaton faculty.[55]

In two other areas, the President persuaded the Board of Trustees to
address long standing faculty concerns. During the first year of his presidency, Dr. Meneely had identified the need for more off-campus faculty
housing for single women faculty as his first priority in terms of building
construction. From the beginning he was clearly every bit as sympathetic
as his predecessor had been to the plight of senior women faculty forced
to live among students in suites located in the dormitories. In 1946, he
brought the long-standing impasse between the administration and Professor Henrietta Jennings to an end, when he persuaded the trustees to
allow him to remove the "living" provisions from her contract, and to
replace it with a cash adjustment in her salary.[56] In 1947, the Board, at
his urging, authorized the development of plans for 16 off-campus units
for women faculty, but the contemplated construction cost of the proposed Georgian style apartments designed by Perry, Shaw & Hepburn
proved far too expensive. In an effort to reduce the per unit cost, the
trustees voted to turn to wood rather than brick construction and engaged
a different Boston architect, Howard Rich, to draw up new plans.[57]

Meanwhile the College embarked on a number of other housing projects. The first floor of The Sem, which had served during the war as the
center for many war related activities, was converted to a faculty apartment. Heeding the President's plea that a lack of available housing in
Norton was hindering his ability to hire male faculty with families, the
College bought three wood frame houses that stood contiguous to College-owned land and renovated them for family occupancy. In addition,
the social rooms in Hebe Parlors, which connected Kilham and Metcalf
dormitories, were converted into suites for four women faculty. Finally,
in March of 1949, the trustees authorized the construction of eight
(rather than the sixteen initially planned) townhouse type units for single
faculty on land at the end of Howard Street. By the following August the
complex, named after former English professor Grace Shepard, had been

completed, and the new occupants moved in early in the fall. Thus by the end of 1949, at an approximate cost of $175,000, the College had added four family and twelve single residential units.[58] Subsequently, in 1954, the old infirmary, renamed Riddell House, was converted into one family and two single apartments.

The pleasure with which the new housing facilities in Hebe and Shepard Court were greeted by the senior women faculty was enormous. "I almost hesitate to let myself think how pleased I would be to live outside the dormitories," Professor of Spanish Frances Burlingame wrote to President Meneely as she enthusiastically responded to his enquiry as to whether she would like one of the new Shepard Court units.[59]

The President's ability to convince the trustees to invest substantially in the purchase, renovation and construction of housing for faculty was primarily due to the fact that he contemplated converting the vacated faculty dormitory suites into student housing. It was estimated that the twelve units vacated by women faculty in 1949 could be utilized to house up to thirty-six additional students, with no major renovations required to the vacated suites. This would provide a much needed permanent increase in revenue flow without any need to construct additional dormitory space.[60]

However, as Dr. Meneely noted in his report to the Board in November, 1947, these many additional students would create an intolerable

The building of Shepard Court was the most important of several actions taken in the late 1940s to address the housing needs of women members of the faculty and staff.

space problem in the Emerson and Everett dining rooms—a problem that could most easily be dealt with by building a separate adjacent dining room for faculty and staff. Doing so, the President commented, would provide not only enough student dining space, but would also do much to improve the morale of unmarried faculty, who had long resented the requirement that they eat with students in the large dining halls.[61]

The result was that in January, 1950, the Board of Trustees authorized the drawing of preliminary plans for a faculty-staff dining room and lounge, which would not only alleviate the overcrowding in the main dining rooms but would also provide a much needed social center for the faculty. The plans were approved in March, and by that fall the new dining room and lounge were open for business. Although single women living in College housing were still required to take some meals in the dining room, by 1954 four different plans covering all meals, all weekday meals, weekday lunches and dinners, or weekday lunches only were made available.[62]

The small quadrangle in front of the new dining hall was named Barrows Green in 1953, in honor of retiring Botanist Florence Barrows. One of the first purchases by the newly created Faculty Lounge Committee was a set of bocci balls, on the rarely fulfilled theory that faculty would relax by bowling on Barrows Green.[63]

Even more important for some faculty was a change in the College's policy regarding faculty occupancy of dormitory suites during vacation periods. From the very beginning of his term in office, President Meneely had urged the Board to address the requirement that all faculty living in dormitories leave campus for the periods when the College was not in session. In November, 1947, the trustees finally authorized him to work out an alternative plan. The President immediately allowed all faculty to remain in their dormitory suites during the Christmas and spring vacations, although they had to take their meals at the Wheaton Inn. By the summer of 1948, Chapin dormitory had been equipped with its own hot water tank, and faculty who desired to remain on campus during the summer months were allowed to take rooms there and eat in the staff dining room, then located in the basement of Emerson.[64]

On two issues President Meneely remained firm in adhering to the policies of his predecessors. Given the fact that women outnumbered men on the faculty by a two to one margin, he sought, whenever possible, to hire men rather than women to positions on the faculty, and generally placed them higher within the salary ranges for each rank than was the case for women. In part this salary differential was due to the general market pressures of the academic world, but it was also because he, like Dr. Park, believed that men should earn more because they were the prime supporters of a family. In Wheaton's case this last was particularly true, since with one exception, English instructor Curtis Dahl, the College adhered to a policy of not hiring single male faculty.[65]

Writing to offer Wheaton alumna Louise Barr MacKenzie a position in the English department in 1947, the President commented that the delay in making the offer had not been because the College questioned her competence or the contribution she could make to Wheaton, but rather "because of a feeling that we should appoint a man if a good one could be found."[66] Mrs. MacKenzie's reply was interesting in terms of her implied acceptance of this policy. "For the sake of the college," she wrote, "I am truly sorry no satisfactory man was available; for my own sake, I am very glad indeed."[67]

President Meneely was also determined that faculty should live near the college. This rule was not gender specific—even leaving College housing to purchase a home in nearby communities such as Mansfield or Foxboro was discouraged. Approving reluctantly a request by Mathematics Professor Hilda Geiringer to live in off-campus facilities, the President also firmly insisted, "I would not be willing to consent to a commuting arrangement since it is particularly desirable for a head of a department to be a resident of the community."[68] Similarly, when August Miller, who taught Political Science, requested permission to be relieved of his contractual arrangement to live in College housing, the President approved only on condition that he purchase a home within a ten to twelve mile radius of Norton. "It would," he wrote to Miller, "be decidedly contrary to the interest of the College to lose the residential character of our faculty."[69] To have very many members of the faculty "nonresident" he commented to the Board of Trustees, was "not in the interest of the College."[70] He was, however, willing to sell College land to faculty who would build their own houses, as long as Wheaton was given a first purchase option if the owner ever decided to sell. Although one professor, Robert Sharp, negotiated at some length regarding this possibility, there is no record that any member of the faculty actually took up this option.[71]

The President was equally insistent that Wheaton-owned family-sized apartments be reserved for married male faculty members. When Chemistry Instructor Bojan Jennings was rehired in 1950, she returned to Norton with a husband and two small children, and was given a one-year rental of a College-owned apartment. However, in his letter confirming this offer President Meneely wrote: "Our Trustees intend and expect that the off-campus apartments should be reserved for married men since we need to have a reasonable number of facilities available for them. I have permitted you and your family to occupy the apartment in question simply because it does not appear that we shall need it for a man with a family next year."[72]

Since most faculty lived on or within walking distance of the campus, small classes and seminars routinely met in faculty dormitory suites or homes, thus alleviating pressure on scarce classroom space. Here Professor Holcombe Austin conducts a philosophy seminar in 1949-50.

In his efforts to improve faculty salaries and benefits, President Meneely was fortunate in having the strong and unswerving support of Richard Chapman, who had taken over as Chairman of the Board of Trustees in the wake of the Art Center controversy. Believing that the main goal of the College should be to improve the quality of both its students and faculty, Chapman recognized the need to provide better salaries, benefits, and working and living conditions in order to attract and retain good faculty.[73]

In retrospect, it is apparent that the well-intentioned and on-going attempts during these years to improve faculty salaries accomplished little other than to lessen the negative impact of the national economic inflationary tendencies of the late 1940s and the 1950s. Nonetheless, there is abundant evidence that most of the faculty recognized and appreciated the efforts that were made. However, the wide range of improvements brought about in the areas of tenure, benefits, and living accommodations did address successfully many long-standing issues of faculty concern. Despite continuing tension regarding required meals in the faculty dining room and the assignment of residential quarters, there was also a distinct lessening of the sense of gender discrimination so long felt among women members of the teaching staff. Overall, the morale of faculty members, and satisfaction with their situation at Wheaton, had improved markedly by the end of President Meneely's first decade in office.

NOTES: CHAPTER 17

1. Staff: Carpenter: Carpenter to Park, 11/22/43.
2. Trustees Minutes: 3/6/44.
3. Trustees: Meadows #9: Meneely to Meadows, 3/26/45.
4. Smart/Park: Park correspondence: Meneely to Park, 3/26/45; see also President's Reports to Trustees: 3/23/45.
5. Staff: Barker: copy, Meneely to McKay, 3/26/45; see also President's Reports to Trustees: 3/23/45.
6. Trustees Minutes: 10/14/44; 3/23/45; 6/3/45; 3/16/46; President's Reports to Trustees: 10/14/44; Trustees: Chase #4: Young to Chase, 4/29/46; Park to Chase, 4/30/46; Chase to Meneely, 5/3/46; Staff: S. B. Young: Packet dealing with remuneration on retirement, 4/30/46. In 1959, the College increased its annual cash supplementary payment to Miss Young from $444 to $1000.
7. President's Reports to Trustees: 6/6/48.
8. The committee was chaired by William Hastings, with Ruth McKay (W1923) and Frances Jordan serving as the other two members.
9. Trustees, General Information: Reports, 1945–55: Report of the Committee on the Survey of Wheaton College, 1/22/49; Memorandum recording decisions taken by the Administration and Finance Committees on the Report of the Trustee Committee, 1/22/49.
10. Ibid.: Meneely to Faculty, 2/4/49. In 1952, the chairmanship of the Committee on Instruction was also changed from the President to the Academic Dean. Faculty Meeting Minutes: 9/17/52. See also Staff: May: Duties of Academic Dean, 9/28/50.
11. Staff: Barker: Barker to Meneely, 1/31/49; Trustees: Chapman #3: Meneely to Chapman, 4/12/49; Trustees Minutes: 6/12/49.
12. Dean May's starting salary was $5000 and meals when on campus, plus the rent free use of Hollyhock House, far less than the $10,000 she had been earning in her most recent positions. Staff: May: Meneely to May, 4/8/49; Trustees Minutes: 6/12/49; President's Reports to Trustees: 6/12/49; Oral History Project: J. Yelle interview, 1983; H. Yelle interview, 1983.
13. Dean Colpitts' salary was $3500 plus meals when on campus, and a rent free apartment. Oral History Project: L. Colpitts interview, 1983; President's Reports to Trustees: 6/12/49. See also Staff: Colpitts: Duties of Dean of Students, 9/28/50.
14. Staff: Colpitts: Colpitts to Meneely, 11/1/49, 12/16/49; President's Reports to Trustees: 6/11/50.
15. Faculty Meeting Minutes: 12/12/49.
16. Oral History Project: E. May interview, 1983.
17. Ibid.
18. Ibid.: L. Colpitts interview, 1983; also E. May interview, 1983.
19. Trustees: Shanks #6: Meneely to Shanks, 12/13/49.
20. Staff: Dearden: Meneely to Dearden, 2/20/50; Trustees Minutes: 3/11/50.
21. Trustees Minutes: 6/8/52; Faculty Meeting Minutes: 9/17/52.
22. Trustees, General Information: Reports, 1945–55: Trustee Survey Committee Report, 1/22/49; President's Reports to Trustees: 6/8/52; Trustees Minutes: 11/1/52; 1/24/53; 3/21/53; *Wheaton News*, 2/5/53; Staff: Sargent; Meneely to Sargent, 8/24/53.

The College Statutes were revised to allow both the Comptroller and the Placement Director to be voting members of the faculty. Faculty Meeting Minutes: 9/23/53.

23. President's Reports to Trustees: 6/11/50; 6/8/52; 6/7/53; 6/6/54; 10/23/54; Trustees Minutes: 11/5/49; 6/8/52; 11/1/52; 3/21/53; 6/7/53; 1/3/54; Staff: Sargent: Sargent to Meneely, 5/26/54. Dr. Duffield's half-time salary was $5000. The infirmary, designed by the new College Architect, Howard Rich, cost $160,481 plus an additional $12,044 for furnishings.

24. For example: Ralph Hidy to the Business History Foundation, William Hunt to Northwestern University, Osborne Earle to Brandeis, Maria Rickers to the University of Connecticut, and Walter Nickerson to Rutgers.

25. Dean May commented later that salaries in this period were terribly low and that the faculty were right to agitate for substantial increases. See Oral History Project: E. May interview, 1983.

26. Trustees: Shanks #7: Meneely to Shanks, 11/13/46.

27. Ibid.: Plimpton #1: Meneely to Plimpton, 1/13/47. See also President's Reports to Trustees: 3/23/45; 6/3/45; 11/3/45; 11/9/46; 3/1/47; 11/6/48. Trustee Maurice Clemence, who was also a member of the School Board in Wellesley, MA, later helped make the case for improving faculty salaries by showing the President and the Board the salary scale for persons holding a Masters degree who taught in the Wellesley public school system. Oral History Project: M. Clemence interview, 1983.

28. Trustees, General Information: Faculty Salary Scales, 1942–66: Report by Norman Malcolm, Jr., 11/24/48; Trustees Minutes: 11/6/48.

29. Trustees: Chapman #2: Chapman to Meneely, 5/21/47.

30. President's Reports to Trustees: 3/6/48; 11/6/48; Faculty Meeting Minutes: 11/15/48; Trustees Minutes: 11/3/45; Trustees, General Information: Reports, 1945–55: Report of Committee on the Survey of Wheaton College, 1/22/49; Memorandum on the Decisions of the Trustee Administration and Finance Committees, 1/22/49; Meneely to Faculty, 2/4/49; Staff: Dunkle: Meneely to Dunkle, 7/31/50.

31. Oral History Project: R. Chapman interview, 1983. See also Meneely/May: Salary Scales: Salary Scales, 1949–62. Beginning in 1957, only the minimum for each rank was established, the maximum was discontinued. Trustees: Meadows #7, Meneely to Meadows, 3/27/50; Faculty: Cressey: Cressey to Meneely, 1/4/52; Meneely to Cressey, 1/10/52; President's Reports to Trustees: 1/20/51; 1/19/52; Faculty Meeting Minutes: 1/15/51; Trustees, General Information: Reports, 1945–55: Meneely to Faculty, 1/25/52; Trustees Minutes: 6/10/51; 1/24/53, which includes a penciled note, "Fin Com reports existing level at top about 20% below that of other colleges in the Northeast."

32. Trustees: Chapman #3: Meneely to Chapman, 7/11/48.

33. President's Reports to Trustees: 3/6/48.

34. Trustees: Chapman #6: Meneely to Chapman, 2/8,10,20/51; Chapman to Meneely, 2/21/51; Winslow #1: Meneely to Winslow, 2/26/51; Cox #2: Meneely to Cox, 2/26/51; Hasting #2: Meneely to Hastings, 3/3/51; 4/19/51; 5/8/51; President's Reports to Trustees: 3/17/51; 6/10/51.

35. Faculty: H. Jennings: Jennings to Meneely, 10/30/50; Meneely to Jennings, 10/16/50; Trustees Minutes: 10/28/50; Trustees, General Information: Reports, 1945–55: Meneely to Faculty, 10/30/50; President's Reports to Trustees: 1/20/51; Faculty: Amen: Meneely to Amen, 10/31/50; Amen to Meneely, 8/7/50; Trustees: Chase #5: Meneely to Chase, 12/28/50; Chapman #5: Chapman to Meneely, 9/14/50; Chapman #6: Meneely to Chapman, 11/5/51; Chapman to Meneely, 11/6/51.

36. See Trustees: Chapman #5: Chapman to Meneely, 6/20/50; Fitzgerald to Chapman, 6/13/50; Meneely to Chapman, 6/26/50.

37. The President of Prudential Insurance was Vice Chairman of the Wheaton Board of Trustees Carroll Shanks.

38. Trustees Minutes: 6/12/49; 11/5/49; Faculty Meeting Minutes: 12/12/49; Staff: M. Clark: Announcement of Group Insurance, 12/22/49; Lincoln: Grounds and Building Department Regulations, 1/31/52; Trustees: Chase #5: Meneely to Chase, 10/18/49; 12/13/49; Shanks #6: Meneely to Shanks, 12/13/49.

39. Trustees Minutes: 6/8/52.

40. Faculty Meeting Minutes: 9/17/52; Trustees Minutes: 11/1/52. Of the twenty-eight persons who chose to place some retirement funds in CREF, two put in 20 percent, seven chose one third of their contribution, while nineteen elected the maximum allowable 50 percent. President's Reports to Trustees: 1/24/53; see also 11/8/47; Trustees: Chase #4: Meneely to Chase, 1/7/48. In 1948, the trustees had voted to require all those with the rank of assistant professor and higher to join TIAA; instructors, however, could only elect to join after three years of service, but even then were not required to do so. Trustees Minutes: 3/6/48.

41. President's Reports to Trustees: Memorandum, Sabbatical Leaves, prepared for meeting 3/11/50; Trustees Minutes: 3/11/50; see also President's Reports to Trustees: 3/6/48; 1/28/50; Faculty Meeting Minutes: 2/26/48; 3/13/50; Faculty: Korsch: Meneely memorandum, 1/15/48; Burton: Burton to Meneely, 11/6/49; 11/29/49.

42. Trustees Minutes: 6/8/52; 11/1/52; Staff: Dunkle: Meneely to Dunkle, 7/7/52.

43. Trustees Minutes: 6/8/47; President's Reports to Trustees: 6/8/47.

44. President's Reports to Trustees: 1/19/52; Trustees minutes: 1/19/52; 6/8/52.

45. Faculty: Chidsey: Chidsey to Meneely, 4/4/52; Meneely to Chidsey, 4/10/52; Shipley: Shipley to Meneely, 6/11/54; Meneely to Shipley 6/17/54; Shipley to Meneely, 6/18/54; Burton: Meneely to Burton, 1/22/51; Burton to Meneely, 1/23/51; 3/10/51.

46. See chs. 13, 15.

47. Faculty: Clewes: Park to Clewes, 4/7/44; Ramseyer: Meneely to Ramseyer, 1/18/45.

48. Trustees: Clark #6: Meneely to Clark, 11/15/44; Meadows #9: Meneely to Meadows, 11/15/44; 4/10/45; Meadows to Meneely, 4/23/45; Trustees Minutes: 3/23/45. In the spring of 1948, writing to newly hired English Instructor Curtis Dahl, the President commented, "We strive to adhere to good academic practice in the matter of tenure." Faculty: Dahl: Meneely to Dahl, 6/15/48.

49. Trustees, General Information: Reports, 1945–55: Report of Trustees Survey Committee, 1/22/49; Memorandum recording decisions taken by the Administration and Finance Committees on the report of the Trustee Survey Committee, 1/22/49; Meneely to Faculty, 2/4/49.

50. Trustees: Hastings #1: Hastings to Meneely, 5/21,23,24/49; Chapman #3: Meneely to Chapman, 5/23/4.

51. Trustees: Chapman #3: Chapman to Meneely, 5/17,24/49; Meneely to Chapman, 5/27/49; Chapman to Meneely, 6/21/49; Trustees Minutes: 3/5/49; 6/12/49; 11/5/49; President's Reports to Trustees: Letter and Data sent to Trustees, 10/26/49.

52. Trustees: Chapman #4: Chapman to Meneely, 12/6/49.

53. Ibid.: Meneely to Chapman, 12/8/49.

54. Trustees Minutes: 1/28/50.

55. In addition to the President, the members of the subcommittee were Ruth McKay and William Chase. See Trustees: Chapman #4: Chapman to Meneely, 12/2/40; 12/6/49; Meneely to Chapman, 12/8/49; President's Reports to Trustees: 1/28/50; Trustees Minutes: 1/28/50; Faculty Meeting Minutes: 3/13/50.

56. See ch 13. Faculty: H. Jennings: Meneely to Jennings, 3/4/46; Jennings to Meneely, 3/6/46.

57. Faculty: Gulley and Amen: Meneely memorandum, 10/26/44; Faculty Meeting Minutes: 9/19/45; 11/29/45; Trustees Minutes: 3/6/48; 6/6/48; President's Reports to Trustees: 6/3/45; 3/6/48.

58. The cost for constructing Shepard Court, including sewer, electrical and landscaping work done by the College work force, came to $114,000. President's Reports to Trustees: 6/3/45; 11/3/45; 3/1/47; 11/5/49; Faculty: Neilson: Meneely to Neilson, 4/23/46; Trustees: Soliday #2: Meneely to Soliday, 4/2/45; Shanks #6: Meneely to Shanks, 3/2/49; Shanks to Meneely, 3/3/49; Meneely to Shanks, 3/7/49; Trustees Minutes: 6/8/47; 3/5/49; 1/28/50; Faculty Meeting Minutes: 9/21/49.

59. Faculty: Burlingame: Burlingame to Meneely, 4/15/49.

60. Trustees, General Information: Reports, 1945–55: Meneely to J. Clark, 3/11/47; Trustees Minutes: 6/8/47; Trustees: Hastings #1: Meneely to Hastings, 11/30/48; President's Reports to Trustees: 3/11/50.

61. President's Reports to Trustees: 11/8/47; Trustees: Chapman #4: Meneely to Chapman, 10/24/49; Faculty Meeting Minutes: 9/21/49.

62. Trustees: Chapman #7: Meneely to Chapman, 1/8/53; Shanks #5: Meneely to Shanks, 2/21/50; President's Reports to Trustees: 10/28/50; 10/24/53; 1/30/54; 3/27/54; Faculty: E. Work: Meneely to Work, 3/18/54; Trustees Minutes: 1/28/50; 1/20/51; 3/11/50; 3/27/54; Faculty Meeting Minutes: 3/13/50. The total cost of the dining room and lounge, including furnishings, was $88,926.

63. Trustees Minutes: 6/7/53; Faculty: Barrows: Meneely to Barrows, 6/9/53; Faculty Meeting Minutes: 9/23/53.

64. Trustees Minutes: 11/8/47; President's Reports to Trustees: 11/3/45; 3/6/48; 6/6/48; Faculty: E. L. White: Meneely to White, 8/7/52.

65. Of the sixty-eight full and part-time faculty actively teaching in 1954–55, twenty-four were men, all married except for one. Dean May commented that President Meneely was reluctant to hire single young men, out of fear that they would seduce students. Oral History Project: E. May interview, 1983. The first question asked the author by Professor E. J. Knapton during my initial interview in May, 1957, at the Harvard History Department Offices, was "Are you married?" The second was "Do you have a car?" Only when the acceptable affirmative answers were provided did the interview turn to a serious discussion of interest and qualifications.

66. Faculty: L. B. MacKenzie: Meneely to MacKenzie, 5/30/47.

67. Ibid.: Mackenzie to Meneely, 6/4/47; see also Sudrann: Sharp to Sudrann, 4/21/47.

68. Faculty: Geiringer: Meneely to Geiringer, 3/10/49.

69. Faculty: Miller: Meneely to Miller, 1/22/52.

70. President's Reports to Trustees: 1/19/52.

71. Faculty: Sharp: Meneely-Sharp correspondence, 1949–56, passim; Trustees Minutes: 11/5/49; President's Reports to Trustees: 11/5/49; Trustees: Cox #2: Meneely to Cox, 11/29/50. Only in the 1960s and 1970s did several faculty negotiate land purchase agreements of this nature.

72. Faculty: B. Jennings: Meneely to Jennings, 5/19/50; Jennings, *Chemistry at Wheaton*, p. 81; see also Oral History Project: J. Chidsey interview, 1983.

73. See, for example, Chapman's strong support for providing summer residence facilities for women faculty. Trustees: Chapman #2: Chapman to Meneely, 2/16/48; see also Oral History Project: R. Chapman interview, 1983.

18
Steady As She Goes, 1946–1954

ONCE THE ENORMOUS TENSIONS induced by the Art Center crisis receded, the College experienced nearly a decade of relative calm and general good will. Although confrontations between the President or the Deans and various faculty members occurred on occasion, with two exceptions they proved to be relatively fleeting in nature. Student activism, so central to the 1945–46 Art Center controversy, also played a preeminent role in bringing about a decision that same year to begin admitting African-American students. After that, however, it totally subsided, and the late 1940s and early 1950s provided generally smooth sailing for both the administration and the College community as a whole.

Perhaps the single most important change during this period was a major revision of the academic requirements mandated for receiving a Wheaton degree. This proved to be a long, tedious, and arduous task, both for the President and for the faculty who participated in it. While President Park had often jump-started new curricular initiatives by independently authorizing them as temporary "experimental" programs or courses, Dr. Meneely insisted that all changes in the curriculum proceed through committee channels to the faculty meeting as a whole, where they were subjected to long and intensive review and debate before being approved.

The issues involved went far beyond reorganizing or repackaging existing courses or programs. Central to the debate was a nationwide revolution in postwar higher education which sought to eliminate the relatively open and free-wheeling elective system of course selection, first championed by President Charles Eliot of Harvard in the 1880s, that had dominated liberal arts programs in colleges and universities during the first four decades of the twentieth century. Now, as President Meneely commented at a Student Council panel discussion in 1946, there was a nationwide trend to replace the free elective system with a specific set of distribution and concentration requirements designed to prevent too great an overconcentration in a single discipline or field by some, as well as too great a dispersion of randomly elected courses by others.[1]

Leading this new trend were curriculums developed at Harvard and

453

Amherst, implemented shortly after the end of the war, which mandated the development of specifically designed broad "general education" courses. Taken together, they would ensure that all students were exposed to the basic principles and concepts inherent in each of the major areas comprising the liberal arts, and would create a relatively uniform educational experience for students during the first two years in college. This would then be followed by work in a major area of concentration, with an upper limit on the number of courses allowed. The major would include seminar work for all, and a greater emphasis on individual research projects for the best students.[2]

With Wheaton's new committee system approved and in place, the President announced to the faculty in October, 1945, that its next major task must be that of a thorough curriculum review. Able to use the elected Committee on Instruction as the development vehicle, rather than the old unwieldy Curriculum Committee which had included all department heads, Dr. Meneely was ready and willing to present his own suggestions for the committee's consideration. Nonetheless, the wheels of change ground fine and very slowly. Proposals generated by the committee were critiqued in enormous detail in faculty meetings and sent back to committee for further consideration. Tentative faculty approval of a new set of requirements was finally attained in April, 1948, with final enactment only coming the following November. In addition to a catalogue statement detailing general graduation standards along with specific distribution and major requirements, the faculty approved (according to the minutes with "loud laughter") a general statement of educational purpose which included that all students were expected to acquire "some knowledge of man in society."[3]

The new requirements followed the national trend. Previously students had been required to take a year of English composition, history, a foreign language, and a science. The new set of distribution requirements specified forty-two rather than twenty-four credits to be taken in seven different classifications: English composition; humanities; foreign language at the 200 level; history; economics, government and sociology; logic, mathematics, natural science and psychology; and a laboratory course in natural science. In only one area was a single course required of all students—History 101, a year course in the history of western civilization from the Middle Ages to the present.[4]

In addition, students were required to complete either a major in one subject or a comprehensive interdepartmental major. The actual number of credits in a major could vary from twenty-four to a maximum of forty-eight credit hours. However, those who completed less than forty-eight hours in their specific discipline were required to take related courses approved by their major department in order to complete a forty-eight hour area concentration. The previous requirement that all students pass a general examination in their major field at the end of the senior year was retained.[5]

In theory this left only thirty hours for free electives; in fact, since courses were allowed to count toward both the distribution and the concentration requirements, the flexibility was somewhat greater than it initially appeared to be. As a final step for the reform package, the faculty also voted to begin using plusses and minuses to record final grades, and passed legislation defining the standards for these new subdivisions of the old straight-letter grading system.[6]

For President Meneely, the faculty's action constituted a moderate step in the right direction. The new requirements as voted were a watered down version of the Committee on Instruction's initial proposal, which had included distribution requirements totalling fifty-four credit hours. "I suspect it would be correct to say that none of us at the College is wholly satisfied with the new revisions," he reported to the trustees. Noting that "few favored a drastic revision and some probably preferred the *status quo*," the President commented that the new curriculum constituted a compromise which was at best "a moderate and unspectacular revision." Nonetheless, "the changes voted represent the best that could be gotten after nearly three years of effort."[7] "What has been approved is far from ideal," he wrote to trustee William Hastings, "but, I believe, it does represent a substantial improvement over what we now have and will be promotive of general education and better balanced programs for our students."[8]

Other than the new distribution requirements, the most important curricular innovation during these years involved a decision to transform the offerings in Education into a program through which Wheaton students could obtain certification as public school teachers. Previously the College had offered a few courses in Education, mainly as an adjunct to the work of the Psychology Department in the College Nursery School. But teacher certification had remained by law the exclusive preserve of the state teachers colleges. Now the Commonwealth of Massachusetts had changed its regulations, and for the first time liberal arts colleges were permitted to develop and implement teacher certification programs. In 1953, Professor Evelyn Banning was recruited to undertake this project. Many faculty were opposed, Dean May recalled, but Professor Banning was "very tactful" in implementing the program. Initially, practice teaching was done in June, after the closing of Wheaton's classes, but eventually it was incorporated into the work of the regular academic year.[9]

The initiative for one of the most successful academic innovations came not from the faculty or administration, but from the Chair of the Board of Trustees, Richard Chapman. In the early 1950s, he began urging the creation of a visiting professorship that would bring to campus each year a distinguished teacher or scholar, who would teach one course each semester, give at least two public lectures, meet with classes taught by others, and consult with faculty as seemed appropriate. Chapman recognized that the salary would have to be considerably higher than that paid any regular member of the teaching staff, but he believed that the positive influence such a person could bring to the whole Wheaton community, plus the favorable general publicity, would more than justify the expense.

Initially, President Meneely was not enthusiastic, but in time he was won over, and in October, 1953, the Board of Trustees approved the plan and authorized a salary of up to $10,000, plus a residence. The President and several trustees were apprehensive about faculty reaction to the higher salary, but when Dr. Meneely announced the plan at a faculty meeting in early November, the response was generally enthusiastic. The result was that in the fall of 1954, nationally renowned poet Richard Eberhart took up his duties as Visiting Professor of English and Poet in Residence, for a salary actually $1500 less than that authorized by the Board.[10]

The appointment turned out to be a great success. Mr. Eberhart's classes "will be almost embarrassingly large," the President reported to the trustees. According to one faculty member, Professor Eberhart's relations with both faculty and students during the year of his appointment "exemplified teaching at its best."[11] The policy of inviting a visiting professor to campus was continued, though not every year, for the next decade.[12]

Other changes also occurred. The faculty approved, first on a trial basis and later permanently, a reading period at the end of each semester for those instructors who wished to use it, in which students were expected to undertake a special independent reading or research project of some type. Classes on the Friday and Saturday after Thanksgiving were given up, and the celebration of Founders Day was moved from the fall to spring because the faculty believed that football weekends, plus the new Thanksgiving break, provided more than enough distractions in the first semester. A proposal to create a calendar that would allow the first semester to end before Christmas received little support in faculty meeting.[13]

A five-day class week also was discussed and rejected by the faculty. Interestingly, in 1953 the *Wheaton News* editorialized against the possible shift to a five-day week, on the grounds that it would be an invitation to all students to leave campus for the entire weekend, which in turn would destroy any sense of the College as a residential community.[14]

Some issues were settled; others were not. In the early 1950s both Paul Cressey and Frank Ramseyer asked permission to teach courses on a regular basis at other institutions in order to supplement income at a time when they had children attending college. Though permission was granted, the Board of Trustees, at the request of the President, approved a policy which stated specifically that all opportunities to teach regular courses at institutions other than Wheaton during the academic year had to be approved annually by the President and could not be done on a long-term continuing basis. An exception was granted to Professor Cressey for a series of five contemporary events lectures to be given each spring at the Katharine Gibbs Secretarial School in Providence.[15]

Unresolved was the request from several individuals and departments that the position of department head be rotated among senior faculty, with limited terms of three years. Suggestions for implementing this policy had actually begun during the latter years of the Park administration. Although the faculty Committee on Conference discussed this with the Administration Committee of the Board of Trustees at length, the President was reluctant to accede, stating that often the small size of departments or the particular personnel involved did not make this practice, however laudable in theory, an appropriate one. As a result, the custom of department heads serving for unspecified terms at the pleasure of the President remained in place.[16]

One other event had a profound effect upon the faculty. Noting that "you do such things superbly well," President Meneely wrote Economics Professor Henrietta Jennings in September, 1947, asking that she take over the position of College Marshal.[17] Miss Jennings agreed, though she commented acerbically that "the form of your request reminded me very much of the way in which my mother used to ask me to iron the men's shirts."[18] For the next eighteen years all academic processions were organized and ruled with her iron hand. Faculty and staff marched by rank in an order of seniority so carefully regimented that for those hired in the same year and rank it was determined by seeking out the date of their letter of appointment. Faculty or staff who failed to be in their proper place five minutes before a procession was to begin were denied the right to march, and had to incur the formidable wrath of Miss Jennings.[19]

Those who wished to be excused from marching in an academic procession for any reason had to make that request to the President at least three days in advance. Such permission was not easily granted. When Biology Professor Jane Chidsey requested in October, 1954, that she be allowed to miss Commencement the following June in order to get an earlier sailing date to Europe, the President refused, stating that he did not want to set a precedent that would force him to excuse others from attending that or other ceremonies.[20]

The loss of Biologist Walter Nickerson, who had been awarded a Guggenheim Fellowship in 1947–48, to Rutgers University, and the retirement of Hilda Geiringer, Professor of Mathematics and widow of the renowned mathematician Richard von Mises, deprived Wheaton of two of its most eminent scholars.[21] However, many within the faculty continued to research, write, and publish on a more modest basis. Faculty spir-

Professor of Economics Henrietta Jennings, College Marshal, leads the 1953 Senior
Class in procession in front of the Library.

its were buoyed by implementation of the tenure system, by the many
improvements in benefits and living conditions, and to an extent by the
real, if not totally successful, efforts by the administration to have salaries keep up with inflation. Overall, the years between 1946 and 1954
proved to be ones in which a much more positive sense of academic and
community well-being existed than had been the case, understandably,
in the years of economic depression and war.

During the first decade of the postwar era, enrollment at Wheaton increased only minimally. Ever since the early 1920s when President Cole
had established 500 as the appropriate size for the College, that guideline had remained firmly in place. In fact, from 1927 to the fall of 1949,
enrollment never attained that magic number, remaining steadily in the
high 400s. Shortly after he attained office, President Meneely expressed
full support for maintaining this standard, commenting to the trustees
that Wheaton should seek to maintain and improve its quality by playing
upon its unique position as the "only small country college for women
carrying on in the liberal arts tradition" among women's colleges in
New England.[22] Despite the subsequent modest increase in the size of
the student body authorized by the Board and made possible by the conversion of former faculty dormitory suites to student housing, in September, 1954, the opening day number of residential students totalled
only 528. However, even with that number of students, the need for a
new classroom building was obvious and pressing. Any expansion substantially beyond the 500 limit for which the campus had been designed
obviously would necessitate major construction projects, not only in

terms of residential housing, but also in academic and support facilities as well.[23]

Lending additional support to the decision to remain a small college of the size envisaged by those who had created it at the beginning of the century were two other factors. The first was the issue of finances. Wheaton had always operated within the basic confines of the fiscal resources of the Wheaton family. With the exception of the Student Alumnae Building and the 1940 addition to the Library, all major construction on the Wheaton campus had been funded either directly by gifts from the Wheaton family, or from income derived from the College's endowment, which again represented almost entirely the financial legacy provided by Eliza Baylies Wheaton's estate.

An attempt to raise additional funds through a capital campaign had failed disastrously in the 1920s, and subsequent more modest attempts through special individual solicitations had been equally unsuccessful, with the exception of three gifts totalling $100,000 to help erect SAB and the Library extension. Time and again Presidents Cole, Park, and Meneely lamented, at times almost incredulously, the inability of Wheaton to raise the kind of funds that other liberal arts colleges seemed able to attract. In March, 1947, in response to the President's statement that Wheaton would need to raise ten to fifteen million dollars in the next ten years, the trustees authorized a subcommittee to examine the feasibility of conducting a capital campaign, though President Meneely himself expressed doubts as to whether the College could even raise one to two million in such an effort.[24]

Two months later the Trustee Committee recommended negatively on the grounds that there was no hope that any large amount could be raised. Instead the Board voted to create a group to be known as the Friends of Wheaton, made up of alumnae and others who would agree to contribute annually to the College. Essentially this involved combining the most loyal contributors to the Annual Alumnae Fund with others who had not attended Wheaton, but who might be willing to contribute to it. Wheaton assumed all annual operational costs of the Alumnae Association, and in turn all proceeds from the Annual Alumnae Fund drive and the Friends of Wheaton campaign went directly to the College.

The whole process was definitely low-keyed; in asking the faculty to recommend nonalumnae who might be contacted the president "emphasized that an effort was being made to avoid the idea of a fund-raising campaign as such."[25] Minimally successful, the Friends of Wheaton failed to attract many who were not alumnae, and while it did contribute in a modest way to gaining funds for the new infirmary, neither it nor the Annual Alumnae Fund drive proved significant as a major fund-raising endeavor. "Fund raising is certainly not an enterprise likely to stimulate the ego or the optimism of an amateur," President Meneely lamented in his report to the Board of Trustees in June, 1950.[26]

In 1950, Wheaton engaged the firm of Marz and Lundy as consultants to assess the prospects for a capital campaign, only to have its hopes completely dashed when the final report estimated that $250,000 was the maximum that the College could hope to raise. Even raising this amount, the consultants stated, would require hiring outside professional supervision of the campaign. The cost of the campaign would be "disproportionately high," because of insufficient public relations efforts by the College in the past. However, the report concluded, conducting a campaign now could lay the basis for a much more successful endeavor in future years, if Wheaton maintained a solid public relations effort in the interim between the two. Faced with this dismal forecast in terms of immediate success, the Board of Trustees decided against engaging a professional fund-raiser, and also rejected an internally run campaign until persons connected with Wheaton could be found to assume key posts in running it. The net result was that no capital campaign was undertaken during the Meneely presidency. In fact, throughout this period, trustee Maurice Clemence later commented, there was no real fund-raising effort of any type, it was just assumed that anybody who wanted to give to Wheaton would do so. Fund-raising, Dean May commented, was "rather quiet and dignified and not very aggressive."[27]

The one remaining possible source for raising additional revenue was to increase the fees levied for tuition, room and board. Since the size of the student body increased only minimally, the inflationary pressures of the postwar and Korean conflict period had to be met solely through increasing charges to students. The result was that between September, 1946 and the fall of 1956, the comprehensive fee rose from $1000 to $1890, with an additional charge ranging from $10 to $75 for a single room. Concomitantly, scholarship awards rose from $26,412 to $51,145. These increases, which were in line with those at other colleges for women, allowed Wheaton to maintain a balanced budget in most years, but provided only very limited funds for capital expenditures beyond what was needed for routine maintenance and repairs to existing facilities.[28]

Clearly, limited increases in enrollment could generate a certain amount of additional revenue. But the decision not to attempt a capital campaign solidified, for the President and most of the Board of Trustees, the attitude that without a real possibility of attracting substantial new funds, any attempt to expand enrollment beyond what the current educational facilities could accommodate would be fiscally imprudent and foolhardy.

The second factor mitigating against a major expansion in the size of the College was considerable doubt as to Wheaton's ability to attract enough good students. In the early 1950s competition among colleges for qualified applicants increased enormously. Institutions which had expanded to meet the educational demands of returning World War II veterans now found that they had to fill those additional spaces from the ranks of new high school graduates. And the number of those finishing high school, representing babies born during the worst of the depression years, was small in comparison to earlier years. Applications for the fall, President Meneely reported in June, 1950, had decreased 25 percent from the previous year.[29]

At the same time, in the early 1950s some coed colleges expanded their admission of women to replace male students lost to the Korean War military draft. In addition, the withdrawal rate of women from colleges and universities reached new heights during the early 1950s, brought on in great part by the tendency toward early marriage that was part of the culture of the immediate postwar generation.[30] The resultant scramble by almost all colleges and universities to preserve both quantity and quality seemed to make it an inauspicious time for a small college such as Wheaton to attempt to expand beyond the limits of the financial base that had successfully nurtured the College through several turbulent decades. Wheaton, President Meneely told the faculty in January, 1951, needed to "batten down the hatches" in order to ride out the financial and admissions storms which lay ahead.[31]

But this policy, supported by both the President and the Board of Trustees, intensified another problem. Over many years, while the student body remained basically the same size, the number of faculty had gradually increased, resulting by 1946 in a student/faculty ratio of seven and a half to one.[32] Shifts in student patterns of course enrollment, particularly a substantial increase of interest in Psychology, plus the addition of offerings in new fields such as Astronomy and Russian had created a staffing situation which seemed, both to the Board and Dr. Meneely, educationally unnecessary and financially unwarranted. The size of the faculty had to be reduced from its less than eight to one ratio, the President wrote to Chemistry Professor Mildred Evans. "It is a ratio that is rare among colleges and one that Wheaton can hardly afford."[33]

Therefore, beginning in the early years of his administration, President Meneely coupled his efforts to improve faculty salaries with a personal commitment to reduce the size of the faculty, a policy that was both endorsed and actively spurred on by the expressed views of the Board of Trustees. In November, 1946, agreeing by formal vote that the faculty, was "unnecessarily large," the trustees urged department heads to cooperate with the President in reducing the size of the faculty within the next three years. Again in 1949, the recommendations of the Trustee Survey Committee specifically called for a "smaller faculty."[34]

This turned out to be more easily said than done. During the late 1940s, President Meneely attempted with limited success to reduce the size of some departments, especially in the foreign languages. He seriously considered abandoning the Physics major because of low enrollment, and forced the permanent termination of the major in American

Civilization. He also negated on financial grounds suggestions for curricular expansion in areas such as Drama. Inevitably, there was faculty opposition. Nonetheless, the President persevered, reducing the size of the French department from nine to eight, denying persistent requests to increase staffing in Russian, refusing to replace the part-time faculty member who taught Italian when she resigned, and cutting back German from a major program to a service department in language instruction, with only one full-time faculty member.[35]

However, it turned out these changes were offset by the need to increase staffing to meet the demands of the new general education requirements, which specified that all students must complete six hours in a number of areas, such as the social sciences, where no general requirement had existed before. The problem, as the President noted, was the differential in teaching loads created by the disparate enrollment in courses offered by different departments. It became apparent that a significant reduction in teaching staff was extremely difficult to achieve because of the need to maintain quality major programs in the areas and disciplines that would enable the College to compete successfully for good students.

The net result was that no real progress was made in reducing the overall size of the faculty; in 1954–55 there were sixty-three full-time teaching faculty as compared with sixty-five in 1946–47, while part-time instructors had increased from three to five. The slight improvement in the student/faculty ratio from 7.5–1 to 8.3–1 was solely attributable to the modest increase in enrollment brought about by student occupation of former faculty suites in dormitories. In 1956 the trustees were still urging that the College strive to achieve a student/faculty ratio of between 9 and 10–1.[36]

However, what the President did have available was a new tool that he could use to terminate faculty at the lower ranks, thereby limiting the number of senior faculty in any given discipline and on the faculty as a whole. This in turn enabled him to tighten controls over the total amount of money allocated for faculty salaries, while at the same time improving the financial compensation for those who had attained senior status. The mechanism for achieving this was the College's adoption in 1949 of the nationally recognized standards and procedures for awarding tenure to senior faculty.

Until 1949, faculty who had been promoted from instructor to assistant professor, or who had received a contract renewal at the latter rank, were regarded as having a form of permanent status on the faculty, particularly if they held the Ph.D. degree. Once the tenure system was in place, the President immediately began using it as a mechanism for intensive review, not only of those holding the rank of assistant professor, but also for assessing the long-term staffing needs of each department as a whole. Many departments were informed that their junior personnel could not hope for promotion to associate professor because of the number of senior tenured faculty already in place.

Openly acknowledging that he would in many cases regard junior appointments as rotating, with little or no hope of permanence, President Meneely was candid not only with his department heads, but also directly and personally with the instructors and assistant professors involved. Often he urged them to begin a search for new employment because there was little likelihood that they could expect a permanent position at Wheaton, no matter how satisfactory their performance in the classroom. In the past faculty had often been kept at lower ranks for years before being promoted. Now, given the nationally recognized guideline of a limited seven-year probationary period, and Wheaton's equation of tenure with the rank of associate professor, this was no longer possible.[37]

The "tenure crunch," as it came to be known generally for junior faculty seeking promotion at Wheaton and elsewhere, sometimes redounded to the College's benefit. Two new members of the faculty arrived in 1952 and 1954 respectively, both having had their promotion to tenure recommended by their departments at Smith College, but denied by President Benjamin Wright because those departments were "fully tenured." For more than twenty years Anne O'Neill and Jane Ruby would provide outstanding teaching and service to Wheaton in the Mathematics and History departments.[38]

The perceived need to reduce the overall size of the faculty, which the President discussed openly in faculty meeting, generated much concern and some anxiety. In meetings with the Committee on Conference with the Trustees, and also with the Executive Committee of the Wheaton chapter of AAUP, Dr. Meneely tried to be reassuring, while still asserting the need to reduce staffing in areas where enrollment had declined substantially. Faculty response, however, was decidedly negative, and on several occasions they offered an alternative, which involved expanding the size of the student body while holding the size of the faculty constant. To counteract these suggestions the President advanced the financial problems that expansion would create and the College's lack of resources to undertake such a project. Inevitably, when discussions regarding a sizeable increase in the student body finally did resume in the mid-1950s, one of the factors involved was a hope that increasing the student body might create efficiencies of scale that would allow development of a student/faculty ratio of 10–1.[39]

Over the years the question of admitting African-American students had not been a major concern at Wheaton. In the mid-nineteenth century the Seminary had turned down one young woman who had written that she would indeed prefer to go someplace else. At the turn of the century President Cole had deemed it necessary to deny admission to the daughter of Booker T. Washington, and in 1919–20 an African-American student had attended Wheaton for one year before transferring to Radcliffe. Other than these three instances, Wheaton had not found itself challenged to confront the issue of admission of "colored" students.[40]

Nonetheless, for some time there had been a general awareness that sooner or later this was a matter that would have to be addressed. In May, 1942, trustee Frederick Page "spoke to the Board of a <u>trend in education</u> which he thinks will develop before many years, whereby more <u>negro students</u> will attend the northern colleges."[41] During the war one letter of inquiry was received with a picture attached, though none was required. After considerable discussion between President Park and Dean of Freshmen and Acting Admissions Director Dorothy Littlefield, the two decided that this was most likely a planned test case, rather than an inquiry from a serious candidate. Therefore, they decided to forward the application forms to the student with no indication that they had received or seen a picture of the person involved. And indeed the forms were never returned. Nonetheless, the experience raised grave concerns within the administration as to how Wheaton students could best be educated to accept an African-American undergraduate. Equally problematical was the question of how, if a qualified applicant did appear, one could at short notice find at least one more person of the same ethnicity to come as well.[42]

On April 20, 1945, Rev. James H. Robinson, Minister of the Church of the Master in Harlem, served as guest speaker at chapel service, following which he engaged in a four-hour discussion with students in Yellow Parlor in SAB. Saying that he was certain that Negro girls could "be happy at Wheaton," he advocated a nationwide campaign to place capable African-American students in American colleges and universities. Noting that many colleges, including Wheaton, reserved special scholarships for foreign students, he urged that similar steps be taken to allow African-American students to attend top-level educational institutions.[43]

His suggestion obviously met with some support, for six weeks later President Meneely reported to the Board of Trustees that there had been "considerable agitation among the undergraduates for the admission to Wheaton of one or more colored students."[44] Noting that no African-American had applied for admission for the upcoming academic year, the President emphasized that it was difficult to determine how widespread this sentiment was within the student body as a whole.

> My own position has been that I would have no objection to the admission of one or more colored students provided they came on the same basis as other students and were treated on campus socially and otherwise in much the same way as other undergraduates. I am inclined to think, how-

ever, that a small country college like Wheaton is probably a less satisfactory place for colored students than the larger colleges like Smith and Wellesley and the urban institutions. Most of these have, I believe, admitted colored students in recent years, and Wheaton might be subjected to notoriety and severe criticism if the college refused to admit colored girls who measured up to our entrance requirements. I should welcome some expression of opinion from the Board for my guidance in this matter.[45]

Following a general discussion on June 3, the trustees voted that they "concurred" with the policies outlined in the President's report, and that applications from qualified African-American students, if and when received, should be favorably considered. Although no official mention was made regarding special scholarships, the opinion of the President and the Board clearly was that such students should compete for funds on an equal basis with all other nonforeign scholarship applicants.[46]

That the President's doubts regarding the general sentiment of the Wheaton student body were well founded is evidenced by the fact that in October, 1945, the students in charge of decorating the new smoker in Metcalf dormitory decided that the motif should be "Nigger Heaven," with paintings of little black devils on the walls.[47] Nonetheless, during that academic year (which was also the year of the Art Center crisis) the drive for admitting African-American students was taken up by the editorial board of the *News* and some faculty members, especially Louise Boas, who was also a strong and vocal supporter of Esther Seaver. The issue came to a head in March, 1946, when, in the matter of a few days students raised $601 dollars for a scholarship to be reserved specifically for an African-American student.[48]

President Meneely, who learned about the drive only when an enterprising student knocked on his door to ask him to contribute, was not in the least happy that the same group which had in his eyes been responsible for generating the Art Center controversy had again acted without informing or consulting him or the Admissions Director. Nonetheless he realized that the cause had to be supported. Writing to trustee Harriet Hughes, however, he could not contain his general irritation both with the process and the perpetrators.

> The disturbing element here on campus confronted me with a new situation a few days ago. . . . Whether it was decided to place me in an embarrassing position or not, I recognized at once that if I repudiated the project, I would be branded anew as a foe of liberalism, and we would have had a new controversy seething on campus. To avoid this I announced in chapel my approval of the project and my willingness to make a personal contribution. This took the wind out of their sails. . . .
>
> Ever since I have been here, there has, of course, been agitation from time to time to admit one or more colored students. We have had no candidates applying for the past three or four years, but there undoubtedly will

be several applying as a result of the campaign being carried on. I myself
have no objection to having one or two colored students. In fact, I think it
would be just as well to let them come, providing they meet the usual entrance requirements. It would tend to put a quietus on the agitation that
arises periodically over this question. It will be a relief to have the present
student agitators graduate in June. I only wish that a couple of the members of the Faculty were going out with them. It would be a boon to
Wheaton College.[49]

Ignoring the fact that the College specifically reserved scholarships
for foreign students, faculty children, and residents of Norton and surrounding towns, a month later the President was still bitter over the specific designation of scholarship money. "It is, of course, a form of
discrimination, but one could not make the parties involved see that
point," he wrote to Miss Hughes. "Fortunately the scholarship received
almost no publicity."[50] Be that as it may, suddenly a number of appropriate applications were received, and two African-American students,
Nadine Lane and Alice Taylor, were admitted as members of the class of
1950. One received the special scholarship; the other was assisted from
the general scholarship fund.[51]

For the next two decades Wheaton appears to have followed an admissions policy for African-American students consistent with that of other
private small New England liberal arts colleges in that era. Generally
one or two students were admitted each year, though occasionally the
number might be slightly higher. Not all graduated; the withdrawal rate
of about one-third of any entering class over four years seemed to hold
true for this group as well. It became the custom by the late 1940s to
provide a special $75 dollar extra scholarship, not based on grade per-
formance, to all African-American students in order that each might
have a single room. Recruitment was made more difficult by existing
College policy, which was to spread the limited amount of scholarship
money available as widely as possible in relatively small individual
amounts. Only when Dean May was able to convince Dr. Meneely to
lump some of the money together to create larger individual scholarships
did Wheaton begin competing successfully with other colleges in minority recruiting.[52]

The greatest number of African-American students to graduate between 1950 and 1970 was four in 1963; in five of those years there were
none. Only beginning with the class of 1971, undoubtedly spurred by
the civil rights movement of the latter 1960s, did the number of African-
Americans receiving Wheaton degrees begin to increase substantially.[53]

∞

Several miscellaneous items from the late 1940s and early 1950s deserve mention. Aside from the building of Shepard court, the faculty/

staff dining room and the new infirmary, construction work on campus during the period between 1945 and 1956 consisted entirely of renovation and repairs. Major work was done to expand and modernize the bathroom facilities in the older dormitories, while condensation between the acoustic tile ceiling and the roof of the swimming pool proved so corrosive that substantial repairs were required. The Board of Trustees authorized a shift from the use of coal to oil in the power plant, and the last of the overhead heating pipes and electric wires that had led to College owned buildings beyond the pond on Pine street were replaced by underground connections. The greenhouse was removed from the east side of Mary Lyon and the wood floors inside Mary Lyon were replaced on the first floor by asphalt tile, which all regarded as a great improvement, both aesthetically and in terms of lessened foot noise. Lamp posts took the place of the light bulbs which had hung from overhead wires along East Main Street; the filter beds in the sewage system were upgraded to meet new state-mandated standards; and in 1948 an engineer was finally retained to do the survey of all college-owned land first authorized by the trustees during the Park administration. Though the President believed that both the Wheaton Inn and his own residence were real assets for the College community, he continually fretted over the "small fortune" that had to be spent to maintain these large, more than century-old edifices.[54]

In 1944, trustee Helen Wieand Cole had suggested to the Board that the Administration Building, built in 1934 but as yet unnamed, should carry that of retiring President J. Edgar Park. Ten years later, the trustees finally took action, and on October 23, 1954, Park Hall was dedicated at a ceremony at which Dr. Park and his wife were present.[55]

Also noteworthy was the decision by the Board of Trustees, upon the recommendation of President Meneely, to appoint Dr. Ruth Capers McKay to a permanent position on the Board when her five year term as Alumnae Trustee expired in 1952. A member of the class of 1923, Mrs. McKay had earned a Ph.D. in English at the University of Pennsylvania and had held a variety of academic and volunteer teaching and administrative positions. Although there had been women trustees appointed to the Board since 1896, generally the regular Board members had tended not to regard the elected alumnae members, with their limited terms of office, particularly highly. However, President Meneely stated that he had come to hold Mrs. McKay in high regard both personally and professionally. Although worried about the possibility of setting an unwanted precedent, Board Chairman Richard Chapman agreed, and on March 29, 1952, the barrier was broken. Over the next twenty-five years, two other elected alumnae trustees, Magdalena Quinby (W1931) and Judge Nancy Holman (W1956), also would be "promoted" to full indefinite-term membership on the Board.[56]

During this period two major items were acquired by the College, one as a gift, the other through purchase. In 1949, E. O. Raabe, the father of a Wheaton alumna, donated his collection of some 520 pieces of nineteenth century American Sandwich glass, on the condition that if in the future his daughter were ever in financial distress the collection should either be sold or the College provide an equivalent amount in aid. And in 1950, President Meneely, himself a historian, seized an opportunity to purchase for the College a set of the original edition of Diderot's famous *Encyclopedie*, at a cost of $350.00 plus shipping.[57]

One other new development that became permanent was the inauguration in 1954–55 of the Shippee Lecture in Art or Art History. This was intended to complement the Shippee collection of art reproductions for student rental that the family had created as a memorial to a daughter who had been killed in an automobile accident in 1936 while a student at Wheaton.[58]

Student life on campus in the latter 1940s and early 1950s mirrored the general attitudes and outlooks of the postwar generation at college

Replete in matching dresses, necklaces, and Wheaton jackets, members of one of the College's two *a capella* singing groups, the Wheatones, performed on the steps of the Library in 1957. Uniformity and conformity, particularly in matters of hair style and dress, was a hallmark of student life on all college campuses in the 1950s.

and university campuses across the country. For many attending eastern women's colleges, marriage to a slightly older college man or recent graduate with good prospects, often before finishing college herself, was seen as normal, even desirable—an acceptable end result of the college experience. The female college graduate expected to work for a relatively brief period of time, but rarely did she think beyond the concept of a job to that of a career. The stereotypical web that Betty Friedan would later characterize as the "feminine mystique" seemed natural and appropriate to most young women.[59] After all, they had only to look at the example set by their older sisters, whose wartime and early postwar marriages to servicemen and veterans anxious to "get on" with their lives seemed to provide an attractive and acceptable model.[60]

Social life, particularly at women's colleges in the northeast, was found off-campus at the weekend athletic events and fraternity parties that dominated social activities at the many comparable men's colleges. Getting "pinned," in other words, being given, and then wearing the fraternity pin of one's serious boyfriend was seen as a major accomplishment and the prelude to formal engagement. A "ring before spring," was the senior-year motto repeated on many campuses; the *Wheaton News* published in most issues wedding and engagement announcements, which could on occasion run as high as 13–15 students, under a column headed "Rings and Bells."[61]

"Dance Lists" were regularly published in the *Wheaton News*, giving the name of the Wheaton student and the man (along with the college he attended) who would be coming to campus to escort her to the Christmas, Valentine, or Spring Weekend dance. On those weekends the floor of the Gymnasium was converted into a bunkhouse for student dates. But with the exception of these major events, weekend social activities occurred elsewhere, mostly at colleges for men, where parietal rules were far more relaxed, and where drinking on campus in fraternities was regarded benevolently by both college and local officials as a means of keeping partying college students off the roads and of minimizing the irritation factor to the surrounding community.[62]

On campus, students were heavily involved in extracurricular activities, so much so that the Wheaton faculty expressed concern on several occasions that the various clubs and student government activities were taking up too much valuable time. In particular the newspaper, yearbook, college choir, and the Outing Club enlisted the participation of many students. The International Relations Club and the Wheaton chapter of the United World Federalists provided outlets for the global concerns of some students, while members of the Cue Club limited themselves to mastering the pool tables in SAB. Theatre productions, especially the student-written and produced annual variety show *Vodvil*, absorbed large amounts of time, energy and creativity.[63]

Athletics played only a limited role, and mostly in an intramural set-

A fixture, often rather painful, of student life at single sex colleges during the 1950s were "mixers," usually for freshmen. Busloads of students of the opposite gender would be imported from other colleges for an evening usually dominated by high levels of anxiety on the part of all. This event was held in Plimpton Hall in September, 1957.

ting. Intercollegiate varsity competition, in which Wheaton had participated during the interwar years, had entirely disappeared. The Head of the Physical Education Department, Christine White, was a strong believer in the tenets of the National Association for Physical Education of College Women, which opposed strenuous athletic activity or varsity-type competition for women. Team sports, a Wheaton student told a group of high school girls in 1955, "should stress the value of having a good time rather than strong competition between teams."[64] When a member of the class of 1958 asked to represent Wheaton in a sailing regatta, she was informed that "women were too fragile for a sport such as sailing."[65]

Occasional informal "playdays" allowed mixed teams of students from different colleges to engage in short "extramural" scrimmages, usually no longer than what would have been a quarter period in a regular game.[66] The Athletics Association also sponsored competition in nonsports activities such as bridge tournaments, dormitory decorations, and ice sculpture. Tritons and the Dance Company continued to prosper. Three hours per week of physical education were mandated for freshmen, and two for sophomores and juniors. All students were required to undergo as freshmen the infamous "posture pictures," which were kept under lock and key and destroyed upon a student's graduation. Freshmen were also required to take a course in Basic Motor Skills designed "to teach the fundamentals of body mechanics, good carriage and body control," among other things.[67] Students learned how to move gracefully while wearing high heels and carrying a suitcase, the proper way to enter a taxi, or how to sit down crosslegged on a floor and then arise without embarrassment.[68]

Parietal rules remained in effect.[69] All dormitories were closed and locked at 10:30 P.M. Monday through Friday, 11:00 on Saturday, and 11:15 on Sunday. Late permissions extending to 1:00 A.M. could be obtained for Friday and Saturday nights if a student had a male escort, or if four unescorted students applied as a group. The number of overnights away from campus was not limited, but parental approval for various forms of off-campus accommodations was required. Students had to sign out and in if they left Norton for more than two hours, or planned to be away after 6 P.M. Seniors were permitted to have cars on campus without restriction; sophomores and juniors were limited to fourteen days each year.

Founded in the 1930s, the Wheaton Dance Company continued to flourish in the postwar period.

Freshmen were required to turn out their lights at the closing of houses up until Thanksgiving, and the number of late permissions for first year students was severely limited. Attendance at classes was voluntary except for first-semester freshman, with the exception that all students were required to be present on "calendar days," which were the first twenty-four hours that classes were in session before or after a vacation period. All students had to attend Convocation and Founders Day ceremonies, as well as all community meetings called by the College Government Association. Attendance at chapel services three times a week was mandatory, with ten cuts allowed each semester.[70]

Despite the fact that class attendance was voluntary for most students, faculty were required to take attendance and report the results periodically to the Registrar's Office. Moreover, the subject of excessive class cutting and extended absences from campus again became a perenniel subject of discussion in faculty committees and at faculty meetings, as it had been in the 1930s. In December, 1951, a faculty resolution stated that students were expected to be in residence on campus during the end-of-semester reading periods, and in 1954, after years of deliberation, class attendance regulations were adopted which set three absences per semester in any course as a "reasonable maximum." Excessive cutting was to be reported to the Academic Dean who was authorized to take "appropriate action." The free cut system, which had been in place since 1931, was effectively ended.[71]

Although most dormitories now had a "smoker," a host of regulations governing smoking on campus and in the town of Norton remained in effect. Writing to Dean Colpitts in September, 1950, President Meneely approved a change that would allow students to smoke in the dining rooms at the conclusion of the evening meal six days a week and after the noon meal on Sunday. "Will you please talk with me," he wrote, "so that we may agree precisely as to what that is, whether it should be with dessert or after dessert."[72] Quiet hours were designated and enforced. Typing in student rooms was forbidden after the closing of houses; those still working on papers had to move to parlors or smokers. Male guests could be entertained in dormitory parlors until houses closed; only fathers, and brothers under the age of ten, were allowed to visit student rooms.

Enforcement of both academic and social regulations was entrusted to the College Government Association. Upon entering Wheaton all students were required to sign a statement pledging to abide by all rules and regulations and to assume collective responsibility for enforcing all aspects of the academic and social honor system that had been installed, with faculty approval, in 1949–50. An individual pledge to observe all academic rules had existed since 1945–46, when an academic honor system that included unproctored examinations had gone into effect. However, the concept of collective responsibility initiated in 1949, which

Senior Hoop Rolling, 1958. The tradition of the Senior hoop rolling contest, begun in
1916, proved to be one of the most durable undergraduate traditions. It was still carried on
in the early 21st century at a coeducational Wheaton.

involved a commitment to take action if one observed violations committed by others, proved to be controversial and always difficult to enforce. All alleged social violations were reviewed first by the Honor
Board of the CGA. The most serious social cases and all academic cases
were heard by the Judicial Board, which included faculty and administrative personnel among its members. "Campusing" for minor infrac-
tions and social probation for major ones were the penalties normally
invoked for violations of social rules. Grade reductions on a paper or
exam, loss of course credit, or possible suspension followed a violation
of academic regulations. Recommendations for suspension or expulsion
had to be approved by the President.[73]

Perhaps the single biggest change in the regulations governing student
life on campus came with the sudden vote by the Board of Trustees in
June, 1952, to abolish the requirement that students (other than those
who were Roman Catholic) attend the Sunday morning nondenominational church services which had been held ever since the Chapel had
opened in 1917. In the years since the end of the war this subject had
become a perennial issue of discussion both in faculty and student government meetings. In 1947, President Meneely had presented the matter

to the Board for its opinion, and the trustees, led by the alumnae on the Board, had overwhelmingly voted to maintain the requirement. However, once the honor system was in place, the taking of attendance at church and chapel services ended, and while attendance at chapel services during the week held up well, there was a noticeable decline in the presence of students on Sunday morning. Seniors had the right to miss as many Sunday services as they wished, but members of others classes were allowed only a few cuts each semester. It was patently evident that the honor system, however effective it might be in others areas, was not working well here.[74]

So acute had the issue become that when the President placed it on the agenda for the Board of Trustees meeting in June, 1952, he indicated that he thought the matter should be studied carefully and a decision reached during the next academic year. Either the present regulations should be enforced effectively by some means, or church attendance should become voluntary. So concerned were Deans May and Colpitts that the Board would legislate a monitoring system that each wrote to President Meneely strongly opposing such a move. Maintaining that such action would run counter to the whole concept of a democratic college and community, both Deans asserted that a majority of both faculty and students were opposed to compulsory attendance, and that enactment of a monitoring system would constitute a severe blow to the whole system of college governance.[75]

Nonetheless, sentiment in the Board meeting initially was strongly in favor of maintaining the requirement, for most believed that removing it would mean such low attendance that the services themselves would have to be discontinued. Suddenly trustee Herbert Gezork, President of Andover-Newton Theological School, and the only minister on the Board, announced that he favored abolishing the requirement. It would be better to hold a service for one student who chose to attend voluntarily, he maintained, than to have a chapel full of those who were compelled by external forces to be there. So persuasive was Dr. Gezork with this argument that, to the amazement of the President and many of the trustees as well, the Board reversed itself and voted, with one abstention, to end the Sunday church attendance requirement immediately.[76]

The announcement of this change was greeted with unmitigated enthusiasm by the students and general approval by the faculty. However, one person who was not in the least happy was the Head of the Religion Department and College Chaplain, Rev. J. Arthur Martin. Although the President had told him that the issue of required Sunday church attendance would be examined during the next academic year, Dr. Martin felt betrayed by the suddenness of the Board's decision, and placed the blame for the swiftness of this action at the feet of the President. In actuality, Dr. Meneely, who in bringing the issue before the Board had stated that he believed the matter should be carefully examined during the next year, was as taken aback as Dr. Martin by the Board's action, but he was unable to persuade Professor Martin of this.[77]

Appointed to his position in 1948, Dr. Martin had already found much to displease him in the religious program at the College. He objected strongly to Dean Colpitts' contention that the Christian Association should be considered one of the many extracurricular clubs on campus. As such, she maintained, it was part of the College Government Association structure, and thus fell within the parameters of her own operational supervision and responsibility. At the same time, she stoutly denied any intention of interfering in or having any say in determining the spiritual or religious aspects of the Association's activities. Nonetheless, Dr. Martin accused both the Dean and the President of wanting to make the religious program of the College "a mere adjunct of the Dean of Students' office," an accusation which the President categorically denied.[78]

Professor Martin also, unbenownst to President Meneely, was furious over an earlier decision in 1950 to convert the large room in the basement of the chapel into facilities to be used by the Art Department. In particular he was resentful that he had not been consulted or informed of this action before it had become an established matter of fact. He believed that the Chapel should be reserved only for religious activities, while Meneely saw the room as available space which could be used to fill any demonstrated need, as had been the case ever since Lower Chapel had served as temporary headquarters for the library between 1918 and 1922.[79]

Over the next five years relations between Professor Martin and President Meneely deteriorated to the point where each assiduously avoided contact with the other. In a meeting in Dr. Meneely's office in 1954, Dr. Martin accused the President of being "disingenuous" and told him that his word was "worthless." Meneely responded by suggesting, as he wrote later in a letter to Dean Colpitts, that "unless he could change his attitude, which I'm sure he can't or won't, it would be best for him and for Wheaton if he found employment elsewhere." Although Martin agreed, the President noted that he would probably remain, "just for spite." "He has developed a virtual obsession against me," Dr. Meneely concluded.[80]

So concerned was the President over this impasse that he felt compelled to consult with the Chairman of the Board, Richard Chapman. "I have lived with this problem for three years and feel the need of further counsel," he wrote in 1955.[81] Thoroughly supportive of the President's position, Mr. Chapman nonetheless eventually, and very reluctantly, found it necessary to take action. Summoning both President Meneely and Dr. Martin to his Boston office in January, 1957, Chapman met with each separately. Reprimanding Martin severely, he remonstrated with him for "unacceptable behavior as a Christian," and suggested that although he could not compel the resignation of a tenured professor, unless Dr. Martin changed his manner, he would be well advised to leave. To the President Chapman commented that he found Dr. Meneely's behavior "childish," stating that his advice was to "shake hands and get on with it."[82]

At a subsequent meeting on February 21, the two adversaries finally achieved a wary and hesitant *modus vivendi*. Agreeing to appoint a second person in religion to assist Martin, who admittedly was carrying an excessive workload, the President proposed that the new younger person should take over the Chaplain's duties. Martin readily agreed. Writing to Chapman, Meneely reported:

> After settling academic matters I invited Martin to tell me something of his sabbatical plans and when he rose to leave I wished him a good journey. To my astonishment he then came over and shook hands! Neither of us made reference to his talk with you, but it is obvious that it proved worthwhile and I thank you very much for what you were able to do.[83]

Years later, Mr. Chapman commented that he believed in time the President did come to forgive Dr. Martin, but that he thought Martin's resentment never truly subsided. It was the only time that as Board Chairman he ever intervened in the internal affairs of the College, Chapman asserted, and he did so only with the greatest reluctance, convinced that there was no alternative mechanism to heal the breach between the two. From that time on both Martin and Meneely were able publicly to work with one another. Whether anything like complete reconciliation took place is doubtful, but clearly Chapman's actions served to resolve this personal impasse well enough to dissipate what had become a mildly disruptive issue for the whole Wheaton community.[84]

The advent of Miss Colpitts as Dean of Students also precipitated a major conflict between her and Choir Director Carl Garabedian. For years the Choir, renowned for its excellence throughout New England, had occupied the preeminent position on campus as far as extracurricular activities were concerned. So dominant had it become that Professor Garabedian had managed to get all other campus organization meetings and public events banned from Monday nights, and also from 7 to 8 P.M. on Thursday evenings, both of which were reserved exclusively for Choir rehearsals. In the same manner, Mr. Garabedian was insistent that no other major social event should occupy a weekend in which a Sunday Choir concert was to occur. The campus should be focussed on this event only, he maintained; moreover, attending a dance or some other event on Saturday night would make it impossible for Choir members to sing at their best on Sunday.[85]

One of the mandates Dean Colpitts had been given when assuming her new position was to improve and make more attractive the weekend

Professor Carl Garabedian rehearsed with students for the 1954 Spring concert.

activities on campus. It was also part of her written job description to "exercise oversight of the college calendar of engagements."[86] Thus, when in 1951 the only viable day for the Christmas dance in terms of the academic and social calendar fell on the same weekend that Mr. Garabedian had scheduled his major Christmas concert, Dean Colpitts saw no problem in having a dance on Saturday night and a concert on Sunday. In fact she regarded each event as enhancing the other by creating a pair of weekend activities that most students would want to attend.[87]

Not so Dr. Garabedian. The persistence with which he issued appeal after appeal to the President, either to extend the academic calendar to include another weekend before the Christmas break, or to cancel or reschedule the dance, was monumental. Equally total was the bitterness with which he attacked Dean Colpitts, and also President Meneely when he backed the Dean. Although the focus of the dispute was the scheduling of a single concert, the underlying issues of rehearsal time monopoly, the authority of the Dean to create an integrated social and public events calendar, and Miss Colpitts' ruling that he could not schedule Choir rehearsals during the January reading period loomed largely just below the surface. Ultimately, with the steadfast support of the President, Dean Colpitts emerged victorious, despite Mr. Garabedian's strenuous insistence that the new College policies in general, and Dean Colpitts in particular, were destroying the Choir.[88]

In the case of both of these disputes, the faculty as a whole watched with a sense of bemusement, but also with quiet, steady support for the President. Most of the faculty had long opposed compulsory student attendance at Sunday church services, and many departments had long chafed at the restrictions on speakers or academic club meetings imposed by the privileged Monday and Thursday Choir rehearsal schedules. In particular, many were not displeased to see, as one faculty member later put it, Dr. Garabedian get his "wings clipped."[89]

Interest in national or regional political or social issues was almost nonexistent, not only on the Wheaton campus but on college and university campuses in general. The student activism that would characterize the latter 1960s and early 1970s was nowhere to be found. Polls conducted by the *Wheaton News* indicated that 94 percent of the students favored Thomas Dewey over Harry Truman in the 1948 Presidential election, while 80 percent supported the candidacy of Dwight Eisenhower in both 1952 and 1956. The Korean War had minimal impact on the campus, other than to create personal emotional concerns for those who had fiances, friends, or brothers in military service.[90]

Nor did the tensions and concerns of the Cold War impinge heavily on the College. At the request of local and state authorities, Wheaton, like most educational institutions and business corporations, developed an "Organization Plan for Civil Defense," which was essentially an update of the old World War II plans for providing shelter for personnel in case of an Air Alert or actual air raid. Although this was the era in which many Americans were constructing underground shelters in their backyards against the possibility of a nuclear attack, no such concerns were evident at Wheaton.[91]

Unlike many colleges and universities, no member of the teaching faculty became involved in the various congressional and other anticommunist hearings and investigations of what later came to be known as the McCarthy witch-hunt era. Interestingly, only Geoffrey May, husband of Academic Dean Elizabeth May, was tinged with a "red" or "pink" paintbrush. The Mays had been good friends of Alger Hiss during their years in Washington, and as a result Mr. May agreed to testify on his behalf during both Hiss trials. When hostile reports of his testimony were printed in the local Attleboro paper, and comments critical of the Mays' continuing connection to Wheaton were received in the mail, Dean May asked President Meneely if he wanted her to resign. "Absolutely not!" was his firm reply.[92]

The President was equally unequivocal in his public opposition to state and federal attempts to get colleges and universities to seek out and dismiss communists or "fellow travelers" on their teaching staffs. He was also clear in his objection to the state mandate that singled out teachers and required them to take loyalty oaths as a condition of employment. Noting that President Park had spoken out firmly in opposition to the law when it had been passed in the 1930s, Dr. Meneely indicated similar sentiments in a speech to the Boston chapter of the American Association of University Women, and also to English instructor Louis Leiter, who protested having to take such an oath after having spent five years in military service during World War II.[93]

More important to students were the conditions that affected their daily lives. Marty's Coffee Shop and the Polo Diner provided off-campus havens for those craving fast food, or desiring to eat at other than established meal times. In 1952, as a cost-saving measure, the College began cafeteria service at breakfast and lunch, a change which students enthusiastically applauded. Not so welcome was the 1953 decision to close down the college laundry. Commercial linen service and laundry cases sent home to mother, which often returned with a box of fudge or home baked cookies nestled among the clean clothes, became the order of the day.[94]

The demise of the Foxboro Bus Company ended commercial bus service to the Mansfield train station and began what would become a perpetual problem of finding means of transportation from Norton to the "outside world." The President steadfastly resisted efforts to have the College start its own bus service, pointing out the many seniors with cars on campus and the general student penchant either to rent taxis as a group, or to hitchhike. Although the College deplored hitchhiking, Dr. Meneely admitted candidly to a trustee that no rule against it would be

For nearly three decades Marty's Coffee House provided an off-campus refuge where students could inject caffeine and fast food, smoke cigarettes, and engage in lingering conversations.

enforceable. "In the light of our experience," he averred, "it would be inadvisable for the College to enter the business since we would almost certainly wind up with a substantial loss and we would have a constant headache on our hands."[95]

In 1946 the population of Norton was 3,200; by 1954 it had grown to 4,850. Most of its residents worked either in several small local factories or for the larger jewelry manufacturers in Attleboro. A fair number of small farms still existed, many of them operated by people of Portuguese descent. The gulf that existed economically and educationally between the majority of Norton residents and the faculty, administration, and students of the College remained as wide as it had ever been.

However, the war had thrown the College and the town together in a number of activities, mainly related to Civil Defense preparations and procedures. As a result a number of Wheaton faculty had become increasingly involved in town affairs. Prior to leaving for military service, History Professor Ralph Hidy was active as a local Boy Scout leader. Professor Caro Lynn of the Classics department was succeeded by Economist Henrietta Jennings as Chair of the Norton Library Board of Trustees. The Ramseyers and Boases were also active in various local activities and organizations. Most significant was the appointment of History Professor E. J. Knapton to fill an unexpired term on the School Committee in 1941, to which position he was reelected for two three-year terms. His wife served for many years as Secretary of the Norton Parent Teachers Association.[96]

Symbolic of the improved relations between the citizens of Norton and Wheaton was the reception given by the Town in honor of the Meneelys at the Norton Grange on January 18, 1945. Nor was it coincidental that heading the organizing committee was Professor Knapton, who had also become Chair of the Norton School Committee. Speakers representing the town's government, churches, businesses and schools all welcomed the Meneelys to Norton on what was described as a snow covered, sparkling winter's evening.[97]

Equally significant in continuing the development of ties between the College and the town was the founding of the Norton Lions Club in 1945, a process in which several members of the faculty and staff were instrumental. Subsequently Paul Cressey, Walter Shipley, Geoffrey May, Jack Knapton, Irving Fillmore, and President Meneely were members, and this service organization did much to facilitate mutual understanding between those associated with Wheaton and the small business and professional group that existed in the town. After three years President Meneely felt compelled to resign because his duties at the College only allowed him to attend meetings irregularly, but the organization refused to accept his withdrawal, instead making him an honorary member. Meneely confessed to being quite moved by this gesture. "I think it is indicative of a healthy town-gown relationship," he wrote to trustee J. K. Clark.[98]

Taking action on a suggestion made originally by Dr. Park, in September 1944, President Meneely authorized Astronomy and Religion Professor Paul Sprague to begin scheduling nights when members of the Norton community could visit the College Observatory, a practice that was still in effect more than a half-century later. In 1950, President Meneely implemented a forgotten 1939 Board action approving the awarding of one half-tuition grant each year to a graduate of Attleboro, Mansfield, and Taunton High Schools. This was in addition to the half-tuition awards available to all graduates of Norton High School whose families had been resident in town for at least three years.[99]

Although Wheaton on occasion contributed funds to support the Norton police or fire departments, requests by various charitable and service organizations for donations to specific causes or fund-raising drives were routinely rejected as a matter of policy. The trustees questioned whether, since Wheaton was a nonprofit, tax-exempt, gift-soliciting institution itself, it could even legally contribute to groups from which (unlike the police and fire departments) it did not receive any services. However, in 1955 the Board of Trustees did authorize a contribution of $500 to the capital campaign drive being conducted by Sturdy Memorial Hospital in Attleboro. The grounds for this exception to the rule were the same as for the 1937 gift to the Norton Fire Department for the purchase of a fire truck—that the direct benefit to Wheaton and Wheaton students was considerable enough to qualify the gift as one of self-interest.[100]

Without a doubt the College's greatest involvement with Norton's governing officials concerned protracted negotiations over the proposed accession of Wheaton-owned land by the town for the purpose of constructing new public schools. In 1946, the public schools were housed in two turn of the century, large, run-down wooden structures, plus the last of Norton's old nineteenth century one-room schools. The need for new schools had been apparent to many in the last years before the war, but efforts to gain Town Meeting approval had proved fruitless.

During the war, primarily at the instigation School Committee Chair E. J. Knapton, the Town Meeting voted annually to put small surpluses in annual revenue into an account specifically designated for new school construction. With the war over, and the population of Norton starting to grow at what was then regarded as an alarming rate, the need became one not just of replacing antiquated facilities, but of having enough space to house the projected increase in the number of students within the system.[101]

In 1938, the College had agreed to donate for school purposes the ten-acre Jackson Lot near Norton Center on the road to Attleboro, which it had received in 1873 from Eliza Baylies Wheaton. In 1946, when the Board of Selectmen approached President Meneely to find out if the offer still stood, the College replied in the affirmative. However, there were doubts raised as to whether under the terms of Mrs. Wheaton's gift of the land to the Seminary, the College had the authority to give the land away outright. Ultimately, in order to avoid having to get a land court judgment on this issue, it was agreed that the town would formally take the land by eminent domain, compensating the College with the nominal sum of $100.[102]

In order to facilitate passage of this measure on the Town Meeting floor, the College also agreed to waive a "right of reversion" clause that existed in the deed by which Mrs. Wheaton had given land to the town in 1902 for the High School. Although the proposed new school would be for elementary level students, it was obvious that a new High School would have to be constructed in the near future. Once it was built, Norton would no longer be using the old site for educational purposes, and it would therefore revert to the College. However, many people in Norton saw such a potential "land swap" as favoring the College, for the old lot, though too small for a modern school, was located centrally and theoretically could be used for other forms of municipal or private development.

Writing privately to the President, Professor Knapton, who was also Secretary of the School Planning Committee, pleaded that the College both give up its right to the old school land and not insert a similar clause in any agreement regarding the new land that the town would acquire. Given the suspicious, even hostile attitude of many townspeople toward the College, it was imperative that Wheaton make it clear that it sought no present or future gain from the transaction. Without such a guarantee, Professor Knapton maintained, "I, along with others, have grave fears that the old attacks on the college will reappear and make our project in its present form almost impossible to achieve."[103] After considerable discussion, the Board of Trustees agreed.[104]

No sooner had the new Norton Elementary School opened in September, 1951, than a new School Building Planning Committee did indeed begin planning for the much needed new six-grade High School. As the plans were developed, they called for the school to be attached to the rear of the auditorium/gymnasium which had been constructed as part of the new elementary school, thus allowing both schools to have use of that facility. To accomplish this, however, the Town needed to obtain additional land that was owned by the College, and in the spring of 1953 town officials again approached President Meneely with a request for an additional fifteen acres of land.[105]

This time the Board of Trustees, though basically receptive, was not willing to forego receiving fair market value for the land, which it established at $5000. However, a Special Town Meeting on November 23,

1953, after approving $800,000 for construction of the new school, followed the recommendation of the Norton Finance Committee and voted to take the land by eminent domain with compensation of only $1500. This time the trustees decided to fight, and informed the Board of Selectmen that the College was prepared to contest the "fair market price" in Superior Court.[106]

Meanwhile, opponents of the new high school were seeking desperately to reverse the action taken on November 23. At a Special Town Meeting called by petition on December 17, a motion to rescind the funding for the school was narrowly defeated. The meeting came the same night as the College's annual formal Christmas banquet. At 7:45 P.M., History Professor Nancy Norton later recalled, a bell was rung in the banquet hall, and all faculty and staff who were registered Norton voters left the banquet and proceeded in their evening gowns and tuxedos to the Town Meeting in order to lend their support for the new high school. One can only imagine the reaction to this spectacle on the part of the working class residents of Norton gathered in the Elementary School gymnasium. A decade later one could still hear sarcastic comments by some residents regarding Wheaton faculty who lived in residences upon which no taxes were paid, and who appeared en masse at meetings in order to vote large sums of other people's money for fancy new schools.[107]

The effort to thwart the new school might have failed in December, but the following March at the Annual Town Meeting the antischool forces took the proponents by surprise and were successful in revoking the previous approval for a new school. However, supporters of the new school regrouped and at a Special Town Meeting on June 3, 1954, a motion for $760,000 received the exact number of votes needed for the two-thirds majority required for bonding. Construction began immediately, and the new High School opened for classes in September, 1955.[108]

Meanwhile, negotiations between College and town officials as to fair compensation for the land upon which the building had already been constructed continued. Only in 1956 was a settlement finally reached. The town accepted the $5000 figure suggested by Wheaton, and the College agreed that an additional 1.5 acres could be added to the original parcel without further compensation.[109]

One other land transaction, convoluted in its development, would have a long term impact on both the town and the College. In 1952, the College was approached by representatives of the Norton Savings and Loan Association. The Association, whose offices were located in Norton Center next to the Unitarian Church, was having difficulties with its landlady, and therefore expressed interest in purchasing a small plot of land on Taunton Avenue between the Wheaton Inn and the Norton Town Hall. The College responded favorably, and in December, 1952, the transaction was completed. However, the Association subsequently was able to purchase the land and buildings it already occupied. By 1956, it was apparent that it had no need for the land it had obtained from the College.[110]

At the same time a crisis of sorts had developed in relation to postal service in the center of Norton. The Norton Center Post Office, one of seven different offices distributing mail in Norton, had for many years been located in one-half of Pratt's General Store, which along with Marty's Coffee Shop was located on Main street between the Wheaton Inn and Howard Street. However, by 1955, the Federal Government had determined not to renew its lease with Pratt's when it expired in 1957, on the grounds that a larger and more modern post office was needed, one which would also allow the consolidation of delivery service and the elimination of a number of the smaller regional distribution offices in the town.

Concerned that the new building might be located some distance from the College, which accounted for 40 percent of the Center Post Office's business, Postmaster Joseph Yelle approached the College in the summer of 1955, with the suggestion that the College erect a post office building on College-owned land and lease it to the Federal Government. The proposal met with a favorable response, particularly because a larger post office next to the Wheaton campus would allow each student to have a personal mail box there, and would permit the College to discontinue its own overcrowded student mail box service located in the Bookstore in the basement of Park Hall.[111]

Originally, plans were drawn to place the new building on the corner of Howard and East Main Streets, but in 1956, as it became apparent that the Savings and Loan Association would not be using the land it had bought, attention shifted to this plot. Still near enough to afford easy access to Wheaton students, the location on Taunton Avenue promised far easier access for the citizens of Norton than did the East Main Street location. As a result the College arranged a repurchase of the land from the Savings and Loan Association. It then negotiated a ten-year lease agreement with the Federal Government, and proceeded to construct a brick post office building to Federal specifications, which opened for business on April 1, 1957.[112]

The opening of the new facility allowed the Federal Government to close all but one of the outlying offices in Norton; the Center Post Office now was responsible for delivering 99 percent of the Norton mail, Mr. Yelle later recalled. Although faculty retained boxes in Park Hall for on-campus mail correspondence, resident faculty and students obtained U.S. mail from personal boxes at the Post Office, which cost each student $2.70 for a nine-month rental. Only Federal mail addressed to College departments was delivered to Park Hall and distributed from there to the various offices. It would be another twenty-nine years before on-campus U.S. mail delivery to faculty and students was restored.[113]

Notes: Chapter 18

1. Meneely: Writings and Speeches: comments at Student Council panel discussion, 1946.

2. The Amherst "new curriculum" brought that college national recognition as a leader in higher education. See G. Kennedy, ed., *Education At Amherst: The New Program* (New York: Harper, 1955); also Synnott, *Half-Opened Door,* pp. 203–4.

3. Faculty Meeting Minutes: 11/15/48; see also 9/19/45; 11/19/47; 11/25/47; 4/27/48; 11/6/48; Meneely: Writings and Speeches: comments at Student Council panel discussion, 1946; President's Reports to Trustees: 11/3/45; 3/6/48; 3/5/49.

4. It should be noted that students at that time carried five three-credit courses each semester, with year-long courses counting for six credits; 120 credits were necessary to obtain a degree, in contrast to the equivalent of 128 credits required in the year 2000.

5. *Wheaton College Bulletin: Catalogue,* 1949–50, pp. 24–27.

6. Faculty Meeting Minutes: 2/14/49; 3/14/49.

7. President's Reports to Trustees: 3/5/49; see also 5/6/48.

8. Trustees: Hastings #1: Meneely to Hastings, 12/8/48.

9. Oral History Project: E. May interview, 1983; E. Banning interview, 1989.

10. President's Reports to Trustees: 10/24/53; 6/6/54; Trustees Minutes: 10/24/53; 3/27/54; Faculty Meeting Minutes: 11/9/53; Trustees: Chapman #7: Meneely to Chapman, 9/8/53; #8: 10/28/54; Burnham: Burnham to Chapman, 11/1/53; Meneely to Burnham, 11/3/53; 11/10/53; Chapman to Burnham, 11/6/53.

11. H. Austin, interview with author, September, 2000.

12. President's Reports to Trustees: 6/6/54.

13. Faculty Meeting Minutes: 10/28/46; 3/10/47; 10/30/47; 11/12/47; 12/9/47; 2/26/48; 1/10/49; President's Reports to Trustees: 3/6/48; 6/10/51.

14. *Wheaton News,* 4/16/53; 5/2/53; see also Faculty Meeting Minutes: 4/13/53; 1/11/54.

15. Faculty: Cressey: Cressey to Meneely, 6/17/53; 10/14/53; Meneely to Cressey, 6/22/53; 10/18/53; 1/10/55; Ramseyer: Meneely to Ramseyer, 5.25.54; 1/10/55; President's Reports to Trustees: 10/24/53; Trustees Minutes: 10/24/53.

16. Faculty: Lange: Biology Department to Meneely, 5/1/47; Lange to Meneely, 10/24/47; Trustees: Chapman #7: Meneely to Chapman, 1/20/53; Chapman to Meneely, 1/22/53.

17. Faculty: H. Jennings: Meneely to Jennings, 9/11/47.

18. Ibid.: Jennings to Meneely, 9/12/47.

19. Ibid.: Meneely memorandum, 11/13/47.

20. Ibid.; also Chidsey: Chidsey to Meneely, 10/14/54; Meneely to Chidsey, 10/15/54; Green: Meneely to Green, 5/27/53.

21. See President's Reports to Trustees: 3/5/49; 10/28/50; Trustees Minutes: 3/27/54.

22. President's Reports to Trustees: 3/23/45.

23. Ibid.; Trustees: Hastings #1: Meneely to Hastings, 11/12/48; Provost/ Registrar: Student enrollment statistics, 1912–73.

24. Trustees Minutes: 3/1/47; President's Reports to Trustees: 11/3/45; 3/1/47.

25. Faculty Meeting Minutes: 2/26/48.

26. For example, the total realized from the two funds after expenses was $15,484 in 1948–49, $23,493 in 1949–50, and $24,968 in 1950–51; in the several subsequent years the amount received from the two funds never exceeded $30,000. Wheaton College Financial Reports, 1949–55, Schedules C-1(a) and (b); President's Report to Trustees: 6/8/47; 6/12/49; 6/11/50; 11/3/51; Alumnae Affairs Office #55: Friends of Wheaton; Trustees Minutes: 6/6/48; 1/24/53; Trustees: Reynolds #15: Trustees Actions Regarding Infirmary, 12/8/52.

27. Oral History Project: E. May interview, 1983; R. Chapman interview, 1983; M. Clemence interview, 1983; President's Reports to Trustees: 10/28/50; 1/20/51; Trustees: Chapman #5: Chapman to Meneely, 12/14/50; Meneely to Chapman, 12/29/50; Trustees Minutes: 3/17/51.

28. The College experienced small deficits in the operational budget in 1946–47 and 1949–50. For information regarding these increased charges to students, see President's Reports to Trustees: 1946–56, passim; Trustees Minutes: 1946–56, passim; also Faculty Meeting Minutes: 10/11/48; 10/9/50; In 1947, the Board of Trustees broke from Wheaton's traditional policy of announcing all fee increases a year in advance, and substituted a policy of considering charges for the next academic year at the March Board meeting of the current year.

29. President's Reports to Trustees: 6/11/50.

30. "Early marriages are causing an increasing number of girls to discontinue," President Meneely commented. President's Reports to the Trustees, 6/6/54.

31. Faculty Meeting Minutes: 1/15/51; President's Reports to Trustees: 3/5/49; 1/28/50; 6/11/50; 1/20/51; 10/23/54; 3/19/55; Trustees: Chapman #5: Meneely to Chapman, 12/11/50; Shanks #5: Meneely to Shanks, 2/21/50; Reynolds #14: Meneely to Reynolds, 10/29/54; 12/1/54; Trustees Minutes: 3/11/50. College Board reporting procedures no longer asked students to indicate college preference, which made it much harder for admissions offices to gauge how many applicants to accept, and encouraged high school seniors to file multiple applications. See President's Reports to Trustees: 11/5/49; Deans Office, Admissions: Reports 1928–61: Report for 1952–53. Trustee Mary Ellen Avery (W1948) later recalled the "enormous pressure" that existed on students in the late 1940s to get married, often before finishing college. Oral History Project: M. E. Avery interview, 1983.

32. Meneely: Writings and Speeches: Meneely letter to Class of 1928, ca. 1946–47; President's Reports to Trustees: 11/9/46.

33. Faculty: Evans: Meneely to Evans, 8/9/45.

34. Trustees Minutes: 11/9/46; Trustees: Hastings #1: Hastings to Meneely, 1/15/49; President's Reports to Trustees: 3/23/45; 11/3/45; Trustees, General Information: Reports, 1945–55: Report of the Committee on the Survey of Wheaton College, January 22, 1949.

35. Faculty: McKee: 1948–49; Korsch: Meneely to Korsch, 1/30/51; 4/21/52; Korsch to Meneely, 11/11/53; Littlefield: Meneely to Littlefield, 4/30/47; Meneely memorandum, 1/31/47; 1/21/52; Trustees Minutes: 3/17/51; Staff: May: Meneely to May, 1/4/50.

36. Trustees Minutes: 3/17/51; 6/3/56; Faculty: Littlefield: Meneely memorandum, 1/31/47; 1/22/48; Rechnitzer: Meneely to Rechnitzer, 3/7/49; Korsch: Meneely to Korsch, 1/30/51; 4/21/52; President's Reports to Trustees: 6/11/50; 11/3/51; 10/23/54; Trustees, General Information: Reports, 1945–55: Data on Size of Teaching Faculty on Active Duty, 10/28/54.

37. For examples of implementation of this policy, see Faculty: Littlefield: Meneely to Littlefield, 4/30/47; Meneely memorandum, 1/23/51; 1/21/52; Pinacola: Meneely memorandum, 2/16/54; Rose: Meneely memorandum, 12/6/50; Miller: Meneely memorandum, 1/30/51; Korsch: Korsch to Meneely, 11/11/53; Peixotto: Meneely to Peixotto, 3/24/45; Reinert: Meneely memorandum, 2/1/55; Vickery: Meneely to Stedman, 2/11/52; President's Reports to Trustees: 1/20/51; 6/10/51; 3/19/52; 3/19/55.

38. Faculty: O'Neill: correspondence, 5/7/52–6/12/52; Ruby: correspondence, 1/30/54–3/9/54.

39. Trustees Minutes: 3/17/51; 3/29/52; 6/3/56; President's Reports to Trustees: 6/6/48; 6/10/51; Faculty Meeting Minutes: 4/27/48; Oral History Project: R. Chapman interview, 1983; G. Hood interview, 1983; E. May interview, 1983.

40. See ch. 7 and 7, n. 12, 13.

41. Trustees Minutes: 5/31/42, emphasis in original.

42. Oral History Project: D. Littlefield interview, 1983.

43. *Wheaton News*, 4/28/45.

44. President's Reports to Trustees: 6/3/45.

45. Ibid.

46. Trustees Minutes: 6/3/45; Trustees: Meadows #9: Meneely to Meadows, 6/26/45.

47. *Wheaton News*, 10/6/45.

48. Ibid., editorial, 10/20/45; 3/23/46; Oral History Project: J. Chidsey interview, 1983.

49. Trustees: Hughes #2: Meneely to Hughes, 3/20/46; Hughes to Meneely, n.d.: see also Meneely: Chapel Talks: 3/19/46.

50. Trustees: Hughes #2: Meneely to Hughes, 4/25/46.

51. President's Reports to Trustees: 6/2/46; see also *Wheaton News*, 4/30/49.

52. Staff: Colpitts: Colpitts to Meneely, 8/22/49; Oral History Project: L. Colpitts interview, 1983; E. May interview, 1983.

53. Deans Office, Admissions: Black Alumnae Advisory Council, 1983, List of Black Alumnae.

54. Trustees, General Information: Reports, 1945–55: I. Fillmore Memorandum, "Postwar Work," June, 1945; Trustees Minutes: 6/6/48; 6/11/50; 3/29/52; President's Reports to Trustees: 3/6/48; 6/11/50; 10/28/50; 6/10/51; 3/29/52; 3/21/53; Meneely: Writing and Speeches: Letter to Class of 1928, 9/11/53. Trustees: Chapman #7: Meneely to Chapman, 5/2/52.

55. Trustees Minutes: 10/14/44; 6/6/54; 10/23/54; Trustees: Meadows #9: Meneely to Meadows, 4/10/45; Chapman #8: Meneely to Chapman, 9/8/54; 9/14/54; Chapman to Park, 9/13/54; Chapman to Meneely 11/7/54.

56. Trustees: Chapman #6: Meneely to Chapman, 1/28/52; Chapman to Meneely, 1/31/52; Trustees Minutes: 3/29/52.

57. President's Reports to Trustees: 11/5/49; Trustees Minutes: 11/5/49; Faculty Meeting Minutes: 5/8/50.

58. President's Report to Trustees: 10/23/54. See ch. 14, n. 55.

59. Friedan, *The Feminine Mystique* (New York: Norton, 1997), Ch. 1.

60. Solomon, *Educated Women*, pp. 194–95; Chafe, *Paradox of Change*, pp. 195–96; Kendall, *Peculiar Institutions,* pp. 208–12; N. Woloch, *Women and the American Experience* (New York: A. A. Knopf, 1984), pp. 474, 483–89; also Oral History Project: M. E. Avery interview, 1983; N. Norton interview, 1983.

61. For examples, see *Wheaton News*, 2/12/49; 2/9/51; 6/10/51; see also President's Reports to Trustees: 10/22/55. For an engaging account of student life at an eastern women's college (Smith) in the latter 1950s, see S. A. Toth, *Ivy Days: Making My Way Out East* (Boston: Little, Brown, 1984).

62. For examples of dance lists, see *Wheaton News*, 5/13/50; 10/20/50; 2/16/51; 2/15/52; 12/4/53; Oral History Project: N. Norton interview, 1983.

63. *Nike*, 1946–54; Faculty Meeting Minutes: 5/8/50; Oral History Project: M. E. Avery interview, 1983.

64. Norton, "Physical Education and Athletics, 1941–1969," p.22.

65. Ibid.: See also, Faculty: C. White: "Girls and Women in Athletics," 4/17/54.

66. Norton, "Physical Education and Athletics, 1941–1969," p. 21.

67. *Wheaton College Bulletin; Catalogue,* 1951–1952, p.72.

68. Norton, "Physical Education and Athletics, 1941–1969," pp. 3–5; Faculty Meeting Minutes: 5/24/48.

69. Rules and regulations of course did not remain totally the same during this period, but what is striking is their consistency, rather than the degree of change. I

have chosen to describe the main provisions found in the *College Handbook* for 1951–52 as a generally accurate portrayal of the system as it existed between 1946 and 1955.

70. Faculty Meeting Minutes: 12/13/50.

71. Ibid.: 3/13/50; 12/10/51; 9/29/52; 10/13/52; 12/13/54.

72. Staff: Colpitts: Meneely to Colpitts, 9/15/50.

73. Faculty Meeting Minutes: 2/6/45; 4/11/45; 4/19/45; 11/29/45; 3/21/49; President's Reports to Trustees: 6/12/49; Meneely: Writings and speeches: Meneely speech at Community Meeting, 9/26/49.

74. Faculty Meeting Minutes: 5/15/47; 9/17/47; Trustees Minutes: 6/8/47; President's Reports to Trustees: 6/8/47; *Wheaton News*, 9/26/52; H. Austin, interview with author, September, 2000.

75. Staff: Colpitts: Colpitts to Meneely, 6/5/52; May: May to Meneely, 6/4/52; President's Reports to Trustees: 6/8/52.

76. Trustees Minutes: 6/8/52; President's Reports to Trustees: 6/8/52; Oral History Project: R. Chapman interview, 1983; K. Burton interview, 1983; L. Colpitts interview, 1983; M. Clemence interview, 1983; Trustees: Gezork: Gezork to Meneely, 10/3/52.

77. H. Austin, interview with author, September, 2000.

78. Staff: Colpitts: Colpitts to Meneely, 9/18/52; Oral History Project: L. Colpitts interview, 1983; Meneely: Writings and Speeches: Special Chapel Talk, 9/19/52; *Wheaton News*, 9/26/52; Faculty: Martin: Martin to Meneely, 9/12/52; 12/4/56; Meneely to Martin, 12/11/56.

79. President's Reports to Trustees: 10/28/50; Staff: Colpitts: Meneely to Colpitts 7/14/54; Trustees: Chapman #8: Chapman to Meneely, 7/23/54.

80. Staff: Colpitts: Meneely to Colpitts, 7/14/54; see also Trustees: Chapman #8: Chapman to Meneely, 7/23/54; McKay #6: McKay to Meneely 8/11/54; Faculty: Martin: Meneely to Martin, 11/23/55.

81. Trustees: Chapman #8: Meneely to Chapman, 9/13/55.

82. Oral History Project: R. Chapman interview, 1983; see also, Faculty: Martin: Meneely to Martin, 1/15/57.

83. Faculty: Martin: Meneely to Chapman, 2/24/57.

84. Oral History Project: R. Chapman interview, 1983; H. Austin, interview with author, 2000.

85. Faculty Meeting Minutes: 5/2/50; Faculty: Garabedian: Meneely to Garabedian, 6/10/50; Garabedian to Colpitts, 5/1/51; Garabedian to Meneely, 7/12/51.

86. Staff: Colpitts: Duties of the Dean of Students, 9/28/50.

87. Faculty: Garabedian: Garabedian to Meneely, 7/22/51.

88. Ibid.: Garabedian to Colpitts, 5/1/51; Garabedian/Meneely correspondence, 6/51–8/51; Johndroe to Garabedian, 7/11/51; Barbie to Mr G, 7/9/51.

89. C. Clewes, comment to author, ca. late 1970s; Faculty: Miller (Maxfield): Miller to Meneely, 12/3/49.

90. *Wheaton News*, 10/28/48; 10/30/52; 11/1/56; Oral History Project: E. May interview, 1983; J. Chidsey interview, 1983.

91. Staff: Colpitts: Memorandum on Suggested Organization for Civil Defense, 12/4/51.

92. Oral History Project: E. May interview, 1983; Staff: May: Newspaper clipping and letter, 12/15/49.

93. A. H. Meneely, "On Academic Freedom," *Wheaton Alumnae Quarterly*, 31:2 (April, 1952), pp. 16–17; Meneely: Writings and Speeches: "Education and Freedom," speech given to Boston chapter of AAUW, 1/15/52; Chapel talk, 9/25/53; *Wheaton News*, 9/28/51; 11/5/53; Faculty: Leiter: Leiter to Meneely, 8/15/57; Meneely to Leiter, 8/19/57.

94. Presidents Reports to Trustees: 11/1/52; *Wheaton News*, 10/15/53.

95. Trustees: Haley: Haley to Meneely, 2/10/53; Meneely to Haley, 2/11/53.

96. Oral History Project: M. Hidy interview, 1985; H. Yelle interview, 1983; Knapton, *Small Figure*, pp. 200–201.

97. Meneely: Inauguration: "Wheaton in Norton," published by the Alumnae Association, March 1945.

98. Trustees: J. K. Clark #8: Clark to Meneely, 10/5/45; Meneely to Clark, 2/10/49; Oral History Project: E. J. Knapton interview, 1983; J. Yelle interview, 1983.

99. Faculty: Sprague: Remick to Sprague, 9/11/44; Staff: Dunkle: Meneely to Dunkle, 7/7/50.

100. President's Reports to Trustees: 6/7/53; 6/5/55; Trustees Minutes: 6/7/53; 6/5/55.

101. Knapton, *Small Figure*, pp. 200–201; President's Reports to Trustees: 3/23/45.

102. Trustees Minutes: 6/2/46; 6/12/49. The necessary two-thirds vote authorizing the land taking was obtained at a Special Town Meeting on May 13, 1949.

103. Town of Norton: Jackson Lot (Norton Center School): Knapton to Meneely, 11/1/47.

104. Trustees Minutes: 3/6/44; 6/8/47; 11/8/47; 3/6/48; 6/6/48; 3/5/49; 6/12/49; President's Reports to Trustees: 11/8/47; Staff: Dunkle: Meneely to Dunkle, 11/23/49.

105. President's Reports to Trustees: 6/7/53.

106. Town of Norton: *Annual Report, Town of Norton, 1953*, pp. 57–59; Trustees Minutes: 1/30/54.

107. N. Norton, interview with author, 8/09/00; Town of Norton: *Annual Report, Town of Norton, 1953*, p.62.

108. Town of Norton: *Annual Report, Town of Norton, 1954*, pp. 41–42, 59–60. Ethelind Austin always credited the victory to the last-minute decision of Admissions Director Barbara Ziegler to leave a dinner engagement in Boston and return to Norton just in time to cast her affirmative vote. E. Austin, interview with author, 2000.

109. Trustees Minutes: 6/7/53; 10/24/53; 1/30/54; President's Reports to Trustees: 6/7/53; 10/24/53; 1/30/54; 1/22/55; 6/3/56. See also Town of Norton: Norton Public Schools, 1902–62: passim. It was also, purely coincidentally, in 1955 that the College discovered that a road it had built from Pine street to the Power House rested partially on land belonging to the House in the Pines School, and the purchase of 2.16 acres from the School was hastily, though amicably, arranged. Trustees Minutes: 1/22/55.

110. Trustees Minutes: 3/29/52; 6/8/52; 11/1/52; 1/24/53; President's Reports to Trustees: 3/29/52; 11/1/52; 1/24/53.

111. President's Reports to Trustees: 10/22/55; Oral History Project: J. Yelle interview, 1983.

112. The cost of the building was $39,658; the annual rental payment for the ten year lease was $3,492. See Town of Norton: Norton Post Office, 1955–57: passim; President's Reports to Trustees: 1/21/56; 3/17/56; 6/3/56; 11/10/56; Faculty Meeting Minutes: 9/18/56; *Wheaton News*, 10/11/56.

113. Oral History Project: J. Yelle interview, 1983.

19

Revolution from Above: The Decision to Expand, 1955–1957

IN MARCH, 1945, nine months after he had assumed office, President Meneely affirmed to the trustees his full support for the 500-student maximum which had been in effect as a matter of policy since the early 1920s.[1] Nine years later he reported again to the Board regarding this issue. He noted that national educational forecasts projected an increase in 1965 college enrollments of 46 percent over that of 1953, rising to 70 percent by 1970, all due to the maturation of the postwar generation later known as "baby-boomers." "Existing colleges and universities," he conceded, "will be under very heavy pressure to expand their facilities and it has been suggested . . . that each institution should face the prospects ahead and plan accordingly. That obligation will rest upon us at Wheaton as well as upon other institutions."[2]

Nevertheless, the President came down foursquare in favor of maintaining the basic status quo. While conceding that Wheaton could perhaps expand from its present 535 students to approximately 600, he pointed out that going beyond that point would mean that "a major expansion of our physical structure would be necessary. . . . The capital outlays involved would appear to be beyond our financial resources unless large sums from presently unknown quarters were made available to us."[3]

During the past ten years persons in virtually all parts of our college constituency have from time to time expressed to me the hope that Wheaton would always remain a small college and thereby preserve its somewhat distinctive character. My own sentiments have run along the same line. I have felt increasingly that there is a place in this region for a college like Wheaton and that there will continue to be. Many young women need or prefer a small college of our type, and we are able to give them a measure of individual attention that is impossible in substantially larger colleges or universities. Moreover, we are able to maintain a campus tone and atmosphere that is, I think, rather uncommon. These and many other values might well be lost or seriously impaired if the college were considerably increased in plant and student body.[4]

Not all members of the Wheaton community were of like mind. The suggestion by many faculty that the problem of a too low faculty/student ratio could best be addressed by increasing enrollment has already been discussed. Moreover, the Chair of the Board of Trustees, Richard Chapman, had attended 850-student Carleton College as an undergraduate, and did not believe that its slightly larger size had in any way impacted negatively on the social and academic benefits of a small college atmosphere. However, as Chapman himself admitted, the preponderance of opinion fully supported President Meneely's position. "If it had been desired to increase the college to a student body of, let's say, 1000 to 1200, then the policies of the past would not have been adequate," he wrote in 1951. "The body of opinion is, however, that an institution of Wheaton's present size has a highly useful place in the academic world; if this has validity then we should concentrate on improving the quality of what we have."[5]

And therein lay the rub. As the decade of the 1950s progressed, and it became evident that neither the faculty/student ratio nor the competitive level of faculty salaries could be improved in substantial fashion despite the College's best endeavors, frustration and unrest on the Board of Trustees began to grow. One could see that the Wheaton family era was coming to an end, trustee Gilbert Hood later commented.[6] It was obvious that there was a desperate need to generate greater income in order to meet the cost of curricular and salary improvements. With a limited endowment and no apparent fund-raising capacity, the College seemed caught "in a straightjacket," Chapman recalled. Convinced that the way to improve quality was first and foremost to attract better faculty by paying higher salaries and providing a good environment to teach in, Chapman believed that a means would have to be found to "lift ourselves by our own bootstraps."[7]

Even the President recognized in 1954 that the coming enrollment crisis would create an enormous competitive demand for qualified faculty. "I shudder to think of the task that will confront college officers in obtaining suitable faculty personnel some years hence," he wrote in the same report in which he expressed his support for maintaining Wheaton's traditional size. "Success will doubtless go to those institutions that can offer the most favorable inducements, financial and otherwise."[8]

Intensifying the questions involving enrollment was the long recognized need to erect a new classroom building, which, with the construction of the infirmary completed, had moved to the top of the priorities list. A variety of preliminary plans had been developed, all involving a site along East Main Street between Mary Lyon (the old classroom building) and Peacock Pond. Rooms that would hold classes of twenty to thirty-five students were desperately needed, given the increased number of specified distribution requirements. Additional seminar rooms were required for the year-long senior seminars that were now a part of almost all major programs. There was also a growing demand for faculty office space. In previous eras few faculty had had individual offices; instead, since almost all lived on or near the campus, they routinely held office hours in their homes or dormitory suites. Now, with more faculty commuting to Norton from a distance, the need for faculty office space was much greater. Finally, In January, 1954, the Board of Trustees authorized preliminary planning for a new classroom building.[9]

The general thinking was that if such a building were constructed, there would be no need to contemplate erecting a center for the arts per se. More room for music and art classes, along with art displays, would be available in Mary Lyon and it was thought that a future addition to the back of Plimpton Hall could turn that auditorium into a serviceable theatre. But all of this was predicated on the proposition that Wheaton's future enrollment would remain approximately the same, which would allow Wheaton to continue operating, as it always had, within the parameters of the fiscal legacy provided by the Wheaton family. There is abundant evidence that in June, 1954, Dr. Meneely was clear in his thinking on this matter, and regarded expansion beyond an upper limit of 600 students as not in the best interest of the College, either fiscally or educationally.[10]

In November, 1953, Academic Dean Elizabeth May wrote to President Meneely requesting a sabbatical leave during the 1955–56 academic year, which would be her seventh at the College. The President refused, responding that he was opposed in principle to the idea that those in administration should have sabbaticals. Administrators were much harder to replace than teaching faculty, he pointed out. Moreover, sabbaticals were not needed by administrators for purposes of professional development. Nonetheless, the general issue of such leaves was discussed at the March, 1954 Board of Trustees meeting, with the President and Mr. Chapman taking opposing views. Subsequently, Dr. Meneely questioned Board Secretary Sylvia Meadow's comment in the minutes of the meeting that the consensus of the Board favored granting administrative sabbaticals. "Perhaps Mr. Chapman will overrule me in connection with the minutes," he wrote.[11]

The matter was discussed again at the June meeting with the result that the Board, against the wishes of the President, approved a permanent policy of paid leaves of absence for the President and both Deans. In October, 1954, they authorized such a leave for the President in the spring of 1955, and approved one for Dean May for the following spring. "The Trustees have put me out to pasture for six months," President Meneely wrote to the Class of 1930.[12]

During the President's absence, Dean May formally assumed the title

Another Wheaton tradition, begun in 1923, which continued into the 21st century were the Candlelight Ceremonies, currently held the first night students arrive on campus as freshmen and again on the night before they graduate. This particular event took place in 1958.

of Acting President. At the first Board meeting she attended, on March 19, 1955, she presented a detailed study regarding the student attrition rate. Over a twenty year period the percentage of entering students who actually had graduated ranged from a high of 75.9 percent in 1949 to a low of 55.4 percent two years later. The projected rate for the spring of 1955 was only 58.2 percent. In the discussion that followed this report, the trustees noted that the major number of withdrawals came during the first two years of college, which "leaves the number of students in some upperclass courses smaller than is desirable. This condition might be benefitted by an increase in the size of the student body."[13]

No action was taken, but the tip of what turned out to be a fast-moving iceberg was already apparent. In her report to the trustees in June, Dean May emphasized that "planning for space should be tied to our concept of the future of our program."[14] At the same Board meeting Chairman Richard Chapman spoke strongly in favor of increasing the size of the College. After considerable discussion the Board voted to authorize its Grounds and Buildings Committee to survey "what steps need to be taken to take care of increasing the size of enrollment to a total of 700–800 students," and requested that the Administration Committee of the

Board "survey the educational needs for a student body of that same size." Both committees were to report at the fall meeting of the Board.[15]

In reality, it was Elizabeth May who undertook to do both of the basic needs assessments, and she did so at the express request of Mr. Chapman. As Acting President, Mrs. May had felt the need to consult with Mr. Chapman frequently, for she did not think she should make any major decision in Dr. Meneely's absence without consulting the Board chairman. Therefore, beginning in February, 1955, she often journeyed to Boston to visit Chapman at his office at the New England Merchants Bank. In their conversations they soon came to an agreement that expansion to at least the 850 student level that Chapman had experienced at Carleton was both feasible and desirable. And it would not, as he later put it, create an environment where "Wheaton would not be Wheaton."[16]

Chapman later recalled that the whole plan of action evolved out of joint discussions between himself and May. "Do you remember how you and I made a revolution?" he said years later to her, and she agreed that it had been that way.[17] At the Board of Trustees meeting in June, 1955, Mrs. May was charged by Mr. Chapman to develop a plan for implementing an expansion. She received little or no guidance from the Board at that time, she later recalled. Mr. Chapman simply said, "Just write out a plan."[18]

Student applications were the highest in history, and, because of the "baby boomers," promised to increase steadily for at least the next fifteen years. Thus, whether enough able students could be attracted to Wheaton was never an issue of great concern. In developing her plan, Dean May started with the premise that all programs offering a major concentration should have two full-time faculty as minimum staffing. Her own view was that the College should expand by 50 percent to 800 students and if that was successful should subsequently do the same again.[19]

In retrospect, it is amazing how little concrete planning was done before the Board authorized the construction of the first of three eighty-student dormitories and voted "to approve in general the proposed plan of expansion" at its meeting in October, 1955. The Trustees Grounds and Buildings Committee met only once, the Administration Committee not at all. On July 26, Acting President May forwarded to the trustees a fifteen page memorandum titled "Expansion of Wheaton College—Preliminary Considerations." In it she raised many questions and provided few answers, mainly outlining issues involving academic policy, staffing, and facilities that required further study. Designating ten existing facilities that needed to be examined, her general conclusion was that most of them could probably accommodate the first phases of expansion, at least on a temporary basis, but that substantial alterations and upgrading would be required down the line. Her comments assumed that a new

Chairman of the Board of Trustees, Richard Chapman was the driving force behind the 1955 decision to increase the size of the College. Here he is shown with Dean Elizabeth May, who was charged by Chapman to develop a plan to implement the expansion.

classroom building would be constructed very shortly, regardless of the decision on expansion. She emphasized the need for an office for every department, along with a departmental seminar room, and the addition of a fair amount of audio visual equipment.[20]

It seems evident that the trustees had informally come to the conclusion that expansion should be undertaken well before the President arrived back from his sabbatical trip to Europe. There is much to indicate that they were ready to take such a decision at the June, 1955, Board meeting, but did not want to act in Dr. Meneely's absence. But there is no doubt that when President Meneely returned in August, 1955, he was greeted with essentially a fait accompli that had temporarily been put on hold. In his report to the Board in preparation for the October meeting, the President expressed his views on the questions and issues raised by Dean May, on the whole taking a less sanguine view regarding the ability of existing facilities to absorb a large influx of students, and suggesting that several more new staff would be needed than the Dean had estimated.

> To do all that would be required for an enrollment increase of approximately 50% would probably involve an eventual outlay of from $2,500,000 to $3,000,000. The ways in which such very substantial sums can be procured constitute a very challenging and awesome problem, but not necessarily an insurmountable one. We need to be reasonably sure that we can obtain the necessary funds before we proceed very far.[21]

The funding needed for construction was anything but secure. Nonetheless, there were some grounds for optimism. For the preceding several years, the College had finished the fiscal year in the black. Every year, trustee Abram Collier commented, President Meneely would show an anticipated deficit through most of the year, which would be "miraculously transformed into a comfortable surplus at the end."[22] Rather than having a relatively large operating surplus show on the books in the year-end audit, Board Chair Richard Chapman and the Treasurer of the Board, William Chase, established several reserve funds, including ones for deferred maintenance and future building, into which the majority of the surplus was diverted each year, so that the final audit showed only a modest favorable balance in revenue over expenditures. Writing to Meneely in 1953, Chapman remarked how pleased he was with the surplus and with the way "the squirrels have chosen to bury the nuts."[23]

The result was that by October, 1955, the funds needed to build the first of a three-dormitory complex recommended by the Grounds and Building Committee at the trustees meeting were already in place. Moreover, the College had discovered a potential major donor in the person of Jeannette Kittredge Watson, who had attended Wheaton Female Seminary in 1901–02, and was the wife of the founder of International Business Machines Corporation (IBM), Thomas Watson. In the spring of 1954, Wheaton awarded Mrs. Watson an honorary degree, and she responded as the College had hoped she would by making a gift of IBM stock worth $30,000 in July. This, it turned out, was the first of many gifts of IBM stock the College would receive from Mrs. Watson over the next few years, culminating in major funding for the Fine Arts Center that would bear her name.[24]

Particularly important was the Board of Trustees' decision to construct the new three-dormitory complex along East Main street on the far side of Peacock Pond, the site originally contemplated in 1938 for

Mrs. Jeannette Kittredge Watson (WSX1902) was greeted by a student at the dedication ceremonies for Watson Fine Arts Center in 1961. Standing between them is Ruth Capers McKay (W1923), the first elected alumnae member of the Board of Trustees to be reappointed by the Board to permanent membership (1952).

the Arts Center. The basic site plan for these dormitories was developed by Howard Rich Associates, who had designed Shepard Court, the Faculty/Staff Dining Room and the Infirmary. However, at the October, 1955, meeting the Board finally approved a long-standing request of Dr. Meneely's that the College hire a landscape architect to draw up a master plan for the location of new buildings. Shortly thereafter the firm of Shurcliff and Shurcliff was retained, and they worked closely with College authorities and the building architects in planning the subsequent development of what would become popularly known as "new" or "lower" campus. The proposed plan of action was to construct the new classroom building after the first of the three dormitories was completed, this to be followed by the other two residence halls and finally a dining room and kitchen to serve the students living on the far side of the pond.[25]

The faculty received the news at its meeting on November 21, 1955, and the student body was informed two days later. Faculty reaction was generally quite positive. Some concern was expressed, particularly within the science departments, as to whether the College could attract enough well qualified students, but that concern was quickly erased as applications continued to escalate in succeeding years. Perhaps the most significant reaction was the faculty's decision to require forty-eight rather than forty-two hours of general distribution courses, beginning with the first expanded class entering in the fall of 1957.[26]

Student and alumnae reaction was amazingly indifferent. While there was some initial concern among students that an increase in size might lessen the relatively close relations between students and faculty, overall both the immediate and long-term reaction of students and alumnae was one neither of hostility nor enthusiasm. Rather both groups seemed to reflect a placid and unquestioning acceptance of the planned changes. Although the *Wheaton News* periodically published stories relating to the design and construction of the new buildings, neither the editorial pages nor the letters to the editor columns reflected particular interest or concern with any other aspect of the College's planned growth.[27]

By the fall of 1956, the initial plans had begun to change. In the interest of generating more revenue from student fees, Mr. Chapman suggested that the College take advantage of low-interest Federal loans available for building residence halls, and proceed immediately with the construction of a second dormitory rather than the new classroom facility. This action would mean very cramped instructional quarters until a new classroom building could be erected, but the additional revenue generated would assist greatly in academic construction projects for which no outside funding assistance was available. After considerable discussion, the Board of Trustees agreed. By June, 1957, it had also been determined that both a classroom building and a fine arts center should be constructed, a decision which necessitated demolishing the existing tennis courts and replacing them with new ones across East Main Street behind the President's House.[28]

The decision to expand also prompted one immediate major change in the administrative structure of the College. In June, 1956, recognizing the now absolute need to create an ongoing systematic fund-raising effort, the Board of Trustees voted to establish for the first time a professionally run Development Office. In order to attract a well-qualified person, and to give him the cachet needed for fund-raising in corporate circles, it became necessary to approve a title of Vice President for Development and Public Relations, which the trustees did with some reluc-

President Meneely shows the architects' sketch of Young Hall (1957), the first of the new three-dormitory complex built on the far side of Peacock Pond.

tance the following November. At the same time they emphasized that the holder of the new office, Charles Adkins, should understand that Dean May was second in command to the President in all College affairs. To this end they authorized a change in Mrs. May's title from Academic Dean to Dean of the College.[29]

In the fall of 1957, the first of the new dormitories, named for former Registrar Sarah Belle Young, opened with a full complement of eighty-one new students. Over the next five years the construction of two more dormitories, a dining room and kitchen, new classroom building, fine arts center, a major expansion of library facilities, and a new bridge over Peacock Pond would all be undertaken. It was the most dramatic and rapid building program since Samuel Valentine Cole's creation of the main campus as he prepared Wheaton for admission to the ranks of four-year colleges in the first decade of the century.

Central to achieving this result were the revenues generated from adding students first and constructing educational facilities second. These monies were augmented by Federal loan funds available for dormitory and dining facilities construction, and the munificence of Mrs. Watson, who time and again responded to the College's needs as plans for the

Watson Fine Arts Center (1961), constructed in the Modernist style, and the new bridge over Peacock Pond, built in 1957.

new fine arts center progressed. "Operation Bootstrap," Board Chairman Richard Chapman later termed it at the 1977 ceremony naming the "new" part of the college campus in his honor.[30] Writing to President Alice Emerson in 1982, Mr. Chapman recalled the summer of 1955:

> Perhaps we did not use his [Dr. Meneely's] absence from the scene with all propriety, however, for Dean May . . . and I spurred each other on to develop what proved to be a steamroller operation to increase the enrollment of Wheaton about 50%, to a level of 800+ students. . . .
>
> After Meneely returned to find this judgment was almost an accomplished fact, with his typical loyalty, Scotch courage, and thrift, he was the one who really made it work. He deserves, I believe, 90% of the kudos for what then transpired.[31]

From the Board of Trustees' perspective, the need for expansion was obvious. A larger enrollment would allow the development of both a fuller curriculum and better academic facilities, which would, it was hoped, make the College more attractive to better qualified students. Equally as important, trustee Maurice Clemence maintained, were the educational efficiencies that an improved faculty/student ratio could create, and the enhanced revenue stream from student fees which would allow a substantial improvement in faculty salaries. The Board's goal, Richard Chapman asserted, was "to pay faculty more nearly a living salary. They [sic] were so abysmally low that I maintained that the faculty was in effect subsidizing the education of the students, to whom they had no such obligation."[32]

Words well spoken and undoubtedly well meant. But in reality, as trustee Abram Collier ruefully noted, the numbers of new faculty roughly paralleled the increase in the student body, with the result that there was little effective change in the faculty/student ratio.[33] Moreover, the additional revenues generated by larger enrollment were swallowed up by increases in general operational expenses, along with the need to extract every possible extra dollar to help pay for the construction of new buildings or additions to old ones. The result was that although annual salary increases were granted, Wheaton's relative position in terms of wages paid at other colleges and the general national rate of inflationary growth failed to improve perceptibly during the last years of the Meneely administration.

What had been created by the time of Dr. Meneely's death in 1961, however, was a larger faculty teaching a curriculum that was both richer and deeper in terms of the courses that could be offered. They did so on a much livelier 785 student campus, one with greatly improved educational facilities. Although the expansion process was hardly complete—it would peak at close to 1200 in 1971—the die had permanently been cast. Wheaton as an educational institution nurtured, but also bound, by the fiscal, attitudinal and emotional ties created by the Wheaton family and its legacy, no longer existed.

Eliza Baylies Wheaton and the Wheaton family had always regarded Wheaton as "theirs" and had fiercely resisted any suggestion that major funding for the institution's needs should come from other than family resources. Even after Mrs. Wheaton's death in 1905, the Seminary and College continued, in terms of student enrollment and academic facilities, to live for the next fifty years essentially within the limits of the endowment legacy provided by the Wheaton family, making few and generally unsuccessful attempts to raise additional funds from outside sources.

In promulgating and then implementing its 1955 decision to begin what turned out to be an ongoing process of expansion, the Wheaton Board of Trustees, and in particular its Chair, Richard Chapman, initiated a process that would in time create the coeducational college of nearly 1600 students that Wheaton would become by the turn of the twenty-first century. But in making that decision the Board also brought to an end what can be regarded as the Wheaton family era of the College's existence. No longer able to live within the financial means provided by the legacy of its founding family, Wheaton was forced for the first time in its history to create a permanent Development Office, and compete both for national recognition and fiscal security with the many other institutions of higher education existing in the United States. How it successfully did so is a story for another volume.

But what was crystal clear in 1955 to Richard Chapman and the Board of Trustees was that it was time for Wheaton to move beyond the gentle but binding fiscal and emotional ties that the Wheaton family had imposed, through their lives and their legacy, on the institution they had founded.[34] These ties had indeed provided primary and essential financial sustenance and support to Wheaton for 120 years, but they had also in various ways involving size, administrative outlook, campus environment, and general self-perception, proved at times to be restrictive on the institution's perspective regarding future growth and development. The initiative undertaken in 1955 by Wheaton's Board of Trustees, assisted by Dean Elizabeth May, indeed involved hard and risky decisions. But the growth and development of Wheaton over the succeeding forty-seven years suggests that, like those who had envisioned a different and greater future for Wheaton Female Seminary in 1897, these men and women too were visionaries who, in the words of the *Wheaton Hymn*, not only "trusted where they could not see," but also, indeed, "builded better than they knew."

NOTES: CHAPTER 19

1. See chs. 9, 18.
2. President's Reports to Trustees: 6/6/54.
3. Ibid.
4. Ibid.
5. Trustees: Chapman #3: Chapman to Meneely, 5/25/48; #5: Chapman to Meneely, 1/3/51; #22: Chapman speech, 10/21/77; Oral History Project: R. Chapman interview, 1983.
6. Oral History Project: G. Hood interview, 1983.
7. Ibid.: R. Chapman interview, 1983. On June 30, 1954, Wheaton's Endowment Fund had a book value of $1,870,830, and a market value of $2,720,979. See Wheaton College Financial Reports, June 30, 1954, p. 34.
8. President's Reports to Trustees: 6/6/54.
9. Trustees Minutes: 1/30/54; President's Reports to Trustees: 11/1/52; 10/24/53; 1/30/54.
10. President's Reports to Trustees: 1/30/54; 6/6/54. Trustee Ruth McKay recalled that President Meneely used to tell her and her husband when discussion of Wheaton's size came up, "I like it just the way it is." Smart/Park: Park, 1926–44: McKay speech, 5/30/77. Dr. William C. H. Prentice, who succeeded Meneely as President, stated that he was told many times over that the decision to expand "was against Dr. Meneely's better judgement." Oral History Project: W. C. H. Prentice interview, 1983. Trustee Gilbert Hood recalled that Mr. Chapman's advocacy of a substantial increase in the size of the College "frightened Dr. Meneely very much." Oral History Project: G. Hood interview, 1983.
11. Trustees: Meadows #6: Meneely to Meadows, 4/14/54; Trustees Minutes: 3/27/54; Staff: May: May to Meneely, 11/22/53; Meneely to May 3/20/54.
12. Meneely: Writings and Speeches: Meneely to Class of 1930, 2/4/55; Trustees Minutes: 6/6/54; 10/23/54; President's Reports to Trustees: 6/6/54.
13. Trustees Minutes: 3/19/55; President's Reports to Trustees: 3/19/55. Meeting with the Board of Trustees was a new experience for the Acting President, since dur-

ing Dr. Meneely's presidency the Academic Dean was, as a matter of policy, "systematically excluded from any participation with Trustees." Oral History Project: E. May interview, 1983.

14. President's Reports to Trustees: 6/5/55.

15. Trustees Minutes: 6/5/55.

16. Oral History Project: R. Chapman interview, 1983.

17. Ibid.: E. May interview, 1983.

18. Ibid.; also E. May conversation with author, August, 1999.

19. Oral History Project: E. May interview, 1983; President's Reports to Trustees: 6/5/55; see also Oral History Project: B. Ziegler interview, 1983.

20. Trustees, General Information: Trustees Reports, 1945–55: E. May memorandum, "Expansion of Wheaton College: Preliminary Considerations," 7/26/55; Trustees Minutes: 10/22/55.

21. President's Reports to Trustees: 10/22/55.

22. Oral History Project: A. Collier interview, 1983.

23. Trustees: Chapman #7: Chapman to Meneely, 9/1/53; see also #6: Chapman to Meneely, 8/16/51; 8/20/51; Trustees Minutes: 10/24/53.

24. Oral History Project: M. Reynolds interview concerning Mrs. Watson, 1984; Trustees: M. Reynolds #14: Reynolds to Meneely, 7/11/54. Years later, Dean May told an interviewer that she was aware that Mrs. Watson was prepared ultimately to give the College $1,000,000 in IBM stock, and that this knowledge was central to the College's planning of the expansion process. Oral History Project: E. May interview, 1983. Mrs. Watson's gifts are documented in Buildings: Watson Fine Arts Center.

25. Trustees Minutes: 10/22/55.

26. Faculty Meeting Minutes: 11/21/55; 3/12/56; 9/18/56; 11/12/56; 9/17/57; Dean's Office, Admissions, #17: Admissions reports: 10/17/58; 9/60; Oral History Project: J. Chidsey interview, 1983; B. H. Jennings interview: 1983.

27. *Wheaton News*, 12/8/55; 10/11/56; 12/6/56; 2/28/57; 3/14/57; 4/28/57; 5/4/57.

28. President's Reports to Trustees: 11/10/56; Wheaton College, *President's Report, June 30, 1957*, pp. 4–5.

29. President's Reports to Trustees: 6/3/56; 11/10/56; Trustees Minutes: 6/3/56; 11/10/56; Staff: Adkins: Meneely to Adkins, 11/16/56; *Wheaton News*, 12/6/56.

30. Trustees: Chapman #22: Speech at Dedication of Chapman Campus, 10/21/77.

31. Ibid.: Chapman #21: Chapman to Emerson, 5/3/82.

32. Ibid.; also Oral History Project: M. Clemence interview, 1983.

33. Oral History Project: A. Collier interview, 1983.

34. Ibid.: G. Hood interview, 1983; R. Chapman interview, 1983.

Bibliography of
Materials Cited in Chapter Endnotes

This bibliography is intended to provide basic reference to the materials cited in the endnotes for each chapter. It does not include the many published sources or archival materials that were examined but not specifically cited. In the case of the Boxed Collections only the main group heading is included—the subsets within the groups are not. However the chapter endnotes provide specific reference to these subsets, and to the specific documents cited. Readers should understand that this bibliography does not constitute a complete list of materials available in the Wheaton Archives covering the 1834 to 1957 period, though to my best knowledge all such materials have been reviewed. Also, anyone interested in using an item cited in this volume should be aware that because so much of the classification work in the College Archives is recent and ongoing, there may be rare instances in which a document location or classification has been shifted since its use in preparing this history.

DOCUMENTS, PAPERS, TAPES, AND PUBLISHED MATERIALS AVAILABLE AT THE MARION B. GEBBIE ARCHIVES AND SPECIAL COLLECTIONS, MADELEINE CLARK WALLACE LIBRARY AT WHEATON COLLEGE

Addison, Daniel D. *Lucy Larcom: Life, Letters and Diary.* Boston: Houghton Mifflin, 1894.

Austin, Holcombe M., and Nancy M. Budd. *Alive and Well Said: Ideas at Wheaton—A Sesquicentennial Anthology.* Norton, MA: Wheaton College, 1984.

Boas, Louise Schutz. *Woman's Education Begins: The Rise of Women's Colleges.* Norton, MA: Wheaton College Press, 1935.

Boxed Collections:
  AAUP
  Academic Council Minutes
  Alumnae Affairs Office
  Alumnae Association
  Anniversaries
  Buildings
  Bursar's Office Correspondence, 1889–1940
  Cole, Helen Wieand (cited in notes as HWC)

Cole, Samuel Valentine (cited in notes as SVC)
Curriculum
Dean's Office, Admissions
Dean's Office, Denkinger
Faculty Before 1910
Faculty Committees
Faculty (Personnel files)
Faculty Meeting Minutes
General Files (Class Years)
Incorporation Papers, Statutes and Seal
Larcom, Lucy
Lyon, Mary
Meneely, A. Howard
Meneely/May
Park, J. Edgar
Phi Beta Kappa
President's Office
President's Reports to Trustees, 1923–74
Principals
Provost/Registrar
SGA (CGA)—(Student Government Association)
Smart/Park
Staff (Personnel files)
Student Groups and Activities
Town of Norton
Treasurer, Reports, 1912–32
Treasurer's Office
Trustees, 1834–1911
Trustees, Board Meeting Minutes, 1834–1961.
Trustees (Personnel files)
Trustees, General Information
Vocational Conferences, 1917–52
Wheaton, Eliza Baylies (cited in notes as EBW)
Wheaton Family
Wheaton Family, Winter Street Property
Wheaton Histories, Seminary
Wheaton Histories, Shepard "Reference History" Notes
Wheaton Histories, Wheaton in World Wars I and II
Clewes, Carolyn. *Wheaton Through the Years: 1835–1960*. Norton, MA: Wheaton
    College, 1960.
Cole, Samuel V. *Concerning Education: Inaugural Address of Rev. Samuel V. Cole as
    President of Wheaton Seminary, given June 23, 1897*. Norton, MA: Wheaton Fe-
    male Seminary, 1897.
———. "Connecting the College with the Home." *The Congregationalist* (July 29,
    1915).

————. "Historical Address." Extracts. *Wheaton Bulletin* 6, no. 3 (June, 1910): pp. 3–13.

————. Letterbook, 1900–1908. Bound, carbon copies.

————. *President's Reports, 1912–1913——-1921–1922.* Norton, MA: Wheaton College, 1913–1922.

————. *Why Did Wheaton Change From Seminary to College.* Norton, MA: Wheaton College, 1920.

Copeland, Jennie. "Judge Laban Wheaton." Incomplete, unpublished manuscript.

Creevey, Caroline Stickney. *A Daughter of the Puritans.* New York: G. Putnam's, 1916.

Cunliff, Emma F. "History of Wheaton College and the Class of 1868." Handwritten unpublished manuscript.

Dahl, Curtis. "Mary Lyon: 1878." *Wheaton Alumnae Magazine* (Fall, 1978): pp. 6–7.

Edwards, Richard. "Mary Jane Cragin." *National Teachers Monthly* 1, no. 6 (April, 1875): pp. 161–66.

Filene, Catherine, ed. *Careers for Women.* 1920. Reprint, Boston: Houghton Mifflin, 1924.

Gilchrist, Beth B. *The Life of Mary Lyon.* Boston: Houghton Mifflin, 1910.

Harris, Hilda. "No Backward Steps: The Wheaton Alumnae Association, 1870–1970." *Wheaton Alumnae Quarterly* 49, no. 2 (Summer, 1970): pp. 4–11.

Helmreich, Paul C. *Wheaton College, 1834–1912: The Seminary Years.* Norton, MA: Wheaton College, 1985.

Hill, William G. *Family Record of Deacons James W. Converse and Elisha S. Converse, Including Some of the Descendants of . . . Robert Wheaton.* Malden, MA, 1887.

Hitchcock, Edward. *The Power of Christian Benevolence: Illustrated in the Life and Labors of Mary Lyon.* 3rd ed. Northampton, MA: Hopkins, Bridgman, 1852.

Holmes, Sylvester. *Sermon Preached at the Funeral of Honorable Laban Wheaton at Norton, March 26, 1846.* Boston, 1846.

Hubbard, George H. "Wheaton Seminary, Norton, Mass." *New England Magazine* 18, no. 1, (March, 1898): pp. 102–15.

Jarvis, Sarah. Letters, 1843–1850. Transcripts.

Jennings, Bojan H. *Chemistry at Wheaton.* Plymouth, MA: Jones River Press, 1999.

Jenny, Herbert J., and Park, J. Edgar. "A Wheaton Hymn."

Knapton, Ernest. J. *Small Figure in a Large Landscape: An Autobiography.* Privately published, 1987.

Kornwolf, James D. "Introduction: The Competitions, the Thirties, and Architectural Issues related to Them, Then and Now." In *Modernism in America 1937–1942: A Catalog and Exhibition of Four Architectural Competitions,* edited by James D. Kornwolf. pp. 1–21. Williamsburg, VA: Joseph and Margaret Muscarelle Museum of Art, 1985.

Larcom, Lucy. Journals. I, November 3, 1859——September 12, 1861; II, October 5, 1861——August 4, 1862.

————. *Wheaton Seminary: A Semi-Centennial Sketch.* Cambridge, MA: Riverside Press, 1885.

Leonard, Jacob. "A Brief Historical Sketch." In *Town of Norton Bi-Centennial, 1711–1911, Souvenir Program.*

McCormick, Thomas J. "Wheaton College: Competition for an Art Center, February 1938–June 1938." In *Modernism in America 1937–1942: A Catalog and Exhibition of Four Architectural Competitions,* edited by James D. Kornwolf, pp. 22–67. Williamsburg, VA: Joseph and Margaret Muscarelle Museum of Art, 1985.

Marshall, Carrie. Letters, 1900–1904.

Meneely, A. Howard. "On Academic Freedom." *Wheaton Alumnae Quarterly* 31, no. 2 (April, 1952): pp. 16–17.

New England Wheaton Seminary Club Scrapbook.

Nike. 1918–1957 student yearbooks.

Norton, Nancy. "Physical Education and Athletics at Wheaton Female Seminary." Unpublished manuscript.

———. "Physical Education and Athletics at Wheaton: The College and the Intercollegiate Years, 1912–1941," Unpublished manuscript.

———. "Physical Education and Athletics at Wheaton: The Christine White Years, 1941–1969." Unpublished manuscript.

Oral History Project Interviews:
  Austin, Holcombe
  Avery, Mary Ellen
  Banning, Evelyn
  Burton, Katherine
  Chapman, Richard
  Chidsey, Jane
  Clemence, Maurice
  Collier, Abram
  Colpitts, Leota
  Ford, Marjorie Person
  Harris, Hilda
  Hidy, Muriel
  Hood, Gilbert
  Jennings, Bojan Hamlin
  Knapton, Ernest J.
  Littlefield, Dorothy
  MacKenzie, Louise Barr
  Mandell, Lena
  May, Elizabeth Stoffregen
  Norton, Nancy
  Park, Rosemary
  Prentice, William C. H.
  Reynolds, Muriel
  Shouse, Catherine Filene
  White, Christine
  Yelle, Henri
  Yelle, Joseph
  Ziegler, Barbara

Orcutt, Sherilyn S. "The Advancement of Physical Education for Women and Girls of the United States During the 1920's." Wheaton College Honors Thesis #594, 1980.

Paine, Harriet. *The Life of Eliza Baylies Wheaton: A Chapter in the History of the Higher Education of Women.* Cambridge, MA: Riverside Press, 1907.

Preservation Resource Group, Inc. "Initial Evaluation for Preservation and Use of Mary Lyon Hall." August, 1980.

Roller, Stephanie G. "Lucy Larcom: A Portrait of 19th Century America." Wheaton College Honors Thesis #182, 1962.

Rushlight. 1855–1960. Published and unpublished years.

Shepard, Grace F. "Reference History of Wheaton College." Unpublished manuscript, 1931.

Stewart, Ruth A. *Portia: The Life of Portia Washington Pittman, The Daughter of Booker T. Washington.* Garden City, NY: Doubleday, 1977.

Town of Norton Bi-Centennial, 1711–1911, Souvenir Program.

Treasurer. "Cash Disbursements Ledger." July, 1913–September, 1918.

Treasurer. "Trial Balance Ledger." 1919–1933.

Wheaton. 1916–1917 student yearbooks.

Wheaton Alumnae News. 1922–1926.

Wheaton Alumnae Quarterly. 1926–1971.

Wheaton Bulletin. 1905–1913.

Wheaton College. *Announcement of Wheaton College, Norton, Massachusetts, 1912.*

———. *Catalogue of Officers and Students.* 1912–1960.

———. *Inauguration of Alexander Howard Meneely, Wheaton College, Norton, Massachusetts, October 14, 1944.*

———. *The President's Report, June 30, 1957.*

———. *The President's Report, the Treasurer's Report to the Board of Trustees, 1939.*

———. *President's Report to the Board of Trustees, 1944.*

———. *Report of the President of Wheaton College, June 22, 1932.*

Wheaton College Alumnae Magazine. 1971–1989.

Wheaton College Bulletin: Alumnae Register Issue, 1959–1960.

Wheaton College Bulletin: Catalogue. 1930–1931—1961–1962.

Wheaton College Bulletin: Catalogue and Announcements. 1912–1913—1929–1930.

Wheaton College Financial Reports. 1921–1960.

Wheaton College Handbook. 1912–1957. Bound volumes of pamphlets variously entitled: *Students' Handbook; Rules and Regulations; Legislation and Practice; Wheaton College Government Association; Wheaton College Handbook;* and *Wheaton College Songbook.*

Wheaton, Eliza B. "Account Book." January 4, 1866–January 16, 1885. "Houses, Repairs, etc." (EBW)

———. "Cash Books," 1867–1905. (EBW)

———. "Incidents in the Life and Brief Account of the Death of Hon. Laban Wheaton." Unpublished manuscript, Wheaton Family Box.

———. Letters (financial) 1865–1873. Bound, carbons. (EBW)

Wheaton Female Seminary. *Annual Catalogue,* 1835–1913.

Wheaton Female Seminary. "Grade Books." 1879–1884; "Record," Vol. 5, Grades, 1899–1911.

Wheaton Female Seminary: Trustees, Faculty, Students, 1834–1912.

Wheaton, Laban Morey. "Cash Receipt Books." (LMW)

———. "Day Book." (LMW)

Wheaton, Laban Morey, and E. B. Wheaton. "Account Books." 1854–1902.

Wheaton News. 1921–1960.

Wheaton Record. 1913–1925.

Wheaton Seminary, 1912.

Wheaton Seminary and College. "Scrapbook of Clippings." 1899–1917.

Wheaton Quarterly. 1989–2000.

Wheaton Traditions. Published by the Class of 1925.

"Where Some of Our Girls are Educated: Wheaton Seminary, Norton, Mass." *Phrenological Journal* 11, no. 3, new series (March, 1875): pp. 173–78.

OTHER ARCHIVAL MATERIALS

Lyon, Mary Lyon. Correspondence. Mount Holyoke College Archives.

———. *Mount Holyoke Female Seminary.* September, 1835. Old South Leaflets #145 (n.d.): pp 425–35. Mount Holyoke College Archives.

———. Printed circular re Proposed Seminary. September 8, 1834, Mount Holyoke College Archives.

"Memorabilia of Mary Lyon: Presented By Amelia Woodward Truesdall, Class of 1858." Statement by Persis Woods Curtis. Unpublished manuscript. Mount Holyoke College Archives.

"Mount Holyoke Female Seminary." Printed but "not published." September, 1835. Mount Holyoke College Archives.

Stevenson, Adlai E. "Commencement Address." June 6, 1955. Smith College Archives.

Trustees of Mount Holyoke Female Seminary. *General View of the Principles and Design of Mount Holyoke Female Seminary.* Boston, 1837. Mount Holyoke College Archives.

Wellesley College Archives. Miscellaneous materials related to Portia Washington.

Wheaton College Alumnae/i Office. Microfilm Records.

PERSONAL INTERVIEWS

Austin, Ethelind

Austin, Holcombe

Burton, Katherine

Clewes, Carolyn

Ford, Marjorie Hill

Goold, Ruth

Heuser, Mary

Jennings, Bojan Hamlin

Knapton, Ernest J.

May, Elizabeth Stoffregen

Norton, Nancy

Yelle, George

Yelle, Henri

Zwicker, Lucille

Other Books and Articles

American Council of Learned Societies. "Ebenezer Bailey," and "Dr. Dudley A. Sargent." In *Dictionary of American Biography,* 20 vols. New York: Scribners, 1928–36.

Bailyn, Bernard, David Davis, David Donald, John Thomas, Robert White, and Gordon Wood. *The Great Republic: A History of the American People.* Boston: Little, Brown, 1977.

Baker, Liva. *I'm Radcliffe! Fly Me!: The Seven Sisters and the Failure of Women's Education.* New York: MacMillan, 1976.

Biographical Directory of the American Congress, 1774–1971. "Judge Laban Wheaton." Washington, D.C.: U.S. Government Printing Office, 1971.

Bowdoin College. *General Catalogue of Bowdoin College, 1794–1950.* Brunswick, ME: Bowdoin College, 1950.

Bunkle, Phillida. "Sentimental Womanhood and Domestic Education, 1830–1970." *History of Education Quarterly* 14, no.1 (Spring, 1974): pp. 13–30.

Cahn, Susan K. *Coming on Strong: Gender and Sexuality in Twentieth-Century Women's Sport.* New York: Free Press, 1994.

Calhoun, Charles C. *A Small College in Maine: Two Hundred Years of Bowdoin.* Brunswick, ME: Bowdoin College, 1993.

Chafe, William H. *The Paradox of Change: American Women in the 20th Century.* New York: Oxford University Press, 1991.

Clark, George F. *A History of the Town of Norton, Bristol County, Massachusetts: From 1669 to 1859.* Boston: Crosby, Nichols and Company, 1859.

Cole, Arthur C. *A Hundred Years of Mount Holyoke College: The Evolution of an Educational Ideal.* New Haven: Yale University Press, 1940.

Conway, Jill. "Perspectives on the History of Women's Education in the United States." *History of Education Quarterly* 14, no. 1(Spring, 1974): pp. 1–12.

Cott, Nancy. *The Bonds of Womanhood: "Woman's Sphere" in New England, 1780–1835.* New Haven: Yale University Press, 1977.

Cowan, Ruth Schwartz. "Ellen Swallow Richards: Technology and Women." In *Technology in America: A History of Individuals and Ideas*, edited by Carroll W. Pursell, Jr. Cambridge, MA: MIT Press, 1981, pp. 142–50.

Degler, Carl. *At Odds: Women and the Family in America from the Revolution to the Present.* New York: Oxford University Press, 1980.

Delamont, Sara and Lorna Duffin, eds., *The Nineteenth Century Woman: Her Cultural and Physical World.* New York: Barnes and Noble, 1978.

Faragher, John M., and Florence Howe, eds. *Women and Higher Education in American History: Essays from the Mount Holyoke College Sesquicentennial Symposia.* New York: Norton, 1988.

Freedman, James O. "Ghosts of the Past: Anti-Semitism at Elite Colleges." *The Chronicle Review: Chronicle of Higher Education* 47, no. 14 (December 1, 2000): pp. B7–B10.

Friedan, Betty. *The Feminine Mystique.* New York: Norton, 1997.

Garraty, John A. *Henry Cabot Lodge: A Biography.* New York: A. A. Knopf, 1953.

Gildersleeve, Virginia C. *Many a Good Crusade: Memoirs of Virginia Crocheron Gildersleeve.* New York: MacMillan, 1954.

Green, Elizabeth A. *Mary Lyon and Mount Holyoke: Opening the Gates.* Hanover, NH: University Press of New England, 1979.

Guild, Reuben A. *Early History of Brown University, Including the Life, Times and Correspondence of President Manning, 1756-1791.* Providence, RI: Snow and Farnham, 1897.

Guttmann, Allen. *From Ritual to Record: The Nature of Modern Sports.* New York: Columbia University Press, 1978.

Hatch, Louis C. *The History of Bowdoin College.* Portland, ME: Loring, Short and Harmon, 1927.

Hawk, Grace E. *Pembroke College in Brown University.* Providence, RI: Brown University Press, 1967.

Helmreich, Paul C. "Lucy Larcom at Wheaton." *New England Quarterly* 63, no. 1 (March, 1990): pp. 109–20.

Historical Statistics of the United States: Colonial Times to 1970. 2 vols. White Plains, NY: Kraus International Publications, 1989.

Horowitz, Helen L. *Alma Mater: Design and Experience in the Women's Colleges from Their Nineteenth Century Beginnings to the 1930s.* 2nd ed. Amherst: University of Massachusetts Press, 1993.

———. *Campus Life: Undergraduate Cultures from the End of the Eighteenth Century to the Present.* New York: A. A. Knopf, 1987.

James, Janet Wilson. "Ellen Swallow Richards." In *Notable American Women, 1607–1950,* vol. 3, pp. 143–46. Cambridge, MA: Belknap Press, 1971.

Katz, Michael B. *The Irony of Early School Reform: Educational Innovation in Mid-Nineteeth Century Massachusetts.* Cambridge: Harvard University Press, 1968.

Kendall, Elaine. *"Peculiar Institutions": An Informal History of the Seven Sister Colleges.* New York: G. Putnam's, 1976.

Kennedy, Gail, ed. *Education at Amherst: The New Program.* New York: Harper, 1955.

Knapton, Ernest J., ed. "The Harvard Diary of Pitt Clarke, 1796–1791." *Sibley's Heir.* In Publications of the Colonial Society of Massachusetts, vol. 59. Boston, 1982.

Lansing, Marion, ed. *Mary Lyon Through Her Letters.* Boston: Books, Inc., 1937.

Lipset, Seymour M., and David Riesman. *Education and Politics at Harvard.* New York: McGraw Hill, 1975.

Lloyd, Susan. *A Singular School: Abbot Academy, 1828–1973.* Andover, MA: Phillips Academy, 1979.

MacLean, Sydney. "Mary Lyon." In *Notable American Women, 1607–1950,* vol. 2, pp. 443–47. Cambridge, MA: Belknap Press, 1971.

Marchalonis, Shirley. *The Worlds of Lucy Larcom, 1824–1893.* Athens: University of Georgia Press, 1989.

Martin, George H. *The Evolution of the Massachusetts Public School System.* New York: D. Appleton, 1902.

Massachusetts, Commonwealth of. *Thirty-Ninth Annual Report of the Board of Education, together with the Thirty-Ninth Annual Report of the Secretary of the Board, 1874–75.* Boston: Massachusetts Board of Education, 1876.

McNeill, William H. *Hutchins' University: A Memoir of the University of Chicago, 1929–1950.* Chicago: University of Chicago Press, 1991.

Monroe, Paul, ed. *A Cyclopedia of Education.* 5 vols. New York: MacMillan, 1913.

Morison, Samuel E. *Three Centuries of Harvard, 1636–1936.* Cambridge: Harvard University Press, 1946.

Newcomer, Mabel. *A Century of Higher Education for American Women.* New York: Harper, 1959.

Oren, Dan A. *Joining the Club: A History of Jews and Yale.* New Haven: Yale University Press, 1985.

Pollard, Lucille A. *Women on College and University Faculties: A Historical Survey and a Study of Their Present Academic Status.* New York: Arno Press, 1977.

Pond, Jean S. *Bradford: A New England Academy.* Bradford, MA: Bradford Academy Alumnae Association, 1930.

The Revolution 2, no. 19 (November, 1868).

Ryan, Mary P. "A Woman's Awakening: Evangelical Religion and the Families of Utica, New York, 1800–1840." In *Women in American Religion,* edited by Janet Wilson James, pp. 89–110. Philadelphia: University of Pennsylvania Press, 1980.

Shea, Lois R. "Sudden, Swift, Silent and Deadly—80 Years Ago, Flu Ravaged New England." *Boston Sunday Globe,* November 1, 1998.

Shepard, Grace F. "Female Education at Wheaton College." *New England Quarterly* 6, no. 4 (1933): pp. 803–24.

Sklar, Kathryn Kish. "The Founding of Mount Holyoke College." In *Women of America: A History,* edited by Carol Ruth Berkin, and Mary Beth Norton, pp. 177–201. Boston: Houghton Mifflin, 1979.

Solomon, Barbara M. *In the Company of Educated Women: A History of Women and Higher Education in America.* New Haven: Yale University Press, 1985.

Stow, Sarah D. *History of Mount Holyoke Seminary, South Hadley Mass., during its First Half Century, 1837–1887.* South Hadley, MA: Mount Holyoke Female Seminary, 1887.

Synnott, Marcia G. *The Half-Opened Door: Discrimination and Admissions at Harvard, Yale, and Princeton, 1900–1970.* Westport, CT: Greenwood Press, 1979.

Taylor, James M., and Elizabeth H. Haight. *Vassar.* New York: Oxford University Press, 1915.

Thorp, Margaret F. *Neilson of Smith.* New York: Oxford University Press, 1956.

Thwing, Charles F. *A History of Higher Education in America.* New York: D. Appleton, 1906.

Toth, Susan A. *Ivy Days: Making My Way Out East.* Boston: Little, Brown, 1984.

Vital Records of Norton, Massachusetts, to the Year 1850. Boston: New England Historic Geneological Society, 1906.

Wechsler, Harold S. *The Qualified Student: A History of Selective College Admission in America.* New York: Wiley, 1977.

Wells, Anna M. *Miss Marks and Miss Woolley.* Boston: Houghton Mifflin, 1978.

Woloch, Nancy. *Women and the American Experience.* New York: A. A. Knopf, 1984.

Woody, Thomas. *A History of Women's Education in the United States.* 2 vols. New York: Science Press, 1929.

World Almanac and Book of Facts for 1927.

Index